American Foreign Policy 11/12
Fifteenth Edition

EDITOR

Glenn P. Hastedt
James Madison University

Glenn Hastedt received his PhD from Indiana University. He is professor of political science at James Madison University, where he teaches courses on U.S. foreign policy, national security policy, and international relations. His special area of interest is on the workings of the intelligence community and the problems of strategic surprise and learning from intelligence failures. In addition to having published articles on these topics, he is the author of *American Foreign Policy: Past, Present, Future;* coauthor of *Dimensions of World Politics;* and editor and contributor to *Controlling Intelligence.* He has also published two volumes of readings, *Toward the Twenty-First Century* and *One World, Many Voices.*

ANNUAL EDITIONS: AMERICAN FOREIGN POLICY, FIFTEENTH EDITION

Published by McGraw-Hill, a business unit of The McGraw-Hill Companies, Inc., 1221 Avenue
of the Americas, New York, NY 10020. Copyright © 2011 by The McGraw-Hill Companies, Inc.
All rights reserved. Previous editions © 2009, 2008, and 2006. No part of this publication may be
reproduced or distributed in any form or by any means, or stored in a database or retrieval system,
without the prior written consent of The McGraw-Hill Companies, Inc., including, but not limited
to, in any network or other electronic storage or transmission, or broadcast for distance learning.

Some ancillaries, including electronic and print components, may not be available to customers
outside the United States.

Annual Editions® is a registered trademark of The McGraw-Hill Companies, Inc.
Annual Editions is published by the **Contemporary Learning Series** group within
the McGraw-Hill Higher Education division.

1 2 3 4 5 6 7 8 9 0 WDQ/WDQ 1 0 9 8 7 6 5 4 3 2 1 0

ISBN 978–0–07–805071–8
MHID 0–07–805071–5
ISSN 1075–5225

Managing Editor: *Larry Loeppke*
Developmental Editor: *Debra A. Henricks*
Permissions Coordinator: *Rita Hingtgen*
Marketing Specialist: *Alice Link*
Project Manager: *Robin A. Reed*
Design Coordinator: *Margarite Reynolds*
Cover Graphics: *Kristine Jubeck*
Buyer: *Laura Fuller*
Media Project Manager: *Yeswini Devdutt*

Compositor: Laserwords Private Limited
Cover Images: DoD photo by Tech. Sgt. James L. Harper Jr., U.S. Air Force/Released
Background: U.S. Navy photo by Logistics Specialist 1st Class Kelly Chastain/Released

Library in Congress Cataloging-in-Publication Data
Main entry under title: Annual Editions: American Foreign Policy, 2011/2012.
  1. U.S. Foreign Relations—Periodicals. I. Hastedt, Glenn P., *comp.* II. Title: American
Foreign Policy.
658'.05

Editors/Academic Advisory Board

Members of the Academic Advisory Board are instrumental in the final selection of articles for each edition of ANNUAL EDITIONS. Their review of articles for content, level, currency, and appropriateness provides critical direction to the editors and staff. We think that you will find their careful consideration well reflected in this volume.

ANNUAL EDITIONS: American Foreign Policy 11/12
15th Edition

EDITOR

Glenn P. Hastedt
James Madison University

ACADEMIC ADVISORY BOARD MEMBERS

Preface

In publishing ANNUAL EDITIONS we recognize the enormous role played by the magazines, newspapers, and journals of the public press in providing current, first-rate educational information in a broad spectrum of interest areas. Many of these articles are appropriate for students, researchers, and professionals seeking accurate, current material to help bridge the gap between principles and theories and the real world. These articles, however, become more useful for study when those of lasting value are carefully collected, organized, indexed, and reproduced in a low-cost format, which provides easy and permanent access when the material is needed. That is the role played by ANNUAL EDITIONS.

This fifteenth edition of *Annual Editions: American Foreign Policy* presents an overview of American foreign policy. Prior to September 11, 2001, the debate over the future of American foreign policy proceeded at a measured pace because few pressing threats to American national security seemed to exist. The foreign policy debate centered on selection strategies and tactics that could guide the United States in the transition period between the end of the Cold War and the emergence of a post–Cold War era. It was a debate largely conducted in the language of academics, and it was one that did not engage large numbers of the American public. All of that has changed. Since September 11, the conduct and content of American foreign policy is seen as important by virtually all Americans.

The immediate issue was combating and eradicating terrorism; the geographic focal point was Afghanistan; and the target was the Taliban government and Osama bin Laden's al Qaeda terrorist organization. Few quarreled with the merits of this military undertaking, either in the United States or abroad. This was not true for the Bush administration's next major foreign policy initiative, when the war against terrorism was expanded to include Iraq with the objective of removing Saddam Hussein from power. This successful military action was followed by an occupation marked by violence and political turmoil. Additional international challenges surfaced in short order. The most noteworthy being revelations concerning the North Korean and Iranian nuclear programs, and growing conflict over trade and monetary matters with China.

As a consequence, we are now witnessing a wide-ranging debate over the strategic and tactical choices open to the United States in an era when it is the dominant (and some would say unchallenged) world power. The Obama administration quickly staked out a position in this debate calling for a "reset" in American foreign policy. One of the key issues in American foreign policy will be the extent to which change or continuity comes to mark his foreign policy.

Annual Editions: American Foreign Policy 11/12 is divided into eight units. The first unit addresses questions of grand strategy. The second unit focuses on selected regional and bilateral relations. In the third unit, our attention shifts inward to the ways in which domestic forces affect the content of American foreign policy. The fourth unit looks at the institutions that make American foreign policy. In the fifth unit, current foreign policy problems and the process by which American foreign policy is made is illustrated through accounts of recent foreign policy decisions. The sixth and seventh units provide an overview of the economic and military issues confronting the United States today. The final unit looks in depth at the issues surrounding the wars in Iraq and Afghanistan and their implications for American foreign policy are examined from a variety of different perspectives.

Together the readings in these eight units provide students with an up-to-date overview of key events in American foreign policy, the forces that shape it, and the policy problems on the agenda. The essays were chosen for their ability to inform students, spark debate, and help them become independent critical thinkers. They are not designed to advance any particular interpretation of American foreign policy.

I would like to thank Ian Nielsen for supporting the concept of an *Annual Editions: American Foreign Policy* many years ago. Also deserving of thanks are the many people at McGraw-Hill/Contemporary Learning Series who worked to make the project a success, and those faculty on the Advisory Board who provided input on the selection of articles. In the end, the success of *Annual Editions: American Foreign Policy* depends upon the views of the faculty and students who use it. I encourage you to let me know what worked and what did not so that each successive volume will be better than its predecessor. Please complete and return the postage-paid *article rating form* at the end of this book.

Glenn P. Hastedt

Editor

Contents

UNIT 1
The United States and the World: Strategic Choices

The concepts in bold italics are developed in the article. For further expansion, please refer to the Topic Guide.

UNIT 2
The United States and the World: Regional and Bilateral Relations

The concepts in bold italics are developed in the article. For further expansion, please refer to the Topic Guide.

UNIT 3
The Domestic Side of American Foreign Policy

The concepts in bold italics are developed in the article. For further expansion, please refer to the Topic Guide.

UNIT 4
The Institutional Context of American Foreign Policy

The concepts in bold italics are developed in the article. For further expansion, please refer to the Topic Guide.

UNIT 5
Foreign Policy Problems and the Policy Making Process

UNIT 6
U.S. International Economic Strategy

The concepts in bold italics are developed in the article. For further expansion, please refer to the Topic Guide.

UNIT 7
U.S. Military Strategy

The concepts in bold italics are developed in the article. For further expansion, please refer to the Topic Guide.

UNIT 8
The Iraq War, Afghanistan, and Beyond

The concepts in bold italics are developed in the article. For further expansion, please refer to the Topic Guide.

The concepts in bold italics are developed in the article. For further expansion, please refer to the Topic Guide.

Correlation Guide

The *Annual Editions* series provides students with convenient, inexpensive access to current, carefully selected articles from the public press. **Annual Editions: American Foreign Policy 11/12** is an easy-to-use reader that presents articles on important topics such as *diplomacy, globalization, military power,* and many more. For more information on *Annual Editions* and other *McGraw-Hill Contemporary Learning Series* titles, visit www.mhhe.com/cls.

This convenient guide matches the units in **Annual Editions: American Foreign Policy 11/12** with the corresponding chapters in one of our best-selling McGraw-Hill Political Science textbooks by Rourke/Boyer.

Annual Editions: American Foreign Policy 11/12	International Politics on the World Stage, Brief, 8/e by Rourke/Boyer
Unit 1: The United States and the World: Strategic Choices	**Chapter 1:** Thinking and Caring about World Politics **Chapter 2:** The Evolution of World Politics **Chapter 10:** National Economic Competition: The Traditional Road
Unit 2: The United States and the World: Regional and Bilateral Relations	**Chapter 1:** Thinking and Caring about World Politics **Chapter 6:** Power, Statecraft, and the National State: The Traditional Structure **Chapter 7:** Intergovernmental Organizations: An Alternative Governance
Unit 3: The Domestic Side of American Foreign Policy	**Chapter 1:** Thinking and Caring about World Politics **Chapter 10:** National Economic Competition: The Traditional Road
Unit 4: The Institutional Context of American Foreign Policy	**Chapter 8:** International Law and Human Rights
Unit 5: Foreign Policy Problems and the Policy Making Process	**Chapter 3:** Level of Analysis and Foreign Policy **Chapter 8:** International Law and Human Rights
Unit 6: U.S. International Economic Strategy	**Chapter 11:** International Economics: The Alternative Road
Unit 7: U.S. Military Strategy	**Chapter 9:** Pursuing Security
Unit 8: The Iraq War, Afghanistan, and Beyond	**Chapter 5:** Globalization: The Alternative Orientation **Chapter 9:** Pursuing Security

Topic Guide

This topic guide suggests how the selections in this book relate to the subjects covered in your course. You may want to use the topics listed on these pages to search the Web more easily.

On the following pages a number of websites have been gathered specifically for this book. They are arranged to reflect the units of this Annual Editions reader. You can link to these sites by going to www.mhhe.com/cls

All the articles that relate to each topic are listed below the bold-faced term.

Internet References

The following Internet sites have been selected to support the articles found in this reader. These sites were available at the time of publication. However, because websites often change their structure and content, the information listed may no longer be available. We invite you to visit www.mhhe.com/cls for easy access to these sites.

Annual Editions: American Foreign Policy 11/12

General Sources

Avalon Project at Yale Law School
www.yale.edu/lawweb/avalon/terrorism/terror.htm

The Avalon Project website features documents in the fields of law, history, economics, diplomacy, politics, government, and terrorism.

Center for Strategic and International Studies (CSIS)
www.csis.org

The Center for Strategic and International Studies (CSIS), which is a nonpartisan organization, has been dedicated to providing world leaders with strategic insights on, and policy solutions to, current and emerging global issues for 40 years. Currently, CSIS has responded to global terrorism threats by developing a variety of well-defined projects and responses that are available at this site.

Congressional Research Service Reports
www.fas.org/sgp/crs/

This site is maintained by the Federation of American Scientists. It contains a collection of foreign policy and national security reports written by the Congressional Research Service for members of Congress. They are not made directly available to the public online but are not classified and generally can be obtained from members of Congress on request.

The Federal Web Locator
www.lib.auburn.edu/madd/docs/fedloc.html

Use this handy site as a launching pad for the websites of federal U.S. agencies, departments, and organizations. It is well organized and easy to use for informational and research purposes.

Foreign Affairs
www.foreignaffairs.org

The Foreign Affairs site allows users to search the magazine's archives and provides access to the field's leading journals, documents, online resources, and so on. Links to dozens of other related websites are possible from here.

International Information Programs
www.america.gov/

This wide-ranging page offered by the State Department provides definitions, related documentation, and a discussion of topics of concern to students of foreign policy and foreign affairs. It addresses today's hot topics as well as ongoing issues that form the foundation of the field. Many Web links are provided.

Oneworld.net
www.oneworld.net/section/partners/

Search this site for information and news about issues related to human sustainable development throughout the world. Information is available by topic or by country.

United Nations Home Page
www.un.org

Here is the gateway to information about the United Nations.

U.S. International Affairs
www.state.gov/www/regions/internat.html

Data on U.S. foreign policy around the world are available here. Some of the areas covered are arms control, economics and trade, international organizations, environmental issues, terrorism, current treaties, and international women's issues.

UNIT 1: The United States and the World: Strategic Choices

The Bulletin of the Atomic Scientists
www.bullatomsci.org

This site allows you to read more about the Doomsday Clock and other issues as well as topics related to nuclear weaponry, arms control, and disarmament.

The Henry L. Stimson Center
www.stimson.org

The Stimson Center, a nonprofit and (self-described) nonpartisan organization, focuses on issues where policy, technology, and politics intersect. Use this site to find assessments of U.S. foreign policy in the post–Cold War world and to research many other topics.

International Network Information Center at University of Texas
http://inic.utexas.edu

This gateway has many pointers to international sites, organized into African, Asian, Latin American, Middle East, and Russian and east European subsections.

ISN International Relations and Security Network
www.isn.ethz.ch

Maintained by the Center for Security Studies and Conflict Research, this site is a clearinghouse for information on international relations and security policy. The many topics are listed by category (Traditional Dimensions of Security and New Dimensions of Security) and by major world regions.

UNIT 2: The United States and the World: Regional and Bilateral Relations

Inter-American Dialogue (IAD)
www.iadialog.org

This IAD website provides data on U.S. policy analysis, communication, and exchange in Western Hemisphere affairs. The organization has helped to shape the agenda of issues and choices in hemispheric relations.

Political Science Resources
www.psr.keele.ac.uk/psr.htm

This is a link to sources available via European addresses. Listed by country name, it includes official government pages, official documents, speeches, elections, and political events.

Internet References

Russian and East European Network Information Center
http://reenic.utexas.edu/reenic/index.html

Information ranging from women's issues to foreign relations and coverage of more than two dozen countries in central and eastern Europe and western Asia may be found here. Also check out University of Texas/Austin's site on Broader Asia (http://asnic.utexas.edu/asnic/index.html) for more insight into bilateral/regional relations.

World Wide Web Virtual Library: International Affairs Resources
www.etown.edu/vl/

Extensive links are available here to help you learn about specific countries and regions, to research for various think tanks, and to study such vital topics as international law, development, the international economy, human rights, and peacekeeping.

UNIT 3: The Domestic Side of American Foreign Policy

American Diplomacy
www.unc.edu/depts/diplomat/

American Diplomacy is an online journal of commentary, analysis, and research on U.S. foreign policy and its results around the world. It provides discussion and information on current news, such topics as Life in the Foreign Service, and A Look Back.

Carnegie Endowment for International Peace (CEIP)
www.ceip.org

One of the most important goals of CEIP is to stimulate discussion and learning among both experts and the public on a range of international issues. This site provides links to the magazine *Foreign Policy*, to the Carnegie Moscow Center, and to descriptions of various programs.

PEW Research Center Reports on Global Affairs/Public Attitudes
http://pewresearch.org/topics/globalattitudesforeignaffairs/

The PEW Research Center is a nonprofit organization that since 2005 has carried out surveys of international public opinion and U.S. public opinion on national security and other foreign policy issues. The Pew Global Attitudes Project website contains international public opinion data drawn from more than 100,000 interviews in more than 50 countries.

RAND
www.rand.org

RAND, a nonprofit institution that works to improve public policy through research and analysis, offers links to certain topics and descriptions of RAND activities as well as major research areas (such as international relations and strategic defense policy).

UNIT 4: The Institutional Context of American Foreign Policy

Central Intelligence Agency (CIA)
www.cia.gov

Use this official CIA page to learn about many facets of the agency and to connect to other sites and resources.

The NATO Integrated Data Service (NIDS)
www.nato.int/structur/nids/nids.htm

NIDS was created to bring information on security-related matters within easy reach of the widest possible audience. Check out this website to review North Atlantic Treaty Organization documentation of all kinds, to read *NATO Review* magazine, and to explore key issues in the field of European security and transatlantic cooperation.

U.S. Department of State
www.state.gov/index.html

This State Department page is a must for any student of foreign affairs. Explore this site to find out what the department does, what services it provides, what it says about U.S. interests around the world, and much more.

United States Institute of Peace (USIP)
www.usip.org

The USIP, which was created by Congress to promote peaceful resolution of international conflicts, seeks to educate people and disseminate information on how to achieve peace.

U.S. White House
www.whitehouse.gov

This official Web page for the White House includes information on the President and Vice President and What's New. See especially The Virtual Library and Briefing Room for Hot Topics and latest Federal Statistics.

UNIT 5: Foreign Policy Problems and the Policy Making Process

Belfer Center for Science and International Affairs (BCSIA)
http://belfercenter.ksg.harvard.edu/

BCSIA is the hub of the John F. Kennedy School of Government's research, teaching, and training in international affairs and is related to security, environment, and technology. This site provides insight into the development of leadership in policy making.

Central Intelligence Agency/Freedom of Information Act Special Documents
www.foia.cia.gov/soviet_estimates.asp

This site, run by the Central Intelligence Agency, offers the contents of a declassified set of national intelligence estimates from 1946–1991 on a range of important topics on national security policy. They provide insight into how crucial policy decisions were arrived at.

The Heritage Foundation
www.heritage.org

This page offers discussion about, and links to, many sites of the Heritage Foundation and other organizations having to do with foreign policy and foreign affairs.

National Archives and Records Administration (NARA)
www.archives.gov/index.html

This official site, which oversees the management of all federal records, offers easy access to background information for students interested in the policy making process, including a search of federal documents and speeches, and much more.

U.S. Department of State: The Network of Terrorism
http://usinfo.state.gov/products/pubs/

This website offers complete coverage from the American government's viewpoint regarding the war against terrorism. It provides a wealth of firsthand documentation and evidence.

UNIT 6: U.S. International Economic Strategy

International Monetary Fund (IMF)
www.imf.org

This website is essential reading for anyone wishing to learn more about this important body's effects on foreign policy and the global economy. It provides information about the IMF, directs readers to various publications and current issues, and suggests links to other organizations.

Internet References

United States Agency for International Development
www.usaid.gov/

Information is available here about broad and overlapping issues such as agriculture, democracy and governance, health, economic growth, and the environment in many regions and countries around the world.

United States Trade Representative
www.ustr.gov

The mission of the U.S. Trade Representative is presented on this site. Background information on international trade agreements and links to other sites may be accessed.

World Bank
www.worldbank.org

News (including press releases, summaries of new projects, and speeches), publications, and coverage of numerous topics regarding development, countries, and regions are provided at this website. It also contains links to other important global financial organizations.

UNIT 7: U.S. Military Strategy

Arms Control and Disarmament Agency (ACDA)
http://dosfan.lib.uic.edu/acda/

This archival ACDA page provides links to information on arms control and disarmament. Researchers can examine texts of various speeches, treaties, and historical documents. For further current information, go to the Bureau of Arms Control page at http://state.gov/t/ac/

Counterterrorism Page
http://counterterrorism.com

A summary of worldwide terrorism events, groups, and terrorism strategies and tactics, including articles from 1989 to the present of American and international origin, plus links to related websites and graphs are available on this site.

DefenseLINK
www.defenselink.mil/news/

Learn about the Department of Defense at this site. News, publications, photos, and other related sites of interest are noted.

Federation of American Scientists (FAS)
www.fas.org

FAS, a nonprofit policy organization, maintains this site to provide coverage of such topics as terrorism and weapons of mass destruction.

Human Rights Web
www.hrweb.org

The history of the human rights movement, text on seminal figures, landmark legal and political documents, and ideas on how individuals can get involved in helping to protect human rights around the world can be found here.

UNIT 8: The Iraq War, Afghanistan, and Beyond

Army Knowledge Online
www.us.army.mil

This website contains publications on U.S. Army strategic thinking and doctrine. One of the most significant documents on this site is FM3-24: Counterinsurgency. This 2006 document coauthored by General David Petraeus is the first major rewriting of U.S counterinsurgency doctrine in 25 years.

White House: Renewal in Iraq
www.whitehouse.gov/infocus/iraq/

View official White House reports, including presidential remarks, on this site.

UNIT 1

The United States and the World: Strategic Choices

Unit Selections

1. **From Hope to Audacity: Appraising Obama's Foreign Policy,** Zbigniew Brzezinski
2. **The World Still Needs a Leader,** Leslie H. Gelb
3. **Hegemony on the Cheap: Liberal Internationalism from Wilson to Bush,** Colin Dueck
4. **The Eagle Has Crash Landed,** Immanuel Wallerstein
5. **Pillars of the Next American Century,** James Kurth
6. **Grand Strategy for a Divided America,** Charles A. Kupchan and Peter L. Trubowitz
7. **Enemies into Friends: How the United States Can Court Its Adversaries,** Charles A. Kupchan

Key Points to Consider

- Make a scorecard of the successes and failures of the Obama administration's foreign policy to date. Defend your choices and explain why these policies turned out the way they did.

- How powerful is the United States today? How should it use its power?

- Make a list of the five most important foreign policy problems facing the United States today. Defend your choices and explain why you ranked them in this order.

- Has the United States become a rogue superpower? Defend your answer.

- What principles do you think should guide American foreign policy in the future?

- How much and what type of responsibility does the United States have for maintaining world order?

- How helpful is the past as a guide in constructing foreign policy strategies for the future?

Student Website
www.mhhe.com/cls

Internet References

The Bulletin of the Atomic Scientists
    www.bullatomsci.org
The Henry L. Stimson Center
    www.stimson.org
International Network Information Center at University of Texas
    http://inic.utexas.edu
ISN International Relations and Security Network
    www.isn.ethz.ch

Choice in foreign policy is always present. This was true even during the Cold War when a general consensus existed within the United States on the need to deter and contain the Soviet Union as policy makers debated how and where to implement these policies. Rolling back the iron curtain was a minority view during the 1950s and cooperation with the Soviet Union also was advocated by some during the immediate post–World War II period. In the late 1960s, a period of détente emerged as a serious competitor to containment and succeeded in supplanting it for a brief period of time.

No single vision of American foreign policy emerged as dominant in the first decade of the post–Cold War era. For some, the 1990s provided the United States with the long-awaited opportunity to walk away from the distracting and corrupting influence of international affairs and focus instead on domestic concerns and embrace traditional American values. For others, the 1990s represented a moment to be seized. Adherents to this perspective were divided over how to proceed. One group advocated replacing the strategies of conflict and confrontation of the Cold War with ones designed to foster cooperation among states and to lift the human condition. A second group saw it as an opportunity to reorder the world in America's image, for it had won the Cold War.

The terrorist attacks of 9/11 ended this debate. Defeating terrorism now was the unchallenged goal of American foreign policy and with it came a secondary goal of removing Saddam Hussein from power and democratizing Iraq. This new foreign policy consensus proved to be short lived. By the end of the George W. Bush administration doubt about the wisdom of becoming engaged in Iraq was widespread. Attention was being redirected to the problem of Afghanistan and its support for terrorism but with little of the enthusiasm for military operations that marked the beginning of the Iraq War. The incoming Obama administration also inherited ongoing foreign policy conflicts with the other two members of Bush's "axis of evil," Iran and North Korea, and a global economic order that was under stress. Progress toward creating a more open international economic order had slowed considerably with the failure of the Doha Talks and the continued emergence of China as a global economic power. A further complicating factor for American foreign policy was that the Bush administration's unilateral approach and belligerent tone had alienated many countries, making it more difficult for the United States to gain their support.

President Obama entered office promising to bring a "reset" to American foreign policy and to reverse the tensions that had arisen between the United States and the world. At the same time he proclaimed the need to move forward. His administration proclaimed that the United States could not go back to Cold War policies of containment, twentieth century balances of power, or nineteenth century concert of powers strategies. What was needed was a new global architecture. While important steps have been taken in "resetting" U.S. relations with the world, little was accomplished in moving relations forward. Agreements with Iran and North Korea remained elusive, as did arms control, and international economic and environmental agreements.

The essays in this unit introduce us to the scope of the contemporary debate over the strategic choices open to the United

Department of Defense/Lee Craker

States. They fall into three groups. The first article, "From Hope to Audacity," provides a generally positive assessment of Obama's foreign policy in his first year as president. The next four essays provide different views of how the United States is positioned in world politics today. Leslie Gelb, author of "The World Still Needs a Leader" argues that the United States is the world's only true leader and that without its leadership other countries cannot solve their problems. In "Hegemony on the Cheap," Colin Dueck criticizes Bush's pursuit of an ambitious Wilsonian agenda without adequate resources. Bush is not the first Wilsonian to err in this regard, argues Dueck. The next article, "The Eagle Has Crash Landed," raises the possibility that the United States has become a powerless superpower. The final article in this group, "Pillars of the Next American Century," looks at the sources of power available to the United States and calls for the reinstitution of these pillars of power. The final two articles in this section examine strategic options open to the United States today in more concrete form. "Grand Strategy for a Divided America" looks inward to divisions in American society for its inspiration, while "Enemies into Friends" looks outward to the dynamics of world politics in making its recommendations.

1

From Hope to Audacity
Appraising Obama's Foreign Policy

ZBIGNIEW BRZEZINSKI

The foreign policy of U.S. President Barack Obama can be assessed most usefully in two parts: first, his goals and decision-making system and, second, his policies and their implementation. Although one can speak with some confidence about the former, the latter is still an unfolding process.

To his credit, Obama has undertaken a truly ambitious effort to redefine the United States' view of the world and to reconnect the United States with the emerging historical context of the twenty-first century. He has done this remarkably well. In less than a year, he has comprehensively reconceptualized U.S. foreign policy with respect to several centrally important geopolitical issues:

- Islam is not an enemy, and the "global war on terror" does not define the United States' current role in the world;
- the United States will be a fair-minded and assertive mediator when it comes to attaining lasting peace between Israel and Palestine;
- the United States ought to pursue serious negotiations with Iran over its nuclear program, as well as other issues;
- the counterinsurgency campaign in the Taliban-controlled parts of Afghanistan should be part of a larger political undertaking, rather than a predominantly military one;
- the United States should respect Latin America's cultural and historical sensitivities and expand its contacts with Cuba;
- the United States ought to energize its commitment to significantly reducing its nuclear arsenal and embrace the eventual goal of a world free of nuclear weapons;
- in coping with global problems, China should be treated not only as an economic partner but also as a geopolitical one;
- improving U.S.-Russian relations is in the obvious interest of both sides, although this must be done in a manner that accepts, rather than seeks to undo, post–Cold War geopolitical realities; and
- a truly collegial transatlantic partnership should be given deeper meaning, particularly in order to heal the rifts caused by the destructive controversies of the past few years.

Obama has shown a genuine sense of strategic direction and a solid grasp of what today's world is all about.

For all that, he did deserve the Nobel Peace Prize. Overall, Obama has demonstrated a genuine sense of strategic direction, a solid grasp of what today's world is all about, and an understanding of what the United States ought to be doing in it. Whether these convictions are a byproduct of his personal history, his studies, or his intuitive sense of history, they represent a strategically and historically coherent worldview. The new president, it should be added, has also been addressing the glaring social and environmental dilemmas that confront humanity and about which the United States has been indifferent for too long. But this appraisal focuses on his responses to the most urgent geopolitical challenges.

Challenges to White House Leadership

Obama's overall perspective sets the tone for his foreign-policy-making team, which is firmly centered in the White House. The president relies on Vice President Joe Biden's broad experience in foreign affairs to explore ideas and engage in informal strategizing. National Security Adviser James Jones coordinates the translation of the president's strategic outlook into policy, while also having to manage the largest National Security Council in history—its over-200-person staff is almost four times as large as the NSC staffs of Richard Nixon, Jimmy Carter, and George H. W. Bush and almost ten times as large as John F. Kennedy's. The influence of Secretary of Defense Robert Gates on national security strategy has been growing steadily. Gates' immediate task is to successfully conclude two wars, but his influence is also felt on matters pertaining to Iran and Russia. Secretary of State Hillary Clinton, who has the president's ear as well as his confidence, is likewise a key participant in foreign policy decisions and is the country's top diplomat. Her own engagement is focused more on the increasingly urgent global issues of the new century, rather than on the geopolitical ones of the recent past.

Finally, Obama's two trusted political advisers, David Axelrod and Rahm Emanuel, who closely monitor the sensitive relationship between foreign and domestic politics, also participate in decision-making. (For example, both sat in on the president's critical September meeting with Israeli Prime Minister Benjamin Netanyahu.) When appropriate, policy discussions also include two experienced negotiators, George Mitchell, who conducts the Middle East peace negotiations, and Richard Holbrooke, who coordinates the regional response to the challenges in Afghanistan and Pakistan. In effect, they are an extension of the president's NSC-centered process.

On this team, Obama himself is the main source of the strategic direction, but, unavoidably, he is able to play this role on only a part-time basis. This is a weakness, because the conceptual initiator of a great power's foreign policy needs to be actively involved in supervising the design of the consequent strategic decisions, in overlooking their implementation, and in making timely adjustments. Yet Obama has had no choice but to spend much of his first year in office on domestic political affairs.

As a result, his grand redefinition of U.S. foreign policy is vulnerable to dilution or delay by upper-level officials who have the bureaucratic predisposition to favor caution over action and the familiar over the innovative. Some of them may even be unsympathetic to the president's priorities regarding the Middle East and Iran. It hardly needs to be added that officials who are not in sympathy with advocated policies rarely make good executors. Additionally, the president's domestic political advisers inevitably tend to be more sensitive to pressures from domestic interest groups. This usually fosters a reluctance to plan for a firm follow-through on bold presidential initiatives should they suddenly encounter a foreign rebuff reinforced by powerful domestic lobbies. Netanyahu's rejection of Obama's public demand that Israel halt the construction of settlements on the West Bank and in East Jerusalem is a case in point.

It is still too early to make a firm assessment of the president's determination to pursue his priorities, as most of the large issues that Obama has personally addressed involve long-range problems that call for long-term management. But three urgent issues do pose, even in the short run, an immediate and difficult test of his ability and his resolve to significantly change U.S. policy: the Israeli-Palestinian conflict, Iran's nuclear ambitions, and the Afghan-Pakistani challenge. Each of these also happens to be a sensitive issue at home.

The Israeli-Palestinian Conundrum

The first urgent challenge is, of course, the Middle East peace process. Obama stated early on that he would take the initiative on this issue and aim for a settlement in the relative near term. That position is justified historically and is in keeping with the United States' national interest. Paralysis over the Israeli-Palestinian conflict has lasted far too long, and leaving it unresolved has pernicious consequences for the Palestinians, for the region, and for the United States, and it will eventually harm Israel. It is not fashionable to say this, but it is demonstrably true that—deservedly or not—much of the current

hostility toward the United States in the Middle East and the Islamic world as a whole has been generated by the bloodshed and suffering produced by this prolonged conflict. Osama bin Laden's self-serving justifications for 9/11 are a reminder that the United States itself is also a victim of the Israeli-Palestinian conundrum.

By now, after more than 40 years of Israeli occupation of the West Bank and 30 years of peace negotiations, it is quite evident that left to themselves, neither the Israelis nor the Palestinians will resolve the conflict on their own. There are many reasons for this, but the bottom line is that the Palestinians are too divided and too weak to make the critical decisions necessary to push the peace process forward, and the Israelis are too divided and too strong to do the same. As a result, a firm external initiative defining the basic parameters of a final settlement is needed to jump-start serious negotiations between the two parties. And that can only come from the United States.

But the necessary outside stimulus has not yet been forthcoming in a fashion consistent with U.S. interests and potential. In raising the issue of the settlements in the spring of 2009 but then later backing off when rebuffed by the Israeli government, the administration strengthened the hard-line elements in Israel and undercut the more moderate elements on the Palestinian side. Then, an opportunity provided by the annual UN General Assembly meeting in September to identify the United States with the overwhelming global consensus about the basic parameters of a peace settlement was squandered. Instead of seizing it, Obama merely urged the Israelis and the Palestinians to negotiate in good faith.

Yet the existing global consensus could serve as a launching pad for serious negotiations on four basic points. First, Palestinian refugees should not be granted the right of return to what is now Israel, because Israel cannot be expected to commit suicide for the sake of peace. The refugees will have to be resettled within the Palestinian state, with compensation and maybe some expression of regret for their suffering. This will be very difficult for the Palestinian national movement to swallow, but there is no alternative.

Second, Jerusalem has to be shared, and shared genuinely. The Israeli capital, of course, would be in West Jerusalem, but East Jerusalem should be the capital of a Palestinian state, with the Old City shared under some international arrangement. If a genuine compromise on Jerusalem is not part of a settlement, resentment will persist throughout the West Bank and the Palestinians will reject the peace process. Although such a compromise will understandably be difficult for the Israelis to accept, without it there cannot be a peace of reconciliation.

Third, a settlement must be based on the 1967 lines, but with territorial swaps that would allow the large settlements to be incorporated into Israel without any further reduction of the territory of the Palestinian state. That means some territorial compensation for Palestine from parts of northern and southern Israel that border the West Bank. It is important to remember that although the Israeli and Palestinian populations are almost equal in number, under the 1967 lines the Palestinian territories account for only 22 percent of the old British mandate, whereas the Israeli territories account for 78 percent.

Fourth, the United States or NATO must make a commitment to station troops along the Jordan River. Such a move would reinforce Israel's security with strategic depth. It would reduce Israel's fears that an independent Palestine could some day serve as a springboard for a major Arab attack on Israel.

Had Obama embraced this internationally favored blueprint for peace when he addressed the UN in September, he would have exerted enormous influence on both the Israelis and the Palestinians and instantaneously gained global support. Failing to endorse this plan was a missed opportunity, especially since the two-state solution is beginning to lose some of its credibility as a viable formula for reconciliation between the Israelis and the Palestinians and within the region. Moreover, there are indications that the United States is already losing the goodwill and renewed confidence of the Arab world that Obama won with his speech in Cairo in June.

The United States is already losing the renewed confidence of the Arab world that Obama won with his speech in Cairo.

The next few months will be critical, and the time for decisive action is running out. Perhaps as a consolation to the Palestinians (and in spite of some opposition within the White House) or perhaps as a reaffirmation of his determination to continue pressing the parties to focus on the key issues, in his UN speech Obama called for final-status negotiations to begin soon and included on the agenda four items similar to these. He also made it explicitly clear that the talks' ultimate goal ought to be "a viable, independent Palestinian state with contiguous territory that ends the occupation that began in 1967." It can be hoped that the president seizes the moment offered by the Oslo ceremony at which the Nobel Peace Prize was awarded (which at the time of this writing had not yet occurred) to give more substance to his Middle East peace initiative. But so far, the Obama team has shown neither the tactical skill nor the strategic firmness needed to move the peace process forward.

The Iranian Challenge

Another urgent and potentially very dangerous challenge, with similarly huge stakes, is confronting Obama in Iran. It involves the true character of the Iranian nuclear program and Iran's role in the region. Obama has been determined to explore the path of serious negotiations with Iran despite domestic (and some foreign) agitation and even some opposition within the second echelon of his team. Without quite saying so, he has basically downgraded the U.S. military option, although it is still fashionable to say that "all options remain on the table." But the prospects for a successful negotiation are still quite uncertain.

Two fundamental questions complicate the situation. First, are the Iranians willing to negotiate—or even capable of doing so—seriously? The United States has to be realistic when discussing this aspect, since the clock cannot be turned back: the Iranians have the capability to enrich uranium, and

they are not going to give it up. But it is still possible, perhaps through a more intrusive inspection regime, to fashion a reasonably credible arrangement that prevents weaponization. Nonetheless, even if the United States and its partners approach the negotiations with a constructive mindset, the Iranians themselves may scuttle any serious prospects for a positive outcome. Already, at the outset of the negotiating process, Iran's credibility was undermined by the convoluted manner in which Tehran complicated a promising compromise for a cooperative Iranian-Russian-French arrangement for processing its enriched uranium.

Second, is Washington willing to engage in negotiations with some degree of patience and with sensitivity to the mentality of the other side? It would not be conducive to serious negotiations if the United States were to persist in publicly labeling Iran as a terrorist state, as a state that is not to be trusted, as a state against which sanctions or even a military option should be prepared. Doing that would simply play into the hands of the most hardline elements in Iran. It would facilitate their appeal to Iranian nationalism, and it would narrow the cleavage that has recently emerged in Iran between those who desire a more liberal regime and those who seek to perpetuate a fanatical dictatorship.

These points must be borne in mind if and when additional sanctions become necessary. Care should be taken to make certain that the sanctions are politically intelligent and that they isolate the regime rather than unify all Iranians. Sanctions must punish those in power—not the Iranian middle class, as an embargo on gasoline would do. The unintended result of imposing indiscriminately crippling sanctions would likely be to give the Iranians the impression that the United States' real objective is to prevent their country from acquiring even a peaceful nuclear program—and that, in turn, would fuel nationalism and outrage.

Sanctions against Iran must punish those in power—not the middle class, as an embargo on gasoline would do.

Moreover, even the adoption of politically discriminating sanctions is likely to be complicated by international constraints. China, given its dependence on Middle Eastern (and particularly Iranian) oil, fears the consequences of a sharpened crisis. The position of Russia is ambiguous since as a major energy supplier to Europe, it stands to benefit financially from a prolonged crisis in the Persian Gulf that would prevent the entrance of Iranian oil into the European market. Indeed, from the Russian geopolitical perspective, a steep rise in the price of oil as a result of a conflict in the Persian Gulf would be most economically damaging to the United States and China—countries whose global preeminence Russia tends to resent and even fear—and would make Europe even more dependent on Russian energy.

Throughout this complicated process, firm presidential leadership will be required. That is particularly so because of the presence of influential voices in the United States, both inside and outside the administration, in favor of a negotiating process that minimizes the possibility of a reasonable compromise. Prior to joining the administration, some senior second-level officials seemed to favor policies designed to force an early confrontation with Iran and even advocated joint military consultations with Israel regarding the use of force. The somewhat sensationalized manner in which the administration revealed in late September that it had been aware for months of the secret Iranian nuclear facility near Qom suggests internal disagreements over tactics.

Ultimately, a larger strategic question is at stake: Should the United States' long-term goal be the evolution of Iran into a stabilizing power in the Middle East? To state the issue even more sharply and simply: Should its policy be designed to encourage Iran to eventually become a partner of the United States again—and even, as it was for three decades, of Israel? The wider the agenda—one that addressed regional security issues, potential economic cooperation, and so on—the greater the possibility of finding acceptable quid pro quos. Or should Iran be treated as if it is fated to remain a hostile and destabilizing power in an already vulnerable region?

As of this writing, an acceptable outcome to the negotiations is obviously still very much in doubt. Assuming they are not aborted, by early 2010 it may be possible to make a calmly calculated judgment as to whether the talks are worth continuing or whether there in fact is no room for reciprocal compromises. At that point, politically intelligent sanctions may become timely. So far, Obama has shown that he is aware of the need to combine strategic firmness with tactical flexibility; he is patiently exploring whether diplomacy can lead to an accommodation. He has avoided any explicit commitment to a precise deadline (unlike France's grandstanding in favor of a December date), and he has not engaged in explicit threats of military action.

Those advocating a tougher stance should remember that the United States would bear the brunt of the painful consequences in the event of an attack on Iran, whether the United States or Israel launched it. Iran would likely target U.S. forces in Afghanistan and Iraq, possibly destabilizing both countries; the Strait of Hormuz could become a blazing war zone; and Americans would again pay steep prices at the gas pump. Iran is an issue regarding which, above all, Obama must trust himself to lead and not to be led. So far, he has done so.

The AFPAK Quagmire

The third urgent and politically sensitive foreign policy issue is posed by the Afghan-Pakistani predicament. Obama has moved toward abandoning some of the more ambitious, even ideological, objectives that defined the United States' initial engagement in Afghanistan—the creation of a modern democracy, for example. But the United States must be very careful lest its engagement in Afghanistan and Pakistan, which still has primarily and most visibly a military dimension, comes to be viewed by the Afghans and the Pakistanis as yet another case of Western colonialism and elicits from them an increasingly militant response.

Some top U.S. generals have recently stated that the United States is not winning militarily, an appraisal that ominously suggests the conflict with the Taliban could become similar to

the Soviet Union's earlier confrontation with Afghan resistance. A comprehensive strategic reassessment has thus become urgently needed. The proposal made in September by France, Germany, and the United Kingdom for an international conference on the subject was helpful and timely; the United States was wise to welcome it. But to be effective, any new strategy has to emphasize two key elements. First, the Afghan government and NATO should seek to engage locally in a limited process of accommodation with receptive elements of the Taliban. The Taliban are not a global revolutionary or terrorist movement, and although they are a broad alliance with a rather medieval vision of what Afghanistan ought to be, they do not directly threaten the West. Moreover, they are still very much a minority phenomenon that ultimately can be defeated only by other Afghans (helped economically and militarily by the United States and its NATO allies), a fact that demands a strategy that is more political than military.

Additionally, the United States needs to develop a policy for gaining the support of Pakistan, not just in denying the Taliban a sanctuary in Pakistan but also in pressuring the Taliban in Afghanistan to accommodate. Given that many Pakistanis may prefer a Taliban-controlled Afghanistan to a secular Afghanistan that leans toward Pakistan's archrival, India, the United States needs to assuage Pakistan's security concerns in order to gain its full cooperation in the campaign against the irreconcilable elements of the Taliban. In this regard, the support of China could be helpful, particularly considering its geopolitical stake in regional stability and its traditionally close ties with Islamabad.

It is likely that before this appraisal hits the newsstands, Obama will have announced a more comprehensive strategy for attaining a politically acceptable outcome to the ongoing conflict—and one that U.S. allies are also prepared to support. His approach so far has been deliberate. He has been careful to assess both the military and the political dimensions of the challenge and also to take into account the views of U.S. allies. Nothing would be worse for NATO than if one part of the alliance (western Europe) left the other part of the alliance (the United States) alone in Afghanistan. Such a fissure over NATO's first campaign initially based on Article 5, the collective defense provision, would probably spell the end of the alliance.

How Obama handles these three urgent and interrelated issues—the Israeli-Palestinian peace process, the Iranian dilemma, and the Afghan-Pakistani conflict—will determine the United States' global role for the foreseeable future. The consequences of a failed peace process in the Middle East, a military collision with Iran, and an intensifying military engagement in Afghanistan and Pakistan all happening simultaneously could commit the United States for many years to a lonely and self-destructive conflict in a huge and volatile area. Eventually, that could spell the end of the United States' current global preeminence.

Key Strategic Relationships

The president, in addition to coping with these immediate challenges, has indicated his intent to improve three key geopolitical relationships of the United States: with Russia, with China, and with Europe. Each involves longer-term dilemmas but does not require crisis management now. Each has its own peculiarities: Russia is a former imperial power with revisionist ambitions but declining social capital; China is a rising world power that is modernizing itself at an astonishing pace but deliberately downplaying its ambitions; Europe is a global economic power devoid of either military clout or political will. Obama has rightly indicated that the United States needs to collaborate more closely with each of them.

Hence, the administration decided to "reset" the United States' relationship with Russia. But that slogan is confusing, and it is not yet clear that Washington's wishful thinking about Moscow's shared interests on such matters as Iran is fully justified. Nonetheless, the United States must think strategically about its long-term relationship with Russia and pursue a two-track policy: it has to cooperate with Russia whenever doing so is mutually beneficial, but in a way that is also responsive to historical reality. The age of closed empires is over, and Russia, for the sake of its own future, will eventually have to accept this.

Seeking to expand cooperation with Russia does not mean condoning Russia's subordination of Georgia (through which the vital Baku-Tbilisi-Ceyhan pipeline passes, providing Europe with access to Central Asian energy) or its intimidation of Ukraine (an industrial and agricultural heartland of the former Soviet Union). Either move would be a giant step backward. Each would intensify Russia's imperial nostalgia and central Europe's security fears, not to mention increase the possibility of armed conflicts. Yet so far, the Obama administration has been quite reluctant to provide even purely defensive arms to Georgia (in contrast to Russia's provision of offensive weaponry to Venezuela), nor has it been sufficiently active in encouraging the EU to be more responsive to Ukraine's European aspirations. Fortunately, Vice President Biden's fall 2009 visit to Poland, Romania, and the Czech Republic did reaffirm the United States' long-term interest in political pluralism within the former Soviet space and in a cooperative relationship with a truly postimperial Russia. And it should always be borne in mind that the survival of the former makes the latter more likely.

A longer-term effort to engage China in a more forthcoming approach to global problems is also needed. China is, as it has proclaimed, "rising peacefully," and unlike Russia, it is patiently self-confident. But one can also argue that China is rising somewhat selfishly and needs to be drawn more broadly into constructive cooperation on global economic, financial, and environmental decisions. It also has growing political influence over geopolitical issues that affect core U.S. interests: North Korea, Iran, Afghanistan and Pakistan, and even the Israeli-Palestinian conflict.

Thus, Obama's decision to develop a top-level bilateral U.S.-Chinese relationship has been timely. Cultivating at the presidential-summit level a de facto geopolitical G-2 (not to be confused with proposals for an economic G-2), highlighted by Obama's November visit to China, is helping develop an increasingly significant strategic dialogue. The leaders of the United States and China recognize that both countries have a major stake in an effectively functioning world system. And they appear to appreciate the historic potential and the respective national interests inherent in such a bilateral relationship.

Paradoxically, despite Obama's expressed desire, there seem to be fewer prospects in the near future for a strategically significant enhancement of the United States' relationship with its closest political, economic, and military partner: Europe. Obama's predecessor left a bitter legacy there, which Obama has greatly redressed in terms of public opinion. But genuine strategic cooperation on a global scale is not possible with a partner that not only has no defined and authoritative political leadership but also lacks an internal consensus regarding its world role.

Hence, Obama's intent to reignite the Atlantic partnership is necessarily limited to dialogues with the three key European states with genuine international clout: the United Kingdom, Germany, and France. But the utility of such dialogues is reduced by the personal and political differences among these countries' leaders—not to mention the British prime minister's grim political prospects, the French president's preoccupation with personal celebrity, and the German chancellor's eastward gaze. The emergence of a unified and therefore influential European worldview, with which Obama could effectively engage, seems unlikely anytime soon.

Domestic Impediments

What then, on balance, can be said of Obama's foreign policy? So far, it has generated more expectations than strategic breakthroughs. Nonetheless, Obama has significantly altered U.S. policies regarding the three most urgent challenges facing the country. But as a democracy, the United States has to base its foreign policy decisions on domestic political consent. And unfortunately for Obama, gaining that support is becoming more difficult because of three systemic weaknesses that impede the pursuit of an intelligent and decisive foreign policy in an increasingly complex global setting.

So far, Obama's foreign policy has generated more expectations than strategic breakthroughs.

The first is that foreign policy lobbies have become more influential in U.S. politics. Thanks to their access to Congress, a variety of lobbies—some financially well endowed, some backed by foreign interests—have been promoting, to an unprecedented degree, legislative intervention in foreign-policy making. Now more than ever, Congress not only actively opposes foreign policy decisions but even imposes some on the president. (The pending legislation on sanctions against Iran is but one example.) Such congressional intervention, promoted by lobbies, is a serious handicap in shaping a foreign policy meant to be responsive to the ever-changing realities of global politics and makes it more difficult to ensure that U.S.—not foreign—interests are the point of departure.

The second, documented by a 2009 RAND study, pertains to the deepening ideological cleavage that is reducing the prospects for effective bipartisanship in foreign policy. The resulting polarization not only makes a bipartisan foreign policy less likely, but it also encourages the infusion of demagogy into policy conflicts. And it poisons the public discourse. Still worse, personal vilification and hateful, as well as potentially violent, rhetoric are becoming widespread in that realm of political debate that is subject to neither fact checking nor libel laws: the blogosphere.

Last but not least, of the large democratic countries, the United States has one of the least informed publics when it comes to global affairs. Many Americans, as various *National Geographic* surveys have shown, are not even familiar with basic global geography. Their knowledge of other countries' histories and cultures is not much better. How can a public unfamiliar with geography or foreign history have even an elementary grasp of, say, the geopolitical dilemmas that the United States faces in Afghanistan and Pakistan? With the accelerating decline in the circulation of newspapers and the trivialization of once genuinely informative television reporting, reliable and timely news about critical global issues is becoming less available to the general public. In that context, demagogically formulated solutions tend to become more appealing, especially in critical moments.

Together, these three systemic weaknesses are complicating efforts to gain public support for a rational foreign policy attuned to the complexity of the global dilemmas facing the United States. Obama's instinct is to lead by conciliation. That has been his political experience, and it has obviously been the key to his electoral success. Conciliation, backed by personal inspiration and the mass mobilization of populist hopes, is indeed the most important impetus for moving a policy agenda forward in a large democracy. In campaigning for the presidency, Obama proved that he was a master both of social conciliation and of political mobilization. But he has not yet made the transition from inspiring orator to compelling statesman. Advocating that something happen is not the same as making it happen.

In the tough realities of world affairs, leadership also requires an unrelenting firmness in overcoming foreign opposition, in winning the support of friends, in negotiating seriously when necessary with hostile states, and in gaining grudging respect even from those governments that the United States sometimes has an interest in intimidating. To these ends, the optimal moment for blending national aspirations with decisive leadership is when the personal authority of the president is at its highest—usually during the first year in office. For President Obama, alas, that first year has been dominated by the economic crisis and the struggle over health-care reform. The next three years may thus be more difficult. For the United States' national interest, but also for humanity's sake, that makes it truly vital for Obama to pursue with tenacious audacity the soaring hopes he unleashed.

ZBIGNIEW BRZEZINSKI was U.S. National Security Adviser from 1977 to 1981. His most recent book is *Second Chance: Three Presidents and the Crisis of American Superpower.*

From *Foreign Affairs,* vol. 89, no. 1, January/February 2010, pp. 16–30. Copyright © 2010 by Council on Foreign Relations. Reprinted by permission. www.ForeignAffairs.com

The World Still Needs a Leader

Leslie H. Gelb

Great powers no longer dominate world politics in the same way they have throughout history. They probably never will again. Today, weaker states are better able to resist the strong. Indeed, strong states rarely consider it worth the cost to conquer weaker states. Further, many of the worst problems in today's world—civil wars, poverty, genocide, failing and failed states, domestic terrorism—occur within nations, rather than between them, and thus are much harder to affect from the outside. At the same time, many growing challenges such as climate change, cyber security, and pandemics are transnational, global, and terribly complex, and thus require the attention of many nations and not just the most powerful. These considerations are all relatively new, and together they have profoundly altered the exercise of international power.

That said, major powers still hold a disproportionate amount of power and remain uniquely capable of either affirmative or blocking action. And among great nations, the United States still stands atop the power ladder—not as a dominant power, but as the leading one. No one seriously questions these propositions except schools of "levelers," who seem to believe that most states are now roughly on the same footing, and "declinists," who never cease to foretell America's fall.

The point is this: The actions of major powers usually turn on the actions of the United States—the one nation capable of exercising leadership on international issues such as security, trade, climate change, and terrorism—and this will remain true for the foreseeable future. The central issue regarding America's role in the world then becomes: How should Washington think about and use its power to either preempt problems or help solve them?

To bring some order to this labyrinth, three sets of questions should be considered. First, how does Washington's power today compare with its power during the cold war? Was the United States really dominant then, as some assert? Second, how is power distributed in the twenty-first–century world? What characterizes the new context for exercising US power; and what kinds of power are effective in various situations? Third, how can American leaders use their power more effectively, toward what goals, and by employing which strategies?

Bipolar Politics

It would be misleading to see the era that began in 1945 and ended with the collapse of the Soviet empire in the late 1980s and early 1990s as a period of US dominance, even though

dominance sometimes occurred. In the bipolar world of the time, the Soviet Union exercised considerable supremacy in its sphere, based almost entirely on military might and a willingness to use force brutally. The United States held sway within its own sphere, largely because of its clear economic superiority and global military capabilities, and because it was the world's sole defender against the spread of communism.

Soviet-US relations amounted to a virtual power stalemate. This was not because the Soviet Union's power actually equaled Washington's; it did not. Moscow's power was mostly military, while Washington's was both broader—military, economic, political—and deeper. When the Soviet Union exercised power beyond its own empire, this was mostly because Washington effectively gave away free power. US political leaders exaggerated Soviet power to the point that Moscow was accorded stature in excess of its actual power. As a result, Washington could not gain bargaining advantages (or other advantages) over Moscow, and vice versa. Relations became more tense than usual during occasional confrontations over Korea, Berlin, or Cuba, and less tense during occasional, mutually useful negotiations. But the United States did not dominate the Soviet Union.

From 1945 until the late 1950s, the United States made substantial efforts to rebuild the economies of Western Europe (particularly Germany) and Japan—indeed, by the end of the cold war, these ruined regions had become leading economic powers. This proved a successful strategy for defending the West against communism. But at the same time that America's new allies gained internal strength, they also gained international position and the power to bargain with Washington.

This was also an era when nation-states exploded in number, going from just a few dozen in the 1940s to nearly 200 as the century closed. Large numbers of former colonies gained independence and statehood during the cold war; almost all were poor and politically weak, making them fertile territory for communist exploitation. Most tests of power involving the two superpowers took place in the developing world.

More tellingly, the new nations (along with traditionally weak states) began to teach major powers unhappy lessons about their power to resist—specifically, that military force could not accomplish what it had once accomplished. Both France and the United States felt the sting of this point in Vietnam, and the Soviets felt it even more devastatingly in Afghanistan. In 1979, the United States was humbled as well by revolutionaries in Iran, who held Americans hostage for well over a year without suffering US military retribution (other than a failed rescue mission).

Once the Soviet empire collapsed, it became fashionable to proclaim a period of US dominance. The trumpeters were wrong. The United States had become the sole superpower, but it still lacked dominance. When true unipolarity did not materialize, fashionable writers dove to the other extreme and pronounced the world multipolar, characterized by an unprecedented leveling of power. Again, they were wrong.

Today's Power Realities

The twenty-first–century world is neither flat nor nonpolar. Rather, it is highly pyramidal. The United States is alone at the pinnacle, with formidable and unique powers of global leadership, but without the power to dominate. Stacked below the United States are many tiers of states, but most power is concentrated in the top tiers, among relatively few states. Nonetheless, states below the top tiers are powerful enough to block action.

In the new pyramid of power, on almost every major issue, the United States still stands as the only country capable of global action and leadership. Its economy, despite its current travails, outstrips all others. Its military, alone among militaries, possesses global reach. And diplomatically, Washington remains at the center of most international transactions.

For all the growth in anti-Americanism over the past decade, most countries distrust the United States far less than they distrust one another, and many still look to Washington for help and protection. Many countries continue to see the United States as a source of balance in their regions as well as their sole protector against potential regional threats, be they China or Iran.

The second tier in the pyramid is occupied by eight major powers: Russia, China, India, Brazil, Japan, Germany, France, and Britain. These countries carry considerable weight in their own regions but also have an international voice. The third tier includes oil-rich states like Saudi Arabia and certain states, such as Canada, that have carved out roles by virtue of their global activities. Nestled throughout the pyramid are significant new international players—international business and nongovernmental organizations. They all have to be factored into strategies for using power effectively.

A New US Strategy

In this new world, the key to an effective US power strategy is not simply for the United States to wield power or to lead, but to use its power toward solving common problems. Washington does not have enough power to compel others to follow its lead—unless other countries think there is something in it for them. This, in turn, means that American leaders have to take the interests of others into account and, beyond that, compromise in their framing of common policies to ensure the participation and cooperation of other states.

This approach does not condemn Washington to a future of denying its own essential interests or compromising away its essential positions. The basis of America's real leverage is

that it is the only world leader. Other nations know they cannot solve *their* problems without US leadership and power. Washington therefore has inherent advantages in bargaining, with which it can readily protect its interests.

Nor is Washington condemned to engaging in a fruitless marathon of multilateralism. American leaders do not need endlessly to increase the number of countries involved in multilateral efforts. Rather, what they should concentrate on is bringing together key countries—mostly the eight major powers, and a few others that are important to whatever matter is at hand. These "power coalitions" can then trigger necessary additional participation from other states.

President Barack Obama's handling of the September 2009 Group of 20 meeting in Pittsburgh was a good example of this approach in the economic sphere. Participants agreed on continued stimulus packages and regulatory reforms—and when countries that make up so much of world GDP take such actions, others will follow.

These power coalitions, however, need to be mindful of how to make the best use of different kinds of power in the new international environment. Foreign policy power is the power necessary to build coalitions. It includes all dimensions of power—stage-setting (which others call "soft power"), military, economic, and political or diplomatic. Getting the job done almost always requires a package of these various powers.

Stage-setting is not itself an exercise of power; it involves preparing the political landscape in a target country with words and deeds designed to increase receptivity to the subsequent exercise of power. It is mostly rhetoric, the kind in which Obama has excelled—in contrast to George W. Bush.

Military power is the most misunderstood form of power. It is not the actual use of force, nor is it mere military capability. It is the use of capabilities and demonstrated prowess to get leaders to do what they would not otherwise do. It is psychological and political, as is all power. US military force is sufficient to conquer the capital cities of most countries, but not countries themselves. That said, military power remains the principal ingredient of the principal security instrument: deterrence. There is no doubt that Iranian and Libyan leaders trembled after America's rapid and total victory over Saddam Hussein. The tragedy was that Bush did not use this fear to negotiate with Iran as he did with Libya. Libya gave up its weapons of mass destruction and its support of terrorism in the bargain.

Economic power is a much more complicated instrument and works much more slowly than force. If military power is the storm, economic power is more like the tide: It takes time for it to eat into the political decisions of target nations.

In today's world, economics is the main means of influencing others. For Washington this presents opportunities, since the US economy is still the largest and most dynamic, and it still produces almost one-quarter of the world's gross output. However, the use of this power presents difficulties as well: Much of America's economic power is not wielded or even controlled by the US government, but by private business.

Political or diplomatic power is the merging of action and language. It requires a depth of knowledge about others' political societies so as to gauge which instruments work and which do not. Equally important, it requires good strategy—that is, a clear sense of threats and opportunities, achievable goals, and a step-by-step plan for moving toward success. Americans usually want everything, yesterday—and do not get it. Consider the ever-repeated example of Washington pushing Israelis and Palestinians to the negotiating table for final status talks, which invariably fail. The power remedy here is to initiate confidence-building measures that establish a political basis for compromise at the discussion table.

Staying on Top

Despite all the new limitations on power, it remains the principal coin of the international realm. Nothing of value gets done without it, and power still comes down to pressure and coercion rather than love and law or newfangled international coalitions.

Despite all the new limitations on power, it remains the principal coin of the international realm.

Most nations still look to Washington and US power to provide the necessary leadership for solving or managing common problems. But the United States is falling short, and falling shorter every day. Its leaders seem to lack the political skills needed to build domestic support for practical applications of power and needed to build necessary patience. Even more worrisome than this is a decline in America's economic strength—a strength that has underpinned US pragmatism and confidence in democratic institutions, and that has enabled America's vast military superiority and its overall influence overseas.

To stay on top and to lead effectively, America's leaders must focus much more on restoring the nation's economic potential and much less on fighting unwinnable wars and pursuing unachievable nation-building goals in the most troublesome countries. Without a new strategic focus, the United States will squander its power and the world will find itself without a leader.

LESLIE H. GELB is president emeritus of the Council on Foreign Relations, a former senior official in the US departments of defense and state, and a former columnist with *The New York Times*. He is the author of *Power Rules: How Common Sense Can Rescue American Foreign Policy* (Harper, 2009).

Hegemony on the Cheap

Liberal Internationalism from Wilson to Bush

COLIN DUECK

One of the conventional criticisms of the Bush administration's foreign policy is that it is excessively and even disastrously unilateralist in approach. According to the critics, the administration has turned its back on a longstanding and admirable American tradition of liberal internationalism in foreign affairs, and in doing so has provoked resentment worldwide.[1] But these criticisms misinterpret both the foreign policy of George W. Bush, as well as America's liberal internationalist tradition. In reality, Bush's foreign policy since 9/11 has been heavily influenced by traditional liberal internationalist assumptions—assumptions that all along have had a troubling impact on U.S. foreign policy behavior and fed into the current situation in Iraq.

The conduct of America's foreign relations has—for more than a hundred years, going back at least to the days of John Hay's "Open Door" Notes and McKinley's hand wringing over the annexation of the Philippines—been shaped, to a greater or lesser extent, by a set of beliefs that can only be called liberal. These assumptions specify that the United States should promote, wherever practical and possible, an international system characterized by democratic governments and open markets.[2] President Bush reiterated these classical liberal assumptions recently, in his speech last November to the National Endowment for Democracy, when he outlined what he called "a forward strategy of freedom in the Middle East." In that speech, Bush argued that "as long as the Middle East remains a place where freedom does not flourish, it will remain a place of stagnation, resentment, and violence ready for export." In this sense, he suggested, the United States has a vital strategic interest in the democratization of the region. But Bush also added that "the advance of freedom leads to peace," and that democracy is "the only path to national success and dignity," providing as it does certain "essential principles common to every successful society, in every culture."[3] These words could just as easily have been spoken by Woodrow Wilson, Franklin Roosevelt—or Bill Clinton. They are well within the mainstream American tradition of liberal internationalism. Of course, U.S. foreign policy officials have never promoted a liberal world order simply out of altruism. They have done so out of the belief that such a system would serve American interests, by making the United States more prosperous, influential, and secure. Americans have also frequently disagreed over how to best promote liberal goals overseas.[4] Nevertheless, it is fair to say that liberal goals and assumptions, broadly conceived, have had a powerful impact on American foreign policy, especially since the presidency of Woodrow Wilson.

The problem with the liberal or Wilsonian approach, however, has been that it tends to encourage very ambitious foreign policy goals and commitments, while assuming that these goals can be met without commensurate cost or expenditure on the part of the United States. Liberal internationalists, that is, tend to define American interests in broad, expansive, and idealistic terms, without always admitting the necessary costs and risks of such an expansive vision. The result is that sweeping and ambitious goals are announced, but then pursued by disproportionately limited means, thus creating an outright invitation to failure. Indeed, this disjuncture between ends and means has been so common in the history of American diplomacy over the past century that it seems to be a direct consequence of the nation's distinctly liberal approach to international relations.

The Bush administration's current difficulties in Iraq are therefore not an isolated event. Nor are they really the result of the president's supposed preference for unilateralism. On the contrary, the administration's difficulties in Iraq are actually the result of an excessive reliance on classically liberal or Wilsonian assumptions regarding foreign affairs. The administration has willed the end in Iraq—and a very ambitious end—but it has not fully willed the means. In this sense, the Bush administration is heir to a long liberal internationalist tradition that runs from Woodrow Wilson, through FDR and Harry Truman, to Bill Clinton. And Bush inherits not only the strengths of that tradition, but also its weaknesses and flaws.

The Lost Alliance

The liberal internationalist pattern of disjuncture between ends and means really begins in earnest with Woodrow Wilson. Wilson, of course, traveled to Europe at the end of 1918, in the wake of the First World War, intending to "make the world safe for democracy" while insisting that a universal League of Nations serve as the linchpin for a new international order. Wilson intended the League to function as a promoter of collective security arrangements, by guaranteeing the territorial integrity and political independence of all member states. But Wilson also intended the League to function, more broadly, as the embodiment of a nascent liberal international order where war would be outlawed and self-determination would remain supreme. The other great powers were to be asked to abandon their imperialistic spheres of influence, their protectionist tariff barriers, their secretive military alliances, and their swollen armories.[5]

Needless to say, in practice, such concessions were hard to extract. The actual outcome at the Paris Peace Conference, contrary to Wilson's desire, was a series of compromises: Japan maintained its sphere of influence in the Chinese province of Shantung; Britain maintained its great navy, as well as its colonial conquests from Germany and Turkey; many of the arrangements negotiated in secret by the Allied powers during the war were in fact observed, though running contrary to Wilson's own pronouncements (including the famous Fourteen Points); and in blatant disregard of Wilson's alleged aversion to "old diplomacy" horse trading, France and Britain had their way vis-à-vis the peace terms imposed on Germany at Versailles while obtaining an explicit security guarantee from the United States.[6] To be sure, Wilson did succeed in winning the assent of the other victorious powers toward common membership in a new League of Nations. Furthermore, it is clear that he took the League's collective security obligations quite seriously. He certainly hoped that future acts of territorial aggression could be prevented through such peaceful means as deterrence, arbitration, and the use of economic sanctions. But in the final analysis, he understood perfectly well that collective security would at times have to be enforced militarily, through the use of armed force on the part of member states. Indeed, Wilson said quite explicitly that the League was meant to function as "a single overwhelming, powerful group of nations who shall be the trustee of the peace of the world."[7] And the United States was to be the leading member of this group.

Still, at the same time that Wilson laid out this extremely ambitious vision, he refused to draw the logical implications for the United States. Obviously, under any sort of meaningful commitment to a worldwide collective security system, the United States would henceforth be obliged to help enforce the peace in areas outside its traditional sphere of influence as proclaimed in the Monroe Doctrine (and subsequent "corollaries")—that is to say, in Europe and Asia. This would necessarily require maintaining a large standing army. Yet Wilson refused to admit that any such requirement existed, just as he disingenuously maintained that the League's covenant would not impinge on America's sovereignty, by insisting that said article carried only a "moral" obligation. In fact, he argued that the League would render a large standing army unnecessary.

Some of Wilson's Republican critics, especially in Congress, far from being isolationist know-nothings, saw through the contradictions in the president's vision, and advocated a pragmatic alternative. Led by Sen. Henry Cabot Lodge, these conservative internationalists called for a straightforward security pact with France and Great Britain as the key to their and America's own postwar security. Lodge and his supporters were willing to enter into the new League of Nations, but not into any global collective security arrangement. These Republican internationalists favored clear but restricted U.S. strategic commitments within Western Europe as the best guarantee of future peace.[8]

Lodge's alternative of a limited, Western alliance actually made perfect sense, strategically speaking. It avoided the impossible implication that America would come to the aid of any state, worldwide, whose territory or integrity was threatened. At the same time, it specified that the United States would defend France from any future attack by Germany while encouraging Britain to do the same. In this way, America's strategic commitments would be based upon concrete, vital national interests, rather than upon vague universalities; and upon real military capabilities, rather than utopian aspirations. The one problem with this alternative vision is that it seems to have been incompatible with domestic liberal pieties. Even Lodge admitted in 1919—at the time of the battle in the Senate over the League—that the idea of a League of Nations was quite popular in America. As Wilson himself suggested, the only way to preserve America's sense of moral superiority, while at the same time bringing its weight to bear in favor of international stability, was through membership in a universal organization, rather than through any particular and "entangling alliances."[9] Lodge and his supporters managed to defeat Wilson's League in the Senate, but they did not succeed in replacing it with a more realistic alternative.

Containment

During the Second World War, Franklin Roosevelt attempted to learn from Wilson's mistakes by carefully building domestic support for American membership in a postwar United Nations. Roosevelt was much more flexible in his approach than Wilson had been. But in terms of his substantive vision for the postwar order, Roosevelt was hardly any less idealistic than Wilson. Roosevelt's "grand design" was that the five major powers fighting the Axis would cooperate in policing the postwar system, each power (more or less) within its own regional sphere of influence. At the same time, however, each great power was to respect such liberal norms as nonaggression, democratic institutions, and free trade within its own sphere.[10] FDR was strikingly successful in nudging the American public toward a new internationalist consensus. His administration laid the groundwork for U.S. postwar leadership of a more liberal international political and economic order. The one great stumbling block to Roosevelt's plans was the Soviet Union. Roosevelt recognized that Moscow would end the war with disproportionate influence over Eastern Europe, but he insisted that such influence be exercised in a benign, democratic, and non-coercive fashion. Stalin, of course, would not accept such conditions, whatever his rhetorical commitments to the contrary. Once this basic clash of interests between Washington and Moscow became visible for all to see, by the end of 1945, American officials were faced with the inevitable dilemma of how to respond to Soviet behavior. To allow the Soviet Union to construct, with impunity, an autarchic, militarized sphere of influence within Eastern Europe—and beyond—would have flown in the face of America's wartime objectives. The United States, under Truman, therefore settled on a strategy of containment in order to curb Soviet power and at the same time preserve FDR's hope for a more liberal world order.

Containment was a pragmatic strategy, but it was also very much influenced by Wilsonian assumptions regarding the nature of international relations. The purpose of containment, after all, was not simply to check or balance the Soviet Union, but also to nurture the long-term vitality and interdependence of an American-led, liberal international order outside of the Communist bloc.[11] The strategists of containment refused to accept permanent Soviet control over Eastern Europe, or to negotiate in earnest with Moscow over the outlines of a general postwar settlement that did not accord with Wilsonian principles. Instead, they hoped to achieve an eventual geopolitical, economic, and ideological victory over the Soviet Union by using every means short of war.[12] The goal was not to learn to coexist with the enemy, but gradually to convert and/or help him destroy himself. It was precisely this ideological, uncompromising tone that gave containment its political viability at home.

During the late 1940s, under the strategy of containment, the United States embarked upon a series of dramatic and unprecedented commitments abroad. Military and economic aid was extended to friendly governments worldwide; anticommunist alliances were formed around the globe; and U.S. troops were deployed in large numbers to Europe and Asia. The Truman Doctrine, the Marshall Plan, and NATO all embodied this new commitment to a forward strategic presence overseas. The problem, however, was that the Truman administration hoped to implement this very ambitious strategy without sacrificing the traditional American preference for limited liability abroad. Defense expenditures, in particular, were at first kept at a level that was exceedingly low, given the diverse and worldwide military commitments the United States had actually undertaken. In effect, the administration gambled that the Soviet Union and its clients would not test America's willingness or ability to contain military aggression by conventional means.[13] With the outbreak of the Korean War in 1950, this gamble proved to be a failure. As a result, in the early 1950s, the United States finally raised defense expenditures to a level commensurate with its strategic commitments overseas. Inevitably, the Wilsonian preference for low-cost internationalism reasserted itself: high levels of defense spending turned out to be politically unsustainable at home, leading the Eisenhower administration to return to a potentially risky reliance on nuclear deterrence. Americans wanted to contain the Soviet Union—an ambitious and in many ways a remarkably idealistic strategy—but they did not necessarily want to bear the full costs of such a strategy. In this sense, even at the height of the Cold War, U.S. foreign policy operated very much within the Wilsonian tradition.

The implementation of containment continued to be characterized by a persistent gap between ambitious liberal ends, and somewhat limited capabilities. In the early 1960s, John F. Kennedy made a concerted effort to close this gap through a strategy of "flexible response," emphasizing conventional and counterinsurgent, as well as nuclear, capabilities. Yet at the same time, Kennedy escalated America's military involvement in Vietnam, without providing any clear idea of how that conflict could be won. The decision to stand by Saigon, on the part of both Kennedy and, later, Lyndon Johnson, was driven primarily by concerns over the credibility of America's worldwide alliance commitments. But this decision was also very much informed by the Wilsonian belief that developing countries such as Vietnam could be reformed, liberalized, and won over to America's side through a vigorous, U.S.-assisted program of nation building.[14] In the words of Walt Rostow, one of Kennedy's leading foreign policy advisors, "Modern societies must be built, and we are prepared to help build them."

In Vietnam, America's willingness to sustain serious costs on behalf of a liberal strategy of containment and nation building was tested to the breaking point. Within the United States, domestic political support for a protracted, expensive, and bloody engagement in Southeast Asia proved to have definite limits. The Johnson administration itself was unwilling to call for maximum effort on behalf of its goals in the region; instead, it tried to achieve them through a process of limited and gradual escalation. The Nixon administration, having inherited this immense commitment, attempted to square the circle through a policy of "Vietnamization." The United States would slowly withdraw its forces from the conflict, relying upon air power and increased military aid to bolster the regime in Saigon. But Nixon's approach was no more able to achieve its stated aims than Johnson's. If Communist forces in Vietnam could not be defeated by half a million American troops, a lower level of American engagement was not going to do the trick. In the end, the United States proved neither willing nor able to bear the costs of meeting its commitments to Saigon—commitments that had been deeply informed by liberal internationalist assumptions.

Even as they experimented with Vietnamization, the Nixon-Kissinger team attempted to place the United States in a more sustainable strategic position by toning down the Wilsonian rhetoric. The new emphasis was on great power relations, rather than on ideological crusades to liberalize or reform the internal politics of other states. As Henry Kissinger put it in 1969, "We will judge other countries, including Communist countries, on the basis of their actions and not on the basis of their domestic ideologies."[15] This more pragmatic approach bore considerable fruit through a relaxation of

tensions with the Soviet Union, as well as a dramatic improvement in relations with China. Despite these successes, Nixon and Kissinger were attacked from both left and right for abandoning America's Wilsonian mission overseas. Both Jimmy Carter, who took office in 1977, and Ronald Reagan, who succeeded him in 1981, criticized the policy of détente from a Wilsonian perspective. Both Carter and Reagan, despite their many differences, insisted that U.S. foreign relations should be rebuilt upon the premise that the United States had a vital practical as well as moral interest in the promotion of a liberal world order. The collapse of the Soviet Union in 1989 seemed to many to have vindicated the Wilsonian approach. But it was the combined economic and military power of the United States and its allies, not Wilsonian idealism, that finally brought the Soviet Union to its knees. In the euphoria over the collapse of communism, the fact that for over 40 years the United States had often pursued a sweeping and ambitious foreign policy with inadequate means was forgotten. The United States had been forced to pay for this strategic mismanagement in both Korea and Vietnam. In the end, the relative weakness of the Soviet Union gave U.S. policy makers considerable room for error. However, the upshot was that Americans misattributed their victory in the Cold War to the unique virtues of the Wilsonian tradition, which only led to a continuing gap between ends and means in the conduct of American foreign policy.

Democratic Enlargement

Following the end of the Cold War, the United States was faced with the choice of either expanding its military and political presence abroad, or retrenching strategically. The Clinton administration decided to do both. Thus it pursued a very ambitious strategy of "democratic enlargement," designed to promote the spread of market democracies worldwide. This included, notably, a new emphasis on humanitarian intervention in civil conflicts of seemingly peripheral interest to the United States. But it also tried to carry out this strategy at an extremely low cost in terms of blood and treasure. Defense expenditures, for example, were kept at a level that was unrealistically low, given the global range of America's military commitments. Just as significantly, Clinton also proved remarkably reluctant to use force in support of his Wilsonian agenda.

Clinton came into office having criticized the foreign policy of George H. W. Bush for being insufficiently true to America's democratic ideals. The new president promised to be more consistent than his immediate predecessor in promoting democracy and human rights in countries such as China, the former Yugoslavia, and Haiti. A leading test of the Clinton administration's rhetorical commitment to the liberal internationalist credo was on the question of humanitarian intervention. Clinton and his advisors repeatedly stated that the United States had a vital humanitarian interest in cases of civil war and disorder. The administration therefore placed a new emphasis on American-led peacekeeping, peacemaking, and nation-building operations.[16] More broadly, foreign policy officials articulated a doctrine of "enlargement," by which they meant that the United States would press for the expansion of free trade, open markets, democratic governments, and human rights worldwide.[17] Their assumption—building on the old Wilsonian gospel—was that such an expansion would encourage an upward cycle of global peace and prosperity, serving American interests and allowing the United States to deemphasize its own military strength.

Under the Clinton administration, the liberal internationalist assumptions of democratic enlargement informed U.S. policy in virtually every region of the globe. In Central Europe, three new members were brought into NATO. In Russia, democratic market reforms were the price demanded for improved bilateral relations with the United States. In China, U.S. diplomats pressed Beijing on human rights issues while working to bring the People's Republic into the international economic system. And in Bosnia, Haiti, Somalia, and Kosovo, Washington undertook to help create or recreate stable, democratic polities, through military intervention, amidst generally unfavorable conditions.[18]

Nevertheless, even as President Clinton laid out his extremely ambitious foreign policy goals, he proved unwilling to support them with the necessary means. In particular, he proved reluctant to support these initiatives with the requisite amount of military force. In one case after another of humanitarian intervention, a pattern emerged: the Clinton administration would stake out an assertive and idealistic public position, then refuse to act on its rhetoric in a meaningful way. Yet in every such case, whether in Somalia, Haiti, Bosnia, or Kosovo, the president was ultimately forced to act, if only to protect the credibility of the United States.[19] The result was a series of remarkably halfhearted, initially low-risk interventions, which only reinforced the impression that the United States was unwilling to suffer costs or casualties on behalf of its stated interests overseas.[20]

It might be argued that the nature of U.S. interventions during the Clinton years was a function of the low geopolitical stakes involved, rather than a reflection of the administration's naiveté. Certainly, the stakes were relatively low. But from a classical realist perspective, the answer would have been to avoid putting America's reputation on the line in the first place—to avoid defining American interests in such an expansive manner as to then call the nation's credibility into question. The fact is that the Clinton administration said, in each case, that the United States had a vital national interest in the pursuit of liberal or humanitarian goals. Then it refused to protect this stated interest with requisite seriousness until American credibility had already been undermined. This may have been partially the result of a presidency characterized by unusual fecklessness on matters of national security. But it was also a pattern of behavior very much in the liberal internationalist tradition: sweeping commitments, too often supported by inadequate means.

Wilson Redux

At first, the inauguration of George W. Bush seemed to indicate, if nothing else, that America's national security capabilities would be brought into line with the nation's strategic commitments. As a candidate for president, Governor Bush had called for significant increases in defense spending. At the same time, he criticized what he termed the "open-ended deployments and unclear military missions" of the Clinton era.[21] Bush was especially critical of employing armed force in nation-building operations overseas; indeed, he suggested that he would not have intervened in either Haiti or Somalia. As Bush phrased it during a debate with Al Gore in October 2000, while referring to the question of intervention, "I would be very guarded in my approach. I don't think we can be all things to all people in the world. I think we've got to be very careful when we commit our troops."[22]

To be sure, neoconservative visions of American primacy always had a certain influence on Bush's thinking, but for the most part, the dominant tone of Bush's foreign policy pre-9/11 was one of "realism." The new administration was determined to be more selective on questions of nation building and humanitarian intervention than its predecessor. American foreign policy was to be refocused on considerations of great power politics and more immediate national interests, and the United States was to play down its pretensions as an international social engineer. Key figures such as Colin Powell and Richard Haass in the State Department and Condoleezza Rice at the National Security Council were well within the tradition of Republican pragmatism on foreign affairs, and hawks such as Vice President Dick Cheney and Secretary of Defense Donald Rumsfeld were either unwilling or unable to press for a comprehensive strategy of primacy across the board.[23] Above all, Bush seemed uninterested in any new, sweepingly ambitious—i.e., Wilsonian—foreign policy departures.

The terrorist attacks of September 11, 2001, changed all of that, coming as a severe shock to the president, his advisors, and the American public at large. These attacks stimulated the search for a new national security strategy. Key advocates of a different approach—at first within the administration, and then including the president himself—took advantage of the opportunity to build support for a new foreign policy agenda. This new national security strategy would be considerably more assertive than before and, in important ways, considerably more idealistic.[24]

Within days of the September 11 attacks, and over the following months, the Bush administration began to outline and articulate a remarkable departure in American foreign policy. The clearest and most elaborate explanation of the new approach came in the National Security Strategy of September 2002. In that document, best known for its embrace of preventive military action against rogue states, the administration began by pointing out that "the United States possesses unprecedented—and unequaled—strength and influence in the world." It renounced any purely realpolitik approach to foreign policy, arguing instead that "the great strength of this nation must be used to promote a balance of power that favors freedom." The promotion of free trade and democratic institutions was held up as a central American interest. Democracy and human rights were described as "nonnegotiable demands." And, interestingly, the possibility of traditional great power competition was played down. Instead, other powers were urged to join with the United States in affirming the global trend toward democracy and open markets.[25]

Of course, this broad affirmation of classical liberal assumptions was no doubt employed, in part, for reasons of domestic political consumption. Liberal arguments have historically been used to bolster strategic arguments of any kind. But the United States had been no less liberal—broadly speaking—in the year 2000, when the nascent Bush team was stressing the need for realism in foreign affairs. So the new rhetoric does seem to have reflected a real shift on the part of the administration toward a more aggressive and, at the same time, more Wilsonian approach.

The implications of this new Wilsonianism were most visible in the decision for war against Iraq. The argument made by the pro-war camp was that a defeated Iraq could be democratized and would subsequently act as a kind of trigger for democratic change throughout the Middle East. As Bush put it in an address last February to members of the American Enterprise Institute, "a new regime in Iraq would serve as a dramatic and inspiring example of freedom for other nations in the region. . . . Success in Iraq could also begin a new stage for Middle Eastern peace, and set in motion progress toward a truly democratic Palestinian state."[26] From the perspective of many leading officials inside the Bush administration, this argument was probably secondary to more basic geopolitical and security concerns. But it did seem to have an effect on the president. And again, 9/11 was the crucial catalyst, since it appeared to demonstrate that U.S. support for authoritarian regimes in the region had only encouraged Islamic fundamentalism, along with such terrorist organizations as al-Qaeda.[27]

Here was a remarkably bold vision for American foreign policy, combining the argument for preventive war with Wilsonian visions of a liberalized or Americanized international system. The goals outlined were so ambitious as to invite intense domestic as well as international criticism. The most common objections to the Bush

Doctrine, at least among foreign policy experts, were that the new national security strategy would lead America into "imperial over-stretch"; that it would trigger antagonism and hostility toward the United States abroad; that it would set a precedent for aggression on the part of other countries; and that it would undermine sympathy and support for the United States overseas. These were the most frequently articulated criticisms, but in fact an even more likely danger was the opposite one: that the Bush team would fail to make good on its promise of a serious commitment to achieving peace, stability, and democratization in Iraq, let alone in the Middle East as a whole.

Certainly the precedent in Afghanistan was not encouraging. There, the United States relied upon proxy forces, supported by air-strikes, special forces operations, and financial aid, in order to over-throw the Taliban. The failure to send in American ground troops early on meant that many members of al-Qaeda were able to escape and reconstitute their terrorist camps along the Afghan-Pakistani border. Worse yet, the Bush administration proved unwilling to con-tribute substantially to the postwar political, military, or economic reconstruction of Afghanistan, leaving its central government with-out effective control over the countryside outside Kabul.[28]

Iraq's postwar reconstruction was even less well considered than Afghanistan's. Certainly, the Bush foreign policy team understood that Saddam Hussein would not be overthrown without a major com-mitment of American ground troops. But in terms of planning for a post-Saddam Iraq, the administration seems to have based its initial actions upon the most optimistic assumptions: ordinary Iraqis would rise up in support of U.S. forces; these same forces would rapidly transfer authority toward a friendly interim government; the oil would flow, paying for reconstruction efforts; and the great majority of American troops would come home quickly. These were never very likely prospects, and with all of the warnings that it received, the administration should have known better. As Bush himself said during the 2000 presidential campaign, nation building is difficult and expensive. The administration's preference has been to avoid nation-building operations—an understandable predilection in itself. But once the administration made the decision to go to war against Saddam Hussein, it was also obliged to prepare for the foreseeable likelihood of major, postwar nation-building operations—not only for humanitarian reasons, but in order to secure the political objec-tives for which it had gone to war in the first place.

The Bush administration's early reluctance to plan for Iraq's post-war reconstruction has had serious and deadly consequences. Once Saddam's government was overthrown, a power vacuum was created, and the United States did not initially step in to fill the void. Wide-spread looting, disorder, and insecurity were the inevitable result. This set the tone for the immediate postwar era. Moreover, because of these insecure conditions, many of Saddam's former loyalists were given the opportunity to develop and pursue a dangerous, low-level insurgency against American forces. The subsequent learning curve within the Bush administration has been steep. By necessity, the president has come a considerable distance toward recognizing how expensive this particular process of nation building is going to be. The approval by Congress of $87 billion for continuing operations in Iraq and Afghanistan is clearly a step in the right direction. Bush has indicated repeatedly that the United States cannot cut and run from its commitments. At the same time, there are disconcerting signs, with American casualties mounting, and the president's reelection loom-ing, that the White House may in fact decide to withdraw American forces from Iraq. Indeed, the administration's latest adjustment seems to be toward a version of Vietnamization: handing over authority to

a transitional government in Baghdad, while encouraging Iraq's own police and security forces to take up the greater burden with respect to counterinsurgency operations. In itself, this approach has certain vir-tues, but if it indicates a comprehensive withdrawal of U.S. resources and personnel from Iraq, then the results will not be benign, either for the United States, or for the Iraqi people. Nation-building operations sometimes fail, even under favorable conditions. But without robust involvement on the part of outside powers, such operations simply cannot succeed. It is an illusion to think that a stable, secure, and democratic Iraq can arise without a significant long-term U.S. invest-ment of both blood and treasure.[29]

The administration responded to the challenge of 9/11 by devising a more assertive, Wilsonian foreign policy. The stated goals of this policy have been not only to initiate "rogue state rollback" but to pro-mote a more open and democratic world order. By all accounts, Bush and his advisors really do believe that 9/11 has offered the United States, in the words of Secretary of Defense Donald Rumsfeld, an "opportunity to refashion the world."[30] The problem is not that the president is departing from a long tradition of liberal international-ism; it is that he is continuing some of the worst features of that tradition. Specifically, in Iraq, he is continuing the tradition of articu-lating and pursuing a set of extremely ambitious and idealistic for-eign policy goals, without providing the full or proportionate means to achieve those goals. In this sense, it must be said, George W. Bush is very much a Wilsonian.

Whatever the immediate outcome in Iraq, America's foreign pol-icy elites are not likely to abandon their longstanding ambition to create a liberal world order. What is more likely, and also more dan-gerous, is that they will continue to oscillate between various forms of liberal internationalism, and to press for a more open and demo-cratic international system, without willing the means to sustain it.

Under the circumstances, the choice between unilateralism and multilateralism, which currently characterizes public debate over U.S. foreign policy, is almost beside the point. Neither a unilat-eral nor a multilateral foreign policy will succeed if Americans are unwilling to incur the full costs and risks that are implied in either case. It is impossible to promote the kind of international system that America's foreign policy elites say that they want without paying a heavy price for it. Iraq is simply the latest case in point. Americans can either take up the burden of acting on their liberal international-ist rhetoric and convictions, or they can keep costs and risks to a minimum by abandoning this ambitious interventionist agenda. They cannot do both. They cannot have hegemony on the cheap.

Notes

1. For representative criticisms in this vein, see David C. Hendrickson, "Toward Universal Empire: The Dangerous Quest for Absolute Security," *World Policy Journal,* vol. 19 (fall 2002), pp. 1–10; G. John Ikenberry, "America's Imperial Ambition," *Foreign Affairs,* vol. 81 (September/October 2002), pp. 44–60; Robert S. Litwak, "The New Calculus of Preemption," *Survival,* vol. 44 (winter 2002), pp. 53–79; and Joseph S. Nye, Jr., *The Paradox of American Power: Why the World's Only Superpower Can't Go It Alone* (New York: Oxford University Press, 2002), pp. 15, 39, 141–63.

2. See Michael H. Hunt, *Ideology and US Foreign Policy* (New Haven: Yale University Press, 1988), pp. 17–18.

3. "Remarks by the President at the 20th Anniversary of the National Endowment for Democracy," Washington, D.C.,

November 6, 2003, available at www.whitehouse.gov/news/releases/2003/11/iraq/20031106-2.html.

4. For a discussion of various schools of thought in the American foreign policy tradition, see Henry R. Nau, *At Home Abroad: Identity and Power in American Foreign Policy* (Ithaca: Cornell University Press, 2002), pp. 43–59; and Walter Russell Mead, *Special Providence: American Foreign Policy and How It Changed the World* (New York: Knopf, 2001).

5. See Arthur S. Link, *Woodrow Wilson: Revolution, War and Peace* (Wheeling, Ill.: Harlan Davidson, 1979), pp. 72–103.

6. In the former Ottoman Empire, for example, Wilson's initial pronouncements in favor of self-determination had raised hopes for postwar national independence among Arabs, Armenians, Jews, and Turks. At Paris, Wilson even promised a U.S. protectorate over an independent Armenia. Yet the eventual settlement in the region, disguised through the creation of League "mandates," closely resembled a classic sphere-of-influence bargain among Europe's great powers. The one major exception was in Turkey itself, where Kemal Atatürk rallied nationalist forces and ejected foreign troops from the Anatolian heartland. In this way, American promises with regard to Armenia were rendered completely irrelevant, even before the Senate's rejection of the Versailles Treaty. For a lively discussion of the postwar settlement within the Middle East, see Margaret MacMillan, *Paris 1919: Six Months That Changed the World* (New York: Random House, 2002), pp. 347–455.

7. Ray Stannard Baker and William Dodd, eds., *Public Papers of Woodrow Wilson,* (New York: Harper and Brothers, 1925–1927), vol. 5, pp. 341–44.

8. William C. Widenor, *Henry Cabot Lodge and the Search for an American Foreign Policy* (Berkeley: University of California Press, 1980), pp. 298, 331.

9. Baker and Dodd, eds., *Public Papers of Woodrow Wilson,* vol. 5, pp. 352–56.

10. See Warren F. Kimball, *The Juggler: Franklin Roosevelt as Wartime Statesman* (Princeton: Princeton University Press, 1991), pp. 63–81, 107–57.

11. See Melvyn P. Leffler, *A Preponderance of Power: National Security, the Truman Administration, and the Cold War* (Stanford: Stanford University Press, 1992), pp. 8–9, 15–18.

12. As George Kennan put it, "Our first aim with respect to Russia in time of peace is to encourage and promote by means short of war the gradual retraction of undue Russian influence from the present satellite area." See George Kennan, NSC 20/1, "US Objectives with Respect to Russia," August 18, 1948, in Thomas H. Etzold and John Lewis Gaddis, eds., *Containment: Documents on American Policy and Strategy, 1945–1950* (New York: Columbia University Press, 1978), p. 184.

13. See Steven L. Rearden, *History of the Office of the Secretary of Defense: The Formative Years, 1947–1950* (Washington, D.C.: United States Government Printing Office, 1984), pp. 532–36.

14. See John Lewis Gaddis, *Strategies of Containment* (New York: Oxford University Press, 1982), pp. 202–03, 217–18, 223–25.

15. Ibid., p. 284.

16. Stephen John Stedman, "The New Interventionists," *Foreign Affairs,* vol. 72 (spring 1993), pp. 4–5.

17. Anthony Lake, Assistant to the President for National Security Affairs, at Johns Hopkins University, September 21, 1993, in *Vital Speeches of the Day, 1993,* vol. 60, p. 15.

18. See Karin von Hippel, *Democracy by Force: U.S. Military Intervention in the Post-Cold War World* (New York: Cambridge University Press, 2000).

19. See, for example, in the case of Bosnia, James Gow, *Triumph of the Lack of Will: International Diplomacy and the Yugoslav War* (New York: Columbia University Press, 1997), pp. 208, 218.

20. Daniel L. Byman and Matthew C. Waxman, *The Dynamics of Coercion: American Foreign Policy and the Limits of Military Might* (New York: Cambridge University Press, 2002), p. 143.

21. Governor George W. Bush, "A Period of Consequences," September 23, 1999, The Citadel, South Carolina, available at www.citadel.edu/pao/addresses/pres_bush.html.

22. Presidential debates, October 3, 2000, at Boston, Massachussetts, and October 11, 2000, at Winston-Salem, North Carolina, available at www.foreignpolicy2000.org/debate/candidate/candidate.html and www.foreignpolicy2000.org/debate/candidate/candidate2.html.

23. For a good exposition of the initially "realist" bent of one of Bush's leading foreign policy advisors, see Condoleezza Rice, "Campaign 2000: Promoting the National Interest," *Foreign Affairs,* vol. 79 (January/February 2000), pp. 45–62.

24. Nicholas Lemann, "Without a Doubt," *The New Yorker,* October 14 and 21, 2002, p. 177.

25. The National Security Strategy of the United States of America (Washington, D.C.: The White House, September 2002), pp. 1, 3–4, 26–28.

26. George W. Bush, "President Discusses the Future of Iraq," February 26, 2003, Washington Hilton Hotel, Washington, D.C., available at www.whitehouse.gov/news/releases/2003/02/iraq/20030226-11.html.

27. George Packer, "Dreaming of Democracy," *New York Times Magazine,* March 2, 2003, pp. 46–49.

28. Anja Manuel and Peter W. Singer, "A New Model Afghan Army," *Foreign Affairs,* vol. 81 (July/August 2002), pp. 44–59.

29. Frederick Kagan, "War and Aftermath," *Policy Review,* no. 120 (August/September 2003), pp. 3–27.

30. "Secretary Rumsfeld Interview," *New York Times,* October 12, 2001.

COLIN DUECK is assistant professor of political science at the University of Colorado, Boulder.

From *World Policy Journal,* Winter 2003/2004, pp. 1–11. Copyright © 2004 by MIT Press. Reprinted by permission.

The Eagle Has Crash Landed

Pax Americana is over. Challenges from Vietnam and the Balkans to the Middle East and September 11 have revealed the limits of American supremacy. Will the United States learn to fade quietly, or will U.S. conservatives resist and thereby transform a gradual decline into a rapid and dangerous fall?

IMMANUEL WALLERSTEIN

The United States in decline? Few people today would believe this assertion. The only ones who do are the U.S. hawks, who argue vociferously for policies to reverse the decline. This belief that the end of U.S. hegemony has already begun does not follow from the vulnerability that became apparent to all on September 11, 2001. In fact, the United States has been fading as a global power since the 1970s, and the U.S. response to the terrorist attacks has merely accelerated this decline. To understand why the so-called Pax Americana is on the wane requires examining the geopolitics of the 20th century, particularly of the century's final three decades. This exercise uncovers a simple and inescapable conclusion: The economic, political, and military factors that contributed to U.S. hegemony are the same factors that will inexorably produce the coming U.S. decline.

Intro to Hegemony

The rise of the United States to global hegemony was a long process that began in earnest with the world recession of 1873. At that time, the United States and Germany began to acquire an increasing share of global markets, mainly at the expense of the steadily receding British economy. Both nations had recently acquired a stable political base—the United States by successfully terminating the Civil War and Germany by achieving unification and defeating France in the Franco-Prussian War. From 1873 to 1914, the United States and Germany became the principal producers in certain leading sectors: steel and later automobiles for the United States and industrial chemicals for Germany.

The history books record that World War I broke out in 1914 and ended in 1918 and that World War II lasted from 1939 to 1945. However, it makes more sense to consider the two as a single, continuous "30 years' war" between the United States and Germany, with truces and local conflicts scattered in between. The competition for hegemonic succession took an ideological turn in 1933, when the Nazis came to power in Germany and began their quest to transcend the global system altogether, seeking not hegemony within the current system but rather a form of global empire. Recall the Nazi slogan *ein tausendjähriges Reich* (a thousand-year empire). In turn, the United States assumed the role of advocate of centrist world liberalism—recall former U.S. President Franklin D. Roosevelt's "four freedoms" (freedom of speech, of worship, from want, and from fear)—and entered into a strategic alliance with the Soviet Union, making possible the defeat of Germany and its allies.

World War II resulted in enormous destruction of infrastructure and populations throughout Eurasia, from the Atlantic to the Pacific oceans, with almost no country left unscathed. The only major industrial power in the world to emerge intact—and even greatly strengthened from an economic perspective—was the United States, which moved swiftly to consolidate its position.

But the aspiring hegemon faced some practical political obstacles. During the war, the Allied powers had agreed on the establishment of the United Nations, composed primarily of countries that had been in the coalition against the Axis powers. The organization's critical feature was the Security Council, the only structure that could authorize the use of force. Since the U.N. Charter gave the right of veto to five powers—including the United States and the Soviet Union—the council was rendered largely toothless in practice. So it was not the founding of the United Nations in April 1945 that determined the geopolitical constraints of the second half of the 20th century but rather the Yalta meeting between Roosevelt, British Prime Minister Winston Churchill, and Soviet leader Joseph Stalin two months earlier.

The formal accords at Yalta were less important than the informal, unspoken agreements, which one can only assess by observing the behavior of the United States and the Soviet Union in the years that followed. When the war ended in Europe on May 8, 1945, Soviet and Western (that is, U.S., British, and French) troops were located in particular places—essentially, along a line in the center of Europe that came to be called the Oder-Neisse Line. Aside from a few minor adjustments, they stayed there. In hindsight, Yalta signified the agreement of both sides that they could stay there and that neither side would use force to push the other out. This tacit accord applied to Asia as well, as evinced by U.S. occupation of Japan and the division of Korea. Politically, therefore, Yalta was an agreement on the status quo in which the Soviet Union controlled about one third of the world and the United States the rest.

Washington also faced more serious military challenges. The Soviet Union had the world's largest land forces, while the U.S. government was under domestic pressure to downsize its army, particularly by ending the draft. The United States therefore decided to assert its military strength not via land forces but through a monopoly of nuclear weapons (plus an air force capable of deploying them). This monopoly soon disappeared: By 1949, the Soviet Union had developed nuclear weapons as well. Ever since, the United States has been reduced to trying to prevent the acquisition of nuclear weapons (and chemical and biological weapons) by additional powers, an effort that, in the 21st century, does not seem terribly successful.

Until 1991, the United States and the Soviet Union coexisted in the "balance of terror" of the Cold War. This status quo was tested seriously only three times: the Berlin blockade of 1948–49, the Korean War in 1950–53, and the Cuban missile crisis of 1962. The result in each case was restoration of the status quo. Moreover, note how each time the Soviet Union faced a political crisis among its satellite regimes—East Germany in 1953, Hungary in 1956, Czechoslovakia in 1968, and Poland in 1981—the United States engaged in little more than propaganda exercises, allowing the Soviet Union to proceed largely as it deemed fit.

Of course, this passivity did not extend to the economic arena. The United States capitalized on the Cold War ambiance to launch massive economic reconstruction efforts, first in Western Europe and then in Japan (as well as in South Korea and Taiwan). The rationale was obvious: What was the point of having such overwhelming productive superiority if the rest of the world could not muster effective demand? Furthermore, economic reconstruction helped create clientelistic obligations on the part of the nations receiving U.S. aid; this sense of obligation fostered willingness to enter into military alliances and, even more important, into political subservience.

Finally, one should not underestimate the ideological and cultural component of U.S. hegemony. The immediate post-1945 period may have been the historical high point for the popularity of communist ideology. We easily forget today the large votes for Communist parties in free elections in countries such as Belgium, France, Italy, Czechoslovakia, and Finland, not to mention the support Communist parties gathered in Asia—in Vietnam, India, and Japan—and throughout Latin America. And that still leaves out areas such as China, Greece, and Iran, where free elections remained absent or constrained but where Communist parties enjoyed widespread appeal. In response, the United States sustained a massive anticommunist ideological offensive. In retrospect, this initiative appears largely successful: Washington brandished its role as the leader of the "free world" at least as effectively as the Soviet Union brandished its position as the leader of the "progressive" and "anti-imperialist" camp.

One, Two, Many Vietnams

The United States' success as a hegemonic power in the postwar period created the conditions of the nation's hegemonic demise. This process is captured in four symbols: the war in Vietnam, the revolutions of 1968, the fall of the Berlin Wall in 1989, and the terrorist attacks of September 2001. Each symbol built upon the prior one, culminating in the situation in which the United States currently finds itself—a lone superpower that lacks true power, a world leader nobody follows and few respect, and a nation drifting dangerously amidst a global chaos it cannot control.

What was the Vietnam War? First and foremost, it was the effort of the Vietnamese people to end colonial rule and establish their own state. The Vietnamese fought the French, the Japanese, and the Americans, and in the end the Vietnamese won—quite an achievement, actually. Geopolitically, however, the war represented a rejection of the Yalta status quo by populations then labeled as Third World. Vietnam became such a powerful symbol because Washington was foolish enough to invest its full military might in the struggle, but the United States still lost. True, the United States didn't deploy nuclear weapons (a decision certain myopic groups on the right have long reproached), but such use would have shattered the Yalta accords and might have produced a nuclear holocaust—an outcome the United States simply could not risk.

But Vietnam was not merely a military defeat or a blight on U.S. prestige. The war dealt a major blow to the United States' ability to remain the world's dominant economic power. The conflict was extremely expensive and more or less used up the U.S. gold reserves that had been so plentiful since 1945. Moreover, the United States incurred these costs just as Western Europe and Japan experienced major economic upswings. These conditions ended U.S. preeminence in the global economy. Since the late 1960s, members of this triad have been nearly economic equals, each doing better than the others for certain periods but none moving far ahead.

When the revolutions of 1968 broke out around the world, support for the Vietnamese became a major rhetorical component. "One, two, many Vietnams" and "Ho, Ho, Ho Chi Minh" were chanted in many a street, not least in the United States. But the 1968ers did not merely condemn U.S. hegemony. They condemned Soviet collusion with the United States, they condemned Yalta, and they used or adapted the language of the Chinese cultural revolutionaries who divided the world into two camps—the two superpowers and the rest of the world.

The denunciation of Soviet collusion led logically to the denunciation of those national forces closely allied with the Soviet Union, which meant in most cases the traditional Communist parties. But the 1968 revolutionaries also lashed out against other components of the Old Left—national liberation movements in the Third World, social-democratic movements in Western Europe, and New Deal Democrats in the United States—accusing them, too, of collusion with what the revolutionaries generically termed "U.S. imperialism."

The attack on Soviet collusion with Washington plus the attack on the Old Left further weakened the legitimacy of the Yalta arrangements on which the United States had fashioned the world order. It also undermined the position of centrist liberalism as the lone, legitimate global ideology. The direct political consequences of the world revolutions of 1968 were minimal, but the geopolitical and intellectual repercussions were enormous and irrevocable. Centrist liberalism tumbled from the throne it had occupied since the European revolutions of 1848 and that had enabled it to co-opt conservatives and radicals alike. These ideologies returned and once again represented a real gamut of choices. Conservatives would again become conservatives, and radicals, radicals. The centrist liberals did not disappear, but they were cut down to size. And in the process, the official U.S. ideological position—antifascist, anticommunist, anticolonialist—seemed thin and unconvincing to a growing portion of the world's populations.

The Powerless Superpower

The onset of international economic stagnation in the 1970s had two important consequences for U.S. power. First, stagnation resulted in the collapse of "developmentalism"—the notion that every nation could catch up economically if the state took appropriate action—which was the principal ideological claim of the Old Left movements then in power. One after another, these regimes faced internal disorder, declining standards of living, increasing debt dependency on international financial institutions, and eroding credibility. What had seemed in the 1960s to be the successful navigation of Third World decolonization by the United States—minimizing disruption and maximizing the smooth transfer of power to regimes that were developmentalist but scarcely revolutionary—gave way to disintegrating order, simmering discontents, and unchanneled radical temperaments. When the United States tried to intervene, it failed. In 1983, U.S. President Ronald Reagan sent troops to Lebanon to restore order. The troops were in effect forced out. He compensated by invading Grenada, a country without troops. President George H.W. Bush invaded Panama, another country without troops. But after he intervened in Somalia to restore order, the United States was in effect forced out, somewhat ignominiously. Since there was little the U.S. government could actually do to reverse the trend of declining hegemony, it chose simply to ignore this trend—a policy that prevailed from the withdrawal from Vietnam until September 11, 2001.

Meanwhile, true conservatives began to assume control of key states and interstate institutions. The neoliberal offensive of the 1980s was marked by the Thatcher and Reagan regimes and the emergence of the International Monetary Fund (IMF) as a key actor on the world scene. Where once (for more than a century) conservative forces had attempted to portray themselves as wiser liberals, now centrist liberals were compelled to argue that they were more effective conservatives. The conservative programs were clear. Domestically, conservatives tried to enact policies that would reduce the cost of labor, minimize environmental Constraints on producers, and cut back on state welfare benefits. Actual successes were modest, so conservatives then moved vigorously into the international arena. The gatherings of the World Economic Forum in Davos provided a meeting ground for elites and the media. The IMF provided a club for finance ministers and central bankers. And the United States pushed for the creation of the World Trade Organization to enforce free commercial flows across the world's frontiers.

While the United States wasn't watching, the Soviet Union was collapsing. Yes, Ronald Reagan had dubbed the Soviet Union an "evil empire" and had used the rhetorical bombast of calling for the destruction of the Berlin Wall, but the United States didn't really mean it and certainly was not responsible for the Soviet Union's downfall. In truth, the Soviet Union and its East European imperial zone collapsed because of popular disillusionment with the Old Left in combination with Soviet leader Mikhail Gorbachev's efforts to save his regime by liquidating Yalta and instituting internal liberalization (perestroika plus glasnost). Gorbachev succeeded in liquidating Yalta but not in saving the Soviet Union (although he almost did, be it said).

The United States was stunned and puzzled by the sudden collapse, uncertain how to handle the consequences. The collapse of communism in effect signified the collapse of liberalism, removing the only ideological justification behind U.S. hegemony, a justification tacitly supported by liberalism's ostensible ideological opponent. This loss of legitimacy led directly to the Iraqi invasion of Kuwait, which Iraqi leader Saddam Hussein would never have dared had the Yalta arrangements remained in place. In retrospect, U.S. efforts in the Gulf War accomplished a truce at basically the same line of departure. But can a hegemonic power be satisfied with a tie in a war with a middling regional power? Saddam demonstrated that one could pick a fight with the United States and get away with it. Even more than the defeat in Vietnam, Saddam's brash challenge has eaten at the innards of the U.S. right, in particular those known as the hawks, which explains the fervor of their current desire to invade Iraq and destroy its regime.

Between the Gulf War and September 11, 2001, the two major arenas of world conflict were the Balkans and the Middle East. The United States has played a major diplomatic role in both regions. Looking back, how different would the results have been had the United States assumed a completely isolationist position? In the Balkans, an economically successful multinational state (Yugoslavia) broke down, essentially into its component parts. Over 10 years, most of the resulting states have engaged in a process of ethnification, experiencing fairly brutal violence, widespread human rights violations, and outright wars. Outside intervention—in which the United States figured most prominently—brought about a truce and ended the most egregious violence, but this intervention in no way reversed the ethnification, which is now consolidated and somewhat legitimated. Would these conflicts have ended differently without U.S. involvement? The violence might have continued longer, but the basic results would probably not have been too different. The picture is even grimmer in the Middle East, where, if anything, U.S. engagement has been deeper and its failures more spectacular. In the Balkans and the Middle East alike, the United States has failed to exert its hegemonic clout effectively, not for want of will or effort but for want of real power.

The Hawks Undone

Then came September 11—the shock and the reaction. Under fire from U.S. legislators, the Central Intelligence Agency (CIA) now claims it had warned the Bush administration of possible threats. But despite the CIA's focus on al Qaeda and the agency's intelligence expertise, it could not foresee (and therefore, prevent) the execution of the terrorist strikes. Or so would argue CIA Director George Tenet. This testimony can hardly comfort the U.S. government or the American people. Whatever else historians may decide, the attacks of September 11, 2001, posed a major challenge to U.S. power. The persons responsible did not represent a major military power. They were members of a nonstate force, with a high degree of determination, some money, a band of dedicated followers, and a strong base in one weak state. In short, militarily, they were nothing. Yet they succeeded in a bold attack on U.S. soil.

George W Bush came to power very critical of the Clinton administration's handling of world affairs. Bush and his advisors did not admit—but were undoubtedly aware—that Clinton's path had been the path of every U.S. president since Gerald Ford, including that of Ronald Reagan and George H.W. Bush. It had even been the path of the current Bush administration before September 11. One only needs to look at how Bush handled the downing of the U.S. plane off China in April 2001 to see that prudence had been the name of the game.

Following the terrorist attacks, Bush changed course, declaring war on terrorism, assuring the American people that "the outcome is certain" and informing the world that "you are either with us or against us." Long frustrated by even the most conservative U.S. administrations, the hawks finally came to dominate American policy. Their position is clear: The United States wields overwhelming military power, and even though countless foreign leaders consider it unwise for Washington to flex its military muscles, these same leaders cannot and will not do anything if the United States simply imposes its will on the rest. The hawks believe the United States should act as an imperial power for two reasons: First, the United States can get away with it. And second, if Washington doesn't exert its force, the United States will become increasingly marginalized.

Today, this hawkish position has three expressions: the military assault in Afghanistan, the de facto support for the Israeli attempt to liquidate the Palestinian Authority, and the invasion of Iraq, which is reportedly in the military preparation stage. Less than one year after the September 2001 terrorist attacks, it is perhaps too early to assess what such strategies will accomplish. Thus far, these schemes have led to the overthrow of the Taliban in Afghanistan (without the complete dismantling of al Qaeda or the capture of its top leadership); enormous destruction in Palestine (without rendering Palestinian leader Yasir Arafat "irrelevant," as Israeli Prime Minister Ariel Sharon said he is); and heavy opposition from U.S. allies in Europe and the Middle East to plans for an invasion of Iraq.

The hawks' reading of recent events emphasizes that opposition to U.S. actions, while serious, has remained largely verbal. Neither Western Europe nor Russia nor China nor Saudi Arabia has seemed ready to break ties in serious ways with the United States. In other words, hawks believe, Washington has indeed gotten away with it. The hawks assume a similar outcome will occur when the U.S. military actually invades Iraq and after that, when the United States exercises its authority elsewhere in the world, be it in Iran, North Korea, Colombia, or perhaps Indonesia. Ironically, the hawk reading has largely become the reading of the international left, which has been screaming about U.S. policies—mainly because they fear that the chances of U.S. success are high.

But hawk interpretations are wrong and will only contribute to the United States' decline, transforming a gradual descent into a much more rapid and turbulent fall. Specifically, hawk approaches will fail for military, economic, and ideological reasons.

Undoubtedly, the military remains the United States' strongest card; in fact, it is the only card. Today, the United States wields the most formidable military apparatus in the world. And if claims of new, unmatched military technologies are to be believed, the U.S. military edge over the rest of the world is considerably greater today than it was just a decade ago. But does that mean, then, that the United States can invade Iraq, conquer it rapidly, and install a friendly and stable regime? Unlikely. Bear in mind that of the three serious wars the U.S. military has fought since 1945 (Korea, Vietnam, and the Gulf War), one ended in defeat and two in draws—not exactly a glorious record.

Saddam Hussein's army is not that of the Taliban, and his internal military control is far more coherent. A U.S. invasion would necessarily involve a serious land force, one that would have to fight its way to Baghdad and would likely suffer significant casualties. Such a force would also need staging grounds, and Saudi Arabia has made clear that it will not serve in this capacity. Would Kuwait or Turkey help out? Perhaps, if Washington calls in all its chips. Meanwhile, Saddam can be expected to deploy all weapons at his disposal, and it is precisely the U.S. government that keeps fretting over how nasty those weapons might be. The United States may twist the arms of regimes in the region, but popular sentiment clearly views the whole affair as reflecting a deep anti-Arab bias in the United States. Can such a conflict be won? The British General Staff has apparently already informed Prime Minister Tony Blair that it does not believe so.

And there is always the matter of "second fronts." Following the Gulf War, U.S. armed forces sought to prepare for the possibility of two simultaneous regional wars. After a while, the Pentagon quietly abandoned the idea as impractical and costly. But who can be sure that no potential U.S. enemies would strike when the United States appears bogged down in Iraq?

Consider, too, the question of U.S. popular tolerance of nonvictories. Americans hover between a patriotic fervor that lends support to all wartime presidents and a deep isolationist urge. Since 1945, patriotism has hit a wall whenever the death toll has risen. Why should today's reaction differ? And even if the hawks (who are almost all civilians) feel impervious to public opinion, U.S. Army generals, burnt by Vietnam, do not.

And what about the economic front? In the 1980s, countless American analysts became hysterical over the Japanese economic miracle. They calmed down in the 1990s, given Japan's well-publicized financial difficulties. Yet after overstating how quickly Japan was moving forward, U.S. authorities now seem to be complacent, confident that Japan lags far behind. These days, Washington seems more inclined to lecture Japanese policymakers about what they are doing wrong.

Such triumphalism hardly appears warranted. Consider the following April 20, 2002, *New York Times* report: "A Japanese laboratory has built the world's fastest computer, a machine so powerful that it matches the raw processing power of the 20 fastest American computers combined and far outstrips the previous leader, an I.B.M.-built machine. The achievement. . . is evidence that a technology race that most American engineers thought they were winning handily is far from over." The analysis goes on to note that there are "contrasting scientific and technological priorities" in the two countries. The Japanese machine is built to analyze climatic change, but U.S. machines are designed to simulate weapons. This contrast embodies the oldest story in the history of hegemonic powers. The dominant power concentrates (to its detriment) on the military; the candidate for successor concentrates on the economy. The latter has always paid off, handsomely. It did for the United States. Why should it not pay off for Japan as well, perhaps in alliance with China?

Finally, there is the ideological sphere. Right now, the U.S. economy seems relatively weak, even more so considering the exorbitant military expenses associated with hawk strategies. Moreover, Washington remains politically isolated; virtually no one (save Israel) thinks the hawk position makes sense or is worth encouraging. Other nations are afraid or unwilling to stand up to Washington directly, but even their foot-dragging is hurting the United States.

Yet the U.S. response amounts to little more than arrogant arm-twisting. Arrogance has its own negatives. Calling in chips means leaving fewer chips for next time, and surly acquiescence breeds increasing resentment. Over the last 200 years, the United States acquired a considerable amount of ideological credit. But these days, the United States is running through this credit even faster than it ran through its gold surplus in the 1960s.

The United States faces two possibilities during the next 10 years: It can follow the hawks' path, with negative consequences for all but especially for itself. Or it can realize that the negatives are too great. Simon Tisdall of the *Guardian* recently argued that even disregarding international public opinion, "the U.S. is not able to fight a successful Iraqi war by itself without incurring immense damage, not least in terms of its economic interests and its energy supply. Mr. Bush is reduced to talking tough and looking ineffectual." And if the United States still invades Iraq and is then forced to withdraw it will look even more ineffectual.

President Bush's options appear extremely limited, and there is little doubt that the United States will continue to decline as a decisive force in world affairs over the next decade. The real question is not whether U.S. hegemony is waning but whether the United States can devise a way to descend gracefully, with minimum damage to the world, and to itself.

For links to relevant websites, access to the *FP* Archive, and a comprehensive index of related Foreign Policy articles, go to www.foreignpolicy.com.

IMMANUEL WALLERSTEIN is a senior research scholar at Yale University and author of, most recently, *The End of the World As We Know It: Social Science for the Twenty-First Century* (Minneapolis: University of Minnesota Press, 1999).

Pillars of the Next American Century

JAMES KURTH

The 20th century was famously called "the American century," yet its being so called occurred in an improbable way. The phrase itself was actually not used until *Time* publisher Henry Luce coined it in a special issue of *Life* magazine in 1941—by which time 40 percent of the 20th century had already passed. Moreover, 1941 was a year in which the superiority of America and of the American way of life appeared decidedly problematic. Only the year before had the United States finally exited, statistically speaking, the decade of the Great Depression. Nazi Germany's armies occupied most of Europe, stretching from the Atlantic coast of France to the heartland of the Soviet Union. At the same time, Imperial Japan's armies occupied most of East Asia, stretching from Manchuria through much of China to Indochina. No objective observer could have been blamed for entertaining a whiff of pessimism about America's prospects.

Nevertheless, Luce was truly prescient. By the end of the 20th century, nearly everyone widely acknowledged that it had, indeed, been the American one. Certainly, no other power and way of life could claim that title. Moreover, as the 20th century passed into the 21st, it seemed reasonable and even self-evident to say that the 21st century, too, would be an American century. In the first couple years of this century there was a little boom in the publication of books and articles—some admiring, some disparaging—that even went so far as to proclaim an American empire. Then, in an amazingly short time, a relentless series of events—almost a staccato burst—perforated and punctured this centennial and imperial dream: the 9/11 attacks, the setbacks of the Iraq war and then of the Afghan War, and particularly the American-originated global economic crisis and Great Recession of 2008–09. The frustrations in Iraq and Afghanistan have largely discredited the American reputation for high moral character and judicious strategic judgment, and the global economic crisis has largely discredited the long-standing U.S. globalization project. More generally, these burdens have raised questions about the applicability abroad of such fundamental American values as liberal democracy and free markets, of "the American way" and "the Washington consensus."

At the same time that confident visions of a second American century and a new American empire (whether benign or not) have dissipated, another great power with its own distinctive culture and way of life has been steadily rising. In the past decade, China's ascent has neatly paralleled America's descent. And so, in the autumn of 2009—one year into the global economic crisis—no one is making a convincing case that the 21st century could still become an American one. Conversely, amid rather a lot of declinist muttering, there is already thoughtful commentary to the effect that this century is more likely to be seen in retrospect as having been a Chinese one.[1]

I doubt it. The United States can still be the most prominent—although not dominant—of the great powers, and it can still offer the most attractive way of life. But to do this, America will have to become more American than it has been in recent years. This means it will have to renovate or reinvent certain pillars that raised the United States to the heights of global power and prosperity in the second half of the 20th century. These pillars remain the only solid and enduring supports for a prominent American role in the 21st century, so we need to be clear about what they are.

Pillars of the First American Century

When discussing power, most international affairs analysts reasonably focus upon military power ("hard power"), in this case America's large-scale and high-tech military forces. The United States first achieved supremacy in vast conventional forces (World War II), then in nuclear weapons (most of the Cold War), and most recently in information-age warfare (the "Revolution in Military Affairs" that began in the 1980s). And when gauging the attractiveness of the American way of life, many analysts focus upon particular American ideas and ideals, or ideological power ("soft power")—in this case, liberal democracy, free markets and the open society. These ideas and ideals have been grouped together and advanced under a variety of slogans, some meant to encompass the globe, some of more limited scope, some emphasizing political and others economic aspects of ideology, to wit: "the Free World," "the Alliance for Progress," the idea of "universal human rights," "the Washington Consensus," "the Freedom Agenda."

There is no doubt that both military power and ideological power were central pillars of the first American century. However, the essential base for these, and for all power in international affairs, remains economic power. (This may sound like economic reductionism or even Marxism, but it is not: I do not argue that economic power is *sufficient* to account for supremacy in world affairs, only that it is *necessary*). Economic power in turn entails strength in three component dimensions: industrial, financial and technological (in other words, manufacturing, banking and innovation). During the first American century, which spanned from the high industrial era to the early information era, the United States obviously led the world in each of these three dimensions.

Industrial superiority. Throughout the 20th century, the United States was the largest industrial or manufacturing economy in the world. Its industrial products were generally competitive in world markets, with the U.S. economy earning substantial foreign exchange from their export. Although the United States lost its competitive advantage successively in older industrial sectors like steel, automobiles and consumer electronics, it demonstrated an extraordinary capacity to innovate whole new industrial sectors like aerospace, computers and telecommunications, each of which then gave the United States a new competitive edge in world markets for several decades.

Of course, many economists argue that as an economy becomes more sophisticated, it can leave behind its manufacturing component altogether and simply move upward into a variety of service sectors (of which finance is one). This argument is partly correct. However, although an economy may cease to produce industrial goods, it will continue to consume them, just as it earlier may have ceased to produce agricultural goods, but it obviously had to continue to consume them. Indeed, as an economy becomes more developed and richer, it may consume even more industrial products than it did before, and these products have to come from somewhere. Indeed, they have to be imported and these imports have to be paid for with exports, which would now have to come in the form of services. But only some services are exportable ("internationally tradable"), of which finance is the most important. Others have turned out to be importable: Advanced service economies are now importing services as well as manufactures, as seen in the outsourcing of data processing and telephone call centers from the United States to India.

The real issue in economic development is not the simple move from manufacturing to services, but rather the more complex move from older, static sectors that are no longer capable of generating export earnings to newer, dynamic sectors that can. Moreover, these new sectors have to be of sufficient scale to cover the costs of all those industrial products now being imported. Some of them might have industrial features, such as the new products of the renewable-energy and biotechnology sectors; some might have service features, such as new processes in the medical field.

Financial superiority. During much of the 20th century, the United States was a creditor nation. It achieved this partly because of its vast foreign-exchange earnings, but also because of political stability (and therefore political predictability) that led to the U.S. dollar becoming the principal international reserve currency. With its own vast amounts of capital and with foreign investors having great confidence in the stability of both the U.S. dollar and U.S. banks, the United States was overwhelmingly the world's leading financial power during most of the 20th century.

Technological superiority. The reason the United States could continually create new industrial sectors was that, for most of the 20th century, it was also the leader in developing new technologies. As late as the 1930s, scientists and engineers in other nations (especially in Britain and Germany) might introduce some new invention, but then Americans would take the lead in expanding this invention into a new innovation and expanding this innovation into a new industry. With World War II, Americans also assumed the lead in new inventions, a lead which has largely continued down to the present.

American technological superiority has been grounded in several unique or unusual features. Most obviously, the United States has long had the largest—and since World War II also the best—university system in the world.[2] This has provided a vast pool of scientists and engineers to develop new inventions and innovations. Second, the American free market system has enabled entrepreneurs to harness these new inventions and innovations to build new industries. Indeed, the combination of advanced universities and energetic entrepreneurs (often headquartered together in metropoles like Boston, the San Francisco Bay area and Silicon Valley) has birthed virtually all the new industrial sectors created in the United States since World War II. Third, the U.S. general population long led the world in average educational level. Although this advantage has disappeared in the past two decades, it was obtained during most of the 20th century. This educated general population of Americans provided a plentiful supply of efficient and productive workers for the new industrial sectors.

From Economic to Military Superiority

The great strength of the American economy enabled the United States to possess great military power, as well. The immense U.S. industrial capacity that existed in 1941, even after a decade of Great Depression, soon overwhelmed Nazi Germany and Imperial Japan with hitherto unimaginable quantities of tanks, artillery, warships, transports, bombers and fighters. Military historians generally acknowledge that the German Army and the Japanese Army were both superb at the level of military operations or "operational art." But the U.S. military trumped their advantage with its own in materiel and logistics. (The U.S. military was also often superior at the level of military strategy, but on this point there is more controversy among historians.)

Military historians have also often discussed what they see as a distinctive "American Way of War." They agree that its two central features are overwhelming mass, in both men and material, and wide-ranging mobility—the projection and sustained support of that overwhelming mass across great distances. But after these features reached their apotheosis in World War II, the American military soon faced the fact that Soviet armies were even more massive than its own. The United States responded to this challenge by drawing upon a third military feature—advanced technology—in which it had recently acquired a substantial advantage. The United States first trumped the large Soviet armies with nuclear technology and weaponry and then, when the Soviets developed their own nuclear weapons, with the computer and telecommunications tools of the information age. These U.S. military innovations amounted to new versions of the American way of war. Just as the American economy kept re-creating itself, so did the American military. Thus, for most of the 20th century no other great power could match America's military power, and the main reason was the dominance of American economic power as manifested in all three of the dimensions of industry, finance and technology.

Beginning with the Vietnam War, however, and again with the wars in Iraq and Afghanistan, the United States has confronted a new problem. Neither its advantages in massive industrial-age armies, nor in nuclear weapons, nor even in high-tech information-age weapons, have been effective in putting down a determined and sustained insurgency (a sort of pre-industrial adversary). And so now, in the first decade of the 21st century, the U.S. military is engaged in inventing yet another effective American way of war. Its success or failure in doing so will play a large role in determining whether the 21st century can become a second American one—as will, of course, the success of American elites in re-creating an effective formula for economic dynamism.

The Pillars Today: America versus China

This review of the pillars of the first American century may occasion some discouraging thoughts. Many of those pillars have been squandered or abandoned—as Daniel Bell foresaw in his *Cultural Contradictions of Capitalism*—by successive generations of Americans during the very decades that comprise much of the golden age of the American century. It is obvious today that two of the economic pillars, the industrial and the financial ones, are particularly diminished. A comparison with China makes this clear.

Although the United States remains the largest manufacturing economy in the world, China is projected to overtake it by 2015 or so. And China, of course, is the largest and often most competitive producer in such basic sectors as steel, shipbuilding and consumer goods. It is rapidly expanding and upgrading its automobile and chemical sectors as well. These have been the basic sectors of any robust industrial economy, and they usually have been the generators of large export earnings. (Along with aircraft production, these sectors enabled the United States to win World War II, and long served as the basis for the American way of war.)

China's industrial superiority, and the export earnings it brings, has of course translated into financial strength. At $2 trillion, China's reserves of foreign currencies—especially the U.S. dollar—now exceed those of any other country. In the past year, the Chinese government has used the leverage afforded by its $800 billion in Treasury securities to pressure the U.S. Treasury and the Federal Reserve with respect to their policies affecting the value of the dollar. Even more important, it has used its financial strength to implement the most successful economic stimulus program any government has yet deployed to address the global economic crisis. In 2009, the world's most effective practitioners of Keynesian fiscal policy are the Chinese.

Indeed, the Chinese government's response to the current global economic crisis is remarkably similar to President Franklin Roosevelt's response to the Great Depression. Like FDR's New Deal, the Chinese version centers on large-scale spending on big infrastructure projects like highways, railroads, bridges, dams, rural electrification and public buildings. These infrastructure projects not only provide steady markets and continuing employment for such basic industries as steel, cement, heavy machinery and construction; they also bring long-term productivity gains to the national economy. In contrast to both the Roosevelt Administration in the 1930s and the Chinese government today, the Obama Administration is spending little on new infrastructure. Most of its stimulus program is directed at simply maintaining existing assets and employment in selected service sectors (and big Democratic Party constituencies), particularly state and local governments and public education.

The similarities between the U.S. response to the Great Depression and the Chinese response to today's global economic crisis are not accidental. Both the United States then and China today possessed a vast industrial structure that suddenly suffered underutilization and excess capacity. With so much of the economy devoted to industry, and with industry thus having so much political influence, it is natural for governments to emphasize the revival of industry and manufacturing. An industry-centered (and industry-influenced) economic recovery program will normally emphasize government spending and some kind of Keynesian fiscal policy.

However, in the United States of recent years, industry has been a much smaller part of the economy than it was in the 1930s and than it is in China now. Rather, finance became the largest single economic sector, along with becoming the most profitable and prestigious one; it is therefore not surprising that finance became the most politically influential economic sector as well. This has meant that the U.S. response to the current economic crisis—first that of the Bush Administration in 2008 and now that of the Obama Administration in 2009—has been finance-centered (and finance-influenced). That is why it has emphasized bailouts of "too big to fail" financial institutions, the manipulation of interest rates and monetary policy (a kind of Friedmanism).

The real, and ominous historical analogue to the U.S. economy and economic policies of today, therefore, is not the United States of the 1930s, but rather the United Kingdom of the 1930s. By then, Britain's decades as "the workshop of the world" were long past; the British economy centered on finance, and British governments devised economic policy accordingly. The City (and Lombard Street) was even more authoritative there than Wall Street has been here. The result was that, during the Great Depression, Britain never saw anything approaching New Deal deficit spending and fiscal policy (never anything like Keynesianism in Keynes's own country). Instead, it experienced a "lost decade" of dreary stagnation, which led in turn to its inability to sustain its world power status thereafter.

In short, if China's present trends and economic policies continue, it will likely make its exit from the current global economic crisis with its economy more developed and diverse than it was when the crisis began. Conversely, if America's own present trends and economic policies continue, it will make its exit from the crisis with its economy more distorted and debilitated than it was before.

Technological Superiority

It is worth remembering that the economic policies of the Roosevelt Administration—both the New Deal and military spending, both civilian Keynesianism and military Keynesianism—resulted in a vast and varied industrial structure that was not just the workshop of the world, but also its wonder (as exemplified in the 1939 New York World's Fair). This industrial structure was fully in place in 1941, and it proved to be the basic foundation of the American century. If we are to make use of the current crisis, we must produce a similar outcome, and we can do so by building on the one strong pillar that remains to us: our long-standing technological superiority.

China is clearly investing a great deal to achieve its own technological strength, rapidly expanding and upgrading universities and research institutes, as well as investing in the rigorous education of the general population. While these measures have been effective in steadily increasing its economic productivity, historically it has taken many years for an economy to translate industrial and financial superiority into technological superiority. (For example, the United States reached industrial superiority in the 1890s and financial superiority in the 1910s, but its universities did not clearly surpass the top British and German ones until World War II.) The central and strategic question about

which country will achieve the technological superiority of the future will turn upon which leads in the new economic sectors of the future.

Today, the most obvious candidates for these sectors are new sustainable or "green" energy sources and uses, new biotechnology-based products and processes, and new medical and health treatments. (One might think that the latter two candidates are not really distinct, but this would be mistaken: The economic implications of biotechnology and uses of biomimicry far surpass medical applications, and not all new medical treatments need be based on biotechnology alone.) It is interesting that the Obama Administration has specified energy and medical-related advances as being at the center of its own vision for America's economic future, and that they, along with the education sector, occupied a prominent place in the Administration's public depiction of its own economic stimulus program and budget priorities.

The potential economic sectors of sustainable energy, biotechnology and medicine/health are clearly of vital importance to vast numbers of people around the world. Moreover, those countries with advanced or advancing economies would be able and willing to spend vast sums to import the new products and processes of these sectors. If the United States can achieve leadership in them, as it did during the 20th century in aerospace, computers and telecommunications, it will have secured a robust pillar for even broader American leadership in the world in the 21st century. The Chinese are not oblivious, however, to the promise of at least one of these new sectors, renewable energy, which they now call a strategic industry. In the past few years, as part of their own economic stimulus program, they have begun to construct large wind power farms and solar power plants and to develop promising battery-powered automobiles.

It should be a prime objective of the U.S. government to maintain and even enhance America's technological superiority, particularly with respect to developing new economic sectors that will be leaders in global markets. This entails encouraging and enabling the traditional bases for U.S. technological superiority: the university system, with its numerous scientists and engineers; the free-market system, with its numerous innovators and entrepreneurs; and the education system for the general population (obviously in great need of improvement).

Some economists have argued that only the quality of top scientists and engineers is important for economic productivity and international competitiveness, and that the education level of the general population is not. However, the inventions of these scientists and engineers have to be transformed and expanded into entire economic sectors. That requires support from a large base of intelligent, skilled and diligent technical, clerical and industrial workers, a base that must continually be reproduced and upgraded by the education system. In any event, the United States is unlikely to continue to enjoy a productive and competitive economy if it must continue to support the large and growing number of its people who are so poorly educated as to be permanently un- and under-employed.

In order to improve general education, it is perhaps time to return to the traditional American value of competition. Numerous attempts to reform the monopolistic public schools (more accurately, government schools) have failed; the solution will come by enabling a large variety of private schools to freely compete with the government ones. All good schools could receive public assistance; none should receive a public monopoly. Unfortunately, since one of the Democratic Party's main constituencies is the public-school teachers' associations, the education policies of the Obama Administration will likely only make things worse.

The Military Corollary

Even if we succeed in revitalizing our economy by depending on scientific-technological leadership, we will still need to re-create a successful American way of war for current circumstances. This begs the question of how we will prevail over insurgent movements and the other slings and arrows of hostile non-state actors.

On the one hand, the dreary (but still debated) U.S. experience with counterinsurgency in Vietnam—which came at the height of the first American century—convinced the U.S. military for more than a generation thereafter that counterinsurgency warfare was incompatible with *any* version of the American way of war. On the other hand, the recent success in Iraq of the new (actually *re*-newed) U.S. counterinsurgency doctrine offers some hope.

The clue to the conundrum posed by insurgent warfare lies in looking even more closely at the features of the American way of war as they have actually been demonstrated in U.S. military history. We have already mentioned the well-known features of overwhelming mass and wide-ranging mobility, along with the later addition of high technology. But when the United States fought wars in the 20th century, it added yet another largely unacknowledged feature: a heavy reliance upon the ground forces of allies. In World War I, these were the French and the British armies; in World War II, the British and Soviet armies; in the Korean War, the South Korean army; and in the Vietnam War, the South Vietnamese army. Even in the Gulf War of 1991, the U.S. military operated with substantial ground units provided by other members of its "coalition of the willing" (for example, those of Britain, France and Saudi Arabia). In short, the "overwhelming mass" of U.S. ground forces has always been something of an illusion; the ground forces of U.S. allies were often more numerous (although less efficient and effective) than the ground forces of the United States itself, and these allied forces often assumed many of the more labor-intensive military tasks. The dirty little secret of the American way of war is that America's allies frequently did much of the dirty work.

It was this secret that the U.S. Army and Marine Corps rediscovered and applied in Iraq in 2006–07. They realized that the key to successful counterinsurgency was to ally with local forces—in this case the Sunni tribes of the "Anbar Awakening"—who had their own reasons for opposing al-Qaeda insurgents. The U.S. military is now trying to apply a similar strategy in Afghanistan by seeking to split various Pashtun tribes from the Taliban insurgents. However, one of the reasons the Sunni tribes allied with the U.S. military in Iraq was that they feared the majority Shi'a government as well as the al-Qaeda insurgents. The Pashtun tribes in Afghanistan lack any comparable fear, and hence any comparable incentive, to push them into alliance with U.S. forces.

The general lesson to be learned about the potential for any American way of counterinsurgency warfare is that the United States will always have to rely upon local forces, whether local militaries or merely local militias, who have their own capabilities for effective counterinsurgency. The U.S. military may be able to add certain essential ingredients or necessary conditions (such as, for example, effective weapons, professional training, mobility and logistics, or simply ample pay), but it can never successfully do the grueling job and dirty work of counterinsurgency all by itself. This means that the United States should not undertake a counterinsurgency campaign until it has developed a thorough knowledge and clear view of local forces and potential allies in a given theater.

In practice, this means too that the United States should normally seek to solve its problems without resorting to using the regular U.S. military for any counterinsurgency operations at all. Rather, the primary focus of the U.S. military should be on deterring war and, if war comes, defeating the military forces of other great powers in all forms of 21st-century warfare. The reason we are now attacked only at sub-conventional levels is not that no motive can exist for attacks against us at other levels; it is because no one dares. If we lose our superiority at these levels, however, someone might well dare.

Popular Culture and American Idealism

The reinvention and renovation of its economic and military pillars would put the United States once again in a position to exercise leadership in the world. However, having recreated its ability to be a world leader, the United States would also have to learn again how to act like one. For almost two decades, U.S. political leaders have often acted toward other nations, and particularly toward other great powers, in a way guaranteed to provoke their annoyance and disdain, and even their anger and contempt. This requires us to pay some attention to both the cultural style of American leadership and the power context in which it is exercised.

With all the talk among American political commentators about "soft power" and the attractiveness of American popular culture to the rest of the world, it is usually forgotten that this popular culture is chiefly popular with the young—particularly those young who are still irresponsible, rebellious and feckless. It does not often attract the mature, particularly those mature enough to be the leaders of their families, communities or countries who are responsible for their security and prosperity. In short, American popular culture is a culture for adolescents, not for adults, and adults around the world know and act upon this truth. If American leaders want to lead the leaders of other countries, they will have to act like mature adults, not like the attention-seeking celebrities of American popular culture.

Similarly, with all the talk among American political leaders and commentators about American "idealism," and the attractiveness of American values to the rest of the world, it is usually forgotten that most of the political leaders in other countries are realistic men making sensible calculations about their nation's interests (and their own). They expect the leaders of other countries, including the United States, to do the same. This is particularly true of the current leaders of China and Russia. Having learned all about the claims of ideology when they were growing up, and having put ideology aside when they became adults, they cannot really believe that U.S. political leaders in turn really believe that American ideals should be promoted for their own sake, for their "universal validity," rather than as a legitimation or cover for U.S. interests. If American leaders want to lead such leaders of other countries, they will have to act in the style of realists, and not in the style of idealists.

Realism requires us to specify the new context of great powers in which the United States would exercise leadership.

That begs a key choice. Realism requires us to specify the new, 21st-century context of great powers in which the United States would exercise leadership. Although rebuilding its economic and military power pillars will make the United States the most prominent power in the world, it will no longer be a dominant one. There will be other great powers as well: some rising, like China and India; some declining, like the European Union and Japan; and some rising in some respects but declining or unstable in others, like Russia, Iran and Brazil. If the United States is to be an effective and constructive leader in world affairs, it must be able to lead at least some of these powers on issues of world importance. These include threats from transnational terrorist networks, nuclear proliferation, the global economy, global epidemics and global warming. In particular, it will have to deal in an effective and constructive way with China, India and Russia,

powers that have risen or revived to the point that they seek to be the pre-eminent or even dominant power in a particular region—which is to say, to have something like a traditional sphere of influence. For China, this is Southeast Asia; for India (not quite yet, but likely within a decade), this will be South Asia and possibly the shores of the Arab Gulf; and for Russia, this is Central Asia and the Caucasus, but also the neighboring Slavic (and Orthodox) states of Belarus and Ukraine.

With respect to these great powers and these regions, the United States will have to make a choice. It can try to lead the small countries in a region in some kind of opposition or even alliance against the aspiring regional power, as the United States has done with Georgia and Ukraine against Russia. Or it can allow the regional power to exercise leadership in its region, while that power in turn allows the United States to exercise a broader leadership on issues of world importance.

Choosing this latter option would not signify anything particularly new or novel. Even when the United States was at its height in the role of a superpower, the United States reluctantly but realistically allowed the Soviet Union to dominate Eastern Europe. However, that kind of intrusive political and economic control went far beyond the traditional norms for a sphere of influence. For the most part, great powers dominant in their particular regions have been satisfied with having their security interests preserved, along with some economic presence, while allowing a large swath of political autonomy within the smaller states. In this regard, it was the Soviet relationship with Finland rather than its relationship with those neighbors upon whom it had imposed Communist regimes that fit the traditional norm. Indeed, the current Russian relationship with most of the former Soviet republics in Central Asia now largely fits this norm as well, suggesting that the traditional pattern (which the Bush and Obama Administrations have derided as *so* 19th century) can be reasonably updated to fit the conditions of the 21st.

The 19th century had its own distinctive features. Some historians have redefined it to be the "century" between 1815 and 1914—between the end of the Napoleonic Wars and the onset of the First World War. That 19th century then becomes an era distinguished by no general wars and by rapid economic growth, a rare era of peace and prosperity. And if any one nation was identified with that peace and prosperity, it was Britain. By the end of the 19th century, it was widely acknowledged that the century had been a British one. Certainly, no other power or way of life could claim that title.

But although Britain was the most prominent of the great powers, it was not a dominant one on the scale that the United States was dominant in the immediate post-World War II period. It certainly dominated the world's oceans with its Royal Navy; it was the leader in the world economy, first in industry and then in finance; and it was the pre-eminent power on many issues of world importance, such as the repression of the slave trade and piracy and the development of international law. But Britain was not a dominant power on any particular continent (except Australia) or in any particular region (except in South Asia during the time of the Raj). Rather, it generally was satisfied with a division of the continents into competing spheres of influence, which then might result in continental-scale balances of power (in Europe, Africa, East Asia and even South America). Britain was the leading world power because it largely allowed other great powers to be the leaders in their own immediate regions. This allowed Britain to be the leader of the leaders without having to ask their explicit permission.

The United States will never again be a dominant power like it was during the American century, particularly in the period from the late 1940s into the early 1970s. Historically, that was an anomalous time in many respects. But a century can still be shaped and defined—and can still be guided toward greater peace and prosperity—by a nation that is only the most prominent of the great powers. And a grateful posterity can later look back upon that century and honor that nation by bestowing upon the century that nation's very own name.

Notes

1. China's potential for rising to global power—with attention to both its strengths and its weaknesses—is debated by Aaron L. Friedberg versus Robert S. Ross, "Here be Dragons: Is China a Military Threat?" *The National Interest* (September/October 2009); and by Minxin Pei versus Jonathan Anderson, "Great Debate: The Color of China," *The National Interest* (March/April 2009).

2. See Itamar Rabinovich, "The American Advantage", *The American Interest* (May/June 2009).

JAMES KURTH is professor of political science and senior research scholar at Swarthmore College.

Grand Strategy for a Divided America

CHARLES A. KUPCHAN AND PETER L. TRUBOWITZ

Mind the Gap

The United States is in the midst of a polarized and bruising debate about the nature and scope of its engagement with the world. The current reassessment is only the latest of many; ever since the United States' rise as a global power, its leaders and citizens have regularly scrutinized the costs and benefits of foreign ambition. In 1943, Walter Lippmann offered a classic formulation of the issue. "In foreign relations," Lippmann wrote, "as in all other relations, a policy has been formed only when commitments and power have been brought into balance. . . . The nation must maintain its objectives and its power in equilibrium, its purposes within its means and its means equal to its purposes."

Although Lippmann was mindful of the economic costs of global engagement, his primary concern was the political "solvency" of U.S. foreign policy, not the adequacy of the United States' material resources. He lamented the divisive partisanship that had so often prevented the United States from finding "a settled and generally accepted foreign policy." "This is a danger to the Republic," he warned. "For when a people is divided within itself about the conduct of its foreign relations, it is unable to agree on the determination of its true interest. It is unable to prepare adequately for war or to safeguard successfully its peace. . . . The spectacle of this great nation which does not know its own mind is as humiliating as it is dangerous." Lippmann's worries would prove unfounded; in the face of World War II and the onset of the Cold War, the bitter partisanship of the past gave way to a broad consensus on foreign policy that was to last for the next five decades.

Today, however, Lippmann's concern with political solvency is more relevant than ever. After the demise of the Soviet Union, the shock of September 11, and the failures of the Iraq war, Republicans and Democrats share less common ground on the fundamental purposes of U.S. power than at any other time since World War II. A critical gap has opened up between the United States' global commitments and its political appetite for sustaining them. As made clear by the collision between President George W. Bush and the Democratic Congress over what to do in Iraq, the country's bipartisan consensus on foreign policy has collapsed. If left unattended, the political foundations of U.S. statecraft will continue to disintegrate, exposing the country to the dangers of an erratic and incoherent foreign policy.

The presidential candidate who understands the urgency and gravity of striking a new balance between the United States' purposes and its political means is poised to reap a double reward. He or she would likely attract strong popular support; as in the 2006 midterm elections, in the 2008 election the war in Iraq and the conduct of U.S. foreign policy are set to be decisive issues. That candidate, if elected, would also enhance U.S. security by crafting a new grand strategy that is politically sustainable, thereby steadying a global community that continues to look to the United States for leadership.

Formulating a politically solvent strategy will require scaling back U.S. commitments, bringing them into line with diminishing means. At the same time, it will be necessary to stabilize the nation's foreign policy by shoring up public support for a new vision of the United States' global responsibilities. Solvency is the path to security; it is far better for the United States to arrive at a more discriminating grand strategy that enjoys domestic backing than to continue drifting toward an intractable polarization that would be as dangerous as it would be humiliating.

Finding the Water's Edge

For Americans who lived through the bipartisan consensus of the Cold War era, the current political warfare over foreign policy seems to be a dramatic aberration. To be sure, Bush has been a polarizing president, in no small part due to the controversial invasion of Iraq and the troubled occupation that has followed. But in fact, today's partisan wrangling over foreign policy is the historical norm; it is the bipartisanship of the Cold War that was the anomaly.

Soon after the republic's founding, political parties formed to help overcome the obstacles that federalism, the separation of powers, and sectionalism put in the way of effective statecraft. With them came partisanship. During the nation's early decades, the main line of partisan competition ran along the North-South divide, pitting the Hamiltonian Federalists of the Northeast against the Jeffersonian Republicans of the South. The two parties disagreed on matters of grand strategy—specifically whether the United States should lean toward Great Britain or France—as well as on matters of political economy.

The Federalists worried that the new republic might fail if it found itself in a conflict with the British; they therefore favored tilting toward Great Britain rather than extending the alliance with France that was struck during the American Revolution. On economic matters, the Federalists defended the interests of the North's aspiring entrepreneurs, arguing for tariffs to protect the region's infant industries. The Republicans, however, continued to lean toward France, hoping to balance Great Britain's power by supporting its main European rival. And as champions of the interests of the nation's farmers, the Republicans clamored for free trade and westward expansion. At George Washington's behest, the two parties found common ground on the need to avoid "entangling alliances," but they agreed on little else.

Partisan passions cooled with the end of the Napoleonic Wars in Europe, and an era of solvency in the conduct of the nation's foreign affairs ensued. The collapse of the Federalist Party and the revival of an economy no longer disrupted by war ushered in what one Boston newspaper called "an Era of Good Feelings." For the first time, the United States enjoyed a sustained period of political consensus. Meanwhile, the peace preserved by the Concert of Europe, coupled with the tentative rapprochement with London that followed the War of 1812, made it possible for the nation's elected officials, starting with James Monroe, to turn their energies to the demands of "internal improvement." Americans focused on the consolidation and westward expansion of the union, limiting the nation's reach to what was sustainable politically and militarily.

This consensus was upended in 1846, when James Polk took the country to war against Mexico in the name of "manifest destiny." The Democrats—the southern heirs to Jefferson's Republicans—championed seizing Mexican territory and saw the war as an opportunity to strengthen their hold on the levers of national power. Fearing exactly that, the northeastern Whigs—the forerunners to modern Republicans—waged a rear-guard battle, challenging the legitimacy of Polk's land grab and the rise of southern "slave power." Polk's war, the United States' first war of choice, unleashed a new round of partisan struggle, aggravating the sectional tensions that would ultimately result in the Civil War.

An uneasy domestic calm set in after the Civil War, but it was soon brought to an end by divisions over the United States' aspirations to great-power status. Over the course of the 1890s, the United States built a world-class battle fleet, acquired foreign lands, and secured foreign markets. Republican efforts to catapult the United States into the front ranks, however, reopened sectional wounds and invited strong Democratic resistance. The Republicans prevailed due to their monopoly on power, but their geopolitical ambitions soon proved politically unsustainable. Starting with the Spanish-American War, the United States engaged in what Lippmann called "deficit diplomacy": its international commitments exceeded the public's willingness to bear the requisite burdens.

After the turn of the century, U.S. foreign policy lurched incoherently between stark alternatives. Theodore Roosevelt's imperialist adventure in the Philippines quickly outstripped the country's appetite for foreign ambition. William Taft tried "dollar diplomacy," preferring to pursue Washington's objectives abroad through what he called "peaceful and economic" means. But he triggered the ire of Democrats who viewed his strategy as little more than capitulation to the interests of big business. Woodrow Wilson embraced "collective security" and the League of Nations, investing in institutionalized partnerships that would ease the costs of the United States' deepening engagement with the world. But the Senate, virtually paralyzed by partisan rancor, would have none of it. As Henry Cabot Lodge, one of the League of Nations' staunchest opponents in the Senate, quipped, "I never expected to hate anyone in politics with the hatred I feel towards Wilson." By the interwar period, political stalemate had set in. Americans shunned both the assertive use of U.S. power and institutionalized multilateralism, instead preferring the illusory safety of isolationism advocated by Warren Harding, Calvin Coolidge, and Herbert Hoover.

The collapse of bipartisanship and liberal internationalism did not start with George W. Bush.

One of Franklin Roosevelt's greatest achievements was overcoming this political divide and steering the United States toward a new era of bipartisanship. With World War II as a backdrop, he built a broad coalition of Democrats and Republicans behind liberal internationalism. The new course entailed a commitment to both power and partnership: the United States would project its military strength to preserve stability, but whenever possible it would exercise leadership through consensus and multilateral partnership rather than unilateral initiative. This domestic compact, although weakened by political struggles over the Vietnam War, lasted to the end of the Cold War.

The nature of the geopolitical threat facing the United States helped Roosevelt and his successors sustain this liberal internationalist compact. Washington needed allies to prevent the domination of Eurasia by a hostile power. The strategic exigencies of World War II and the Cold War also instilled discipline, encouraging Democrats and Republicans alike to unite around a common foreign policy. When partisan passions flared, as they did over the Korean War and the Vietnam War, they were contained by the imperatives of super-power rivalry.

The steadiness of bipartisan cooperation on foreign policy was the product not just of strategic necessity but also of changes in the nation's political landscape. Regional divides had moderated, with the North and the South forming a political alliance for the first time in U.S. history. Anticommunism made it politically treacherous to stray too far to the left, and the public's worries about nuclear Armageddon reined in the right. The post–World War II economic boom eased the socioeconomic divides of the New Deal era, closing the ideological distance between Democrats and Republicans and making it easier to fashion a consensus behind free trade. Prosperity and affluence helped nurture the United States' political center, which served as the foundation for the liberal internationalism that lasted a half century.

A Nation Redivided

Contrary to conventional wisdom, the collapse of bipartisanship and liberal internationalism did not start with George W. Bush. Bipartisanship dropped sharply following the end of the

Cold War, reaching a post–World War II low after the Republicans gained control of Congress in 1994. Repeated clashes over foreign policy between the Clinton administration and Congress marked the hollowing out of the bipartisan center that had been liberal internationalism's political base. The Bush administration then dismantled what remained of the moderate center, ensuring that today's partisan divide is every bit as wide as the interwar schism that haunted Lippmann. Democratic and Republican lawmakers now hold very different views on foreign policy. On the most basic questions of U.S. grand strategy—the sources and purposes of U.S. power, the use of force, the role of international institutions—representatives of the two parties are on different planets.

Most Republicans in Congress contend that U.S. power depends mainly on the possession and use of military might, and they view institutionalized cooperation primarily as an impediment. They staunchly back the Bush administration's ongoing effort to pacify Iraq. When the new Congress took its first votes on the Iraq war in the beginning of this year, only 17 of the 201 Republicans in the House crossed party lines to oppose the recent surge in U.S. troops. In the Senate, only two Republicans joined the Democrats to approve a resolution calling for a timetable for withdrawal. In contrast, most Democrats maintain that U.S. power depends more on persuasion than coercion and needs to be exercised multilaterally. They want out of Iraq: 95 percent of House and Senate Democrats have voted to withdraw U.S. troops in 2008. With the Republicans opting for the use of force and the Democrats for international cooperation, the bipartisan compact between power and partnership—the formula that brought liberal internationalism to life—has come undone.

To be sure, the Republican Party is still home to a few committed multilateralists, such as Senators Richard Lugar (of Indiana) and Chuck Hagel (of Nebraska). But they are isolated within their own ranks. And some Democrats, especially those eyeing the presidency, are keen to demonstrate their resolve on matters of national defense. But the party leaders are being pushed to the left by increasingly powerful party activists. The ideological overlap between the two parties is thus minimal, and the areas of concord are superficial at best. Most Republicans and Democrats still believe that the United States has global responsibilities, but there is little agreement on how to match means and ends. And on the central question of power versus partnership, the two parties are moving in opposite directions—with the growing gap evident among the public as well as political elites.

In a March 2007 Pew Research Center poll, over 70 percent of Republican voters maintained that "the best way to ensure peace is through military strength." Only 40 percent of Democratic voters shared that view. A similar poll conducted in 1999 revealed the same partisan split, making clear that the divide is not just about Bush's foreign policy but also about the broader purposes of U.S. power. The Iraq war has clearly widened and deepened ideological differences over the relative efficacy of force and diplomacy. One CNN poll recorded that after four years of occupying Iraq, only 24 percent of Republicans oppose the war, compared with more than 90 percent of Democrats. As for exporting American ideals, a June 2006 German Marshall

Fund study found that only 35 percent of Democrats believed the United States should "help establish democracy in other countries," compared with 64 percent of Republicans. Similarly, a December 2006 CBS News poll found that two-thirds of Democrats believed the United States should "mind its own business internationally," whereas only one-third of Republicans held that view.

Fueled by these ideological divides, partisanship has engulfed Washington. According to one widely used index (Voteview), Congress today is more politically fractious and polarized than at any time in the last hundred years. After Democrats gained a majority in Congress in the 2006 midterm elections, many observers predicted that having one party control the White House and the other Congress would foster cooperation, as it often has in the past. Instead, the political rancor has only intensified. The White House, despite its initial pledge to work with the opposition, has continued its strident ways, dismissing the Democrats' call for a timetable for withdrawal from Iraq as a "game of charades." Just after capturing the House and the Senate, the Democrats also promised to reach across the aisle. But as soon as the 110th Congress opened, they gave Republicans a taste of their own medicine by preventing the minority party from amending legislation during the initial flurry of lawmaking.

Partisan confrontation is a recipe for political stalemate at home and failed leadership abroad.

The sources of this return to partisan rancor are international as well as domestic. Abroad, the demise of the Soviet Union and the absence of a new peer competitor have loosened Cold War discipline, leaving the country's foreign policy more vulnerable to the vicissitudes of party politics. The threat posed by international terrorism has proved too elusive and sporadic to act as the new unifier. Meanwhile, the United States' deepening integration into the world economy is producing growing disparities in wealth among Americans, creating new socioeconomic cleavages and eroding support for free trade.

Within the United States, the political conditions that once encouraged centrism have weakened. Regional tensions are making a comeback; "red" America and "blue" America disagree about what the nature of the country's engagement in the world should be as well as about domestic issues such as abortion, gun control, and taxes. Moderates are in ever shorter supply, resulting in the thinning out of what Arthur Schlesinger, Jr., aptly labeled "the vital center." Congressional redistricting, the proliferation of highly partisan media outlets, and the growing power of the Internet as a source of campaign financing and partisan mobilization have all contributed to the erosion of the center. A generational change has taken its toll, too. Almost 85 percent of the House was first elected in 1988 or after. The "greatest generation" is fast retiring from political life, taking with it decades of civic-minded service.

With the presidential campaign now building up to full speed and the domestic landscape already deeply etched along regional and ideological lines, the partisan confrontation is poised to intensify—a recipe for political stalemate at home and failed leadership abroad.

Restoring Solvency

In the early twentieth century, deep partisan divisions produced unpredictable and dangerous swings in U.S. foreign policy and ultimately led to isolation from the world. A similar dynamic is unfolding at the beginning of the twenty-first century. The assertive unilateralism of the Bush administration is proving politically unsustainable. Eyeing the 2008 elections, the Democrats are readying ambitious plans to breathe new life into international institutions. But they, too, will find their preferred grand strategy politically unsustainable. The Republican Party, virtually bereft of its moderates after the 2006 elections, has little patience for cooperative multilateralism—and will gladly deploy its power in the Senate to block any programmatic effort to bind Washington to international agreements and institutions. Especially amid the domestic acrimony spawned by the war in Iraq, partisanship and stalemate at home could once again obstruct U.S. statecraft, perhaps even provoking an unsteady retreat from abroad.

The U.S. electorate already appears to be heading in that direction. According to the December 2006 CBS News poll, 52 percent of all Americans thought the United States "should mind its own business internationally." Even in the midst of impassioned opposition to the Vietnam War, only 36 percent of Americans held such a view. Inward-looking attitudes are especially pronounced among younger Americans: 72 percent of 18- to 24-year-olds do not believe that the United States should take the lead in solving global crises. If Washington continues to pursue a grand strategy that exceeds its political means, isolationist sentiment among Americans is sure to grow.

The United States needs to pursue a new grand strategy that is politically solvent. In today's polarized landscape, with Democrats wanting less power projection and Republicans fewer international partnerships, restoring solvency means bringing U.S. commitments back in line with political means. Finding a new domestic equilibrium that guarantees responsible U.S. leadership in the world requires a strategy that is as judicious and selective as it is purposeful.

First, a solvent strategy would entail sharing more burdens with other states. Great powers have regularly closed the gap between resources and commitments by devolving strategic ties to local actors. The United States should use its power and good offices to catalyze greater self-reliance in various regions, as it has done in Europe. Washington should build on existing regional bodies by, for example, encouraging the Gulf Cooperation Council to deepen defense cooperation on the Arabian Peninsula, helping the African Union expand its capabilities, and supporting the Association of Southeast Asian Nations' efforts to build an East Asian security forum. Washington should urge the European Union to forge a more collective approach to security policy and assume greater defense burdens. The United States also ought to deepen its ties to emerging regional powers, such as Brazil, China, India, and Nigeria. Washington would

then be able to better influence their behavior so that it complements rather than hinders U.S. objectives.

Second, where the war on terrorism is concerned, U.S. strategy should be to target terrorists rather than to call for regime change. This would mean focusing military efforts on destroying terrorist cells and networks while using political and economic tools to address the long-term sources of instability in the Middle East. Recognizing that reform in the Arab world will be slow in coming, Washington should pursue policies that patiently support economic development, respect for human rights, and religious and political pluralism. It should also fashion working partnerships with countries prepared to fight extremism. Pursuing regime change and radical visions of transforming the Middle East will only backfire and continue to overextend U.S. military power and political will.

Third, the United States must rebuild its hard power. To do so, Congress must allocate the funds necessary to redress the devastating effect of the Iraq war on the readiness, equipment, and morale of the U.S. armed forces. The Pentagon should also husband its resources by consolidating its 750 overseas bases. Although the United States must maintain the ability to project power on a global basis, it can reduce the drain on manpower by downsizing its forward presence and relying more heavily on prepositioned assets and personnel based in the United States.

Fourth, the United States should restrain adversaries through engagement, as many great powers in the past have frequently done. In the nineteenth century, Otto von Bismarck adeptly adjusted Germany's relations with Europe's major states to ensure that his country would not face a countervailing coalition. At the turn of the twentieth century, the United Kingdom successfully engaged the United States and Japan, dramatically reducing the costs of its overseas empire and enabling it to focus on dangers closer to home. In the early 1970s, Richard Nixon's opening to China substantially lightened the burden of Cold War competition. Washington should pursue similar strategies today, using shrewd diplomacy to dampen strategic competition with China, Iran, and other potential rivals. Should U.S. efforts be reciprocated, they promise to yield the substantial benefits that accompany rapprochement. If Washington is rebuffed, it can be sure to remain on guard and thereby avoid the risk of strategic exposure.

The fifth component of this grand strategy should be greater energy independence. The United States' oil addiction is dramatically constricting its geopolitical flexibility; playing guardian of the Persian Gulf entails onerous strategic commitments and awkward political alignments. Furthermore, high oil prices are encouraging producers such as Iran, Russia, and Venezuela to challenge U.S. interests. The United States must reduce its dependence on oil by investing in the development of alternative fuels and adopting a federally mandated effort to make cars more efficient.

Finally, the United States should favor pragmatic partnerships over the formalized international institutions of the Cold War era. To be sure, international collaboration continues to be in the United States' national interest. In some areas—fighting climate change, facilitating international development, liberalizing international trade—institutionalized cooperation is likely to endure, if not deepen. It is already clear, however, that congressional support for the fixed alliances and robust institutions that were created after World War II is quickly waning. Grand visions of a global alliance of democracies need to be tempered by political reality. Informal groupings, such as the "contact group" for the Balkans, the Quartet, the participants in the six-party talks on North Korea, and the EU-3/U.S. coalition working to rein in Iran's nuclear program, are rapidly becoming the most effective vehicles for diplomacy. In a polarized climate, less is more: pragmatic teamwork, flexible concerts, and task-specific coalitions must become the staples of a new brand of U.S. statecraft.

Far from being isolationist, this strategy of judicious retrenchment would guard against isolationist tendencies. In contrast, pursuing a foreign policy of excessive and unsustainable ambition would risk a political backlash that could produce precisely the turn inward that neither the United States nor the world can afford. The United States must find a stable middle ground between doing too much and doing too little.

Break on through to the Other Side

Former Secretary of State Dean Acheson once claimed that 80 percent of the job of foreign policy was "management of your domestic ability to have a policy." He may have exaggerated, but he expressed an enduring truth: good policy requires good politics. Bringing ends and means back into balance would help restore the confidence of the American public in the conduct of U.S. foreign policy. But implementing a strategic adjustment will require dampening polarization and building a stable consensus behind it. As Roosevelt demonstrated during World War II, sound leadership and tireless public diplomacy are prerequisites for fashioning bipartisan cooperation on foreign policy.

The next president will have to take advantage of the discrete areas in which Democrats and Republicans can find common

purpose. Logrolling may be necessary to circumvent gridlock and facilitate agreement. Evangelicals on the right and social progressives on the left can close ranks on climate change, human rights, and international development. Democrats might support free trade if Republicans are willing to invest in worker retraining programs. The desire of big business to preserve access to low-wage labor may be consistent with the interests of pro-immigration constituencies; building a bridge between the two groups would reconcile corporate interests in the North with immigrant interests in the Southwest. Democrats who support multilateralism on principle can team up with Republicans who support institutions as vehicles for sharing global burdens. Although these and other political bargains will not restore the bipartisan consensus of the Cold War era, they will certainly help build political support for a new, albeit more modest, grand strategy.

So will more efforts to reach across the congressional aisle. Roosevelt overcame the Republicans' opposition to liberal internationalism by reaching out to them, appointing prominent Republicans to key international commissions and working closely with Wendell Willkie, the candidate he defeated in the 1940 election, to combat isolationism. The next administration should follow suit, appointing pragmatic members of the opposition to important foreign policy posts and establishing a high-level, bipartisan panel to provide regular and timely input into policy deliberations. Form will be as important as substance as U.S. leaders search for a grand strategy that not only meets the country's geopolitical needs but also restores political solvency at home.

CHARLES A. KUPCHAN is Professor of International Affairs at Georgetown University, a Senior Fellow at the Council on Foreign Relations, and Henry A. Kissinger Scholar at the Library of Congress. PETER L. TRUBOWITZ is Associate Professor of Government at the University of Texas, Austin, and a Senior Fellow at the Robert S. Strauss Center for International Security and Law.

From *Foreign Affairs*, July/August 2007, pp. 71–83. Copyright © 2007 by Council on Foreign Relations, Inc. Reprinted by permission of Foreign Affairs. www.ForeignAffairs.org

Enemies into Friends

How the United States Can Court Its Adversaries

CHARLES A. KUPCHAN

In his inaugural address, U.S. President Barack Obama informed those regimes "on the wrong side of history" that the United States "will extend a hand if you are willing to unclench your fist." He soon backed up his words with deeds, making engagement with U.S. adversaries one of the new administration's priorities. During his first year in office, Obama pursued direct negotiations with Iran and North Korea over their nuclear programs. He sought to "reset" relations with Russia by searching for common ground on arms control, missile defense, and Afghanistan. He began scaling back economic sanctions against Cuba. And he put out diplomatic feelers to Myanmar (also called Burma) and Syria.

Over a year into Obama's presidency, the jury is still out on whether this strategy of engagement is bearing fruit. Policymakers and scholars are divided over the merits and the risks of Obama's outreach to adversaries and over how best to increase the likelihood that his overtures will be reciprocated. Debate continues on whether rapprochement results from mutual concessions that tame rivalries or rather from the iron fist that forces adversaries into submission. Equally controversial is whether the United States should pursue reconciliation with hardened autocracies or instead make engagement contingent on democratization. And disagreement persists over whether diplomacy or economic engagement represents the most effective pathway to peace.

Many of Obama's critics have already made up their minds on the merits of his outreach to adversaries, concluding not only that the president has little to show for his efforts but also that his pliant diplomacy demeans the United States and weakens its hand. Following Obama's September 2009 speech to the United Nations General Assembly, in which he called for "a new era of engagement based on mutual interest and mutual respect" and "new coalitions that bridge old divides," the conservative commentator Michelle Malkin charged that the president had "solidified his place in the international view as the great appeaser and the groveler in chief."

The historical record, however, makes clear that such skepticism is misplaced and that Obama is on the right track in reaching out to adversaries. Long-standing rivalries tend to thaw as a result of mutual accommodation, not coercive intimidation. Of course, offers of reconciliation are sometimes rebuffed,

requiring that they be revoked. But under the appropriate conditions, reciprocal concessions are bold and courageous investments in peace. Obama is also right to ease off on democracy promotion as he engages adversaries; even states that are repressive at home can be cooperative abroad. Moreover, contrary to conventional wisdom, diplomacy, not trade, is the currency of peace; economic interdependence is a consequence more than a cause of rapprochement.

If tentative engagement with U.S. adversaries is to grow into lasting rapprochement, Obama will need to secure from them not just concessions on isolated issues but also their willingness to pursue sustained cooperation. Doing so will require Washington to make its own compromises without dangerously dropping its guard. Obama must also manage the domestic political perils that will inevitably accompany such diplomacy. Not only will he have to weather Republican complaints about his "apology tours" abroad, but Obama will need to make sure that Congress is ready to support any deals that result from his diplomatic efforts. Should foreign governments take up Washington's offers of cooperation, they, too, will face dangers at home. In fact, Obama is in the difficult position of seeking peace with regimes whose viability may well be undermined if they reciprocate the United States' overtures. Washington is off to a good start in seeking to turn enemies into friends, but the task at hand requires exceptional diplomacy both abroad and at home.

Diplomatic Courtship

Some of the recalcitrant regimes Obama is seeking to engage will surely refuse to reciprocate. With such states, Washington, after a decent interval, should suspend the offer of accommodation in favor of a strategy of isolation and containment. But other regimes are likely to take up the offer. Thus far, Russia, Iran, North Korea, Cuba, and Myanmar have all demonstrated at least a modicum of interest in engagement with the United States. Russia has worked with the United States on arms control, stepped up its effort to contain Iran's nuclear program, and expanded access to Russian territory and airspace for military supplies headed to Afghanistan. Enveloped in domestic turmoil since its June 2009 election, Iran has taken an on-again, if mostly off-again approach to negotiations with the United States. It is clearly tempted by the offer to compromise on the scope of its nuclear program as a means of avoiding—or at least delaying—a confrontation with the West. North Korea has been similarly tentative in engaging with Washington over its nuclear program. Meanwhile, Cuba has been expanding its diplomatic dialogue with the United States, and last fall Myanmar welcomed a visit from a high-ranking U.S. diplomat and allowed him to meet with the opposition leader Aung San Suu Kyi.

These glimmers of progress notwithstanding, critics insist that trying to make deals with extremists is appeasement by another name. Drawing on British Prime Minister Neville Chamberlain's infamous capitulation to Hitler at Munich in 1938, opponents of engagement claim that it will invite only intransigence and belligerence. As U.S. President George W. Bush told the Knesset in 2008, negotiating with radicals is simply "the false comfort of appeasement, which has been repeatedly discredited by history." Bush was certainly correct that accommodation had no place in dealing with a Nazi regime bent on conquest and genocide, but Chamberlain's fateful blunder should not tar all offers of accommodation as naive bouts of appeasement.

On the contrary, the historical record reveals that the initial accommodation of an adversary, far from being an invitation to aggression, is an essential start to rapprochement. Such opening bids are usually the product of necessity rather than altruism: facing strategic overcommitment, a state seeks to reduce its burdens by befriending an adversary. If the target country responds in kind, an exchange of concessions can follow, often setting the stage for the rivalry and mutual suspicion to abate. In the final stage of rapprochement, top decision-makers bring around bureaucracies, legislative bodies, private interest groups, and ordinary citizens through lobbying and public outreach. Broader societal engagement is needed to ensure that rapprochement does not unravel when the leaders that brought it about leave office.

To be sure, offers of accommodation may need to be balanced with threats of confrontation. Nonetheless, the historical record confirms that accommodation, not confrontation, is usually the essential ingredient of successful rapprochement. The United States and Great Britain were antagonists for decades; after the Revolutionary War and the War of 1812, their geopolitical rivalry continued until the end of the nineteenth century. The turning point came during the 1890s, when the United Kingdom's imperial commitments began to outstrip its resources. London made the opening move in 1896, acceding to Washington's blustery demand that it submit to arbitration a dispute over the border between Venezuela and British Guiana—an issue the United States deemed within its sphere of influence. The United States responded in kind to London's gesture, agreeing to bring to arbitration a disagreement over sealing rights in the Bering Sea. Soon thereafter, the two countries amicably settled disputes over the construction of the Panama Canal and the border between Alaska and Canada. The United Kingdom was the only European power to support the United States in the 1898 Spanish-American War, and it went on to welcome U.S. expansion into the Pacific.

As diplomacy dampened the rivalry, elites on both sides of the Atlantic sought to recast popular attitudes through ambitious public relations campaigns. Arthur Balfour, leader of the House of Commons, proclaimed in 1896 that "the idea of war with the United States of America carries with it something of the unnatural horror of a civil war." In a speech at Harvard in 1898, Richard Olney, U.S. secretary of state from 1895 to 1897, referred to the United Kingdom as the United States' "best friend" and noted "the close community . . . in the kind and degree of the civilization enjoyed by both [countries]." With the help of lobbying groups such as the Anglo-American Committee, these changes in the public discourse ensured that by the early 1900s the United Kingdom had succeeded in befriending the United States. In 1905, President Theodore Roosevelt informed London, "You need not ever be troubled by the nightmare of a possible contest between the two great English-speaking peoples. I believe that is practically impossible now, and that it will grow entirely so as the years go by."

How Peace Breaks Out

Other instances of rapprochement followed a similar trajectory—as was the case with rapprochement between Norway and Sweden. As part of the territorial settlement at the end of the Napoleonic Wars, Denmark ceded control over Norway to Sweden in 1814. The Swedes promptly invaded Norway to put down a revolt against their rule, and the resulting union between Norway and Sweden that formed in 1815 led to decades of Norwegian estrangement from the Swedish. Rivalry between the two parties began to abate in 1905, when Sweden, confronted with resource constraints and pressure from Europe's great powers, accepted Norway's unilateral secession from the union. Norway reciprocated by dismantling its border defenses, and the two countries proceeded to resolve their outstanding territorial disputes. Their cooperation during World War I consolidated rapprochement, setting the stage for the eventual consolidation of peace throughout Scandinavia after World War II.

Peace came to Southeast Asia in a comparable fashion. A militarized rivalry between Indonesia and Malaysia began in 1963, when Jakarta opposed the formation of Malaysia—a federation among Malaya, Sabah, Sarawak, and Singapore. In 1966, General Suharto took power in Indonesia and proceeded to back away from confrontation with Malaysia, primarily to redress the deteriorating economic conditions brought on by Jakarta's refusal to trade with Malaysia and by the international sanctions imposed in response to Indonesian belligerence. The two countries then exchanged concessions on a number of issues and teamed up with their neighbors to form the Association of Southeast Asian Nations in 1967, which has helped preserve peace in Southeast Asia ever since.

Rapprochement between Argentina and Brazil followed a similar pattern. After decades of rivalry that had begun in the colonial era, mutual accommodation started to clear the way for reconciliation in the late 1970s. Argentina faced the prospect of a war with Chile and needed to reduce its other strategic commitments, and Brazil's more moderate leaders viewed rapprochement with Argentina as a way of undercutting the growing power of hard-liners in Brazil's security and intelligence apparatus. Argentina made the opening move in 1979 by finally reaching an accord with Brazil and Paraguay on the construction of a hydroelectric dam across the Paraná River, which flows through the three countries. During the 1980s, Argentina and Brazil exchanged concessions, cooperated on their nuclear programs, and deepened their political, scientific, and cultural ties. In 1991, they launched a regional trade pact—Mercosur—and soon thereafter engaged in joint military exercises, which brought Brazilian troops to Argentine territory for the first time since the 1860s.

As these and many other episodes of rapprochement make clear, Obama is on firm ground in seeking to resolve long-standing rivalries through engagement rather than confrontation. This strategy is all the more attractive at a time when the United States is overstretched by the wars in Afghanistan and Iraq and by economic distress at home. Obama's outreach certainly entails risks and comes with no guarantee of success. But U.S. President Richard Nixon had no guarantee of a breakthrough when he went to Beijing in 1972, nor did Egyptian President Anwar al-Sadat when he went to Jerusalem in 1977. Even George W. Bush, who initially forswore dialogue with members of the "axis of evil," was by the end of his second term negotiating with North Korea, sending U.S. envoys to meet Iranian officials, and allowing U.S. forces to cooperate with the Sunni insurgents in Iraq who had spent the preceding years trying to kill Americans. When it is handled correctly, engagement is not appeasement; it is sound diplomacy.

When it is handled correctly, engagement is not appeasement; it is sound diplomacy.

Getting Rapprochement Right

As Obama pursues rapprochement with a host of different rivals, he faces two main challenges: how to handle the sequence and substance of the negotiations and how to manage the political fallout at home and abroad. As for sequence and substance, Washington should be prepared to exchange concessions that are timely and bold enough to send signals of benign intent; otherwise, each party will be unconvinced that the other is sincere in its quest for reconciliation. At the same time, Washington should not move too quickly or too boldly: overshooting could make the United States and its potential partners strategically vulnerable, intensify domestic opposition, and prompt both parties to retreat to safer ground.

History also provides useful guidance on these matters. Anglo-American rapprochement started slowly, with the United Kingdom and the United States first focusing on second-order issues: borders in Central America and sealing rights in the Bering Sea. Only after testing the waters were London and Washington ready to strike bolder bargains—over borders in North America, the building of the Panama Canal, and U.S. expansion into the Pacific. The exchange of concessions began in 1896, but it was not until 1906 that the last units of British regulars left Canada. Similarly, Norway and Sweden dropped their guards only gradually. Rapprochement began in 1905, but in 1907, still wary of the potential for Swedish aggression, Norway concluded a treaty with France, Germany, Russia, and the United Kingdom to guarantee its territorial integrity. Not until World War I did the residual suspicions abate. In August 1914, Norway and Sweden issued a joint declaration of neutrality. After that, a memorial stone to King Oscar I, the king of Norway and Sweden in the mid-nineteenth century, was placed on the Norwegian-Swedish border. The inscription quotes the monarch: "Hereafter is war between the Scandinavian brothers impossible."

In contrast, attempts at rapprochement have foundered when they have gone too far too fast. China and the Soviet Union fashioned a remarkably close strategic partnership during the 1950s, but it unraveled at the end of the decade in part because Beijing suddenly found itself exposed by its heavy reliance on Soviet advisers and economic assistance. In 1958, when Moscow proposed a joint submarine force and a joint naval communications headquarters, Mao Zedong told Russia's ambassador to China, "Well, if [you] want joint ownership and operation [of the submarines], how about having them all—let us turn into joint ownership and operation our army, navy, air force, industry, agriculture, culture, education. . . . With a few atomic bombs, you think you are in a position to control us." The same dynamic scuttled a partnership between Egypt and Syria. After a long history of rivalry, the two countries formed the United Arab Republic in 1958, but it collapsed in 1961 when Syria rebelled against Egyptian dominance within the union. Syrian officers carried out a coup against the Cairo-controlled government in Damascus and proceeded to secede from the United Arab Republic on the grounds that Egypt had "humiliated Syria and degraded her army."

Such historical examples offer at best a loose comparison with the rivalries Washington currently hopes to tame. Nonetheless, they suggest that the Obama administration should pursue rapprochement incrementally and carefully sequence its concessions, strictly conditioning each more ambitious step on reciprocity. Through this strategy, mutual antagonism can gradually give way to mutual accommodation without the risk of exploitation: each side lets down its guard only in step with the other.

So far, the Obama administration's handling of relations with Russia has followed just such an approach. Washington has backed up its call for resetting relations with Moscow by pursuing nuclear arms control, addressing Russian concerns about U.S. missile defense, and establishing bilateral working groups on a range of issues. The Kremlin has reciprocated, enabling progress in negotiations on arms reductions, diplomacy toward Iran, and access to Afghanistan. Should the momentum behind rapprochement continue to build, the stage may be set for tackling more difficult issues, such as NATO enlargement, the independence of Kosovo, the status of Abkhazia and South Ossetia, and Russia's place in the Euro-Atlantic security architecture.

Obama's outreach to Cuba has been even more incremental. Washington made the opening move by loosening some sanctions and tentatively expanding diplomatic and cultural engagement. Cuba has undertaken only modest economic reforms, and Obama has conditioned a wider opening on Havana's readiness to advance political and economic liberalization. Similarly, Washington cautiously reached out to Myanmar through a high-level dialogue but is now awaiting clearer signs that its generals are prepared to loosen their grip on power before pursuing deeper engagement.

Iran and North Korea, because of their nuclear programs, are particularly tough cases. Washington is justifiably intent on neutralizing the nuclear threats they pose. But both countries appear unwilling to give up their nuclear programs, which they deem necessary to maintain their security and bargaining leverage. The tightening of sanctions could help change the political calculus in Tehran and Pyongyang. Nonetheless, the logic of incrementalism would suggest that Washington should also pursue negotiations on a set of broader issues to help build the levels of mutual confidence needed to tackle the nuclear question. With Tehran, the United States could seek cooperation on Afghanistan, particularly on curbing the drug trade there, which flows into Iran. Washington could also discuss with Tehran the potential for a new security architecture in the Persian Gulf, which is of particular importance as U.S. forces prepare to exit Iraq. With Pyongyang, a dialogue on economic assistance, energy supplies, and the normalization of relations may help clear the way for a deal on North Korea's nuclear program.

It was precisely this kind of step-by-step approach that allowed Argentina and Brazil to reach a final accord on their nuclear programs in 1985, after several years of building confidence through presidential visits, scientific exchanges, and technical accords. The nuclear agreement, which committed both countries to the renunciation of nuclear weapons and provided each unfettered access to the other's nuclear sites, then served as a breakthrough, clearing the way for lasting rapprochement. In a similar fashion, Tehran and Pyongyang may not agree to constraints on their nuclear programs and rigorous international monitoring until engagement with Washington has begun to dampen the mutual antagonism. A deal on the nuclear issue may well need to be part of a broader strategic realignment with the United States, not a precondition for that realignment.

The Hostile Home Front

Obama's second main challenge is to manage the domestic backlash that regularly accompanies the accommodation of adversaries—one of the key stumbling blocks in past efforts at rapprochement. Anglo-American rapprochement in the nineteenth century on several occasions almost foundered on the shoals of domestic opposition. The U.S. Senate, for example, rejected a general arbitration treaty with the United Kingdom in 1897. Meanwhile, the British government, fearful of a nationalist revolt against its accommodating stance toward Washington, hid from the public its readiness to cede naval superiority in the western Atlantic to the United States. General Suharto, well aware that accommodation with Malaysia risked provoking Indonesian hard-liners, moved slowly and

cautiously—as did General Ernesto Geisel when Brazil opened up to Argentina. As the Nixon administration discovered in the 1970s, these governments were wise to be cautious. Détente between the United States and the Soviet Union stalled in part because the White House failed to lay the groundwork for it at home and ran up against congressional resistance. In 1974, for example, Congress passed the Jackson-Vanik amendment, which imposed trade restrictions in order to pressure the Soviet Union to allow emigration.

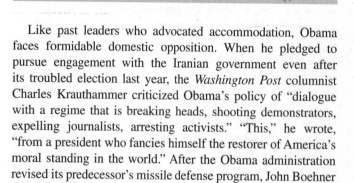

Obama must manage the domestic backlash that accompanies the accommodation of adversaries.

Like past leaders who advocated accommodation, Obama faces formidable domestic opposition. When he pledged to pursue engagement with the Iranian government even after its troubled election last year, the *Washington Post* columnist Charles Krauthammer criticized Obama's policy of "dialogue with a regime that is breaking heads, shooting demonstrators, expelling journalists, arresting activists." "This," he wrote, "from a president who fancies himself the restorer of America's moral standing in the world." After the Obama administration revised its predecessor's missile defense program, John Boehner (R-Ohio), the House minority leader, claimed that "scrapping the U.S. missile defense system in Poland and the Czech Republic does little more than empower Russia and Iran at the expense of our allies in Europe."

An even bigger challenge than parrying these rhetorical blows will be ensuring that the concrete bargains struck in the service of rapprochement pass muster with Congress. If the United States is to ratify a deal on nuclear weapons reductions with Moscow and embrace the Comprehensive Nuclear Test Ban Treaty, two-thirds of the Senate will have to approve. Even without a single defection from the Democratic caucus, the White House will need a healthy measure of support from the Republican Party, which has moved considerably to the right since it last shot down the Comprehensive Nuclear Test Ban Treaty, in 1999. Scaling back sanctions against Cuba, Iran, or Syria would similarly require congressional action, which also would not come easily; Congress would no doubt balk at the prospect of ending the isolation of Havana, Tehran, or Damascus. Jackson-Vanik, after all, is still on the books, even though the Soviet Union is no more and Russia ended its restrictive emigration policies long ago. In the face of such congressional hurdles, Obama should develop a legislative strategy that supports his diplomacy sooner rather than later.

To complicate matters further, Obama has to worry about domestic obstacles to rapprochement in other countries as well. From Iranian President Mahmoud Ahmadinejad to Russian leaders Dmitry Medvedev and Vladimir Putin to Cuban President Raúl Castro, Obama's negotiating partners as a matter of course play the anti-American card to bolster their rule. Even if they want to compromise with the United States, they might find themselves hemmed in by the popular resentment of

Washington that they have already stirred up. Obama can lend a hand by using public diplomacy to lessen popular animosity toward the United States. His superb oratorical skills are an important asset: his frequent efforts at public outreach—such as his speeches in Ankara, Cairo, and Moscow and his video greeting to the Iranians on their New Year—may well help give foreign leaders the room they need to reciprocate U.S. overtures. Far from showboating or squandering his presidential prestige, Obama is wisely deploying his popularity in the service of peace.

Myth Busting

Building congressional support for Obama's outreach to adversaries will mean debunking three myths that often distort public debate about strategies of engagement. The first is the presumption that Washington compromises its values and power by seeking rapprochement with autocratic regimes. U.S. officials and opinion-makers on both sides of the aisle share a commitment to democratization for both principled reasons (democracies respect the rights of their citizens) and pragmatic ones (democracies are peaceful and cooperative, whereas autocracies are presumably belligerent and unreliable partners). Accordingly, even if the United States succeeded in striking a deal with the Iranian, the Russian, or the Syrian government, critics would charge that Washington's behavior was morally tainted (for rewarding and strengthening autocrats) and naive (because such governments cannot be trusted to keep their commitments).

But Obama is fully justified in putting the democratization agenda on the back burner and basing U.S. diplomacy toward other states on their external behavior, not their regime type. Even repressive regimes can be reliably cooperative when it comes to their conduct of foreign policy. Argentina and Brazil embarked on the path of rapprochement when they were both ruled by military juntas. Suharto oversaw a campaign of brutal repression at home but nonetheless ended Indonesia's belligerent stance toward Malaysia and helped found the Association of Southeast Asian Nations as a pact to preserve regional peace.

Striking bargains with repressive regimes does require making moral compromises. Doing so is justified, however, by the concrete contributions to international stability that can result. Washington should speak out against violations of human rights and support political liberalization around the world. But when nuclear weapons, terrorism, and matters of war and peace are on the line, responsible statecraft requires pragmatic compromise, not ideological intransigence.

A second misconception, often affirmed by opponents of engagement, is that pursuing rapprochement with an adversary means abandoning hope that its government will change. On the contrary, doing business with autocracies has the potential to bring about regime change through the backdoor by weakening hard-liners and empowering reformers. Engagement with Iran, for example, could undermine a government that relies on confrontation with the United States to rally popular support and disarm the opposition.

Belligerent governments have frequently been the victims of rapprochement. Sweden's aristocracy and military lost power to the country's liberals as rapprochement with Norway advanced. Military juntas governed Argentina and Brazil when their reconciliation began in 1979; by 1985, both countries were democracies. In none of these cases was rapprochement the only factor that helped bring about regime change, but the more benign strategic environment that accompanied reconciliation certainly strengthened the hand of reformers.

Should Obama's outreach succeed in winning over adversaries, the anti-American pedigree of such leaders as Ahmadinejad, Castro, and Putin may well do more to compromise their credibility than to enhance their popularity. Over the long run, working with recalcitrant autocrats may undermine them far more effectively than containment and confrontation.

Diplomacy before Dollars

A final misconception is that economic interdependence is usually a precursor to rapprochement. Proponents of a "commercial peace" contend that trade and investment encourage amity between rivals by bringing their economic and political interests into alignment. By trading with China, Cuba, and other autocracies, the United States can pursue joint gains and advance political liberalization, which will in turn promote peaceful relations. Supporters of this view call for economic integration not only between the United States and its rivals but also between China and Japan, the Israelis and the Palestinians, and Bosnian Serbs and Bosnian Muslims.

Rapprochement, however, is the product of diplomacy, not commerce. Although commercial integration can help deepen reconciliation, primarily by enlisting the support of industrialists and financiers, the diplomats must first lay the political foundation. Anglo-American trade declined in relative terms between 1895 and 1906, the critical decade of rapprochement. Big business on both sides of the Atlantic did help improve relations, but only after the key diplomatic breakthroughs that occurred between 1896 and 1898. Argentina and Brazil enjoyed minimal bilateral commerce during the 1980s—their era of reconciliation. Only after the founding of Mercosur in 1991 did commercial integration take off.

Moreover, strong commercial ties by no means guarantee comity. By 1959, after a decade of economic integration, 50 percent of China's exports were going to the Soviet Union, and China had become the Soviet Union's top trading partner. But this extraordinary level of commercial interdependence did nothing to prevent the return of geopolitical rivalry after the break between Beijing and Moscow. By 1962, bilateral commerce had dropped by 40 percent. Politics was in command.

The lesson for the Obama administration is to keep its eye on the fundamentals. Under pressure from its critics, the White House might be tempted to sidestep the core security issues at stake and seek to pursue reconciliation with adversaries primarily through economic means. But as the Sino-Soviet case illustrates, unless commercial integration is pursued within the context of a consensus on major geopolitical issues, it will be a distraction at best. To be sure, Washington can wield important leverage by loosening economic sanctions against Cuba, Iran, and Syria. The main benefit of such action, however, would be the political signal it sends, not the purportedly pacifying effects of commercial integration. Growing economic ties can help lock in rapprochement, but only after a political settlement is at hand.

Delivering the Goods

If the Obama administration's tentative engagement with the United States' rivals is to be more than a passing flirtation, Washington will have to conduct not only deft statecraft abroad but also particularly savvy politics at home. Progress will be slow and incremental; it takes years, if not decades, to turn enmity into amity. The problem for Obama is that patience is in extraordinarily short supply in Washington. With midterm elections looming in November, critics will surely intensify their claims that Obama's outreach has yet to pay off. In preparation, Obama should push particularly hard on a single front, aiming to have at least one clear example that his strategy is working. Rapprochement with Russia arguably offers the best prospects for near-term success. Washington and Moscow are well on their way toward closing a deal on arms control, and their interests intersect on a number of other important issues, including the need for stability in Central and South Asia. Moreover, the United States can piggyback on the progress that the European Union has already made in reaching out to Russia on issues of trade, energy, and security.

It takes years to turn enmity into amity. The problem for Obama is that patience is in short supply in Washington.

Obama also needs to start laying the groundwork for congressional support. To help clear the legislative hurdles ahead, Obama should consider including in his stable of special envoys a prominent Republican—such as former National Security Adviser Brent Scowcroft, former Senator Chuck Hagel, or former Secretary of State James Baker—to lend a bipartisan imprimatur to any proposed deals that might come before Congress. He must also be careful not to overreach. For example, his call to eliminate nuclear weapons altogether, however laudable in theory, may scare off centrist senators who might otherwise be prepared to ratify the Comprehensive Nuclear Test Ban Treaty. Obama should also be mindful of the order in which he picks his fights. If advancing rapprochement with Russia is a priority for 2010, it makes sense to put off heavy lifting with Cuba until the following year. It is better to shepherd a few key items through Congress than to ask for too much—and risk coming back empty-handed.

Despite the numerous obstacles at home and abroad, the Obama administration should stick to its strategy of engaging U.S. adversaries. Rapprochement usually takes place in fits and starts and, under the best of circumstances, requires painstaking diplomacy and persistence. But when it works, it makes the world a much safer place. That realization alone should help buy Obama at least some of the time that he will need if he is to succeed in turning enemies into friends.

CHARLES A. KUPCHAN is Professor of International Affairs at Georgetown University and a Senior Fellow at the Council on Foreign Relations. This essay is adapted from his book *How Enemies Become Friends: The Sources of Stable Peace* (Princeton University Press, 2010).

From *Foreign Affairs,* vol. 89, no. 2, March/April 2010, pp. 120–134. Copyright © 2010 by Council on Foreign Relations, Inc. Reprinted by permission of Foreign Affairs. www.ForeignAffairs.org

UNIT 2

The United States and the World: Regional and Bilateral Relations

Unit Selections

Key Points to Consider

- Construct a list of the top five regional or bilateral problems facing the United States. Justify your selections. How does this list compare to one that you might have composed 5 or 10 years ago?

- What is the most underappreciated regional or bilateral foreign policy problem facing the United States? How should the United States address it?

- How much weight should the United States give to the concerns of other states in making foreign policy decisions? Should we listen to some states more than others? If so, whom should we listen to?

- What should the United States expect from other states in making foreign policy decisions?

- Five years from now, what do you expect will be the most important regional or bilateral issue facing the United States?

- What is the major complaint other states have about U.S. foreign policy today? How should the United States respond to this complaint?

Student Website

www.mhhe.com/cls

Internet References

Inter-American Dialogue (IAD)
www.iadialog.org
Political Science Resources
www.psr.keele.ac.uk/psr.htm
Russian and East European Network Information Center
http://reenic.utexas.edu/reenic/index.html
World Wide Web Virtual Library: International Affairs Resources
www.etown.edu/vl/

Possession of a clear strategic vision of world politics is only one requirement for a successful foreign policy. Another is the ability to translate that vision into coherent bilateral and regional foreign policies. What looks clear-cut and simple from the perspective of grand strategy, however, begins to take on various shades of gray, as policymakers grapple with the domestic and international realities of formulating specific foreign policy. This will be particularly true in seeking the support of others in pursuing one's foreign policy goals. Cooperation will often come at a price. That price may be as simple as increased access to U.S. officials, or it may carry very real military and economic price tags. It may also take the form of demands for American acquiescence to the foreign or domestic policies of others.

No single formula exists to guide presidents in constructing a successful foreign policy for dealing with other states and organizations. Still, it is possible to identify three questions that should be asked while formulating a foreign policy. First, what are the primary problems that the United States needs to be aware of in constructing its foreign policy toward a given country or region? Second, what does the United States want from this relationship? That is, what priorities should guide the formulation of that policy? Third, what type of "architecture" should be set up to deal with these problems and realize these goals? Should the United States act unilaterally, with selected allies, or by joining a regional organization?

Each succeeding question is more difficult to answer than the previous one. Problems are easily cataloged. The challenge is to distinguish between real and imagined ones. Prioritizing goals is more difficult because it forces us to examine critically what we want to achieve with our foreign policy as well as what price we are willing to pay. Constructing an architecture is even more difficult because of the range of choices available and the inherent uncertainty of whether the chosen plan will work.

The readings in this section direct our attention to some of the most pressing bilateral and regional problem areas in American foreign policy today. During the Cold War, relations with Europe and the Soviet Union always dominated this list. Today, in spite of disagreements with its European allies over the conduct of the Iraq War and its aftermath, the bilateral and regional relations with Europe are relatively calm. Relations with Russia remain more contested. More and more it is relations with Asia that are garnering high level attention in Washington. Relations with the South continue to occupy a low priority except in periods of crisis.

The first readings in this unit examine United States relations with Russia. "Will Moscow Help with Trouble Spots?" asserts that Russia cannot be counted upon to help manage, much less solve, the central problems facing the United States today. The next essay, "Russia and the West: Mutually Assured Distrust," argues that a central problem in United States-Russia relations is the way the two sides view domestic developments in Russia. While the United States and the West are highly critical of movement away from democratic and free market reforms, Russians see them as necessary corrections of past efforts for reform. The result is increasing mistrust between the two sides.

Department of Defense/U.S. Navy Petty Officer 1st Class Chad J. McNeeley

The next section examines U.S. foreign policy toward Asia. The first two essays in this section look at United States-China relations. "Emerging Strategic Dilemmas in United States-Chinese Relations" argues that the time has come for the U.S. to create a strategic policy directed toward China and not become distracted by Russian power or other problems. "China's Challenge to U.S. Hegemony" sees the relationship between the two states as potentially being destabilizing for the region and the world. It argues that this is not inevitable and the crucial factor in determining the future will be U.S. foreign policy. The final essay on Asia examines North Korea's pursuit of nuclear weapons. "Let's Make a Deal" calls for a policy of sustained engagement with North Korea in order to ensure that the North Korea problem does not undermine the more central U.S. foreign policy relationships with China, Japan, and South Korea.

The final set of readings examines the complex issues of dealing with the South. "Requiem for the Monroe Doctrine" deals with U.S. foreign policy toward Latin America and warns against attempts to resurrect the Monroe Doctrine in an era of globalization. "Mirror-Imaging the Mullahs" is critical of U.S. foreign policy for its failure to appreciate the role that religion plays in the decision making calculus used by leaders in the Middle East. It argues that the days of pro-American secular elites are long gone and will not return. "After Iran Gets the Bomb" examines the strategic options open to the United States should the named event happen. It argues the Cold War policy of containment will not offer much guidance and identifies three key areas where deterrence needs to be practiced.

The next essay, "U.S. Africa Command," explains why the United States has established a new military command in Africa at this time and argues that a close and underappreciated relationship exists between security and development. The final essay, "Bottom-Up Nation Building," calls for a fundamental re-evaluation of how the United States approaches the named problem. Rather than proceed by imposing grand designs, the author calls for a bottom-up strategy that starts with supporting trends on the ground.

Will Moscow Help with Trouble Spots?

"Russia is content to play a parasitic role regarding the world's trouble spots and Western—above all, American—involvement in them."

YURY E. FEDOROV

Those who view international politics through the pragmatic lens of realpolitik might observe of the Obama administration's offer to hit the "reset" button in relations between Washington and Moscow that it simply amounted to proposing a deal.

In return for Russia's help in ending Iran's nuclear program and achieving stability in Afghanistan, the United States would conclude a new strategic arms treaty with Russia, scrap its plans for ballistic missile defense in Central Europe, and perhaps not push too hard for Ukrainian and Georgian membership in NATO. And as for Russian democracy? The White House and the State Department have long since decided that if Russians enjoy living under an authoritarian regime so much, it is a waste of time and effort to try convincing them of democracy's advantages.

Indeed, what really matters to the United States is not how well or badly the Kremlin treats its subjects but whether Moscow is capable of making rational foreign policy decisions. This approach, though cynical, has its logic. Yet it takes two to tango. The question is: Will Moscow seriously help with trouble spots such as Iran, Afghanistan, North Korea, and the Middle East, in return for a more conciliatory American posture on other issues? And if not, why not?

Accommodating Iran

So far, Russia has thrown cold water on US suggestions that Moscow might assist in ending Iran's nuclear program. In February 2009, just after it became clear what sort of reset the US administration was proposing, Russian Deputy Foreign Minister Sergei Ryabkov said that Russia's "stance on the Iranian nuclear program has no elements which could be interpreted as a toughening of approach." A few weeks later Ryabkov announced that Moscow saw no evidence that Iran was trying to build nuclear weapons. And Russian President Dmitri Medvedev—in April, on the eve of his first meeting with President Barack Obama—himself rejected linking the Iranian nuclear issue to the problem of missile defense in Europe. "I don't think that any trade-offs are possible in this respect," he said. "This is not serious talk."

Russia's claims that Iran is not trying to develop nuclear weapons are not at all convincing. All these claims prove is that—at least from Moscow's point of view—Iran's nuclear ambitions do not run counter to Russia's own interests. Thus, Russia does not intend to rethink its approach to the Iranian nuclear issue, nor will it support effective sanctions against Tehran. Some experts suggest this attitude recalls the Soviet Union's stance on Iraq's nuclear efforts nearly 30 years ago. Oleg Grinevsky, a former high-ranking Soviet and Russian diplomat, has described the reaction of then–Soviet Foreign Minister Andrei Gromyko to news about Saddam Hussein's nuclear activities at the beginning of the 1980s:

> "Development of nuclear weapons, if of course Saddam Hussein is able to do this, will change the Middle East conflict significantly," Gromyko said to his trusted subordinates. "Yet . . . is this really dangerous for us? Can we imagine the circumstances under which an Iraqi atomic bomb threatens us? I do not see such a situation. But for the Americans and for Israel, which is an American ally, it will cause a strong headache. The Middle East conflict will flame up with a new strength and they will be on their knees begging us to help them to settle it."

Today, just as then, Russia would like to see the United States and Israel on their knees. Yet Moscow does not actually want a nuclear-armed Iran. A nuclear Iran, unlike the Iraq of 30 years ago, might actually threaten Russia. Such an Iran would create dramatic and mostly undesirable changes in the strategic environment of regions near Russia's southern borders.

In particular, a nuclear Iran might become a source of tension in the Caspian region and in Central Asia, and could encroach on Russian interests in those areas, which Moscow regards as its own backyard. On the other hand, the possibility of a US or Israeli "military option" to prevent Iran's nuclearization, an option whose likelihood is growing as Iran approaches the ability to produce nuclear weapons, is highly unwelcome in Russia.

Rightly or wrongly, many in Israel see a nuclear Iran as an existential threat, one that could be neutralized only by destruction of its nuclear assets. However, if a military strike against

Iran were to be launched, Tehran would immediately respond through asymmetrical means, including massive terror attacks against the United States and Europe. Thus, it would be necessary not merely to eliminate Iran's nuclear and missile facilities but also to paralyze the country's governance through massive air and missile strikes.

Such a mission could only be performed by American forces. A war of this nature would result in complete chaos in Iran, and probably a division of the country along ethnic lines. A hotbed of Shiite extremism would emerge near Russia's borders. In all likelihood, Azerbaijan would unite with the Azeri-populated areas of northern Iran and create a large Azeri state in the South Caspian, a state that would maintain close links with Turkey and the United States. For Russia, all of these prospects are decidedly undesirable.

No, No, and No

At the same time, and for a number of reasons, Moscow does not want to see a political resolution to the Iranian nuclear issue. Theoretically, such a resolution could come about if Tehran halted its nuclear program in exchange for massive Western investment, security guarantees, and recognition of Iran as the West's principal partner in the Islamic world. In reality, especially in view of the turmoil surrounding Iran's recent presidential election, this outcome hardly seems possible.

However, if it were to come about, Moscow would no longer be able to use the Iranian problem as a bargaining chip in its relations with the West. The Central Asian and Caspian states would acquire new pipeline options for exporting their energy resources, allowing them to bypass Russia. And Iran might once again play the geopolitical role that it played under the Shah—something that Moscow definitely does not want.

The Kremlin prefers for US and European resources, both political and military, to be focused on Iran, and not on the post-Soviet states that Moscow considers within its zone of "privileged interest," as Medvedev has termed it. The Kremlin also prefers for the government-controlled Gazprom, Europe's largest supplier of natural gas, not to face competition from Iranian gas fields. In addition, Moscow has a major investment in Iran's nuclear program: The Russian Ministry of Atomic Energy was closely involved in building Iran's $1 billion Bushehr nuclear power plant, and the Russian nuclear industry seeks more such projects.

As a result, Moscow has developed an approach to the Iran issue that may be characterized as "the three noes": no to a nuclear Iran, no to a military option, and no to a diplomatic resolution of the problem. Effectively, the Kremlin wants to freeze the status quo. With this in view, Russia as a permanent member of the United Nations Security Council vetoes all effective sanctions against Tehran. In the long term, Russia is concerned that such sanctions might lead to a political solution. In the short term, Moscow is worried that effective sanctions would cut off its ability to supply arms to Iran and to pursue further cooperation in the nuclear field.

Russia uses Iran's nuclear program as a trump card in its zero-sum game with the West. The strategy has produced some tactical gains to date. But the longer Moscow plays this trump, the deeper may be an "Iranian trap" for Russia: Moscow will be challenged either by a nuclear-armed Iran or by the consequences of a military operation against Tehran.

No glimmer of hope exists that Moscow and Washington will cooperate to thwart Iran's nuclear ambitions by diplomatic means.

In light of all this, Moscow was deeply satisfied with the June reelection of Iranian President Mahmoud Ahmadinejad and with Iran's brutal crackdown on election protesters. Just after the voting, Ahmadinejad participated as an observer at a summit of the Shanghai Cooperation Organization (SCO), a body created to assure Russian-Chinese dominance in Central Asia. The Russian Foreign Ministry declared that "Russia respects the choice of the Iranian people and is ready to continue developing mutually beneficial cooperation with Iran." No glimmer of hope exists that Moscow and Washington will cooperate to thwart Iran's nuclear ambitions by diplomatic means. Thus Tehran carries on with its nuclear program, convinced that its actions will go unpunished.

Welcome to the Quagmire

Along with Iran, Afghanistan is among the most critical issues on the West's security agenda. Stabilization in Afghanistan is seen as the key proving ground for NATO's capacity to address the emerging strategic realities of the twenty-first century. A failure there, rightly or wrongly, would be considered a strategic defeat for NATO and the United States, and would signal a dramatic reduction of the West's power and influence. This would have long-term global consequences. Many in Washington believe that if the war in Afghanistan is lost, Al Qaeda would regain its strength and strike the United States again. The Obama administration considers the struggle against Islamist extremists in Afghanistan a principal strategic goal.

In this light, Russia's support of Western efforts in Afghanistan is a practical indicator of Moscow's readiness (or lack of readiness) to reset its relationship with the United States and NATO. This is especially the case when it comes to Russia's approach toward the Western military presence in Central Asia, of which a critical element is communication lines that supply the international coalition's troops in Afghanistan.

Then–President Vladimir Putin's dramatic decision in September 2001 to support the US-led war in Afghanistan was widely interpreted at the time as a departure from the Kremlin's Soviet-style policy of treating international relations as a zero-sum game. It was believed that Russia might pursue long-term cooperation with the West on the issues of Islamist terrorism, nuclear proliferation, drug trafficking, and other shared threats. But the conciliatory decisions made by Putin at the beginning of his presidency did not result from any change in the basic attitudes of Russia's ruling cohort. Rather, the decisions were made because Russia lacked resources to confront the West and because Russia's economic situation at the beginning of this decade was frightful.

Although Moscow officially supports the international operation in Afghanistan, since 2005 it has been working to bring about the withdrawal of the Western military forces from Central Asia. Thus Moscow initiated an SCO declaration in 2005 which said it was "essential that the relevant members of the antiterror coalition fix time limits [on] the temporary use of . . . infrastructure and [on] the length of the military contingents' stay on the territories of SCO member states." In Russia this declaration was interpreted by mass media close to the Kremlin as a demand by the SCO members for an immediate termination of the West's military presence in Central Asia. This idea was wishful thinking, since the document did not mention the withdrawal of military forces, only the need to fix time limits. It may be that Russian negotiators and Putin himself tried to persuade the leaders of the other SCO countries to approve a much tougher statement, but failed.

In 2005 the Karshi-Khanabad air base in Uzbekistan, known as K2, was evacuated of US forces following American criticism of the host country's brutal suppression of a popular uprising. This was seen in Moscow as a great political triumph. Afterwards, America's withdrawal from the Manas Air Base in Kyrgyzstan became a priority of Russian policy. This base is a crucial facility for operations in and around Afghanistan. The international coalition relies on it heavily for supply, logistics, troop rotations, and refueling of aircraft—especially in view of growing problems associated with supplying Afghanistan via Pakistan.

The Russian aim of ending US use of the Manas Air Base has been frustrated by the fact that US payments for use of the base represent a substantial financial resource for Kyrgyzstan. In addition, the Kyrgyz government—like the governments of other Central Asian states—has good reason to believe that if US and NATO troops are not able to defeat Islamist extremists in Afghanistan, then sooner rather than later Islamists will become active in Central Asia, possibly igniting widespread popular unrest there. Nonetheless, a group of Kyrgyz politicians, including a few within the inner circle of President Kurmanbek Bakiyev, in recent years became receptive to Russia's campaign for immediate US withdrawal from the base.

Tensions over the air base came to a head in February 2009—just after Medvedev had made conciliatory remarks regarding Russia's attitude toward Western military operations in Afghanistan. Speaking in Uzbekistan in January, Medvedev had announced that Moscow was ready to cooperate with the new US administration and with NATO. Medvedev welcomed Obama's plans to review US policy in Afghanistan, and voiced his hope that "the new US administration will have greater success than the previous one in resolving the Afghanistan issue." He also said Russia would work with NATO on transit routes for the delivery of nonmilitary goods to Afghanistan. This was seen as a signal that Moscow was rethinking its hostile attitude toward the United States and NATO and was ready to turn over a new leaf in Russian-US relations.

A Peculiar Understanding

It turned out very quickly, however, that the Kremlin had a peculiar understanding of what it meant to help the United States fight terrorism. Just a few days after his Uzbekistan statement,

Medvedev managed to twist Bakiyev's arm into ordering the United States to withdraw from Manas. The Kyrgyz president, speaking in Moscow after a lengthy haggling session in which he had secured a $2 billion loan from Russia, said that the Americans would be given six months to withdraw.

If the loan was not inducement enough for Bakiyev to do the Kremlin's bidding, another factor motivated him: He faced the prospect of presidential elections in July 2009. If he was unresponsive to Moscow's pressure, the Kremlin would support his rivals, financially and otherwise. Although the Kremlin denied there was a Russian hand behind Bakiyev's decision, the Russian propaganda machine implied exactly that, with great satisfaction. Moscow had demonstrated its dominating influence in Central Asia.

But Russia's apparent success in closing the American air base at Manas proved a short-lived phenomenon. First, in May, Uzbek President Islam Karimov announced that a cargo airport in the Uzbek city of Navoi could be used for airborne transport of NATO supplies to Afghanistan, and that a major renovation at that airport would turn it into a world-class airfreight hub. Then, a few weeks later, the Kyrgyz government announced a deal with the United States that would allow the Americans to continue using the Manas Air Base as a transit center. The deal represented a significant defeat for Russian policy in Central Asia.

The deal was probably a major reason that the Kremlin in July agreed to allow the United States to transport troops and weapons across Russian airspace en route to Afghanistan. That agreement, signed during a Russian-US summit in Moscow, permits 4,500 American flights per year and saves the US government an annual $133 million. For Russia, it appears, the deal amounted to making the best of a bad situation. Because the United States had managed to maintain transit arrangements to Afghanistan via Central Asia, it had become meaningless for Russia to continue pursuing its objective of cutting off US supply lines.

At the same time, America's war in Afghanistan is definitely in Russia's interest, and the new air transit corridor across Russia only deepens US involvement in Afghanistan—reinforcing Washington's determination to fight there until final victory, even if that goal is unattainable. Another benefit of the agreement from Moscow's perspective is that it suggests Russia still holds the keys to US and NATO military transit.

Certain segments of Russia's political and military circles hope to see NATO and the United States atrophy because of defeat in Afghanistan.

The zigzags and inconsistencies in Moscow's approach to the US war effort in Afghanistan result from opposing viewpoints that persist in the top echelons of Russian government. Certain segments of Russia's political and military circles hope to see NATO and the United States atrophy because of defeat in Afghanistan. They see America and NATO as greater potential dangers to Russian interests than the threat of Islamic jihadism that might result from the restoration of the Taliban regime in Afghanistan. Indeed, they entertain a paranoid perception that the United States poses a military threat to Russia because of its presence in Central Asia.

Others in the top echelons understand that if the international coalition fails in Afghanistan, serious consequences might develop not only in Central Asia but in the northern Caucasus too. However, they are not interested in US and NATO success in Afghanistan but rather in their long-term, large-scale involvement there. The Kremlin hopes that the United States and NATO, by committing an increasing number of troops to operations in Afghanistan, will severely limit their strategic capabilities in other regions, such as the Black Sea, the Caspian, Ukraine, and other areas of Russia's "privileged interest." Moreover, as long as US and NATO forces remain in Afghanistan, the Taliban and Al Qaeda cannot gain control of the country and thus do not present a substantial threat to Russia's allies in Central Asia.

In this light, military transit via Russian territory makes a withdrawal of US and European troops from Afghanistan less probable, especially given the tense situation in Pakistan and the Khyber Pass area. At the same time, it stops the West from developing an alternate supply route across the Black Sea, the southern Caucasus, the Caspian, and Turkmenistan.

Nuclear Dominoes

Recent developments on the Korean peninsula have put Russia in a ticklish position. North Korea's nuclear test in May 2009, along with its subsequent missile launches, shows that the Korean nuclear crisis is escalating. The crisis threatens far-reaching strategic changes in East Asia, in particular a game of "nuclear dominoes," which would be highly unwelcome in Russia.

The next domino to fall could be Japan. That country is concerned not only about North Korea's nuclear weapons but also about America's strategic focus on the greater Middle East, something that weakens Tokyo's confidence in US security guarantees and that is stimulating deep changes in Japan's strategic attitudes. Japan is capable of quickly building its own nuclear arsenal if it decides to go that route. A nuclear Japan, on top of a nuclear North Korea, might cause South Korea and Taiwan to develop nuclear weapons as well. In the meantime, Japan, Taiwan, and South Korea might, together with the United States, accelerate the development of an antimissile defense system.

In this context, China would increase its arsenal of nuclear missiles, further stimulating a regional arms race. In response, Washington would increase its military presence in Northeast Asia. This increased presence would include warheads and delivery platforms for limited nuclear attack, improved ballistic missile defense systems, and precise conventional counterforce capabilities.

As part of this vicious cycle, a new strategic configuration would emerge in East Asia. At one pole would be the United States and its allies—Japan, South Korea, and Taiwan. These countries would combine America's extended deterrence with development of their own military capabilities, both conventional and nuclear. China would have no option but to constitute the other pole in this system.

This of course would have significant negative consequences for Russia's strategic posture in the northern Pacific. An arms race would change the ratio of the military forces in the region, and not in Moscow's favor. In fact, Russia already is concerned about its military position in the region. Its Pacific fleet is degrading. Its ground forces in Siberia and the Russian Far East are outnumbered more than three to one by Chinese ground forces deployed in military districts adjacent to Russia. Russia's main military asset in the region is nuclear weapons. But a game of nuclear dominoes, along with deployment of missile defense systems and a high-tech arms race, could diminish the significance of Russia's nuclear arsenal.

Finally, as nuclear dominoes fell, the probability of a military conflict on the Korean peninsula might increase. This would carry severe economic and sociopolitical consequences for the Russian Far East. Prospects for the realization of some large economic projects that promise critical benefits to Russia would come to a definitive end, and foreign investment in the development of oil and gas deposits in eastern Siberia would be blocked.

All this makes Russia interested in resolving the Korean nuclear crisis as soon as possible. The longer the situation remains unresolved, the higher the probability that Russian interests will suffer. Theoretically, this opens a path for Russia to cooperate constructively with the United States. But Russia, like China, wishes to resolve the nuclear crisis in a way that will not strengthen American influence on the Korean peninsula and in the North Pacific. Moscow understands that a political solution to the North Korean crisis would most probably result in a fundamental improvement of North Korea's relations with the United States. This is highly unappetizing to the Kremlin.

In addition, as soon as Pyongyang abandoned its nuclear program, rapprochement between North and South Korea would begin. This might eventually result in the unification of the two Korean states and the rise of a strong new international actor that could diminish Russian influence in the region and threaten territory close to Russia's strategically important sea terminals on the Pacific.

In any case, Russia as a practical matter has virtually no instruments with which to influence the nuclear crisis. Russian military intervention in an armed conflict on the Korean peninsula virtually defies imagination. Such an intervention could occur only if conflict in Korea spread to Russian territory, which is highly unlikely. Similarly, Russia's ability to render economic aid to North Korea is minimal. Large Russian-North Korean joint projects are impractical due to a dearth of Russian funding. And Russia cannot use its trade with North Korea to exert political influence—in 2008, trade between the two countries comprised only 2.3 percent of North Korea's total foreign trade.

Because of competing motives and a lack of levers, Russia's Korea policy is incoherent.

Because of competing motives and a lack of levers, Russia's Korea policy is incoherent. On one hand, Moscow uses its status as a permanent member of the UN Security Council to block effective international sanctions against North Korea. Such sanctions are the only means available to force Pyongyang to give up its nuclear weapons, and Russia's actions only stimulate North Korea's nuclear ambitions and discourage Pyongyang from rethinking its approach toward relations with the United States and South Korea. Indeed, Russia's actions increase the probability of a nuclear arms race in the North Pacific.

On the other hand, Russia routinely calls for a resumption of the six-party talks (involving Russia, China, Japan, the two Koreas, and the United States) on North Korea's nuclear program. Participation in these talks creates for Moscow the illusion that it has political influence on the Korean peninsula and in a wider regional strategic context. However, North Korea's recent nuclear test and its missile launches prove that these talks are not an effective instrument.

Capitalizing on Conflict

Since the fall of the Soviet Union, Russian policy regarding the Israeli-Palestinian conflict has been essentially constant. In place of the rigid anti-Israel strategy of the Soviet days, which was driven by confrontation with the United States (Israel's primary patron and sponsor) as well as by the antisemitism that was typical of Soviet ruling circles, Moscow has pursued a more sophisticated and balanced policy.

Today, Russian elites do not see the Middle East as a principal area of strategic rivalry with the West, as they did during the days of the cold war. Russia has developed a pragmatic relationship with Israel, and in some ways a cooperative one, motivated by economic concerns and, many believe, a common interest in fighting Islamist terrorism. It might seem that Russia has replicated the US policy of maintaining relations with both Israel and the Arab states, playing a role both as mediator and as a guarantor of security. If this view of Russian policy were correct, there would be a substantial chance that the United States and Russia can cooperate to resolve the Israeli-Palestinian conflict and help stabilize the region.

But this perception of Russian behavior in the Middle East is not accurate. Unlike America and Europe, which are actually interested in resolving the Israeli-Palestinian conflict and believe that the conflict's end would strengthen their position in the region, Moscow's goal is to capitalize on the conflict—as well as on conflicts between Israel and Syria, and between Israel and Iran.

Russian policy in the Middle East calls into question Moscow's willingness to partner with the United States in fighting Islamist-led terrorism. Russia supplies Syria and Iran with armaments, which then fall into the hands of Hezbollah and Hamas, two of the region's most dangerous organizations. Indeed, Russia invites Hamas leaders to Moscow, treating them as legitimate political figures. This strengthens the radicals' position and hinders moderate Palestinian forces from compromising with Israel. The logic of the Russian position is quite simple. Moscow retains very few levers of political influence in the Middle East, so it uses the one it has—which is to manipulate conflicts between Israel and its enemies.

Policy makers in the West need to realize that in no case will Russia be their partner in resolving Iran's nuclear program, in providing practical support (other than flyover rights) to the international military operation in Afghanistan, or in other trouble spots. Moscow cannot be called a rival to the West in these areas either. The Kremlin does not want, and has no resources, to force the West out of Afghanistan or the Middle East, to take on responsibility for resolving the North Korean nuclear crisis, or to impose its own solution on the Israeli-Palestinian conflict. Instead, Russia is content to play a parasitic role regarding the world's trouble spots and Western—above all, American—involvement in them.

YURY E. FEDOROV is an associate fellow at the Royal Institute of International Affairs (Chatham House) in London.

Russia and the West: Mutually Assured Distrust

"In their determination to validate their recovery and return to world leadership, the Russians sometimes overreact, even if in the process this means straining relations with the West."

MARSHALL I. GOLDMAN

A story is told that goes something like this. Before President Vladimir Putin's July 2007 visit to former President George H. W. Bush's home in Kennebunkport, Maine, a television reporter sought to interview a White House aide for a brief comment on Russian relations with the West, particularly the United States. But the reporter's producer cautioned him that, because of time constraints, all he could record was a one-word answer. Meeting with a member of the White House staff, the reporter asked for a one-word characterization of US-Russian relations. "Good," the official replied.

Just then the program's producer realized that he had a bit more time and so he told the reporter he could actually have a two-word answer. The question was asked again. "How in two words would you describe Russian relations with the West?" "Not good."

The Responsible Power

Paradoxically, this joke does seem to characterize the current diplomatic climate between Russia and the West. On the good side, Russia has not only been admitted to the Group of Seven (making it the G-8), but in 2006 Putin chaired the group's May meeting—convening it in St. Petersburg, his hometown. In an unusually warm gesture, this year Putin was invited to meet with President George W. Bush at the home of the president's father in Kennebunkport, the first foreign leader to have been invited there by the current president.

This unusual welcome was in part a reflection of the close bond the two men have established. In part it also reflected recognition of Russia's cooperation in preventing the trafficking of nuclear and radioactive materials and, even more important, Moscow's sharing with Western countries intelligence about Islamist terrorist activities in Afghanistan and the Middle East. Indeed, to help facilitate the United States' response to the 9-11 attacks, Russia erected no obstacles when Washington sought to establish military bases in Kyrgyzstan and Uzbekistan in support of operations in Afghanistan.

Following the meeting in Maine, Putin flew on to Guatemala, where he appealed in English and French to the International Olympic Committee to select Sochi, Russia, as the site of the 2014 Winter Olympics. Putin's appearance in person (he was the only world leader to attend) and his promise to provide necessary financing impressed the committee so much that, against almost all predictions, Russia won and Sochi was selected. The Olympic Committee apparently accepted Putin's guarantee that Russia would be able to absorb the costs, handle the logistics and scheduling, and meet other international responsibilities that come with hosting the Olympics. The committee made its decision even though, at the time of the decision, no facilities in Sochi were in place. Russia's backers were right to claim this represented a vote of confidence in Russia and its international standing as a responsible country.

That the West has accepted Russia is proven further by the rush of Western businesses and banks seeking to set up operations there. Whereas during the 1990s, capital flight from Russia averaged $1 billion a month, in 2006 an estimated $41 billion flowed *into* Russia—that is more than $3 billion a month. Thirty-one billion dollars of that total came in foreign direct investment, meaning that foreign companies were confident enough of the business and political climate to set up mining, manufacturing, and service operations in Russia. For its part, Russia has committed itself to the West as a major energy supplier. Its natural gas and petroleum pipelines now provide on average 25 percent of the gas that Western Europe imports and about the same percentage of oil.

Rising Tensions

Winning the right to hold the Olympics, plugging into the world's gas and oil network, attracting large sums of foreign direct investment, joining the G-8—these are all reflections of Russia's good standing in the world community. But not everything is so positive. Indeed, signs of mutual tension, distrust, and even hostility are serious and seem to be growing. In response to Moscow's refusal to extradite the prime suspect in the murder of Alexander Litvinenko, a Putin critic and former KGB agent who had been living in London, Great Britain in July expelled four Russian diplomats, alleged to be spies. Russia subsequently expelled four British diplomats from Moscow, while Russian bombers threatened to overfly British airspace. And this is hardly the only evidence of worsening relations between Russia and the West.

Although something even more dramatic than the mutual expulsion of suspected spies could happen tomorrow, perhaps the most threatening sign of the growing tension was Putin's announcement on July 14, 2007, that Russia intended to withdraw within five months from the 1999 Conventional Forces in Europe treaty. This treaty committed signatories, both Russia and members of the NATO alliance, to limit the number of tanks and combat aircraft deployed in Europe. Officially, Russia explained that it was renouncing the treaty because, while it had ratified an amended version of the treaty, too many NATO countries had not.

This was but one of Russia's grievances. Russian officials were also upset that, not only had the United States itself announced in 2002 that it was withdrawing from the Anti-Ballistic Missile (ABM) treaty that was intended to mark the end of the cold war, but in 2007 the Americans sought to install a radar unit in the Czech Republic and an actual battery of antiballistic missiles in Poland. The Russians brushed aside official US insistence that this ABM system was intended to protect the West from Iran and North Korea or that the system had not been successfully tested. Given NATO's past broken promises—that former members of the Warsaw Pact would not be recruited into NATO, nor would NATO station offensive military forces in Eastern Europe (as it then did in Bulgaria and Romania)—the Russians suspect that the purportedly anti-Iranian, anti–North Korean system would in fact turn out to be an anti-Russian system.

It was in order to provoke opposition in the West to both the withdrawal from the ABM treaty and the plan to install antiballistic missiles in Eastern Europe that Putin threatened to withdraw from the Conventional Forces in Europe treaty. Sergei Ivanov, his former minister of defense, also warned that if the United States were to install its ABM system in Eastern Europe, Russia would respond by again targeting its missiles on Western Europe, just as it did during the cold war. If each side carries out its plans, this would amount to a scary replay of the mutual-destruction nightmare that characterized the cold war.

While the West may disapprove of Putin's policies, clearly most Russians do not.

Western Grievances

Such disputes reflect the growing contempt with which each side views the other side's behavior and political and social mores. For its part, the West has become more and more critical of what it sees as the continual undoing of market reforms and democratic reforms that were introduced after the col-

lapse of the communist system. The Russians see the situation differently. They regard Putin's changes as an effort to correct reforms that were too far-reaching. As they see it, during Boris Yeltsin's years as president their country fell into chaos, which the people abhorred.

One priority for Russians, then, was to reexamine the results of privatization. Whatever the official purpose of the privatization program of the 1990s, most Russians now view the transfer of state-owned entities to private owners as something just short of highway robbery. Not surprisingly, while the West views Putin's renationalization of many of these assets, especially the valuable energy companies, as a step backward, to the Russians it represents a rectification of serious errors.

This explains why, within Russia, there is today widespread approval of the fact that the share of crude oil produced by state-controlled companies has increased from under 20 percent at the peak of privatization in 2000 to approximately 50 percent in 2007. Moreover, under Putin, even companies in which the state has no or only a minority share again act as if they were agents of the state—or national champions, as Putin calls them. What observers in the West see is a form of state capitalism.

There is also widespread criticism outside Russia of the way Putin's government has been in effect nationalizing property theoretically owned by Western companies. When the state forced the Russian oil company Yukos into bankruptcy, broke it up, and renationalized most of it as a subsidiary of state-owned Rosneft, that could in part be rationalized as an internal matter. Yukos and its owners were accused of all manner of illegal acts, from tax evasion to buying votes in the Duma to murder. It was clear that Russian courts, in finding guilty the chief owner of Yukos, Mikhail Khodorkovsky, were merely doing the Kremlin's bidding. But at the same time, Yukos and Khodorkovsky were not innocent victims.

The state's treatment of foreign oil companies is another matter. Shell Oil, for example, has been charged with polluting a work site and as a consequence has been forced to surrender majority ownership of its multibillion-dollar exploration effort on the island of Sakhalin to Gazprom, the state-owned gas monopoly. It is not that there was no pollution, but in comparison with the way most Russian companies ignore pollution regulations, Shell was far from the most serious offender. This is simply a case where the Russian government wanted to reclaim oil and gas fields that it had leased to foreign companies in the 1990s when no Russian firm had the wherewithal to operate in such challenging conditions. Nor is Shell the only Western company to see its original concessions and contracts nullified. Virtually every foreign energy business operating in Russia in difficult and hostile geological conditions has been forced to sell out or accept Gazprom as a partner. Those affected include BP of the United Kingdom, Exxon-Mobil of the United States, and Total of France.

Kremlin officials who justify this renationalization argue that the original agreements were made when Russia was under undue duress and that Western companies at the time took unfair advantage. Now that Russia is stronger and better able to protect its interests, it has the right to restore the proper balance. Besides, the Western companies had indeed created pollution. And in the case of Shell, the company without warning suddenly claimed that its total cost of operation in Sakhalin had soared from $10 billion to $20 billion. Since Shell was operating under a production-sharing agreement that allowed the company to recoup all of its expenses before it had to share revenues with Russia, this increase in costs was viewed as a scheme by Shell to prevent Russia from sharing the profits of the operation for years to come.

The state's takeover of Russia's major television networks has worked much the same way, with the owners claiming theft and the government asserting that too much was given away too readily and cheaply in the 1990s. In particular, Putin justified the return of media outlets to state control by pointing out that the oligarchs who came to own these assets were using them not to provide fair and unbiased coverage of the news, but instead to carry out their own private vendettas and corporate battles.

The leaders who have recently come to power in Europe appear initially to be much more critical of Russia and especially Putin.

Nor have many Russians opposed what observers in the West view as a step backward in democratization: the abolition of direct elections for governor. Most Russians accept Putin's argument that the whole process had become a farce and that the wealthy were using their money to buy up voters and corrupt the elections. Putin insists that, as president, he is in a much better position to weed out the corrupt and appoint more capable and honest officials. Of course, the democratic process in the United States also has room for improvement. (Some still say that corruption in Chicago in the 1960 presidential election swung Illinois from Richard Nixon to John Kennedy. Others still question the 2000 vote count in Florida, the state that put George W. Bush over the top against Al Gore. Putin has often cited the latter election to demonstrate that the United States has nothing to brag about.) Still, the American system appears more in tune than the Putin version with what the West generally considers to be democracy. As Putin has begun to act arbitrarily in more and more circumstances, he has replaced the rule of law with what seems to be the law of the ruler.

Despite all this, it is the assassination of the former KGB agent Litvinenko that seems to have drawn the most concern from the public in the West, especially in Great Britain. Many were particularly troubled that the killer used polonium 210, a radioactive isotope, to commit the murder. That seemed an unusually nasty thing to do, more so than a run-of-the-mill gunshot killing. As the newly installed British Foreign Minister David Miliband pointed out, Litvinenko's "murder put hundreds of others, residents and visitors, at the risk of radioactive contamination."

Radioactive poisoning triggers a whole new set of concerns and makes the person who committed the crime (British authorities allege it is a former KGB agent, Andrei Lugovoi) appear to be particularly reckless and diabolical. It certainly did nothing for Russia's image that Litvinenko's death came as a series of political and media figures who had been critical of Putin and Kremlin policies were murdered. Some murders are just ordinary crimes, but others clearly carry a political connotation and seem more ominous, especially in the West.

The Pride of Russia

It is not that the Russians take pride in these assassinations. But what is galling to them is that, ever since the 1980s, they have been continually harangued about this and other so-called shortcomings by Western officials, moralists, and former Sovietologists. This hectoring has had a devastating impact on their national ego. It was bad enough that they had ceased to be a military and economic superpower. Beginning in the 1990s, nobody seemed to seek their input or care about them. At the time, one could only guess how humiliating all this was to the public psyche. Now as the country has regained its footing, at least in the economic sphere, we are finding out just how deeply felt was Russia's temporary fall from prominence and influence.

There are an embarrassing number of illustrations. For example, in response to the British demand that the Russian government extradite Lugovoi, Konstantin Kosachyov, the chairman of the Duma's Foreign Affairs Committee and an otherwise reasonable legislator, complained about British arrogance. "You can act this way toward a banana republic, but Russia is not a banana republic," he said. Valentina Matviyenko, the governor of St. Petersburg, has expressed a similar view, arguing that Russia will no longer tolerate being treated as an inferior. In a July 2007 interview in the weekly newspaper *Argumenty I Fakty,* she boasted that "Russia has now regained a sense of self-respect. We spent so many years feeling there was something wrong with us—others lecturing us on how we should live and where we should go. But we have overcome our inferiority complex."

If only it were so. Based on recent behavior, it seems as if Putin and other Russian officials are still seeking to prove themselves. Putin has been particularly outspoken. In a June 2007 speech in St. Petersburg, he went so far as to challenge the way the World Trade Organization, the International Monetary Fund, and the World Bank are run. He called them "archaic, undemocratic, and awkward," largely because they are too dependent on the European Union, the United States, and Japan—and by implication, not Russia. This, he insisted, disadvantaged developing countries. Even more pointedly, Putin suggested that the world should have more than two reserve currencies, implying that the dollar and the euro are not enough. As he sees it, now that oil exports have made Russia so prosperous, the ruble should fill the same role.

In an even more revealing initiative, Putin earlier this year announced his support for a new textbook for Russian schools. It is time to reassert the correctness of Russia's behavior in the past, he declared. Putin attacked the West for suggesting that Russia should be ashamed of such things as the Stalinist purges, collectivization, and the subjugation of national groups in the former Soviet Union and Eastern Europe. If anything, he argued, it is the West that should be ashamed.

As an example, Putin agreed with the new textbook that Stalin's "Great Terror" of 1937, in which at least 700,000 people were executed, was not as bad as the Americans' use of atomic bombs in Japan, not to mention the use of chemical weapons (napalm) against civilians in Vietnam. Putin has accused the United States of using its campaign to spread democracy to create a global empire under American control. In a May 2007 speech, he seemed to compare the United States with Nazi Germany, though he later denied it. Putin's speech described a "global threat in which, as in the time of the Nazi Third Reich, we saw the same contempt for human life, the same claims to world exclusivity and diktat."

A Nation That Matters

In their determination to validate their recovery and return to world leadership, the Russians sometimes overreact, even if in the process this means straining relations with the West. A good example is the way the Russians reacted this spring to Estonia when it relocated a statue dedicated to Soviet military heroism against German troops in World War II. The Moscow police, disregarding international protocol, stood by while members of a Russian youth group demonstrated outside the Estonian embassy and harassed Estonian diplomats. Protesters also attacked the Swedish ambassador's car. (On another occasion, after he attended a meeting of dissidents, the British ambassador to Russia was similarly harassed.) In addition, the government suspended the flow of petroleum to Estonia and stood by while Russian hackers assaulted Estonian computers and websites in an effort to disrupt communications to and from the country and within it.

The Russians seemed to be acting as if Estonia were still a subservient republic of the Soviet Union and not a sovereign independent nation. Moscow assumed that it had license to treat Estonia as it pleased and ignore not only Estonian protests but also complaints from Estonia's fellow members in the European Union and NATO. To some extent, Russians even seem to welcome such criticism, taking it as a sign that the outside world has begun to take notice of their country again and that what Russia thinks and does matters, even if it is to be condemned.

Moscow has also taken to harassing Lithuania, Estonia's close Baltic neighbor. Russian authorities suspended pipeline shipments of petroleum to Lithuania's Mazeikiai refinery after Russian companies were unable to buy the refinery. (Lithuania wanted to sell it to a Polish group of buyers because they were not Russian and, in addition, they offered a higher price.) Again, there was the implication that Lithuania had no choice but to keep this refinery, which was built in the Soviet era, within what used to be the Soviet family.

Some Russian actions are reflexive responses expressing historic Russian positions that date back to the czarist era. One example is how Russia has opposed Kosovo's independence from Serbia. Russia traditionally has viewed itself as the protector of the Serbs and their Christian Orthodoxy against encroachments from the Muslim world. This is not something new—Russia reacted that way in the nineteenth century when it sought to protect Serbia from the Ottoman Empire. It is trying to do the same in the twenty-first century by protecting Serbs in Kosovo from the Muslim Albanians there who make up the vast majority of the population.

Not everything that upsets present-day Russia is an overreaction. It is easy to see that Putin, sitting in the Kremlin, would be upset by the behavior of some nongovernmental organizations—particularly NGOs financed by groups and governments outside Russia, ones that seek to build up political parties that are independent of the state. Kremlin officials see this as interference in the internal affairs of another country. They point to political upheaval in Georgia and Ukraine that was sparked by various NGOs, some financed by the US government and private foundations that have openly announced that their next target will be Russia. Arguably, it would have been irresponsible for Putin to have ignored such a possibility.

It is the assassination of the former KGB agent Litvinenko that seems to have drawn the most concern from the public in the West.

This explains to a substantial degree Putin's support for a youth group like Nashi (Ours), which backs the president and his political party and is willing to risk confrontation with anti-Putin protesters. The group's loyalty is to Putin more than to the party, and its actions are often patterned more after the Komsomol (the Soviet-era Young Communist League) or even the Hitler Youth than after the Girl or Boy Scouts. In the same way, the government's heavy-handed use of riot police to suppress only opposition demonstrations—especially when the protests are as disorganized and inconsequential as they have been—comes across as antidemocratic.

Hectoring Hypocrites

While there have indeed been instances of antidemocratic actions in Russia, the Russians regard the United States as hypocritical when it demands good behavior from Russia while disregarding America's own shortcomings. What gives the United States the right to preach to Russia about corporate governance and the way Gazprom behaves, the Russians ask, when some US corporations seem equally if not more in need of lessons in proper governance? Are the senior executives at MMM or SBS-Agro (companies whose executives have had to face charges of illegal behavior) any more in need of corporate ethics lessons, or more deserving of jail sentences, than their American counterparts such as Kenneth Lay of Enron or Bernard Ebbers of WorldCom?

Russians extend the same criticism to US attacks on the inadequacy of Russian law, human rights, and individual safeguards. What gives the United States and Western Europe the right to criticize Russia when Western countries ban demonstrations or their police fire rubber bullets to suppress rioters, as happened outside Paris in the fall of 2005? How do those who call for human rights accept the jailing of British bombing suspects even though no formal charges have been lodged against them? As for the United States, how can it reconcile detention without trial of Islamic terror suspects for months, even years, at its Guantánamo prison facility? Whatever happened to habeas corpus? US federal courts have decreed that certain government practices violate the American constitution, yet they seem to continue.

Of course, not all such criticisms of the United States and its behavior are unique to Russia. Many Europeans, not to mention Arabs, oppose what they see as America's unilateral behavior, be it in Iraq or in Eastern Europe, where the United States seeks to install the missiles referred to previously. Others worry that NATO expansion to the east and to Russia's borders, even if it is important for Eastern European and Baltic states as a sign that they are no longer part of the Soviet empire, is unduly provocative. Many Europeans can understand, along with the Russians, why the Kremlin would regard as a hostile act any effort to extend NATO further into Georgia and Ukraine.

The Challenge Ahead

Prediction is always hazardous—particularly, as Yogi Berra noted, when it deals with the future. Yet it has to be said that prospects for relations between Russia and the West are not especially promising. The leaders who have recently come to power in Europe—Angela Merkel in Germany, Nicolas Sarkozy in France, and Gordon Brown in Britain—appear initially to be much more critical of Russia and especially Putin than were their predecessors. Certainly there is not yet the personal warmth or bond between Putin and this group that all three of their predecessors had with him.

Given the criticisms Democrats have leveled at President Bush's policies, and the likelihood that a Democrat will succeed Bush in the White House, it is to be expected that there will also be less tolerance in the United States for Russian behavior after the 2008 presidential election than there has been in the seven years corresponding with the Bush and Putin administrations. For that matter, Putin himself is due to leave office in March 2008. There is a strong probability he will be succeeded by someone even more determined to restore Russia's place in the world as an independent force and as a check on America's role as a unilateral actor.

Regardless of whether leaders from the East and West bond personally, there is likely to be greater concern within the European Union over what some will see as a return to cold war antagonisms. Many aspects of the old communist-versus-capitalist class struggle may no longer be relevant. Yet it is a bit of a surprise to see how some of the issues dividing East and West today so resemble the dividing philosophies of the cold war. The Kremlin under Putin, as it did in the Soviet era, has effectively eliminated meaningful democracy and has come close to eliminating criticism in the media, especially on television. As the power of the state has grown, the rights of individuals have been sharply constrained. While there is still private business, state controls are considerably more intrusive than they were in the mid-1990s.

To be clear, these increased state powers fall far short of what the Soviet state had. Yet the trend in Russia today is not encouraging for those who support a restricted role for the state and reasonably expansive rights for the individual. A return to something closer to authoritarianism, stripped of the ideology of the cold war, may reflect widespread nostalgia among Russians for their country's long czarist history and the czar's strong hand—particularly after what many saw as a laissez-faire attitude during Yeltsin's 1990s.

With over 70 percent of polled Russians approving of his administration, Putin seems to be doing something right. While the West may disapprove of Putin's policies, clearly most Russians do not. Many of them do not accept the notion that Putin is backing away from democracy. And if he is, they do not seem to care. For that matter, Putin himself asserts over and over again that what the West calls democracy is flawed, and that what he is fashioning comes closer to true democracy. His response to a German reporter in a June 1, 2007, press conference is typical. When asked if he considered himself a pure democrat, Putin laughed and said:

> Am I a pure democrat? Of course I am, absolutely. But do you know what the problem is? Not even a problem but a real tragedy? The problem is that I am all alone, the only one of my kind in the whole wide world. Just look at what's happening in North America. It's simply awful: torture, homeless people, Guantánamo, people detained without a trial and investigation. Just look at what's happening in Europe: harsh treatment of demonstrators, rubber bullets and tear gas. . . . There is no one to talk to since Mahatma Gandhi died.

All of this was said with a straight face. In a follow-up question, the same reporter sought confirmation. "And your country is not moving at all back toward a totalitarian regime?" Putin replied: "There is no truth in that. Do not believe what you hear."

Relations between the East and West are not hot or cold, but neither are they warm. At a time when Russia and the West have such different interpretations of democracy, it will take great effort to reduce tensions. Without great skill, even simple matters that would pose no problem between members of the EU or NATO are likely to lead to misunderstandings and hostility between Russia and the West. As Russia continues to prosper with its oil exports and the United States remains entangled in Iraq and Afghanistan, no matter who the new presidents of the United States and Russia turn out to be, keeping a civil tone in US-Russian as well as Russian-EU relations is likely to be a continuing challenge, more than it has been in the past two decades.

Marshall I. Goldman, a senior scholar at Harvard University's Davis Center for Russian and Eurasian Studies, is a professor emeritus at Wellesley College and author of the forthcoming *Petroleum, Putin, and Power* (Oxford University Press, 2008).

From *Current History,* October 2007, pp. 314–320. Copyright © 2007 by Current History, Inc. Reprinted by permission.

Emerging Strategic Dilemmas in U.S.-Chinese Relations

Since the Cold War, arms control negotiations have been strictly a bilateral affair between Washington and Moscow. But as times have changed, so must this dynamic. Enter China.

JOSHUA POLLACK

President Barack Obama's April 5 speech in Prague made it official: Arms control is back. The United States and Russia already are pursuing a new bilateral nuclear arms reduction treaty to replace the Strategic Arms Reduction Treaty, or START, which expires on December 5. Work toward a second, more ambitious bilateral treaty is expected to follow. Another early goal of the administration is to secure Senate ratification of the Comprehensive Test Ban Treaty. All of these steps, it is hoped, will smooth the path for a successful 2010 Nuclear Non-Proliferation Treaty (NPT) Review Conference.

> **The U.S.-Chinese relationship remains dogged by the potential for conflict that emanates from the 60-year contest over the status of Taiwan. Major defense acquisitions on both sides seem inexorably to be justified in terms of this scenario, spurring mutual fear and suspicion.**

The administration's agenda is driven both by the START calendar and by a belief that rapid progress will build momentum for strengthening the nonproliferation regime. But amid these urgent plans, it pays to recall something equally important. Traditionally, arms control has two fundamental purposes—to contain the risks of war and to prevent the spiral of mistrust driven by arms races, either numerical or technological. Neither of these goals can be achieved without a parallel arms control agenda, one focused on the United States and China. Today, there is no longer a plausible war scenario between the United States and Russia. But the U.S.-Chinese relationship remains dogged by the potential for conflict that emanates from the

60-year contest over the status of Taiwan. Major defense acquisitions on both sides seem inexorably to be justified in terms of this scenario, spurring mutual fear and suspicion.

The good news is that since Taiwan elected President Ma Jingyeou in March 2008, the "Taiwan question" has gone into remission, at least temporarily. The governments of mainland China and Taiwan have renewed contacts and reached new understandings on economic ties. Recently, Beijing has even consented to Taiwanese participation as an observer in the U.N. World Health Assembly, under the guise of "Chinese Taipei." The easing of tensions across the Taiwan Strait could create a favorable atmosphere for reaching new U.S.-Chinese understandings on military issues.

But the present calm is not guaranteed to last. Two waves of confrontation between the United States and China took place in the strait, in the 1950s and in the 1990s. Serious tensions have come and gone, depending on developments in China, Taiwan, and beyond. Moreover, in the decade since the U.S. Air Force accidentally bombed China's embassy in Belgrade in March 1999, military developments on both sides of the Pacific have drifted into unfamiliar and potentially dangerous waters. What political scientist Christopher Twomey aptly calls an "interlocking pattern" of new or upgraded strategic forces increases tensions and risks for both sides.[1] In future war scenarios, the interactions of strategic forces may encourage preemptive moves that risk even more serious forms of escalation.

Current risks—already a source of discomfort—are only liable to grow as China and the United States continue to modernize their strategic forces. Each side tends to draw ominous inferences about the other's intentions for new weapons developments, which justifies countermoves and, most of all, injects considerable suspicion and antagonism into a centrally important international relationship. The particular crisis, war, and escalation scenarios that animate this security dilemma are outweighed in significance by their potential to confound cooperation on crucial global challenges: financial stabilization, trade relations, economic recovery, and climate change. But this outcome can be avoided. China and the United States should seize on the current lull in cross-strait tensions to quell the prospect of a trans-Pacific strategic arms race before it becomes self-fulfilling.

A Delicate Transition

U.S.-Chinese strategic military interactions do not resemble a numerical nuclear arms race along Cold War lines. The two sides' arsenals are unevenly matched. The United States has a mature strategic triad, rivaled only by Russia's, with thousands of warheads ready to launch within minutes of receiving an order. China's Second Artillery Force has a relatively slender silo-based force, with an even smaller handful of new road-mobile missiles added in recent years. The new strategic submarine force of the People's Liberation Army Navy is just starting to take shape. Even as the Second Artillery and the navy are expanding and modernizing their respective nuclear capabilities, there is no indication that they will seek to match U.S. or Russian force levels, absent dramatic cuts by the two other powers.

U.S.-Chinese strategic military interactions do not resemble a numerical nuclear arms race along Cold War lines. The United States has a mature strategic triad, rivaled only by Russia's. Meanwhile, China's Second Artillery Force has a relatively slender silo-based force, with an even smaller handful of new road-mobile missiles added in recent years.

The differences in these arsenals stem from their divergent purposes. For the United States, the strategic nuclear triad is a source of power, advantage, and respect worthy of the world's sole super-power. It is alert, survivable, and accurate, standing behind unparalleled U.S. conventional forces and underwriting a global network of alliances. Through a studied ambiguity about when U.S. nuclear forces might be employed, the nuclear arsenal is even believed to provide the United States, its conventional military forces, and its allies with a measure of security against chemical or biological attack.

By comparison, China's relatively modest strategic nuclear forces are designed to assert the country's status as a recognized major power, immune to the sort of episodes of nuclear coercion that punctuated the 1950s. To convince Washington (and Moscow) that its nuclear force had some ability to survive an attack and retaliate, Beijing's deterrence strategy originally depended on maintaining ambiguity about how many weapons it had. But technological progress is enabling a new approach. As China develops and fields a new generation of solid-fueled, long-range ballistic missiles, mobility has begun to replace uncertainty as the mainspring of credible retaliatory capability. The force remains small, but it is becoming considerably more sophisticated.

This situation seems benign on its face. China is neither maintaining a large force on high alert nor racing to catch up to the United States numerically. The United States, therefore, feels little pressure to stay ahead of China. But two issues complicate the picture: (1) the unpredictable effect of emerging Chinese doctrine and operational practices in a crisis; and (2) the emergence on both sides of new strategic weapons, primarily based on ballistic missile technology but adapted to purposes other than nuclear attack or retaliation. In a crisis or a limited conflict, these new weapons would have the potential to interact with both conventional forces and strategic nuclear forces, creating a pathway for escalation. Furthermore, each side's acquisition of non-nuclear strategic forces has begun to justify the other side's acquisition of its own.

Chinese nuclear doctrine has consistently been articulated as retaliatory in character, exemplified by the no-first-use pledge that Beijing's leaders supported even before the country's first nuclear test in 1964.[2] (Periodic calls by Chinese military analysts to revisit this commitment have gone unheeded by policy makers.) Despite Beijing's commitment to no-first-use, its transition to road-mobile and submarine-based missiles raises concerns about the outcome of the next potential crisis. In particular, it is unclear when the navy or Second Artillery might be ordered to engage in "alert operations," mobilizing nuclear submarines or missiles with the intention of advertising their ability to survive and retaliate in the event of a first strike.[3] According to the 2008 edition of a white paper on national defense issued by China's State Council, "If China comes under a nuclear threat, the nuclear missile force of the Second Artillery Force will go into a state of alert and get ready for a nuclear counterattack to deter the enemy from using nuclear weapons against China."[4] But it is difficult to anticipate what words or actions would constitute a "nuclear threat" in China's eyes. It is also unclear how the United States would interpret and react to such moves, especially since some U.S. experts believe that China's no-first-use doctrine contains unresolved ambiguities, and alert operations may not be clearly distinguishable from launch preparations.[5]

The transition to a mobile nuclear deterrent also raises a new set of operational questions connected to the appearance of China's first generation of fully deployable nuclear ballistic missile submarines. According to the New America Foundation's Jeffrey Lewis, the U.S. intelligence community believes that nuclear warheads are stored separately from the Second Artillery's land-based missiles, including mobile missiles.[6] It is difficult to imagine how comparable arrangements could be made at sea. Submarines can be expected to hold missiles with warheads attached, as there will not be opportunities to mate these systems underwater. Strategic submarines also may be expected to conduct long-range ocean patrols. All of these conditions call for rigorous communications, command, and control arrangements, seemingly beyond anything in China's experience to date.[7]

The initial deployments of China's nuclear-armed submarines will raise unsettling questions: Under what circumstances will submarine commanders be authorized to launch? During an intense crisis or a conventional military conflict, what sort of communications will they be able to maintain with the chain of command onshore? The problem extends in the other direction as well: If a submarine is lost at sea during a crisis—or simply falls out of communication—would leaders onshore perceive it as the opening shot of a preemptive attack on its strategic nuclear forces?[8] The South China Sea incident in March, when Chinese boats harassed a U.S. Navy ocean surveillance vessel, hints at the Chinese Navy's growing sensitivity to the threat of U.S. antisubmarine warfare.[9]

Entanglement with Theater Missiles

As troublesome as these problems may be, they are familiar in their outlines thanks to interactions between U.S. and Soviet strategic forces in the early days of the Cold War. Other characteristics of U.S.-Chinese relations are less well understood. For example, the addition of more than one thousand conventional theater ballistic missiles to the Second Artillery's arsenal during the last two decades complicates the picture. While nuclear missiles are deterrent weapons, conventional missiles are available for use in the early stages of an armed conflict. In such an event, the United States would have incentives to attack Second Artillery command-and-control nodes, raising difficult questions about the precise boundaries of China's no-first-use pledge.

According to the 2008 white paper, the conventional missile force "is charged mainly with the task of conducting medium- and long-range precision strikes against key strategic and operational targets of the enemy."[10] The annual U.S. Defense Department report on China's military anticipates the potential use of these missiles against Taiwan, either to close off the island to shipping or to attack key targets in the event of war. It also anticipates the development of anti-ship ballistic missiles designed to disable (or sink) U.S. aircraft carriers.[11] At least some Chinese sources describe conventional missile strikes as a means of demonstrating the willingness and ability of the Second Artillery to employ its weapons against a nuclear-armed enemy.[12]

The idea of China demonstrating resolve during a conflict by attacking high-value U.S. targets introduces—for both sides—the classic dilemma of when to act assertively in order to give pause to a foe, and when to act with restraint in order to avoid dangerous escalation. U.S. intelligence analyst Lonnie Henley has expressed concern that the writers of Chinese military doctrine tend to gaze past this problem, underestimating the unpredictability of crises by presuming that adversaries will understand each other's motives clearly. Chinese doctrine, Henley concludes, contains "little consideration of the possibility that what China considers a resolute response to maintain the political initiative, the opponent might misconstrue as alarming preparations for aggressive military action."[13]

Operational and organizational factors complicate matters further. Once mobile missiles have been dispersed into the field, they become notoriously difficult to locate; the most effective way to suppress their fire would be to silence the command-and-control centers that issue launch orders. Yet conventional theater ballistic missiles appear to share command-and-control channels with land-based nuclear ballistic missiles, as both are the property of the Second Artillery. According to Stanford University scholars John Lewis and Xue Litai, the Second Artillery maintains a General Communications Station in Beijing through which all of its coded messages flow.[14] Unlike the army, navy, and air force, the Second Artillery also is subject to the direct authority of a senior civilian body, the Central Military Commission (CMC) and "strictly follows the orders of the CMC."[15] Lewis and Xue report that the CMC communicates to the Second Artillery through the General Staff's communications department.[16]

As a consequence of these arrangements, attempts to "decapitate" Chinese command-and-control capabilities for conventional missiles could implicate China's nuclear deterrent force, and even its entire military establishment. This places U.S. planners in a bind. Targeting central command-and-control nodes could threaten China's nuclear deterrent and might be interpreted as a prelude to—or equivalent to—a nuclear first strike. (It is difficult to ascertain what Second Artillery bases are instructed to do if the General Communications Station were to fall silent, or whether there are backup stations.) Yet it is difficult to imagine that, in the event of an armed conflict, a U.S. commander would be content to absorb a barrage of precision strikes. Absent some means of protection, such as plentiful and reliable theater missile defenses, the U.S. side therefore may be faced with a choice between either striking early at undispersed mobile missiles or keeping aircraft carriers at a safe distance from the conflict zone.

Entanglement with Non-Nuclear Strategic Forces

Thanks to the emergence of new weapon types on both sides of the Pacific, the problems surrounding theater missiles are increasingly paralleled in the strategic domain. These innovative non-nuclear strategic forces overlap with both conventional weapons and strategic nuclear weapons, creating additional pressure to deliver strikes early in a conflict against targets associated with the other side's non-nuclear strategic forces.

One of these new "entangling" weapons is the U.S. Ground-Based Midcourse Defense system, the only strategic ballistic missile defense system deployed by the United States. Although the U.S. Missile Defense Agency states that the system is designed exclusively to counteract emerging threats from North Korea and Iran, Chinese officials and experts take a skeptical view of these claims. And in theory, the system—in combination with theater defense systems—could provide U.S. leaders with the ability to blunt China's threat of retaliation should they choose to threaten a U.S. nuclear first strike.

With this added edge, or so Beijing might conclude, Washington could return to the "bullying" that originally motivated China's acquisition of nuclear weapons. This possibility has been cited as driving some aspects of China's intercontinental ballistic missile modernization, including the development of decoys and counter-measures to overcome defenses. But as long as Beijing perceives the Ground-Based Midcourse Defense system as emboldening Washington, Chinese military planners will be tempted to consider the system a legitimate target, especially because it is not a nuclear target.[17]

The expected deployment of the U.S. Space Tracking and Surveillance System (STSS) satellites could increase the system's effectiveness and heighten Chinese concerns. According to the manufacturer, STSS will provide "unique capability to track and discriminate missiles in midcourse; report on post-boost vehicle maneuvers, reentry vehicle deployments, and the use of various types of decoys; and provide hit/kill assessment."[18] If Chinese officials lack confidence that their new generation of missiles could overcome a U.S. missile defense system enhanced by STSS, or even if they believed that STSS would provide *unwarranted* U.S. confidence in the system's effectiveness, they might plan to disable or destroy the satellites during a crisis before nuclear threats could come into play. To attack the satellites, the Chinese would rely on a second category of entangling weapons: antisatellite weapons, either involving ground-based lasers or direct ascent (i.e., attack with a ballistic missile).[19]

Partly as a counter to this potential threat, U.S. defense officials have turned to the idea of deploying "conventional prompt global strike" weapons. To protect important imaging and communications assets in orbit, these weapons would stand ready to strike antisatellite systems preemptively, by attacking their sensors, command-and-control facilities, or launchers.[20] In a potential conflict with China, this third type of entangling weapon could be called upon to strike valuable targets deep inside China from platforms traditionally associated with strategic nuclear capabilities. All of these circumstances implicitly require great confidence in the integrity of the Chinese no-first-use pledge under extreme and confusing circumstances.

Attacking the systems and networks that support antisatellite weapons could raise similar concerns to those associated with attacking theater ballistic missiles. If antisatellite command-and-control arrangements overlap with those for nuclear forces then the stakes involved in attacking them are considerably greater than simply the security of a satellite constellation. The direct-ascent antisatellite weapon tested by China in January 2007 was reportedly fired from a mobile launcher of the type associated with the DF-21 theater ballistic missile, presenting some of the same difficult choices as conventional theater ballistic missiles.[21]

Revisiting Assumptions

These new strategic military trends and interactions have emerged during a period of relative calm in the U.S.-Chinese relationship. For most of the past decade, the interests of the two countries have aligned behind economic ties and a common rhetoric of fighting terrorism. But seemingly lacking a coherent alternative, both sides have continued to develop their military capabilities and planning against each other. Starting in 1999 with the Cox Commission report on "U.S. National Security and Military/Commercial Concerns with the People's Republic of China" and the Belgrade embassy bombing, a series of espionage allegations and military incidents have deepened mistrust between the two countries and hobbled efforts at dialogue.

For most of the past decade, the interests of Washington and Beijing have aligned behind economic ties and a common rhetoric of fighting terrorism. But seemingly lacking a coherent alternative, both sides have continued to develop their military capabilities and planning against each other.

The Obama administration's ambitious arms control agenda and the positive trend in cross-Taiwan Strait relations creates an opportunity to shift away from these unwelcome trends in the U.S.-China strategic arena. But to achieve progress, both sides must revisit some of the assumptions that have brought them to this point. In the United States, strategic thinking appears to labor under an unstated belief that decisions about different classes of strategic systems can be made without reference to each other and to no more than one potential adversary at a time. U.S. nuclear forces have been sized to match or exceed Russian forces, a stance codified in the 2002 Moscow Treaty; initial deployments of strategic missile defense systems have been postured against North Korea. Relatively little thought appears to have been given to how Chinese officials might perceive either of these decisions, let alone the two in combination.

In China, meanwhile, the elite juggle two competing and seemingly incompatible views. The first is that U.S. national security strategy is inexorably focused on restraining or opposing China.[22] The second is that China should avoid high-level bilateral negotiations about nuclear or strategic weapons, a situation that would be too reminiscent of Cold War summitry. Chinese participants at international conferences often express the view that Beijing's participation in arms reduction talks can be deferred until Russia and the United States reach China's low force levels. China's preferred venue for arms control proposals has been the U.N. Conference on Disarmament in Geneva, a broadly multilateral format.

Another way of describing the relationship is that U.S. strategic force planners see China as neither as big as Russia nor as unpredictable as North Korea, and therefore, judge it not to be their first concern. (Conventional force planners plainly do not share this perspective.) Chinese policy makers, for their part, seem to see the United States as too big and strong for China to face on its own. This combination of U.S. distraction and Chinese aloofness has allowed the two sides to slide into dangerous strategic interactions.

The present situation not only engenders risk but deepens suspicions when the opposite is needed. Considering that even limited, conventional conflict would entail profound and unacceptable harm for everyone involved, trying to cut a firebreak between the cataclysmic and the merely catastrophic might seem like a misallocation of national energies.

The present situation not only engenders risk but deepens suspicions when the opposite is needed. Considering that even limited, conventional conflict would entail profound and unacceptable harm for everyone involved, trying to cut a firebreak between the cataclysmic and the merely catastrophic might seem like a misallocation of national energies. But the single greatest benefit of quashing an incipient strategic arms race may simply be to interrupt the cycle of suspicion and antagonism that lends an adversarial cast to relations and makes war scenarios seem plausible at all.

Both to ease mutual suspicions and to minimize escalation pressures, it is in the interests of both sides to negotiate arrangements to manage, verifiably limit, or ban entirely classes of non-nuclear weapons—such as non-nuclear applications for ballistic missiles and directed-energy weapons—which interact with nuclear weapons and with each other. Separately, the United States and China should consider negotiating a "code of conduct" for maritime operations in the Pacific, potentially along the lines of the U.S.-Soviet Incidents at Sea Agreement of 1972.

Arms control advocates should not expect too much too soon from U.S.-Chinese relations. Russia currently dominates the U.S. arms control agenda, and economic issues occupy center stage between Washington and Beijing. The April 1 joint statement between presidents Hu Jintao and Barack Obama affirmed a process of continuous dialogue with both a "strategic track" and an "economic track," but economic concerns can be expected to receive the bulk of high-level attention for the time being, and there is no similarly prominent military track. (On the U.S. side, the "strategic track" is chaired by the secretary of state.) Even in the best case, it may take years to build up a level of mutual comfort for serious discussions on strategic affairs. The record of bilateral arms control talks is relatively scant.

In the meantime, the countries can pursue a number of working-level activities to develop greater mutual familiarity and promote understanding of each side's concerns. Expanding military-to-military dialogue would be valuable, as would resuming the laboratory-to-laboratory exchanges that have been suspended for more than a decade. Renewed lab-to-lab contacts could help to build a common understanding of verification technology, information barriers, and other technical aspects of arms control practice. Arms control expert Lewis Dunn also has put forth a useful proposal to hold consultations with Chinese officials during the course of the ongoing Nuclear Posture Review and to provide briefings on the results.[23]

Whatever mechanisms U.S. and Chinese officials settle on, it is important for them to start early and to continue even in the event of one of the periodic incidents that tend to perturb the U.S.-Chinese relationship. Without a dialogue aimed at developing agreements to regulate military interactions and limit forces, mutual risk and suspicion will only grow.

Notes

1. Christopher P. Twomey, "Chinese-U.S. Strategic Affairs: Dangerous Dynamism," *Arms Control Today,* January/February 2009.

2. John Wilson Lewis and Xue Litai, *China Builds the Bomb* (Stanford, CA: Stanford University Press, 1988), p. 194.

3. Jeffrey Lewis, *The Minimum Means of Reprisal: China's Search for Security in the Nuclear Age* (Cambridge, MA: American Academy of Arts and Sciences, 2007).

4. Information Office of the State Council of the People's Republic of China, "China's National Defense in 2008" (Beijing: January 2009), p. 29. Pagination follows the version of the document assembled by the Federation of American Scientists. Available at www.fas.org/programs/ssp/nukes/2008DefenseWhitePaper_Jan2009.pdf.

5. Evan S. Medeiros, "Evolving Nuclear Doctrine," in Paul J. Bolt and Albert S. Willner, eds., *China's Nuclear Future* (Boulder, CO: Lynne Rienner Publishers, 2006), pp. 39–78.

6. Jeffrey Lewis, "Chinese Nuclear Posture and Force Modernization," in Christina Hansell and William C. Potter, eds., *Engaging China and Russia on Nuclear Disarmament* (Monterey, CA: Monterey Institute of International Studies, 2009), pp. 43–45.

7. Andrew S. Erickson and Michael Chase, "An Undersea Deterrent?" *Proceedings,* Vol. 135/6/1,276 (June 2009). Available at www.usni.org/magazines/proceedings/story.asp?STORY_ID=1907.

8. "Chinese Nuclear Posture and Force Modernization," pp. 43–45.

9. Hans Kristensen, "U.S.-Chinese Anti-Submarine Cat and Mouse Game in South China Sea," *FAS Strategic Security Blog,* March 9, 2009. Available at www.fas.org/blog/ssp/2009/03/incident.php.

10. *China's National Defense in 2008,* p. 29.

11. Office of the Secretary of Defense, *Annual Report to Congress: Military Power of the People's Republic of China: 2009* (Washington, D.C.: March 2009), pp. 20–22, pp. 43–44.

12. "Evolving Nuclear Doctrine," p. 61.

13. Lonnie D. Henley, "Evolving Chinese Concepts of War Control and Escalation Management," in Michael D. Swaine, Andrew N. D. Yang, and Evan S. Medeiros with Oriana Skylar Mastro, eds., *Assessing the Threat: The Chinese Military and Taiwan's Security* (Washington, D.C.: Carnegie Endowment for International Peace, 2007), p. 97.

14. John Wilson Lewis and Xue Litai, *Imagined Enemies: China Prepares for Uncertain War* (Stanford, CA: Stanford University Press, 2006), pp. 198–199.

15. *China's National Defense in 2008,* p. 29.

16. Lewis and Xue, *Imagined Enemies,* pp. 198–199.

17. *The Minimum Means of Reprisal.*

18. Northrop Grumman, "Space Tracking and Surveillance System (STSS)." Available at www.northropgrumman.com/ missiledefense/ProgramInfo/STSS.html.

19. *Military Power of the People's Republic of China: 2009,* p. 27.

20. William B. Scott, "Wargames Zero In On Knotty Milspace Issues," *Aviation Week & Space Technology,* January 29, 2001; "Transcript: Hearing of the Strategic Forces Subcommittee of the Senate Armed Services Committee," *Federal News Service,* March 28, 2007.

21. Phillip C. Saunders and Charles D. Lutes, "China's ASAT Test: Motivations and Implications," *INSS Special Report,* June 2007.

22. Chu Shulong, "Chinese Views of American Strategic Development in Asia," in Jonathan D. Pollack, ed., *Asia Eyes America: Regional Perspectives on U.S. Asia-Pacific Strategy in the Twenty-First Century* (Newport, RI: Naval War College Press, 2007), pp. 95–112.

23. Lewis A. Dunn, "Reshaping Strategic Relationships: Expanding the Arms Control Toolbox," *Arms Control Today,* May 2009.

JOSHUA POLLACK is a consultant to the U.S. government on arms control, proliferation, and deterrence issues.

From *Bulletin of the Atomic Scientists,* July/August 2009, pp. 53–63. Copyright © 2009 by Bulletin of the Atomic Scientists. Reprinted by permission.

China's Challenge to U.S. Hegemony

"If the United States tries to maintain its current dominance in East Asia, Sino-American conflict is virtually certain. . . ."

CHRISTOPHER LAYNE

The Soviet Union's collapse transformed the bipolar cold war international system into a "unipolar" system dominated by the United States. During the 1990s, the U.S. foreign policy community engaged in lively debate about whether America's post–cold war hegemony could be sustained over the long haul or was merely a "unipolar moment." More than 15 years after the cold war's end, it is obvious that American hegemony has been more than momentary. Indeed, the prevailing view among policy makers and foreign policy scholars today is that America's economic, military, and technological advantages are so great that it will be a long time before U.S. dominance can be challenged.

There is mounting evidence, however, that this view is mistaken, and that, in fact, the era of American hegemony is drawing to a close right before our eyes. The rise of China is the biggest reason for this. Notwithstanding Washington's current preoccupation with the Middle East, in the coming decades China's great power emergence will be the paramount issue of grand strategy facing the United States.

Whether China will undergo a "peaceful rise"—as Beijing claims—is doubtful. Historically, the emergence of new poles of power in the international system has been geopolitically destabilizing. For example, the rise of Germany, the United States, and Japan at the end of the nineteenth century contributed to the international political frictions that culminated in two world wars. There is no reason to believe that China's rise will be an exception.

However, while it is certainly true that China's rise will cause geopolitical turmoil, a Sino-American war is not inevitable. Whether such a conflict occurs will hinge more on Washington's strategic choices than on Beijing's.

Rise of a Great Power

From the mid-1980s through the late 1990s China's economy grew at a rate of approximately 10 percent a year. From the late 1990s until 2005 its economy grew at 8 percent to 9 percent annually. In 2006 China's annual growth rate was above 11 percent, as it is projected to be for 2007. China's phenomenal economic growth is driving its emergence as a great power—and

this is a familiar pattern in international politics. The economic power of states grows at different rates, which means that some states are always gaining power and some are losing power relative to others. As Paul Kennedy demonstrated in his 1987 book *The Rise and Fall of the Great Powers,* time and again these relative economic shifts have "heralded the rise of new great powers which one day would have a decisive impact on the military/territorial order."

The leadership in Beijing understands the link between economic strength and geopolitical weight. It realizes that, if China can continue to sustain near–double digit growth rates in the early decades of this century, it will surpass the United States as the world's largest economy (measured by gross domestic product). Because of this astonishing economic growth, China is, as journalist James Kynge has put it (with a nod to Napoleon), truly shaking the world both economically *and* geopolitically. Studies by the U.S. Central Intelligence Agency and others have projected that China will be a first-rate military power and will rival America in global power by 2020.

Engage or Contain?

In fact, China's rise has been on the radar screens of U.S. foreign policy experts since the early 1990s. Broadly speaking, the debate about how the United States should respond to China's emergence as a great power has focused on two policy alternatives: engagement and containment.

Engagement assumes that, as China's contacts with the outside world multiply, its exposure to Western (that is, mostly American) political and cultural values will result in evolutionary political change within China. The proponents of engagement believe that the forces of domestic political liberalization and economic globalization will temper Beijing's foreign policy ambitions and lead to a peaceful Sino-American relationship.

On the economic side, the logic of engagement is that, as China becomes increasingly tied to the international economy, its interdependence with others will constrain it from taking political actions that could disrupt its vital access both to foreign markets and capital and to high-technology imports from the

United States, Japan, and Western Europe. This was the claim made in the 1990s by the Clinton administration and its supporters during a debate about whether the United States should extend permanent normal trade relations to China and support Beijing's accession to the World Trade Organization.

Proponents of engagement have also argued that the United States can help foster political liberalization in China by integrating the country into the international economy and embedding it in the complex web of international institutional arrangements. A China so engaged, it is said, will have strong interests in cooperation and will not be inclined to pursue security competition with America or with its Asian neighbors.

Engagement is a problematic strategy, however, because it rests on a shaky foundation. The conventional wisdom notwithstanding, there is little support in the historical record for the idea that economic interdependence leads to peace. After all, Europe never was more interdependent (not only economically but also, among the ruling elites, intellectually and culturally) than before World War I. It was famously predicted, on the eve of World War I, that the economic ties among Europe's great powers had ushered in an era in which war among them was unthinkable. Yet, as we know, the prospect of forgoing the economic gains of trade did not stop Europe's great powers from fighting a prolonged and devastating war.

Beijing's actual foreign policy furnishes a concrete reason to be skeptical of the argument that interdependence leads to peace. China's behavior in the 1996 crisis with Taiwan (during which it conducted missile tests in waters surrounding the island in the run-up to Taiwan's presidential election) suggested it was not constrained by fears that its muscular foreign policy would adversely affect its overseas trade.

Of course, during the past decade, China has been mindful of its stake in international trade and investment. But this does not vindicate the U.S. strategy of engagement. China's current policy reflects the fact that, for now, Beijing recognizes its strategic interest in preserving peace in East Asia. Stability in the region, and in Sino-American relations, allows China to become richer and to catch up to the United States in relative power. For a state in China's position vis-à-vis the United States, this is the optimal realpolitik strategy: buying time for its economy to grow so that the nation can openly balance against the United States militarily and establish its own regional hegemony in East Asia. Beijing is pursuing a peaceful policy today in order to strengthen itself to confront the United States tomorrow.

The era of American hegemony is drawing to a close right before our eyes.

The belief that a democratic—or more liberal—China would be pacific and collaborative in its external policies is similarly dubious. This view rests on the so-called "democratic peace theory" which is near and dear to many U.S. foreign policy experts. In fact, the democratic peace theory is another one of those bits of foreign policy conventional wisdom that is based on flimsy evidence. The historical record demonstrates that when vital national interests have been at risk, democratic states have routinely practiced big-stick diplomacy against other democracies (including threats to use force). In other words, when the stakes are high enough, great powers act like great powers even in their relations with other democracies. Thus, even if China does undergo political liberalization in the future, there is no reason to believe that its foreign policy behavior would be fundamentally affected.

A U.S. containment strategy for China differs from engagement in that it relies mostly on the traditional "hard power" tools of military might and alliance diplomacy to thwart China's great power emergence. Containment calls for the United States to emulate its anti-Soviet cold war strategy by assembling a powerful coalition of states sharing a common interest in curbing rising Chinese power—particularly by tightening the U.S. security relationship with Japan while simultaneously investing that alliance with an overtly anti-Chinese mission. Containment would require the United States to pledge explicitly to defend Taiwan while bolstering Taiwanese military capabilities. Some containment advocates also argue that the United States should engage in covert operations to destabilize China, especially by fomenting unrest among China's ethnic minorities.

To contain China, the United States would maintain both its nuclear and conventional military superiority over China, and would develop a credible first strike option based on a combination of robust offensive nuclear capabilities and effective ballistic missile defenses. Advocates of containment hope that the various measures encompassed by this strategy could halt China's rise and preserve American dominance in East Asia. However, as argued for example by Missouri State University's Bradley A. Thayer, if these steps failed to stop China's great power emergence, the United States would have to consider "harsher measures." In other words, the United States should be prepared to engage in a preventive war against China. Containment, therefore, is a strategy that at best would result in an intense Sino-American security competition. At worst, it could lead to war.

The Actual Strategy

Engagement and containment are "ideal type" grand strategies toward China. In the real world, Washington's actual approach fashions elements of both engagement and containment into a hard-edged grand strategy that requires China to accept U.S. geopolitical and ideological hegemony—or else. In this respect, American policy toward China is the specific manifestation of overall U.S. grand strategy, which rests on both strategic and idealistic pillars.

Strategically, the goal of post–cold war U.S. strategy has been to prevent the emergence of new great powers (or, as the Pentagon calls them, "peer competitors"). This strategy was first articulated in March 1992 in the initial draft of the Pentagon's *Defense Planning Guidance* document for fiscal years 1994–1999. It stated that the goal of U.S. grand strategy henceforth would be to maintain America's preponderance by preventing new great powers from emerging. The United States, it declared, "must maintain the mechanisms for deterring potential competitors from even aspiring to a larger regional or global role."

The Clinton administration similarly was committed to the perpetuation of U.S. preponderance. And the administration of George W. Bush has embraced the hegemonic strategy of its two immediate predecessors. The 2002 *National Security Strategy of the United States* promises that America will act to prevent any other state from building up military capabilities in the hope of "surpassing, or even equaling, the power of the United States."

Ideologically, U.S. grand strategy amounts to "real-politik-plus," to borrow Brandeis University professor Robert Art's phrase. As such, national interests are defined in terms of both hard power and the promotion of American ideals. As the *National Security Strategy* puts it, U.S. grand strategy is "based on a distinctly American internationalism that reflects the union of our values and our national interests."

Some observers have described this formula as "liberal realism," "national security liberalism," or (as neoconservative pundit Charles Krauthammer puts it) "democratic realism." This sort of liberalism is more muscular and offensive than idealistic. The spread of democracy and economic openness are imbedded in American grand strategic thought because policy makers believe that U.S. power, influence, and security are enhanced in a world comprised of "free market democracies."

America's post–cold war strategy is based firmly on these twin pillars of military superiority and liberal internationalist ideology. And because domestic ideology is the fundamental driver of U.S. grand strategy, America's geopolitical aims transcend those traditionally associated with power politics. Not only does the emergence of a powerful challenger in general threaten America's ability to control its environment, but China in particular is seen as a threat because its politico-economic system challenges America's need for a world compatible with—and safe for—its own liberal ideology. China's rise threatens to close East Asia to U.S. economic and ideological penetration.

Liberalize—Or Else

Because of ideology, engagement has a role in U.S. strategy, but it is engagement with (bared) teeth. The United States is willing to give China the opportunity to integrate itself into the U.S.-led international order—on Washington's terms. Thus, as a Pentagon document has put it, the United States wants China to become a "responsible member of the international community." Responsibility, however, is defined as Beijing's willingness to accept Washington's vision of a stable international order. As President Bush declared in a November 2005 speech in Kyoto, responsibility also requires China to achieve political liberalization and develop as a free market economy firmly anchored to the international economy.

Indeed, U.S. policy makers believe that, over the long term, peaceful relations are possible with Beijing *only* if China undergoes domestic political and economic liberalization. As a result, the United States aims to promote China's internal transformation. As the Bush administration's *National Security Strategy* declares: "America will encourage the advancement of democracy and economic openness" in China, "because these are the best foundations for domestic stability and international order."

As then-Deputy Secretary of State Robert Zoellick said in 2005, "Closed politics cannot be a permanent feature of Chinese society."

U.S. officials believe that nations such as China that do not adopt American-style political and economic systems, and that do not play by the rules of the American-led international order, are *ipso facto* threats to U.S. interests—threats to which America must be prepared to respond aggressively.

Here is where America's willingness to employ the hard fist of military power against China comes into play. The Bush administration has said it "welcomes a confident, peaceful, and prosperous China that appreciates that its growth and development depend on constructive connections with the rest of the world." At the same time, however, Washington has made crystal clear that it will not countenance a China that emerges as a great power rival and challenges American primacy. The 2002 *National Security Strategy* enjoins Beijing from challenging the United States militarily and warns that, "In pursuing advanced military capabilities that can threaten its neighbors in the Asia-Pacific region, China is following an outdated path that, in the end, will hamper its own pursuit of national greatness. In time, China will find that social and political freedom is the only source of that greatness."

As Washington sees it, China has no justifiable grounds for regarding the U.S. military presence in East Asia as threatening to its interests. Then–Defense Secretary Donald Rumsfeld made this point in 2005 when he stated that any moves by China to enhance its military capabilities necessarily are signals of aggressive Chinese intent. According to Rumsfeld, China's military modernization cannot possibly be defensive because "no nation threatens China." Rumsfeld's view was echoed in the administration's 2005 report on *The Military Power of the People's Republic of China,* which stated that "China's military modernization remains ambitious," and warned that in coming years "China's leaders may be tempted to resort to force or coercion more quickly to press diplomatic advantage, advance security interests, or resolve disputes."

Similarly, at an October 2007 conference on Sino-American relations Admiral Timothy Keating, the commander in chief of the U.S. Pacific Command, made three points with respect to America's China strategy. First, the United States will seek to maintain its present military dominance over China. Second, America will, through arms sales, ensure there is a cross-Strait military balance between Taiwan and China. Third, the United States will not allow China to change the status quo in Taiwan by force. In short, the United States is determined both to make sure that China does not emerge as a peer competitor and to impose itself as an obstacle to China's overriding national goal of reunification with Taiwan.

Strangling the Baby

China's rise affects the United States because of what international relations scholars call the "power transition" effect: Throughout the history of the modern international state system, ascending powers have always challenged the position of the dominant (hegemonic) power in the international system—and these challenges have usually culminated in war. Notwithstanding Beijing's talk about a "peaceful rise," an ascending China inevitably will challenge the geopolitical equilibrium in East Asia. The doctrine of peaceful rise thus is a reassurance strategy employed by Beijing in an attempt to allay others' fears of growing Chinese power and to forestall the United States from acting preventively during the dangerous transition period when China is catching up to the United States.

Does this mean that the United States and China are on a collision course that will lead to a war in the next decade or two? Not necessarily. What happens in Sino-American relations largely depends on what strategy Washington chooses to adopt toward China. If the United States tries to maintain its current dominance in East Asia, Sino-American conflict is virtually certain, because U.S. grand strategy has incorporated the logic of anticipatory violence as an instrument for maintaining American primacy. For a declining hegemon, "strangling the baby in the crib" by attacking a rising challenger preventively—that is, while the hegemon still holds the upper hand militarily—has always been a tempting strategic option.

An Alternative Plan

Washington, however, faces perhaps a last chance to adopt a grand strategy that will serve its interests in ensuring that Chinese power is contained in East Asia but without running the risk of an armed clash with Beijing. This strategy is "offshore balancing," a concept that is finding increasing favor with a group of influential American scholars in the field of security studies. According to this strategy, the United States should deploy military power abroad only in the face of direct threats to vital American interests. The strategy recognizes that Washington need not (and in fact cannot) directly control vast parts of the globe, that it is better off setting priorities based on clear national interests and relying on local actors to uphold regional balances of power. The idea of offshore balancing is to husband national power for maximum effectiveness while minimizing perceptions that this power represents a threat.

By adopting an offshore balancing strategy, the United States could better preserve its relative power and strategic influence.

As an offshore balancer in East Asia, the United States would embrace a new set of policies regarding Sino-American economic relations, political liberalization in China, the defense of Taiwan, and America's strategic posture in the region.

An offshore balancing strategy would require the United States to approach economic relations with China based on a policy of strategic trade rather than free trade. A strategic trade policy would seek to curtail the flow of high technology and direct investment from the United States to China. It also would require a shift in current U.S. trade policy to drastically reduce the bilateral trade deficit, which is a de facto American subsidy of the very economic growth that is fueling China's great power emergence.

Second, the United States would abandon its efforts to effectuate political liberalization in China. This policy is a form of gratuitous eye-poking. Because the United States lacks sufficient leverage to transform China domestically, the primary effect of trying to force liberalization on China is to inflame Sino-American relations.

An offshore balancing strategy also would require a new U.S. stance on Taiwan, a powder-keg issue because China is committed to national reunification and would regard a Taiwanese declaration of independence as a *casus belli*. If U.S. policy fails to prevent a showdown between China and Taiwan, the odds are that America will be drawn into the conflict because of its current East Asia strategy. There would be strong domestic political pressure in favor of U.S. intervention. Beyond the arguments that Chinese military action against Taiwan would constitute aggression and undermine U.S. interests in a stable world order, powerful incentives for intervention would also arise from ideological antipathy toward China, concerns for maintaining U.S. "credibility," and support for a democratic Taiwan in a conflict with authoritarian China.

Notwithstanding these arguments, which are underpinned by a national security discourse that favors American hegemony, the issues at stake in a possible showdown between China and Taiwan simply would not justify the risks and costs of U.S. intervention. Regardless of the rationale invoked, the contention that the United States should go to war to prevent Beijing from using force to achieve reunification with Taiwan (or in response to a unilateral declaration of independence by Taipei) amounts to nothing more than a veiled argument for fighting a "preventive" war against a rising China.

Sharing the Burden

The final element of a U.S. offshore balancing strategy would be the devolution from the United States to the major powers in Asia of the responsibility for containing China. An offshore balancing strategy would rely on the balance-of-power dynamics of a twenty-first century multipolar global order to prevent China from dominating East Asia. The other major powers in Asia—Japan, Russia, and India—have a much more immediate interest in stopping a rising China in their midst than does the United States.

In a multipolar system, the question is not whether balancing will occur, but which state or states will do the heavy lifting. Because the United States is geographically distant from China—and protected both by the expanse of the Pacific Ocean and by its own formidable military (including nuclear) capabilities—the United States has the option of staying out of East Asian security rivalries (at least initially) and forcing Beijing's neighbors to assume the risks and costs of stopping China from attaining regional hegemony. Because its air and naval power is based on long-range strike capabilities, the United States can keep its forces in an over-the-horizon posture with respect to East Asia and limit itself to a backstopping role in the unlikely event that the regional balance of power falters.

It is hardly surprising—indeed, it parallels in many ways America's own emergence as a great power—that China, the largest and potentially most powerful state in Asia, is seeking a more assertive political, military, and economic role in the region, and even challenging America's present dominance in East Asia. However, this poses no direct threat to U.S. security. Japan, India, and Russia, on the other hand, are worried about the implications of China's rapid ascendance for *their* security. They should bear the responsibility of balancing against Chinese power.

An incipient drift toward multipolarity—which is the prerequisite for the United States to adopt an offshore balancing strategy—is already apparent in East Asia. Driven by fears of U.S. abandonment in a future East Asian crisis, Japan has embarked on a buildup of its military capabilities and has even hinted that it is thinking about acquiring nuclear weapons. Moreover, the past several years have seen a significant escalation in tensions between China and Japan, fueled both by nationalism and by disputes over control of the South China and East China seas (which may contain large energy deposits).

> **Great powers that seek hegemony are always opposed—and defeated—by the counterbalancing efforts of other states.**

From the standpoint of offshore balancing, Japan's military buildup in response to its fear of China is a good thing if it leads to Japan's reemergence as an independent geopolitical actor. However, Japan's military resurgence is not so good (for the United States) if it takes place under the aegis of the U.S.-Japan security alliance, and if the United States remains in the front lines of the forces containing China. Under those conditions, the United States could find itself ensnared in an Asian conflict; its alliance with Japan risks dragging it into a war with China in which American strategic interests would not be engaged. The idea of an offshore balancing strategy is to get the United States out of China's crosshairs, not to allow it to remain a target because of its present security commitments to allies in the region.

The wisdom of risking war with China to maintain U.S. hegemony in East Asia is all the more doubtful because America's predominance in the region is ebbing in any event. One indication of this is that U.S. economic supremacy in East Asia is waning as China rises. China is emerging as the motor of the region's economic growth.

While the United States has been preoccupied with Iraq, Iran, and the so-called war on terrorism, China has used its burgeoning economic power to extend its political influence throughout East and Southeast Asia. Indeed, most of the smaller states in Southeast Asia are gradually slipping into Beijing's political orbit because their own prosperity is ever more closely tied to their relations with China.

America's strategy of trying to uphold the geopolitical status quo in East Asia clashes with the ambitions of a rising China, which has its own ideas about how East Asia's political and security order should be organized. If the United States puts itself in the forefront of those trying to contain China, the potential for future tension—or worse—in Sino-American relations can only increase. By pulling back from its hegemonic role in East Asia and adopting an offshore balancing strategy, the United States could better preserve its relative power and strategic influence. It could stand on the sidelines while that region's great powers enervate themselves by engaging in security competitions.

The Temptation of Power

If American strategy were determined by the traditional metrics that have governed the grand strategies of great powers—the distribution of power in the international system, geographic proximity of rivals, and military capabilities—China would not be considered much of a threat to the United States. The wellspring of U.S. grand strategy lies elsewhere, however: in Wilsonian ideology. This is why the United States remains wedded to a strategy of upholding its predominance in East Asia, as well as in Europe and the Middle East.

One of the few ironclad lessons of history is that great powers that seek hegemony are always opposed—and defeated—by the counterbalancing efforts of other states. Yet the prevailing belief among the American foreign policy community is that the United States is exempt from the fate of hegemons. This belief, really a form of American exceptionalism, is wrong. If Washington gives in to the temptation of hegemonic power, dangerous times lie ahead.

CHRISTOPHER LAYNE is a professor at Texas A&M University's George H. W. Bush School of Government and Public Service. He is author of *The Peace of Illusions: American Grand Strategy from 1940 to the Present* (Cornell University Press, 2006), and (with Bradley A. Thayer) *American Empire: A Debate* (Routledge, 2007).

Let's Make a Deal

Leon V. Sigal

President George W. Bush gets little credit in Washington these days, but he did achieve one major accomplishment in Asia: He resisted pressure from the Republican Right to confront China. U.S. cooperation with China and maintenance of U.S. alliances with Japan and South Korea are the pillars of future security in Asia. Contrary to popular wisdom, these are the primary U.S. equities in the region; what happens in and to North Korea is secondary.

That said, uncontrolled North Korean nuclear and missile programs will shake these pillars. They will generate demands that China do more to bring the DPRK to its knees, if not compel its collapse, which Beijing does not judge to be in its interest. Such pressure will hardly advance U.S. cooperation with China. They will also sow further doubts in Tokyo and Seoul about relying on Washington for security. A Japan that acts more independently of the United States under its newly elected government will move to accommodate China. It should be encouraged to. But if Japan's rivalry with China heats up nonetheless, it could rekindle its interest in nuclear weapons. That would raise alarms in South Korea, perhaps stimulating Seoul's own interest in nuclear arms. None of these outcomes would benefit U.S. security.

That is why the denuclearization of the Korean peninsula matters. On its own terms, it is an issue of but modest import, but its capacity to roil U.S. interests with the region's major players makes it a high priority. That is why President Bush authorized bilateral talks with North Korea within three weeks of Pyongyang's October 2006 nuclear test, and why President Obama approved former President Bill Clinton's trip to Pyongyang in August.

So far, the nuclear issue is sub-critical. North Korea has not restarted its reactor to produce more plutonium or armed its missiles with nuclear warheads, a development that would require it to conduct another nuclear test or two, as well as test-launches of its medium- and long-range missiles. As we know from experience, however, the DPRK could move to take these steps. So the top priority is to keep North Korea from doing so. The Obama Administration's current course, unfortunately, will not achieve that goal.

The Administration has successfully mustered a coalition of states to contain and isolate North Korea. Tougher sanctions and inspections of suspect shipments may impede proliferation, but they will not stop North Korea from making more fissile material or conducting more nuclear and missile tests. Quite the contrary, such actions, which Pyongyang regards as evidence of continued U.S. hostility, will only provoke further arming. They will also strengthen Kim Jong-il's legitimacy, which rests on asserting Korea's sovereignty and his willingness to stand up to all the powers in the region.

Isolation and containment concede not only that North Korea remains nuclear-armed but also that its weapons programs run free. Disengagement also misses an opportunity to encourage positive internal change during the leadership transition in Pyongyang, which, despite the apparent improvement in the Dear Leader's health, is currently underway.

To roll back the North's nuclear and missile efforts and change its behavior, Washington needs to resume negotiations, bilaterally if need be, and expand engagement with Pyongyang—the sooner, the better. Bill Clinton's success in obtaining the release of the two American journalists has created an opening for doing just that.

For negotiations to succeed, however, U.S. policymakers need to learn the lessons of nuclear diplomacy with North Korea over the past two decades. Though much about the DPRK is uncertain, this much is known: Contrary to the conventional wisdom in Washington, Pyongyang has demonstrated significant restraint in its nuclear and missile efforts over that period. Until now, the only way it had to make the fissile material it needed for nuclear weapons was to remove spent nuclear fuel rods from its reactor at Yongbyon and reprocess them to extract the plutonium. Yet North Korea stopped reprocessing in fall 1991, three years before it signed the 1994 Agreed Framework with the United States, and it did not resume reprocessing until 2003. It stopped again in 2007 and did not resume until now. And it did not make enough fuel rods for more than a handful of weapons. Similarly, the only way for it to perfect missiles for delivering nuclear warheads on Japan or the United States is to keep testing them until they work with a modicum of reliability and accuracy. Yet, until 2006, it had conducted just two test launches of medium- or long-range missiles.

The timing of the North's starts and stops in its nuclear effort and its missile tests over the past two decades suggests that it has pursued a two-edged strategy to ease its insecurity: on the one hand, arm to deter the threat of attack; on the other, refrain from arming as inducement for a fundamentally new political, economic and strategic relationship with the United States. We do not know if that remains its strategy. We need to find out.

Pyongyang says that as long as Washington remains its foe, it feels threatened and will acquire nuclear weapons and missiles to counter that threat. But if Washington, along with Seoul and Tokyo, moves to reconcile, it will no longer feel threatened and will not need these weapons.

All the speculation that Kim will never give up his nuclear arms only encourages him to think he won't have to.

Does Pyongyang mean what it says? Many observers doubt it, but the fact is that, with the possible exception of Kim Jong-il himself, nobody knows. Again, we need to find out. And we need to find out exactly what he wants in return. The only way to do that is to probe through sustained diplomatic give-and-take, offering the DPRK meaningful steps toward a new political, economic and strategic relationship in return for steps toward verified denuclearization. All the speculation that Kim will never give up his nuclear arms only encourages him to think he won't have to. Worse, it encourages our allies to think we are abandoning our goal of complete denuclearization.

A second major source of uncertainty is the future of the North Korean regime if Kim Jong-il should suddenly die or become incapacitated. Lack of evidence has not squelched speculation that something is amiss in the transition underway in Pyongyang. One thing is clear: Doubts about Kim Jong-il's health make diplomatic give-and-take more urgent. Why take chances that his successor might be less able to make and keep a nuclear or missile deal, or control North Korea's nuclear weapons and material? Managing or ignoring North Korea, as some in Washington favor, is not a prudent policy, especially if the North becomes inherently less manageable.

Why might Kim still be interested in a deal? For the past few years he has been promising his people a "strong and prosperous country" by 2012, the centenary of his father's birth. Prosperity requires a political accommodation with Washington, Seoul and Tokyo that would allow him to reallocate resources from military to civilian use and open the door to outside aid and investment. Although he claims that nuclear weapons have made his country strong, they do not make it secure. Only a demonstrated end to U.S., Japanese and South Korean enmity will do that. Until he is assured of that, he cannot afford to give up arming.

Instead of dealing with Pyongyang's insecurity, Washington has repeatedly accused it of wrongdoing and tried to punish it. The crime-and-punishment approach has failed to build much trust or give either side much of a stake in living up to any agreement, leaving Kim Jong-il free to use his nuclear and missile leverage. And use that leverage he has. Whenever he believed the United States was not keeping its side of the bargain, he was all too quick to retaliate tit for tat: in 1998 by seeking the means to enrich uranium and by testing a longer-range Taepodong-1 missile; in 2003 by resuming his plutonium program and giving nuclear aid to Syria; in 2006 by test-launching

a Taepodong-2, along with six other missiles, and by conducting a nuclear test; and in 2009 by test-launching Taepodong-2 technology in the guise of trying to put a satellite into orbit, and then conducting six more medium-range missile tests and a nuclear test. The lesson he learned from 1998, 2003, 2006 and 2009, but that Washington has not, is that we lack the leverage to force him to do what we want or to punish Pyongyang for its transgressions—and that we cannot be counted on to fulfill our side of agreements.

We need a new negotiating strategy that focuses sharply on the aim of reducing North Korea's leverage while adding to our own. We can achieve this by easing its insecurity and expanding engagement with cultural, educational and scientific exchanges, and agricultural, energy and infrastructure aid. Aid can be provided bilaterally, multilaterally and through non-governmental organizations and international financial institutions. Deepening engagement is the only way to encourage change in North Korea. It is also our only way to enhance our potential leverage. For those reasons, some engagement and exchanges should be pursued unconditionally.

Pyongyang may be willing to trade away its plutonium, enrichment and missile programs brick by brick. Washington should be willing to offer it much more, in return for much more. That includes diplomatic recognition and an Obama-Kim summit meeting as the DPRK dismantles its fuel fabrication plant, reprocessing facility and reactor at Yongbyon and allows its plutonium declaration to be verified. It also includes the prompt start of a peace process with a declaration signed by the United States, North Korea, South Korea and China, in which Washington reaffirms it has no hostile intent toward Pyongyang and formally commits itself to signing a peace treaty ending the Korean War when the North is nuclear-free. It also means commencing a regional security dialogue that puts the DPRK at the top table and eventually provides negative security assurances (a formal multilateral pledge not to introduce nuclear weapons into the Korea Peninsula or threaten it with nuclear or conventional attack) and other benefits to its security. Such a comprehensive set of actions, each of them linked to reciprocal steps by the North to denuclearize, would also give the United States its first real leverage: Washington could withhold or reverse these steps if, and only if, Pyongyang fails to follow through on commitments to give up its nuclear programs and arms.

In 2008 Japan and South Korea tried to prevent President Bush from negotiating with North Korea along these or any other lines. Will the allies go along now? Whatever their misgivings about U.S. diplomatic give-and-take with the DPRK, failing to constrain and reverse North Korea's nuclear and missile programs will only aggravate alliance relations over time, adding to Japanese and South Korean unease about relying on Washington for security. Allied unhappiness with our North Korea policy can best be addressed neither by deferring to their wishes nor by running roughshod over them, but by frank and thorough consultation. That means having serious discussions not only about our negotiating proposals, but also about their security needs as long as North Korea remains nuclear-armed. Above all, it means making clear to our allies that we will not accept a nuclear-armed North Korea and that we remain committed to our goal of complete denuclearization of the Korean peninsula.

Rollback of North Korea's nuclear arming, not containment, is needed for Asia's security, and that goal calls for sustained engagement. We've tried almost everything else and shown that it doesn't work. We need to go "all in" diplomatically. If we do, we may discover that genuine engagement will ultimately bring about the changes we desire.

LEON V. SIGAL is director of the Northeast Asia Security Project at the Social Science Research Council and author of *Disarming Strangers: Nuclear Diplomacy with North Korea.*

From *The American Interest*, January/February 2010, pp. 83–85. Copyright © 2010 by American Interest. Reprinted by permission.

Requiem for the Monroe Doctrine

"The era when the United States could treat Latin America and the Caribbean as its backyard . . . is receding ever faster into history."

DANIEL P. ERIKSON

The United States has long been suspicious of foreign powers that meddled in the Western Hemisphere. In recent years, Latin America's increasingly diverse international relations have stoked such fears anew, as the region has drawn closer to Washington's global rivals at a moment when US influence is facing unprecedented challenges. The alliance forged between Venezuela's Hugo Chávez and Iranian President Mahmoud Ahmadinejad is only the most dramatic example of a new trend that has seen Latin America and the Caribbean seek greater independence from the United States while deepening ties with emerging powers outside the hemisphere such as China, India, and Russia.

Many US policy makers understand intellectually that this increasingly complex mosaic of international relationships is the product of a more globalized world. Still, there is an underlying current of unease that American primacy in the Western Hemisphere is being threatened in subtle but important ways.

Of course, a precept of US foreign policy has long existed to address precisely this problem. It is called the Monroe Doctrine, after its creator President James Monroe, and it constitutes the iconic assertion of the United States' right to oppose foreign powers in the Western Hemisphere. Like a cat with nine lives, the Monroe Doctrine has died many times since its first articulation in 1823, only to reemerge in slightly different forms at different historical moments. Most recently, the Monroe Doctrine was buried with full honors at the end of the cold war in the early 1990s, when the collapse of the Soviet Union left the United States without an enemy to fight in Latin America.

But today the ghost of President Monroe, once a secretary of state himself, continues to stalk the halls of Foggy Bottom, and suspicions of foreign encroachment in the hemisphere are growing. The realities that formed the basis for the Monroe Doctrine have fundamentally changed, yet the United States has been slow to adjust its attitudes accordingly. If Washington wishes to be effective in Latin America, it must resist the temptation to revive the Monroe Doctrine and instead work to restore trust in inter-American relations as the region adapts to an increasingly globalized era.

What Bush Owes Monroe

If President George W. Bush were given the opportunity to go back in time and meet any historical figure, it is a safe bet that Monroe would not top his list. At first blush, the fifth and forty-third presidents appear to have little in common. Elected in 1816, Monroe was by most accounts a detail-oriented pragmatist whose nonpartisan approach to politics ushered in the "Era of Good Feelings." Bush, by contrast, preferred after his election in 2000 to focus on the big picture while leaving the details to others, and his early promises to be a "uniter not a divider" have fallen prey to rancorous partisanship and an era of unease.

Monroe did, however, lay claim to a "big picture" achievement that Bush could surely envy: creating a doctrine, bearing his name, that guided American foreign policy for well over a century. December 2, 2008, will mark the 185th anniversary of the Monroe Doctrine, the declaration by President Monroe that the United States would no longer tolerate the meddling of European powers in Latin America. Speaking in his seventh State of the Union address to Congress, Monroe declared that "the American continents, by the free and independent condition which they have assumed and maintain, are henceforth not to be considered as subjects for future colonization by any European powers. . . . We should consider any attempt on their part to extend their system to any portion of this hemisphere as dangerous to our peace and safety."

Monroe's words outlived the parochial concerns of that era to provide the philosophical underpinning for US foreign policy for decades to come. During the cold war, the doctrine was reinterpreted to support American efforts to contain the expansion of Soviet influence into the hemisphere. In 1962, for example,

President John F. Kennedy defended US actions against Cuba by saying that "the Monroe Doctrine means what it has meant since President Monroe and John Quincy Adams enunciated it, and that is that we would oppose a foreign power extending its power to the Western Hemisphere." Ronald Reagan was perhaps the last US president whose policies toward Latin America so clearly reflected the Monroe Doctrine's core principles, demonstrated especially by his administration's support for the rebels fighting against the Sandinistas—and, by proxy, the Soviets—in Nicaragua.

The Monroe Doctrine has become the phantom limb of America's posture in the hemisphere.

Presidents George H. W. Bush and Bill Clinton worried less about containing foreign powers in Latin America, instead emphasizing democratic consolidation, the war on drugs, and economic integration as the cornerstones of US policy in the region. The elder Bush presided over the last unilateral US military action in the hemisphere: the 1989 invasion of Panama to arrest the military dictator Manuel A. Noriega, an American ally turned embarrassing drug trafficker. Five years later, when Clinton staked US credibility on a well-intentioned but ultimately ill-fated effort to restore democracy to Haiti, he first asked the United Nations for permission. The Monroe Doctrine remained an animating idea in the national security consciousness, but with the end of the cold war it no longer provided a serious source of foreign policy guidance.

When George W. Bush arrived at the White House, he found a hemisphere that was increasingly democratic and market-friendly, and the specter of rival powers competing in the Americas seemed a thing of the past. On September 11, 2001, when the United States was struck by terrorist attacks, Secretary of State Colin Powell was in Lima, Peru, signing the Inter-American Democratic Charter along with representatives of 33 other democratic countries in the hemisphere.

Within a year, President Bush had made a series of major foreign policy pronouncements that came to be known collectively as the Bush Doctrine. It essentially asserted an American right to exercise unilateral military power to respond preemptively to threats from wherever they might emanate. The administration's ex post facto justifications for the Iraq War expanded the Bush Doctrine to incorporate sweeping calls to liberate the world from tyranny. In Latin America and the Caribbean, this all sounded hauntingly familiar.

It was not only the United States' southern neighbors who perceived links between the Monroe Doctrine and the Bush Doctrine. When Washington unveiled its strategy for preemptive war in 2002, a number of analysts heard echoes of the earlier doctrine. A Canadian commentator, Paul Knox, wrote in the *Toronto Globe and Mail* that "One way to read the National Security Strategy that Mr. Bush unveiled last week is as a Monroe Doctrine for the entire planet. It proposes explicitly to maintain overwhelming military supremacy around the globe."

The foreign affairs editor of London's *The Observer* argued that the Bush Doctrine recalled the Monroe Doctrine, except that "in the following 180 years, America has moved from local to regional and then to global superpower. . . . The country that once challenged those renewing their imperial ambitions in its orbit is now declaring in this document the 'manifest destiny' of Americans to exercise good across the world."

The comparisons of the two doctrines continued into Bush's second term. Reflecting on the president's second inaugural speech in January 2005, the author Tom Wolfe wrote an essay in *The New York Times* entitled "The Doctrine That Never Died." Recalling how Theodore Roosevelt dragged the Monroe Doctrine into the twentieth century by proclaiming that the United States had a right to reshape hemispheric nations guilty of "chronic wrongdoing," Wolfe argued that Bush had issued a new corollary to the Monroe Doctrine. "The notion of a sanctified Western Hemisphere depended upon its separation from the rest of the world by two vast oceans, making intrusions of any sort obvious," he wrote. "By Mr. Bush's Inauguration Day, the Hemi in Hemisphere had long since vanished, leaving the Monroe Doctrine with—what?—nothing but a single sphere . . . which is to say, the entire world." Bush, in short, wanted to update the Monroe Doctrine for the twenty-first century by extending its messianic mission around the globe.

Alas, it was not to be. The flame of the Bush Doctrine burned brightly for a few years, but its failures have extinguished much of its light. The US military experience in Iraq will likely dampen any enthusiasm for future preemptive wars, and the prospects for the United States' provoking another global wave of democratization look increasingly dim. Despite its sweeping rhetoric against tyranny, the Bush administration has failed to advance liberty in countries like Myanmar, Belarus, Pakistan, and Russia.

Meanwhile, if the Bush Doctrine was intended to raise the Monroe Doctrine to a higher plane, the result has been to crush the original doctrine's foundations. In Latin America and the Caribbean, the practical effects of the Bush Doctrine, far from revitalizing US sway in the region, have instead distracted the United States from hemispheric affairs, alienated its closest neighbors, and left Washington ill-equipped to prevent rivals from gaining a foothold in its sphere of influence. And this has occurred at a moment when Latin America is more independent and self-assured, and when the heavyweights of the developing world are seeking to cultivate alliances with countries in the region.

In recent years, China has charged into South American commodity markets to snap up goods including oil.

The New Assertiveness

The 9-11 attacks and their aftermath caused the Bush administration largely to neglect Latin America, but Washington's absence did not make the region's heart grow fonder. Instead, during the past six years virtually every country in Latin America and the

Caribbean has responded by forging its own path, showing ever less regard for US preferences. The new geopolitical environment in fact accelerated what had been a gradual trend under way in the region. This movement toward greater political independence has occurred quickly in many of the nations of South America, and more slowly in Mexico, Central America, and the Caribbean, but all countries in the region have come to grips with the post–9-11 reality.

Of course, the United States remains the dominant economic partner and an important political reference for all of Latin America and the Caribbean. Trade between the United States and the region totaled more than $550 billion in 2006, and the more than 20 million Latino immigrants who live in the United States send back another $45 billion in remittances annually. This process of integration makes it all the more ironic that Washington's views now carry far less weight in the region than at any other point in recent memory.

The decline of US influence in Latin America is driven by a confluence of positive and negative trends. The most favorable change is that the Western Hemisphere has arrived at a consensus on democratic norms, a consensus ratified by the Inter-American Democratic Charter. Setting aside the troubling case of Cuba, the spread of democracy has increased the political legitimacy of governments throughout the hemisphere—including those that dislike the United States. Washington's foes, such as Venezuela's Chávez and Nicaragua's Daniel Ortega, now have a level of democratic legitimacy that did not exist during the region's long periods of military dictatorship. The United States helped democracy take root in Latin America and the Caribbean in the 1990s, but this has created new limits on Washington's ability to intervene in these countries to pursue its own interests.

Since his election in 1998, Chávez has been the leader who poses the most severe test for US power in the region. Chávez rejects the United States' historical leadership role (which he terms "imperialism") and has strived to create a network of alliances and institutions independent of US influence. He wants to replace the International Monetary Fund and the World Bank in the region with the Latin America–dominated Banco del Sur, and exchange the Free Trade Area of the Americas for a social trade pact known as the Bolivarian Alternative for Latin America. He has funded a new Spanish-language news station, Telesur, as an alternative to American media sources. Chávez has won a limited following for these ideas in the region, and despite his recent defeat in a constitutional referendum, he still benefits from high oil prices and has five years left in his presidential term.

In an interview with *Time* magazine shortly after he called President Bush "the devil" in a speech before the United Nations in 2006, Chávez described his "Bolivarian Revolution" in the following way: "For two centuries in this hemisphere we've experienced a confrontation between two theses: America's Monroe Doctrine, which says the US should exercise hegemony over all the other republics, and the doctrine of Simón Bolívar, which envisioned a great South American republic as a counter-balance. Bush has spread the Monroe thesis globally, to make the US the police of the world—if you're not with us, he says, you're against us. We're simply doing the same now with the Bolívar thesis, a doctrine of more equality and autonomy among nations, more equilibrium of power."

Brazil, with the world's fifth-largest population and tenth-largest economy, is similarly interested in a realignment of global power that recognizes its own political and economic heft. Unlike Venezuela, however, Brazil has sought to avoid conflict and instead strengthen its global influence in tandem with its ties to the United States. Indeed, Brazilian President Luiz Inácio Lula da Silva enjoys one of the warmest relationships with President Bush of any Latin American leader, and their two nations have agreed to cooperate on a new ethanol initiative.

Still, Brazilian opposition to the Free Trade Area of the Americas helped cause its demise in 2005. And the country, as a leader of the G-20 group of developing countries, which also includes China, India, and South Africa, has clashed with the United States in world trade talks. Brazil's aggressive bid to win a permanent seat on the UN Security Council has led Lula on an international tour to drum up support for his country's global aspirations. Such diplomacy has included special outreach to the Middle East: Brazil hosted the first-ever summit between South American and Arab countries in 2005—and pointedly left Washington off the invitation list.

This independent streak is increasingly apparent throughout South America. Leaders in Ecuador, Bolivia, and Argentina have all taken steps to distance themselves from the United States. Chile and Peru have signed free trade agreements with the United States but are increasingly focused on building trade relationships in the Asia-Pacific region. Colombia remains reliant on US military aid but its stalled free trade deal in Washington has clearly soured relations with the government of Alvaro Uribe. In Mexico, Central America, and the Caribbean, economic interconnectedness with the United States remains the dominant fact of politics in the region. Mexican President Felipe Calderón has pledged to work closely with the United States to solve the problem of drug-related insecurity along the border, and El Salvador maintains troops in Iraq. Still, all Latin American countries are experiencing a diversification of political relationships, and the Caribbean is looking increasingly to China and Venezuela as key partners.

The result is that the United States can no longer dictate decisions that were once considered solely in its purview. In the 2005 election for the secretary general of the Organization of American States, the region rebuffed Washington's preferred candidates from El Salvador and Mexico, forcing it to accept Chilean socialist José Miguel Insulza as the consensus candidate. In 2006, US officials disapproved of awarding a first-round election victory to presidential candidate René Préval in Haiti when his vote tally fell just short of the 50 percent margin required for outright victory. But the Bush administration's reluctance to join the UN mission in Haiti left Latin American nations like Brazil, Argentina, and Chile in the driver's seat, and they brushed aside US concerns to deliver a quick victory to Préval. Even in Cuba, the United States vowed to block Fidel Castro's succession strategy, only to watch from the sidelines as Raúl Castro consolidated his power and renewed the island's relations with Europe, Latin America, and Asia. The power dynamic in the Western Hemisphere has tilted away from the United States, but Washington has been reluctant to adapt its playbook accordingly.

Expanding Horizons

Latin America and the Caribbean in recent years have sought to capitalize on booming commodity prices in global markets to diversify their trade ties beyond the United States, especially with Europe and Asia. In 2006, total trade between the European Union and Latin America reached a record $177 billion. Although this equals only one-third of US–Latin American trade, the EU's share is growing at a fast pace, led by Germany, Spain, Italy, and the Netherlands. Currently, the EU's top trading partners in the region are Brazil, Mexico, Chile, Argentina, and Venezuela. The union is also negotiating a trade agreement with the Central American countries, and is in preliminary discussions with the Andean Community and the South American Common Market (Mercosur). In December, Mercosur signed a free trade agreement with Israel, its first with any country outside the Western Hemisphere, and Brazil's foreign minister declared that the trade bloc "is open to the world."

In Asia, Japan remains one of Latin America's biggest investors and trading partners. Japanese officials, worried that trade growth is languishing, are focusing on reactivating the economic relationship with the region. China is already having a big impact on Latin American economies. India, also scouring the region for investments in the oil sector, is the next giant on the horizon.

Even Russia is renewing ties with Latin America that had been virtually dormant since the collapse of the Soviet Union. In June 2004, Vladimir Putin made the first-ever visit to Mexico by a Russian president for talks focusing on military sales. Later that year he attended the Asia-Pacific Economic Cooperation summit in Chile, and then visited Brazil to initiate cooperation in satellite technology and oil exploration. In 2007, the Russian leader attended an international Olympics meeting in Guatemala and then promised to cooperate with that country on electricity production, prompting then-President Oscar Berger to describe Putin as "one of the brightest leaders in today's world."

As a network of ties emerges between Iran and Latin America, Chávez is vowing to "unite the Persian Gulf and the Caribbean."

Russian arms sales to the region amounted to only $300 million for the period from 1998 to 2001, but they have since escalated dramatically. In 2006, Russia's military sales to Venezuela alone totaled $3 billion (including 100,000 Kalishnikov assault rifles), and hundreds of millions more in weapons were sold to other Latin American countries. If the pace of military trade continues, Russia's arms sales to Latin America will soon surpass the records set by the Soviet Union.

But perhaps no country has flummoxed US policy makers as much as the People's Republic of China, which has established itself as the new power to be reckoned with in the Western Hemisphere.

China's Inroads

China's emerging role in Latin America and the Caribbean perfectly encapsulates the new challenge facing US policy makers in the hemisphere as they wrestle with the legacy of the Monroe Doctrine. On one hand, China is viewed as a growing rival that is seeking to achieve economic and military parity with the United States and must therefore be treated with caution. On the other hand, the United States and China have deep economic ties, including one of the largest trade relationships in the world, and the two countries cooperate on a wide range of issues.

In recent years, China has charged into South American commodity markets to snap up goods including oil, agricultural products, and heavy metals, and has used promises of trade and aid to win over most of Taiwan's remaining allies in the region. Just a decade ago, China was viewed as a peripheral actor in the Western Hemisphere. Today, though far from being a dominant player, China is a top-five trading partner of most Latin American countries, and has become a relevant actor in hemispheric affairs.

In 2001, Chinese President Jiang Zemin's landmark visit to the region was followed by a wave of exchanges among Chinese and Latin American senior officials and business leaders to discuss political, economic, and military concerns. Jiang's successor, Hu Jintao, traveled to Argentina, Brazil, Chile, and Cuba in 2004 and visited Mexico in 2005. The presidents of all of these countries (and several others) have subsequently paid reciprocal visits to China. Growing political engagement has accompanied the skyrocketing volume of trade between China and the region, which totaled an estimated $80 billion in 2007. China has also become a strong competitor with the United States in sales of manufactured goods, making deep inroads into markets in Mexico and Central America and, more recently, in Brazil and Argentina.

Rising Chinese influence in Latin America has prompted some US officials and members of Congress to view China as the most serious challenge to US economic and security interests in the region since the end of the cold war. American policy makers cite concerns about stable access to the Panama Canal, the deployment of Chinese peace-keepers in Haiti, China's support for Castro, and Beijing's growing claims to Venezuelan oil. In 2004, when President Hu's three-week tour through Latin America sparked feverish speculation about how this new relationship would affect US interests, a rash of publications warned of the "China threat" on America's southern flank.

There is little question that Chinese competition for Latin America's energy resources has created a new and uncertain dynamic for US policy makers. Even the most benign interpretation of Chinese penetration into Latin American markets—that China is growing and needs resources, while the region is searching for new customers—implies a potential loss for US business interests. Some analysts in 2004 ominously warned of an emerging anti-American alliance, led by China and Venezuela, that might include other energy-exporting nations in Latin America and elsewhere. Others argued that China's new role could benefit both Latin America and the United States by fueling the region's economic growth.

Seeking to defuse the growing wariness about Chinese intentions in Latin America, the United States has shifted course to engage China from a more cooperative stance. In 2004, China became an observer at the Organization of American States, and discussions are ongoing about bringing the country into the Inter-American Development Bank. In the spring of 2006, US Assistant Secretary of State Thomas Shannon traveled to Beijing for a first round of dialogue with Chinese officials on Latin American affairs, and follow-up talks were held in Washington in November 2007. The United States even persuaded China to back a one-year extension of the UN peacekeeping mission in Haiti (which includes 125 Chinese riot police), despite the fact that Haiti's recognition of Taiwan remains a sore spot for Beijing.

Only time will tell if the State Department's vision of converting China from a potential threat into a responsible stakeholder in Latin America will be achieved. Still, the new emphasis on diplomacy offers a novel strategy for dealing with rival powers in the US sphere of influence, replacing containment with mechanisms for cooperation. Whether this would leave Monroe nodding his approval or spinning in his grave is anyone's guess.

Mullahs in the Backyard

Washington's China fever had barely dissipated when a new and more ominous specter raised its head in Latin America—in the form of the Islamic Republic of Iran. In September 2007, the Bush administration's efforts to curtail Iran's nuclear ambitions had brought the two countries to the brink of confrontation at the United Nations. By that time, Iran had already succeeded in cultivating a range of new allies in Latin America, most prominently Chávez. President Ahmadinejad encountered a hostile reception in New York during his September trip to speak at the UN, but afterwards he flew directly to Caracas, where Chávez warmly greeted him.

The Venezuelan president praised Ahmadinejad's Columbia University speech, which had followed a harshly critical introduction by the university's president. "An imperial spokesman tried to disrespect you, calling you a cruel little tyrant," Chávez told him. "You responded with the greatness of a revolutionary." From Venezuela, Ahmadinejad traveled to Bolivia. That country's president, Evo Morales, had just days earlier appeared on "The Daily Show with Jon Stewart," during which he said, "Please don't consider me part of the 'axis of evil.'" But back in Bolivia, Morales met with Ahmadinejad for five hours, established diplomatic relations between the two countries, and signed an economic cooperation agreement worth $1 billion over five years.

Ahmadinejad's most recent trip to Latin America highlighted the Iranian government's ambitious diplomatic efforts to create new allies in the traditional US sphere of influence. Chávez has emerged as the godfather and relationship manager, striving to draw in other allies such as Bolivia, Ecuador, and Nicaragua. Iran's courtship is moving quickly. In September 2006, Ahmadinejad attended the Non-Aligned Movement summit in Havana and met with Chávez in Caracas. In

January 2007, the Iranian president was treated as an honored guest in Venezuela, Nicaragua, and Ecuador. Chávez called him a "hero of the struggle against American imperialism." Nicaraguan President Daniel Ortega met with him to discuss "common interests, common enemies, and common goals." Ecuadorian President Rafael Correa exchanged warm words with Ahmadinejad as well.

Chávez and Ahmadinejad see political benefits to their alliance, and they also claim economic benefits. The two countries have signed 180 agreements since 2001, in areas such as gas and oil exploration and petrochemical and agricultural production. Officials claim the agreements are worth $20 billion, though bilateral trade has been less than $20 million annually. Chávez recently granted Iran observer status in the Bolivarian Alternative for the Americas, his leftist trade-pact group. Iran and Venezuela have also announced a $2 billion development fund for "anti-imperialist" countries, though the money has been predictably slow to materialize. And Tehran has promised to finance a $350 million deep-water port and build 10,000 houses in poverty-stricken Nicaragua, whose president has defended Iran's nuclear program at the UN.

To be sure, Ahmadinejad remains an unwelcome figure in other parts of Latin America—including Argentina, where Iran was allegedly involved in the 1994 bombing of a Jewish community center in Buenos Aires; and in Brazil, where Lula has repeatedly rebuffed meeting requests. Even so, the United States has been at a loss about how to counter Iran's growing influence in the region, or even how to fully calculate its impact on US interests.

Clearly, Iran is neither a benign force in world affairs nor a major power capable of posing a threat on par with the Soviet Union during the cold war. Iran's interest in Latin America could just be an example of normal state-to-state diplomacy or an attempt to lay the foundation for more sinister plans. But the fact that it is occurring at all unearths latent fears associated with the Monroe Doctrine. It also underlines that the United States has limited options in its efforts to counteract foreign powers in the Western Hemisphere, with intelligence collection and diplomacy taking precedence over unilateral military action. Meanwhile, as a network of ties emerges between Iran and Latin America, Chávez is vowing to "unite the Persian Gulf and the Caribbean."

Is There a Doctrine in the House?

President Bush entered office vowing to strengthen and intensify US relations with Latin America. His administration instead has presided over an era that paradoxically has seen expanded economic ties between the United States and Latin America while leaving Washington's political influence in the hemisphere greatly reduced. Still, the United States has much to be happy about in Latin America. To some degree, US policy has been a victim of its own success in ensuring that democratic norms have taken hold throughout the region. Moreover, Latin American peoples have largely elected leaders whose respect for democracy and commitment to market economics are in sync with the United States.

Frictions on trade policy and immigration continue to plague US relations with the two largest countries in the region—Brazil and Mexico—but this has not prevented constructive ties on a wide range of issues. US relations with the Caribbean and much of Central and South America remain positive on balance. Venezuela's Chávez will continue to be a thorn in the side of the United States for the foreseeable future, but his "Bolivarian Revolution" shows signs of reaching its natural limits.

Latin America's increasing connectedness with the rest of the world does not inherently undermine US interests, but Washington will continue to find these links disturbing in certain cases. Despite the current calm, China's role in the Western Hemisphere will become increasingly controversial as that country evolves into a major world power in the coming decades. Iran is a new factor to contend with, and broader links between Latin America and the Middle East are certain to grow. Putin's Russia is selling billions of dollars' worth of weapons in the region, and other nontraditional actors likely will emerge in the years to come. Even the "hermit kingdom" of North Korea has opened talks with the Dominican Republic and Guatemala.

What does all this mean for President Monroe's doctrine? The Bush Doctrine may share an intellectual heritage with the Monroe Doctrine, but the practical implementation of Bush's foreign policy has created a climate that has eviscerated what was left of the Monroe Doctrine's relevance in Latin America. The United States has been distracted at a time when rivals like China, Iran, and Russia are newly emboldened to seek alliances in the region. Economic globalization in any event has assured Latin America's increasing connectivity to nations across the oceans, essentially rendering obsolete Monroe's vision of a hemisphere under US tutelage. In 2008, the Monroe Doctrine has become the phantom limb of America's posture in the hemisphere: US policy makers still occasionally feel its tingle, but no weight can be put on it.

The major candidates for the American presidency have all vowed, with varying degrees of enthusiasm and specificity, to reverse the perception of US neglect and reenergize relationships with Latin America and the Caribbean. The change in presidential administrations will undoubtedly introduce fresh thinking that will be helpful to US-Latin American relations, whoever wins the White House. President Bush's successor, however, will find a region that has changed dramatically since the 1990s, in ways both good and bad, and that is increasingly reluctant to resume its dependence on US leadership.

Given all the pressing challenges elsewhere in the world that will confront the next administration, prospects for developing a major new doctrine to replace the Monroe Doctrine as a guide for US policy in the hemisphere seem remote at best. With serious engagement and intelligent policy choices, the next US president will still have the opportunity to help guide the hemispheric community of nations. But the era that began 185 years ago with the declaration of the Monroe Doctrine—the era when the United States could treat Latin America and the Caribbean as its backyard—is receding ever faster into history.

DANIEL P. ERIKSON is a senior associate for US policy and director of Caribbean programs at Inter-American Dialogue.

From *Current History*, February 2008, pp. 58–64. Copyright © 2008 by Current History, Inc. Reprinted by permission.

Mirror-Imaging the Mullahs
Our Islamic Interlocutors

REUEL MARC GERECHT

In 1993, Bernard Hourcade, a geographer, sociologist, and Persianist who was the head of Iranian studies at the Centre National de la Recherche Scientifique, got a bit of a shock. After completing lengthy negotiations on the first cultural and scientific exchange between France and the Islamic Republic, the Iranian delegation demanded the agreement open with the words: *Bismillah ar-Rahman ar-Rahim* ("In the Name of God, the Compassionate and the Merciful"). The negotiations were supposed to be a friendly *arrangement,* something less formal than an *accord.* So the French were aghast that the Iranians, whom Hourcade and the other French scholars and diplomats had known for years, would demand the Koranic invocation. The Iranians understood well the secular ethos of France. Ali Akbar Hashemi-Rafsanjani, then the president of the Islamic Republic, was even then making a determined pitch for more French investment and trade.

Exasperated and operating independently from the French foreign ministry, Hourcade responded that Tehran would either withdraw this stipulation or Paris would begin booting Iranian scholars and scientists from France. Within twenty-four hours, the Iranians informed Hourcade that the Islamic Republic would not object to the removal of the Koran's most famous lines.

The episode, like the contretemps provoked by President Mohammad Khatami when he visited France in 1999 and Spain in 2002, and insisted that wine not be served at official banquets (the French and the Spanish cancelled the dinners rather than forego the wine), conveys a truth not so easy for Westerners to accept. Even on *minor* issues, religion—and in particular, the devout version of Islam that governments like Iran's embrace—can intrude, distort, and paralyze. The Koran says nothing about banning wine for non-believers, let alone non-believers living in their own lands, or that wine by its mere presence compromises the faithful. Ayatollah Ruhollah Khomeini, who spent most of his life explicating and defending the Holy Law, upheld the religious right of Iranian Christians in Iran to produce and drink wine in their homes and in their churches. Yet here we were seventeen years later listening to a reformist cleric, who had loudly promoted a "dialogue of civilizations," demand that Frenchmen abstain from their national drink.

There is a lesson here: God may be kaput in most of the West, but he has hardly been reduced to the status of personal philosophy in Islamic lands. And, yet, our God-diminishing, mirror-imaging impulse keeps blinding us to Islam's place at the center of the political realm. The tendency to view Muslims through secular eyes, or to recast them and their faith into a version of Christianity ("Islam is a religion of peace"), is perhaps the greatest impediment to rational American policy. Whether it be clerical Iran's nuclear program, Pakistan on the brink, the Israeli-Palestinian imbroglio, Saudi Arabia and its Wahhabis, or Egypt's ice-cold relations with Israel, religion offers the one indispensable prism through which to peer into the region. For if we cannot see the Middle East first and foremost on its own terms, which means, among other things, never forgetting that Muslim states define themselves as exactly that, then we will surely find ourselves caught in binds worse than Iraq.

In March 2003, the State Department and the Central Intelligence Agency—the two institutions that enjoyed the most contact with Iraqis under Saddam Hussein—viewed Iraq as the most secular nation in the Arab world. Influential Iraqi expatriates, among them Ayad Allawi, Ahmed Chalabi, Adnan Pachachi, and Kanan Makiya, bolstered this view, suggesting further that a free Iraq could and should be led by Westernized Iraqis not known for their religious beliefs. In truth, Iraq under Saddam Hussein had become a profoundly religious place for Sunnis and Shiites alike. That no one seemed to realize this owes something to the fact that Iraqi intellectuals, usually smitten with some variation of Arab nationalism, socialism, or Communism, were not inclined to linger on antiquated topics such as religion. Western scholars, usually possessed of the same progressive mindset, avoided probing too deeply. Regional experts, for example, considered Hanna Batatu's magisterial work, *The Old Social Classes and New Revolutionary Movements of Iraq,* published in 1978, to be the bible of contemporary Iraq studies. It is also a wasteland. We can read that enormous work and come away thinking that modern Iraq, one of the central lands of Islamic history, and key to the development of Shiite identity, is a country of irreversibly fading faith. If the Bush administration, for one, had understood that the opposite was true, it would have also understood that election plans that ignored Grand Ayatollah Ali Sistani, the country's preeminent Shiite jurisprudent, were doomed; it would have recognized at the outset how rich Sunni soil was for al-Qaeda and other Islamic extremists; it would have gleaned the depth of the Sunni-Shiite divide; and it would have sent more troops.

Then again, we always make the same mistakes. In the nine years (1985–1994) that I spent in the Central Intelligence Agency working on Middle Eastern issues, especially on the "Iranian target," I cannot recall a single serious conversation about Islam as a faith, and about why a glimpse of the divine inspired an entire generation of young Iranian men to draw closer to God through war and death. In part this was because the organization veered toward "hard-fact" reporting. Intelligence services need to know about the size, disposition, and quality of soldiers and their material, about potentially lethal imports and exports, and about technical progress in the drive for weapons of mass destruction. Needless to say, few Iranians with a passionate commitment to the Almighty associated with the CIA. Serving Allah and serving Langley was a difficult philosophical proposition.

The CIA, like the State Department, is a secular institution where officers typically do not discuss their faith (or, more to the point, lack thereof) or the faith of others. Friends at Langley tell me that even today there remains little sustained attention to the question of how believing Muslims, country by country, view the outside world, or how Saudi-supported militant Salafi teachings have gobbled up mosques and religious schools throughout the once virulently anti-Wahhabi lands of the eastern Mediterranean. For spooks, such "hearts and minds" reporting belongs in the arena of covert action, not "foreign intelligence" collection, where proper case officers ply their trade. And covert action, never a large-scale enterprise in the Middle East as it was in Cold War Europe, is dead as a doornail at Langley.

More broadly, educated Westerners tend to assume that, like themselves, well-educated Middle Eastern Muslims possess too much common sense for religion to determine their political behavior. People naturally associate with their own kind. Secularists attract secularists. Westerners usually don't seek out devout Muslims, at least not for long. The effect of all this on our image of the Muslim Middle East has been substantial. The American-educated Iranian political scientist, Mohammad Hadi Semati, who until recently worked at the Woodrow Wilson Center, had a significant impact on Washington's Iran analysts. A delightful fellow who socialized easily with Americans, Semati, who has since returned to the University of Tehran, offered up a treasure trove of information about the Westernized Iranians who hover around the clerical elite's "pragmatists" and reformers. For Washington's Iran-lookers, who rarely if ever travel to the Islamic Republic because the regime won't issue them visas (or because it will imprison them), Semati provided what Western journalists rarely do: detailed, colorful, and delicious gossip about the players in Tehran.

Yet, Semati and his fellow Iranian progressives, precisely because they think and dream more or less as we do, have also been among the most errant analysts of their homeland. Iran's liberal intellectual elite, whose members flourished briefly under Mohammad Khatami's presidency, and who have become devotees of former president Ali Akbar Hashemi Rafsanjani, labor mightily to depict an Iran that is beyond a Thermidorian Reaction. Real innovative religious discussions—the kind of anti-clerical philosophical commentary that one used to hear from the lay (and now downtrodden) Islamist Abd al-Karim Soroush—don't figure in this progressive crowd simply because the religious dimension has too much salience. Thus, Semati didn't anticipate Mahmoud Ahmadinejad being a serious contender in Iran's 2005 presidential election. Instead, he predicted another victory by Rafsanjani, the ultimate pragmatist. "All of my friends thought Rafsanjani was going to win," Semati remarked to me after Ahmadinejad crushed the *gorbeh* (the cat), Iran's most politically adept and probably most despised cleric. In the progressive telling, Ahmadinejad was just too religious, too coarse to prevail in "post-revolutionary" Iran, which, the progressives assured us, was more prepared to make peace with America than America was prepared to make peace with it.

Not surprisingly, then, their American friends assumed no differently. When I was an advisor to the Iraq Study Group, the overwhelming majority of my colleagues thought that America under George W. Bush, not Iran under Ali Khamenei, deserved more blame for delaying the restoration of "normalcy" between the two states. In its deliberations and its final recommendations, the ISG barely acknowledged Islam. Read a stack of essays and op-eds about the Middle East by Bush père's former national security advisor, Brent Scowcroft, one of America's preeminent realists, and the words "Islam" and "Muslim" seldom appear, much less any discussion of how Islam as understood and practiced by Iran's rulers could affect American diplomacy—which, in Scowcroft's eyes, really ought to be able "to assuage Iran's security concerns and temper its urge to acquire a nuclear capability." (Realists have a way of making devout Muslims sound as if they mostly require a sympathetic and reassuring psychotherapist.) For his part, Zbigniew Brzezinski prefers to see contemporary "Islamism" as a movement "led by secular intellectuals," which combines "militant populism with a religious gloss."

Islamism, however, comes much closer to being an authentic expression of Islam than Brzezinski realizes. Devout Muslims probably constitute a majority in every Muslim country in the Middle East. Iran may—just may—be the exception, twenty-eight years of theocracy having dampened the average Iranian's attachment to his faith and its clerical custodians. Who, then, qualifies as devout? Someone who believes the Koran embodies the literal word of God and that the Holy Law, the *Sharia,* ought to be revered and obeyed. Devout Muslims can pick and choose to an extent, allowing local customs, man-made legislation, and human weaknesses to intrude into their everyday lives. But the Sacred Law remains the beloved ideal.

A devout Muslim also loves history. He may do so selectively, ignoring the complexity and diverse strains of medieval and modern Islam in favor of the imagined clarity of early Islam under the Prophet Mohammad. The glories of Islam, foremost among them the faith's unrivaled military conquests, endure vividly for the believer. So, too, memories of the Christian counterattack in the Levant and Andalusia (memories revived, ironically, by Western Orientalists; Saladin has a special place in contemporary Muslim literature not least because Christians recall, seldom accurately, Richard the Lionheart, not because Muslims have always revered Saladin). Memories notwithstanding, devout Muslims can certainly be sincere and devoted friends of Americans. They can, in the right circumstances, even be America's friends.

But it is neither a natural nor easy friendship. In the congressionally sponsored 2003 report on Public Diplomacy for the Arab and Muslim World, "Changing Minds Winning Peace," former ambassador Edward Djerejian, the chairman of the advisory group, avers that "Our adversaries' success in the struggle of ideas is all the more stunning because American values are so widely shared. As one of our Iranian interlocutors put it, 'Who has anything against life, liberty, and the pursuit of happiness?'" Odds are extraordinarily good that this Iranian is highly Westernized, doesn't pray often or at all, and would be hard-pressed to discuss the Koran in detail. For a devout Muslim, "happiness" derives exclusively from the believer's faithfulness to God's commandments and hence his odds of going up, not down, in the afterlife. The idea of "fun" is something difficult for him to digest fully.

If the urge to pursue "happiness" is not a self-evident truth, as Djerejian implies, neither is the Western concept of liberty—that is, the rights that the individual can claim against government, and the corollary freedom to follow one's curiosity and dreams so long as they do not impinge on the autonomy of others. Having banished religion from their conversation, American and European elites are supremely confident—devout Muslims would say mistakenly so—that their enlightened ideas and values have universal resonance. Yet, it is preposterous to suggest, as some in the West do, that only Taliban-like Muslims oppose what we label as basic human or "universal" rights. Hard-core fundamentalists aren't the only Muslims who understand that the Koranic injunction, "commanding the right and forbidding the wrong," probably the defining ethical commandment in the Muslim Holy Book, is inherently incompatible with modern Western sentiment and law.

In the Islamic world, moreover, the personal really is political. Although Muslim governments often have awful relations with each other, and friendlier relations with Washington, this isn't a reality they advertise with pride. The contemporary Muslim ideal, as expressed in the Organization of the Islamic Conference, tends to be highly traditional on this count: Muslims ought to have closer relations with one another than they have with non-believers. Sayyid Qutb, one of the primary theoreticians behind today's Islamic revival, was hardly alone among Muslims in reacting to America's pulsating culture with both fascination and horror. As Osama bin Laden knows well, Saudis, among the most repressed Muslims on the planet, constantly bounce between this yin and yang. Believing Muslims who have no intention whatsoever of becoming holy warriors frequently react to American permissiveness and consumerism with the same mixture of curiosity and revulsion.

To be sure, exposure to the West has colored the dreams, professional expectations, and worldly knowledge of Muslims. The Islamic World has always been highly syncretistic—up to a point. When the Mongols nearly buried Islam in the thirteenth century, the Mameluks, the resolutely devout slave soldiers of Egypt who stopped the Mongol advance in 1260 at Ayn Jalut, acquired many of the trappings of Mongol culture. Since the eighteenth century, the Islamic World has absorbed Western language, thought, manners, architecture, food, furniture, and clothes. But that does not mean Muslims became any less Muslim. It does mean that today's devout Muslims comprehend Western concepts—and Western challenges—better than their forefathers. Ayatollah Mohammad Taqi MesbahYazdi, the so-called spiritual advisor to Ahmadinejad, who can expatiate endlessly on the poisonous nature of the West, can easily give the Karl Popper–obsessed Mohammad Khatami a run for his money in his appreciation of Plato, Aristotle, and the philosophical foundations of Western thought. Men of unquestionable faith can be "populists" or calm, black-eyed lawyers who connect in solitary ways with God; they can be pacifists and warriors. As much as Saint Augustine or Saint Thomas Aquinas, the Algerian Islamist leaders Abbassi Madani and Ali Belhadj, or Iran's Mohammad Khatami and Mesbah-Yazdi, view themselves as God's men trying to keep the faithful on the "straight path." Their brand of Islam has no less authenticity than a spinning Sufi dervish whose spiritual roots lie in pagan and Christian neo-Platonism.

Members of the U.S. foreign policy bureaucracy tend to see these members of the ruling Iranian elite as bearded versions of themselves—men who do not believe that morality and other "abstract" ideas have much of a role in foreign affairs. They have the hardest time seeing the obvious: When Khamenei, a man of principle and integrity, calls the United States the "enemy of God," he means it.

The Islamic Republic, itself based on the idea that Iran exists to further the cause of Islam, has always taken substantial risks in the name of its mission. It seized American hostages and kept them for a year; it aided and abetted the killing of 241 American servicemen in Lebanon; it sent or supported assassination teams around the globe during the 1990s to murder Jews and dissidents in the very same countries where it was trying to promote trade ties; in 1996, it murdered nineteen American airmen in Saudi Arabia three weeks before making its formal application to the World Trade Organization; and it granted, according to the 9/11 Commission Report, free passage to members of al-Qaeda after the 1998 bombing of the U.S. embassies in Africa.

American and European realists tend to ignore this last episode since it unravels the conceit that the Islamic Republic has become, for all its theological eccentricities and deplorable behavior at home, a country you can do business with. Or, if absolutely necessary, contain. Regardless of what one thinks of the latest National Intelligence Estimate, those prone to substituting Communism for Iran's militant faith and suggesting that, like the Soviet Union or Red China before it, Iran's clerical regime can be deterred from reckless conduct abroad and overwhelmed by its own internal contradictions, ought to recall that the Soviet Union as a going philosophical proposition lasted fewer than seven decades. The jihadist impulse in Islam has lasted almost 1400 years. Communism was a post-Christian, Western materialist dream: it did not aim to save men's souls. It promised to improve their mundane lives—and could be graded accordingly. Is it really necessary to point out that Islam, by contrast, is not about economics? When Iran's rulers refer to the United States as the "enemy of God," they aren't taking their cues from the dialectic.

To Iran's clerics, the obstacle to closer relations is fairly straightforward: America epitomizes the anti-Islamic. For Rafsanjani, Khomeini and Ahmadinejad, who view Iran, like their beloved teacher Khomeini, as the sword and shield of God's will on earth, mutually beneficial relations between the United States and the Islamic Republic do not fall within the realm of theological possibility. Short-term compromises can be found only on issues that do not raise existential questions. For example, Tehran encouraged the Sunni Dari-speaking Afghan Tajiks to cooperate with the non-Taliban, American-backed Pashtuns in establishing a government in Kabul. (Primary benefit to the clerical regime: One million–plus much-disliked Sunni Afghan refugees could go home.) But the occasional compromise does not mean that Iran has forsaken its faith and will to expend blood and treasure—to the outsider's eye, often with irrational zeal—to advance its causes. Saudi Arabia and Iran have spent billions of dollars—at times when neither country was flush with funds—to advance their respective visions of Islam. The issues that animate the Islamic Republic's *mission civilisatrice*—support to Hizbollah, Hamas and Islamic Jihad, or the radicalization of the Iraqi Shia, which counts, with the possible exception of the quest for nuclear weaponry, as the most important foreign policy goal of the clerical regime—are not up for negotiation.

Viewing the Middle East through an Islamic lens leaves us uneasy, though not in complete despair. The Islamic revival, which has been vigorously underway since the 1960s, shows no signs of diminishing; there exists scant evidence that the dictatorships and kingdoms, which have done so much to encourage the trend, can reverse it now. Unlike Christianity, Islam dominates the public square, and until Muslims begin to battle openly about the proper scope of public discourse, reforming the theory and practice of Islamic law and governance seems extremely unlikely.

Even if Iraq stabilizes and democracy in the country gains depth, anti-Americanism will still be a staple of the Iraqi street. However, anti-American excuses and conspiracy theories can only go so far in electoral politics. In the end, democracy in Iraq ought to be a significant check at least on the holy-warrior virus. Elsewhere, as the Islamic identity grows stronger in the Arab heartland, a lasting Israeli-Palestinian accommodation will recede further into the future. A more self-consciously Islamic Egypt, the great intellectual engine of anti-Americanism in the Arab world, will continue to pump out hatred of America and the West, and behind the scenes, for both religious and selfish reasons, do what it can to sabotage Israeli–Palestinian negotiations. And Pakistan, perhaps the most dynamic Islamist stronghold, where first-rate minds with first-rate educations espouse ever-harsher ideologies, could radicalize even further under an impossible burden: To be a nation-state defined exclusively by Islamic identity when only Islamists really have any firm idea of what this means. (One thing it certainly means is that the United States can expect to be fighting in neighboring Afghanistan for a *very* long time.)

On the upside of the ledger, modernity, especially the female side of it, continues to rearrange the ethics of Muslim homes and communities. The Westernization of Muslim women appears to be unstoppable, although it's not so clear how this will play out. Highly Westernized Muslim women in Europe and the Middle East are, like their brothers, rediscovering their Islamic identities and re-segregating themselves from men. But modernization

could eventually modify this arrangement, and one has to suspect that the fundamentalist critics of Western rights for women have it right: they will reorder Islamic societies as they exist today.

Also on the personal scale, the Islamic conception of each believer as a deputy of God—the certainty that every Muslim can discern the beauty and superiority of his faith—contains within it the seeds of religious reformation and possibly even democratic growth. Grand Ayatollah Sistani's call to Muslims to exercise their God-given right to vote amounts to a variation of this theme. In particular, modern Sunni Islam's profound egalitarianism—the insistence that God and His law treat all men equally and a distaste for state-controlled religious authority—seems tailor-made for a system of representative government. Restored democracy in Pakistan—the protesting lawyers in Pakistan today should give us hope—could break and reverse the country's radicalization, as Muslims of all stripes debate the relationship between Man, God, and parliamentary legislation.

For the most part, this is not a liberal debate, as we witnessed with the Islamic Salvation Front in Algeria. It is simply a debate about how believing Muslims can encourage legitimate governance. The dialogue in the Arab Middle East is, if anything, part of the region's growing religiosity. Unintentionally, the Islamic Republic of Iran has accelerated the trend by making everything public have a religious dimension. What would be everyday civic criticism in the West assumes religious overtones in Iran. In fact, many clerical dissidents see political pluralism as a means of salvaging the faith. The clerical regime still boasts many hard-core adherents who define happiness as wounding America. But the live-to-die drive, which al-Qaeda has in spades, seems attenuated among most Iranians, if not their rulers.

Alas, Islamic terrorism of the 9/11 variety remains an omnipresent possibility, at least until the Islamist wave recedes among Sunnis and from the halls of power in Tehran. Until things do calm down, it would be good to recall what Bernard Hourcade knew in 1993: the West can intimidate and deter Islamic militants if the West responds to them with sufficient force, and soon enough—before they conclude, as they often have, that the West won't do anything at all. We should not deceive ourselves into believing that Muslim societies express themselves hypocritically: if Wahhabis or Khomeinists dominate political culture at home, they will dominate foreign policy abroad. The secular, "pro-American" autocratic political cultures that have defined much of the Middle East since World War II are dying, if not dead. The United States would do well not to pretend otherwise.

REUEL MARC GERECHT is a resident fellow at the American Enterprise Institute. He is the author of *Know Thine Enemy: A Spy's Journey into Revolutionary Iran* and *The Islamic Paradox: Shiite Clerics, Sunni Fundamentalists, and the Coming of Arab Democracy.*

From *World Affairs*, Winter 2008, pp. 91–100. Copyright © 2008 by World Affairs Institute. Reprinted by permission. www.WorldAffairsJournal.org

After Iran Gets the Bomb
Containment and Its Complications

JAMES M. LINDSAY AND RAY TAKEYH

The Islamic Republic of Iran is determined to become the world's tenth nuclear power. It is defying its international obligations and resisting concerted diplomatic pressure to stop it from enriching uranium. It has flouted several UN Security Council resolutions directing it to suspend enrichment and has refused to fully explain its nuclear activities to the International Atomic Energy Agency. Even a successful military strike against Iran's nuclear facilities would delay Iran's program by only a few years, and it would almost certainly harden Tehran's determination to go nuclear. The ongoing political unrest in Iran could topple the regime, leading to fundamental changes in Tehran's foreign policy and ending its pursuit of nuclear weapons. But that is an outcome that cannot be assumed. If Iran's nuclear program continues to progress at its current rate, Tehran could have the nuclear material needed to build a bomb before U.S. President Barack Obama's current term in office expires.

The dangers of Iran's entry into the nuclear club are well known: emboldened by this development, Tehran might multiply its attempts at subverting its neighbors and encouraging terrorism against the United States and Israel; the risk of both conventional and nuclear war in the Middle East would escalate; more states in the region might also want to become nuclear powers; the geopolitical balance in the Middle East would be reordered; and broader efforts to stop the spread of nuclear weapons would be undermined. The advent of a nuclear Iran—even one that is satisfied with having only the materials and infrastructure necessary to assemble a bomb on short notice rather than a nuclear arsenal—would be seen as a major diplomatic defeat for the United States. Friends and foes would openly question the U.S. government's power and resolve to shape events in the Middle East. Friends would respond by distancing themselves from Washington; foes would challenge U.S. policies more aggressively.

Such a scenario can be avoided, however. Even if Washington fails to prevent Iran from going nuclear, it can contain and mitigate the consequences of Iran's nuclear defiance. It should make clear to Tehran that acquiring the bomb will not produce the benefits it anticipates but isolate and weaken the regime. Washington will need to lay down clear "redlines" defining what it considers to be unacceptable behavior—and be willing to use military force if Tehran crosses them. It will also need to reassure its friends and allies in the Middle East that it remains firmly committed to preserving the balance of power in the region.

Containing a nuclear Iran would not be easy. It would require considerable diplomatic skill and political will on the part of the United States. And it could fail. A nuclear Iran may choose to flex its muscles and test U.S. resolve. Even under the best circumstances, the opaque nature of decision-making in Tehran could complicate Washington's efforts to deter it. Thus, it would be far preferable if Iran stopped—or were stopped—before it became a nuclear power. Current efforts to limit Iran's nuclear program must be pursued with vigor. Economic pressure on Tehran must be maintained. Military options to prevent Iran from going nuclear must not be taken off the table.

But these steps may not be enough. If Iran's recalcitrant mullahs cross the nuclear threshold, the challenge for the United States will be to make sure that an abhorrent outcome does not become a catastrophic one. This will require understanding how a nuclear Iran is likely to behave, how its neighbors are likely to respond, and what Washington can do to shape the perceptions and actions of all these players.

Messianic and Pragmatic

Iran is a peculiarity: it is a modern-day theocracy that pursues revolutionary ideals while safeguarding its practical interests. After three decades of experimentation, Iran has not outgrown its ideological compunctions. The founder of the Islamic Republic, Ayatollah Ruhollah Khomeini, bequeathed to his successors a clerical cosmology that divides the world between oppressors and oppressed and invests Iran with the mission of redeeming the Middle East for the forces of righteousness. But the political imperative of staying in power has pulled Iran's leaders in a different direction, too: they have had to manage Iran's economy, meet the demands of the country's growing population, and advance Iran's interests in a turbulent region. The clerical rulers have been forced to strike agreements with their rivals and their enemies, occasionally softening the hard edges of their creed. The task of governing has required them to make concessions to often unpalatable realities and has sapped their revolutionary energies. Often, the clash of ideology and pragmatism has put Iran in the paradoxical position of having to secure its objectives within a regional order that it has pledged to undermine.

To satisfy their revolutionary impulses, Iran's leaders have turned anti-Americanism and a strident opposition to Israel into pillars of the state. Tehran supports extremist groups, such as Hamas, Hezbollah, and the Islamist militias opposing U.S. forces in Iraq. The mullahs have sporadically attempted to subvert the U.S.-allied sheikdoms of the Persian Gulf. But the regime has survived because its rulers have recognized the limits of their power and have thus mixed revolutionary agitation with pragmatic adjustment. Although it has denounced the United States as the Great Satan and called for Israel's obliteration, Iran has avoided direct military confrontation with either state. It has vociferously defended the Palestinians, but it has stood by as the Russians have slaughtered Chechens and the Chinese have suppressed Muslim Uighurs. Ideological purity, it seems, has been less important than seeking diplomatic cover from Russia and commercial activity with China. Despite their Islamist compulsions, the mullahs like power too much to be martyrs.

Iran's nuclear program has emerged not just as an important aspect of the country's foreign relations but increasingly as a defining element of its national identity. And the reasons for pursuing the program have changed as it has matured. During the presidencies of Hashemi Rafsanjani and Muhammad Khatami, nuclear weapons were seen as tools of deterrence against the United States and Saddam Hussein's regime, among others. The more conservative current ruling elite, including President Mahmoud Ahmadinejad and the Revolutionary Guards, sees them as a critical means of ensuring Iran's preeminence in the region. A powerful Iran, in other words, requires a robust and extensive nuclear infrastructure. And this may be all the more the case now that Iran is engulfed in the worst domestic turmoil it has known in years: these days, the regime seems to be viewing its quest for nuclear self-sufficiency as a way to revive its own political fortunes.

Going nuclear would empower Iran, but far less than Tehran hopes. Iran's entry into the nuclear club would initially put Tehran in a euphoric mood and likely encourage it to be more aggressive. The mullahs would feel themselves to be in possession of a strategic weapon that would enhance Iran's clout in the region. They might feel less restrained in instigating Shiite uprisings against the Arab sheikdoms in the Persian Gulf. But any efforts to destabilize their Sunni neighbors would meet the same unsuccessful fate as have similar campaigns in the past. Iran's revolutionary message has traditionally appealed to only a narrow segment of Shiites in the Persian Gulf. Sporadic demonstrations in Bahrain and Saudi Arabia have not sought to emulate Iran's revolution; rather, they have been an outlet for Shiites to express their economic and political disenfranchisement.

A nuclear Iran might also be tempted to challenge its neighbors in the Persian Gulf to reduce their oil production and limit the presence of U.S. troops on their territories. However, obtaining nuclear weapons is unlikely to help Iran achieve these aims, because nuclear weapons, by definition, are such a narrow category of arms that they can accomplish only a limited set of objectives. They do offer a deterrent capability: unlike Saddam's Iraq, a nuclear Iran would not be invaded, and its leaders would not be deposed. But regime security and power projection are two very different propositions. It is difficult to imagine Sunni regimes yielding to a resurgent Shiite state, nuclear or not; more likely, the Persian Gulf states would take even more refuge under the U.S. security umbrella. Paradoxically, a weapon that was designed to ensure Iran's regional preeminence could further alienate it from its neighbors and prolong indefinitely the presence of U.S. troops on its periphery. In other words, nuclear empowerment could well thwart Iran's hegemonic ambitions. Like other nuclear aspirants before them, the guardians of the theocracy might discover that nuclear bombs are simply not good for diplomatic leverage or strategic aggrandizement.

Likewise, although the protection of a nuclear Iran might allow Hamas, Hezbollah, and other militant groups in the Middle East to become both more strident in their demands and bolder in their actions, Israel's nuclear arsenal and considerable conventional military power, as well as the United States' support for Israel, would keep those actors in check. To be sure, Tehran will rattle its sabers and pledge its solidarity with Hamas and Hezbollah, but it will not risk a nuclear confrontation with Israel to assist these groups' activities. Hamas and Hezbollah learned from their recent confrontations with Israel that waging war against the Jewish state is a lonely struggle.

The prospect that Iran might transfer a crude nuclear device to its terrorist protégés is another danger, but it, too, is unlikely. Such a move would place Tehran squarely in the cross hairs of the United States and Israel. Despite its messianic pretensions, Iran has observed clear limits when supporting militias and terrorist organizations in the Middle East. Iran has not provided Hezbollah with chemical or biological weapons or Iraqi militias with the means to shoot down U.S. aircraft. Iran's rulers understand that such provocative actions could imperil their rule by inviting retaliation. On the other hand, by coupling strident rhetoric with only limited support in practice, the clerical establishment is able to at once garner popular acclaim for defying the West and oppose the United States and Israel without exposing itself to severe retribution. A nuclear Iran would likely act no differently, at least given the possibility of robust U.S. retaliation. Nor is it likely that Iran would become the new Pakistan, selling nuclear fuel and materials to other states. The prospects of additional sanctions and a military confrontation with the United States are likely to deter Iran from acting impetuously.

A nuclear Iran would undeniably pose new dangers in the Middle East, especially at first, when it would likely be at its most reckless. It might thrash about the Middle East, as it tried to press the presumed advantages of its newfound capability, and it might test the United States' limits. But the mullahs will find it difficult to translate Iran's nuclear status into a tangible political advantage. And if Washington makes clear that rash actions on their part will come at a high cost, they will be far less likely to take any.

The Ripples in the Region

In assessing the consequences of Iran's nuclearization, it is important to consider not only how Iran is likely to act but also how other states will react to this outcome—and what the United States could do to influence their responses. Iran's nuclearization would not reduce Washington to passively observing events in the region. Washington would retain considerable ability to shape what Iran's neighbors do and do not do.

The nightmare scenario that could be unleashed by Iran's nuclearization is easy to sketch. Israel would go on a hair-trigger alert—ready to launch a nuclear weapon at a moment's notice—putting both countries minutes away from annihilation. Egypt, Saudi Arabia, and Turkey would scramble to join the nuclear club. The Nonproliferation Treaty (NPT) would collapse, unleashing a wave of nuclear proliferation around the globe.

Such a doomsday scenario could pan out. Whether it did would depend greatly on how the United States and others, starting with Israel, responded to Iran's nuclearization. Whether Israeli Prime Minister Benjamin Netanyahu forgoes a preventive strike against Iran's nuclear facilities or opts for launching an attack and it fails, the Israeli government will continue to regard the Iranian regime as an existential threat to Israel that must be countered by any means possible, including the use of nuclear weapons. Given Israel's unique history and Ahmadinejad's contemptible denials of the Holocaust, no Israeli prime minister can afford to think otherwise.

The riskiness of a nuclear standoff between Israel and Iran would vary with the nature and size of Tehran's nuclear arsenal. An Iran with only the capability to build a nuclear weapon would pose a far less immediate threat to Israel than an Iran that possessed an actual weapon. Iran's possession of a bomb would create an inherently unstable situation, in which both parties would have an incentive to strike first: Iran, to avoid losing its arsenal, and Israel, to keep Tehran from using it. The Israeli government's calculations about Iran would depend on its assessment of the United States' willingness and ability to deter Iran. Israel's decision-making would be shaped by a number of factors: the United States' long-standing support for Israel, Israel's doubts about U.S. leadership after Washington's failure to stop Iran from going nuclear, and Washington's response to Iran's nuclearization.

Another danger that would have to be countered would be nuclear proliferation in the Middle East. Iran's regional rivals might try to catch up with it. History suggests, however, that states go nuclear for reasons beyond tit for tat; many hold back even when their enemies get nuclear weapons. China's pursuit of the bomb in the 1960s prompted fears that Japan would follow, but nearly half a century later, Japan remains nonnuclear. Although Israel has more than 200 nuclear weapons, neither its neighbors—not even Egypt, which fought and lost four wars with Israel—nor regional powers, such as Saudi Arabia or Turkey, have followed its lead.

An Iranian nuclear bomb could change these calculations. The U.S. National Intelligence Council concluded in a 2008 report that "Iran's growing nuclear capabilities are already partly responsible for the surge of interest in nuclear energy in the Middle East." And nuclear energy programs can serve as the foundation for drives for nuclear weapons. But it would not be easy for countries in the region to get nuclear weapons. Many lack the infrastructure to develop their own weapons and the missiles needed to deliver them. Egypt and Turkey might blanch at the expense of building a nuclear arsenal. The Pakistanis were willing to "eat grass" for the privilege of joining the nuclear club, as the Pakistani leader Zulfikar Ali Bhutto once famously put it, but not everyone is.

Cost considerations aside, it would take years for nuclear aspirants to develop indigenous nuclear capabilities. They would need to build nuclear reactors, acquire nuclear fuel, master enrichment or reprocessing technologies, and build weapons and the means to deliver them. While they tried, the United States and other states would have ample opportunity to increase the costs of proliferation. Indeed, the economic and security interests of Egypt, Saudi Arabia, and Turkey, unlike those of Iran, are tied to the United States and the broader global economy, and developing nuclear weapons would put those interests at risk. Egypt would jeopardize the $1.5 billion in economic and military aid that it receives from Washington each year; Saudi Arabia, its implicit U.S. security guarantee; and Turkey, its place in NATO. Given their extensive investments in and business ties to the United States and Europe, all three countries would be far more vulnerable than Iran is to any economic sanctions that U.S. law imposed, or could impose, on nuclear proliferators.

States seeking nuclear weapons might try to sidestep these technological and political hurdles by buying, rather than making, the weapons. Saudi Arabia's clandestine acquisition of medium-range ballistic missiles from China in the 1980s suggests that even countries that depend on U.S. security guarantees might be tempted to buy their way into the nuclear club. Although neither the five acknowledged nuclear powers nor India would be likely to sell nuclear weapons to another state, Pakistan and North Korea could be another matter. Both countries have a history of abetting proliferation, and Pakistan has warm ties with its fellow Muslim-majority countries. But selling complete nuclear weapons would come at great political cost. Pakistan might forfeit U.S. foreign assistance and drive the United States into closer cooperation with India, Pakistan's mortal enemy. North Korea would endanger the economic aid it gets from China, which the regime needs to stay in power.

If a buyer did manage to find a seller, it would have to avoid a preventive strike by Israel—which would be likely if the sale became known before the weapon was activated—and then handle the inevitable international political and economic fallout. (In 1988, Saudi Arabia avoided a major rift with Washington over its missile deal with China only by finally agreeing to sign and abide by the NPT.) Furthermore, any country that bought a nuclear weapon would have to worry about whether it would actually work; in global politics, as in everyday life, swindles are possible. Obtaining a nuclear weapon could thus put a country in the worst of all worlds: owning a worthless weapon that is a magnet for an attack.

If Iran's neighbors decided against trying to get nuclear weapons, they could pursue the opposite approach and try to appease Tehran. The temptation would be greatest for small Persian Gulf states, such as Bahrain and Kuwait, which sit uncomfortably close to Iran and have large Shiite populations. Such a tilt toward Iran would damage U.S. interests in the region. The U.S. Fifth Fleet is based in Bahrain, and U.S. military bases in Bahrain, Kuwait, and the United Arab Emirates are crucial to projecting U.S. power and reassuring U.S. allies in the region. But as long as these governments believe that Washington is committed to their security, appeasement will be unappealing. Pursuing that strategy would mean casting aside U.S. help and betting on the mercy of Tehran. In the absence of a U.S. security guarantee, however, Iran would be free to conduct in those countries the very subversive activities that their governments' appeasement was intended to prevent.

Although Iran's nuclearization would probably not spell the end of efforts to halt proliferation in other parts of the world, it would undeniably deal the nonproliferation regime a setback, by demonstrating that the great powers are unable or unwilling to act collectively to stop proliferators. On the other hand, most states adhere to the NPT because they have compelling national reasons to do so. They may not feel threatened by a nuclear power; they may be covered by the nuclear umbrella of another state; they may lack the financial or technological wherewithal to build a bomb. Iran's success in developing a nuclear weapon would not change these calculations. Nor would it prevent Washington from pushing ahead with its efforts to strengthen the Proliferation Security Initiative (a U.S.-led multinational effort launched by the Bush administration that seeks to stop trafficking in weapons of mass destruction), impose a cutoff on the further production of fissile material, tighten global rules on trade in nuclear materials, and otherwise make it more difficult for nuclear technologies to spread.

Iran's acquisition of a nuclear bomb could have disastrous consequences in the Middle East. But Washington would have considerable opportunities to influence, and constrain, how Iran's neighbors reacted to its new status. It would matter whether Washington reassured Israel or fueled its fears. It would matter whether Washington confronted regional proliferation efforts or turned a blind eye, as it did with Pakistan in the 1980s. It would matter whether Washington pushed ahead with efforts to strengthen the NPT regime or threw in the towel. To keep the nightmare scenario at bay, the United States will need to think carefully about how to maximize its leverage in the region.

I Say No, No, No

Tehran is an adversary that speaks in ideological terms, wants to become a dominant regional power, and is capable of acting recklessly. But it is also an adversary that recognizes its limitations, wants to preserve its hold on power, and operates among wary neighbors. Its acquiring a nuclear bomb, or the capacity to make a nuclear bomb, need not remake the Middle East— at least not if the United States acts confidently and wisely to exploit Iran's weaknesses.

Tehran's acquiring a nuclear bomb need not remake the Middle East—if Washington wisely exploits Tehran's weaknesses.

Any strategy to contain Iran must begin with the recognition that this effort will have to be different from that to contain the Soviet Union. Iran poses a different threat. During the early years of the Cold War, U.S. policymakers tried to protect like-minded countries against a Soviet invasion that would have imposed communist rule, or against widespread economic dislocation, which could have produced a communist takeover from within. Their strategy was to turn to the NATO alliance and launch the Marshall Plan. The United States' containment strategy toward Iran must reflect different realities today. Iran does not seek to invade its neighbors, and its ideological appeal does not rest on promises of economic justice. It seeks to establish itself as the dominant power in the region while preserving political control at home.

Deterrence would by necessity be the cornerstone of a U.S. strategy to contain a nuclear Iran. Success is by no means guaranteed. Deterrence can fail: it nearly did during the Cuban missile crisis, in 1962, and at several other critical junctures of the Cold War. Iran's revisionist aims and paranoia about U.S. power may appear to make the country uniquely difficult to deter. But that conclusion conveniently—and mistakenly—recasts the history of U.S. confrontations with emerging nuclear powers in a gentler light than is deserved. At the start of the Cold War, U.S. officials hardly saw the Soviet Union as a status quo power. In the 1960s, China looked like the ultimate rogue regime: it had intervened in Korea and gone to war with India, and it repressed its own people. Mao boasted that although nuclear war might kill half the world's population, it would also mean that "imperialism would be razed to the ground and the whole world would become socialist."

Today, the challenge for U.S. policymakers devising a deterrence strategy toward Iran will be to unambiguously identify what behavior they seek to deter—and what they are willing to do about it. When Washington publicly presents its policy on how to contain a nuclear Iran, it should be explicit: no initiation of conventional warfare against other countries; no use or transfer of nuclear weapons, materials, or technologies; and no stepped-up support for terrorist or subversive activities. It should also make clear that the price of Iran's violating these three prohibitions could be U.S. military retaliation by any and all means necessary, up to and including nuclear weapons.

The pledge to deter a conventional attack would be the easiest of the three prohibitions to enforce. Iran's ability to project sustained military power outside its borders is limited. And it is unlikely to grow substantially anytime soon: even more arms embargoes would likely be imposed on Iran if it crossed the nuclear threshold. At their current level, U.S. troops in the region are more than sufficient to deter Iran from undertaking incursions into Iraq or amphibious operations across the Persian Gulf—or to stop them if they occurred.

Deterring Iran from using or threatening to use nuclear weapons would present a different set of challenges. So long as Iran lacks the ability to strike the United States with a nuclear-tipped missile, the United States can credibly threaten to retaliate militarily if Iran uses or threatens to use a nuclear bomb against anyone. But that could change if Iran developed long-range missiles. Tehran might also try to deter the United States by threatening to attack Europe, which would raise well-known concerns about the viability of so-called extended deterrence, the ability of one state to deter an attack on another. These possibilities highlight the importance of developing robust, multi-layered ballistic missile defenses. The Obama administration's decision to reorient U.S. missile defenses in Europe to protect against shorter-range missiles while continuing to develop defenses against longer-range missiles is just the right approach.

A tougher challenge would be to ensure stable deterrence between Iran and Israel. With regard to this issue, too, the Iranian nuclear program's ultimate degree of development would be pivotal: an Iran armed with nuclear weapons would present a significantly more dangerous threat than one that merely had the capacity to build them. It is thus essential that Washington continue to apply diplomatic and economic pressure to keep Tehran, should it manage to complete the nuclear fuel cycle, from taking the final step. The United States should also publicly pledge to retaliate by any means it chooses if Iran uses nuclear weapons against Israel; this would in effect supplement whatever second-strike capability Israel has. If the Israelis need a formal commitment to be more reassured, this pledge could be made in an executive agreement or a treaty. As a tangible expression of its commitment, Washington should also be prepared to deploy U.S. troops on Israeli soil as a tripwire, which would show that the United States would be inextricably bound to Israel in the event of any Iranian attack.

Washington should also inform Tehran that it would strike preemptively, with whatever means it deemed necessary, if Iran ever placed its nuclear forces on alert. And it should bring both Israel and Israel's Arab neighbors fully under its missile defense umbrella. The more aggressive Iran is, the more inclined its neighbors will be to work with Washington to construct missile defenses on their territories.

Deterring Iran from transferring nuclear weapons, materials, and technologies to state and nonstate actors would require another set of measures. For the most part, Iran has reasons not to pursue such perilous activities, but it could be tempted to exploit the difficulty of tracking the clandestine trade in nuclear materials. The United States and its allies would need to act decisively to prevent Tehran from seeking to profit in the international nuclear bazaar, for example, through the Proliferation Security Initiative and through UN resolutions that imposed additional sanctions on Iran and its potential business partners. To impress on Iran's ruling mullahs that it is singularly important for them to control whatever nuclear arsenal they may develop or obtain, Washington should hold Tehran responsible for any nuclear transfer, whether authorized or not; Tehran cannot be allowed to escape punishment or retaliation by pleading loss of control. Increased investments in monitoring and spying on Iran would be critical. The United States must improve its ability to track nuclear weapons, materials, and debris and prove and publicize whether they came from Iran (or any other country, for that matter). Such nuclear forensics is crucial to determining who is responsible for nuclear transfers and would be crucial to building support for any U.S. retaliation against Iran, if it were the culprit.

Deterring Iranian support for terrorist and subversive groups—the third redline prohibition that the United States should impose—would be difficult. Such activities take place secretly, making it hard to establish precisely who is complicit. That complication places a premium on improving the ability of the U.S. intelligence community, acting alone and in concert with its counterparts abroad, to track Iran's clandestine activities.

Whats and What Nots

In addition to holding Iran accountable for violating any of the three noes, the United States' containment strategy should seek to influence and, where necessary, constrain Iran's friends in the Middle East. An energetic diplomacy that softened the disagreements between Israel and its neighbors would undermine Iran's efforts to exploit anger in the region. A concerted push, diplomatic and economic, to improve the lives of the Palestinians would limit Iran's appeal among them. Drawing Syria into a comprehensive Israeli-Palestinian peace process could not only attenuate Tehran's links with Damascus but also stem Iran's ability to supply weapons to Hezbollah. Washington should seek to further limit Iran's strategic reach by strengthening the institutional and military capabilities of Afghanistan and Iraq. It should reassure the Persian Gulf states that it is committed to preserving the existing balance of power, which would require expanding trade agreements, enhancing their security and intelligence apparatuses, and developing a more integrated approach to defense planning in the region. At the same time, the United States will need to dissuade these governments from further suppressing their Shiite minorities, a practice that inadvertently aids Tehran. And it should work assiduously to prevent more countries in the Middle East from going nuclear; the United States cannot look the other way again, as it did with Pakistan during the 1980s.

Tone and conviction will matter. Washington must keep in mind that Iran's entry into the nuclear club would be read by Israel and Arab states as a failure of the United States' political will and a demonstration of the limits of U.S. power. Washington cannot afford to compound its credibility problem by hesitating or vacillating. An indecisive U.S. response would undermine the efforts both to deter Iran and to reassure U.S. friends and allies in the region.

Washington should also push other major powers to contain the Iranian threat. The five permanent members of the UN Security Council have sponsored numerous resolutions demanding that Iran cease its nuclear activities and cooperate with the International Atomic Energy Agency. They should have a vested interest in punishing Iran, an original signatory to the NPT, if it reneges on its decades-old pledge to remain a nonnuclear power. Doing nothing would substantially undermine the UN Security Council's authority and with it their status as permanent members of the council. Europe should be pressed to commit troops and naval vessels to preserve the free flow of traffic through the Persian Gulf. Russia should cease its nuclear cooperation with and its conventional arms sales to Iran. China should be pressed to curtail its investment in Iran's energy sector, which does so much to fuel Iran's belligerence. The United States would have to do much of the heavy lifting in containing a nuclear Iran, but any concerted containment strategy must have not just regional support but also an international complexion.

Just as important as what Washington should do to contain Iran is what it should not do. If Iran gets a nuclear bomb, the United States might be tempted to respond by substantially expanding the presence of U.S. troops in the Middle East. But this would not appreciably increase Washington's ability to deter Iran from launching a nuclear or conventional attack; there are already enough U.S. forces in the region for that. It could, however, play into the hands of Tehran's proxies by inflaming anti-American sentiment and fanning civil unrest in the Persian Gulf.

Washington might also be tempted to seek to further undermine Iran's economy by imposing broad-based economic sanctions, an idea that enjoys considerable support on Capitol Hill. But such measures would wind up punishing only Iran's disenfranchised citizenry (which is why Iranian opposition leaders have strenuously opposed them). The wiser course of action would be to strengthen and better monitor existing export controls, in order to make certain that Iran's nuclear and defense industries do not have access to dual-use technologies, and to reinforce targeted sanctions against the Iranian leadership and the business enterprises controlled by the Revolutionary Guards. Washington should push, both inside and outside the UN, for travel bans on Iranian leaders and measures denying Iran access to capital markets, for example. It should also find ways to penalize foreign businesses that invest in Iran's dilapidated oil industry. Smart sanctions of this kind would punish Iran's leaders but spare ordinary Iranians, who have no say over the regime's actions.

The United States should refrain from greatly expanding the range of weaponry it sells to the Persian Gulf states, which see the United States as a military guarantor and their chief arms supplier. To some extent, increasing arms sales will be necessary: the Arab governments of the region would regard such sales as a tangible sign of the strength of Washington's commitment to their defense, and if Washington holds back, these governments will look for weapons elsewhere. On the other hand, throwing the doors of the armory wide open would do little to secure the buyers and might even increase instability in the region. A smart U.S. arms sales policy would focus on offering weapons systems that are designed to deter or help counter an Iranian attack, such as missile defense systems and command-and-control systems, which would provide advance notice of Iranian actions.

Finally, Washington should resist any urge to sign mutual security treaties with Arab countries in the Middle East. (Israel, whose relations with Iran are fundamentally different from those of every other power in the region, is a special case.) Such

efforts would do little to enhance deterrence and could do a lot to undermine it. Many members of the U.S. Senate, which would have to vote on any alliance treaty, would question whether the United States should further tie itself to authoritarian regimes that many Americans find odious. The spectacle of that debate would exacerbate doubts in the Middle East about the depth of the United States' commitment. Efforts to construct formal alliances might also lead Iran to believe that any country left out of these agreements is fair game for intimidation or attack. Washington should be mindful not to invite a replay of North Korea's calculation in 1950 that South Korea lay outside the U.S. defense perimeter.

Instead, the U.S. government should encourage the formation of a regional alliance network that would marshal Arab states into a more cohesive defense grouping. The network could be organized along the lines of the Middle East Treaty Organization (then the Central Treaty Organization), a security arrangement among Iran, Pakistan, Turkey, the United Kingdom, and, for a time, Iraq (with the United States participating in the organization's military and security committees) that existed from 1955 to 1979. An alliance of this kind would secure all the benefits of a regionwide commitment to deterrence without exposing the United States and its allies to the complexities of formal bilateral or multilateral security treaties.

Dangerous Times

Iran's nuclearization would make the Middle East a more dangerous place: it would heighten tensions, reduce the margin for error, and raise the prospect of mass catastrophe. The international community should not let up on its efforts to stop Iran's progress. But given the mullahs' seeming indifference to the benefits of engagement, U.S. policymakers must consider now what to do if Iran does get the bomb.

Containment would be neither a perfect nor a foolproof policy. The task of foiling Iran's support for Hamas and Hezbollah would be difficult, as would countering Iran's support for terrorist and subversive groups in the region. The need to gain favor with Arab dictatorships would likely tempt Washington to shelve its calls for domestic political reforms in those countries—even though such reforms could diminish Iran's ability to meddle there by improving the lot of local minority Shiites who might otherwise be susceptible to Tehran's influence. Maintaining great-power support for pressure on Iran could require overlooking objectionable Chinese and Russian behavior on other matters. Containment would not be a substitute for the use of force. To the contrary, its very success would depend on the willingness of the United States to use force against Iran or threaten to do so should Tehran cross Washington's redlines. Applying pressure without a commitment to punishing infractions is a recipe for failure—and for a more violent and dangerous Middle East.

Containment could buy Washington time to persuade the Iranian ruling class that the revisionist game it has been playing is simply not worth the candle. Thus, even as Washington pushes to counter Iran, it should be open to the possibility that Tehran's calculations might change. To press Tehran in the right direction, Washington should signal that it seeks to create an order in the Middle East that is peaceful and self-sustaining. The United States will remain part of the region's security architecture for the foreseeable future, but it need not maintain an antagonistic posture toward Iran. An Islamic Republic that abandoned its nuclear ambitions, accepted prevailing international norms, and respected the sovereignty of its neighbors would discover that the United States is willing to work with, rather than against, Iran's legitimate national aspirations.

James M. Lindsay is Senior Vice President, Director of Studies, and Maurice R. Greenberg Chair at the Council on Foreign Relations. **Ray Takeyh** is a Senior Fellow at the Council on Foreign Relations and the author of *Guardians of the Revolution: Iran and the World in the Age of the Ayatollahs.* For an annotated guide to this topic, see "What to Read on Iranian Politics" at www.foreignaffairs.com/readinglists/iran and "What to Read on Nuclear Proliferation" at www.foreignaffairs.com/readinglists/nuclear-proliferation.

U.S. Africa Command
A New Strategic Paradigm?

Sean McFate

This new command will strengthen our security cooperation with Africa and help to create new opportunities to bolster the capabilities of our partners in Africa. Africa Command will enhance our efforts to help bring peace and security to the people of Africa and promote our common goals of development, health, education, democracy, and economic growth in Africa.[1]

—President George W. Bush

On 6 February 2007, the president announced the establishment of a tenth unified combatant command called Africa Command, or "AFRICOM." Its area of responsibility will cover Africa, and it will have an unprecedented number of interagency civilians in leadership roles (including a civilian deputy commander). This new command's objective will be to enhance Department of Defense (DOD) efforts to assist African partners in achieving a more stable environment through security cooperation.

Yet questions abound. AFRICOM's vision, as outlined by the president on the day of its public unveiling, is anomalous among unified commands. Words like "development, health, education, democracy, and economic growth" are atypical of military missions, which traditionally center on fighting and winning wars. In many ways, AFRICOM is a post-Cold War experiment that radically rethinks security in the early 21st century based on peace-building lessons learned since the fall of the Berlin Wall. Will it work? This article explores possibilities by analyzing AFRICOM's origins, timing, strategy, and composition as well as the early challenges that will confront the nascent command.

Why AFRICOM?

AFRICOM originated as an internal administrative change within DOD that remedies "an outdated arrangement left over from the Cold War," in the words of Secretary of Defense Robert Gates.[2] Or, in the words of Ambassador Robert Loftis, the former senior State Department member of the AFRICOM transition team, it was created because "Africa is more important to us strategically and deserves to be viewed through its own lens."[3] That lens is the new unified command.

Unified commands, or combatant commands, were instituted during the Cold War to better manage military forces for possible armed confrontation with the Soviet Union and its proxies. Today, they are prisms through which the Pentagon views the world. Each command is responsible for coordinating, integrating, and managing all Defense assets and operations in its designated area of responsibility, per the Unified Command Plan. This plan is regularly reviewed, modified as required, and approved by the president.

The unified command design has proven problematic for DOD's involvement in Africa, a continent not viewed as strategically significant during the Cold War. That DOD never designated a unified command for Africa evinces the want of concern for one of the largest and most conflict-prone continents on the planet. Instead, DOD divided African coverage between three unified commands: European Command (EUCOM), Central Command (CENTCOM), and Pacific Command (PACOM). This lack of focus had several deleterious effects.

The first effect is that Africa was never a number-one priority for any unified command. Each viewed its strategic imperative as being elsewhere, leaving Africa as a secondary or even tertiary concern. For example, EUCOM's strategic center of gravity has always been Europe, with the overwhelming majority of its forces, staff, and resources dedicated to that continent, even after the fall of the Berlin Wall.

Second, the three-part division of responsibility violates the principle of unity of command, increasing the likelihood of an uncoordinated DOD effort in Africa. This disunity can occur especially at the "seams" between unified commands; for instance, a hypothetical U.S. military response to the crisis in the Darfur region might be complicated because the area of interest straddles the EUCOM and CENTCOM boundary, causing coordination challenges.[4]

Third, owing to historical disinterest, DOD never developed a sizable cadre of dedicated African experts. Only within the past decade has DOD invested in the Africa Center for Strategic Studies (a think tank akin to the George C. Marshall European Center for Security Studies in Germany) to support the development of U.S. strategic policy towards Africa.

Lastly, Africa has never benefited from the advocacy of a four-star commander whose undiluted mandate includes helping policy-makers understand the perspectives of African countries and formulate effective African security policy.

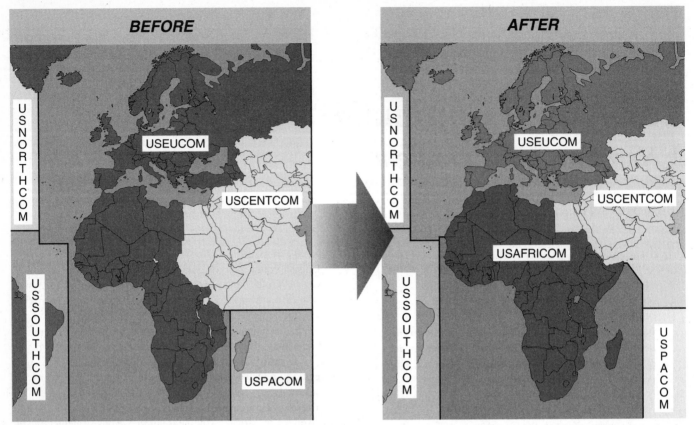

Figure 1 AFRICOM (right) will take over responsibility for all of Africa (except Egypt) from EUCOM, CENTCOM, and PACOM (left) in October 2008.

Taken together, these four deficiencies resulted in a disjointed and hindered approach towards Africa that lacked primacy within the Pentagon and, by extension, U.S. interagency networks.

Partly in response to this unwarranted lack of attention, DOD decided to redraw the unified command landscape by creating AFRICOM (see Figure 1). As Secretary Gates testified before the Senate, creating AFRICOM "will enable us to have a more effective and integrated approach than the current arrangement of dividing Africa between [different unified commands]."[5] AFRICOM combines under a single unified command all but one of the countries conventionally considered "African." (Egypt is the exception, owing to its relationship with the Middle East in general and Israel in particular. It remains covered by CENTCOM).

AFRICOM will be a distinct unified command with the sole responsibility of Africa.[6] A four-star general will command it and its approximately 400–700 staff members. It will be temporarily located in Stuttgart, Germany, as a sub-unified command, but is scheduled to move to Africa (place to be determined) and be operational by 1 October 2008.[7] Its four-star commander will be able to enhance policy decisions regarding Africa by advocating for African security issues on Capitol Hill and raising the military's strategic awareness of the continent.

DOD intends AFRICOM's presence to be innocuously transparent to African countries. Ryan Henry, the principal deputy under secretary of defense for policy, continually reiterates: "The goal is for AFRICOM not to be [sic] a U.S. leadership role on the continent but rather to be supporting the indigenous leadership efforts that are currently going on."[8] The theme of partnership is ubiquitous in

DOD's dealings with AFRICOM and Africa. The department has, for example, conducted high-level delegations to African countries to discuss the creation of the command. As Theresa Whelan, deputy assistant secretary of defense of African affairs, explains, "If we take partnership seriously, then we must go out in a way never done before and consult with the nations affected. This manner of approaching partnership was not done with EUCOM, PACOM, or CENTCOM."[9]

Why Now?

AFRICOM is more than just an administrative change within DOD; it responds to Africa's increased geopolitical importance to U.S. interests. As Deputy Under Secretary Henry has stated, "Africa . . . is emerging on the world scene as a strategic player, and we need to deal with it as a continent."[10] U.S. strategic interests in Africa are many, including the needs to counter terrorism, secure natural resources, contain armed conflict and humanitarian crisis, retard the spread of HIV/AIDS, reduce international crime, and respond to growing Chinese influence.

Counterterrorism dominates much of U.S. security policy as the U.S. prosecutes its War on Terrorism. In a stark reversal of Cold War thinking, the 2002 *National Security Strategy* asserts that "America is now threatened less by conquering states than . . . by failing ones."[11] From the U.S. perspective, the inability or unwillingness of some fragile states to govern territory within their borders can lead to the creation of safe-havens for terrorist organizations. Government recalcitrance was indeed the case with Afghanistan in the late

1990s, when the Taliban permitted Al-Qaeda to operate unfettered within its boundaries, leading to the events of 11 September 2001. Africa contains the preponderance of fragile states in the world today, placing it squarely in the crosshairs of the War on Terrorism. AFRICOM will oversee current U.S. counterterrorism programs in Africa, such as Operation Enduring Freedom: Combined Joint Task Force-Horn of Africa (CJTF-HOA), and the Trans Sahara Counterterrorism Initiative (TSCTI).[12]

America is also interested in Africa's natural resources, especially in terms of energy security. As instability in the Middle East grows and international demand for energy soars, the world—and the United States in particular—will become increasingly beholden to Africa's ability to produce oil, an inelastic commodity. Central Intelligence Agency estimates suggest Africa may supply as much as 25 percent of imports to America by 2015.[13] Already by 2006, sub-Saharan African oil constituted approximately 18 percent of all U.S. imports (about 1.8 million barrels per day). By comparison, Persian Gulf imports were at 21 percent (2.2 million barrels per day).[14]

At present, Nigeria is Africa's largest supplier of oil and the fifth largest global supplier of oil to the United States.[15] However, instability in the Niger Delta region has reduced output periodically by as much as 25 percent, escalating world oil prices. For instance, the price of oil jumped more than $3 per barrel in April 2007 after Nigeria's national elections were disputed, and it spiked again in May after attacks on pipelines in the delta. To help control this volatility, AFRICOM may become increasingly involved in the maritime security of the Gulf of Guinea, where the potential for deep-water drilling is high. "You look at West Africa and the Gulf of Guinea, it becomes more focused because of the energy situation," General Bantz Craddock, EUCOM Commander, told reporters in Washington. Safeguarding energy "obviously is out in front."[16]

Stemming armed conflict and mitigating humanitarian catastrophe also remain important U.S. objectives. Africa has long endured political conflict, armed struggle, and natural disasters, all of which have exacted a grave toll on Africans and compromised international development efforts. The direct and indirect costs of instability are high in terms of human suffering and economic, social, and political retardation. Although Africa is afflicted by fewer serious armed conflicts today than it was a decade ago, it hosts a majority of the United Nations peacekeeping operations.[17]

African militaries make up a sizable contingent of the African peacekeeping operations conducted by the UN and such regional organizations as the African Union and the Economic Community of West African States (ECOWAS). Despite a willingness to participate in these operations, many African militaries lack the command, training, equipment, logistics, and institutional infrastructure required for complex peacekeeping, leaving the onus of support on the international community. This burden has prompted some donor countries to help build the capacity of African militaries, thereby enhancing their ability to participate in peacekeeping operations. In 2004 the G-8 introduced its Global Peace Operations Initiative (GPOI), a multilateral program that plans to create a self-sustaining peacekeeping force of 75,000 troops, a majority of them African, by 2010. The U.S. Department of State manages GPOI, as it does the Africa Contingency Operations Training Assistance (ACOTA) program, which also trains peacekeepers.[18] According to Chip Beck, who heads ACOTA, "Our job is to help African countries enhance their capabilities to effectively take part in peacekeeping operations."[19] Although AFRICOM will not manage GPOI

or ACOTA, it should offer technical assistance to such programs and partner with African states in security sector reform (SSR).

HIV/AIDS is the leading cause of death on the continent, and controlling its global spread remains a critical concern for the U.S. In 2004, then-Secretary of State Colin Powell described HIV/AIDS as "the greatest threat of mankind today."[20] According to the UN, nearly 25 million Africans were HIV-positive in 2006, representing 63 percent of infected persons worldwide.[21] The rate of infection in some African security forces is believed to be high (between 40 and 60 percent in the case of the Democratic Republic of the Congo), raising concerns that those forces may be unable to deploy when needed and may even be vectors of the disease's spread.[22]

International crime in Africa is also a U.S. interest, especially the narcotics trade. West Africa has become the newest center for trafficking drugs. In the past year Nigeria, West Africa's economic hub, has made 234 drug-trafficking arrests at the Lagos airport, which is just grazing the surface, according to government officials.[23] Guinea-Bissau, another West African country, is quickly developing into a narco-state. Its soldiers have been caught facilitating the transfer of narcotics to mostly European markets.[24] To suggest the scale of this emerging problem, there were two seizures of over 600 kilos of cocaine, worth over $30 million each, during the past year. In Guinea-Bissau, narcotics trafficking accounts for almost 20 percent of GDP.[25] African trade in contraband such as narcotics, small arms, and human beings is a continuing global concern.

The People's Republic of China's (PRC) expanding influence in Africa is also a continuing worry for the United States. The continent is quickly emerging as a competitive battlefield in what some U.S. defense intellectuals are describing as a proxy economic cold war with China, especially in the quest for resources.[26] China's insatiable appetite for oil and other natural resources is the product of its own success. The PRC's economy has maintained an incredible average of 9 percent growth per annum over the last two decades, nearly tripling the country's GDP during that time. African oil fuels this growth. Until 1993, China was a net exporter of oil; now it is the world's second-largest energy consumer, obtaining 30 percent of its oil from African sources, especially Sudan, Angola, and Congo (Brazzaville).[27] Competition for natural resources, and oil in particular, is a strategic concern for the United States.

China is also seeking new markets for its goods. As its policy paper on Africa bluntly asserts: "The Chinese Government encourages and supports Chinese enterprises' investment and business in Africa, and will continue to provide preferential loans and buyer credits to this end."[28] Currently, over 700 Chinese state companies conduct business in Africa, making China the continent's third largest trading partner, behind the United States and France, but ahead of Britain. A series of diplomatic initiatives buttress these commercial ventures, aimed initially not only at isolating Taiwan but also at broader policy objectives. The PRE has diplomatic relations with 47 of Africa's states and offers limited, but not inconsiderable, development assistance in exchange for diplomatic support. China also engages in multilateral efforts to build strategic partnerships in Africa. In 1999, then-president Jiang Zemin petitioned the Organization of African Unity (now the African Union) to create a Forum on China-Africa Cooperation. A year later the first ministerial conference took place in Beijing with 44 African states participating. In 1995, two-way trade between Africa and China hovered at less than U.S. $1 billion. By the end of 2006, it exceeded U.S. $50 billion.

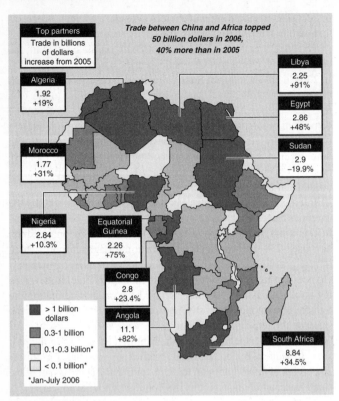

Top partners
Trade in billions of dollars increase from 2005

Trade between China and Africa topped 50 billion dollars in 2006, 40% more than in 2005

Libya
2.25
+91%

Algeria
1.92
+19%

Egypt
2.86
+48%

Morocco
1.77
+31%

Sudan
2.9
−19.9%

Nigeria
2.84
+10.3%

Equatorial Guinea
2.26
+75%

Congo
2.8
+23.4%

Angola
11.1
+82%

South Africa
8.84
+34.5%

- > 1 billion dollars
- 0.3-1 billion
- 0.1-0.3 billion*
- < 0.1 billion*

*Jan-July 2006

China Africa trade.

Source: China Ministry of Commerce

At the core of China's rapid push into African markets is its drive to forge strategic alliances. African countries constitute the largest single regional grouping of states within any international organization, accentuating their importance to Chinese diplomacy. Furthermore, in multilateral settings such as the UN, African countries tend to engage in bloc-voting, an effective tactic for influencing rules formulation, multilateral negotiations, and other international processes. China has relied on African support in the past to overcome staunch international criticism. For example, African votes were crucial to blocking UN Commission on Human Rights resolutions that condemned Chinese human rights abuses.[29] In the words of Premier Wen Jiabao: "China is ready to coordinate its positions with African countries in the process of international economic rules formulation and multilateral trade negotiations."[30] Strategic relationships with Africa will give China, at relatively low cost, the means to secure its position in the World Trade Organization and other multilateral venues.

This clout rankles the United States, which has admonished the PRC not to support "resource-rich countries without regard to the misrule at home or misbehavior abroad of those regimes."[31] Nevertheless, Beijing has secured many African alliances, public and private, through direct aid and concessionary loans with "no political strings" attached. As Premier Wen told African delegates at the 2003 China-Africa Cooperation summit at Addis Ababa, "We do offer our assistance with the deepest sincerity and without any political conditions."[32]

Perhaps the best-known beneficiary of China's "don't ask, don't tell" policy is Sudan. China is both the largest direct foreign investor in, and the largest customer of, Sudan's petroleum production. The PRC owns 13 of the 15 largest companies working in Sudan

and purchases more than 50 percent of Sudan's crude oil.[33] In return, China is arming the Sudanese regime: according to recent Amnesty International reports, it is violating the UN arms embargo by illegally exporting weapons—including fighter jets—to Khartoum at the height of the Darfur conflict. By Amnesty's estimation, the PRC has exported $24 million worth of arms and ammunition, nearly $57 million worth of parts and military equipment, and $2 million worth of helicopters and airplanes to Sudan.[34] If this estimate is correct, then China's implicit willingness to abet genocide puts it squarely at odds with multiple U.S. positions, especially in terms of national security policy. As a permanent member of the UN Security Council, China must realize that its actions contravene the council's own mandatory arms embargo.

In sum, U.S. security interests in Africa are considerable, and Africa's position in the U.S. strategic spectrum has moved from peripheral to central. In 2006, EUCOM's then-commanding general James Jones said that his staff was spending more than half its time on African issues, compared to almost none three years prior.[35] The current EUCOM commander, General Craddock, was unequivocal in his written testimony for Congress: "The increasing strategic significance of Africa will continue to pose the greatest security stability challenge in the EUCOM AOR [Area of Responsibility]. The large ungoverned area in Africa, HIV/AIDS epidemic, corruption, weak governance, and poverty that exist throughout the continent are challenges that are key factors in the security stability issues that affect every country in Africa."[36]

This relatively new interest in Africa is not confined to EUCOM, which currently covers the majority of the continent for the military. The president, for one, has mandated increased interest in Africa. The March 2006 U.S. *National Security Strategy* affirms that "Africa holds growing geo-strategic importance and is a high priority of this Administration," and that "the United States recognizes that our security depends upon partnering with Africans to strengthen fragile and failing states and bring ungoverned areas under the control of effective democracies."[37] AFRICOM is a product of this broad policy. More than a mere map change, it represents a response to the early 21st century's new security environment.

A New Strategic Paradigm

How should AFRICOM help secure Africa, a continent in crisis? It must begin by adopting a new security paradigm, one that regards security and development as inextricably linked and mutually reinforcing. This linkage is the nucleus of the security-development nexus, the strategic paradigm most likely to produce more durable security in Africa.

Since the Cold War's end, development donors have come to realize that if the security sector operates autonomously—with scant regard for the rule of law, democratic principles, and sound management practices—then sustainable, poverty-reducing development is nearly impossible to achieve. Africa has been the recipient of several Marshall Plans worth of foreign aid since World War II's end, yet it remains arguably as impoverished today as it was in 1946. This situation partly stems from the World Bank, U.S. Agency for International Development (USAID), and other organs of development traditionally eschewing security-related development, allowing the cycle of violence in Africa's fragile states to continue.

As U.S. problems in Iraq have shown, if there is a single lesson to be learned from recent nation-building experiences, it is that security is a precondition of development.[38] This axiom should play a central role in formulating a new security strategy for Africa, the most underdeveloped continent on Earth. Sadly, however, U.S. security and development institutions have long been divorced from one another in terms of perspective, operations, and outcomes. USAID is prohibited by law from supporting defense-oriented reform, resulting in a strained toleration of corrupt police forces and abusive militaries that tend to spoil the fruits of development. DOD traditionally shuns noncombat missions, limiting its involvement to narrow venues such as the Joint Combined Exchange Training and Foreign Military Financing programs, which are necessary but insufficient for wholesale security sector transformation. Over time, the schism between these two communities has ossified into interagency intransigence, lack of interoperability, and absence of strategic coordination, all of which have contributed to Africa's failure to develop despite decades of dedicated resources.

AFRICOM's mission should not be development, but the failures of development may drive AFRICOM. This paradoxical relation stems from the principal threats to African security, which are not interstate but intrastate in nature. For example, the largest threat to Liberian security is not a Sierra Leonean blitzkrieg across its border, but internal: guerilla warfare, insurgency, *coup d'etat,* or terrorism. Full-scale invasions of one country by another are uncommon in African military history. African conflicts have sprung mostly from domestic armed opposition groups. Such groups find it easier to change governments through violence rather than through the legitimate means of democracy, given the political exclusion many regimes practice, the paltry rule of law, easy access to small arms, and expanses of ungoverned territory in which to find sanctuary.

Domestic armed groups do have a weakness: they must rely upon local popular support to hide, survive, and thrive within the borders of a country. To attain this support, they must gain public sympathy by exploiting public grievances—real or perceived—that often can be attributed to failures of development. Common grievances include disproportionate distribution of wealth, lack of social justice, political exclusion of some groups, ubiquitous economic hardship, ethnic violence, inadequate public security, and failure of democracy.

To deny the sanctuary in which armed groups incubate and thereby stave off internal conflict, governments must address the root causes of public grievances. These grievances are development based; therefore, the security solution must be development based. The best weapons against intrastate threats often do not fire bullets; in fact, large, idle security forces can incite violence as much as check it. As Jacques Paul Klein, the former special representative of the secretary general for the United Nations mission in Liberia, has quipped, not entirely tongue-in-cheek, many African armies "sit around playing cards and plotting coups."[39]

Only by addressing the challenges of development can security be achieved and maintained. This is the core of the security-development nexus. Failure to heed this linkage results in a "security-development gap," where the lack of security prevents development from taking root, thus perpetuating conflict and compromising development in a vicious cycle. AFRICOM's strategic mandate must be to narrow the security-development gap.

Securing Development

Narrowing the security-development gap does not mean militarizing development. Nor does it mean transforming DOD into an aid agency. Narrowing the gap means shifting military strategic priorities from combat to noncombat operations; it means focusing on conflict prevention rather than conflict reaction. For some, the idea of a military command without a combat orientation is heretical. To others, AFRICOM represents an experiment in early 21st-century security, and potentially serves as a prototype for post-Cold War unified commands. As Deputy Assistant Secretary of Defense Whelan explains, "Ultimately we [were] simply reorganizing the way we do business in DOD. But then we saw an opportunity to do new things, to capture lessons observed since the fall of the Berlin Wall, to create an organization designed for the future and not the past."[40] In many ways, AFRICOM is an opportunity to institutionalize and operationalize peace-building lessons captured over the past 15 years.[41]

The first lesson is that strategic priority should be given to conflict prevention rather than reaction. Owing to the size and complexity of Africa, concentrating on fragile states before they fail or devolve into conflict represents an economy of force. Intervening only after a crisis festers into conflict, as in Somalia in 1993, is costly in terms of American blood, treasure, and international standing. Moreover, such military interventions rarely achieve durable peace because they fail to address the root causes of conflict.

By focusing on pre-conflict operations, AFRICOM will help "prevent problems from becoming crises and crises from becoming conflicts," as the 2006 *Quadrennial Defense Review* advocates.[42] Military campaigns are conventionally understood to proceed in four stages: phase I-"deter/engage," phase II-"seize initiative," phase III-"decisive operations," and phase IV-"transition/stability operations." Recently, military thinkers have introduced an additional phase, "phase zero," which encompasses all activities prior to the beginning of phase I. In other words, phase zero is purely preventative in nature, focusing on everything that can be done to avert conflicts from developing in the first place.[43] In a shift of traditional unified command strategy, AFRICOM should adopt conflict prevention as its primary mission, as Ryan Henry makes clear: "The purpose of the command is . . . what we refer to as anticipatory measures, and those are taking actions that will prevent problems from becoming crises, and crises from becoming conflicts. So the mission of the command is to be able to prevent that."[44]

The second lesson informing AFRICOM is that phase IV, transition/stability operations, may eclipse combat operations when it comes to determining "victory." The situations in Iraq and Afghanistan have made it patently evident that lethal force alone is no longer the decisive variable in military campaigns. To this end, in 2005 the White House issued "National Security Presidential Directive 44," which recognizes the primacy of reconstruction and stabilization operations.[45] Although a rudimentary document, it forms the foundation for interagency coordination of all stability and reconstruction programs. Additionally, that same year the Pentagon issued *DOD Directive 3000.05,* which defines stability operations as a "core U.S. military mission" that "shall be given priority comparable to combat operations."[46] This definition marks a revolution in military strategy for a military that has traditionally focused on fighting and winning wars. Moreover, these new policies are influencing DOD,

State, USAID, and others' funding and program development for 2008 and beyond. This new focus represents a seismic shift in military thought, as it prioritizes noncombat functions above traditional warfighting missions in the pursuit of durable security.

A Civilian-Heavy Military Command

The shift of strategic focus from combat to noncombat missions will require a commensurate shift in how unified commands function. If AFRICOM is expected to supervise an array of missions that are a hybrid of security and development, then it must forge interagency modalities, fusing the capabilities of DOD with State, USAID, and other civilian organizations. This coordination will prove difficult. As Ambassador Loftis puts the challenge, "How do you create a structure that is both a military Unified Command but needs to incorporate enough civilian inputs yet does not appear to take over these agencies and authorities?"[47] Issues concerning organizational structure, institutional culture, lines of authority, funding sources, best practices, and perspectives will mire efforts to create synthesis. Moreover, there are fears—both inside and outside the U.S. Government—that AFRICOM signals the militarization of U.S. foreign aid. Pentagon officials object to this perception, stressing that DOD will not be crossing into "other people's lanes" but simply wants to work more effectively with other agencies, recognizing the symbiotic relationship between it and the interagency in peace-building missions.[48] Only time will tell.

Forging particular interagency modalities will be a gradual process with few shortcuts. The effort was initiated by a decision to staff AFRICOM heavily with interagency civilians, many of them in key decision-making positions and not just traditional liaison roles. In fact, AFRICOM will be the most civilian-heavy unified command in history. In an unprecedented break from tradition, one of two deputy commanders will be a civilian, most likely an ambassador.[49] That DOD sees AFRICOM as becoming a "combatant command plus," with the plus being the exceptionally high number of civilians from other agencies, indicates the department's commitment to addressing security challenges on the continent in a thoroughly interagency manner.[50] But again, this process will take time. As Theresa Whelan confirms, "The command will continue to evolve over time, and will ultimately be an iterative process. It will not become a static organization in October 2008, but will continue to be a dynamic organization, as circumstances merit."[51]

Security Sector Reform

Moving beyond a strategy of conflict prevention and post-conflict transition, the best tactic for narrowing the African security-development gap is SSR. Security sector reform is the essence of "security cooperation," as it builds indigenous capacity and professionalizes the security sector so that African governments can effect development for themselves. As a senior USAID official and member of the AFRICOM transition team with extensive experience in Africa explains, "Security sector reform could contribute to a security architecture that ensures that citizens are provided with effective, legitimate, and democratically accountable external and internal security. What is needed is security sector reform that professionalizes forces for the protection of civilians and enables development. This would be a significant contribution."[52]

SSR is the complex task of transforming organizations and institutions that deal directly with security threats to the state and its citizens. SSR's ultimate objective is to create a security sector that is effective, legitimate, and accountable to the citizens it is sworn to protect. This objective is the essence of "cooperative security," as it can only be achieved in partnership with the host nation, civil society, and other indigenous stakeholders. SSR programs can range from building the capacity of a single military unit, such as a joint-combined exchange training mission, to the total reconstitution of a country's armed forces and ministry of defense, as in the Joint U.S.-Liberia Security Sector Reform Program. SSR is crosscutting transformation, requiring a multidisciplinary, "whole-of-government" approach by the U.S. Government.

DOD's role in SSR is essential but not all-inclusive. Building security-sector capacity and professionalizing actors requires many kinds of expertise, which fundamentally dictates an interagency effort. For example, DOD is not the best agency to train border control forces or set up criminal courts, two parts of the security sector. Rather, the Department of Homeland Security is best suited to train customs and immigration agencies, while the Department of Justice can assist with criminal justice reform. DOD's strong suit is transforming the military sector, which goes far beyond current train-and-equip programs and may entail a comprehensive, soup-to-nuts approach, especially in failed states.

Lastly, institutional transformation is key to SSR, since all institutions must rise together. DOD, for instance, cannot begin to train indigenous soldiers until the ministry of finance has the capacity to pay their salaries, which may be dependent on training from the U.S. Treasury Department. Failure to synchronize development may cause a relapse into conflict, as unpaid soldiers and police forces are a precipitant to violence. AFRICOM will be dependent on other agencies to implement SSR, hence its civilian-heavy nature.[53]

African Perceptions of AFRICOM

Despite DOD's exceptional campaign of consultations on the continent, American efforts to headquarter AFRICOM in Africa have met with resistance. A sampling of headlines from African newspapers is revealing: "Stop AFRICOM;" "New U.S. Command Will Militarise Ties with Africa;" "Wrong for Liberia, Disastrous for Africa;" "Why U.S.'s AFRICOM Will Hurt Africa;" "AFRICOM— the Invasion of Africa?" "Southern Africa says 'No' to U.S. Military Bases In Region;" and "We're Misunderstood, Says U.S."[54] Regional superpowers Nigeria and South Africa have refused to give the U.S. permission to establish AFRICOM on their soil, and they have warned their neighbors to do the same. Morocco, Algeria, and Libya, too, have reportedly refused U.S. requests to base AFRICOM forces in their countries. Member states of such regional organizations as the 14-country Southern African Development Community (SADC) have also agreed not to host AFRICOM, and there is discussion within the 16-country ECOWAS to do the same.[55] South African Defense Minister Mosiuoa Lekota summarizes the sentiment of many countries: "If there was to be an influx of armed forces into one or other of the African countries, that might affect the relations between the sister countries and not encourage an atmosphere and a sense of security." He warns that it would be better for the United States not "to come and make a presence and create uncertainty here."[56]

There are other reasons behind the suspicion and refusals. To name a few, AFRICOM has been equated with CENTCOM, which is fighting wars in Iraq and Afghanistan; the U.S. interest in African oil is well known and perceived to be predatory; and Africa's colonial past has ingrained distrust in its leaders.

Some of the opposition may also be in response to AFRICOM's inability, despite its consultative approach, to articulate its message to Africans. Rwandan General Frank Rusagara, former secretary general of the Rwandan Defense Ministry and top policymaker for Rwanda's military development, expresses a frustration common among military officers on the continent: "The lack of information [about AFRICOM] has resulted in people not knowing what it is and how it will relate to Africa." This statement is especially worrisome because Rusagara is no stranger to U.S. military operations and doctrine: he attended military courses at the U.S. Naval Post-Graduate School in Monterey, California, and the Africa Center for Strategic Studies in Washington, DC. Rusagara thinks that if AFRICOM wants to contribute to African security, it must do three things. First, it must embrace new strategic thinkers and innovative concepts of security, such as "human security," for peace-building in Africa. Second, U.S. officers must explain AFRICOM to their African peers—the command cannot simply rely on senior DOD officials to brief senior African government officials. Third, AFRICOM must enhance African capacity for peacekeeping operations.[57]

Not all African countries have turned their backs on AFRICOM, however. Some, such as Liberia, see it as a boon to the continent. Having just emerged from a brutal 14-year civil war, Liberia has a significant perspective on African security. Liberian Minister of Defense Brownie Samukai explains that AFRICOM has the potential to "build partnerships, lead to the convergence of strategic interest, prevent conflict, and conduct operations other than war." He also believes that professionalizing African militaries through SSR will promote good governance, buttress development, and enhance peacekeeping operations. Samukai adds that supporting AFRICOM does not indicate naiveté about U.S. interests in Africa, but rather shows a willingness to find synergies of interest between the U.S. and African countries. Owing to this understanding, he says, "ECOWAS stands to benefit most in terms of cooperation, interest and intervention, if necessary."[58] Liberia not only supports AFRICOM, but has also offered to host it.

Working with External Organizations

Another major challenge is courting nontraditional military partners early, such as non-government organizations (NGOs) and private voluntary organizations (PVOs).[59] These organizations often know the African lay of the land better than DOD, have decades' worth of operational know-how, are development experts, and have access to places that may be denied to the U.S. military. Moreover, NGOs (both developmental and humanitarian) and DOD have complementary interests in terms of securing development and providing support for complex humanitarian crisis response. Their responses to the 2004 tsunami in Indonesia and the 2005 earthquake in Pakistan demonstrate their convergence.

However, there are several challenges facing this partnership, each of which deserves examination. First, many NGOs are uneasy about working with the U.S. military, believing it puts their people at risk of violent reprisals from groups targeted by U.S. combat operations. As Jim Bishop of InterAction, a large umbrella organization for many NGOs, explains: "Humanitarian organizations

may want to keep some distance between themselves and the U.S. military, especially in environments with potential for violent opposition to the U.S."[60] Second, some NGOs believe that aligning themselves with the military impugns their neutrality or impartiality, sometimes their only guarantee of safety in conflict-prone areas. Similarly, working with neutral or impartial NGOs may prove incompatible for AFRICOM, since "neutral" NGOs do not take sides and "impartial" NGOs give assistance where needed most, even if that conflicts with U.S. interests. Third, Defense's understanding of the complexly diverse NGO community remains limited, and it risks viewing that community as a monolithic whole, which would have adverse consequences. Fourth, AFRICOM might find it difficult to partner with NGOs since they often receive money (and mandates) from multiple countries and sources, do not operate like contractors, and typically demand relative autonomy over program management and outcomes.

Still, there is reason to be hopeful. Currently, both DOD and elements of the NGO community are working to bridge the military-NGO divide. Defense is sensitive to NGO concerns regarding neutrality, as Theresa Whelan acknowledges: "We recognize that their [NGOs'] safety depends upon their neutrality, and we are looking for mechanisms that allow all of us to work together without undermining their mission."[61] Mechanisms under consideration include the African Center for Strategic Studies and the U.S. Institute of Peace (USIP), either of which could function as a "neutral space" for the government and NGOs to jointly explore opportunities for partnership.

Another alternative is working through NGO umbrella organizations like Global Impact or InterAction, which could act as credible interlocutors. Global Impact represents more than 50 U.S.-based international charities (e.g., the overseas Combined Federal Campaign), has worked with DOD in the past, and has even participated in AFRICOM planning cells. InterAction is a coalition of approximately 150 humanitarian organizations that provide disaster relief, refugee assistance, and sustainable development programs worldwide. On 8 March 2005, representatives from DOD, State, USAID, and InterAction met at USIP to launch a discussion of U.S. armed forces and NGO relations in hostile or potentially hostile environments. The meeting yielded pragmatic guidelines that could serve as a foundational model for AFRICOM.[62]

Lastly and perhaps most importantly, AFRICOM should draw on USAID's considerable experience and expertise working with NGOs. USAID staff can help translate perspectives, objectives, and best practices for both NGOs and AFRICOM, thereby deconflicting efforts on the ground and mitigating misunderstanding. As a senior USAID member of the AFRICOM transition team explains, "Effective and agreed upon mechanisms for dialogue could help keep each other informed about each other's efforts and [help everyone] . . . coordinate differing approaches as appropriate. Such dialogue could also provide an opportunity for NGOs to discuss pressing concerns or issues."[63] Although many challenges persist to forging a functional NGO-AFRICOM relationship, there are also many avenues for potential cooperation.

Conclusion: Will It Work?

Skeptics consider achieving durable security in Africa a sisyphusian task, and it probably is, if dependent upon the dominant security paradigm. Therefore AFRICOM must eschew this paradigm and adopt a new strategic focus that links security with development and regards them as inextricably linked and mutually reinforcing—the core of the security-development nexus. In Africa, most armed threats are intrastate in nature and reliant upon the support of the local population to hide, survive, and thrive within the borders of a country. To attain this, they exploit public grievances, real or perceived, that result from the failures of development. However, by "securing development" and narrowing the security-development gap, AFRICOM will deny armed groups their sanctuary, thus fostering durable security on the continent.

Strategically, AFRICOM will narrow this gap by prioritizing conflict prevention and post-conflict transition over traditional "fighting and winning wars." This represents a major shift in military strategy, and it requires a holistic interagency approach to security, hence AFRICOM's extraordinary civilian-heavy structure and unprecedented civilian deputy commander. Tactically, AFRICOM will narrow the gap through security sector reform and other programs that professionalize forces, promote good governance, and help Africans improve their own security. Security sector reform is at the center of AFRICOM's conflict prevention and security cooperation mandate.

Will it work? Clearly it is too early to tell, with major challenges ahead, including instituting interagency best practices, addressing African concerns, and attracting NGO/PVO partners. These challenges may not be resolved by October 2008, but that does not mean AFRICOM will ultimately fail in its bid to stabilize the continent. The strategy it will employ is a promising one, suggesting that there is sufficient reason to be hopeful.

Notes

1. The White House Office of the Press Secretary, "President Bush Creates a Department of Defense Unified Combatant Command for Africa," 6 February 2007.
2. Robert Gates, secretary of defense, in testimony before the Senate Armed Services Committee, 6 February 2007.
3. Robert G. Loftis, ambassador in the State Department's Bureau of Political and Military Affairs and a member of the Africa Command transition team, personal interview, 27 June 2007.
4. It should also be noted that the issue of "seams" is not unique to DOD. The Department of State also divides Africa between sub-Saharan Africa and northern Africa/Middle East, rather than treat the continent as an organic whole. The Bureau of African Affairs is responsible for sub-Saharan Africa and the Bureau of Near Eastern Affairs is responsible for northern Africa and the Middle East.
5. Gates testimony.
6. AFRICOM Public Brief, United States Department of Defense, 2 February 2007.
7. Lauren Ploch, "Africa Command: U.S. Strategic Interests and the Role of the U.S. Military in Africa," CRS Report for Congress, 16 May 2007, 9.
8. Ryan Henry, Principal Deputy Under Secretary of Defense, Office of the Secretary of Defense, DOD News press briefing, 23 April 2007.
9. Theresa M. Whelan, Deputy Assistant Secretary of Defense of African Affairs, Office of the Secretary of Defense, personal interview, 9 July 2007.
10. Henry press briefing.
11. The National Security Strategy United States of America (September 2002), 1.
12. For more information, see Peter Pham, "Next Front? Evolving United States–African Strategic Relations in the 'War on Terrorism' and Beyond," Comparative Strategy 26 (2007): 39–54.
13. Central Intelligence Agency, Global Trends 2015: A Dialogue About the Future With Non-government Experts, December 2000.
14. Edward Harris, "Oil Boom, Politics Shape Africa's Future," Associated Press, 29 June 2007.
15. Ploch, CRS Report, 12.
16. Tony Capaccio, "Securing African Oil a Major Role for New Command (Update1)," Bloomberg.com, 18 May 2007.
17. "Progress Report of the Secretary-General: Causes of Conflict and the Promotion of Durable Peace and Sustainable Development in Africa," UN Report A/59/285, 20 August 2004.
18. For more information about GPOI/ACOTA and U.S. interest, see Nina M. Serafino, "The Global Peace Operations Initiative: Background and Issues for Congress," CRS Report RL32773, 11 June 2007.
19. Jim Fisher-Thompson, "US Military Training Program Benefits African Peacekeepers," U.S.INFO, 20 March 2007, <http://usinfo.state.gov> (14 July 2007).
20. Colin L. Powell, Secretary of State, speech at the Gheskio Clinic, Port-au-Prince, Haiti, 5 April 2004.
21. UNAIDS, AIDS Epidemic Update, December 2006.
22. Kevin A. O'Brien, "Headlines Over the Horizon: AIDS and African Armies," Atlantic Monthly 292, no. 1, July/August 2003.
23. "That's all they needed," The Economist, 8 December 2007.
24. "Guinea-Bissau: Pushers' Paradise," The Economist, 7 June 2007.
25. CIA World Factbook, Guinea-Bissau, <https://www.cia.gov/library/publications/the-world-factbook/geos/pu.html> (13 July 2007).
26. Donovan C. Chau, "Political Warfare in Sub-Saharan Africa: U.S. Capabilities and Chinese Operations in Ethiopia, Kenya, Nigeria, and South Africa" (monograph, Strategic Studies Institute, 26 March 2007).
27. Capaccio.
28. See <http://news.xinhuanet.com/english/2006-01/12/content_4042521_3.htm> (14 July 2007).
29. Chris Alden, "Emerging countries as new ODA players in LDCs: The case of China and Africa," Institut du développement durable et des relations internationales, 01/2007.
30. BBC Monitoring Asia, 15 December 2003.
31. National Security Strategy, 42.
32. Peoples Daily, 16 December 2003, <www.englishpeopledaily.com.cn>.
33. Peter Pham, "China Goes on Safari," World Defense Review, 24 August 2006.
34. Amnesty International Report, AI Index: AFR 54/019/2007, May 2007, Amnesty International Report, AI Index: ASA 17/030/2006, June 2006.
35. Greg Mills, "World's Biggest Military Comes to Town," Business Day, 9 February 2007.
36. Bantz J. Craddock, General, Commander U.S. Southern Command, Testimony to the Senate Armed Services Committee, 19 September 2006.

37. *National Security Strategy.*

38. For more information on the preconditions of nation-building see James Dobbins, Seth G. Jones, Keith Crane, Beth Cole, "The Beginner's Guide to Nation-Building," *RAND Corporation Monograph MG-557,* 2007.

39. Jacques Paul Klein, Special Representative of the Secretary General, UN Mission in Liberia, statement made 5 November 2003.

40. Whelan interview.

41. In some ways, Southern Command (SOUTHCOM) is a model for AFRICOM, as it has incorporated some of the security-development lessons learned since the end of the Cold War. However, AFRICOM is envisaged to expand this model significantly.

42. *Quadrennial Defense Review,* 6 February 2006, 17.

43. General Charles Wald, "The Phase Zero Campaign," *Joint Force Quarterly* 43 (4th Quarter 2006).

44. Henry, press briefing. See also, *Quadrennial Defense Review,* 17.

45. President, "National Security Presidential Directive 44: Management of Interagency Efforts Concerning Reconstruction and Stabilization," 7 December 2005.

46. *DOD Directive 3000.05: Military Support for Stability, Security, Transition, and Reconstruction (SSTR) Operations,* 28 November 2005.

47. Loftis interview.

48. Whelan interview.

49. Henry press briefing.

50. "Pentagon: AFRICOM Won't Boost U.S. Troop Presence on the Continent," *Inside the Army,* 12 February 2007.

51. Whelan interview.

52. USAID senior conflict mitigation advisor and member of the AFRICOM Transition Team, personal interview, 16 August 2007.

53. Currently, the U.S. Institute of Peace is working with DOD and other U.S. agencies to develop a "whole of government" approach to SSR.

54. Editorial, "Stop AFRICOM," *Leadership* (Abuja), 28 September 2007, Salim Lone, "New U.S. Command Will Militarise Ties with Africa," *Daily Nation,* 9 February 2007; Ezekiel Pajibo and Emira Woods, "AFRICOM: Wrong for Liberia, Disastrous for Africa," *Foreign Policy in Focus,* 26 July 2007; Michele Ruiters, "Why U.S.'s AFRICOM Will Hurt Africa," *Business Day* (Johannesburg), 14 February 2007; Obi Nwakanma, "AFRICOM—the Invasion of Africa?" *Vanguard* (Lagos), 18 November 2007; Isdore Guvamombe, "Southern Africa says 'No' to U.S. Military Bases In Region," *The Guardian,* 26 September 2007; Oyedele Abuja, "'We're Misunderstood,' Says U.S.," *This Day* (Lagos), 30 November 2007.

55. Guvamombe.

56. Shaun Benton, "Africa opposed to U.S. command base," *BuaNews,* 29 August 2007.

57. General Frank Rusagara, Rwanda Defence Forces, personal interview, 1 December 2007.

58. Brownie Samukai, Liberian Minister of Defense, personal interview, 30 November 2007.

59. For the purposes of this discussion, NGOs and PVOs will be treated as the same.

60. Jim Bishop, Vice President for Humanitarian Policy and Practice InterAction, personal interview, 29 June 2007.

61. Whelan interview.

62. *Guidelines for Relations Between U.S. Armed Forces And Non-Governmental Humanitarian Agencies,* <http: www.usip.org/pubs.guidelines_pamphlet.pdf> (21 August 2007).

63. USAID senior conflict mitigation advisor interview.

SEAN MCFATE is an expert in African security policy. He was a principal architect of U.S. peace-building efforts in Liberia, Burundi, and Sudan, including the Liberian Security Sector Reform Program. Previously, he served as an officer in the U.S. Army's 82nd Airborne Division. Mr. McFate holds a master of public policy from Harvard University's Kennedy School of Government and dual bachelor's degrees from Brown University.

From *Military Review,* January/February 2008, pp. 10–21.

Bottom-Up Nation Building

AMITAI ETZIONI

The tired debate between those who believe in nation-building and those who scoff at it glosses over a major difference between top-down and bottom-up society building. The starting point for a bottom-up approach is the communitarian recognition that societies—even modern, so-called "mass" societies—are not composed of just millions upon millions of individual citizens. Instead, most societies are communities of communities. Most people come in social packages. They are greatly influenced by the communities of which they are members and by their natural leaders. These communities are not necessarily residential—the traditional village—but may be ethnic, religious, or based on national origin.

This is not to suggest that individuals do not have degrees of freedom or that their behavior is determined in full by their communities. It merely points out that communities have a profound effect on what seem like individual choices, from voting to purchasing to eating and beyond. Moreover, American national society was formed to a significant extent only after the Civil War. Before that, most Americans' prime loyalty was to the colony, state, or region in which they lived. When asked overseas, "Where are you from?" Americans used to answer, "I am Virginian" or "I am Bostonian." Only after the 1870s did more and more Americans respond, "I am American." Only during the Reconstruction period did the Supreme Court stop referring to the United States as a plurality ("The United States are") and start referring to the nation as a singular entity ("The United States is"). It took a very bloody war and a generation of society building afterwards to make the South and the North into one political community—a process that is still ongoing. Many other countries we now know as nations were similarly cobbled together, including the United Kingdom, Germany, Italy, and Switzerland.

I point to these familiar pieces of sociological history because we tend to ignore them when we deal with countries that have not yet made much progress along these society building, communitarian lines—whether or not they are called nations or have flags, seats at the United Nations, and diplomatic representatives in the capitals of the world. For instance: Iraq, Pakistan, and above all, Afghanistan.

Think Tribes, Not a Nation

Given the power and import of communities (often referred to as "tribes"), the issue here is not whether we can or should avoid engaging in nation building, but how we proceed. Do we make our starting point the notion that there is a central national government, whose troops and police we can train as a national force and whose administration of justice and social services we can improve? Or, do we realize that such a center-to-periphery approach is unworkable, and that we need to build from the periphery to the center? This does not mean that we should go find individual citizens to "empower" and work with them. Instead, we should look at places like Afghanistan as lands in which several tribes lie next to each other. (I use the term "tribes" loosely, referring to ethnic and confessional communities whose members have tribe-like ties to one another, ties they do not have to members of other communities.) In other words, there are many societies in which nation building cannot start from the center—and those who insist otherwise pay a heavy price.

Howard Hart, a member of the CIA clandestine service for 25 years and former CIA Chief of Station in Islamabad, observes that "Afghan" is purely a geographic distinction and that "there is not, and never has been, anything remotely approaching a shared national identity." He finds that tribal loyalties in the region are paramount, and "warlords" (or tribal chiefs) are loath to subordinate themselves to a higher authority, especially one fostered by foreign powers. I would temper this argument a bit and suggest that these tribal leaders have some sense of national citizenship. However, and this is the crucial point, when their tribal loyalty conflicts with their national one, their tribal loyalty tends to prevail. J. Alexander Thier, the Director for Afghanistan and Pakistan at the U.S. Institute of Peace, and Jarat Chopra, a former professor at Brown University, write that in Afghanistan, "family and tribal affiliations outweigh all others." And according to a recently published article in *Special Warfare,* a quarterly of the United States Army, "[tribal elders] are not willing to place a united Afghanistan over advancement of their particular tribe."

This tribal primacy is in part due to the fact that many of these nations were created by foreign powers drawing lines on a map that clumped several tribes, who had little in common and much separating them, into a single territory. These tribes were not asking for a more encompassing community—for a nation—but were forcibly joined by colonial powers. Moreover—as in several countries that we now consider well-established nations—the tribes are now vying with one another, in part through civil wars, for control over the nature and leadership of the union-to-be. I am not saying that such strife is to be welcomed or that, to the extent possible, one should not seek to find nonviolent ways for, say, the Shia and Sunni or the Pashtuns, Tajik, Uzbek, and Hazara to work out their differences and form stable communities of communities. However, anyone familiar with the history of Western nations should not act as if these nations did not pass through similar violent phases.

Design versus Trends

In discussing the ways in which Afghanistan and other such unstable states can become the kind of nation that we hold is best for them (and us), we tend to start with what political scientists call "design questions." Implicit is the notion that we are builders and have the needed raw material to build regimes following a blueprint we lay out. Typically, we seek a modern state with a strong national army and police force, a low level of corruption, a proficient civil service, a trustworthy justice system, democratic institutions, and open markets. And we take it for granted that loyalty to the central government will take precedence over loyalty to any member community, to any tribe.

This position is sometimes associated with the policy of nation building that Governor George W. Bush scoffed at and then promoted once he became the president of the United States, pursuing it relentlessly in Iraq. President Obama's first strategic review of the situation in Afghanistan, completed in March 2009, set much more limited goals, namely "to disrupt, dismantle, and defeat al Qaeda in Pakistan and Afghanistan and to prevent their return to either country in the future." However, the advocates of nation building soon interpreted this as necessitating winning the hearts and minds of the population, which in turn requires providing them with security, economic development, and an efficient, functioning government.

One of the most important advisers to General Stanley McChrystal, Anthony H. Cordesman, a senior scholar at the Center for Strategic and International Studies, calls for the U.S. forces "to 'hold' and keep the Afghan population secure, and 'build' enough secure local governance and economic activity to give Afghans reason to trust their government and allied forces." Representative Jane Harman, a leading member of the House Intelligence Committee, believes that "it's too early to abandon a strategy focused on protecting the population and rebuilding the country." General McChrystal believes that we must ". . . promote good local governance, root out corruption, reform the justice sector, pursue narcotics traffickers, [and] increase reconstruction activities."

Instead of starting with such a "design" approach, though, we must first ask what the reality on the ground looks like and in what direction it is changing before we intervene. The main reason we must adopt this focus is that our leverage is much smaller than we tend to imagine. Hence, we must focus the use of those resources that are available to ride trends that are unfolding anyhow and seek to redirect them somewhat, rather than seeking to fashion new ones out of whole cloth. Thus, we should ask at what stage in their sociological history are these failing states? What kind of societal structures do they have? What are their innate dynamics? Then we will be ready to seek ways to build on these existing structures and trends.

One of the greatest insights of the neoconservatives, one which carried them forward for a long time both as public intellectuals and as political counselors, was the recognition that there are great limits to social engineering, that societies tend to be highly resistant to change, and that design drives initiated by governments are prone to failure. Sadly, they ignored the fact that the same grand insight that applied to Los Angeles, Chicago, and New York also applies in full to Helmand and Kandahar, Basra and Swat.

Cases in Point

In Iraq, it is all too obvious, most citizens' main loyalties are to major "tribal" groups, especially the Sunni, Shia, and Kurds, and a few other smaller ones (Arabs and Turkmens). Within each of these, there are subcommunities (or clans) that tend to rival each other. These communities command a strong sense of loyalty from their members. They have a clear and strong sense of "do's" and "don'ts" specific to their community and duties to the common—tribal—good. They have distinct religious beliefs and rituals, tribal leaders, and tribal councils. And they have armies, arms, and ways of raising revenue.

We will probably never find out to what extent the surge in the number of American troops in Iraq in 2007 served as a turning point in the war there, and to what extent a tribal deal made the difference. However, a strong case can be made that a major part of the success attributed to the surge was actually due to the deal the United States made with a group of Sunni sheikhs—a deal known as the "Awakening"—which turned them from a major force of insurgency to one that supported the regime and fought for security. In other parts of Iraq, working with local tribes or clans has also made a considerable difference. For instance, in June 2007, U.S. and Iraqi forces reached agreements with ten Iraqi tribes in the Baghdad area to help in the fight against al Qaeda. In October of that year, the U.S. military reported that attack levels were steadily declining.

Most dramatically, there were next to no American or other coalition forces in northern Iraq, the area in which Kurdish tribes dominate, and yet the area was peaceful. This was the case because the Kurds used their very sizeable armed force, the peshmerga, to maintain security. In a February 2007 interview. Major General Benjamin Mixon, the commanding officer of U.S. forces in northern Iraq and Kurdistan, told *60 Minutes* that of the 20,000 troops under his command, a mere 60 or 70 were stationed in Kurdistan. Because Kurdish areas are patrolled by Kurdish troops, "there's no need" for an American presence in Kurdistan. The U.S. and its allies suffered next to no casualties in this sizable area.

In Pakistan, which is more of a cohesive nation than either Iraq or Afghanistan, there are still major tribal forces at play.

In Pakistan, which is more of a cohesive nation than Iraq and Afghanistan, there are still major tribal forces at play. It is well known that there are seven tribes in Waziristan that govern themselves, have considerable armed forces, and do not recognize the Pakistani government. Beyond that, there is also much tension between the Punjabi-dominated government and the Pashtun tribes in the mountainous borderlands, some of which had an autonomous status until 2002 and seek to be integrated into an, at least, semi-independent Pashtun province. In short, what seems to Westerners a fight between the central government and some rebellious citizens is, to a significant extent, a confrontation between Punjabis and Pashtuns. Thus, even here, in a nation that is more unified than Afghanistan, an analysis of where we are and the ways in which we can proceed should start with an examination of the tribal tensions and the means by which their differences may be worked out (e.g., greater autonomy for the Pashtuns), rather than from the assumption that there is or can be in the short order an effective national government that will command the loyalty of most of its citizens.

In Afghanistan, the Taliban were defeated in 2001, with very few American casualties. During the 2001 air and ground campaign that drove the Taliban out of major Afghan cities, only 12 American service members were lost. The war was instead won by an American-supported coalition of several tribes, mainly Tajik, Uzbek, and Hazara, known as the Northern Alliance.

Security: Tribal Bests National

The implications of the cases just briefly visited are especially important for the formation of native security forces. Americans tend to take for granted that these ought to be national forces, although even in the United States, much police work is locally and not nationally controlled. The National Guard can be called up only by the governors of the various states and each unit primarily serves its own state. Yet, in Iraq, after American-led coalition forces removed the Saddam regime, the United States and its allies tried to create a national force in Iraq by insisting that Sunni, Shia, and Kurdish units either disarm or integrate. Moreover, the United States positioned Shia forces in Sunni areas and Sunni forces in Shia areas, on the grounds that they should cease to view themselves as tribal forces and start acting like "Iraqis." The result was often increased bloodshed. (One may argue that Saddam had a national army. However, it was in effect dominated by one tribal grouping, the Sunnis, with most officers drawn from one clan, Albu Ghafour. The Shia majority felt alienated and oppressed. Indeed, both the Shia and the Kurds fought against Saddam's "national" army.)

A similar development took place in Afghanistan. In the aftermath of the defeat of the Taliban in 2001, the new Afghan government sought to disarm the tribal forces that had ousted the Taliban, what the government referred to as the AMF (Afghan Militia Forces), in favor of fashioning a new Afghan national army. As a result of this Disarmament, Demobilization, and Reintegration (DDR), about 63,000 militiamen were disarmed by 2005. However, there are still a great number of unofficial tribal forces. Estimates of their size run between 65,000 and 180,000.

Moreover, according to Selig Harrison, the United States has helped the Tajik minority gain control of many key levels of government, including the armed forces and important security agencies. These forces often operate in the Pashtun areas in which the Taliban are particularly strong, due to their proximity to Pakistan (the Pashtun are concentrated in southeastern Afghanistan) and because the Pashtun are more supportive of the Taliban than other tribes. The UN reports that Tajiks comprise 70 percent of the battalion commanders in the army, and many of the army units sent to Pashtun areas are composed mainly of Tajiks who do not speak Pashto. And while the U.S. supported Karzai in order to put a Pashtun face on the government, other Pashtuns consider him a turncoat, a sort of Uncle Tom.

As Seth Jones, a political scientist at the RAND Corporation, testified before the House of Representatives Foreign Affairs Committee,

> The United States and others in the international community have focused the bulk of their efforts since 2001 in trying to create a strong central government capable of establishing security and delivering services. This goal is ahistorical in Afghanistan and it is not likely to be effective. In addition, the local nature of power in Afghanistan—including in Pashtun areas of the country which are populated by a range of tribes, sub-tribes, clans, and qawms—makes this objective unpopular among many Afghans, who remain skeptical of a strong central government.

Beyond the very serious issue of loyalty, the center-to-periphery nation building approach runs into difficulties because of especially high levels of corruption and attempts to hold the new national forces to Western standards. When local Afghans deal with members of the national police or army, they report that they are exploited, subjected to endless demands for cash and goods, and given little protection. This is due to a culture in which corruption is endemic and to the fact that the soldiers and police are not locals. They take their cut and are soon assigned elsewhere.

In contrast to the national forces, members of tribal forces live with their fellow tribe members, who are often related to them as kin, and while they are far from free of corruption, they tend to show more self-restraint. They have also shown a willingness to fight for their own kind, while members of the national forces often do not show up and avoid fighting. Furthermore, national forces demonstrate a remarkable level of disloyalty to the nation. There are reports of members of the national police selling to the Taliban arms provided by the West, of members of the national army delaying American military operations to give the Taliban time to set up ambushes, and of other betrayals of their government and their Western allies.

The vision of building a central national police and army also suffers because of sociological ignorance. Western trainers and advisers are trying to convert the Afghan army and police forces into units that adhere to Western ethical and legal standards of professionalism. Thus, a Western trainer cannot stand by if an Afghan trainee does not show the proper attitude toward women, suspects, or minors. No wonder, given the deep and strong differences between Afghan and Western culture, that after eight years, the number of successfully trained police officers is still rather small. The training of the army has progressed more successfully, but for the same reasons it is still far below the level needed if national forces are to be relied upon.

All this suggests that the U.S. and its allies in Afghanistan should work with the local tribal forces and their natural leaders, and shift major resources currently dedicated to the national army and police to help shore up the local forces rather than seeking to dismantle them. Each local force can be responsible for security in the areas of its tribe.

Such suggestions are challenged by the observation that the Afghans do not want a decentralized government. James Dobbins of the RAND Corporation has noted that Afghans want a central government, but a very weak one. Barnett Rubin, professor at New York University, who has studied Afghanistan for 26 years, writes that he does not know any Afghans who want decentralization. Moreover, the constitution that Afghanistan adopted in 2004 does not accommodate a federation.

These are all well-taken points—if one approaches the subject from the viewpoint of a legal scholar or a political scientist. However, speaking as a sociologist, one notes that Afghans already have a de facto societal federation (or even a confederation) in terms of the ways they govern themselves. In effect, Afghans have a high level of regional, cultural, social, and even political self-determination. They reject the government in Kabul, especially because it was fashioned by foreigners and has lost much of whatever legitimacy it had due to association with drug lords and the heavy-handed manipulation of the 2009 elections. In the long run, one may work with the tribal leaders to integrate their armies into a national force and to slowly move towards implementing Western standards with regards to individual and minority rights and professional, modern modes of fighting. In the short run, working with sizable tribal armies seems much more likely to succeed: This is what I mean by moving from the periphery to the center rather than from the center to the periphery. Instead of trying to break the tribal authorities and undermine tribal loyalties and structures, we must build upon them and move towards coalition building, which may gradually lead to society-wide commitments and forces.

Recently the United States and its allies faced an unfortunate development: The tribes united against the United States.

Recently the U.S. and its allies, reluctant to deal with tribal leaders, faced an unfortunate development: The tribes united *against* the U.S. In the summer of 2009, Admiral Michael Mullen reported that the situation in Afghanistan was "serious" and "deteriorating." In September 2009, General McChrystal echoed these sentiments, writing, "Although considerable effort and sacrifice have resulted in some progress, many indicators suggest the overall effort is deteriorating." One of the main reasons: Many Tajiks (led by, among others, warlord Ghulam Yahya), who previously were relatively supportive of the U.S. and the Karzai government have now joined the Pashtun in opposing both.

Natural Leaders and Elected Leaders

An essential feature of a stable and adaptable political system is the availability of institutions that can be used to settle differences without resorting to violence. We tend to assume that these political institutions will be democratic and that various particularistic interests will be represented by elected officials. In this way, as the saying goes, ballots will replace bullets. In Iraq and Afghanistan, the United States and its allies invested considerable effort into introducing free and fair elections, in part to serve the purpose of absorbing intertribal conflicts into political institutions.

Given that the format of the introduced institutions was greatly influenced by the United States, however, they often did not reflect the preferences of the Iraqi or Afghani people. For instance, when it came time to draft an interim constitution for Iraq, L. Paul Bremer, head of the Coalition Provisional Authority, stated that he would veto any document that made Islam the sole source of legislation, despite the fact that the two main Shia parties called for the institution of sharia. The differences between American requirements and local preferences resulted in odd compromises in both the interim and final constitutions of Iraq. For example, Article II of the constitution stipulates that "No law may be enacted that contradicts the established provisions of Islam" and that "No law may be enacted that contradicts the rights and basic freedoms stipulated in this Constitution." Additionally, the United States pushed to give more authority to the national government and opposed greater autonomy for regional bodies that largely parallel the tribes, a federalism preferred by many Iraqis. In Afghanistan, the U.S. insisted that the constitution be drafted and approved by consensus before the election of the National Assembly and national officials, and it promoted Karzai as the national leader. None of these moves helped lend legitimacy to political institutions that were imported and alien to begin with.

Often, native people have their own institutions and ways of selecting leaders and resolving conflicts—tribal councils, for instance, or community elders. Religious authorities also serve to guide, influence policies, and resolve differences. That is, the people often rely on natural leaders—those who rose to power due to their charisma, persuasive powers, lineage, or religious status, but who were not elected in the Western way. Initially, one had best try to work with them, rather than expect that they could be replaced by elected officials in short order. The same holds for tribal councils and intertribal bodies.

To understand the influence of natural leaders, one could consider the case of Ismail Khan. After the defeat of the Taliban, Ismail Khan, a warlord in Herat, Afghanistan, became governor of the area. Despite his ability to maintain security. Khan's support of Iran and his refusal to send the tax revenues he collected to the central government, coupled with a wish to strengthen Karzai, led the United States to urge for his removal. Khan was removed from his local post in 2004, a move that resulted in violent protests, sectarian violence, increased crime, and the Taliban making inroads into Herat. Similarly, Governor Gul Agha Shirzai of the Nangarhar province was removed from a previous gubernatorial position for his autocratic, warlord style, but is now seen as necessary to stabilize the province.

While the United States, at least until very recently, tended to avoid working with tribal chiefs, Karzai has been courting them assiduously.

While the United States, at least until very recently, tended to avoid working with tribal chiefs, Karzai has been courting them assiduously. Indeed, they played a key role in mobilizing various tribes to support his reelection. (Working with tribal leaders raises ethical questions that require separate treatment. One should note, though, that even if the U.S. and its allies avoid them, the national government the West is propping up does not. That is, they are prominently in the picture, one way or the other.)

Seth Jones reports that a strategy that seeks to build a strong central government and to hold territory with foreign forces is unlikely to work in Afghanistan. He reports that the national presidential elections in 2004 and parliamentary elections in 2005 did little to diminish the power of regional warlords and tribal militias. Even efforts that were made to relocate such leaders and wrest them from their regional power bases were unsuccessful. Instead of attempting (and failing) to break these solid ties, strategists should draw upon them to promote security in Afghanistan. Jones points out that a successful bottom-up strategy must strengthen the local tribal and religious leaders who understand their communities best, so that they may provide security and services. Indeed, he writes, "the most effective bottom-up strategy in Afghanistan is likely to be one that already taps into existing local institutions . . . Local tribal and religious leaders best understand their community needs."

Similarly, Clare Lockhart, an expert on Afghanistan, told the Senate Foreign Relations Committee, that what was needed was a "'light touch' form of governance . . . where formal structures . . . can 'mesh' with local and traditional networks and social organizations . . . Networks of traditional birth attendants, hawala dealers, traders, ulema, and teachers can all be mobilized or partnered with for different tasks." In a 2008 survey, the Asia Foundation found that local representative bodies (both traditional ones such as the shura and jirga and newer ones such as the Community Development Councils and Provincial Councils) enjoy the support of about two-thirds of the population. In addition, almost 70 percent said that religious leaders should be involved in local government decision-making.

The reluctance of the United States to build on the tribal power structure is one major reason its attempts to break away the moderate Taliban from the insurgents in Afghanistan have failed. According to Fotini Christia, assistant professor of political science at MIT, and Michael Semple, a regional specialist focusing on Afghanistan and Pakistan, individual fighters are generally "operating within their home provinces, where their relationship to the local population is defined by their tribal status and political back-ground." In Iraq, it was sheikhs who played the major role in the Sunni Awakening movement (and not the Sunni's elected representatives in Baghdad), and they were the leaders the U.S. commanders turned to in the Anbar region (which includes Fallujah). These sheikhs were the leaders who decided to cooperate with the United States in taking on al Qaeda in Iraq, routing them from the region.

The necessity of working with tribal leaders in Afghanistan is a lesson the British learned in the 1800s.

The necessity of working with tribal leaders in Afghanistan is a lesson the British learned in the 1800s, when efforts at colonization were failing. Instead of continuing to engage in a military undertaking, the British paid subsidies to the tribal leaders on the borders but otherwise let them control their own areas, thus turning them away from those who threatened British interests. Working with tribal leaders is still a strategy, albeit in a modifled form, which current British officials support.

Working with tribal and religious leaders will not only help us establish security but also lead to a much more efficient use of aid money. To date, USAID projects have been poorly planned and badly administered, reflecting American unfamiliarity with Afghan culture and terrain. In the summer of 2009, Richard Holbrooke called the campaigns to eradicate poppy crops and USAID's alternative employment programs the "most wasteful, most ineffective program I have ever seen." To provide one example, in late 2005, USAID funded a project which put people to work building cheap, but labor-intensive cobblestone roads. When the project was completed, the contractor learned that the local leaders objected: Cobblestone hurt camels' hooves, and they wanted gravel and asphalt roads.

Again, it is not necessary to ally oneself with tribal chiefs no matter how authoritarian they are, although the question stands to what extent a foreign power should intervene in the internal political development of these countries, on both principled and pragmatic grounds. However, it is essential to make the leaders in place the cornerstone of *starting* an alliance.

Religious authorities can play this role. The United States must overcome its reluctance to work with religious leaders and instead embrace and even favor them—but only those who reject violence, of course. A prime example is Grand Ayatollah Sayyid Ali al-Husayni al-Sistani, the most important Shia cleric in Iraq. He is very influential among the largest Iraqi confessional group (some 60 percent of Iraqis are Shia) and a strong advocate of nonviolence. Initially, the United States sought to marginalize him. The reasons are telling: He is not elected by voters, and thus does not fit the democratic model. The U.S. believes that separation of religion and state should be promoted in other nations despite the fact that many democracies do not draw such a line, and the U.S. is increasingly finding ways to bridge the two worlds at home. American agencies acting overseas, especially the State Department, are very uneasy when they have to deal with religious figures, both because many American civil servants are not devout, and because they believe that it would violate the law to use U.S. taxpayer money to support religious authorities. However, if one returns to what I suggested is the essential prerequisite for sound policies—that one start from where people are, not from where we believe they ought to be—one cannot ignore that many of the most influential people in the countries in which terrorists thrive are religious authorities.

Seeking to marginalize or dismiss these leaders merely undermines much that the U.S. seeks to accomplish—regardless of whether or not it should be in the business of promoting secular regimes in the first place. In short, building up from the periphery means initially accepting the tribal groups and their natural leaders, traditional and religious leaders included.

Ultimately, the question of the extent to which one should rely on tribal forces, and not on a national police or army, to maintain order depends on the goals foreign powers set for themselves. If the main goal is to build a stable democracy and a modern economy, promoting national forces is called for though still in the gradual, transitional way already indicated. However, pursuing these goals, given the high level of corruption and the lack of commitment of Afghanistan's leaders to a democratic state makes it likely that the U.S. and its allies will have to stay in that country for decades and commit a large amount of resources there. Thomas Friedman, who is a master at putting things succinctly, wrote in the *New York Times,* "This is State-Building 101: our partners, the current Afghan police and government, are so corrupt that more than a few Afghans prefer the Taliban. With infinite time, money, soldiers and aid workers, we can probably reverse that. But we have none of these."

In contrast, if the purpose of U.S. policy is, as President Obama concluded in March 2009, "to disrupt, dismantle, and defeat al Qaeda in Pakistan and Afghanistan and to prevent their return to either country in the future," much can be done by relying on tribal forces, their natural leaders, and intertribal coalitions. At least, communitarians would argue, this is the level at which all restructuring of failing states like Afghanistan must be started.

AMITAI ETZIONI is University Professor and Professor of International Affairs at the George Washington University.

UNIT 3

The Domestic Side
of American Foreign Policy

Unit Selections

Key Points to Consider

- Should policymakers listen to the U.S. public in making foreign policy decisions? Defend your answer.

- What types of foreign policy issues are the American public most informed about?

- Conduct a public opinion poll to measure the relative support for internationalism and isolationism among students. What did you expect to find? Were your expectations correct?

- In what ways is U.S. foreign policy true to traditional American values?

- What is the most effective way for Americans to express their views on foreign policy to policymakers?

- What important foreign policy issues are not being talked about today?

- Does global involvement threaten to destroy American national values? If so, what steps might be taken to prevent this from happening?

Student Website
www.mhhe.com/cls

Internet References

American Diplomacy
    www.unc.edu/depts/diplomat/
Carnegie Endowment for International Peace (CEIP)
    www.ceip.org
PEW Research Center Reports on Global Affairs/Public Attitudes
    http://pewresearch.org/topics/globalattitudesforeignaffairs/
RAND
    www.rand.org

Conventional political wisdom holds that foreign policy and domestic policy are two very different policy arenas. Not only are the origins and gravity of the problems different, but the political rules for seeking solutions are dissimilar. Where partisan politics, lobbying, and the weight of public opinion are held to play legitimate roles in the formulation of health, education, or welfare policy, they are seen as corrupting influences in the making of foreign policy. An effective foreign policy demands a quiescent public, one that gives knowledgeable professionals the needed leeway to bring their expertise to bear on the problem. It demands a Congress that unites behind presidential foreign policy doctrines rather than one that investigates failures or pursues its own agenda. In brief, if American foreign policy is to succeed, politics must stop "at the water's edge."

This conventional wisdom has never been shared by all who write about American foreign policy. Two very different groups of scholars have dissented from this inclination to neglect the importance of domestic influences on American foreign policy. One group holds that the essence of democracy lies in the ability of the public to hold policymakers accountable for their decisions, and therefore, elections, interest group lobbying, and other forms of political expression are just as central to the study of foreign policy as they are to the study of domestic policy. A second group of scholars sees domestic forces as important because they feel that the fundamental nature of a society determines a country's foreign policy. These scholars direct their attention to studying the influence of forces such as capitalism, American national style, and the structure of elite values.

The terrorist attack of September 11, 2001, altered the domestic politics of American foreign policy at least for the short run. Unity replaced division in the aftermath of the attacks as the public rallied behind President Bush. This unity began to fray somewhat as the Bush administration made its case for war with Iraq, but overall it remained in place. Domestic political forces began to reassert themselves after President Bush declared that major fighting had ended. Now issues such as the cost of the war, the length of time American forces would remain in Iraq, the constant attacks on American occupying forces, and the handling of prewar intelligence came under close scrutiny. By June 2004, for the first time, public opinion polls showed a majority of Americans (54.6%) saying sending troops to Iraq was a mistake and that the war had made the United States less safe from terrorism.

As Barack Obama began his presidency, the influence of domestic politics on the conduct of American foreign policy was quite evident—although not as intense as that which was found in the last years of the Bush administration, which saw a growing split among the American public over the legitimacy and purpose of the war in Iraq. Additionally, revelations of administration approved spying by the National Security Agency on Americans in the name of the war on terrorism brought forward charges that Bush had overstepped his constitutional powers as president. Obama's foreign policy honeymoon was brief.

Department of Defense/U.S. Air Force photo by Staff Sgt. Larry E. Reid Jr.

The lengthy decision making process his administration entered into over Afghanistan provided an opportunity for criticism across the political spectrum on his handling of foreign policy. His decision to send additional troops seemed to please few, although it aroused little opposition. Republicans wished for a stronger statement and Democrats, while supportive, were largely unsupportive of the war. A coup in Honduras was opposed by the administration and most governments in Latin America, but supported by Republicans who used it as an opportunity to block administration foreign policy appointments to the region. The Copenhagen global environmental summit, which in the end produced little by way of an agreement, brought forward a warning about entering into agreements that did not adequately protect American interests. It does not appear that the next years of Obama's administration will see a significant reduction in partisan political conflict. The global economic slowdown makes free trade a volatile issue and arms control agreements are scheduled to be a major item on the administration's agenda.

The readings in this section provide us with an overview of the ways in which U.S. domestic politics and foreign policy interact. The first reading in this unit, "The War We Deserve," takes a critical look at how Americans view the government and argues that the problems encountered in Iraq exemplify the tendency of Americans to expect much of their government, while at the same time being unwilling to sacrifice. It asserts that under these conditions a global war on terrorism cannot succeed. The second reading, "The Evangelical Roots of U.S. Africa Policy," examines the role that religion and religious groups play in the formation and implementation of U.S. foreign policy to Africa. The final essay, "Waiting Games: The Politics of U.S. Immigration Reform," addresses the political impasse over immigration reform. It looks at what Congress has tried to do, identifies the major political groupings that have formed around this issue, and presents suggestions on how to proceed.

The War We Deserve

It's easy to blame the violence in Iraq and the pitfalls of the war on terror on a small cabal of neocons, a bumbling president, and an overstretched military. But real fault lies with the American people as well. Americans now ask more of their government but sacrifice less than ever before. It's an unrealistic, even deadly, way to fight a global war. And, unfortunately, that's just how the American people want it.

ALASDAIR ROBERTS

There's an uncomplicated tale many Americans like to tell themselves about recent U.S. foreign policy. As the story has it, the nation was led astray by a powerful clique of political appointees and their fellow travelers in Washington think tanks, who were determined even before the 9/11 attacks to effect a radical shift in America's role in the world. The members of this cabal were known as neoconservatives. They believed the world was a dangerous place, that American power should be applied firmly to protect American interests, and that, for too long, U.S. policy had consisted of diplomatic excess and mincing half measures. After 9/11, this group gave us the ill-conceived Global War on Terror and its bloody centerpiece, the war in Iraq.

This narrative is disturbing. It implies that a small cadre of officials, holding allegiance to ideas alien to mainstream political life, succeeded in hijacking the foreign-policy apparatus of the entire U.S. government and managed to skirt the checks and balances of the U.S. Constitution. Perversely, though, this interpretation of events is also comforting. It offers the possibility of correcting course. If the fault simply lies in the predispositions of a few key players in the policy game, then those players can eventually be replaced, and policies repaired.

Unfortunately, though, this convenient story is fiction, and it's peddling a dangerously misguided view of history. The American public at large is more deeply implicated in the design and execution of the war on terror than it is comfortable to admit. In the six years of the war, through an invasion of Afghanistan, a wave of anthrax attacks, and an occupation of Iraq, Americans have remained largely unshaken in their commitment to a political philosophy that demands much from its government but asks little of its citizens. And there is no reason to believe that the weight of that responsibility will shift after the next attack.

The Path of Least Resistance

Since at least the election of Ronald Reagan in 1980, a political philosophy known as neoliberalism has dominated the American political landscape. Defined by a commitment to tax reduction, discipline in fiscal and monetary policy, light regulation of the private sector, and free trade, it has risen above party politics. Leading Democrats have advocated the neoliberal creed, even if they did not use the phrase. It was former President Bill Clinton, after all, who promised the American people in 1996 that "the era of big government [was] over"; that the federal bureaucracy would shrink; and that the federal government would adhere to a program of fiscal balance, regulatory restraint, and trade liberalization.

This neoliberal philosophy is built on a bedrock of skepticism about the role of central government and the effectiveness of grand governmental projects. As a consequence, politics got small. Political leaders learned to shy away from policies that threatened to disrupt the status quo and make great demands of the American polity. A hallmark of the Clinton administration in its later years, after the Democrats' drubbing in the 1994 midterm elections, was its enthusiasm for "micropolicies"—initiatives that could be linked to great themes but did not incur great costs.

The rejection of sacrifice on a national scale contributed to the bungled war the United States finds itself in today.

This rejection of sacrifice on a national scale contributed to the bungled war the United States finds itself in today. The war on terror is not simply a neoconservative project. It is as much a neoliberal project, shaped by views about the role of government that enjoy broad public support.

It may seem extraordinary, given the experience of the past six years, to suggest that President George W. Bush's administration pursued a Clinton-style strategy of accommodation to neoliberal realities. After all, key Bush advisors flaunted their determination to throw off the constraints that bound the executive branch. And the Bush administration's policies have had cataclysmic consequences—in Iraq alone, there are tens of thousands dead and more than a million people displaced. How can we call this "small politics"?

However, we must first recognize the critical distinction between what the Bush administration intended to do, and what actually transpired. The material point about the planned invasion of Iraq was that it appeared to its proponents to be feasible with a very small commitment of resources. It would be a cakewalk, influential Pentagon advisor Kenneth Adelman predicted in February 2002. The cost of postwar reconstruction would be negligible. Former Deputy Secretary of Defense Paul Wolfowitz suggested that it might even be financed by revenues from the Iraqi oil industry.

Of course, there were critics inside and outside the U.S. government who warned that these forecasts were unduly optimistic. But the administration's view was hardly idiosyncratic. There were many Americans who believed, based on the experience of the previous decade—including the first Gulf War, subsequent strikes on Iraq, and other interventions such as Kosovo—that the U.S. military had acquired the capacity to project force with devastating efficiency. Consequently, it wasn't hard to imagine that the invasion and occupation of a nation of 27 million, more than 6,000 miles away, could be accomplished without significant disruption to American daily life.

Even the larger war on terror remains a relatively small affair, asking for little from its masters. Although U.S. defense expenditures have grown substantially during the Bush administration—by roughly 40 percent in inflation-adjusted terms between 2001 and 2006—it is growth from a historically low base. In the five years after 9/11, average defense expenditure as a share of gross domestic product (3.8 percent) was little more than half of what it was during the preceding 50 years (6.8 percent). The proportion of the U.S. adult population employed in the active-duty military (roughly 0.6 percent) remained at a low not seen since before the attack on Pearl Harbor.

This determination to execute policy without disrupting daily life was maintained even as it became clear that the war on terror was faltering. The U.S. "surge" of troops in Iraq beginning in January 2007, designed to wrest control of the country from insurgents, was advertised as a substantial increase in U.S. commitments in Iraq. In August, the *New York Times* called it a "massive buildup." But by historical standards, it has been negligible. The United States had more boots on the ground in Japan 10 years after its surrender in 1945 and in Germany at the end of the Cold War. It deployed twice as many troops in South Korea and three times as many in Vietnam.

In 2003, the conflict in Iraq might reasonably have been described as George W. Bush's war. In 2007, however, it has become a bipartisan war—that is, a conflict whose course is shaped by the actions of a Republican president and by Democratic majorities in Congress. The stakes are substantial: Continued failure in Iraq is bound to have tremendous human and diplomatic costs. Yet the range of policy options is still arbitrarily limited to a token "surge" or various forms of "phased withdrawal." No major political actor, Democrat or Republican, dares to contemplate a genuine surge that would raise the U.S. commitment in Iraq to the level said to be essential by several military leaders before the invasion. Similarly, there has been no serious consideration of a return to the draft, despite strains on the U.S. military. This, the *New York Times* said—echoing the argument made by Milton Friedman during Vietnam—would be inconsistent with the "free-choice values of America's market society."

Follow the Money

It isn't just in Iraq where this preference for small-scale politics has shaped the war on terror. Vice President Dick Cheney claimed in 2005 that the Bush administration had been "very aggressive . . . using the tools at our disposal" to defend the U.S. home-land against terrorism. But the administration has not been aggressive in imposing regulatory burdens on the private sector, which owns many of the United States' most vulnerable targets. In 2002, for example, it declined to assert that the Clean Air Act gave it authority to impose safety requirements on U.S. chemical facilities. Instead, it encouraged voluntary corporate efforts to improve security in this and other sectors of the economy.

First and foremost, the aim was to keep the economy humming. "One of the great goals of this nation's war," President Bush said immediately after 9/11, "is to restore confidence in the airline industry." His administration quickly launched a "pro-consumption publicity blitz" (in the words of the *Boston Globe*) on behalf of the U.S. travel industry. The president starred in a campaign by the Travel Industry Association of America, designed, as one industry executive put it, to "link travel to patriotic duty." Many Americans interpreted the campaign as a call to spend more money to boost the economy. "The important thing, war or no war, is for the economy to grow," then White House Press Secretary Ari Fleischer said in 2003.

The extension of such pro-growth policies in a declared time of war has created jarring rhetorical inconsistencies. Historically, war has been regarded—by definition—as a grand project, requiring deep societal shifts and the subordination of other priorities. Traditionally, presidents had the responsibility to remind citizens of this fact. They called on Americans to "make the sacrifices that the emergency demands," as President Franklin D. Roosevelt did less than a year before Pearl Harbor.

President Bush feigns continuing this tradition when he tells Americans that "a time of war is a time of sacrifice." But this attempt to link the war on terror and earlier campaigns fails, precisely because today the state is not able to demand comparable sacrifices from its constituents. Asking for real sacrifices and tax hikes doesn't go over well at the ballot box. And so, when President Bush was asked in 2001 precisely how Americans should contribute to fighting the war on terror, he replied: "Well,

I think the average American must not be afraid to travel. . . . They ought to take their kids on vacations. They ought to go to ball games. . . . Americans ought to go about their business."

Another sad attempt at analogy was made by the new Transportation Security Administration (TSA), which launched a research-and-development program to achieve "revolutionary" improvements in methods for screening airline passengers and baggage. Part of this program was coined the "Manhattan II Project"—an homage to the crash program that produced a nuclear bomb in the Second World War. But the original Manhattan Project was a vast and expensive enterprise. It consumed 1 percent of GDP (in contemporary terms, one quarter of the annual defense budget); employed 130,000 people; enlisted scientists and engineers from leading universities and private industry; and continued until an atomic weapon had been successfully detonated. Manhattan II, by contrast, expended $6 million in its first two years—or less than one ten-thousandth of 1 percent of U.S. GDP.

The TSA's research-and-development program eventually fell prey to "competing priorities in a tight budget environment." In 2003, the agency cut its R&D budget by half to meet shortfalls elsewhere in the agency. R&D was just one of many areas in which investments in homeland security clashed fatally with fiscal constraints. "From Day One," said Clark Kent Ervin, the former inspector general of the Department of Homeland Security (DHS), attempts to improve domestic security were compromised by a "lack of money."

Conservatives often countered that one consequence of the war on terror has been a complete loss of budgetary discipline in Washington. It is a gross exaggeration. On the contrary, a remarkable feature of post-9/11 budgeting is the extent to which federal expenditures continued long-standing patterns, even as policymakers profess commitment to a "total war" on terrorism. Federal spending rose from 18.5 percent of GDP in 2001 to 20.3 percent of GDP in 2006, but it was not an extraordinary shift: The average for the 40 years ending in 2006 was 20.6 percent of GDP. Spending on non-entitlement domestic programs, including DHS programs, remains well within historical parameters. Indeed, the largest increase in annual federal outlays between 2000 and 2006 was not on non-defense discretionary spending (a change of $177 billion) or even on defense ($225 billion), but on Social Security, Medicare, Medicaid, and other forms of mandatory spending ($461 billion).

Broadly speaking, three familiar forces have shaped federal budgets since 9/11. The first is the continuing weight of the doctrine of fiscal discipline, which discredits the idea of borrowing to fund security needs. The second is the continued difficulty of entitlement reform, evidenced by the Bush administration's failed attempt to reform Social Security in 2005, and thus the inability to control growth in mandatory spending.

The third consideration is a resistance to taxation. As a share of GDP, federal taxes increased to their highest level in modern history during the later Clinton years, and popular resentment about federal taxes grew right alongside them. As a consequence, the popularity of the Bush administration's tax cuts endured after 9/11. One month after the attacks, three quarters of respondents told a Gallup poll that they wanted the first round of tax cuts, introduced in June 2001, to take effect immediately. More than 60 percent favored additional cuts.

Bush's tax reforms reduced the overall tax burden to the historical average. The result, however, has been another stark discontinuity between the rhetoric of the war of terror and the realities on the ground. President Bush claimed that the United States had undertaken a "historic mission" after 9/11. But this was a highly unusual security crisis—one in which the tax burden imposed by the federal government *declined.* The president even defended the tax cuts as a critical component of protecting the home front in the war on terror, designed to safeguard an economy targeted by al Qaeda. Tax cuts, said Bush, would "make sure that the consumer has got money to spend in the short term." The effects of this pro-consumption policy have sometimes been perverse. For example, containerized maritime imports rose by 64 percent after 9/11, even as policymakers wrung their hands about weaknesses in container and port security.

Liberty for Some

So, if taxes have declined, a draft has been avoided, and regulatory burdens have been minimized, were there any other ways in which the broad mass of the American public might have carried a heavier load after 9/11?

Civil libertarians certainly think Americans have paid a large if intangible price in the rollback of their civil liberties. Here, critics also reach for analogies between the war on terror and earlier conflicts. They accuse the Bush administration of trampling on civil liberties in the name of national security, just as the government had during the First and Second World Wars, the Cold War, and the domestic turmoil of the late 1960s and early 1970s. The steps taken after 9/11 were "chillingly familiar," reported the *San Francisco Chronicle*. The historian Alan Brinkley said the government's treatment of civil liberties was a "familiar story." In 2002 *The Progressive* said, "We've been here before."

But we haven't been here before. Infringement of Americans' rights after 9/11—that is, actual rather than anticipated infringements—were different in type and severity than those suffered in earlier crises. Citizens were not imprisoned for treason, as they were during the First World War. Thousands of citizens were not detained indefinitely, as they were during the Second World War. Citizens were not deported, or denied passports, or blacklisted, as they were during the Red scares.

Were there serious issues about the denial of citizens' rights after 9/11? Undoubtedly. But those violations often had a distinctly postmillennial character. New surveillance programs were launched in secrecy and designed so that their footprint could not be easily detected. In effect, government was adapting to political realities, searching for techniques of maintaining domestic security that did not involve obvious disruptions of everyday life.

Foreigners, in contrast, had a much rougher time. The second distinguishing feature of the war on terror, insofar as basic rights are concerned, is the extent to which the heaviest burdens were sent abroad. The most obvious and grievous harms—kidnapping, secret detention, abusive interrogation, denial of habeas corpus—have been deliberately perpetrated against foreigners rather than citizens.

Indeed, the spirit of sacrifice doesn't even permeate the Bush administration itself. The president's first choice as head of the Federal Emergency Management Agency resigned 15 months after 9/11 to head a consulting business that would "take advantage of business opportunities in the Middle East following the conclusion of the U.S.-led war in Iraq." By 2006, two thirds of the Department of Homeland Security's senior executives had departed, often taking more lucrative positions as lobbyists for DHS contractors. A 2007 report for the Homeland Security Advisory Council worried about a "Homeland Security 'meltdown'" because of turnover in DHS leadership.

Some have borne serious costs in this war on terror, though, beginning of course on Day One. And as of today, more than 4,000 U.S. soldiers have been killed in Iraq and Afghanistan, and more than 13,000 have been injured so severely that they could not return to duty. At least 70,000 Iraqis have died since March 2003. Immigrant communities within the United States complain of surveillance and the abusive application of immigration laws. These pains are substantial but concentrated, often on politically marginal constituencies.

In fact, some of these costs are aggravated precisely because the Bush administration wants to avoid policies that incur more broadly distributed burdens. "We're fighting the enemy abroad," the Bush White House said in 2005, "so that we don't have to fight them here." This course of action has been presented as a matter of national security—a sensible form of forward defense. However, it's also good domestic politics. "Fighting them here" would mean higher taxes, bigger bureaucracies, tighter regulation, clearer challenges to civil liberties, and more impediments to trade. The Bush administration did not want that, because it understood correctly that most Americans did not want it, either.

But the consequences of this basic policy decision have been profoundly harmful to U.S. interests. The United States has failed to take steps domestically that would enhance security. It has stumbled into overseas conflicts marred by poor planning and vague objectives. Its standing as a champion of human rights has been badly damaged. It has left itself open to charges of hypocrisy—using the language of sacrifice to cloak a policy of business as usual.

Meanwhile, Americans are still as committed to the principles of fiscal discipline, low taxes, light regulation, and free trade as they were on Sept. 10, 2001. They remain deeply skeptical of "big government" and federal bureaucracy. Indeed, a 2006 Gallup poll found that a large majority of Americans, Republicans and Democrats alike, believed that "big government" posed the biggest threat to the country in the future, ahead of both "big business" and "big labor."

Was the war on terror devised and promoted by a small cadre of neoconservatives? Perhaps. But it was also a response to crisis that recognized and largely respected the well-defined boundaries of acceptable political action in the United States today. In important ways, the war on terror is not their war but our war. The desires and preferences of the American people have shaped the war on terror just as profoundly as any neoconservative doctrine on the conduct of U.S. foreign policy.

So Americans can keep reciting their favorite myth—even as the broad currents of U.S. politics remain unchanged. But the next time the war suffers a setback or a terror attack hits home, we shouldn't expect the country's response to differ much from the war the Bush administration launched six years ago. Americans might try to pin their problems on a few powerful neocons. In truth, though, they must shoulder some of the blame.

ALASDAIR ROBERTS is professor of public administration at the Maxwell School of Citizenship and Public Affairs at Syracuse University and author of the forthcoming book *The Collapse of Fortress Bush: The Crisis of Authority in American Government* (New York: New York University Press, 2008).

The Evangelical Roots of US Africa Policy

Asteris Huliaras

About a quarter of US citizens claim to be evangelicals, or 'born-again' Christians.[1] While this broad term covers a number of different denominations and movements,[2] in general evangelicals are theologically conservative, viewing the Bible as the sole authority of faith and strongly promoting preaching and evangelism. While they were once considered America's staunchest isolationists (with the exception of their strong anti-communist views and their unconditional support for Israel),[3] in recent years their political agenda has shifted away from a strict focus on domestic issues to encompass a greater interest in foreign affairs. They have come to play a significant role in the making of US foreign policy, especially with respect to developing countries.

Until the late 1970s, evangelicals tended not to take part in US politics. A large proportion of them did not even vote in presidential elections. However, through a process of gradual politicisation initiated mainly by their strong interest in contested domestic issues such as abortion and gay marriage, and strengthened by Republican officials looking for new constituencies,[4] the evangelical presence in US political life increased spectacularly.[5] By the late 1990s, evangelicals had become a recognised voting bloc, mobilised most effectively by George W. Bush in the 2000 presidential election.[6] More recently, the evangelical lobby has been a major driving force in placing African issues on the US government agenda.

Saving the Third World

It is no coincidence that US evangelicals have become increasingly interested in the Third World. Evangelical Christianity has grown tremendously in the global South, to the point where Third World Christians greatly outnumber their counterparts in the North. In 1900 only 7% of the world's evangelicals lived in the Third World. By 1985 this share had shifted to 66%.[7] In 2002 evangelicalism had nearly 800 million adherents worldwide, of whom some 500m resided in the global South.[8] And it is in Africa where evangelicalism (especially its Pentecostal and charismatic variants) is growing most spectacularly.[9]

Still, demographic changes do not fully account for the relatively sudden interest of US evangelical Christians in the Third World. Also of importance are the missionary activities that have brought increasing numbers of evangelicals into direct contact with the people of Africa and other developing areas. Until the early 1950s, the majority of US Protestant missions in the Third World were drawn from mainline denominations.[10] By the late 1980s, however, 90% were evangelical.[11] A combination of growing self-confidence and impressive economic resources (more than $2 billion annually) explain this

shift. Evangelical missions have become a particularly big industry in Africa. In the early 1990s there were at least 1,300 American protestant missionaries in Kenya alone.[12] In the second half of the 1990s, the number of US evangelicals fanning out across the globe on proselytising missions reached record levels. According to some estimates, nearly 350,000 Americans undertook such missions in 2001, eight times as many as in 1996.[13] In 2002, the Southern Baptist Convention, one of the most important US evangelical denominations, spent $290m abroad, mainly in Asia and Africa, establishing more than 8,000 churches and baptising more than 421,000 converts.[14] In 2005, the BBC's *Focus on Africa* reported:

> Africa is being colonised and Christianised all over again. The colonisers this time are Americans, not Europeans, and the brand of belief they are bringing to Africa is Evangelical Christianity.[15]

Evangelical missionaries returning to the United States were acutely aware of the poverty and oppression they had encountered in the less-developed countries they had visited. Above all, they were concerned with the persecution of Christians in countries such as Myanmar and Sudan. They played a crucial role in persuading their organisations to mobilise in support of their persecuted co-believers. As a result of their interest in the 'suffering church' in Third World countries, evangelical groups attempted to re-direct American foreign policy in defence of Christian minorities worldwide. In 1996 the National Association of Evangelicals embarked upon a highly coordinated campaign that included public gatherings, strong media coverage and private meetings with officials in Washington aimed at changing US foreign policy towards countries that were seen as persecuting Christians.[16] The association finally persuaded a reluctant Clinton administration to introduce the International Religious Freedom Act in 1998. Although government officials initially tried to underplay its importance, the act created three significant government bodies to monitor and respond to violations of religious freedom: the State Department Office of International Religious Freedom, the Commission on International Religious Freedom and the Special Advisor on International Religious Freedom within the National Security Council.[17]

Another factor that played a crucial role in increasing evangelical interest in foreign affairs was the violence of 11 September 2001. In the three presidential elections prior to 2004, fewer than 2% of evangelicals mentioned foreign policy as 'the most important issue' that the United States was facing. However, after 11 September attitudes changed markedly: by 2004 about a third of evangelical Christians named foreign policy as the most important issue on the country's agenda.[18] But the events of 11 September not only changed the views of the evangelical community, they changed those of the US administration. America was now at war. And it was not just a war of revenge but a war of ideals, including the spread of democracy worldwide. As liberal evangelical Jim Wallis observed, the terrorist attacks transformed Bush from a 'self-help Methodist' to a 'messianic Calvinist.'[19] If the United States had decided to become the world's 'moral leader,' a 'force of good' in global politics aiming to 'export democracy and freedom' in an unruly world, then evangelicals clearly had a role to play.

Other, more structural changes also affected evangelical interest in international affairs. With the growth of interdependence among nations and increasingly porous borders, a new concern for distant and different peoples appeared among evangelicals as among other Americans.[20] Technological advances also played a crucial role. The development of transnational television networks and the capacity for 'real-time' coverage of international crises unleashed an 'electronic internationalism.'[21] Barriers of citizenship, religion, race and geography that once divided the international moral space broke down, creating an emergent 'global conscience.'[22] The rapid expansion of the Internet provided not only an important means for acquiring information but also a critical networking and organising tool. US domestic factors were also important: a new emphasis on norms and values in the conduct of US foreign policy helped reanimate the notion of the 'persecuted church' that had energised anti-communist Christian networks in the Cold War period.[23]

Growing US evangelical interest in foreign affairs has led to attempts, particularly within the last ten years, to launch initiatives aimed at fighting global poverty and injustice, especially in Africa. In the words of the *Economist:*

> If the European campaign for aid for Africa is dominated by bleeding-heart liberals, poring over the *Guardian* and *l'Humanité,* the American campaign is dominated by Bible-believing Christians.[24]

For example, in October 2004, the National Association of Evangelicals issued a document entitled 'For the Health of the Nation: An Evangelical Call to Civic Responsibility' that called upon evangelicals to seek justice for the poor, protect human rights and seek global peace:

> We believe that care for the vulnerable should extend beyond our national borders. American foreign policy and trade policies often have an impact on the poor. We should try to persuade our leaders to change the patterns of trade that harm the poor and to make the reduction of global poverty a central concern of American foreign policy.[25]

Pat Robertson appeared alongside Brad Pitt and Tom Hanks.

In Washington, Richard Cizik, the vice-president for governmental affairs of the National Association of Evangelicals, has supported the large evangelical aid organisations World Relief and World Vision in lobbying for a major increase in US foreign aid.[26] In California, Rick Warren, an influential pastor (he was given top billing in *Time* magazine's list of the 25 most important evangelicals[27]), sent thousands of volunteers to combat poverty in Africa.[28] 'I've never been involved in partisan politics . . . and don't intend to do so now,' Warren said. 'But global poverty is an issue that rises far above mere politics. It is a

moral issue . . . a compassion issue, and because Jesus commanded us to help the poor, it is an obedience issue'.[29] (In August 2008, Warren did host an important political event—the Saddleback Civil Forum on Leadership and Compassion—where he questioned presidential candidates John McCain and Barack Obama on faith and values issues.) In 2005, leading evangelicals and faith-based organisations joined humanitarian non-governmental organisations (NGOs) and Hollywood celebrities to form the ONE campaign to 'make poverty history.' The diversity of ONE supporters impressed many observers: in a public-service announcement, Rev. Pat Robertson appeared alongside actors Brad Pitt and Tom Hanks.[30] Among other initiatives, the ONE campaign called on the US government to raise by 1% of the federal budget the amount of aid it provides to Africa.

Several observers have argued that Bush's decision to greatly increase US aid to Africa was partly a response to evangelical demands.[31] In autumn 2006, Secretary of State Condoleezza Rice said that President Bush 'should be known for increasing—doubling development assistance and tripling it to Africa after a period in which [it] was essentially flat for decades.'[32] He should also be known, she said, 'for the largest single investment in AIDS and malaria, the biggest health investment of any government program ever.'[33] It is true that the presidential initiative reflected in part priorities related to the growing strategic importance of Africa.[34] But there is evidence that the influence of the evangelical community also played an important role.

The content of the US programme on AIDS, for example, was heavily influenced by the president's evangelical backers. It has been reported that when Bush spoke to his evangelical speech-writer Michael Gerson about the feasibility of a plan to spend $15bn fighting AIDS, Gerson told him, 'if this is possible, and we don't do it, we will never be forgiven.'[35] In 2003, under pressure from evangelical lobby groups like Focus on the Family, the US administration decided to introduce a three-pronged strategy to fight AIDS, based on promoting abstinence, monogamy and, under certain limited circumstances, the use of condoms.[36] The programme has faced heavy criticism from many activists and health experts: the UN secretary-general's special envoy for HIV/AIDS in Africa has argued that its emphasis on abstinence has contributed to a shortage of condoms in some African countries.[37] 'To impose a dogma-driven policy that is fundamentally flawed is doing damage to Africa,' said the UN official.

The influence of evangelicals was also evident in US development-assistance programmes that did not focus on AIDS. For decades, US policy avoided intermingling aid programmes and religious proselytising. However, in December 2001 Bush created a new Center for Faith-Based and Community Initiatives within the United States Agency for International Development (USAID).[38] Gradually, the percentage of US aid going to faith-based organisations doubled and, according to many observers, the separation between religious services and donor activities became increasingly blurred.[39] Some restrictions imposed at the request of Congress in order to separate USAID-funded programmes from religious activities seemed to lose their effectiveness as many religious organisations could easily argue that they were using private and not public money for proselytising. In 2006, the US Government Accountability Office examined 13 federally financed faith-based organisations and concluded that four of them 'did not appear to understand the requirements to separate these activities in time or location from their program services.'[40] 'By the early years of the new millennium,' concluded development scholar Gerard Clarke, 'an effective nexus between the Bush administration and the US Christian right had become an important feature of US policy in international development.'[41]

Some analysts argued that the evangelicals' broadening of their agenda to include Third World poverty was more a tactical move, a reaction to a growing resentment among the American public of conservative Christians' support for the Republican Party and their perceived political influence over Bush's decisions.[42] In March 2005 a poll by the Pew Research Center for the People and the Press showed that 34% of Americans held an 'unfavourable' view of Christian conservatives, compared with 29% in 2002.[43] Several leading evangelicals have since tried to distance themselves from the Bush administration. David Neff, the editor of *Christianity Today,* the magazine of the National Association of Evangelicals, argued in a July 2005 editorial that:

> George Bush is not Lord. The Declaration of Independence is not an infallible guide to Christian faith and practice . . . The American flag is not the Cross. The Pledge of Allegiance is not the Creed. 'God bless America' is not the Doxology. Sometimes one needs to state the obvious—especially at times when it's less and less obvious.[44]

Other observers have argued that the evangelical emphasis on poverty was also intended to deflect attention from a number of scandals that 'have blown away the careers of several of the religious right's darlings,' including Ted Haggard, Tom Delay, Jack Abramoff and Ralph Reed.[45] Although there is some truth in this claim, it tends to underestimate the depth of the discussion within the evangelical community that shows a clear *structural* shift in priorities.

Not all evangelicals agree with their movement's focus on poverty or endorse with the same enthusiasm the broadening trend in their foreign-policy agenda. It has been reported, for example, that Joel Hunter, the president-elect of the Christian Coalition of America, stepped down in December 2006 because of 'his frustration at the group's refusal to adopt a broader social agenda.'[46] And the Rev. Richard Cizik has identified Focus on the Family head James Dobson as a leader of 'isolationist' evangelicals who refuse to 'extend support of the community to addressing poverty'; Cizik has characterised this refusal as the 'Empire strikes back.'[47] It also seems that grassroots evangelicals do not always share the zeal of their leaders: according to a recent poll, only 8% of white evangelicals and 20% of African-American evangelicals said that helping to improve the standard of living in less-developed countries is 'extremely important.'[48] Nevertheless, these controversies and disagreements show that the evangelical anti-poverty call is not just a response to a growing negative image but has real substance, reflecting a clear new focus that may have a long-term impact on the US foreign-policy agenda.

Sudan

Of course, just because evangelicals became interested in US foreign policy did not necessarily mean they would be able to exert real influence over it. Evangelicals exerted an unprecedented level of influence in the Bush administration,[49] but neither their interest in foreign policy nor the Bush administration's receptiveness to their demands can fully explain their success. A further reason why evangelicals were able to exert political leverage was because they began collaborating with non-evangelical groups, particularly Jewish organisations. Michael Horowitz, a former Reagan administration official and a senior fellow at the Hudson Institute, was important in bringing about this alliance.[50] On 5 July 1995, Horowitz published an editorial in the *Wall Street Journal,* 'New Intolerance between the Crescent and the Cross,' calling for an intervention to stop the persecution of Christians in Africa and the Middle East.[51] 'Christians are the Jews of the 21st century,' he claimed, going on to call them the 'victims of choice for thug regimes.' Horowitz asked for a new foreign policy that would make ending the persecution of Christians a high priority.

Horowitz initiated a mass campaign that crucially secured the involvement of the National Association of Evangelicals. In 1996, the association issued a 'Statement of Conscience' that called on its members 'to work tirelessly to bring about action by our government to curb worldwide religious persecution.'[52] The campaign introduced a very successful idea: an 'International Day of Prayer for the Persecuted Church.' The first such day was estimated to include 60,000 congregations.[53] Despite his being Jewish, Horowitz was named one of the ten most influential Christians of the year (together with Mother Teresa and Billy Graham) by *Southern Baptist Magazine* in 1997. The influential *Christianity Today* called him the 'Jew who is saving Christians.'[54] Jewish organisations such as the Union of American Hebrew Congregations and the Anti-Defamation League joined the evangelicals in the campaign for religious freedom in Africa and elsewhere.[55]

Topping Horowitz's list of global outrages was 'the imprisonment, beating, torture and selling into slavery of thousands of Christians in Sudan by the Islamic radical regime.'[56] Sudan quickly became the focus of the evangelical campaign for religious freedom. In April 2001 Horowitz was arrested (along with radio talk-show host Joe Maddison and former Congressman Walter E. Fauntroy) after he chained himself to the fence in front of the Sudanese Embassy in Washington to protest slavery and 'anti-Christian genocide.'[57] Steady campaigning by evangelicals concerned about the Sudanese government's efforts to impose its will on the predominantly Christian and animist southern part of the country played a prominent role in a US government diplomacy to end Sudan's civil war, a war that had claimed more than 2m lives.

Evangelicals became involved in an anti-slavery movement.

Many evangelicals also became involved in an anti-slavery movement that emerged in the early 1990s, originally led by the Boston-based American Anti-Slavery Group.[58] For evangelical groups such as Christian Solidarity International, slavery in Sudan became a central issue. A systematic effort to 'redeem' southern Sudanese slaves believed to be Christians from 'Arab Muslim' raiders/masters gained momentum in the mid 1990s. Steady campaigning on the slavery issue at the Christian grassroots level and fund-raising through appeals to 'buy back' slaves by evangelical congregations helped to upgrade interest in Sudan's civil war,[59] which was portrayed in simplistic terms as a 'biblical conflict' between Arab Muslims of the North and African Christians of the South. Gradually, evangelical groups started to show a strong interest in US foreign policy towards Sudan.

Growing US evangelical interest in Sudan coincided with the increasing anger of humanitarian and development NGOs at the continued interference of the Sudanese government in the workings of Operation Lifeline Sudan (a consortium providing humanitarian assistance to the southern part of the country). Although NGOs often held very different views on what the US response to the Sudanese civil war should be, all of them were outraged by the aerial bombings of civilians by the Khartoum regime in southern Sudan.[60] The Rev. Franklin Graham, founder of the faith-based Samaritan's Purse organisation, which runs a hospital in southern Sudan that was bombed by Sudanese government aircraft seven times in 2000, stated that he was persuaded that Khartoum's government was genocidal and that Islam itself was 'evil and wicked.'[61] Graham tried to publicise the plight of Sudan by flying Republican Senator Bill Frist to Sudan's most desolate outposts. A few days before becoming president, George W. Bush took a break from the campaign in Florida to meet Graham (whose father, Billy, had persuaded Bush to 'recommit' his life to Christ). The two prayed together, and Graham made one request: 'Governor, if you become president, I hope you put Sudan on your radar.'[62]

Shortly after Bush took office, a group of activists came to see presidential adviser Karl Rove, who had masterminded Bush's electoral strategy. The group included born-again Christians and liberal Jewish activists, and its objective was to ask the new administration to intercede in the Sudanese civil war. Rove, according to participants in the meeting, was 'unusually receptive.'[63] The need to retain evangelical voter support was an important factor in persuading the new administration to show a strong interest in Sudan's civil war. While the evangelicals' demands were a headache for many career State Department officials, Rove saw an opportunity to encourage cooperation between evangelicals and African-American lobbyists.

For African-American activists, building alliances with other lobby groups was highly desirable, considering that their influence on US foreign policy was in decline.[64] The retreat from public life owing to illness of Black Muslim leader Louis Farrakhan, who was a defender of the Islamic government of Sudan, helped encourage rapprochement between African Americans and evangelicals.[65] African-American groups such as the National Black Leadership Committee and the National Association for the Advancement of Colored People (NAACP) banded with evangelical groups, and the anti-Khartoum coalition became a significant political force.

In March 2001, the US Commission on International Religious Freedom, an independent government entity created by the International Religious Freedom Act, issued a report calling Sudan 'the world's most violent abuser of the right to freedom of religion and belief' and summoned the administration to intervene.[66] That same month, then Secretary of State Colin Powell told the Congress that 'there is perhaps no greater tragedy on the face of the earth today than the tragedy that is unfolding in the Sudan.' He added: 'The only way to deal with that tragedy is to end the conflict.'[67] One week after these comments, Powell commissioned a review of US policy toward Sudan.

Shortly after coming to power, Bush had announced that he would abandon Clinton's practice of assigning special envoys, but under pressure from evangelicals and their allies, the administration changed its position. In August 2001, Bush appointed John Danforth, a moderate Episcopalian priest and former senator, as US special envoy for Sudan's peace process. The appointment ceremony took place in the White House Rose Garden on 6 September and was attended by then Secretary of State Colin Powell, then National Security Advisor Condoleezza Rice and many leading evangelicals.

Two months earlier, in June 2001, Congress had passed the Sudan Peace Act, a bill that made available to Bush up to $10m per year in non-lethal aid to rebel-controlled areas. The act also threatened further sanctions against Sudan if the country's president could not certify every six months that the regime was negotiating in good faith. The act was praised as an expression of unity among a diverse group of lobbyists. Democratic Congressman Charles Rangel joked that in all his 30 years in Congress he had never before been on the same platform with his Republican colleague Dick Armey. 'I will not forget Sudan,' Bush promised when he signed the Sudan Peace Act into law. 'And if I do,' he added, 'I know that you will prod me.' It was, concludes a commentator, a clear acknowledgement of the power of the faith-based movement.[68]

In early 2002, Danforth reported to the president and advocated continued US engagement in Sudan. In July, under strong pressure from Washington, Khartoum and the rebels finally reached an agreement in Machakos, Kenya, that acknowledged the right of the southern Sudanese to self-determination. Five other protocols were signed in

the next two years, under which Sudan became a federal state with two regional governments that shared the country's newly found oil resources. Finally, in 2005, the two sides signed the Comprehensive Peace Agreement that paved the way for the arrival of UN forces to monitor the transition process. Of course, not all the factors that contributed to the agreement can be attributed to US diplomacy. But according to many analysts, the peace deal would never have been sealed if the United States had not brought such leverage to the process.[69] The agreement was a diplomatic achievement and a great victory for evangelical activists.

Powell described the Darfur tragedy as genocide.

However, US efforts to bring peace to southern Sudan were complicated by developments in the western parts of the country. In February 2003 the Sudanese government, facing another insurgency in the western region of Darfur, launched a ground and aerial assault that killed many civilians. Despite considerable progress in North-South negotiations, the Darfur crisis gradually escalated, killing hundreds of thousands and leaving more than 2m refugees. In April 2004, the US Holocaust Memorial Museum issued its first-ever 'genocide alert,' citing conditions in Darfur.[70] The American Jewish World Service and 100 evangelical and human-rights groups joined forces to form the Save Darfur Coalition. The coalition's campaign seemed capable of exerting some influence on foreign policy, especially with the US election approaching. In July 2004, the US Congress adopted a resolution branding the attacks by militias allied with the Sudanese government as 'genocide.' Powell also described the Darfur tragedy as genocide, the first time Congress or such a senior official had labelled a crisis with the term.[71] In August 2004, 35 evangelical leaders signed a letter urging the president to provide massive humanitarian aid and consider sending US troops to stop the killing.[72]

This time, no Christian victims were involved: it was a Muslim-against-Muslim affair. In January 2005 the UN published the results of its own investigation into the Darfur atrocities, concluding that the violent attacks on civilians stemmed from counter-insurgency tactics and that, despite the claims of evangelical activists and the US administration, genocide was not committed. Nevertheless, the evangelical activists continued with their campaign. On 26 April 2006, five members of Congress were arrested after protesting outside the Sudanese Embassy in Washington over atrocities in Darfur. That same day the president met with Darfur advocates in the White House and lent his support to rallies planned in more than a dozen cities around the United States: 'The genocide in Sudan is unacceptable,' Bush told them.[73] In autumn 2006, a group called Evangelicals for Darfur, created and backed by Richard Land of the Southern Baptist Convention and the National Association of Evangelicals, asked Bush to take the lead in sending a peacekeeping force to western Sudan.[74]

In short, the evangelical community played a crucial role not only in placing Sudan on the US government agenda but also in affecting its actual policy toward this African country. And it continued to do so even after the signing of the North–South peace accord. As Danforth put it, Sudan became 'a very, very high priority . . . something that was of personal interest' to Bush.[75] This does not mean, however, that evangelical influence over US Africa policy will decline once Bush leaves the White House. On the contrary, there is reason to expect that evangelicals will continue to shape US policies even after Barack Obama is sworn in as US president on 20 January 2009.

The Future

Several observers seriously question the practice of treating evangelicals as a single group. It is a great mistake, some argue, to lump all evangelicals 'together into one mass and then confound the lumping by quoting the wackiest people you can find.'[76] In a recent article, one leading evangelical noted that by putting all evangelicals 'into one indistinguishable mass we cede to the religious Right more weight and power than it deserves.'[77]

However, in the case of evangelical interest in US policy towards Africa, this argument partly loses its analytical power. Here, the evangelical community is less divided than on any other domestic or foreign-policy issue.[78] And relative unity means greater potential for influence. Evangelical campaigns to address African poverty and the conflict in Sudan show clearly that the movement's influence over US Africa policy is not only real but is probably much deeper, more consistent and more able to survive a change of US administration than the evangelical impact on any other area of US external relations.

Some commentators argue that the evangelical interest in US foreign policy is and will continue to be circumstantial and inconsistent. Mark Galli, editor of the leading evangelical magazine *Christianity Today,* recently claimed that US evangelicals are only interested in 'specific problems that affect specific people in specific ways.' 'We will continue to have flashes of international genius,' he added, 'but in all, our unique contribution to the world lies elsewhere.'[79] However, the African and global-poverty agendas have the potential to become exceptions. It is in relation to these agendas that the evangelical 'flashes of international genius' are more likely to appear in the near future. Moreover, these flashes have probably more potential to influence *real* foreign-policy decisions than US evangelical interest in any other region or country (including Israel). There are three reasons for this.

Firstly, in their interest in these issues evangelicals are not alone. The themes of Africa and global poverty offer ample opportunities for cooperation not only with other religious groups (such as Roman Catholics) but with other segments of civil society, including left-wing activists, humanitarian NGOs and ethnic (such as the African-American) lobbies. Common cause can also be made with African governments: several African leaders, such as Olusegun Obasanjo of Nigeria and Yoweri Museveni of Uganda, have already used their evangelical credentials to build support in Washington.[80]

Secondly, in relation to Africa and its development, any US administration is susceptible to the demands of public opinion. As Africa was—and still is—more marginal in US foreign policy than probably any other world region, any president, regardless of political affiliation, can satisfy evangelical demands for policy change relatively easily, avoiding the need for compromise with other domestic interests or foreign-policy objectives. This is often not the case with other regions or countries. The *Economist* reported, for example, that Bush 'brushed aside evangelical worries about government persecutions of Christians' in China.[81] Here, strategic objectives, realist calculations and business interests superseded evangelical worries.

Thirdly, in a period which has seen the international image of the United States decline, evangelicals in Africa are one of the strongest pro-American groups in the less-developed world. Although African evangelicals can be stubbornly independent and often align themselves with the African left,[82] they generally hold a very positive view of the United States. In the words of liberal evangelical and Oklahoma State Senator Andrew Rice,

> Grateful for years of patronage by their American brethren, bound by a sense of fellowship to the nation where the contemporary evangelical movement was formed, and respectful of

born-again President Bush, these Africans represent a growing constituency of friends.[83]

The US evangelical community's international connections are important for any American government. They wield a kind of soft power that neither a Republican nor a Democratic president could ignore. Although Americans will see many changes in US policy when President Obama takes office in January 2009, a change in the country's Africa policy is unlikely to be among them. In short, evangelical influence on US foreign policy towards Africa is here to stay.

Notes

1. A. Kohut, J.C. Green, S. Keeter and R.C. Toth (eds), *The Diminishing Divide: Religion's Changing Role in American Politics* (Washington, DC: Brookings Institution Press, 2000), p. 18; Pew Forum on Religion and Public Life, *The American Religious Landscape and Politics,* 2005, http://pewforum.org/publications/surveys/green.pdf.

2. Given this variety, some analysts have expressed doubts whether the concept 'evangelical' is analytically useful [see George Marsden (ed.), *Evangelicalism and Modern America* (Grand Rapids, MI: Eerdmans, 1984]; Donald W. Dayton, 'Some Doubts about the Usefulness of the Category "Evangelical,"' in Donald W. Dayton and Robert K. Johnston (eds), *The Variety of American Evangelicalism* (Downers Grove, IL: InterVarsity Press, 1991), pp. 245–51). Nevertheless, most observers continue to use the term, claiming that there is 'unity in diversity' and that evangelical Christianity in the United States can be regarded as an 'extended family' [see, among others: D. Michael Lindsay, *Faith in the Halls of Power: How Evangelicals Joined the American Elite* (Oxford: Oxford University Press, 2008)]. After all, US evangelical denominations are largely represented by the National Association of Evangelicals, an umbrella organisation founded in 1942 that claims to speak for 30 million Christians.

3. Martin Durham, 'Evangelical Protestantism and Foreign Policy in the United States after September 11', *Patterns of Prejudice,* vol. 38, no. 2, 2004, pp. 147–54; Jeremy D. Mayer, 'Christian Fundamentalists and Public Opinion Toward the Middle East: Israel's New Best Friends?,' *Social Sciences Quarterly,* vol. 85, no. 3, September 2004, pp. 695–710.

4. Jeffrey Haynes, *An Introduction to International Relations and Religion* (London: Pearson/Longman, 2007), pp. 243–4.

5. Several Christian grassroots organisations with a political agenda appeared in the early 1980s. Probably the most important was Moral Majority, an organisation led by the evangelical preacher Jerry Falwell, whose rallying cry of 'get 'em saved, get 'em baptised, get 'em registered' marked the beginning of the contemporary era of politicisation. By the mid 1980s, partly reflecting a disappointment with President Ronald Reagan's lack of interest in banning abortion and reinstating school prayer, Moral Majority was replaced by a number of politically more active evangelical organisations such as the Christian Coalition of the cable-television mogul Pat Robertson and Focus on the Family, led by radio broadcaster James Dobson. See William Martin, *With God On Our Side: The Rise of the Religious Right in America* (New York: Broadway, 1997); William Martin, 'The Christian Right and American Foreign Policy,' *Foreign Policy,* vol. 114, Spring 1999, pp. 66–80.

6. 'The Triumph of the Religious Right—American Values', *Economist,* 11 November 2004, www.economist.com/world/displaystory.cfm?story_id=3375543. Evangelical voters played a significant role in the 2000 presidential election, especially in the states President Bush won in the electoral college. In total, 78% of all evangelicals voted Republican, bringing to the White House an evangelical president (see 'The Triumph of the Religious Right—American Values'). Many observers viewed George W. Bush as an exceptionally religious president (Stephen Mansfield, *The Faith of George W. Bush* (New York: Tarcher, 2003), pp. xvii–xviii). There was ample evidence for this: the new president prayed often, read the Bible every day and argued that his faith formed his general 'frame of mind, and attitude and outlook' (Interview with Steve Waldman, *Beliefnet,* October 2000, www.beliefnet.com/story/47/story_4703_3 .html). His first major appointees included several born-again Christians such as Condoleezza Rice, speechwriter Michael Gerson, and Attorney General John Aschroft. Moreover, the new president established an Office of Faith-Based and Community Initiatives in the White House. In March 2003, *Newsweek* characterised his presidency as the 'most resolutely "faith based" in modern times' (Howard Fineman, 'Bush and God,' *Newsweek,* 10 March 2004, p. 25). Not unexpectedly, evangelical voters became Bush's most ardent supporters, securing him a second term in 2004, when about one-third of the extra votes he received were cast by the evangelical community. 'The Republican Party does not have the head count . . . to elect a president without the support of the religious right,' Jerry Falwell said confidently in 2004 (Quoted in Frances FitzGerald, 'The Evangelical Surprise,' *New York Review of Books,* vol. 54, no. 7, 26 April 2007, www.nybooks .com/articles/20131). This seems to be a correct statement: it is estimated that evangelicals now account for more than 40% of the Republican voter base (see 'The Triumph of the Religious Right—American Values').

7. Jan Nederveen Pieterse (ed.), *Christianity and Hegemony: Religion and Politics on the Frontier of Social Change* (Oxford: Berg Publishers, 1992).

8. Timothy S. Shah, 'The Bible and the Ballot Box: Evangelicals and Democracy in the "Global South,"' *SAIS Review,* vol. 24, no. 2, Summer–Fall 2004, p. 120, http://muse.jhu.edu/login?uri=/journals/sais_review/vo24/24.2shah.html.

9. *Ibid.,* p. 121.

10. Julie Hearn, 'The "Invisible NGO": US Evangelical Missions in Kenya,' *Journal of Religion in Africa,* vol. 32, no. 1, 2002, p. 39.

11. *Ibid.,* p. 40.

12. *Ibid.,* p. 41.

13. Peter Waldman, 'Evangelicals Give US Foreign Policy an Activist Tinge,' *Wall Street Journal,* 26 May 2004, available at www.religionandsocialpolicy.org/article_index/article_print .cfm?id=1552.

14. 'Right On: Bob Geldof and Bono Have Some Unlikely Friends in America,' *Economist,* 30 June 2005, available at http://findarticles.com/p/articles/mi_hb5037/is_200507/ai_n18255818.

15. Leslie Goffe, 'God, Gospel, Dollar,' *BBC Focus on Africa,* July–September 2005, pp. 11–12.

16. Elizabeth Castelli, 'Praying for the Persecuted Church: US Christian Activism in the Global Arena,' *Journal of Human Rights,* vol. 4, no. 3, 2005, pp. 321–51.

17. J. Mertus, 'Raising Expectations? Civil Society's Influence on Human Rights and US Foreign Policy,' *Journal of Human Rights,* vol. 3, no. 1, March 2004, p. 32.

18. John C. Green, *The American Religious Landscape and Political Attitudes: A Baseline for 2004* (Akron, OH: Ray C. Bliss Institute, University of Akron, 2005).

19. Jim Wallis, 'Dangerous Religion: George W. Bush's Theology of Empire,' *Sojourners,* September–October, pp. 20–6, www .sojo.net/index.cfm?action=magazine.article&issue=sojo309&article=030910.

20. Robert David Sack, *Homo Geographicus: A Framework for Action, Awareness and Moral Concern* (Washington DC: Johns Hopkins University Press, 1997), p. 257.

21. Michael Ignatieff, *The Warrior's Honor: Ethnic War and the Modern Conscience* (New York: Henry Holt, 1997), p. 10.

22. *Ibid.,* p. 11.

23. Haynes, *An Introduction to International Relations and Religion,* p. 253.

24. 'Right On: Bob Geldof and Bono Have Some Unlikely Friends in America.'

25. National Association of Evangelicals, 'For the Health of the Nation: An Evangelical Call to Civic Responsibility,' October 2004, pp. 9–10, www.nae.net/images/civic_responsibility2.pdf. The document goes on to express support for Christian and American foreign-policy initiatives aimed at addressing such problems as 'extreme poverty, lack of health care, the spread of HIV/AIDS, inadequate nutrition, unstable and unjust economies, slavery and sexual trafficking, the use of rape as a tool for terror and oppression, civil war and government cronyism' around the world.

26. Frances FitzGerald, 'The Evangelical Surprise,' *New York Review of Books,* vol. 54, no. 7, 26 April 2007, www.nybooks .com/articles/20131.

27. 'The 25 Most Influential Evangelicals in America,' *Time,* 1 February 2005, available at www.time.com/time/covers/1101050207/.

28. In 2005, on the occasion of the 25th anniversary of his church, Warren brought the president of Rwanda to a stadium filled with tens of thousands of the pastor's supporters. The president took the microphone to thank Warren for helping 'rebuild his country.' See Malcolm Gladwell, 'The Cellular Church: How Rick Warren Built his Ministry,' *New Yorker,* 12 September 2005, www.newyorker.com/archive/2005/09/12/050912fa_fact_gladwell.

29. Quoted in Pauline J. Chang, 'Celebrities and Evangelicals Unite to Make Poverty History,' *Christian Today,* 11 June 2005, www.christiantoday.com/article/celebrities.evangelicals.unite.to.make.poverty.history/3128.htm.

30. Holly Lebowitz Rossi, 'Evangelicals Embrace New Global Priorities,' *Beliefnet,* 2005, www.beliefnet.com/story/168/story_16822_1.html.

31. Daniel Bergner, 'The Call,' *New York Times Magazine,* 29 January 2006, www.nytimes.com/2006/01/29/magazine/29missionaries.html.

32. Michael A. Fletcher, 'Bush Has Quietly Tripled Aid to Africa,' *Washington Post,* 31 December 2006, www.washingtonpost.com/wp-dyn/content/article/2006/12/30/AR2006123000941.html.

33. Fletcher, 'Bush Has Quietly Tripled Aid to Africa.'

34. Herman J. Cohen, 'The United States and Africa: Non-vital Interests also Require Attention,' *American Foreign Policy Interests,* vol. 25, no. 1, February 2003, p. 19, available at www.unc.edu/depts/diplomat/archives_roll/2003_07-09/cohen_africa/cohen_africa.html.

35. Elisabeth Bumiller, 'White House Letter: Last-minute Touches for Bush's Speech Writer,' *International Herald Tribune,* 17 January 2005, www.iht.com/articles/2005/01/16/news/letter.php; 'Right On,' *Economist.*

36. Michael Kranish, 'Religious Right Wields Clout: Secular Groups Losing Funding Amid Pressure,' *Boston Globe,* 9 October 2006, www.boston.com/news/nation/articles/2006/10/09/religious_right_wields_clout/.

37. Jeevan Vasagar and Julian Borger, 'Bush Accused of AIDS Damage to Africa,' *Guardian,* 30 August 2005, www.guardian.co.uk/world/2005/aug/30/usa.aids.

38. Gerard Clarke, 'Donors, Faith-based Organisations and International Development,' *Third World Quarterly,* vol. 28, no. 1, 2007, pp. 82–3.

39. Farah Stockman, Michael Kranish, Peter S. Canellos and Kevin Baron, 'Bush Brings Faith to Foreign Aid,' *Boston Globe,* 8 October 2006, www.boston.com/news/nation/articles/2006/10/08/bush_brings_faith_to_foreign_aid/.

40. *Ibid.*

41. Clarke, 'Agents of Transformation?'.

42. Nina J. Easton, 'With Antipoverty Call, Evangelicals Seek New Tone: Respond to Concerns on Negative Image,' *Boston Globe,* 5 July 2005, www.boston.com/news/nation/washington/articles/2005/07/05/with_antipoverty_call_evangelicals_seek_new_tone/.

43. *Ibid.*

44. 'Editorial: Worship as Higher Politics', *Christianity Today,* vol. 49, no. 7, July 2005, p. 16.

45. Robert Lanham, 'America's Religious Right: God's Own Country,' *The Independent,* 16 December 2006, www.independent.co.uk/news/world/americas/americas-religious-right-gods-own-country-428485.html.

46. *Ibid.*

47. Rossi, 'Evangelicals Embrace New Global Priorities.'

48. Adelle M. Banks, 'Poll: Evangelicals See Themselves as Part of Mainstream, Still Beleaguered,' *Religious News Service,* 14 April 2004, available at http://pewforum.org/news/display.php?NewsID=3267.

49. Esther Kaplan, *With God On Their Side: George W. Bush and the Christian Right* (New York: New Press, 2004).

50. David Aikman, 'Avoiding a Holocaust,' *Charisma,* 1 July 1996, available at www.eppc.org/publications/pubID.243/pub_detail.asp.

51. Joshua Green, 'God's Foreign Policy,' *Washington Monthly,* November 2001, p. 28, www.washingtonmonthly.com/features/2001/0111.green.html.

52. Stuart Croft, ' "Thy Will be Done": The New Foreign Policy of America's Christian Right', *International Politics,* vol. 44, no. 6, November 2007, p. 694.

53. *Ibid.*

54. Michael Cromartie, 'The Jew Who is Saving Christians,' *Christianity Today,* 1 March 1999, www.christianitytoday.com/ct/1999/march1/9t3050.html?start=1.

55. Allen D. Hertzke and Daniel Philpott, 'Defending the Faiths,' *The National Interest,* Fall 2000, p. 75, available at http://findarticles.com/p/articles/mi_m2751/is_2000_Fall/ai_65576877.

56. Michael Horowitz, 'New Intolerance Between Crescent and Cross,' *Wall Street Journal,* 5 July 1995, p. A1.

57. Al Kamen, 'Sudan Protest Makes Odd Bedfellows,' *Washington Post,* 30 April 2001.

58. Walid Phares, 'The Sudanese Battle for American Opinion,' *Middle East Quarterly,* vol. 5, no. 1, March 1998, www.meforum.org/article/383.

59. Human Rights Watch, 'Slavery and Slave Redemption in Sudan,' March 2002, www.hrw.org/backgrounder/africa/sudanupdate.htm; Richard Miniter, 'The False Promise of Slave Redemption,' *Atlantic Monthly,* July 1999, www.theatlantic.com/issues/99jul/9907sudanslaves.htm.

60. Matthias Muindi, 'Sudan: Christian Right Might Inflame War, Observers Fear,' *Africannews,* May 2001, available at http://southsudanfriends.org/News/Africanews62May2001.html.

61. Raymond L. Brown, *American Foreign Policy Toward the Sudan: From Isolation to Engagement* (Washington DC: National War College, National Defense University, 2003), p. 24.

62. *Ibid.;* Farah Stockman, 'Christian Lobbying Finds Success: Evangelicals Help to Steer Bush Efforts,' *Boston Globe,* 14 October 2004, www.boston.com/news/nation/articles/2004/10/14/christian_lobbying_finds_success/.

63. Elisabeth Bumiller, 'Religious Lobby Finds a Good Friend in Bush,' *International Herald Tribune,* 27 October 2003.

64. Adekeye Adebajo, 'Africa, African Americans, and the Avuncular Sam,' *Africa Today,* vol. 50, no. 3, Spring 2004, p. 99.

65. Human Rights Watch, *Sudan, Oil and Human Rights* (London: Human Rights Watch, 2003), p. 486.

66. 'Report of the US Commission on International Religious Freedom on Sudan,' Washington DC, 21 March 2001, www.uscirf.Gov/reports/21Mar01/sudan_21Mar01.php3.

67. 'USA/Sudan: Caution, Lobbies at Work,' *Africa Confidential,* vol. 42, no. 7, 6 April 2001.

68. Allen D. Hertzke, *Freeing God's Children:. The Unlikely Alliance for Global Human Rights* (New York: Rowman & Littlefield, 2004), p. 292.

69. Peter Woodward, *US Foreign Policy and the Horn of Africa* (Aldershot: Ashgate, 2006), p. 132; Asteris C. Huliaras, 'Evangelists, Oil Companies and Terrorists: The Bush Administration's Policy Towards Sudan,' *Orbis,* vol. 50, no. 4, Autumn 2006, pp. 709–24.

70. Scott Straus, 'Darfur and the Genocide Debate,' *Foreign Affairs,* vol. 84, no. 1, January–February 2005, p. 128.

71. *Ibid.,* p. 129.

72. Alan Cooperman, 'Evangelicals Urge Bush to do More for Sudan,' *Washington Post,* 3 August 2004, www.washingtonpost .com/wp-dyn/articles/A35223-2004Aug2.html.

73. Andrew Miga, '5 Lawmakers Arrested At Darfur Protest,' *Washington Post,* 28 April 2006, www.washingtonpost.com/ wp-dyn/content/article/2006/04/28/AR2006042800893.html.

74. Mark Totten, 'A New Agenda for US Evangelicals,' *Christian Science Monitor,* 18 December 2006, www.csmonitor .com/2006/1218/p09s02-coop.html.

75. John Danforth, Interview, BBC, 3 July 2005.

76. 'Foreign Policy: In the World of Good and Evil,' *Economist,* www.economist.com/world/unitedstates/displaystory .cfm?story_id=7912626.

77. Peggy L. Shriver, 'Evangelicals and World Affairs,' *World Policy Journal,* vol. 23, no. 3, 2006, p. 58, www .mitpressjournals.org/doi/abs/10.1162/wopj.2006.23.3.52.

78. Warren Vieth, 'Churches Join to Urge Aid to Africa,' *Los Angeles Times,* 28 August 2005, http://articles.latimes .com/2005/jun/28/world/fg-africaaid28.

79. Mark Galli, 'Evangelical DNA and International Affairs,' *Review of Faith & International Affairs,* vol. 4, no. 3, Winter 2006, pp. 54–5.

80. Mead, 'God's Country?,' pp. 24–6.

81. 'Foreign Policy: In the World of Good and Evil.'

82. Shah, 'The Bible and the Ballot Box', p. 130.

83. Andrew Rice, 'Evangelicals vs. Muslims in Africa: Enemy's Enemy,' *New Republic,* 9 August 2004, p. 19, available at www .siu.edu/~anthro/adams/pages/565/EvangelicalsvMuslims_in_ Africa-Rice.htm.

ASTERIS HULIARAS is Associate Professor in the Department of Geography, Harokopion University of Athens, Greece.

Acknowledgments—An earlier version of this paper was presented at the 6th Pan-European International Relations Conference, Torino, Italy, September 2007. The author would like to thank the participants for useful comments.

Waiting Games: The Politics of US Immigration Reform

"What the United States needs now is comprehensive reform achieved incrementally to ensure the effectiveness and test the impact of new approaches. Such a strategy has a better chance of convincing skeptics on both sides of the debate."

SUSAN F. MARTIN

Repeated efforts to achieve a new binational approach to immigration between the United States and Mexico have all ended in failure. So have recurring attempts to enact comprehensive US immigration reform that would include new temporary worker programs and legalization of unauthorized migrants, along with enhanced enforcement of immigration laws and border security. It is too soon to tell how immigration reform will fare in the young administration of Barack Obama, or with a more dominantly Democratic US Congress. But swift passage of new legislation does not seem a likely prospect. For the foreseeable future, in any event, migration from Mexico appears likely to remain a contentious and vexing issue in American politics.

Although migration has long existed between Mexico and the United States, the North American Free Trade Agreement (NAFTA), implemented in 1994, heralded a new era of cooperation and consultation on migration management. Until the 1990s, each government saw migration from its own perspective, and did little to understand the position of the other or to negotiate common approaches. The US government pursued largely unilateral policies. While many recognized that changes in immigration policies might have a disproportionate effect on migrants from Mexico, there was no interest in designing Mexico-specific policy responses. Rather, legislation such as the Immigration Reform and Control Act of 1986 provided legal status to Mexican undocumented aliens on the same basis as to those who came from other countries.

The Mexican government, for its part, chose until the late 1980s to maintain a "policy of no policy" on migration to the United States. During the 1990s, however, that position changed and Mexico's government became more visibly engaged. Mexican authorities began to lobby in the United States on political and economic matters, something they had not done before the NAFTA negotiating process. Today the Mexican government no longer operates solely via its Secretariat for Foreign Relations and the US Department of State, but rather fans out across the spectrum of US private interest groups, public agencies, and Congress. The increased closeness of the US-Mexico economic relationship, and that relationship's salience for Mexican economic recovery and growth, also increase the need to handle other problems in ways that avoid harming economic cooperation. Among these "other problems," immigration is the most significant.

In the long term, when economic progress reduces income disparities among the three countries in NAFTA, freer movement of people will likely follow the already recognized benefits of freer movement of goods, services, and capital. At present, however, such integration of the labor markets is unlikely to occur, given the large differences in wages. The United States will continue to be a magnet for Mexicans seeking higher wages and more stable employment. And parts of Mexico will continue to rely heavily on remittances from workers in the United States for support of families and contributions to economic development.

Immigration reform is needed that will deter future illegal migration while regularizing the status of those already living in the United States.

The United States and Mexico share the goal of improving management of migration between the two countries. It is in neither country's interest that hundreds of thousands of people risk their lives each year to cross illegally into the United States. Nor is the continued presence of millions of unauthorized migrants, living and working in the shadows, of benefit to either country. Immigration reform is needed that will deter future illegal migration while regularizing the status of those already living in the United States.

During the 1990s, the US-Mexico Binational Commission created a Working Group on Migration and Consular Affairs, which provided tangible opportunities for enhanced cooperation on immigration and border issues. In 1997 President Bill Clinton signed a joint statement pledging improved bilateral cooperation on managing migration. This engagement has led to a number of actions, both unilateral and cooperative. Fast lanes, for example, were set up to reduce waits at border crossings into the United States. Cooperation to prevent drug smuggling at the border has increased. And both sides have taken steps to reduce the smuggling of immigrants.

The higher cost and greater risk of crossing the border have encouraged unauthorized migrants to remain for longer periods in the United States.

But the enhanced consultation has not always yielded positive results, and migration has remained a tense issue in the bilateral relationship. The economic situation in both countries in the 1990s—a boom in the United States, a very slow recovery from a 1994 bust in Mexico—led record numbers of Mexicans to enter the United States during the second half of that decade. Over the past 10 years, a much-publicized increase in border enforcement has done little to stem the tide. And the higher cost and greater risk of crossing the border have encouraged unauthorized migrants to remain for longer periods in the United States.

Congressional Gridlock

At the same time, comprehensive reform bills proposed in the US Congress have gone nowhere. The most recent Senate legislation died as opposition from the Republican right and, to a lesser degree, from the Democratic left prevented the congressional leadership from even bringing the bill to a vote. Washington essentially entered a holding pattern on immigration policy with the start of the long campaign season that culminated last year in Obama's election. What accounts for America's repeated failure to achieve comprehensive reform?

Part of the explanation is the controversial nature of the immigration issue in US politics. The issue sparks intense reactions on both sides of the political spectrum. Different groups are equally committed to ensuring, on the one hand, that unauthorized migrants are kept out of the country and do not receive amnesty if they have entered illegally; and on the other hand, that those who provide needed work gain the fullest access possible to employment opportunities, benefits, and citizenship.

In the fierce debate concerning immigration reform and temporary worker proposals, a number of questions keep recurring. For instance: Should separate guest worker programs exist for agricultural workers and for nonagricultural workers, or should the same program cover both groups? Should eligible participants in guest worker programs be limited to aliens currently within the United States, aliens outside the country, or both?

What about a legalization or "earned adjustment" program that would lead to legal permanent residency in the United States? Should criteria for legalization include multi-year work requirements? Or would that exclude many short-term agricultural workers, and lead to exploitation of workers who fear being fired? And should a new guest worker program offer derivative status to family members, or is it better to eliminate such measures to encourage eventual return to the country of origin?

Also, should numerical limits be placed on the numbers of individuals eligible to participate in a new guest worker program? Would it be wise to enforce return to the participant's country of origin—for example, through deportation—at the end of the program? Or could there be financial incentives to return home? And how can the operation of a guest worker program protect homeland security, ensuring that individuals who pose a security threat are not allowed into the country?

For the most part, the debate in Congress has not envisioned a separate or special migration agreement with Mexico. Rather, the reforms proposed would apply universally. Nevertheless, there is recognition that Mexicans constitute the largest source of both unauthorized and legal immigration into the United States. Hence, the changes would have disproportionate impact on Mexico—for better or worse.

In the 110th Congress, a comprehensive reform bill in the Senate represented a compromise, one that lifted elements from previous legislative attempts while also introducing new policies. It failed in part because of sustained opposition from both conservative Republicans and liberal Democrats. On the right, the concerns were about earned regularization for unauthorized migrants, a policy referred to as amnesty throughout the debate. Drawing on grassroots opposition to "rewarding illegality," opponents argued for an enforcement-only approach that more closely mirrored sentiment among Republicans in the House of Representatives.

On the left, the opposition took two forms. First was opposition to an expansive temporary worker program, which, it was argued, would weaken labor standards protection and reduce wages for already resident workers. Second was opposition to changes proposed in the admission of permanent residents, particularly the elimination of certain categories of family admissions. At the same time, business groups expressed concern about potential difficulties in obtaining green cards for valued employees who might not qualify under proposed regularization rules. When the presidential campaign heated up, political observers declared immigration reform dead, at least for the time being.

Quotas and Commissions

In fact, comprehensive immigration reform has been the exception, not the rule, in American politics. Until 1875, there were few laws regulating immigration to the United States. From then until 1921, the Congress put into effect a series of rules that excluded immigrants from certain countries or races (primarily through the Chinese, Japanese, and other Asian exclusion acts) and restricted others on the basis of their health, morals, likelihood to become public charges, and other similar factors.

During the last decades of the nineteenth century and into the early twentieth century, the debate on immigration heated up as the number of immigrants from Southern and Eastern Europe increased dramatically. As would be the case in later reform efforts, the Congress established a commission to assess the impact of immigration and make recommendations. At first the debate focused on a literacy test that proponents thought would restrict immigration to those with higher levels of education. After passage of the literacy requirements in 1917 failed to shift immigration origins and numbers as expected, opponents of mass migration turned to a more comprehensive approach that resulted in the National Origins quota system. It was enacted in 1921 and refined into its definitive form in the National Origins Act of 1924.

The National Origins Act placed overall numerical restrictions on immigration from the Eastern Hemisphere and set per-country quotas based on the percentage of Americans in the 1890 Census who originated from specific countries. Because the 1890 Census preceded the mass migration from Southern and Eastern Europe, higher quotas went to the United Kingdom and northwestern Europe. The annual quotas for Italy, Poland, and Greece were 4,000, 6,000, and 100, respectively; by contrast, in 1907 alone, more than 285,000 Italians had entered the United States.

The National Origins laws stayed in place until 1965 despite great criticism in the period after World War II and a series of bills that enabled admission of refugees and displaced persons outside of the quotas. The Congress, overriding President Harry Truman's veto, renewed the National Origins quotas in the 1952 McCarran-Walter Act. That act also established a system of preferences for skilled workers and the relatives of US citizens and permanent residents. In the context of the emerging cold war, the legislation tightened security as well, barring admission on a number of ideological grounds.

In 1952, Truman established a commission that issued a report the following year entitled "Whom We Shall Welcome." It recommended that national origins quotas be eliminated and that criteria based on broader US interests be established instead. The commission held that US immigration laws "flout fundamental American traditions and ideals, display a lack of faith in America's future, damage American prestige and position among other nations, [and] ignore the lessons of the American way of life."

But it was not until 1965 that a comprehensive overhaul of US immigration policy took place. Introduced in the context of the broader civil rights movement, the 1965 amendments ˹iminated national origins quotas, replacing them with a limit ˹0,000 visas per country and an overall ceiling of 160,000

for the Eastern Hemisphere. The legislation also established the first ceiling on Western Hemisphere migration, set at 120,000 visas per year. Immediate family (spouses, minor children, and parents) of US citizens would be admitted outside of the numerical limits. Within the numerically limited categories, a preference system was established that permitted admission of relatives, foreign workers, and refugees. Subsequent legislation established a global ceiling of 290,000, eliminating the separate ceilings for the Eastern and Western hemispheres.

No Rush on Refugees

Legislation regarding admission of refugees underwent a similarly lengthy process before reform was achieved. During the 1930s and early 1940s, many refugees had been rejected for admission to the United States. The most extreme case was that of the *St. Louis,* a ship full of Jewish refugees that was turned back by the United States (and other countries) and forced to return to Europe, where many of the passengers died in the Holocaust. After the war, the United States admitted thousands of displaced persons via a series of presidential rulings and ad hoc laws.

In 1951, the UN Convention Relating to the Status of Refugees was adopted, but the United States did not ratify the convention despite participating in its drafting. Only in 1969 did the United States ratify the 1967 Protocol to the Refugee Convention. And it was not until 1980 that the country passed legislation adopting the UN definition of "refugee" and putting in place a permanent system for refugee resettlement and asylum proceedings. Previously, refugees from Hungary, Cuba, Indochina, and the Soviet Union were admitted through the parole authority of the Attorney General because those emergency admissions exceeded the 17,000 refugee visas included in the regular immigration legislation.

When unauthorized migration grew in the 1970s, Congress considered legislation but failed to reach consensus. Instead, it formed the bipartisan Select Commission on Immigration and Refugee Policy (SCIRP), a time-honored way, as we have seen, to navigate the complexities and emotions of immigration policy. Its final report, issued in 1981, recommended a three-legged stool that included enhanced enforcement, particularly in the form of sanctions against employers who hired illegal workers; legalization for the estimated 3 million to 6 million unauthorized migrants already in the country; and reforms in legal admissions programs that would increase dramatically the number of immigrants to be admitted on the basis of their skills.

The basics of the SCIRP proposals were taken up by successive Congresses. The employer sanctions and legalization recommendations were finally enacted in the 1986 Immigration Reform and Control Act (IRCA) by a narrow vote in a lame duck Congress. The legal admission reforms were not enacted until the 1990 Immigration Act. As unauthorized migration grew again after implementation of IRCA, the Congress asked still another commission to advise it on immigration reforms. While some of the Commission on Immigration Reform's recommendations were adopted by administrative action and in 1996 immigration legislation, its recommendation for an electronic employment verification system—the heart of its 1994 report to Congress—was never fully implemented.

In the context of these historical trends, the recent congressional failure to enact comprehensive reform despite strong bipartisan agreement on many points is not surprising. Major changes in immigration policy generally require years of preparation and negotiation. Even the imprimaturs of blue ribbon commissions do not ensure quick passage of new approaches.

Strange Bedfellows

The nature of the political coalitions that form around immigration explains some of the difficulty of gaining consensus. I have found it helpful to identify four different groups in the debate, characterized by varying attitudes about immigration levels on the one hand and immigrant rights on the other.

The first group, the *advocates,* is favorable to high levels of immigration, as measured by numbers of admissions, and is committed to the protection of the rights of immigrants. Its preference is for permanent admissions that provide access to citizenship. The second group, the *free marketers,* also supports high levels of immigration, but its members are willing to restrict the rights of those admitted. Free marketers prefer large-scale temporary worker programs, limitations on access to public welfare programs, and measures that permit quick removal of any migrants who commit criminal or other offenses. The third group, the *restrictionists,* also supports limits on the rights of migrants, but in the context of limitations on the numbers to be admitted. The fourth group, *integrationists,* sees rights as paramount. But it is comfortable with numerical limits on admissions, especially in categories that inherently limit the capacity of migrants to exercise their rights (for example, temporary worker programs and unauthorized migration).

In debates over immigration reform, these groups often form coalitions in support of specific provisions. For example, the supporters of high levels of immigration (advocates and free marketers) will often join together to defeat efforts to restrict movements. But they break apart when issues regarding the rights of immigrants come up for votes; at such times, the free marketers will often join the restrictionists. Such shifting interests create strange bedfellows who find it difficult to achieve consensus on comprehensive reforms, even if they are able to agree on many elements of immigration policy.

Making the process of reform even more difficult is a basic ambivalence within the American public regarding immigration. Many Americans speak fondly and nostalgically about their own immigrant forebears who, in their mind, created this nation of immigrants. At the same time, they are fearful that today's immigrants are somehow different and less likely to contribute and assimilate—that is, to become true Americans. This ambivalence is by no means new. Benjamin Franklin worried that the Germans immigrating to Pennsylvania in the eighteenth century would never learn English.

The result of this ambivalence is the absence of any strong consensus among the public about changes in immigration policy. A small group that knows what it opposes can often preempt action—as witnessed in immigrant rallies that derailed House Republican enforcement measures, and talk radio shows that derailed Senate regularization measures. But pressure for positive changes is too often lacking. The safe decision for politicians is no decision—at least until there is no choice but to act.

The Way Forward

Recent top-down reform efforts failed in large part because they sought to achieve too much too quickly. What the United States needs now is comprehensive reform achieved incrementally to ensure the effectiveness and test the impact of new approaches. Such a strategy has a better chance of convincing skeptics on both sides of the debate.

As a first step, the Congress must address the work magnet that stimulates illegal migration. The highest priority is a more secure method of verifying the authorization of would-be employees to work in the United States. The pilot employment verification program mandated in the 1996 Immigration Act is still in testing mode, hampered by false negatives that question the right to work of authorized workers and false positives that allow unauthorized workers to assume the identities of those who are legally authorized to work. Congress should invest considerable resources now toward improving the data used to verify work authorization and testing the use of biometrics and other mechanisms to reduce abuse. These measures are needed precursors for universal implementation of the verification program.

Second, Congress should establish targeted employment programs for foreign workers in business sectors that are now highly dependent on unauthorized workers. There is no need now for the type of large-scale, open-ended temporary worker program that was included in the most recent Senate legislation. New programs should be tailored to the specific situation of those sectors of the economy that can demonstrate current shortages of domestic workers even when reasonable wages and working conditions are offered. Employers participating in foreign-worker programs should be required to participate in the pilot employment verification initiative.

If the labor is seasonal or short-term, as in agriculture, temporary worker programs may be appropriate. If the work is of indefinite duration, however, the programs should allow for transition to permanent residence. And current employees, regardless of their legal status, should be given the opportunity to apply for the new worker programs and receive their work permits inside the United States without being forced to rotate back to their home countries. Otherwise, there is little chance that these programs will serve as effective substitutes for unauthorized migration. Employers will not want to lose tested and valuable employees, and unauthorized migrants will not risk leaving the country to reenter as legal workers.

The Dependence Problem

In addressing the need for new admission programs for less-skilled workers, Congress should test mechanisms to help reduce future dependence on foreign workers. In too many cases, access to cheap labor impedes investment in a higher-skilled workforce, or in mechanization, which may improve productivity. Fees paid by employers who hire foreign workers could usefully be targeted toward exploring alternatives.

One program could test a method for reducing the dependence of US agriculture on Mexican migrants and spur development in migrant communities of origin. Recent legislative proposals would grant temporary legal status to unauthorized migrants who do US farm work, allow them to earn an immigrant status with continued farm work, and simplify procedures for farmers to obtain additional guest workers. If this is all that is done, individuals will have their status legalized, but US agriculture will remain dependent on foreign workers.

An agricultural pilot guest worker program could test methods to use the payroll taxes collected from guest workers and US employers to encourage worker returns to their home countries, as well as to promote the mechanization made increasingly necessary because of global competition in labor-intensive commodities, especially from China. Farm employers who hire migrants are usually well organized in associations that already collect fees (assessments) to support research and marketing of particular commodities. A pilot program could allow employers to have guest workers admitted more easily in exchange for fees that would be used to subsidize mechanization and encourage worker returns.

Another program could test ways for meatpackers and other industries that hire large numbers of unauthorized Mexicans to obtain legal guest workers. Employers who agree to participate in the pilot employment verification program for all new hires could be allowed to hire guest workers under a pilot temporary worker program even if the jobs were year-round, which would test the concept of rotating guest workers through year-round jobs. Guest worker returns to their home country could be encouraged by isolating and refunding worker and employer payments made on behalf of guest workers for Social Security and unemployment insurance benefits, or crediting the guest workers for these contributions in the Mexican social security system.

Third, Congress should fix the most egregious problem in the permanent admissions program—long backlogs that separate family members for years. Of most concern are the delays for immediate relatives of permanent residents. Spouses and minor children of legal immigrants from Mexico, for example, must wait five years or longer to enter the United States. Few US natives would tolerate such long separations. Not surprisingly, many family members instead wait for their visas in the United States. Clearing these backlogs within the next year could significantly reduce the stock of unauthorized migrants. Eliminating numerical quotas on these close family members would also help reduce the flow of future unauthorized migrants who are only seeking to be with their spouses and parents.

Fourth, the administrative capacities of the immigration bureaus within the Department of Homeland Security, the State Department, and the Labor Department should be beefed up and professionalized. The Senate legislation would have placed tremendous pressures on these agencies. It is not enough to tell

them to implement massive new requirements. They must be given the time and resources to build their capacity to take on new challenges.

Once these steps are implemented, Congress should then revisit immigration reform to determine the residual unauthorized population and assess the extent to which the new, targeted programs have achieved their aims. Once the inflow of unauthorized migrants has been reduced significantly and the impacts of new, targeted admission programs are known, a broader legalization and further reforms in legal admissions may well be needed. By that time, however, the public may have gained more confidence in the ability of the government to manage immigration.

Prospects for Reform

How will US immigration reform fare in general under President Obama and with a Congress more heavily controlled by Democrats? Several factors would appear to argue against quick enactment of comprehensive legislation. First and foremost, the financial crisis and a deepening recession bode ill for passage of any measures not directly related to economic recovery. Indeed, until the short- and medium-term impact of the recession on migration patterns becomes more apparent, it would be foolhardy to enact legislation that might keep out workers whom the United States needs in the short to medium term, or that might bring in workers whom the economy cannot quickly absorb.

Although some evidence suggests that the inflow of Mexican migrants is slowing with the downturn in the economy, and some migrants have relocated from hard-hit sectors such as construction into other work, there is little evidence to date that migrants are returning home in sizeable numbers. Whether these patterns will persist with a deepening and broadening of the recession is anyone's guess at present.

Too often economic crises have led to backlashes against immigrants, who are seen as taking jobs from natives.

If the worst-case scenario of a deep and lengthy recession comes to pass, there will be a second reason to postpone comprehensive immigration reform. Too often economic crises have led to backlashes against immigrants, who are seen as taking jobs from natives, even if they are not competing in the same labor markets. Since comprehensive reform would likely include measures to legalize at least a portion of the undocumented population, such legislation could combine with economic concerns to increase the likelihood of violent reactions to immigrants. Some reliable observers, such as the Southern Poverty Law Center, report that hate crimes against immigrants in the United States have increased in the past couple of years, in no small part because the debate over comprehensive immigration reform and the prospect of a large-scale amnesty program generated a backlash. The fear is that attacks against immigrants could increase as the economy worsens and unemployment increases.

A third impediment to swift passage of legislation rests with the congressional leadership on immigration reform. Since 1965, Senator Edward Kennedy of Massachusetts has led the Senate on all immigration reform initiatives. He has been for decades the chair or ranking member of the immigration subcommittee in the Judiciary Committee. Because of his worsening health, however, he had to step down from that position. His successor, Senator Charles Schumer of New York, is familiar with immigration issues, having played an important role in negotiating the Immigration Reform and Control Act of 1986, but there will be an inevitable learning curve as he takes over the committee and determines the direction in which he would like immigration reform to go.

Meanwhile, even if comprehensive reform seems unlikely in this term of Congress, incremental steps could be taken to address specific problems and issues. Somewhat surprisingly, given the economic crisis, Congress recently passed legislation guaranteeing the eligibility of legal immigrant children for the State Children's Health Insurance Program. Congress, reversing policies adopted in 1996 that restricted the access of legal immigrants to federally funded services for their first five years in the country, indicated a willingness to protect immigrant children along with natives—as long as they are in the country legally.

In a similar vein, limited provisions to legalize certain farm workers—and to provide legal status to undocumented children who attend college or enter the military—have had high levels of bipartisan support, and may fare better in the Congress than would more sweeping efforts at reform.

The Perfect and the Good

Proponents of comprehensive reform are correct that the US immigration system is badly broken. The Commission on Immigration Reform established a useful yardstick for measuring the credibility of immigration policies: "People who should get in, do get in; people who should not get in are kept out; and people who are judged deportable are required to leave." The large number of unauthorized migrants, in combination with the lengthy backlogs in the legal immigration system, demonstrates that US immigration policy fails this simple test.

For years, however, a "grand bargain" of regularization and increased legal admissions in exchange for enhanced enforcement and border security has eluded enactment. Pursuing the "perfect" of immediate and comprehensive reform may in fact have become the enemy of achieving "good," if imperfect, policy reforms that would reduce unauthorized migration while serving the national need for a credible legal admissions system. Perhaps now is the time to do something instead of nothing.

SUSAN F. MARTIN is an associate professor at Georgetown University and director of the Institute for the Study of International Migration at Georgetown's Edmund A. Walsh School of Foreign Service. She is also the former executive director of the US Commission on Immigration Reform. This article is adapted from a chapter she contributed to a book she coedited with Augustín Escobar Latapí, *Mexico-US Migration Management: A Binational Approach* (Lexington, 2008).

From *Current History,* April 2009, pp. 160–166. Copyright © 2009 by Current History, Inc. Reprinted by permission.

UNIT 4

The Institutional Context of American Foreign Policy

Unit Selections

Key Points to Consider

- How relevant is the Constitution to the conduct of American foreign policy? Do courts have a legitimate role to play in determining the content of U.S. foreign policy?

- To what extent should the United States adjust its foreign policy and laws according to the decisions made by international bodies such as the World Trade Organization or the International Criminal Court?

- What is the proper role of Congress in making foreign policy?

- How much power should the president be given in making foreign policy?

- Which foreign affairs bureaucracy is most important? Which one is most in need of reform? Which is most incapable of being reformed?

Student Website
www.mhhe.com/cls

Internet References

Central Intelligence Agency (CIA)
    www.cia.gov
The NATO Integrated Data Service (NIDS)
    www.nato.int/structur/nids/nids.htm
U.S. Department of State
    www.state.gov/index.html
United States Institute of Peace (USIP)
    www.usip.org
U.S. White House
    www.whitehouse.gov

Central to any study of American foreign policy are the institutions responsible for its content and conduct. The relationship between these institutions is often filled with conflict, competition, and controversy. The reasons for this are fundamental. Edwin Corwin put it best: The Constitution is an "invitation to the president and Congress to struggle over the privilege of directing U.S. foreign policy." Today, this struggle is not limited to these two institutions. At the national level, the courts have emerged as a potentially important force in the making of American foreign policy. State and local governments have also become highly visible players in world politics.

The power relationships that exist between the institutions that make American foreign policy are important for at least two reasons. First, different institutions represent different constituencies, and thus advance different sets of values regarding the proper direction of American foreign policy. Second, decision makers in these institutions have different time frames when making judgments about what to do. The correct policy on conducting a war against terrorism looks different to someone coming up for election in a year or two than it does to a professional diplomat.

This close linkage between institutions and policies suggests that if American foreign policy is to successfully conduct a war against terrorism, policymaking institutions must also change their ways. Many commentators are not confident of their ability to respond to the challenges of the post-September 11 foreign policy agenda. Budgetary power bases and political predispositions that are rooted in the Cold War are seen as unlikely to provide any more of a hospitable environment for a war against terrorism than they were for promoting human rights or engaging in peacekeeping operations. The creation of the Department of Homeland Security was a first institutional response to the terrorist attacks of September 11. The appointment of a Director of National Intelligence, a post advocated by investigative reports of why 9/11 happened and how intelligence was handled in the lead up to the Iraq War, was a second.

We can organize the institutions that make American foreign policy into three broad categories. The first composes of elected officials and their staffs: the president and Congress. One topic of enduring interest is the relationship between these bodies. Considerable variation has existed over time with such phrases as the "imperial presidency," "bipartisanship," and "divided government" being used to describe it. A more contemporary issue that has raised considerable concern is the ability of elected officials to manage and organize their appointed staffs effectively, so as to retain control over, and responsibility for, making decisions.

Bureaucratic organizations constitute a second set of institutions that need to be studied when examining American foreign policy. The major foreign policy bureaucracies are the State Department, the Defense Department, and the Central Intelligence Agency. Often agencies with more domestic focus such as the Commerce Department and the Treasury Department also play important foreign policy roles in highly specialized areas. The Department of Homeland Security might be described as the first foreign policy bureaucracy to have a domestic mandate. Bureaucracies play influential roles in making foreign policy by supplying policymakers with information, defining problems, and

Library of Congress, Prints and Photographs Division (LC-USZ62-13039).

implementing the selected policies. The current international environment presents these bureaucracies with a special challenge. Old threats and enemies have declined in importance or disappeared entirely and new ones have arisen. To remain effective, these institutions must adjust their organizational structures and ways of thinking, or risk being seen by policymakers as irrelevant anachronisms.

The final institutional actor of importance in making American foreign policy are the courts. Their involvement tends to be sporadic and highly focused. Courts serve as arbitrators in the previously noted struggle for dominance between the president and Congress. A key issue today is one that involves determining the jurisdictional boundary of the American legal system and international bodies such as an International Criminal Court and the World Trade Organization. Another is one which involves determining the boundary of legitimate national security concerns and Constitutional rights and protections of those accused or suspected of engaging in terrorist activities.

The essays in this section survey recent developments and controversies surrounding the key institutions that make American foreign policy. The first two essays examine the contemporary presidency. "The Carter Syndrome" examines how Barack Obama and recent presidents compare to their predecessors in terms of their thinking about the proper role of the United States in world affairs.

The second article on the president is an excerpt from the National War Powers Commission Report. In 1973 Congress passed, over President Nixon's veto, the War Powers Resolution. It was designed to control presidential actions in taking the United States into war. No president has ever recognized its constitutionality. President George W. Bush did not make reference to it after 9/11 in sending troops to Afghanistan or Iraq and President Barack Obama did not go to Congress for authorization to send U.S. forces into Afghanistan. The Commission proposed a new War Powers Consultation Act to take its place. The key features of this act and the logic behind it are presented here.

The next series of essays look at the bureaucracy. "The Homeland Security Hash" takes a critical look at the operation of the Department of Homeland Security and recommends ways to improve its performance. Richard Kohn, in "Coming Soon," directs our attention to the growing rift between civilians and professional military officers. He argues that four areas stand out in need of attention: ending the Iraq War, reorganizing for 21st century military operations, overcoming budget problems, and dealing with social issues such as gays in the military. The next bureaucracy essay, "Lost for Words," looks at the challenges facing the intelligence community in carrying out intelligence analysis and presenting its findings to policymakers. The author suggests that we might model intelligence analysis on the field of medicine and think of intelligence analysis in terms of a medical diagnosis. The final bureaucracy essay is written by three former administrators of the U.S. Agency for International Development. It looks at the problems facing U.S. foreign aid policy and calls for bureaucratic reforms as a key step in correcting them.

The final essay in this section looks at Congress. "When Congress Stops Wars" presents the argument that Congress is not powerless in dealing with presidents, but that it tends only to challenge presidential war powers when there exists a partisan divide between the party that controls the White House and the party that controls the Congress.

The Carter Syndrome

Barack Obama might yet revolutionize America's foreign policy. But if he can't reconcile his inner Thomas Jefferson with his inner Woodrow Wilson, the 44th president could end up like No. 39.

WALTER RUSSELL MEAD

Neither a cold-blooded realist nor a bleeding-heart idealist, Barack Obama has a split personality when it comes to foreign policy. So do most U.S. presidents, of course, and the ideas that inspire this one have a long history at the core of the American political tradition. In the past, such ideas have served the country well. But the conflicting impulses influencing how this young leader thinks about the world threaten to tear his presidency apart—and, in the worst scenario, turn him into a new Jimmy Carter.

Obama's long deliberation over the war in Afghanistan is a case study in presidential schizophrenia: After 94 days of internal discussion and debate, he ended up splitting the difference—rushing in more troops as his generals wanted, while calling for their departure to begin in July 2011 as his liberal base demanded. It was a sober compromise that suggests a man struggling to reconcile his worldview with the weight of inherited problems. Like many of his predecessors, Obama is not only buffeted by strong political headwinds, but also pulled in opposing directions by two of the major schools of thought that have guided American foreign-policy debates since colonial times.

In general, U.S. presidents see the world through the eyes of four giants: Alexander Hamilton, Woodrow Wilson, Thomas Jefferson, and Andrew Jackson. Hamiltonians share the first Treasury secretary's belief that a strong national government and a strong military should pursue a realist global policy and that the government can and should promote economic development and the interests of American business at home and abroad. Wilsonians agree with Hamiltonians on the need for a global foreign policy, but see the promotion of democracy and human rights as the core elements of American grand strategy. Jeffersonians dissent from this globalist consensus; they want the United States to minimize its commitments and, as much as possible, dismantle the national-security state. Jacksonians are today's Fox News watchers. They are populists suspicious of Hamiltonian business links, Wilsonian do-gooding, and Jeffersonian weakness.

Moderate Republicans tend to be Hamiltonians. Move right toward the Sarah Palin range of the party and the Jacksonian

influence grows. Centrist Democrats tend to be interventionist-minded Wilsonians, while on the left and the dovish side they are increasingly Jeffersonian, more interested in improving American democracy at home than exporting it abroad.

Some presidents build coalitions; others stay close to one favorite school. As the Cold War ended, George H.W. Bush's administration steered a largely Hamiltonian course, and many of those Hamiltonians later dissented from his son's war in Iraq. Bill Clinton's administration in the 1990s mixed Hamiltonian and Wilsonian tendencies. This dichotomy resulted in bitter administration infighting when those ideologies came into conflict—over humanitarian interventions in the Balkans and Rwanda, for example, and again over the relative weight to be given to human rights and trade in U.S. relations with China.

More recently, George W. Bush's presidency was defined by an effort to bring Jacksonians and Wilsonians into a coalition; the political failure of Bush's ambitious approach created the context that made the Obama presidency possible.

Sept. 11, 2001, was one of those rare and electrifying moments that waken Jacksonian America and focus its attention on the international arena. The U.S. homeland was not only under attack, it was under attack by an international conspiracy of terrorists who engaged in what Jacksonians consider dishonorable warfare: targeting civilians. Jacksonian attitudes toward war were shaped by generations of conflict with Native American peoples across the United States and before that by centuries of border conflict in England, Scotland, and Ireland. Against "honorable" enemies who observe the laws of war, one is obliged to fight fair; those who disregard the rules must be hunted down and killed, regardless of technical niceties.

When the United States is attacked, Jacksonians demand action; they leave strategy to the national leadership. But Bush's tough-minded Jacksonian response to 9/11—invading Afghanistan and toppling the Taliban government that gave safe haven to the plotters—gave way to what appeared to be Wilsonian meddling in Iraq. Originally, Bush's argument for overthrowing Saddam Hussein rested on two charges that resonated powerfully with Jacksonians: Hussein was building weapons of mass destruction, and he had close links with al Qaeda. But the war dragged on, and as Hussein's fabled hoards of WMD failed to appear and the links between Iraq and al Qaeda failed to emerge, Bush shifted to a Wilsonian rationale. This was no longer a war of defense against a pending threat or a war of retaliation; it was a war to establish democracy, first in Iraq and then throughout the region. Nation-building and democracy-spreading became the cornerstones of the administration's Middle East policy.

Bush could not have developed a strategy better calculated to dissolve his political support at home. Jacksonians historically have little sympathy for expensive and risky democracy-promoting ventures abroad. They generally opposed the humanitarian interventions in Somalia, Bosnia, and Haiti during the Clinton years; they did not and do not think American young people should die and American treasure should be scattered to spread democracy or protect human rights overseas. Paradoxically, Jacksonians also opposed "cut and run" options to end the war in Iraq even as they lost faith in both Bush and the Republican Party; they don't like wars for democracy, but they also don't want to see the United States lose once troops and the national honor have been committed. In Bush's last year in office, a standoff ensued: The Democratic congressional majorities were powerless to force change in his Iraq strategy and Bush remained free to increase U.S. troop levels, yet the war itself and Bush's rationale for it remained deeply unpopular.

Enter Obama. An early and consistent opponent of the Iraq war, Obama was able to bring together the elements of the Democratic Party's foreign-policy base who were most profoundly opposed to (and horrified by) Bush's policy. Obama made opposition to the Iraq war a centerpiece of his eloquent campaign, drawing on arguments that echoed U.S. anti-war movements all the way back to Henry David Thoreau's opposition to the Mexican-American War.

Like Carter in the 1970s, Obama comes from the old-fashioned Jeffersonian wing of the Democratic Party.

Like Carter in the 1970s, Obama comes from the old-fashioned Jeffersonian wing of the Democratic Party, and the strategic goal of his foreign policy is to reduce America's costs and risks overseas by limiting U.S. commitments wherever possible. He's a believer in the notion that the United States can best spread democracy and support peace by becoming an example of democracy at home and moderation abroad. More than this, Jeffersonians such as Obama think oversize commitments abroad undermine American democracy at home. Large military budgets divert resources from pressing domestic needs; close association with corrupt and tyrannical foreign regimes involves the United States in dirty and cynical

alliances; the swelling national-security state threatens civil liberties and leads to powerful pro-war, pro-engagement lobbies among corporations nourished on grossly swollen federal defense budgets.

While Bush argued that the only possible response to the 9/11 attacks was to deepen America's military and political commitments in the Middle East, Obama initially sought to enhance America's security by reducing those commitments and toning down aspects of U.S. Middle East policy, such as support for Israel, that foment hostility and suspicion in the region. He seeks to pull U.S. power back from the borderlands of Russia, reducing the risk of conflict with Moscow. In Latin America, he has so far behaved with scrupulous caution and, clearly, is hoping to normalize relations with Cuba while avoiding collisions with the "Bolivarian" states of Venezuela, Ecuador, and Bolivia.

Obama seeks a quiet world in order to focus his efforts on domestic reform—and to create conditions that would allow him to dismantle some of the national-security state inherited from the Cold War and given new life and vigor after 9/11. Preferring disarmament agreements to military buildups and hoping to substitute regional balance-of-power arrangements for massive unilateral U.S. force commitments all over the globe, the president wishes ultimately for an orderly world in which burdens are shared and the military power of the United States is a less prominent feature on the international scene.

While Wilsonians believe that no lasting stability is possible in a world filled with dictatorships, Jeffersonians like Obama argue that even bad regimes can be orderly international citizens if the incentives are properly aligned. Syria and Iran don't need to become democratic states for the United States to reach long-term, mutually beneficial arrangements with them. And it is North Korea's policies, not the character of its regime, that pose a threat to the Pacific region.

At this strategic level, Obama's foreign policy looks a little bit like that of Richard Nixon and Henry Kissinger. In Afghanistan and Iraq, he hopes to extract U.S. forces from costly wars by the contemporary equivalent of the "Vietnamization" policy of the Nixon years. He looks to achieve an opening with Iran comparable to Nixon's rapprochement with communist China. Just as Nixon established a constructive relationship with China despite the radical "Red Guard" domestic policies Chinese leader Mao Zedong was pursuing at the time, Obama does not see ideological conflict as necessarily leading to poor strategic relations between the United States and the Islamic Republic. Just as Nixon and Kissinger sought to divert international attention from their retreat in Indochina by razzle-dazzle global diplomacy that placed Washington at the center of world politics even as it reduced its force posture, so too the Obama administration hopes to use the president's global popularity to cover a strategic withdrawal from the exposed position in the Middle East that it inherited from the Bush administration.

This is both an ambitious and an attractive vision. Success would reduce the level of international tension even as the United States scales back its commitments. The United States would remain, by far, the dominant military power in the world, but it would sustain this role with significantly fewer demands on its resources and less danger of war.

Yet as Obama is already discovering, any president attempting such a Jeffersonian grand strategy in the 21st century faces many challenges. In the 19th-century heyday of Jeffersonian foreign policy in American politics, it was easier for U.S. presidents to limit the country's commitments. Britain played a global role similar to that of the United States today, providing a stable security environment and promoting international trade and investment. Cruising as a free rider in the British world system allowed Americans to reap the benefits of Britain's world order without paying its costs.

As British power waned in the 20th century, Americans faced starker choices. With the British Empire no longer able to provide political and economic security worldwide, the United States had to choose between replacing Britain as the linchpin of world order with all the headaches that entailed or going about its business in a disorderly world. In the 1920s and 1930s, Americans gave this latter course a try; the rapid-fire series of catastrophes—the Great Depression, World War II, Stalin's bid for Eurasian hegemony—convinced virtually all policymakers that the first course, risky and expensive as it proved, was the lesser of the two evils.

Indeed, during Franklin D. Roosevelt's first two terms, the United States pursued essentially Jeffersonian policies in Europe and Asia, avoiding confrontations with Germany and Japan. The result was the bloodiest war in world history, not a stable condominium of satisfied powers. Since that time, Jeffersonians have had to come to terms with the vast set of interlocking political, economic, and military commitments that bind the United States to its role in the postwar era. Jeffersonian instincts call for pruning these commitments back, but it is not always easy to know where to cut.

The other schools are generally skeptical about reducing American commitments. Wilsonians interpret Jeffersonian restraint as moral cowardice. Why, they ask, did Obama refuse to meet the sainted Dalai Lama on his way to kowtow to the dictators in Beijing? Jacksonians think it is cowardice pure and simple. And why not stand up to Iran? Hamiltonians may agree with Jeffersonian restraint in particular cases—they don't want to occupy Darfur either—but sooner or later they attack Jeffersonians for failing to develop and project sufficient American power in a dangerous world. Moreover, Hamiltonians generally favor free trade and a strong dollar policy; in current circumstances Hamiltonians are also pushing fiscal restraint. Obama will not willingly move far or fast enough to keep them happy.

The widespread criticism of Obama's extended Afghanistan deliberations is a case in point. To a Jeffersonian president, war is a grave matter and such an undesirable course that it should only be entered into with the greatest deliberation and caution; war is truly a last resort, and the costs of rash commitments are more troubling than the costs of debate and delay. Hamiltonians would be more concerned with executing the decision swiftly

and with hiding from other powers any impression of division among American counsels. But Obama found harsh critics on all sides: Wilsonians recoiled from the evident willingness of the president to abandon human rights or political objectives to settle the war. Jacksonians did not understand what, other than cowardice or "dithering," could account for his reluctance to support the professional military recommendation. And the most purist of the Jeffersonians—neoisolationists on both left and right—turned on Obama as a sellout. Jeffersonian foreign policy is no bed of roses.

In recent history, Jeffersonian foreign policy has often faced attacks from all the other schools of thought. Kissinger's policy of détente was blasted on the right by conservative Republicans who wanted a stronger stand against communism and on the left by human rights Democrats who hated the cynical regional alliances the Nixon Doctrine involved (with the shah of Iran, for example). Carter faced many of the same problems, and the image of weakness and indecision that helped doom his 1980 run for re-election is a perennial problem for Jeffersonian presidents. Obama will have to leap over these hurdles now, too.

It is not only Americans who will challenge the new American foreign policy. Will Russia and Iran respond to Obama's conciliatory approach with reciprocal concessions—or, emboldened by what they interpret as American weakness and faltering willpower, will they keep pushing forward? Will the president's outreach to the moderate majority of Muslims around the world open an era of better understanding, or will the violent minority launch new attacks that undercut the president's standing at home? Will the president's inability to deliver all the Israeli concessions Arabs would like erode his credibility and contribute to even deeper levels of cynicism and alienation across the Middle East? Can the president execute an orderly reduction in the U.S. military stake in Iraq and Afghanistan without having hostile forces fill the power vacuum? Will Venezuelan leader Hugo Chávez be so impressed with American restraint under Obama that he moderates his own course and ceases to make *anti-Yanquismo* a pillar of his domestic and international policy? Will other countries heed the president's call to assume more international responsibility as the United States reduces its commitments—or will they fail to fulfill their obligations as stakeholders in the international system?

A Jeffersonian policy of restraint and withdrawal requires cooperation from many other countries, but the prospect of a lower American profile may make others less, rather than more, willing to help the United States.

There is an additional political problem for this president, one that he shares with Carter. In both cases, their basic Jeffersonian approach was balanced in part by a strong attraction to idealistic Wilsonian values and their position at the head of a Democratic Party with a distinct Wilsonian streak. A pure Jeffersonian wants to conserve the shining exceptionalism of the American democratic experience and believes that American values are rooted in U.S. history and culture and are therefore not easily exportable.

Jeffersonians

Famous Jeffersonians: John Quincy Adams, Dwight D. Eisenhower, George F. Kennan, J. William Fulbright

Likes: limiting overseas entanglements, prioritizing domestic reform, warning of "imperial overstretch"

Dislikes: bloated military budgets, imposing American values abroad, close alliances with foreign regimes

"[W]e must guard against the acquisition of unwarranted influence . . . by the military-industrial complex. The potential for the disastrous rise of misplaced power exists and will persist."

—Dwight D. Eisenhower,
farewell address, Jan. 17, 1961

Hamiltonians

Famous Hamiltonians: Daniel Webster, Henry Clay, Theodore Roosevelt, George H. W. Bush

Likes: economic frameworks for prosperity, G-20 summits, American power used to advance the national interest, opening foreign markets for American business, realism regarding U.S. goals and capabilities

Dislikes: expending resources on humanitarian missions, undue focus on the domestic politics of foreign allies, international human rights watchdogs

"One class of our citizens indulges in gushing promises to do everything for foreigners, another class offensively and improperly reviles them; and it is hard to say which class more thoroughly misrepresents the sober, self-respecting judgment of the American people as a whole. The only safe rule is . . . to 'speak softly and carry a big stick.'"

—Theodore Roosevelt,
An Autobiography, 1913

Wilsonians

Famous Wilsonians: Eleanor Roosevelt, John F. Kennedy, Paul Wolfowitz, Christopher Hitchens

Likes: spreading democratic values as a prerequisite for international stability, the United Nations, human rights

Dislikes: isolationism, alliances with unsavory regimes, making policy based on narrow economic interests, balance-of-power politics

"Let every nation know, whether it wishes us well or ill, that we shall pay any price, bear any burden, meet any hardship, support any friend, oppose any foe to assure the survival and the success of liberty. This much we pledge—and more."

—John F. Kennedy,
1961 inaugural address

Jacksonians

Famous Jacksonians: William Tecumseh Sherman, George S. Patton, Jesse Helms, Ronald Reagan, Sarah Palin

Likes: muscular expansion of American power, unapologetic defense of U.S.

Dislikes: international treaties, the United Nations, timidity, undue concern with human rights and other countries' sovereignty

"Americans love a winner. Americans will not tolerate a loser. Americans despise cowards. Americans play to win all the time. I wouldn't give a hoot in hell for a man who lost and laughed. That's why Americans have never lost nor will ever lose a war, for the very thought of losing is hateful to an American."

—George S. Patton,
speech to the 3rd Army, June 5, 1944

For this president, that is too narrow a view. Like Abraham Lincoln, Woodrow Wilson, and Martin Luther King Jr., Barack Obama doesn't just love the United States for what it is. He loves what it should—and can—be. Leadership is not the art of preserving a largely achieved democratic project; governing is the art of pushing the United States farther down the road toward the still-distant goal of fulfilling its mission and destiny.

Obama may well believe what he said in his inaugural speech—"we reject as false the choice between our safety and our ideals"—but as any president must he is already making exactly those tradeoffs. Why else refuse to meet the Dalai Lama? Why else pledge support to the corrupt regime of President Hamid Karzai in Afghanistan or aid Pakistan despite the dismal track record of both the civil and military arms of the Pakistani government when it comes to transparent use of U.S. resources? Did the administration not renew its efforts to build a relationship with the regime in Tehran even as peaceful democratic protesters were being tortured and raped in its jails? Is Obama not taking "incentives" to Khartoum, a regime that has for more than a decade pursued a policy in Darfur that the U.S. government has labeled genocidal?

It is hard to reconcile the transcendent Wilsonian vision of America's future with a foreign policy based on dirty compromises with nasty regimes.

It is hard to reconcile the transcendent Wilsonian vision of America's future with a foreign policy based on dirty compromises with nasty regimes. If the government should use its power and resources to help the poor and the victims of injustice at home, shouldn't it do something when people overseas face extreme injustice and extreme peril? The Obama administration cannot easily abandon a human rights agenda abroad. The contradiction between the sober and limited realism of the Jeffersonian worldview and the expansive, transformative Wilsonian agenda is likely to haunt this administration as it haunted Carter's, most fatefully when he rejected calls to let the shah of Iran launch a brutal crackdown to remain in power. Already the Wilsonians in Obama's camp are muttering darkly about his failure to swiftly close the Guantánamo prison camp, his fondness for government secrecy, his halfhearted support for investigating abuses of the past administration, and his failure to push harder for a cap-and-trade bill before the Copenhagen summit.

Over time, these rumblings of discontent will grow, and history will continue to throw curveballs at him. Can this president live with himself if he fails to prevent a new round of genocide in the Great Lakes region of Africa? Can he wage humanitarian war if all else fails? Can he make these tough decisions quickly and confidently when his closest advisors and his political base are deeply and hopelessly at odds?

The Jeffersonian concern with managing America's foreign policy at the lowest possible level of risk has in the past helped presidents develop effective grand strategies, such as George Kennan's early Cold War idea of containment and the early 19th-century Monroe Doctrine. If successful, Obama's restructuring of American foreign policy would be as influential as these classic strategic designs.

Recent decades, however, have seen diminishing Jeffersonian influence in U.S. foreign policy. Americans today perceive problems all over the world; the Jeffersonian response often strikes people as too passive. Kennan's modest form of containment quickly lost ground to Dean Acheson's more muscular and militarized approach of responding to Soviet pressure by building up U.S. and allied forces in Europe and Asia. The Nixon-Kissinger policy of détente was repudiated by both the Republican and Democratic parties. Carter came into the White House hoping to end the Cold War, but by the end of his tenure he was supporting the resistance to the Soviet occupation of Afghanistan, increasing the defense budget, and laying the groundwork for an expanded U.S. presence in the Middle East.

In the 21st century, American presidents have a new set of questions to consider. The nature of the international system and the place of the United States in it will have to be rethought as new powers rise, old ones continue to fade, and attention shifts from the Atlantic to the Pacific. The rapid technological development that is the hallmark of our era will reshape global society at a pace that challenges the ability of every country in the world to manage cascading, accelerating change.

With great dignity and courage, Obama has embarked on a difficult and uncertain journey. The odds, I fear, are not in his favor, and it is not yet clear that his intuitions and instincts amount to the kind of grand design that statesmen like John Quincy Adams and Henry Kissinger produced in the past. But there can be no doubt that American foreign policy requires major rethinking.

At their best, Jeffersonians provide a necessary element of caution and restraint in U.S. foreign policy, preventing what historian Paul Kennedy calls "imperial overstretch" by ensuring that America's ends are proportionate to its means. We need this vision today more than ever: If Obama's foreign policy collapses—whether sunk by Afghanistan or conflicts not yet foreseen—into the incoherence and reversals that ultimately marked Carter's well-meaning but flawed approach, it will be even more difficult for future presidents to chart a prudent and cautious course through the rough seas ahead.

WALTER RUSSELL MEAD is Henry A. Kissinger senior fellow at the Council on Foreign Relations and author of *Special Providence: American Foreign Policy and How It Changed the World.* He blogs at The-American-Interest.com.

Reprinted in entirety by McGraw-Hill with permission from *Foreign Policy,* January/February 2010, pp. 58–64. www.foreignpolicy.com. © 2010 Washingtonpost.Newsweek Interactive, LLC.

National War Powers Commission Report

MILLER CENTER OF PUBLIC AFFAIRS

Whether to go to war is perhaps the most serious decision a country can make. In this section, we will provide a summary of (1) the constitutional basis for executive and congressional claims to primacy in war making; and (2) a cursory view of two centuries of the American experience about going to war.

The Constitutional Framework

The extent of the authority of both the President and Congress to take the country to war is far from clear. Put simply, the Executive and Legislative Branches do not agree about the scope of their powers; our history provides no clear line of precedent; and the Supreme Court has provided no definitive answer to this fundamental question.

Advocates on both sides find the answer obvious. Each of their claims to power, however, is met with contrary legal authority, historical counterexamples, and countervailing policy arguments. The only branch of government capable of resolving these disputes—the Judicial Branch—has consistently declined to do so, largely on the ground that questions of war and peace present political questions within the exclusive purview of the other two branches. So, unlike the rich tapestry of case law interpreting other provisions of the Constitution, such as freedom of speech or interstate commerce, the constitutional interpretation of war powers has largely been left to a competition between the Executive and Legislative Branches. As a result, the debate has sometimes focused more on process rather than on the merits of going to war and how best to prosecute it.

In these debates over process, many argue that the Constitution is perfectly clear, depending on which branch of government one supports. Proponents of congressional authority point to Article 1, Section 8 of the Constitution, which provides that "Congress shall have power . . . to declare War" and "grant Letters of Marque and Reprisal." Proponents of this view say that by vesting Congress with the power to declare war, the framers stripped the Executive of the powers the English king enjoyed. They say the framers placed the powers to decide to go to war in the hands of Congress because it is the branch most deliberate by design, most in touch with the American people, and thus least inclined to commit soldiers to the battlefield.

Advocates of congressional power further argue that after Congress has authorized or declared war, the President then—but only then—has the power to conduct war through his role as Commander in Chief of the armed services. They say the President can initiate war without congressional authorization only in limited circumstances, such as when the President does not have time to secure congressional approval because the country has been invaded or American citizens abroad are in imminent danger. Advocates of congressional power also note that Congress, once it has authorized a war, has many tools at its disposal to shape its conduct and duration. For example, Congress can define narrowly what military objectives the President may pursue. And, they also note, Congress can terminate an armed conflict in a variety of ways.

For their part, proponents of presidential authority point to the "Executive powers" and "Commander in Chief" clauses in the Constitution. They say that the framers wanted to put the authority for making war in the hands of the government official who has the most information and the best ability to execute—the President. According to their argument, congressional advocates overstate the significance of Congress's power to "declare" war. The power to "declare" war, as advocates of executive power interpret the Constitution, does not include the power to decide whether to go to war. Instead, it merely provides Congress the power to recognize that a state of war exists. These advocates argue that the President need not seek or obtain congressional approval before committing the country to military campaigns. Although it may be politically expedient for the President to obtain such popular support, they argue that the Constitution does not require it.

According to this view, Congress should exercise its constitutional powers if it wishes to check the President's actions. First, Congress can use its constitutional "power of the purse" to cut off funding. Second, Congress may impeach the President in an effort to change policy and conclude hostilities. The most ardent proponents of executive power argue that short of exercising one of these two options, Congress cannot regulate when or how the President wages war. They reason that the President has extensive unilateral powers to protect national security. . . .

The War Powers Resolution of 1973 attempted to resolve the fundamental constitutional questions that had been debated for almost two centuries, but it has failed to do so. The Resolution purports to formalize a role for Congress in making the decision whether to go to war. While it seeks to limit presidential power, the Resolution—either because of drafting error or political miscalculation—arguably invites Presidents to wage any military campaign they wish for up to 90 days. Once a conflict begins, however, the President is required under the Resolution to terminate it within 90 days if Congress has not authorized it. . . .

Every President since Ford has questioned the constitutionality of the War Powers Resolution and submitted reports that are "consistent with," but not "pursuant to" the statute. In President Reagan's September 23, 1987 report to Congress on activity in the Persian Gulf, he noted he was "mindful of the historical differences between the legislative and executive branches of government, and the positions taken by all of my predecessors in office, with respect to the interpretation and constitutionality of certain of the provisions of the War Powers Resolution." Reagan's White House Counsel, A. B. Culvahouse, reflecting on the War Powers Resolution of 1973, has noted: "There's a real Kabuki dance that's done here. You send a notice up to the Hill while protesting all the time that you're not really providing notice and that it's all unconstitutional." Democratic officials have expressed similar views.

Despite these and similar sentiments, Congress as a whole has never sought to compel the President to comply with the War Powers Resolution of 1973 or file a report under Section 4(a) of the Resolution. Individual members of Congress have, at times, filed lawsuits seeking to enforce the Resolution, by compelling, for example, the President to file Section 4(a)(1) reports and to start the Section 5(b) clock running. The courts have dismissed every such case.

Critics of the Resolution further note that it allows both branches to justify inaction. They point out that Presidents have regularly involved the country's armed forces in what are clearly "hostilities" under the terms of the statute, while claiming the statute is unconstitutional or not triggered in that particular case and therefore largely ignoring it. Critics further contend that Congress is only too willing to let the President navigate around the statute this way, because if the statute were triggered Congress might need to vote up or down on the conflict. Some defenders of the Resolution say, with scant supporting evidence, that despite all its flaws, it still acts to keep Presidents from unwisely rushing into military campaigns.

In sum, we encountered broad dissatisfaction with the 1973 Resolution. Unsurprisingly, there have been widespread bipartisan efforts over the years to amend or replace the statute. Arguments for repealing the statute and putting nothing in its place come mainly from staunch advocates of executive power. Conversely, arguments to give it real bite come from those who believe in congressional predominance. Still others suggest more modest reforms.

No proposal has gotten very far. (Several past reform efforts are discussed in Appendix 1, posted on the Commission's website at www.millercenter.org/warpowers.) Those advocating outright repeal—and, in their view, restoring the constitutional balance—have been met with the objection that their proposal too greatly favors the President and is unconstitutional. Those advocating significantly strengthening the Resolution to check executive power—and in so doing, in the congressionalists' view, restoring the constitutional balance of power—have been met with similar claims of unconstitutionality and the threat of veto. Still other proposals set forth detailed ways in which members of Congress, U.S. military personnel, and others would be authorized to bring suit to enforce their putative rights under the War Powers Resolution of 1973, some new statute they propose, or the Constitution. Although many argue it would be worthwhile to involve the courts to add some clarity to this body of law, these judicial review proposals have not been successful.

Even amidst these conflicting approaches, a unifying theme emerges: the need for greater consultation between the President and Congress. Indeed, many of the proposals would establish specific consultation groups with which the President would meet, as well as when and how these meetings should occur. (Examples of such consultative groups are collected in the table at Appendix 2 on the Miller Center website.)

Our Commission repeatedly heard calls for better communication between the President and Congress in regards to war. These views reflect the observations of constitutional scholar Alexander Bickel, who once said: "Singly, either the President or Congress can fall into bad errors. . . . So they can together too, but that is somewhat less likely, and in any event, together they are all we've got." Indeed, even President Nixon, in vetoing the War Powers Resolution called for further study about how Congress and the President could better consult. In so doing, he argued: "The responsible and effective exercise of the war powers requires the fullest cooperation between the Congress and the Executive and the prudent fulfillment by each branch of its constitutional responsibilities." . . .

WAR POWERS CONSULTATION ACT OF 2009

WHEREAS, the War Powers Resolution of 1973 has not worked as intended, and has added to the divisiveness and uncertainty that exists regarding the war powers of the President and Congress; and,

WHEREAS, the American people want both the President and Congress involved in the decision-making process when United States armed forces are committed to significant armed conflict, and such involvement of both branches is important in building domestic understanding and political support for doing so and ensuring the soundness of the resulting decision; and,

WHEREAS, past efforts to call upon the Judicial Branch to define the constitutional limits of the war powers of the Executive and Legislative Branches of government have generally failed because courts, for the most part, have declined jurisdiction on the grounds that the issues involved are "political questions" or that the plaintiffs lack standing; and,

WHEREAS, it harms the country to have the War Powers Resolution of 1973, the centerpiece statute in this vital area of American law, regularly and openly questioned or ignored; and,

WHEREAS, the country needs to replace the War Powers Resolution of 1973 with a constructive and practical way in which the judgment of both the President and Congress can be brought to bear when deciding whether the United States should engage in significant armed conflict, without prejudice to the rights of either branch to assert its constitutional war powers or to challenge the constitutional war powers of the other branch.

NOW THEREFORE BE IT RESOLVED:

Section 1. Short Title.

The War Powers Resolution of 1973, Pub. L. No. 93-148, is hereby repealed. This Act shall be cited as the War Powers Consultation Act of 2009.

Section 2. Purpose.

The purpose of this Act is to describe a constructive and practical way in which the judgment of both the President and Congress can be brought to bear when deciding whether the United States should engage in significant armed conflict. This Act is not meant to define, circumscribe, or enhance the constitutional war powers of either the Executive or Legislative Branches of government, and neither branch by supporting or complying with this Act shall in any way limit or prejudice its right or ability to assert its constitutional war powers or its right or ability to question or challenge the constitutional war powers of the other branch.

Section 3. Definitions.

3(A). For purposes of this Act, "significant armed conflict" means (i) any conflict expressly authorized by Congress, or (ii) any combat operation by U.S. armed forces lasting more than a week or expected by the President to last more than a week.

3(B). The term "significant armed conflict" shall not include any commitment of United States armed forces by the President for the following purposes: (i) actions taken by the President to repel attacks, or to prevent imminent attacks, on the United States, its territorial possessions, its embassies, its consulates, or its armed forces abroad; (ii) limited acts of reprisal against terrorists or states that sponsor terrorism; (iii) humanitarian missions in response to natural disasters; (iv) investigations or acts to prevent criminal activity abroad; (v) covert operations; (vi) training exercises; or (vii) missions to protect or rescue American citizens or military or diplomatic personnel abroad.

3(C). The "Joint Congressional Consultation Committee" consists of:

(i) The Speaker of the U.S. House of Representatives and the Majority Leader of the Senate;

(ii) The Minority Leaders of the House of Representatives and the Senate;

(iii) The Chairman and Ranking Minority Members of each of the following. Committees of the House of Representatives:

(a) The Committee on Foreign Affairs,

(b) The Committee on Armed Services,

(c) The Permanent Select Committee on Intelligence, and

(d) The Committee on Appropriations.

(iv) The Chairman and Ranking Minority Members of each of the following Committees of the Senate:

(a) The Committee on Foreign Relations,

(b) The Committee on Armed Services,

(c) The Select Committee on Intelligence, and

(d) The Committee on Appropriations.

3(D). The Chairmanship and Vice Chairmanship of the Joint Congressional Consultation Committee shall alternate between the Speaker of the House of Representatives and the Majority Leader of the Senate, with the former serving as the Chairman in each odd-numbered Congress and the latter serving as the Chairman in each even-numbered Congress.

Section 4. Consultation and Reporting.

4(A). The President is encouraged to consult regularly with the Joint Congressional Consultation Committee regarding significant matters of foreign policy and national security.

4(B). Before ordering the deployment of United States armed forces into significant armed conflict, the President shall consult with the Joint Congressional Consultation Committee. To "consult," for purposes of this Act, the President shall provide an opportunity for the timely exchange of views regarding whether to engage in the significant armed conflict, and not merely notify the Joint Congressional Consultation Committee that the significant armed conflict is about to be initiated. If one of the military actions described in Section 3(B) of this Act becomes a significant armed conflict as defined in Section 3(A), the President shall similarly initiate consultation with the Joint Congressional Consultation Committee.

4(C). If the need for secrecy or other emergent circumstances precludes consultation with the Joint Congressional Consultation Committee before significant armed conflict is ordered or begins, the President shall consult with the Joint Congressional Consultation Committee within three calendar days after the beginning of the significant armed conflict.

4(D). Before ordering or approving any significant armed conflict, the President shall submit a classified report, in writing, to the Joint Congressional Consultation Committee setting forth the circumstances necessitating the significant armed conflict, the objectives, and the estimated scope and duration of the conflict.

4(E). If the need for secrecy or other emergent circumstances precludes providing such a report before significant armed conflict is ordered or begins, such a report shall be provided to the Joint Congressional Consultation Committee within three calendar days after the beginning of the significant armed conflict.

4(F). For the duration of any significant armed conflict, the President shall consult with the Joint Congressional Consultation Committee at least every two months.

4(G). On the first Monday of April of each year, the President shall submit a classified written report to the Joint Congressional Consultation Committee describing (i) all significant armed conflicts in which the United States has been engaged during the previous year; (ii) all other operations, as described in Section 3(B) of this Act, other than covert operations, in which the United States was engaged in the same time period.

4(H). Congress shall employ a permanent, bi-partisan joint professional staff to facilitate the work of the Joint Congressional Consultation Committee under the direction of its Chairman and Vice Chairman. The members of the Joint Congressional Consultation Committee and the professional staff shall be provided all relevant national security and intelligence information.

Section 5. Congressional Approval or Disapproval.

5(A). If Congress has not enacted a formal declaration of war or otherwise expressly authorized the commitment of United States armed forces in a significant armed conflict, then within 30 calendar days after the commitment of United States armed forces to the significant armed conflict, the Chairman and Vice Chairman of the Joint Congressional Consultation Committee shall introduce an identical concurrent resolution in the Senate and House of Representatives calling for approval of the significant armed conflict.

5(B). Such a concurrent resolution shall be referred to the House of Representatives Committee on Foreign Affairs and Senate Committee on Foreign Relations and the Committees shall report on the concurrent resolution within seven calendar days. When the Committees so report, the concurrent resolution may be called up by any Senator or Representative, shall be highly privileged, shall become the pending business of both Houses, shall be voted on within 5 calendar days thereafter, and shall not be susceptible to intervening motions, except that each house may adjourn from day to day.

5(C). If the concurrent resolution of approval is defeated, any Senator or Representative may file a joint resolution of disapproval of the significant armed conflict, and the joint resolution shall be highly privileged, shall become the pending business of both Houses, shall be voted on within five calendar days thereafter, and shall not be susceptible to intervening motions, except that each house may adjourn from day to day. The effect of the passage of this joint resolution shall not have the force of law unless presented to the President and either signed by the President or subsequently approved by Congress over the President's veto, but Congress may specify the effect of the joint resolution of disapproval in the internal rules of each House of Congress.

5(D). Nothing in this Section 5 alters the right of any member of Congress to introduce a measure calling for the approval, disapproval, expansion, narrowing, or ending of a significant armed conflict.

Section 6. Treaties.

The provisions of this Act shall not be affected by any treaty obligations of the United States.

Section 7. Severability.

If any provision of this Act is held invalid, the remainder of the Act shall not be affected thereby.

The Homeland Security Hash

The Department of Homeland Security gets little credit for the fact that terrorists have not staged an attack on American soil since 2001, and it is an open question whether it deserves much. Conceived in haste and crippled by its design, the newest addition to the cabinet desperately needs an overhaul.

PAUL C. LIGHT

Four years after it opened its doors, the Department of Homeland Security is by general agreement one of the most troubled cabinet-level agencies in the federal government. Hardly a day goes by without some fresh report on a contract gone bad, a new technology that does not work, a new Coast Guard cutter that is not seaworthy, or more cargo that slips through port without inspection. Year after year, virtually every assessment, including those by Congress, the 9/11 Commission, and the department's own inspector general, has given the department the same mediocre grades. "While the terrorists are learning and adapting, our government is still moving at a crawl," said 9/11 Commission chairman Thomas Kean in December 2005.

Homeland Security's personnel agree. According to the federal government's latest survey of its own employees, the department is the worst place to work in the government. It received the lowest ratings of 36 federal agencies for job satisfaction, management, and leadership. It is plagued by high turnover, internal bureaucratic struggles, and a variety of structural handicaps stemming from its creation in the aftermath of the 9/11 attacks.

As a result, the department is far behind in achieving many goals. It still needs funding to inspect more cargo shipments; the authority to regulate and protect chemical plants and railroad cars; a clear strategy for protecting bridges, roads, trains, subways, and other critical infrastructure; more personnel to reduce the backlog of immigration cases; an effective screening program for airport employees; better technology for detecting hidden explosives; an accurate watch list of potential terrorists; and perhaps most important, improved intelligence capabilities.

If destiny is largely determined by birth, this is a federal bureaucracy destined to stumble, and perhaps to fail. The product of the largest and most complex governmental merger since the creation of the Department of Defense in 1949, it was cobbled together by White House aides in just a few frenzied weeks.

With 180,000 employees and a $43 billion budget, the department is a collage of 22 distinct government agencies drawn from different corners of the federal organization chart and glued together into a single, largely dysfunctional unit. Even as they continue doing all the unrelated tasks they brought with them—from screening airline passengers for weapons and explosives to administering the national flood insurance program and rescuing boaters in distress—its component agencies have been directed to make defending the nation against terrorism their top priority. It is as if a group of widget makers were brought together in a private-sector merger and told they must now start producing software.

Homeland Security is a collage of 22 distinct government agencies glued together into a single, largely dysfunctional unit.

Homeland Security is still striving simply to win the hearts and minds of its own employees. Many of them do not doubt that defending against terrorism is an important mission, but they do not necessarily see it as the primary job of their particular unit. It is no wonder they think this way. Only 65 percent of the department's budget is spent on programs properly defined as homeland security. That points toward the fundamental problem. The Department of Homeland Security includes bureaucratic pieces that do not belong in an organization designed to protect the nation from terrorism. It may have a mission statement, but it lacks a unified mission.

Secretary Michael Chertoff recently reminded Congress that it took 40 years for the Department of Defense to finally come together—and that was after the first secretary committed suicide. But the nation does not have four decades to wait for the Department of Homeland Security to succeed. There are important steps that can be taken now.

H omeland Security was born in the wake of 9/11 in a climate of fear and shared determination to prevent fresh terrorist attacks, but political considerations were never far from the forefront. Congress and President George W. Bush agreed on the need to coordinate the agencies that would caulk the borders and track those the president had labeled the "evil-doers." Yet the administration hoped to deflect calls for what Vice President Dick Cheney dismissed as a "big government" approach by recruiting former Pennsylvania governor Tom Ridge in October 2001 to head a tiny White House Homeland Security Council.

Ridge himself soon concluded that his office was not strong enough to do the job and began pushing for a merger of the Border Patrol, the Customs Service, and the Immigration and Naturalization Service (INS). As Ridge later told *The Washington Post,* "The only person at the time that thought it was a good idea was yours truly."

The Democrat-controlled Senate was already well ahead of Ridge. The Senate Governmental Affairs Committee held its first hearings on the need for reorganization the day after the 9/11 attacks, and in the spring of 2002 recommended the creation of a cabinet-level department. The proposal focused primarily on border security, with elements of the Border Patrol, the Coast Guard, the Customs Service, the Federal Emergency Management Agency (FEMA), and the INS at its core.

Much as it opposed a new department, the Bush administration felt it could not let the Senate Democrats take the lead on homeland security, especially not with the congressional elections looming in November. By early spring, the White House had decided to design its own merger.

It could not be just any merger, however. According to a 2005 retrospective by *Washington Post* reporters Susan B. Glasser and Michael Grunwald and a study last year by four researchers at the Naval Postgraduate School's Center for Defense Management Reform (*Legislating Civil Service Reform: The Homeland Security Act of 2002*), the White House concluded that if it wanted to take back the homeland security issue, nothing but the biggest merger in modern history would do. Ignoring warnings of bureaucratic train wrecks and a clash of cultures, the administration put five White House aides to work on designing a maximum merger.

Selected for their loyalty more than their collective knowledge of government reorganization, the Gang of Five—or the G-5, as its members liked to call themselves—included a future Internal Revenue Service commissioner, a National Guard major general, and three other mid-level aides. But experienced or not, the G-5 was given firm instructions to think big. "The overriding guidance" G-5 member Bruce M. Lawlor later told the *Post,* "was that everything was on the table for consideration."

The members of the G-5 took their mandate seriously, and began searching the federal organization manual for merger targets. Although the G-5 used the Senate proposal as a foundation and certainly knew enough to get started, the planners soon strayed far from the notion that the new department should be built around agencies with similar missions. What about adding the Federal Bureau of Investigation (FBI)? The Secret Service?

The National Guard? The Drug Enforcement Administration? The Federal Aviation Administration?

The choices seemed endless. The G-5 even considered detaching the Lawrence Livermore nuclear research laboratory from the Department of Energy and slipping it into Homeland Security. Richard Falkenrath, a G-5 member, simply called up a friend and asked which laboratory might fit: "He goes, 'Livermore.' And I'm like, 'All right. See you later.' Click."

It was all part of the maximum-merger zeitgeist. More agencies equaled a better reorganization.

The secrecy came at a price. As the G-5 proposal took shape in the White House basement, it was shielded from what could have been useful scrutiny.

Even Cheney offered suggestions. According to Lawlor, the G-5 started out with the eight agencies already in the Senate bill. "Then the vice president came along and said, 'You've got to do something more about bioterrorism.'" Other White House aides also weighed in, later leading one anonymous insider to criticize the merger as the work of "people who didn't know a whole lot about the boxes they were moving around."

Throughout the process, the G-5 operated in secrecy. That provided what one G-5 member called "freedom of deliberation" and protected the group from attack, especially by the affected agencies. "Everybody realized the agencies were not going to look at mission first; they were going to look at turf first," Lawlor recalled.

The secrecy came at a price. As the G-5 blueprint took shape in the White House basement, it was shielded from what could have been useful scrutiny. As Falkenrath remembered, there were dozens of questions during his first encounters with congressional staff after weeks of hush-hush tinkering. "Every one of these staffers had some little angle on something that we hadn't thought of. I was like, 'We better go figure out what we've missed here.'"

The secrecy also showed in the holes in the department's organization chart, notably in the failure to provide for a high-level policy planning unit of the kind normally found in a cabinet department. Policy planning staffs typically look at department-wide issues and take a longer-term perspective than bureaucrats charged with day-to-day responsibilities. When they work well, they can serve as the strategic brain trust of a department. Lacking such a unit, which was not created until a Chertoff-sponsored reorganization in 2005, the new department would be able to implement strategic plans, but not make them.

The G-5 also forgot to create the post of chief intelligence officer. Without a top official to provide leadership, the department's tiny intelligence unit drifted for its first three years. That post, too, was finally created in 2005, but a second handicap remains. The department is not authorized to collect intelligence on its own but must rely on the FBI, the Central Intelligence Agency, and a host of other sources in order to create a picture of potential threats to the homeland and plan its next moves.

June 6, 2002, was a very important day for the White House. Not only was it the date chosen to announce the creation of the new department, but it was also to be the moment when FBI agent Coleen Rowley would testify before the Senate Judiciary Committee about her office's aborted efforts to investigate Zacarias Moussaoui, who had paid cash to train on a Boeing 747 flight simulator in Minnesota less than a month before 9/11. Rowley had been rebuffed by her supervisors when she asked for permission to seek a warrant to search Moussaoui's laptop computer.

It was precisely the kind of testimony that would dominate the front pages. But the story was easily eclipsed by the White House proposal. Under the Bush administration's rollout strategy, Ridge released the proposal the morning of the 6th, an assortment of White House aides and enthusiastic members of Congress made the rounds of the major television outlets in the afternoon, and Bush made a nationally televised speech at 8 PM. By the next morning, the president was back in charge of the homeland security issue. He signed the White House bill into law on November 25.

When the new Department of Homeland Security formally opened for business in March 2003, the facts of geography revealed an unhappy truth about its position in the Washington power matrix. At his new headquarters in an old Navy annex building tucked away in the northwest corner of Washington, Secretary Tom Ridge was miles away from the White House, the Capitol, and the headquarters of other federal departments, not to mention the nearly two dozen separate organizations that were now part of his new department.

Even Ridge came to wonder about the scope of the reorganization. "The notion that everyone was going to join hands and sing 'Kumbaya,'" he later told *The Washington Post,* "I don't think anybody in our leadership expected that to happen. And it didn't." It still hasn't. Turf wars over budgets and staffing rage inside the department, especially among the remnants of the Customs Service and the INS, which have similar missions. On Capitol Hill, congressional committees and subcommittees refused to reshape their jurisdictions to match all the organizational shifts that occurred when agencies were wrenched out of their old homes. Last year, as a result, department officials were required to testify before 70 different congressional units. And in the federal budget process, top administrators have been forced to fight for every spending increase.

There is nothing quite like the Homeland Security merger in the history of the federal government. The creation of the Defense Department after World War II involved more people, but the Homeland Security merger involved many more agencies, split and recombined many of their component parts, and, astoundingly, demanded that they focus on a mission almost none of them had ever dealt with before: combatting terrorism.

Moreover, Congress wanted the new department to operate without any budget or personnel increases. Savings were supposed to come from the elimination of duplication and

A Big Agenda

Weapons of Mass Destruction

This is "the gravest danger facing America," according to the Department of Homeland Security. Plans include a ring of radiation detectors 50 miles from Manhattan. Technology is a limitation: Today's detectors can be triggered by banana peels and often miss nuclear materials. The multibillion-dollar Project BioShield effort to create defenses against viruses, toxins, and chemicals has produced few results.

Aviation

DHS screens 730 million people traveling on commercial airlines each year—and all 700 million pieces of their checked luggage. But federal investigators with bomb-making materials successfully passed security at all 21 airports tested last year.

Critical Infrastructure

This year, DHS will award $445 million in grants to protect everything from ports to commuter rail lines against threats such as bombs and biological weapons.

Border Protection

Though the spotlight shines on the Mexican border, terrorists have sought to enter the United States from the north. Each day, 18,000 trucks cross the Canada-U.S. border. No passport is necessary until 2009.

Pandemic Outbreak

Avian flu is a top concern. In February a Food and Drug Administration panel endorsed the first vaccine, though it had been successful in less than half of the clinical trials.

Cyber Security

Viruses and other forms of attack on computer networks cost some $50 billion worldwide each year. The National Cyber Security Division of DHS leads collaboration between the public and private sectors to combat technological infiltration.

Natural and Manmade Disasters

Nine of the 10 most costly presidentially declared disasters have been natural—either hurricanes or earthquakes. September 11, number two on the list after Hurricane Katrina, is the sole exception.

overlap. The department's different agencies were expected to incorporate the war on terrorism into their existing missions, and somehow find enough dollars and employees to add it to their already complicated mandates.

The merger combined some of the best and worst agencies in the federal government. Indeed, some of the pieces of the Homeland Security collage were thrown in chiefly to ensure that the department was not composed only of sub-par performers. In its "Government Performance Project" series, which concluded just before the merger, *Government Executive* magazine rated the Coast Guard one of Washington's most successful agencies, applauding its planning, esprit de corps, and ability to do more with less. It also rated FEMA near the top of the class. But the magazine's reporters rated the Customs Service as average at best, citing its antiquated information technology and problems collecting and accounting for duties, taxes, and fees. And they reserved their harshest assessment for the INS, noting among other things its long history of mismanagement, top-heavy bureaucracy, and decaying detention facilities. The Transportation Security Administration (TSA), with its 43,000 airport security screeners and other personnel, was too new to be rated.

Homeland Security's leaders have less access to information than many state and local security offices.

Adding to the turmoil, Homeland Security has experienced extraordinary personnel turnover. In its first four years, the department has gone through two secretaries (Ridge resigned late in 2004), three deputy secretaries, eight under secretaries, three FEMA administrators, four TSA administrators, a dozen assistant secretaries, hundreds of senior executives, and nearly 100,000 civil servants, many of whom left the baggage and screener lines in search of higher pay.

It is surprising that a department built around this uneven inventory of assets and liabilities was able to design a logo and seal, let alone create a sense of common identity across its agencies. It is even more surprising given the 22 personnel offices, 19 financial systems, 13 contracting units, and eight payroll processes that its agencies brought with them, along with every uniform color in the spectrum, from Coast Guard blue to Border Patrol green.

Many of Homeland Security's problems came to the fore in the summer of 2005, during Hurricane Katrina, when virtually everything that could go wrong did. FEMA was late in responding to the catastrophe, and the White House ignored the obvious need for action. It is well known that FEMA was led by a group of inexperienced political appointees headed by Michael Brown, fresh from an unsuccessful stint as commissioner of the International Arabian Horse Association. But there were other factors involved. FEMA's natural disaster budget was in shreds after three years of cutbacks designed to free money for antiterrorism efforts. It had lost dozens of experienced senior executives. Buried deep in the new department's organization chart, FEMA lacked the direct access to the White House it had once enjoyed. Moreover, the agency had been stripped of its responsibility for preparing the nation for natural and terrorist disasters only weeks before Katrina as part of Chertoff's reorganization, so its executives lacked the key connections with state and local officials that might have accelerated its response.

Although Congress recently restored at least part of FEMA's independence, including its direct line to the president and its

preparedness duties, terrorism still consumes three-quarters of its budget, leaving few resources for the next Katrina.

It is still too early to declare the Homeland Security merger a failure. While we do not know how much credit the department can claim, the United States has not suffered another terrorist attack on its soil. The department has produced notable gains in border security. Most U.S. seaports will have radiation detectors within three years, airplane cockpit doors are impenetrable, and the Border Patrol is still catching illegal immigrants. The department has regained at least some of the productivity its components lost at the start of the merger, and it has built some of the missing parts the G-5 neglected to create.

It is also making progress in its partnerships with state and local governments, particularly through the "fusion" centers that blend information from state and local law enforcement with intelligence from federal sources. Secretary Chertoff's reorganization in 2005 finally gave the department two essentials, a policy planning staff and an intelligence chief, as well as a much greater sense of shared purpose.

Yet Homeland Security still falls short. In coping with the great uncertainty involved in defending against terrorism, four characteristics are vital: alertness, agility, adaptability, and alignment around a core mission. Alertness depends on access to information, and the department is still fighting for that. It has been forced to rely on the cooperation of strangers in the intelligence community to find out what it needs to know, a disadvantage that has been compounded by the fact that the community's own reorganization under the national director of intelligence has been highly contentious. The department is often the last to know, and its leaders have less access to information than many state and local security offices (which, ironically, are funded by the department itself).

Despite the TSA's quick reaction to last summer's terrorist plot to bomb U.S.-bound airplanes with liquid explosives, the department as a whole has a well-deserved reputation for poor agility and missed deadlines. The long-promised "virtual border" composed of drones, pole-mounted cameras, satellite monitors, and 700 miles of two-layered fence at selected points along the U.S.-Mexico border is years away from implementation; new technology for inspecting seaborne cargo containers is proving much more expensive than expected; and a promised "bioshield" for protecting the nation from biological attacks and pandemics is still an expensive dream. And none of these projects will necessarily prove effective.

In its lagging effort to improve adaptability, the department is still looking for a reasonable rate of return on the billions it has spent seeking new technologies to further its mission, including radiation detectors for the borders, information technology for tracking foreign tourists and students as they enter and exit the country, and cameras that can detect illegal immigrants as they cross the border. Homeland Security's research directorate, with a limited staff and an inadequate $800 million budget, is still struggling to integrate the eight research programs that were merged under its authority.

Finally, the department has yet to resolve the tensions among the competing missions its agencies brought into the merger. Just visit the Coast Guard's homepage (www.uscg.mil) on any given day and read its news summary, which reports such things as emergency rescues, ice-breaking work, and environmental protection efforts, but rarely anything about terrorism. To be a truly unified department, Homeland Security will need to create a department-wide identity around one all-encompassing mission.

The department's creation followed standard Washington procedure in moments of national crisis. New missions demand new bureaucracy, and the bigger the mission, the bigger the bureaucracy. The conventional wisdom also holds that a seat at the president's cabinet table provides a fulcrum to leverage greater coordination while creating the high visibility that is needed to get big jobs done.

Sometimes a new bureaucracy *is* essential to success. Every one of the federal government's greatest achievements of the past half-century involved at least some new bureaucracy—the National Aeronautics and Space Administration helped the United States win the space race in the 1960s, the Environmental Protection Agency opened a new era in clean air and water in the 1970s, and dozens of other agencies such as the Centers for Disease Control and Prevention and the National Institutes of Health have produced stunning gains in Americans' lifespan. But sometimes a new bureaucracy can turn out badly. Thirty years after its launch, the Energy Department is still in disarray, and still searching for a coherent policy to end the nation's addiction to foreign oil.

The Coast Guard's modernization efforts have produced an undue number of horror stories about delays, cost overruns, and bad management.

Congress and the president now face a simple choice. They can either hope the merger will eventually work out or undertake an ambitious new reorganization. The chief goal would be to tighten the department's focus on a single core mission of preventing terrorism, with the related task of dealing with natural and terrorist disasters. There are three ways to do it:

Give some agencies back to their original owners. Although all Homeland Security agencies share at least part of the same mission, many share so little common ground that they should go.

There is no reason that the Secret Service should stay in Homeland Security, for example. In addition to protecting the president and other top officials, it guards against counterfeiting and financial fraud. It was perfectly comfortable as a quasi-independent agency housed in the Treasury Department, as was the Federal Protective Service, which guards federal office buildings, as part of the General Services Administration, the

Federal Law Enforcement Training Center, as part of Treasury, and elements of the Animal and Plant Health Inspection Service as part of Agriculture.

All could easily move home, thereby reducing the span of the department to a more manageable number of agencies and offices.

Reduce the number of agencies through internal mergers. Assuming that it rebuilds quickly, FEMA could easily absorb the department's entire preparedness bureaucracy, including the Fire Administration, which helps local fire departments buy new equipment and educate the public on fire prevention, as well as the $3 billion state and local grants program, which provides the dollars for preparedness for both natural disasters and terrorist attacks.

The department could also merge two of its other bureaus, Customs and Border Protection and Immigration and Customs Enforcement. Both share law enforcement responsibilities, focus on the same entry points, and undergo similar training. Although such an internal merger would introduce its own costs in lost productivity in the short term, the longer-term benefits for border security would outweigh the costs. The two agencies have been squabbling for the past four years about budgets and responsibilities, in part because they overlap so much.

Set some agencies free. After more than 200 years of operating first within the Treasury Department and later within the Transportation Department without a break in performance, the Coast Guard has earned its independence. It not only has one of the broadest missions in government, it also has some of the most pressing needs for modernization. Its efforts so far have produced an undue number of horror stories about delays, cost overruns, and bad management by the Coast Guard and the rest of the Department of Homeland Security. Given its freedom, the Coast Guard could pursue modernization without constant worries about the antiterrorism agenda.

The more one looks at the Department of Homeland Security, the more one admires the parsimony of Tom Ridge's original proposal for an agency with a highly focused border security agenda. Instead of taking on a host of unrelated missions, such an organization could spend its time and resources on a much more sharply defined mission. Ridge may have been the only one who thought it made sense, but it looks more and more like the kind of department that could work.

Homeland Security can still become one of the federal government's success stories. This organization born in a fever of necessity and politics can be repaired if common sense is allowed to prevail. The price of failure is too high for the country to shoulder.

PAUL C. LIGHT, the Paulette Goddard Professor of Public Service at New York University's Robert F. Wagner School of Public Service, has frequently testified before Congress on the Homeland Security merger. He is the author of *The Four Pillars of High Performance* (2005).

Coming Soon
A Crisis in Civil-Military Relations

RICHARD H. KOHN

When Bill Clinton won the presidency in November 1992, few could have anticipated that his first crisis would be a full-blown clash with the armed forces, unhinging his administration even before it took office. His, after all, was to be a domestic presidency. Clinton inherited a military rebuilt from its Vietnam nadir, led by generals and admirals jubilant from success in the Persian Gulf and cheered on by an admiring public. When Clinton pushed for the right of homosexuals to serve in uniform, the brass revolted, culminating in the spectacle of a president forced to surrender to his own generals.

Fast forward to 2008. The president elected in November will inherit a stinking mess, one that contains the seeds of a civil-military conflict as dangerous as the crisis that nearly sank the Clinton team in 1993. Whether the new president is a Republican or Democrat makes only a marginal difference. The issues in military affairs confronting the next administration are so complex and so intractable that conflict is all but inevitable.

When a new president takes office in early 2009, military leaders and politicians will approach one another with considerable suspicion. Dislike of the Democrats in general and Bill Clinton in particular, and disgust for Donald Rumsfeld, has rendered *all* politicians suspect in the imaginations of generals and admirals. The indictments make for a long list: a beleaguered military at war while the American public shops at the mall; the absence of elites in military ranks; the bungling of the Iraq occupation; the politicization of General David Petraeus by the White House and Congress; an army and Marine Corps exhausted and overstretched, their people dying, their commitments never-ending. Nearly six years of Donald Rumsfeld's intimidation and abuse have encouraged in the officer corps a conviction that military leaders ought to—are obliged to—push back against their civilian masters. Egged on by Democrats in Congress—and well-meaning but profoundly mistaken associates who believe the military must hold political leaders accountable for their mistakes—some flag officers now opine publicly and seemingly without hesitation. Though divided about Iraq strategy, the four-stars unite in their contempt for today's political class and vow not to be saddled with blame for mistakes not of their own making.

For its part, the new administration will enter office mindful and jealous of the military's iconic status in the public mind, even if, ironically, the rhetoric of politicians does much to inflate that prestige. In truth, increasing politicization of the armed forces has generated considerable cynicism and distrust among elected officials of every stripe, kept private only out of fear of appearing not to support the troops. The new administration, like its predecessors, will wonder to what extent it can exercise civilian "control." If the historical pattern holds, the administration will do something clumsy or overreact, provoking even more distrust simply in the process of establishing its own authority.

In the background, as always, will be the legacy of civil-military tensions going back to the beginning of the Republic, but magnified whenever a new administration comes to office. One four-star general put it this way in 2001 at the outset of the Bush presidency: "It's like waking up in the morning, looking across the bed, and discovering you've got a new wife. You've never met her, you don't know what she wants or what she's thinking, and you have no idea what will happen when she wakes up." He added, "we on this side of the river don't have to take it, either."

The problem here is not the ordinary friction between the military and its political bosses. That is understandable and, to a degree, typical and functional; the two sides come from different worlds, with different perspectives and different requirements. No decision in war, no military policy proposed to or considered by the Congress, no military operation—nothing in the military realm—occurs that does not derive in some way from the relationship between civilians, to whom the U.S. Constitution assigns responsibility for national defense, and the military leadership, which manages, administers, and leads the armed forces.

When the relationship works—when there is candor, argument, and mutual respect—the result aligns national interest and political purpose with military strategy, operations, and tactics. The collaboration between Franklin Roosevelt, his secretaries of war and navy, and the heads of the two armed services is considered the model in this regard. Each side kept the other mostly informed; the military were present at all the major allied conferences; Army Chief of Staff George C. Marshall spoke candidly with the president and consulted daily with Secretary of War Henry Stimson. When the relationship does not work—when the two sides don't confer, don't listen, don't compromise—the decisions and policies that follow serve neither the national interest nor conform to the bitter realities of war. The distrust, manipulation, and absence of candor that colored relations between President Lyndon Johnson, Defense Secretary Robert McNamara, and his senior military advisors offers a case in point; to this day Robert Strange McNamara arouses hatred and contempt among military officers who were not even born when he ruled the Pentagon.

While civil-military relations at the beginning of the Republic involved real fears of a coup, for the last two centuries the concern has revolved around relative influence: can the politicians (often divided among themselves) really "control" the military? Can the generals and admirals secure the necessary resources and autonomy to accomplish the government's purposes with minimal loss of blood and treasure? Until World War II, the influence of the regular military even in its own world was limited. After the war, the integration of foreign and military policies, the creation of the intelligence community, new weapons systems, and other elements of the Cold War national security establishment decidedly enhanced the military's say in policy deliberations. The end of the Cold War and an operational *tour de force* in the first Persian Gulf War cemented the military's position as the public's most trusted and esteemed institution. During the Clinton administration, the military leadership had a virtual veto over military policy, particularly the terms and conditions of interventions overseas. The power of the military has waxed and waned since the 1940s, but not a single secretary of defense has entered office trusting the armed forces to comply faithfully with his priorities rather than their own.

Four problems, in particular, will intensify the normal friction: the endgame in Iraq, unsustainable military budgets, the mismatch between twenty-first century threats and a Cold War military establishment, and social issues, gays in the military being the most incendiary.

As to the first of these, Iraq confounds the brightest and most knowledgeable thinkers in the United States. George W. Bush has made it clear that he will not disengage from Iraq or even substantially diminish the American military presence there until the country can govern, sustain, and defend itself. How to attain or even measure such an accomplishment baffles the administration and war critics alike. That is precisely why a majority of the American people supports withdrawing.

It follows that no candidate will be elected without promising some sort of disengagement. An American withdrawal would probably unleash the all-out civil war that our presence has kept to the level of neighborhood cleansing and gangland murder. Sooner or later that violence will burn itself out. But a viable nation-state that resembles democracy as we know it is far off, with the possibility that al-Qaeda will survive in Iraq, requiring American combat forces in some form for years to come.

In the civil-military arena, the consequences of even a slowly unraveling debacle in Iraq could be quite ugly. Already, politicians and generals have been pointing fingers at one another; the Democrats and some officers excoriating the administration for incompetence, while the administration and a parade of generals fire back at the press and anti-war Democrats. The truly embittered, like retired Army Lieutenant General Ricardo Sanchez, who commanded in Iraq in 2003–04, blame everyone and everything: Bush and his underlings, the civilian bureaucracy, Congress, partisanship, the press, allies, even the American people. Last November, Sanchez went so far as to deliver the Democrats' weekly radio address—and, with it, more bile and invective. Thomas Ricks, chief military correspondent of the *Washington Post,* detects a "stab in the back narrative . . . now emerging in the U.S. military in Iraq. . . . [T]he U.S. military did everything it was supposed to do in Iraq, the rest of the U.S. government didn't show up, the Congress betrayed us, the media undercut us, and the American public lacked the stomach, the nerve, and the will to see it through." Ricks thinks this "account is wrong in every respect; nonetheless, I am seeing more and more adherents of it in the military."

If the United States withdraws and Iraq comes apart at the seams, many officers and Republicans will insist that the war was winnable, indeed was all but won under General David Petraeus. The new administration will be scorned not only for cowardice and surrender, but for treachery—for rendering meaningless the deaths, maiming, and sacrifice of tens of thousands of Americans in uniform. The betrayed legions will revive all of the Vietnam-era charges, accusing the Democrats of loathing the military and America and of wishing defeat. The resentments will sink deep into the ranks, at least in the army and the Marines, much as the Praetorian myths about Vietnam still hold sway today in the Pentagon. The response—namely, that the war was a strategic miscalculation bungled horribly by the Bush administration—will have no traction. There will only be a fog of anger, bitterness, betrayal, and recrimination.

The second source of civil-military conflict will revolve around the Pentagon budget. The administration's request for the coming year, nearly $650 billion, is plainly unsustainable, although it accounts for only 20 percent of the federal budget and less than 4.5 percent of the gross domestic product. The figure understates true costs by excluding veterans affairs, homeland security, and other national security expenditures, which could boost the total upward of $850 billion, more than the rest of world combined spends on defense and larger than any military budget since World War II. This will be a red flag to a Democratic Congress, and certainly to a Democratic White House. However eager they may be to deflect charges of being weak on national defense, the Democrats will have no choice but to cut, and over time, cut deeply.

That is because the dilemma is substantially worse than even these figures suggest. The bill does not include the wearing out of military equipment, from overworked transport jets to tanks and trucks, or the expansion of ground forces. Then, too, there is the need for additional spending on homeland security, which several presidential candidates have vowed to do. Port defense, transportation, border integrity, the stockpiling of vaccines—the ability of the United States to respond to and recover from a successful nuclear or biological attack remains rudimentary, and by consensus underfunded. Finally, the Pentagon budget will have to compete with domestic spending priorities: for roads, water systems, and other infrastructure; for the FBI, the air traffic control system, the IRS, and other national agencies; for Social Security and Medicare to support the flood of retiring baby boomers; and for expanding and reforming health care. Claims on the national treasury could arise suddenly, like the hundred billion–plus dollars promised to New Orleans. A Republican administration could press for further tax cuts. (Some years ago, before 9/11, I asked Newt Gingrich whether Republicans, if they had to choose, favored tax reduction or a stronger national defense. He answered: tax cuts.) Expanding deficits could relentlessly drive up interest costs. A recession in turn would diminish tax receipts and raise the deficit even higher, setting in motion a downward spiral that would challenge any Congress, administration, or Federal Reserve chairman.

When presented with these fiscal challenges, military leaders are likely to cede nothing. They are at war around the world. They are charged not only with national defense, but with the stewardship of institutions rooted in past glory and expected to triumph over any and all foes. Officers recognize their historic role and they embrace it. Every year when budgets arise in discussion at war colleges, student officers—the up-and-comers in each service, many destined for flag rank—demand more money. In September, the air force asked for an additional $20 billion for aircraft. The Joint Chiefs and the combatant commanders understand the squeeze. New weapons systems must be funded and the cost of recruiting and retention bonuses has jumped to more than one billion dollars a year for the army alone. One petty officer recently told me that the navy paid him $80,000 to re-enlist, something he intended to do anyway. Some specialties command $150,000 in douceurs. And even these fees do not suffice. "I have in the last several years arrived at a point," Chairman of the Joint Chiefs of Staff Admiral Mike Mullen said recently, "where I think as a country we're just going to have to devote more resources to national security in the world that we're living in right now." Needless to say, Mullen was hardly speaking for himself alone.

The ways out of this jam all invite some sort of conflict. Least controversial would be to tackle that old bugbear, Pentagon waste. Several of the presidential candidates have vowed to do exactly this. But the gold-plated weapons systems always survive. And, clichés notwithstanding, the actual savings would be minimal in any case. Another perennial favorite is centralization or consolidation, an impulse that led to the creation of the Defense Department in 1947 and something attempted regularly ever since. Certainly, there are more opportunities here. Are six war colleges really still necessary? Does each service really need its own weather, chaplain, medical, and legal corps? Do both the navy and Marine Corps need their own air forces, since they fly many of the same aircraft, all

of them integrated on aircraft carriers? Are military academies a necessity? A larger percentage of ROTC graduates than of West Pointers stay in the army past the ten-year mark.

Yet imagine the outcry any one of these proposals would provoke, and the resistance it would generate from the services, agencies, and congressional committees whose ox was being gored. The delegation or defense company about to lose a base or a weapons contract would certainly howl—and mobilize. Organizational change in any bureaucracy provokes enormous and almost always successful resistance. In the Pentagon, the battles have been epic.

The world has a say in all this, too. The next administration will take office nearly twenty years after the fall of the Berlin Wall. Yet the American military establishment is essentially the same one created in the 1940s and 1950s to deter the Soviet Union. The United States today boasts four independent armed services with the same weapons, upgraded and more capable to be sure, as those known to George Marshall, Dwight Eisenhower, Chester Nimitz, and Curtis LeMay. Not only are the ships, planes, tanks, vehicles, and guns similar, but they are organized similarly, performing virtually the same roles and missions assigned them in the late 1940s.

The United States after 1989 did not demobilize. It "downsized." Successive administrations cut the budget by ten percent and the size of the force by about 25 percent, while the Pentagon substituted regional threats for the Soviet menace in its planning. Even in the midst of a "Global War on Terrorism," neither the generals nor their bosses in the White House and Congress have been able to rethink the purpose, organization, command and control, or even operation of the armed forces. Two decades is a long time. The decades between 1895 and 1915, 1935 and 1955, and 1975 and 1995 all involved paradigm shifts in America's role in the world and in its national security requirements. Today's security situation differs no less radically from the Cold War for which today's military establishment was devised. Are these the armed forces we really need?

Bitter fights over strategy, budgets, weapons, and roles and missions dating back sixty-plus years suggest the question may not be answerable in any practical sense. To understand fully just how difficult it will be to raise fundamental concerns about defense policies, consider the recent confusion over what exactly the role and purpose of the National Guard and reserves ought to be. A week before 9/11, I participated in a roundtable discussion of the subject for the Reserve Forces Policy Board. There was general agreement that reserve forces should concentrate more on homeland defense and less on backstopping active duty forces on the battlefield. Yet the former head of the National Guard Bureau insisted, without evidence and in the face of great skepticism, that the Guard and reserves could do both. The past five years have proved him wrong; reserve forces are underequipped and stretched thinner than the active duty army and Marine Corps.

Today, a congressionally chartered commission on the National Guard and reserves still struggles with how to shape and organize the reserves (particularly the National Guard, which reports to each state governor unless summoned for federal service). Admittedly, the National Guard and reserves possess unusual political power and since 1789 have been more resistant to rational military policy than any other part of the national security community. Robert McNamara, who transformed American defense more than any other Pentagon leader, failed utterly to budge the Guard and reserve. None of his successors possessed the nerve even to try. But the problem cannot be avoided. As the commission wrote in bureaucratic understatement, in March 2007, "the current posture and utilization of the National Guard and Reserve as an 'operational reserve' is not sustainable over time, and if not corrected with significant changes to law and policy, the reserve component's ability to serve our nation will diminish."

All the more so because Iraq and Afghanistan compose the first substantial, extended military conflicts the United States has fought with a volunteer force in more than a century. Today's typical combat tour of fifteen months is the longest since World War II. Expensive procurement programs are underway, but sooner or later they will be robbed to pay for other costs, such as war operations, the expansion of ground forces, or medical and veterans costs. Already, the Project on Defense Alternatives has proposed cutting two Air Force wings, two Navy wings, and two aircraft carriers for a total savings of more than $60 billion over the next five years. Eventually, the bill comes due, either in blood, defeat, or political crisis. As the old Fram oil filter advertisement put it, "Pay me now, or pay me later."

L ast on the list of issues certain to provoke civil-military tension is social concerns, two of which will surely arise in a Democratic administration and also may be unavoidable in a Republican one.

At a time when the Pentagon spends huge sums of money annually to recruit and retain soldiers, it makes no sense to eject hundreds of fully trained, dutifully serving volunteers, many of whom—the several dozen Arab linguists forced out in the last few years come to mind—possess skills in short supply in the military. The old arguments about gays undermining unit cohesion or threatening discipline have lost credibility; foreign militaries allow homosexuals to serve at all levels, including in command and at flag rank, without detrimental effect. Young people today, even from the more conservative demographics likely to enlist, express little concern about serving alongside gays. But for many older men in uniform, it's a different story, as recently-retired Chairman of the Joint Chiefs of Staff Marine General Peter Pace made clear when he labeled homosexuality immoral. All the Democratic presidential candidates support lifting the ban; sooner rather than later Democrats in Congress are likely to try to change the law. Both sides will drag in the armed services, reviving the emotional debate of the early 1990s, escalating tensions within the military's leadership and between it, Congress, and the administration. Not all of this will make the newspapers, but within the Pentagon the disagreements will provoke tension, anger, mistrust, and perhaps open dissent.

Another issue bound to cause friction involves the right of evangelical chaplains to pray at public events in the name of Jesus Christ, and of evangelical officers to proselytize according to the principles of their faith. The issue pits freedom of religion against the duty of chaplains to minister to a diverse military in an ecumenical fashion, for their units comprise people of many faiths (and sometimes none), with varying degrees of commitment. The historian of religion Ann Loveland, now retired from the history department at Louisiana State University, has documented the evangelical mission to the military first undertaken in World War II. Believing that military service could debauch American youth, the Christian evangelical movement sought to spread the gospel inside the services by encouraging its clergy to become chaplains, founding and supporting organizations to support and spread evangelical faith, and working to boost the number of evangelicals in the military leadership. In the early 1980s these efforts began to generate anxiety in the officer corps. Commanders who held prayer breakfasts and Bible readings for their officers were sometimes suspected of favoring their fellow worshippers in the yearly evaluations so critical to promotion and assignment. Early in this decade, a scandal erupted at the U.S. Air Force Academy when it was discovered that the football coach, commandant of cadets, and faculty and chaplains were subtly pressing cadets to join the faith, and disparaging others who did not. Just last year, four generals were recommended for reprimand for participating in uniform in a video used by an evangelical organization to proselytize.

Now, it could be argued that none of these four great problems will trigger a crisis. Republicans, for example, might not risk a break with the evangelical community by strictly enforcing policies against proselytizing. And they would be only too happy to continue lavishing funds on the Pentagon. But how will they reconcile tax cuts, balanced budgets, and robust defense spending? Iraq, for which Republican presidential candidates have offered no solution beyond more of the same, makes the election of a Republican administration unlikely in any case. Yet, if elected, it too would have to disengage, lest the army and Marines become so exhausted and alienated that their leaders go public with their resentments.

The Democrats would surely prefer to finesse these dilemmas and, with them, charges of weakness on national defense. Hillary Clinton has labored assiduously to gain the trust of the military, mindful of how it nearly crippled her husband's administration. Yet escape will be impossible, particularly when it comes to Iraq and the budget. Significantly, Clinton has made no promises to the military, not even a ritualistic pledge to maintain a strong national defense. Civil-military relations under Democratic administrations, from Truman to Kennedy to Johnson to Carter to Clinton, became more toxic with each. The leading Democratic contenders today have no military experience or feel for military culture. All would find themselves under extraordinary pressure from their constituencies to exit Iraq, cut the budget, allow gays to serve without prejudice, and apply the separation of church and state with rigor. None would wish to expend political capital on less sexy, but more consequential, questions related to the proper roles, missions, scope, and resources of the military establishment. Nor would the Congressional Democrats. Yet if they don't set the terms of the debate, the military will do it for them.

However it begins, a clash between the next administration and the armed forces need not metastasize into a full-blown crisis. Military leaders should start to consider how they will react to civilian demands, and which of their traditions they will choose. Will they acquiesce after due advice and consultation, as the Constitution and our tradition of civilian control suggests? Or will they resist, employing techniques borne of decades of inside-the-beltway maneuvering? Will they confine dissent to the appropriate channels? Or will they go public, enlisting their allies in Congress, industry, and veterans groups? Will they collaborate with their new civilian superiors? Or will they work to thwart every recommendation harmful to their service? Much will depend on the capacity of military leaders to establish a workable relationship with their civilian superiors and to embrace their own tradition of professionalism.

Civilians have equal obligations. Will they tackle thorny defense issues in a serious, nonpartisan way, or will they succumb to their own posturing? Will they box themselves in with their campaign promises? Will they apply Band-Aids to the Pentagon budget, or will they address the more fundamental problem of reorganizing a Cold-War military for an age of asymmetric threats? Will they consider seriously, if not always heed, the counsel of military expertise?

A crucial intermediary here will be the next secretary of defense. Someone in the mold of Melvin Laird or James Schlesinger or William Perry will be indispensable—that is, someone knowledgeable and politically skilled who can gain and keep the confidence of the military, Congress, and the president. Whoever wins the job must wear his or her authority without bluster or arrogance, and lead firmly while holding the military to account. Above all, the secretary must act with courtesy, fairness, and decisiveness. A new administration might even ask Robert Gates to stay on; he has presided over the Pentagon with a calming, steady hand after Rumsfeld's departure.

Staffing decisions at less senior levels will be nearly as important. Neither party can afford to populate the Defense Department with politicians on the make, congressional staffers beholden to special interests, or young know-nothings looking to plus-up their résumés. These positions require knowledgeable people from the business community, the federal bureaucracy, and other professions who understand and respect the military but will not be awed by medals and campaign ribbons. The service secretaries have the closest relationship with the military leadership and have a critical say in picking senior leaders for advancement into the key commands and the Joint Chiefs. Finding the right individuals for these slots will be essential. The new secretary of defense would do well to assemble his deputy, under secretaries, and service secretaries into a cohesive executive committee that would formulate an agenda, rethink policy, and oversee its implementation.

The next administration should also act quickly to insulate the military leadership from partisan politics. The first act will be, after due consideration, the reappointment of Admiral Mullen as chairman. Then there should be a concerted search within the services for loyal but independent thinkers who understand the American system of civilian control but also know how to be dead honest in their advice. The recent appointment of General James Mattis of the Marines to head Joint Forces Command sends exactly the right message. Whoever comes into office in January 2009, in turn, needs to make clear up front that he or she will not hide behind the military, that he or she will not compromise the military's professional ethos by delivering partisan speeches in front of uniformed audiences or trotting out the brass to market administration policies.

Last of all, the new president ought to reach out to the armed forces in their own communities: visiting bases, praising the military with genuine sincerity, addressing veteran's care, making certain that as troops are withdrawn from Iraq, no blame falls unfairly on them for what follows. The political leadership will have to consult widely about changes, cuts, consolidations, and other modifications to the defense establishment. The next administration will need to establish a precedent for strict civilian control from the outset, all the while spending political capital on national defense and boosting the morale of what will likely be an anxious force. Consistent and vocal praise for military (and public) service would go a long way—easy for a Republican who abandons the demonization of government, difficult for a Democrat accustomed to ignoring or criticizing the military.

Soldiers and civilians alike will have momentous decisions to make. Politicians will have to choose whether to lead or to hide, whether in the name of maintaining or establishing their bona fides as "supporters of the military" they will put off decisions that upend the current and unsustainable order of things. Military leaders face their most important choice in more than half a century: whether to cooperate and assist in this effort, or to resist past the point of advice and discussion, to the detriment of their service, national defense, and indeed their professional souls.

RICHARD H. KOHN is Professor of History and Peace, War, and Defense at the University of North Carolina at Chapel Hill. He was Chief of Air Force History for the USAF, 1981–1991. Last year, he was the Omar N. Bradley Professor of Strategic Leadership at Dickinson College and the U.S. Army War College.

From *World Affairs*, Winter 2008, pp. 69–80. Copyright © 2008 by World Affairs Institute. Reprinted by permission. www.WorldAffairsJournal.org

Lost for Words
The Intelligence Community's Struggle to Find Its Voice

Josh Kerbel

In the wake of the 9/11 attacks and the Iraq intervention, most of the national security components of the US government have had some—mostly overdue—introspective moments. Such reviews can only be considered healthy. For as Sun Tzu, the Chinese military and intelligence theorist, said, "Know the enemy and know yourself; in a hundred battles you will never be in peril."[1] The fact is, however, that many of those governmental components did not necessarily like what they saw looking back at them from the mirror. This result was particularly true of the intelligence community, which found its own self-identity issues staring back with an unnerving intensity.

To be blunt, the intelligence community, which for the purposes of this article refers mainly to the analytic component, still does not "know itself." That is to say, 60-plus years after its creation as a "community"—making the point that this identity crisis is not solely the product of post-9/11 and Iraq soul-searching—America's intelligence analysts still cannot agree on an answer to that most fundamental question of analytic identity: What exactly is intelligence analysis?

Quite possibly, this analytic identity crisis has been summarized best in writing by the intelligence community itself. In 2005, the Central Intelligence Agency's Center for the Study of Intelligence published an unclassified ethnographic study of the community's analytic component which, based on hundreds of interviews with analysts and countless hours watching them work, found that "heterogeneous descriptions and definitions of intelligence analysis as a professional discipline were consistent findings." Consequently, the study went on to conclude, there still "needs to be a clear articulation and dissemination of the identity and epistemology of intelligence analysis."[2]

Art or Science?

In terms of overall analytic identity, perhaps no question is more fundamental or divisive than the question of whether intelligence analysis is art or science. On one side of this debate is the "analysis as science" school of thought whose adherents favor a less individualistic or idiosyncratic and more "rigorous" approach to analysis. On the other side of the divide are the "analysis as art" adherents who argue for an analytic approach that places greater value on experience, intuition, and "feel" versus some artificially sterile scientific approach.

For the science adherents, perhaps the most persuasive outlet so far has been the 2005 CIA study which meticulously examined not only how the community came to perceive analysis as art, but also what intelligence agencies might do to make it more of a science. That study argues that the notion of analysis as art is deeply rooted in the concept of tradecraft, which is defined as "practiced skill in a trade or art." It elaborates by explaining that in interviews, "analysts, managers, instructors, and academic researchers employed the word 'tradecraft' as a catchall for the often-idiosyncratic methods and techniques required to perform analysis." Moreover, the study asserts that while the term might be appropriate for describing the activities of the operational side of the intelligence community, "the analytic community's adoption of the concept to describe analysis and analytic methods is not [appropriate]. The obvious logical flaw with adopting the idea of tradecraft as a standard of practice for analytic methodology is that, ultimately, analysis is neither craft nor art." To the contrary, the study contends that analysis is—or at least should be—"part of a scientific process."[3]

The CIA study is not alone in its assessment. Putting a vivid exclamation point on the debate, an article in the journal *Survival* asserts that "putative CIA tradecraft . . . promotes the cultivation of a kind of 'Pinball Wizard,' the deaf, dumb, and blind kid from the rock opera *Tommy*, who instinctively avoids distractions, plays by intuition, and always achieves success." The article goes on to argue that "boosting analytical effectiveness requires more than the serendipitous cultivation of analytical wizards, whose skills and methods are rarely if ever subjected to testing, validation, and broader organizational application."[4]

Clearly disturbed by this unscientific approach to analysis, the CIA study argues that "intelligence analysis can be reconstructed in the context of a scientific method, which is merely an articulated formal process by which scientists, collectively and over time, endeavor to put together a reliable, consistent, and nonarbitrary representation of some phenomena." Moreover, the study asserts that "the data collected through both interviews and observation indicated that there were, in fact, general methods that could be formalized and that this process would then lead to the development of intelligence analysis as a scientific discipline." That said, however, the study also notes that "the idea that intelligence analysis is a collection of scientific methods encounters some resistance in the intelligence community."[5]

Adherents of the "analysis as art" school of thought have also been active in the debate. In one notable *The New York Times* op-ed that was widely circulated and discussed within the intelligence community, it was argued that in a misguided effort to be scientific, the intelligence community—as exemplified by the CIA—has over-reached into the realm of scientism. More specifically, the article argued that this scientism emerged from a fashionable post-war belief that "human affairs could be understood scientifically, and that the social sciences could come to resemble hard sciences like physics." It went on to lament that even some five decades later, one can still sense how this scientism "has factored out all those insights that may be the product of an individual's intuition and imagination."[6] It is important to recognize that *The New York Times* is not alone in its lament. A *Washington Times* column that also received extensive distribution and discussion in the intelligence community argued that "producing useful, useable intelligence is an art . . . a grand exercise in data interpretation, pattern recognition, and intuition."[7]

Interestingly, unlike the science adherents who seem almost uniformly inclined to blame the intelligence community itself, the art adherents appear more divided on who is to blame. For instance, some seem inclined to place the blame for "false scientism" on the community, especially via the pernicious influence of the CIA's "father of analysis," Sherman Kent. Others, however, apparently feel that policymakers must bear much responsibility. Again, the column in *The Washington Times* asserted that "[i]t seems very few leaders understand that [intelligence is an art—not science]."[8] Consequently, this line of thinking goes, policymakers expect and demand analyses characterized by a degree of precision and certainty that only a science could provide.

Undoubtedly, the issue of blame is debatable. What is not debatable is the fact that the notion of "analysis as art," like the notion of "analysis as science," meets considerable resistance from the ranks of analysts themselves. For evidence of this, one need only read the comments engendered by the posting of *The New York Times* op-ed on one internal analyst discussion board: "Gibberish," "A rant," "[The author] just doesn't understand what we do."

Alloying Analysis

Notwithstanding the ambivalence of intelligence analysts, both of these perspectives have real merit. To be fair, most adherents of a particular perspective will accept that the question is not a zero-sum, all-or-nothing issue. Rather, what they are really advocating is an analytic approach that—if not dominated by their preferred perspective—at least tempers the perceived excesses of the other. In other words, most advocates of a particular perspective will usually acknowledge, if only begrudgingly, that intelligence analysis is truly a matter of complements, with the real question being one of relative weight.

The necessity for such a balanced perspective was perhaps most articulately acknowledged by the presidential commission investigating intelligence related to Iraqi weapons of mass destruction. Interestingly, however, rather than lament an imbalance in the proportion of art to science in community analyses of Iraq, the commission instead regretted the fundamentally poor application of each perspective. Thus, with regard to the scientific school's argument for a more formalized and rigorous analytic process, the commission's report agreed when it found "the (*2002 Iraq National Intelligence Estimate* [NIE]) fully met the standards for analysis that the community had set for itself. That is the problem." On the other hand, however, the commission's report also agreed with the art advocates when it concluded that the 2002 NIE "displayed a lack of imagination" that precluded the asking of "the questions that could have led the intelligence community closer to the truth."[9] In sum, according to the commission, the problem was not so much an imbalance of perspectives but an across-the-board deficiency in practice.

Given this finding, it is clearly necessary for the analytic community to find a new conceptual model, one that raises the level by which both artistic and scientific approaches are applied while simultaneously blending them into a sort of complementary "alloy." Ideally, this new model would integrate art and science and yet forsake high art and hard science pretensions. Admittedly, this formula may prove a difficult mix to create. Only by formulating it, however, will the intelligence community find the analytical "sweet-spot" that resides somewhere between the prevailing perceptions, which are antagonistic (art *or* science) on the one hand and alchemic (wizardry and scientism) on the other.

A Better Model

One such alloyed model that has been proposed is a medical one, since intelligence analysis and medical diagnosis are similar in many ways.[10] For example, both intelligence analysts and medical doctors are confronted with problem sets—the international system and living systems respectively—that are highly dynamic and uncertain. Analysts and doctors also follow cyclical procedures that while differing in specific terminology (collection versus testing; analysis versus diagnosis; and dissemination versus prognosis), have details that are fundamentally similar. For the purposes of this article, however, perhaps the greatest similarity is that both intelligence analysis and medicine—done well—require their practitioners to blend art and science.

At present, the medical community appears much more accepting of this need for balance than the intelligence community. There is almost universal acceptance amongst doctors, whether general practitioner or specialist, that the practice of medicine is both art and science. One practicing physician who also is a student of medical intelligence has noted, "While much of clinical medicine is firmly grounded in basic science research, there is a substantial practical component to medical practice which cannot be found in any textbook, and is instead passed down from attending physicians to resident physicians to medical students."[11] This, of course, is not to say that the medical community does not continue to fight over this—it does—as the increasingly vocal "evidence-based" movement, which was originally known as the "science-based" movement, makes abundantly clear. That fight, however, is largely one about the relative weighting each approach should get—not the need for a blend in the first place.

In contrast, the intelligence community continues to wrestle with a fundamental need for both perspectives, never mind what the proper balance between them should be. For evidence of that perspective think back to the resistance from analysts to both the "analysis as art" and "analysis as science" arguments presented earlier in this article. If that is not deemed sufficient evidence, one might consider the extreme swings in managerial emphasis—between the imperative for generalists (with a synthetic macro-perspective that values the ability to connect the proverbial "dots") and the imperative for experts (with a more analytic micro-perspective that values mastery of a specific "account")—that periodically sweep across the analytic community. Ideally, the intelligence community would view these unique perspectives in a highly complementary light, much as the medical community has with its embrace of both the general practitioner and the specialist. Alas, the intelligence community—particularly the line analysts, when compared to the analytical methodologists—continues to bicker over the need for a mixed approach that precludes the discussion from addressing the real issue of the proper mixture.

This is where the adoption of a medical model could really help the intelligence community. The need for an appropriate art and science blend, at least in medicine, is a notion that resonates strongly, if unconsciously, with most people—including intelligence analysts. After all, most people when choosing a doctor tend to look for one who is not only familiar with the "basic science," but is also in possession of the "practical component" that comes with experience and intuition. Consequently, by modeling the practice of intelligence analysis on the practice of medicine it may be possible to use that unconscious resonance as a means of fostering a similar desire for a balance of art and science amongst analysts.

Finding the "Right" Words

Recognition of the powerful analogy between medicine and intelligence analysis is not new. Historian Walter Laqueur wrote about it more than 20 years ago, and it has been a thin but enduring theme in the literature of intelligence ever since.[12] What has not been sufficiently addressed in that literature is the need for more than just a useful analogy. More specifically, what is now required is much more attention on the linguistic aspects of the analogy, the metaphors.

At a fundamental level metaphors are models.[13] Which is to say, they are much more than mere "rhetorical flourish—a matter of extraordinary rather than ordinary language."[14] Rather, "our conceptual system [i.e., the way one defines everyday reality] is largely metaphorical."[15] Consequently, metaphors fundamentally "structure how we perceive, how we think, and what we do."[16]

Given this fact that the metaphors analysts use directly reflect and reinforce their thinking, metaphors are key focal points in any effort to examine analytic mindsets and subsequently

formulate a cohesive analytic identity. This is a point that while not entirely lost on the intelligence community—like the need for an art and science balance—is more readily recognized by the analytic methodologists rather than the line analysts. For evidence of this, one need only consult the CIA study on analytic culture—written by an anthropologist, not an analyst—which noted that "language is a key variable in anthropology and often reveals a great deal about the cognition and culture of a community of interest. The adoption by members of the analytic community of an inappropriate [operational] term [i.e., tradecraft] for the processes and methods employed in their professional lives obfuscates and complicates the reality of their work."[17]

Despite this acknowledgment, the fact remains that the predominant linguistic metaphor for intelligence analysis, like that for the larger national security debate of which it is a part, is essentially an unrealistic one. That is to say, it is a mechanical metaphor built upon such terms and concepts as tension, inertia, momentum, leverage, and trajectory that unrealistically portray the international system as a sort of machine that behaves linearly: is fully understandable, predictable, and certain. The truth, however, is that the international system is simply not a machine. Rather, it is an organism in that it is made up of "living" beings (people, states, etc.) that learn, change, and adapt to changing circumstances which machines, of course, do not.

To accurately describe and think about such an organism in a way that captures, or at least accepts, the uncertainty that is inherent in its behavior, it is necessary to employ a more realistic nonlinear metaphor. In this case, that would mean a biological one, or more specifically a medical one—using terms such as susceptibility, symptomatic, ripeness, side effects, etc.—that is well-suited to describing an organic problem set. In sum, if intelligence analysts are to start thinking more biologically than mechanically, they need to start communicating more like physicians than the physicists they have long tended to mimic.

Ultimately, it is vitally important that the intelligence community, when considering language, begin to focus on the metaphorical aspects versus the stylistic aspects that it has traditionally tended to emphasize. In particular, for too long when the intelligence community has talked about precision of language it has really meant concision—the quest to say things with even fewer words and more "white space." In contrast, what the intelligence community truly needs to appreciate is that precision of language needs to be about using language, the actual words (even if it means more of them) that accurately reflect and reinforce how it conceptualizes its subject matter and, by extension, itself.

A Hard Pill to Swallow

For the intelligence community, the linear mechanical metaphor remains the dominant linguistic and consequently mental model; it is the default setting. This is not surprising considering the powerful historical experiences that have foisted it upon the community. First, and at a most general level, American culture—rooted as it is in western philosophical and intellectual tradition—remains saddled with the heavy weight of Newtonianism. Sir Isaac Newton's legacy—one of pure science overflowing into alchemy (wizardry and scientism)—continues to fundamentally shape prevailing western perspectives of the universe and how it works.[18] Newton may have credited his extraordinary vision to his "standing on the shoulders" of the scientific giants who preceded him, but the West has never managed to climb out from under him. Nowhere is this more manifestly evident than in the way American intelligence analysts talk, write, and think about the world.

At a second, more community-specific level, it is important to understand that the "unified" intelligence community's formative experience was the relatively linear Cold War. As one former professor at the National War College noted, the Cold War was essentially a two-body problem and "two-body problems lie generally in the linear to mildly nonlinear range. In other words, the Cold War marked by the interaction of two world powers habituated participants to an essentially linear environment."[19] In turn, this history contributes to one of the community's most vexing post–Cold War problems: how to provide adequate numbers of mentors versed in nonlinear thinking for the legions of new analysts when the pool of potential mentors is populated by senior analysts comfortable with highly linear perspectives.

Finally, if one adds to this mix the linear scientism exemplified by Sherman Kent, it is easy to see how the lexicon of linear reductionism—and the corresponding mindset that it, again, reflects and reinforces—is now so infused into the US national security/intelligence discussion so as to seem beyond question. Indeed, it is rather rare to read an American article on foreign affairs, international relations, or national security—not just intelligence analyses—that does not employ mechanical terminology. Consequently, assertions that such terminology is now somehow unsuitable are inevitably met by an almost reflexive resistance.

Aligning Capabilities and Expectations

Given how thoroughly infused the mechanical metaphor is in the US national security and intelligence dialogue, the adoption of a new metaphor and commensurate mindset that accepts uncertainty cannot be done by the intelligence community in a vacuum. Rather, it will require the complicity and cooperation of the community's beneficiaries and benefactors (i.e., policymakers and the public) whose unrealistic expectations are also rooted in a linear metaphor/mindset. Consequently, any genuine effort in this vein will require a conscious process of education aimed at bringing expectations of policymakers, the general public, and the intelligence community into accordance. In particular, all concerned parties need to come to a mutual understanding that it is simply impossible to expect the intelligence community to predict the behavior of nonlinear systems with certainty and precision, especially over long periods of time. Rather, what should be expected from the community are better (allowing for uncertainty) models for understanding and anticipating—but not predicting—the potential behavior of the complex systems which it is tasked to

watch. Presumably, policymakers should find significant value in this perspective. After all, as noted economist and complex systems theory pioneer Brian Arthur observed, "An awful lot of policymaking has to do with finding the appropriate metaphor. Conversely, bad policymaking almost always involves finding inappropriate metaphors."[20]

Given that observation, it is not unreasonable to think that the adoption of a more biological metaphor might help in the changing of those expectations. For instance, no reasonable person expects a physician to predict with precision and certainty the details (time, severity, lingering impact, etc.) of a patient's heart attack. Rather, the physician is expected to help the patient identify risk factors and conditions (hereditary, eating habits, smoking, exercise, stress level, cholesterol level, etc.) that might potentially contribute to the onset of a heart attack (or other problems) and help the patient formulate a proper mitigating response. In other words, the expectations are understood to be limited. At a fundamental level, it is the language of medicine, with its inherent uncertainty, that greatly contributes to those limited expectations. Moreover, it directly contributes to a doctor's credibility in its evident honesty and realism. Analysts, then, need to understand this approach and be as "linguistically true" with policymakers and the public as—ideally—physicians are with their patients. For only then will policymakers and the public come to accept that intelligence analysts are not miracle workers and that they do not have the proverbial crystal ball.

Of course, some will argue that it is not the intelligence community's place to educate the public (after all, it is a secret community) or that it has no business telling policymakers (its bosses) what they should and should not expect. Rather these voices argue that if policymakers (and the public) want certainty, the community can provide it—given sufficient (greater) resources, new analytical tools, and such. Should the community adopt such a mentality, however, and consequently do nothing to disabuse policymakers and the public of their illusions then it will be surrendering itself to fate. For it is then guaranteed that these unreasonable and unrealistic expectations will endure, that another surprise will occur at some point, and that a new round of debilitating recriminations will undoubtedly result. If a greater degree of openness, outreach, and candor—with both its customers and itself—can help the community avoid such a fate, it ought to actively seek those opportunities. A better metaphor is a good place to start.

From Ambivalence to Self-Awareness

Given what has been argued here, it might be possible to answer the fundamental question of analytic identity asked at the outset of this article—it is in fact both art and science. The fact that the community remains ambivalent suggests it does not like that answer and suspects customers will not like it either. After all, this is just the type of duality that is often difficult for an individual, never mind an entire community, to effectively reconcile. Nonetheless, there are several fundamental steps that the intelligence community—again, learning from the medical community—could take in conjunction with "metaphor reform" to better prepare the ground for growing a cohesive analytic identity.

First, the community can cultivate a more scientific and analytic perspective via an extensive training and education regimen that is focused on critical thinking. The ability to think critically is key to the provision of "better answers" and requires analysts—just as it does medical interns and residents—to master the systematic processing and analysis of evidence such as is possible via so-called "structured analytic methods" (timeline-building, weighted ranking, analysis of competing hypotheses, etc.). Also worth considering is a requirement for analysts to explicate, for managers if not necessarily policymakers, the particular methodological approaches and thought processes they employed in formulating any particular analysis. Too often, analysts approach their jobs in an entirely ad hoc fashion—the so-called pinball wizard approach, as it were—since most receive minimal training in, and have minimal requirements to employ, structured analytic techniques.

Additionally, the complementary artistic (creative) aspect of analysis, actually synthesis, must also be cultivated. One method for doing this would be to require senior analysts, or anyone aspiring to such a title, to mentor junior analysts in how they develop hypotheses (ask better questions) for testing. Structured synthetic methods, as distinct from structured analytic methods, for doing this include scenario-development; brainstorming; modeling, gaming, and simulation; and red-teaming. Unfortunately, mentorship also remains a highly ad hoc community practice that needs to be both institutionalized and mandated. Quite simply, it should be made an absolute promotion requirement for more experienced analysts to systematically share their experience and intuition—their pattern-recognition and synthetic thinking skills—with the burgeoning crop of junior analysts currently flooding the analytical ranks. In turn, senior analysts will benefit from exposure to fresh perspectives that they otherwise might never consider. In many ways this process would mirror the medical community's practice of having interns and residents learn and work under the supervision of senior physicians.

Beyond this complementary approach to the education of analysts, a similar approach to recruitment is also crucial. More specifically, analytic recruitment should explicitly emphasize the attraction of the critical, analytic, and scientific, as well as the creative, synthetic, and artistic thinkers. Currently, the intelligence community appears to be more attuned to attracting the former, which should not be surprising since the prevailing recruitment terminology describes the job, like the problem sets, in almost exclusively analytic terms. If the community sincerely desires to inject a greater measure of synthetic capability into the analytical mix, it needs to use appropriate and accurate language to convey that objective. In other words, perhaps it is time for the community's human capital components to begin recruiting with both "analytic/specialist" and "synthetic/practitioner" aptitude and inclinations clearly in mind.

That last point brings us back to the fundamental importance of accurate language and metaphors to the analytic community's effort to develop a cohesive analytic identity—to "know"

itself. Again, the linguistic metaphors that one uses directly, if subconsciously, reflect and reinforce the underlying thought. Consequently, if the community continues to speak and write in exclusively analytic, reductionist, linear, and mechanical terms it will continue to think almost exclusively in those terms as well. Moreover, expectations will continue to unproductively focus on "did the intelligence community get it right" versus "did the intelligence community usefully inform." In sum, the old saying that "you are what you eat, drive, and wear . . . " is not quite true. The essential role that language plays in thinking means that "you are what you say." Actions do not always speak "louder" than words . . . often it is the words that really do matter.

We conclude then by coming full circle. It is worth noting that Sun Tzu went on to say, "When you are ignorant of the enemy but know yourself, your chances of winning or losing are equal. If ignorant both of your enemy and of yourself, you are certain in every battle to be in peril."[21] Presumably, Sun Tzu left out the variation of knowing one's enemy but not knowing oneself because he saw it for the impossibility that it is. This implied admonition should be of particular concern to the intelligence community, whose primary task is to help policymakers "know" others. For until the intelligence community "knows" itself it will not be able to reliably fulfill that fundamental mission.

Notes

1. Sun Tzu, *The Art of War,* Samuel B. Griffith, trans. (Oxford, U.K.: Oxford Univ. Press, 1963), 84.

2. Rob Johnston, *Analytic Culture in the U.S. Intelligence Community* (Washington: Central Intelligence Agency, Center for the Study of Intelligence, 2005), 27.

3. Ibid., 17.

4. Dennis Gormley, "The Limits of Intelligence: Iraq's Lessons," *Survival,* 46 (Autumn 2004), 16.

5. Johnston, 19–20.

6. David Brooks, "The C.I.A.: Method and Madness," *The New York Times,* 3 February 2004.

7. Austin Bay, "Fixing Intelligence," *The Washington Times,* 9 December 2005.

8. Ibid.

9. Commission on the Intelligence Capabilities of the United States Regarding Weapons of Mass Destruction, *Report to the President of the United States* (Washington: The White House, 31 March 2005), 12–13.

10. Jonathan D. Clemente and Stephen Marrin, "Improving Intelligence Analysis by Looking to the Medical Profession," *International Journal of Intelligence and Counter Intelligence,* 18 (January 2005), 708–16.

11. Stephen Marrin, "Intelligence Analysis: Turning a Craft into a Profession" (paper presented at the International Conference on Intelligence Analysis, McLean, Va., 4 May 2005), https://analysis.mitre.org/proceedings/Final_Papers_Files/97_Camera_Ready_Paper.pdf

12. Clemente and Marrin, 707.

13. Thomas Czerwinski, *Coping with the Bounds: Speculations on Nonlinearity in Military Affairs* (Washington: National Defense University, 1998), 64.

14. Mark Johnson and George Lakoff, *Metaphors We Live By* (Chicago: Univ. of Chicago Press, 1980), 3.

15. Ibid.

16. Ibid.

17. Johnston, 18.

18. "Alchemy," Wikipedia, http://en.wikipedia.org/wiki/Alchemy.

19. Czerwinski, 9–10.

20. M. Mitchell Waldrop, *Complexity: The Emerging Science at the Edge of Order and Chaos* (New York: Simon and Schuster, 1992), 334.

21. Sun Tzu, 84.

JOSH KERBEL is a fourteen-year veteran of the intelligence community, including service in the ODNI, CIA, and naval intelligence. The views expressed in this article are his own and do not imply endorsement by any US government agency.

From *Parameters,* by Josh Kerbel, Summer 2008, pp. 102–112. Published by U.S. Army War College. Reprinted by permission.

Arrested Development
Making Foreign Aid a More Effective Tool

J. Brian Atwood, M. Peter McPherson, and Andrew Natsios

Washington's foreign aid programs have improved in many ways during the Bush presidency. Official development assistance has increased from $10 billion in 2000 to $22 billion in 2008, funding two dozen presidential initiatives, many of them innovative and groundbreaking. At the same time, however, the organizational structures and statutes governing these programs have become chaotic and incoherent thanks to 20 years of accumulated neglect by both Republicans and Democrats in the executive and legislative branches. The president has elevated development to a theoretically equal place with defense and diplomacy in what is considered the new paradigm of national power: "the three Ds." But this vision has not been realized because of organizational and programmatic chaos. The Defense Department's massive staff has assumed roles that should be performed by the State Department and the U.S. Agency for International Development (USAID), and the Pentagon's $600 billion budget has eclipsed those of the civilian agencies.

The Pentagon recognizes this problem. In November 2007, Secretary of Defense Robert Gates called for a "dramatic increase in spending on the civilian instruments of national security." Gates pointed to the "asymmetric-warfare challenge" U.S. forces face in the field and insisted that "success will be less a matter of imposing one's will and more a function of shaping the behavior of friends, adversaries, and, most importantly, the people in between." In March 2008, retired Marine Corps General Anthony Zinni and Navy Admiral Leighton Smith, representing a group of more than 50 retired flag and general officers, testified before the Senate Foreign Relations Committee in support of a budget increase for the State Department and USAID. Zinni and Smith said, "We know that the 'enemies' in the world today are actually conditions—poverty, infectious disease, political turmoil and corruption, environmental and energy challenges."

The U.S. foreign assistance program has traditionally sought to support U.S. national security and promote economic growth, poverty reduction, and humanitarian relief abroad. Modern foreign aid efforts began with the Marshall Plan, which was justified as a national security measure, a humanitarian contribution, and an effort to build markets for U.S. exports. In the intervening years, the policy rationale for aid has not changed much, and it remains as compelling now as it was then.

> **Washington cannot win the hearts and minds of the world's people with only an anemic USAID presence in the developing world.**

Effective foreign aid programs, therefore, can and should be a crucial component of U.S. foreign policy. To ensure that taxpayer dollars are well spent on a single, coherent foreign aid bureaucracy under one chain of command, the next president will have to push through major institutional reforms. But as many recent studies have demonstrated, U.S. development efforts lack coherent policy guidance and are spread across myriad agencies with little coordination among them. Such a sad state of affairs did not always exist. We can testify to this from our own experience, having collectively run USAID for 16 years, under both Democratic and Republican administrations. We share the concern that our civilian capacities have eroded at a time when they are most needed. The United States cannot win the hearts and minds of the world's people with only an anemic USAID presence in the developing world. The situation will not improve without sensible presidential leadership to support an independent, vigorous, and restructured USAID or a new federal department devoted to development.

Downsizing Development

During the Cold War, USAID's presence abroad was far more significant than it is today. Leaders realized that the agency's staff was one of the most powerful instruments of soft power the U.S. government had at its disposal. In many places, USAID is the most visible face of the U.S. government; its influence at the level of civil society is far greater than the State Department's or the Pentagon's, whose representatives tend to remain in capital cities. USAID officers have daily interactions with civil-society leaders, government officials, members of local legislative bodies, businesspeople, and ministries that deal with development issues.

For much of its existence, USAID had substantial resources and autonomy, but in recent decades these have largely been stripped away. For example, the State Department was given responsibility for U.S. foreign assistance programs in central and eastern Europe in 1989 and in the former Soviet Union in 1992, with USAID placed in a subordinate role. Eventually, in 2001, the State Department took over USAID's account and its direct relationship with the Office of Management and Budget. As a result, USAID lost staff, programmatic flexibility, and influence with Congress, other government departments, other aid donors, and recipient nations.

Policymakers began to look for other vehicles to implement their development initiatives. When the Millennium Challenge Corporation was set up in 2004, the secretary of state—rather than the USAID administrator—was named to chair it. At first, the MCC was discouraged from even working with USAID; when the President's Emergency Plan for AIDS Relief (PEPFAR) was set up in 2003, it was placed in the State Department, with USAID and the Department of Health and Human Services given only supporting roles.

Organizational chaos has significantly increased the costs of implementing foreign aid programs.

Many new players in the foreign assistance arena—the Centers for Disease Control, the MCC, and now even the Defense Department, through its new Africa Command—have created independent organizational structures to carry out their programs. Not surprisingly, this has led to policy incoherence, a lack of integration across programs and issue areas, inefficient and overlapping bureaucracies, and endless conflicts over roles and responsibilities—not to mention confusion among recipients and among other donors about who represents Washington on development issues. These new development players are now even using the same contractors as USAID. All of this organizational chaos has significantly increased the costs of implementing foreign aid programs, delayed their implementation, and reduced their impact. There is no evidence that this broad array of new development agencies has done any better than the old, more unified USAID, and much evidence that this organizational structure has done worse.

The most recent reorganization of Washington's development apparatus was announced in 2006. USAID was effectively folded into the State Department and given its allocations through a State Department–controlled budget process, and its administrator was asked to wear two bureaucratic hats: director of foreign assistance at the State Department and head of USAID. Many thought this was a mistake. The practical and policy problems that have resulted have only confirmed their views. Dozens of studies on foreign aid show that aid programs rarely succeed when they are not customized to the poor countries they are designed to help and built on local ownership. The centralization of the U.S. government's aid programs in Washington may satisfy the needs of key players in both the executive and the legislative branches for command and control, but it increases the risk of program failure and invites attacks from critics, who insist foreign aid is ineffective.

USAID has also suffered over the years from crippling staff cuts. In 1980, the agency had 4,058 permanent American employees. By 2008, the number had dropped to 2,200. Resources for staff training were also slashed dramatically. These cuts have had several detrimental effects. Most important, they forced the closing of 26 overseas missions in the 1990s. USAID's field presence used to be a real source of strength for the United States. Other countries often looked to the agency for leadership and donor coordination on the ground, and USAID's decentralized structure made its programs more responsive to local conditions and needs and allowed the agency to move faster than its foreign counterparts. Downsizing also resulted in a dramatic loss of technical expertise. For example, the agency now has only six engineers and 16 agriculture experts, far fewer than in the 1980s.

The reduced staff and loss of expertise has limited the agency's technical competency and its managerial control over projects, making USAID increasingly dependent on larger and larger grants and contracts to spend its budget. This has transformed USAID from a creative, proactive, and technically skilled organization focused on implementation to a contracting and grant-making agency. This, in turn, has translated into less policy coherence, reduced flexibility, diminished leverage with other donors, and an increasingly risk-averse bureaucracy.

On a policy level, meanwhile, large presidential initiatives and congressional earmarks for health care, HIV/AIDS, K-12 education, microfinance, and the environment have in recent years crowded out other development interventions, such as anticorruption measures, agricultural assistance, democracy-promotion programs, and infrastructure-enhancement measures. The narrower, more focused programs are politically appealing because they appear to have a direct, measurable impact on identifiable individuals. But such a concentration on the short-term delivery of goods and services comes at the expense of building sustainable institutions that promote long-term development. For example, resources devoted to postconflict transitions now exceed development investments in peaceful nations. And the transfer of goods and services, such as in PEPFAR, has not always included the long-term human and institutional infrastructure so important to sustaining an effort. (Thankfully, the congressional reauthorization of PEPFAR recently signed by President George W. Bush requires the training of more than 100,000 local health-care workers in developing countries.)

The impact of this approach to development can best be understood at the country level. Ethiopia, one of the poorest countries in the world, has a largely agricultural economy and suffers from periodic famines. Yet in 2007, about 50 percent of U.S. assistance to Ethiopia went to HIV/AIDS prevention, 38 percent to emergency food relief, and 7 percent to child survival, family planning, and malaria prevention and treatment. Only 1.5 percent went to agriculture, 1.5 percent to economic growth, 1.5 percent to education, and 1 percent to improving governance. Such distorted profiles of development aid are unfortunately quite common.

Strategic needs on the ground should dictate the nature of the programs, but currently, allocation decisions are determined by earmarks, presidential initiatives, or diplomatic pressures.

Reconstructing Aid

The problems with current U.S. development efforts cannot be fixed without major organizational reforms. The time has come to recognize that the semimerger of USAID and the State Department has not worked. The missions and personnel requirements of the two organizations are different. The State Department often has to deal with pressing issues and naturally views development dollars as only one of the possible tools at hand. State Department officers are superb diplomats, negotiators, political observers, and policy analysts. USAID, in contrast, is an operational and program-management agency focused on achieving sustainable economic growth abroad; its staffers are aid professionals with the technical and managerial skills to get their work done. With USAID and the State Department merged, the urgency of the State Department's mission and the collective mindset of its personnel end up dominating, to the detriment of the development agenda. The problem lies not in individuals but in clashing organizational cultures, management systems, and time horizons.

There are two proposed approaches to fixing the problem: integrating USAID even more completely into the State Department and granting it significantly more independence, either as its own cabinet-level department or as a strong autonomous agency whose head reports directly to the secretary of state. The first option would make things even worse than they are now. In a full merger with the State Department, USAID would lose its development mission altogether, as that mission would continually lose out to the State Department's more traditional diplomatic priorities. The right approach is to find some way of restoring USAID's autonomy and vitality. The real question is whether USAID should be an independent agency reporting to the secretary of state or a new cabinet department. Both routes have advantages and disadvantages, but either would be preferable to the current setup.

A cabinet-level department would give USAID much greater stature and allow it to influence policy on trade, investment, and the environment while improving existing assistance programs. This approach is the predominant model used in wealthy donor countries. The United Kingdom moved in this direction in the mid-1990s. The United Kingdom's Department for International Development has used its perch to achieve greater influence on development matters throughout the British government by helping to shape trade, finance, and environmental policy at the cabinet level. As a result, the Department for International Development has become the most prominent government aid agency in the world, even though London spends far less on aid than Washington does.

The chief argument against a cabinet-level development department in the United States is that the secretary of state needs to have some policy involvement and oversight when it comes to foreign aid. Moreover, the secretary of state is always going to be a more powerful member of the cabinet than a development czar. USAID often relies on the active support of the secretary of state in order to get the funding and legislation it needs to carry out its mission. For these reasons, many observers believe that a strong agency reporting to the secretary of state would be preferable.

Regardless of which option the next administration chooses, there are several policies that must be implemented in order to strengthen the United States' development capabilities. First, the new USAID must have budgetary independence, and its operating account—which pays for buildings, salaries, and technology—should be dramatically increased in order to boost the size of the permanent staff, invest in training, and increase the agency's technical expertise. This will enable the new USAID to reopen missions that were permanently closed and to staff them adequately.

Second, the head of the new USAID should be a statutory member of the National Security Council and serve as part of the president's international economic advisory team on the National Economic Council. There are compelling security and macroeconomic arguments for foreign aid. As Paul Collier's acclaimed book *The Bottom Billion* demonstrates, countries with high poverty rates descend into civil war far more often than more prosperous nations. These conflicts kill thousands and destroy the political and economic institutions of the states in which they occur, leaving the international community to pick up the enormous tab for rescue, relief, and reconstruction. Likewise, development success is closely related to investment, trade, and finance policies; U.S. policy and developing-country policies on these matters are as important as the volume of foreign assistance. U.S. agricultural subsidies, trade protectionism, and subsidies for ethanol all hurt poor countries by distorting food markets. Yet within the U.S. government, decisions concerning international trade and finance are all too often made without any regard for reducing poverty or stimulating economic growth in poor countries. Making the new USAID an integral part of the interagency process would allow it to influence policymaking and take direction from the State Department, the Pentagon, and other agencies on matters involving foreign policy and national security. It would be a two-way street.

Third, the new USAID will need a new congressional mandate. The Foreign Assistance Act of 1961—which has not been amended in any meaningful way since 1985—is a Cold War artifact that has become obsolete. The eligibility criteria for the MCC could serve as the basis for new legislation. The MCC uses 17 indicators in three broad development categories—"ruling justly, economic freedom, and investing in people"—to determine a nation's eligibility to receive development aid. A new congressional mandate would make the executive branch accountable for results and provide a new framework for legislators who wish to earmark funds for specific purposes.

Civilian Casualties

As the division of labor among the Pentagon, the State Department, and USAID has become blurred, military bureaucracies have eclipsed their civilian counterparts, thanks largely to their vastly greater resources and greater organizational capacity. Few in Washington, including Secretary Gates, like this situation or think it serves U.S. interests. But nothing will change unless the next president works with Congress to oversee significant institutional reform. Revitalizing the U.S. approach to development assistance should be viewed as a crucial part of the broader effort to revitalize the government's civilian institutional capacities.

To streamline and strengthen the State Department bureaucracy and restore USAID's authority over aid programs, all humanitarian and development programs now assigned to the State Department—such as refugee programs, PEPFAR, and the programs implemented by the new bureau for postconflict reconstruction—should be placed under the aegis of the new USAID. Likewise, democracy-promotion programs and the Defense Department's aid programs around the world should largely return to civilian control, with the relevant authority and resources assigned to the new USAID. Many cabinet departments understandably have policy interests abroad, but those interests should not include managing their own, independent foreign aid programs. From the early 1960s to 1992, the Office of Management and Budget aggressively enforced a rule mandating that all foreign aid programs and spending must go through USAID (except when USAID chose to contract with other federal agencies in cases for which it lacked specific technical expertise). It is time to return to that model.

Furthermore, the head of the new USAID must have the authority to devise an overall U.S. government strategy on humanitarian and development programs and to coordinate the activities of other departments at the global, country, and regional levels. In addition to presiding over a White House interagency committee on foreign assistance, the new USAID's head (instead of the secretary of state) should chair the MCC board. The MCC is one of the United States' most innovative foreign aid programs; it is free of earmarks and promotes genuine partnership with recipient countries. The MCC should be protected from political pressures in Washington that might compromise its eligibility criteria. At the same time, a new, strengthened USAID should be given the authority to help recipient nations design proposals, facilitate the implementation of programs, and evaluate their effectiveness.

Finally, the next president should establish a civilian equivalent to the Joint Chiefs of Staff that would include the most senior career officers of the State Department, the new USAID, the Treasury Department, and the Office of the U.S. Trade Representative. Chaired by a senior Foreign Service officer, this statutory institution would offer advice to the political leadership on diplomacy, development, and crisis prevention. This group would also provide a source of independent judgment on development issues to agency heads and to the National Security Council, just as the Joint Chiefs do on military matters.

Of course, there will be areas of overlapping jurisdiction between the defense, diplomatic, and development institutions. One example is the provision of security assistance in countries recovering from conflict; in these difficult environments, the State Department's diplomatic mission is crucial, and the Defense Department is needed for training and logistics. The key is who controls the money for noncombat activities. This authority belongs with the diplomatic mission. But when foreign aid payments are involved, the authority should rest squarely with the new, revamped USAID, whether it attains the status of a cabinet-level department or simply greater autonomy as an agency reporting to the secretary of state.

It is official U.S. policy to build strong and effective defense, diplomatic, and development institutions working together to advance U.S. national security and foreign policy. This goal has not yet been achieved. The civilian agencies today are simply not capable of pulling their weight. The next president will have to dramatically overhaul the foreign aid establishment during his first year. The United States' national security and its global leadership position will depend on it.

J. BRIAN ATWOOD is Dean of the Hubert H. Humphrey Institute of Public Affairs at the University of Minnesota and was Administrator of USAID from 1993 to 1999. **M. PETER MCPHERSON** is President of the National Association of State Universities and Land-Grant Colleges; he was President of Michigan State University from 1993 to 2004 and Administrator of USAID from 1981 to 1986. **ANDREW NATSIOS** is Distinguished Professor in the Practice of Diplomacy at Georgetown University and a Senior Fellow at the Hudson Institute; he was Administrator of USAID from 2001 to 2005.

From *Foreign Affairs,* vol. 87, no. 6, November/December 2008, pp. 123–132. Copyright © 2008 by Council on Foreign Relations, Inc. Reprinted by permission of Foreign Affairs. www.ForeignAffairs.org

When Congress Stops Wars
Partisan Politics and Presidential Power

WILLIAM G. HOWELL AND JON C. PEVEHOUSE

For most of George W. Bush's tenure, political observers have lambasted Congress for failing to fulfill its basic foreign policy obligations. Typical was the recent Foreign Affairs article by Norman Ornstein and Thomas Mann, "When Congress Checks Out," which offered a sweeping indictment of Congress' failure to monitor the president's execution of foreign wars and antiterrorist initiatives. Over the past six years, they concluded, Congressional oversight of the White House's foreign and national security policy "has virtually collapsed." Ornstein and Mann's characterization is hardly unique. Numerous constitutional-law scholars, political scientists, bureaucrats, and even members of Congress have, over the years, lamented the lack of legislative constraints on presidential war powers. But the dearth of Congressional oversight between 2000 and 2006 is nothing new. Contrary to what many critics believe, terrorist threats, an overly aggressive White House, and an impotent Democratic Party are not the sole explanations for Congressional inactivity over the past six years. Good old-fashioned partisan politics has been, and continues to be, at play.

It is often assumed that everyday politics *stops* at the water's edge and that legislators abandon their partisan identities during times of war in order to become faithful stewards of their constitutional obligations. But this received wisdom is almost always wrong. The illusion of Congressional wartime unity misconstrues the nature of legislative oversight and fails to capture the particular conditions under which members of Congress are likely to emerge as meaningful critics of any particular military venture.

The partisan composition of Congress has historically been the decisive factor in determining whether lawmakers will oppose or acquiesce in presidential calls for war. From Harry Truman to Bill Clinton, nearly every U.S. president has learned that members of Congress, and members of the opposition party in particular, are fully capable of interjecting their opinions about proposed and ongoing military ventures. When the opposition party holds a large number of seats or controls one or both chambers of Congress, members routinely challenge the president and step up oversight of foreign conflicts; when the legislative branch is dominated by the president's party, it generally goes along with the White House. Partisan unity, not institutional laziness, explains why the Bush administration's Iraq policy received such a favorable hearing in Congress from 2000 to 2006.

The dramatic increase in Congressional oversight following the 2006 midterm elections is a case in point. Immediately after assuming control of Congress, House Democrats passed a resolution condemning a proposed "surge" of U.S. troops in Iraq and Senate Democrats debated a series of resolutions expressing varying degrees of outrage against the war in Iraq. The spring 2007 supplemental appropriations debate resulted in a House bill calling for a phased withdrawal (the president vetoed that bill, and the Senate then passed a bill accepting more war funding without withdrawal provisions). Democratic heads of committees in both chambers continue to launch hearings and investigations into the various mishaps, scandals, and tactical errors that have plagued the Iraq war. By all indications, if the government in Baghdad has not met certain benchmarks by September, the Democrats will push for binding legislation that further restricts the president's ability to sustain military operations in Iraq.

Neither Congress' prior languor nor its recent awakening should come as much of a surprise. When they choose to do so, members of Congress can exert a great deal of influence over the conduct of war. They can enact laws that dictate how long military campaigns may last, control the purse strings that determine how well they are funded, and dictate how appropriations may be spent. Moreover, they can call hearings and issue public pronouncements on foreign policy matters. These powers allow members to cut funding for ill-advised military ventures, set timetables for the withdrawal of troops, foreclose opportunities to expand a conflict into new regions, and establish reporting requirements. Through legislation, appropriations, hearings, and public appeals, members of Congress can substantially increase the political costs of military action—sometimes forcing presidents to withdraw sooner than they would like or even preventing any kind of military action whatsoever.

The Partisan Imperative

Critics have made a habit of equating legislative inactivity with Congress' abdication of its foreign policy obligations. Too often, the infrequency with which Congress enacts restrictive statutes is seen as prima facie evidence of the institution's failings. Sometimes it is. But one cannot gauge the health of the U.S. system of governance strictly on the basis of what Congress does—or does not do—in the immediate aftermath of presidential initiatives.

After all, when presidents anticipate Congressional resistance they will not be able to overcome, they often abandon the sword as their primary tool of diplomacy. More generally, when the White House knows that Congress will strike down key provisions of a policy initiative, it usually backs off. President Bush himself has relented, to varying degrees, during the struggle to create the Department of Homeland Security and during conflicts over the design of military tribunals and the prosecution of U.S. citizens as enemy combatants. Indeed, by most accounts, the administration recently forced the resignation of the chairman of the Joint Chiefs of Staff, General Peter Pace, so as to avoid a clash with Congress over his reappointment.

To assess the extent of Congressional influence on presidential war powers, it is not sufficient to count how many war authorizations are enacted or how often members deem it necessary to start the "war powers clock"—based on the War Powers Act requirement that the president obtain legislative approval within 60 days after any military deployment. Rather, one must examine the underlying partisan alignments across the branches of government and presidential efforts to anticipate and preempt Congressional recriminations.

During the past half century, partisan divisions have fundamentally defined the domestic politics of war. A variety of factors help explain why partisanship has so prominently defined the contours of interbranch struggles over foreign military deployments. To begin with, some members of Congress have electoral incentives to increase their oversight of wars when the opposing party controls the White House. If presidential approval ratings increase due to a "rally around the flag" effect in times of war, and if those high ratings only benefit the president's party in Congress, then the opposition party has an incentive to highlight any failures, missteps, or scandals that might arise in the course of a military venture.

After all, the making of U.S. foreign policy hinges on how U.S. national interests are defined and the means chosen to achieve them. This process is deeply, and unavoidably, political. Therefore, only in very particular circumstances—a direct attack on U.S. soil or on Americans abroad—have political parties temporarily united for the sake of protecting the national interest. Even then, partisan politics has flared as the toll of war has become evident. Issues of trust and access to information further fuel these partisan fires. In environments in which information is sparse, individuals with shared ideological or partisan affiliations find it easier to communicate with one another. The president possesses unparalleled intelligence about threats to national interests, and he is far more likely to share that information with members of his own political party than with political opponents. Whereas the commander in chief has an entire set of executive-branch agencies at his beck and call, Congress has relatively few sources of reliable classified information. Consequently, when a president claims that a foreign crisis warrants military intervention, members of his own party tend to trust him more often than not, whereas members of the opposition party are predisposed to doubt and challenge such claims. In this regard, Congressional Democrats' constant interrogations of Bush administration officials represent just the latest round in an ongoing interparty struggle to control the machinery of war.

Congressional Influence and Its Limits

Historically, presidents emerging from midterm election defeats have been less likely to respond to foreign policy crises aggressively, and when they have ordered the use of force, they have taken much longer to do so. Our research shows that the White House's propensity to exercise military force steadily declines as members

of the opposition party pick up seats in Congress. In fact, it is not even necessary for the control of Congress to switch parties; the loss of even a handful of seats can materially affect the probability that the nation will go to war.

The partisan composition of Congress also influences its willingness to launch formal oversight hearings. While criticizing members for their inactivity during the Bush administration, Ornstein and Mann make much of the well-established long-term decline in the number of hearings held on Capitol Hill. This steady decline, however, has not muted traditional partisan politics. According to Linda Fowler, of Dartmouth College, the presence or absence of unified government largely determines the frequency of Congressional hearings. Contrary to Ornstein and Mann's argument that "vigorous oversight was the norm until the end of the twentieth century," Fowler demonstrates that during the post-World War II era, when the same party controlled both Congress and the presidency, the number of hearings about military policy decreased, but when the opposition party controlled at least one chamber of Congress, hearings occurred with greater frequency. Likewise, Boston University's Douglas Kriner has shown that Congressional authorizations of war as well as legislative initiatives that establish timetables for the withdrawal of troops, cut funds, or otherwise curtail military operations critically depend on the partisan balance of power on Capitol Hill.

Still, it is important not to overstate the extent of Congressional influence. Even when Congress is most aggressive, the executive branch retains a tremendous amount of power when it comes to military matters. Modern presidents enjoy extraordinary advantages in times of war, not least of which the ability to act unilaterally on military matters and thereby place on Congress (and everyone else) the onus of coordinating a response. Once troops enter a region, members of Congress face the difficult choice of either cutting funds and then facing the charge of undermining the troops or keeping the public coffers open and thereby aiding a potentially ill-advised military operation.

On this score, Ornstein and Mann effectively illustrate Bush's efforts to expand his influence over the war in Iraq and the war on terrorism by refusing to disclose classified information, regularly circumventing the legislative process, and resisting even modest efforts at oversight. Similarly, they note that Republican Congressional majorities failed to take full advantage of their institution's formal powers to monitor and influence either the formulation or the implementation of foreign policy during the first six years of Bush's presidency. Ornstein and Mann, however, mistakenly attribute such lapses in Congressional oversight to a loss of an "institutional identity" that was ostensibly forged during a bygone era when "tough oversight of the executive was common, whether or not different parties controlled the White House and Congress" and when members' willingness to challenge presidents had less to do with partisan allegiances and more to do with a shared sense of institutional responsibility. In the modern era, foreign-policy making has rarely worked this way. On the contrary, partisan competition has contributed to nearly every foreign policy clash between Capitol Hill and the White House for the past six decades.

Divided We Stand

Shortly after World War II—the beginning of a period often mischaracterized as one of "Cold War consensus"—partisan wrangling over the direction of U.S. foreign policy returned to Washington, ending a brief period of wartime unity. By defining U.S. military involvement in Korea as a police action rather than a war, President Truman effectively freed himself from the constitutional requirements regarding war and established a precedent for all subsequent presidents to circumvent Congress when sending the military abroad. Although Truman's party narrowly controlled both chambers, Congress hounded him throughout the Korean War, driving his approval ratings down into the 20s and paving the way for a Republican electoral victory in 1952. Railing off a litany of complaints about the president's firing of General Douglas MacArthur and his meager progress toward ending the war, Senator Robert Taft, then a Republican presidential candidate, declared that "the greatest failure of foreign policy is an unnecessary war, and we have been involved in such a war now for more than a year. . . . As a matter of fact, every purpose of the war has now failed. We are exactly where we were three years ago, and where we could have stayed."

On the heels of the Korean War came yet another opportunity to use force in Asia, but facing a divided Congress, President Dwight Eisenhower was hesitant to get involved. French requests for assistance in Indochina initially fell on sympathetic ears in the Eisenhower administration, which listed Indochina as an area of strategic importance in its "new look" defense policy. However, in January 1954, when the French asked for a commitment of U.S. troops, Eisenhower balked. The president stated that he "could conceive of no greater tragedy than for the United States to become involved in an all-out war in Indochina." His reluctance derived in part from the anticipated fight with Congress that he knew would arise over such a war. Even after his decision to provide modest technical assistance to France, in the form of B-26 bombers and air force technicians, Congressional leaders demanded a personal meeting with the president to voice their disapproval. Soon afterward, Eisenhower promised to withdraw the air force personnel, replacing them with civilian contractors.

Eventually, the United States did become involved in a ground war in Asia, and it was that war that brought Congressional opposition to the presidential use of force to a fever pitch. As the Vietnam War dragged on and casualties mounted, Congress and the public grew increasingly wary of the conflict and of the power delegated to the president in the 1964 Gulf of Tonkin resolution. In 1970, with upward of 350,000 U.S. troops in the field and the war spilling over into Cambodia, Congress formally repealed that resolution. And over the next several years, legislators enacted a series of appropriations bills intended to restrict the war's scope and duration. Then, in June 1973, after the Paris peace accords had been signed, Congress enacted a supplemental appropriations act that cut off all funding for additional military involvement in Southeast Asia, including in Cambodia, Laos, North Vietnam, and South Vietnam. Finally, when South Vietnam fell in 1975, Congress took the extraordinary step of formally forbidding U.S. troops from enforcing the Paris peace accords, despite the opposition of President Gerald Ford and Secretary of State Henry Kissinger.

Three years later, a Democratic Congress forbade the use of funds for a military action that was supported by the president—this time, the supply of covert aid to anticommunist forces in Angola. At the insistence of Senator Dick Clark (D-Iowa), the 1976 Defense Department appropriations act stipulated that no monies would be used "for any activities involving Angola other than intelligence gathering." Facing such staunch Congressional opposition, President Ford suspended military assistance to Angola, unhappily noting that the Democratic-controlled Congress had "lost its guts" with regard to foreign policy.

In just one instance, the case of Lebanon in 1983, did Congress formally start the 60-day clock of the 1973 War Powers Act. Most scholars who call Congress to task for failing to fulfill its constitutional responsibilities make much of the fact that in this case it ended up authorizing the use of force for a full 18 months, far longer than the 60 days automatically allowed under the act. However, critics often overlook the fact that Congress simultaneously forbade the president from unilaterally altering the scope, target, or mission of the U.S. troops participating in the multinational peacekeeping force. Furthermore, Congress asserted its right to terminate the venture at any time with a one-chamber majority vote or a joint resolution and established firm reporting requirements as the U.S. presence in Lebanon continued.

During the 1980s, no foreign policy issue dominated Congressional discussions more than aid to the contras in Nicaragua, rebel forces who sought to topple the leftist Sandinista regime. In 1984, a Democratic-controlled House enacted an appropriations bill that forbade President Ronald Reagan from supporting the contras. Reagan appeared undeterred. Rather than abandon the project, the administration instead diverted funds from Iranian arms sales to support the contras, establishing the basis for the most serious presidential scandal since Watergate. Absent Congressional opposition on this issue, Reagan may well have intervened directly, or at least directed greater, more transparent aid to the rebels fighting the Nicaraguan government.

Regardless of which party holds a majority of the seats in Congress, it is almost always the opposition party that creates the most trouble for a president intent on waging war. When, in the early 1990s, a UN humanitarian operation in Somalia devolved into urban warfare, filling nightly newscasts with scenes from Mogadishu, Congress swung into action. Despite previous declarations of public support for the president's actions, Congressional Republicans and some Democrats passed a Department of Defense appropriations act in November 1993 that simultaneously authorized the use of force to protect UN units and required that U.S. forces be withdrawn by March 31, 1994.

A few years later, a Republican-controlled Congress took similar steps to restrict the use of funds for a humanitarian crisis occurring in Kosovo. One month after the March 1999 NATO air strikes against Serbia, the House passed a bill forbidding the use of Defense Department funds to introduce U.S. ground troops into the conflict without Congressional authorization. When President Clinton requested funding for operations in the Balkans, Republicans in Congress (and some hawkish Democrats) seized on the opportunity to attach additional monies for unrelated defense programs, military personnel policies, aid to farmers, and hurricane relief and passed a supplemental appropriations bill that was considerably larger than the amount requested by the president. The mixed messages sent by the Republicans caught the attention of Clinton's Democratic allies. As House member Martin Frost (D-Tex.) noted, "I am at a loss to explain how the Republican Party can, on one hand, be so irresponsible as to abandon our troops in the midst of a military action to demonstrate its visceral hostility toward the commander in chief, and then, on the other, turn around and double his request for money for what they call 'Clinton's war.' " The 1999 debate is remarkably similar to the current wrangling over spending on Iraq.

Legislating Opinion

The voice of Congress (or lack thereof) has had a profound impact on the media coverage of the current war in Iraq, just as it has colored public perceptions of U.S. foreign policy in the past. Indeed, Congress' ability to influence executive-branch decision-making extends far beyond its legislative and budgetary powers. Cutting funds, starting the war powers clock, or forcing troop withdrawals are the most extreme options available to them. More frequently, members of Congress make appeals designed to influence both media coverage and public opinion of a president's war. For example, Congress' vehement criticism of Reagan's decision to reflag Kuwaiti tankers during the Iran-Iraq War led to reporting requirements for the administration. Similarly, the Clinton administration's threats to invade Haiti in 1994 were met with resistance by Republicans and a handful of skeptical Democrats in Congress, who took to the airwaves to force Clinton to continually justify placing U.S. troops in harm's way.

Such appeals resonate widely. Many studies have shown that the media regularly follow official debates about war in Washington, adjusting their coverage to the scope of the discussion among the nation's political elite. And among the elite, members of Congress—through their own independent initiatives and through journalists' propensity to follow them—stand out as the single most potent source of dissent against the president. The sheer number of press releases and direct feeds that members of Congress produce is nothing short of breathtaking. And through carefully staged hearings, debates, and investigations, members deliberately shape the volume and content of the media's war coverage. The public posturing, turns of praise and condemnation, rapid-fire questioning, long-winded exhortations, pithy Shakespearean references, graphs, timelines, and pie charts that fill these highly scripted affairs are intended to focus media attention and thereby sway the national conversation surrounding questions of war and peace. Whether the media scrutinize every aspect of a proposed military venture or assume a more relaxed posture depends in part on Congress' willingness to take on the president.

Indeed, in the weeks preceding the October 2002 war authorization vote, the media paid a tremendous amount of attention to debates about Iraq inside the Beltway. Following the vote, however, coverage of Iraq dropped precipitously, despite continued domestic controversies, debates at the United Nations, continued efforts by the administration to rally public support, and grass-roots opposition to the war that featured large public protests. Congress helped set the agenda for public discussion, influencing both the volume and the tone of the coverage granted to an impending war, and Congress' silence after the authorization was paralleled by that of the press.

Crucially, Congressional influence over the media extended to public opinion as well. An analysis of local television broadcast data and national public-opinion surveys from the period reveals a strong relationship between the type of media coverage and public opinion regarding the war. Even when accounting for factors such as the ideological tendencies of a media market (since liberal markets tend to have liberal voters and liberal media, while conservative districts have the opposite), we found that the airing of more critical viewpoints led to greater public disapproval of the proposed war, and more positive viewpoints buoyed support for the war. As Congress speaks, it would seem, the media report, and the public listens.

As these cases illustrate, the United States has a Congress with considerably more agenda-setting power than most analysts presume and a less independent press corps than many would like. As the National Journal columnist William Powers observed during the fall of 2006, "Journalists like to think they are reporting just the facts, straight and unaffected by circumstance." On the contrary, he recognized, news is a product of the contemporary political environment, and the way stories are framed and spun has little to do with the facts. In Washington, the party that controls Congress also determines the volume and the tone of the coverage given to a president's war. Anticipating a Democratic Congressional sweep in November 2006, Powers correctly predicted that "if Bush suffers a major political setback, the media will feel freed up to tear into this war as they have never done before."

With the nation standing at the precipice of new wars, it is vital that the American public understand the nature and extent of Congress' war powers and its members' partisan motivations for exercising or forsaking them. President Bush retains extraordinary institutional advantages over Congress, but with the Democrats now in control of both houses, the political costs of pursuing new wars (whether against Iran, North Korea, or any other country) and prosecuting ongoing ones have increased significantly.

Congress will continue to challenge the president's interpretation of the national interest. Justifications for future deployments will encounter more scrutiny and require more evidence. Questions of appropriate strategy and implementation will surface more quickly with threats of Congressional hearings and investigations looming. Oversight hearings will proceed at a furious pace. Concerning Iraq, the Democrats will press the administration on a withdrawal timetable, hoping to use their agenda-setting power with the media to persuade enough Senate Republicans to defect and thereby secure the votes they need to close floor debate on the issue.

This fall, the Democrats will likely attempt to build even more momentum to end the war in Iraq, further limiting the president's menu of choices. This is not the first instance of heavy Congressional involvement in foreign affairs and war, nor will it be the last. This fact has been lost on too many political commentators convinced that some combination of an eroding political identity, 9/11, failures of leadership, and dwindling political will have made Congress irrelevant to deliberations about foreign policy.

On the contrary, the new Democratic-controlled Congress is conforming to a tried-and-true pattern of partisan competition between the executive and legislative branches that has characterized Washington politics for the last half century and shows no signs of abating. Reports of Congress' death have been greatly exaggerated.

WILLIAM G. HOWELL and JON C. PEVEHOUSE are Associate Professors at the Harris School of Public Policy at the University of Chicago and the authors of *While Dangers Gather: Congressional Checks on Presidential War Powers*.

From *Foreign Affairs*, vol. 86, no. 5, September/October 2007. Copyright © 2007 by Council on Foreign Relations. Reprinted by permission. www.ForeignAffairs.com

UNIT 5

Foreign Policy Problems and the Policy Making Process

Unit Selections

Key Points to Consider

- Construct an ideal foreign policy making process. How close does the United States come to this ideal? Is it possible for the United States to act in the ideal manner? If not, is the failing due to the individuals who make foreign policy or the institutions in which they work? Explain.

- What is the single largest failure of the foreign policy making process? How can it be corrected? What is the single largest strength of the foreign policy making process?

- What changes, if any, are necessary in the U.S. foreign policy making process for the United States to act effectively with other countries in multilateral efforts?

- What advice would you give to the president who is considering undertaking military action?

- How would you run a meeting organized to respond to a terrorist act? Whom would you invite? What would you expect of those you invite? How much dissent would you permit?

Student Website
www.mhhe.com/cls

Internet References

Belfer Center for Science and International Affairs (BCSIA)
http://belfercenter.ksg.harvard.edu/

Central Intelligence Agency/Freedom of Information Act Special Documents
www.foia.cia.gov/soviet_estimates.asp

The Heritage Foundation
www.heritage.org

National Archives and Records Administration (NARA)
www.archives.gov/index.html

U.S. Department of State: The Network of Terrorism
http://usinfo.state.gov/products/pubs/

There is no such thing as a standard foreign policy problem. Problems come in many different shapes and sizes. Some are inherited from past administrations. Others are due to the current administration's miscalculations or mishandling of the issue. Foreign policy problems may stand alone, or they may be part of a bundle of problems in which efforts to address one topic seem to worsen the others. And, while some problems seem to race to the top of the foreign policy agenda, others seem to get lost and never receive serious attention.

Recognizing the immense variety in the nature of foreign policy problems is only a start for coming to an understanding of the way in which the foreign policy decision making process operates. We also must shed the notion that there is an underlying rationality at work in the conduct of foreign policy. In this view, once a foreign policy problem is identified, then goals are established, policy options are listed, the implications of competing courses of action are assessed, a conscious choice is made as to which policy to adopt, and then the policy is implemented correctly. This assumption is comforting because it implies that policymakers are in control of events and that solutions do exist. Moreover, it allows us to assign responsibility for policy decisions and hold policymakers accountable for the success or failure of their actions.

As comforting as this assumption is, it is also false. Driven by domestic, international, and institutional forces, as well as by chance and accident, perfect rationality is an elusive quality. This is true regardless of whether the decision is made in a small group setting or by large bureaucracies. Small groups are created when the scope of the foreign policy problem appears to lie beyond the expertise of any single individual. This is frequently the case in crisis situations. The essence of the decision making problem here lies in the overriding desire of group members to get along with each other. Determined to be a productive member of the team and not rock the boat, individual group members suppress personal doubts about the wisdom of what is being considered and become less critical of the information before them than they would be if they alone were responsible for the decision. They may stereotype the enemy, assume that the policy cannot fail, or believe that all members of the group are in agreement on what must be done.

The absence of rationality in decision making by large bureaucracies stems from their dual nature. On the one hand, bureaucracies are politically neutral institutions that exist to serve the president and other senior officials by providing them with information and implementing their policies. On the other hand, they have goals and interests of their own that may not only conflict with the positions taken by other bureaucracies, but may be inconsistent with the official position taken by policymakers. Because not every bureaucracy sees a foreign policy problem in the same way, policies must be negotiated into existence, and implementation becomes anything but automatic. Although it is essential for building a foreign policy consensus, this exercise in bureaucratic politics robs the policy process of much of the rationality that we look for in government decision making.

The problem of trying to organize the policy process to conduct a war against terrorism is an especially daunting task.

© Brand X Pictures/PunchStock

In part, this is because the enormity of the terrorist attacks and the language of war embraced by the Bush administration lead to expectations of an equally stunning countermove. Rationality is also strained by the offsetting pressures for secrecy and the need for a speedy response on the one hand, and the need to harmonize large numbers of competing interests on the other. Finally, no matter how many resources are directed at the war against terrorism, there will continue to be the need to balance resources and goals. Priorities will need to be established and trade-offs accepted, as is evidenced by the debate over the legality and value of domestic spying programs in support of the war on terrorism. There is no neutral equation or formula by which this can be accomplished. It will be made through a political process of bargaining and consensus building, in which political rationality rather than any type of substantive rationality will triumph.

The readings in this unit provide insight into the process by which foreign policy decisions are made by highlighting some of the key problems that are on the foreign policy agenda (or trying to get on it), and the activities involved at different points in the policy making process. The first essay, "Law, Liberty and War," presents a debate between Anne-Marie Slaughter and Jeremy Rabkin over the proper constitutional balance between Congress and the president in conducting foreign policy in the war against terrorism and the Iraq War. The second essay, "Neo-Conservatives, Liberal Hawks, and the War on Terror," speaks of the importance of the ideas that shape American foreign policy. It is critical of both neo-conservatives and liberal hawks for holding utopian visions of what goals American foreign policy might pursue, and unrealistic ideas about the potential uses of American power. The final essay by Wesley Clark and Peter Levin, "Securing the Information Highway," leads us through an examination of a new policy area, cyberwarfare, that has yet to establish a secure place for itself in the policy making process. The authors review the nature of the problem and compare it to the process by which dangerous biological diseases can spread out of control if not managed properly.

Law, Liberty and War
Originalist Sin

Has the Bush Administration run roughshod over American civil liberties and distorted Constitutional balances during the Global War on Terror? *You bet it has,* argues Anne-Marie Slaughter. *No way,* says Jeremy Rabkin.

ANNE-MARIE SLAUGHTER

How historical periods are defined depends on the purposes of the definer. Geologists look to rock structure, demarking eras such as the Cretaceous, Jurassic, Triassic, Mesozoic and Paleozoic. Economists look to the primary source of wealth: the Iron Age, the Bronze Age, the Industrial Age and now the Information Age. Chroniclers of foreign affairs look to catastrophes: While their business is war *and* peace, their timelines are chiefly defined by wars. Consider how we talk and write about the 20th century: World War I, the interwar period, World War II, the Cold War. After the Cold War came the post-Cold War period, until 9/11, which marked the beginning of the War on Terror. The military is currently planning for "The Long War" against terrorism—and, if there is such a long war, it is a good bet that decades hence historians and political analysts will still be defining time in the cadences of war.

But why not focus instead on naming periods of peace? John Lewis Gaddis has written about "the long peace", describing how United States and the Soviet Union managed to get through over four decades of the Cold War without fighting one another directly. Yet proclaiming peace has not caught on, notwithstanding occasional references to Pax Americana, Pax Britannia and Pax Romana. The reason is not hard to find: Telling citizens that they live in wartime is good for boosting defense budgets. It is also good for expanding presidential power. "War makes the state", wrote celebrated sociologist Charles Tilly, "and the state makes war."

Such ruminations make a worthy backdrop for reading and assessing John Yoo's provocative book, *Powers of War and Peace: The Constitution and Foreign Affairs After 9/11*. Yoo writes to rectify an awkward legal contradiction for political conservatives. Ardent advocates of originalism—a school of Constitutional interpretation that prizes the intent of the Framers and literal reading of the text of our founding document—have heretofore found themselves arguing against the seemingly clear Constitutional text granting Congress the power to declare war. And they must explain away contemporaneous accounts in the *Federalist Papers* making clear that the Framers wanted to give the Executive authority to make war, but only once Congress had decided to go to war in the first place. As Thomas Jefferson put it, "We have . . . given . . . one effectual check to the Dog of war by transferring the power of letting him loose from the Executive to the Legislative body, from those who are to spend to those who are to pay." In foreign affairs debates, therefore, liberal constitutionalists like Louis Henkin and Harold Koh have been able to claim the originalist high ground, while conservatives have instead made sweeping claims about how the evolving nature of war and new threats to American national security require that the Constitution be interpreted in light of two centuries of practice—the very argument anathema to them in, say, constitutional debates over abortion or the death penalty.

No longer. Yoo offers an originalist understanding of a vast Executive foreign affairs power, checked not by the Constitution itself but only by Congress' ability to push back. The Framers, according to Yoo, designed "a flexible system for making foreign policy in which the political branches could opt to cooperate or compete." In this system, the roles of Congress and the courts are narrowly confined to the specific powers granted them in Articles I and III, respectively. Article II, on the other hand, which defines the Executive's powers, "effectively grants to the president any unenumerated foreign affairs powers not given elsewhere to the other branches."

Yoo's book reads as a long footnote to a Supreme Court brief.

The Powers of War and Peace offers the theoretical grounding for this expansive view of Executive power based on evidence from practice in early U.S. history, the intent of the Framers, and the text and structure of the Constitution. The book reads as a long footnote to a Supreme Court brief upholding the Bush Administration's controversial claims to lawfully detain U.S. citizens as enemy combatants or disregard treaties that have become inconvenient. With Yoo in hand, the Bush Administration need not argue to the courts that it must push out the boundaries of our Constitution in this national emergency. Giving such enormous power to the president in foreign affairs was what the Framers intended in the first place: Congress could fend for itself, Yoo writes, "[s]imply by refusing to do anything, by not affirmatively acting to vote funds or to enact legislation. . . . [T]he appropriations power and the power to raise the military gives Congress a sufficient check on presidential warmaking."

The key point, of course, is that the Framers wrote in a time of no standing armies, no established political parties and relatively little difficulty in demarcating the line between foreign and domestic affairs. Without standing armies, the Congressional power of the purse was necessary to put soldiers in the field, a very real check on executive war-mongering. But with 1.4 million men and women on active duty in the military today and another 860,000 in the reserves, the Executive branch tends to shoot first and ask Congress to fund later, when our young men and women in uniform are already on the front lines. The political calculus, as any modern president well knows, overwhelmingly favors lining up behind the troops once they are in the field—a decision, according to Yoo, that is entirely up to the president.

Without entrenched partisan politics, it was possible to imagine members of Congress serving as a genuine voice of the people in opposition to the Executive. But with the most partisan system the nation has seen in a century, the President's party votes with him, and it is the opposition alone that must face accusations of starving the troops in the field.

Without shrinking oceans, instant communications and a global economy it was at least possible to limit even a broad Executive foreign affairs power to distinctively and definably "foreign" affairs. But in an age of terrorism practiced by non-state groups both within the territory of the United States and without, by aliens and citizens alike, through a complex system of financing and support that travels through a tangled trail of domestic and foreign transactions, what a president can do abroad—wiretapping, for instance—he can also presume to do at home.

Yoo's history is, to say the least, highly selective. Despite his central claim that the Framers clearly intended a unified executive, Yoo's historical chapter about the writing of the Constitution opens with an admission of the Framers' "silence" about the separation of powers in foreign affairs. Manfully, Yoo tries to explain away messy historical facts—such as the Constitutional Convention's rejection of amendments that would have added to the Constitution explicit language setting out Yoo's own unconventional understanding of the treaty and war powers.

(Though these amendments failed, Yoo takes pains to note that at least some of the Framers agreed with him.)

But by filling pages with every shred of evidence from the Founding period that might support a unified executive in foreign affairs, Yoo misses the real story. The Framers' animating purpose in abandoning the loose Articles of Confederation for our Constitution was not to resurrect the British monarchy's tradition of a dominant executive. Rather, the Framers were far more concerned about creating a strong central government to harmonize the dissonant foreign policies of the states, which had left the infant United States vulnerable in the 18th-century world of marauding mercantilist great powers. To the extent that the Framers sought what Alexander Hamilton called "energy in the executive", as Stanford's Pulitzer Prize-winning historian Jack Rakove writes in "Making Foreign Policy: The View from 1787", the constitutional provisions "that laid the strongest foundation for a major executive role in foreign policy are more safely explained as a cautious reaction against the defects of exclusive senatorial control of foreign relations than as a bold attempt to convert the noble office of a republican presidency into a vigorous national leader in world affairs."

In light of George Washington's difficulties with a war run by committee during the Revolution, the Framers explicitly chose not to give Congress the power to "make war", that is, to actually conduct it. But they equally explicitly gave Congress the power to "declare war", that is, to start it. Indeed, at the Constitutional Convention, when Pierce Butler of South Carolina formally proposed giving the president the power on his own to start war, Elbridge Gerry of Massachusetts said he "never expected to hear in a republic a motion to empower the executive to declare war." The Constitutional Convention quickly rejected Butler's motion.

Yoo's version of the Constitution is both disingenuous and dangerous.

Moreover, the practice of early presidents confirms this understanding. In 1801, facing depredations by the Barbary pirates, President Jefferson took certain defensive actions but went before the Congress to explain himself. He told the Congress that anything beyond defensive action was for them to authorize. Four years later, during a dispute with Spain, Jefferson put the matter as plainly as possible: "Congress alone is constitutionally vested with the power of changing our situation from peace to war."

By contrast, Yoo's version of the Constitution is both disingenuous and dangerous. Take the striking inconsistency between Yoo's understanding of "flexibility" in the Constitution's treatment of the War Powers and Treaty powers. Yoo argues that "[t]he Constitution did not intend to institute a fixed, legalistic process" in foreign affairs, and goes to great lengths to explain why Articles I and II do not actually restrict the president's war powers in the way historians and legal scholars have long understood. But, flexibility for Yoo does not extend to the treaty power, even though treaties are clearly instruments of foreign affairs. Instead, Yoo insists that treaties must not only satisfy the requirements of Article II, but that they also be subject to additional rigid legal requirements to have the force of law. Yoo infers such "fixed, legalistic process" for implementing treaties in the United States even though no specific language in the Constitution sets out such requirements. This conveniently allows the president to dispose of a host of inconvenient treaties that might restrain his power if their terms had the force of domestic law. And despite Yoo's own history describing the Framers' concern with the states ignoring treaties, he even questions how much the Federal government today can require the states to follow U.S. treaty obligations. Such conclusions leave the reader wondering how much of this book is pure Constitutional interpretation, and how much a manual for the Bush Administration's vision of American unilateralism.

Yoo's most sweeping and dangerous claim is hidden as a legal technicality.

Given Yoo's recent service in an intensely ideological administration, his partisanship here is hardly surprising and easy to spot. Yoo's most sweeping—and most dangerous—claim is hidden as a legal technicality. "Article II", he writes, "effectively grants to the president any unenumerated foreign affairs powers not given elsewhere to the other branches." In other words, whatever is not explicitly granted ("enumerated") to Congress or the courts belongs to the Executive. All that is necessary is to identify a particular power as a "foreign affairs power."

The danger of this view is that the president can claim any new threat to American national security—and those appear all the time—as one he alone is empowered to address. Take the war on terror. The Bush Administration has claimed that the president has the power to declare any American citizen an "enemy combatant", to keep such combatants in jail indefinitely without bringing criminal charges, and to try them through a separate court system without the core protections of the Bill of Rights. Even judges in President Bush's conservative camp are unwilling to trust a president that much. In 2003 the Supreme Court—in an opinion joined by Antonin Scalia—rejected Bush's claim that the president's war powers meant that enemy combatants could not challenge their detention in court. And this past December, a conservative appellate judge once on Bush's Supreme Court short-list (Michael Luttig of the Fourth Circuit) wrote a biting opinion holding that the Bush Administration could not move a U.S. citizen in and out of the protections of the criminal justice system simply by invoking the shibboleth of terrorism and national security.

Yoo's position not only threatens our civil liberties; it is equally dangerous to our national security. He is right about the profound changes America faces in the world and the resulting need for a flexible framework governing foreign affairs powers—a push and pull between the Executive and Congress, with periodic intervention by the courts. But rather than

expanding Executive power while pretending that Congress can cut funding to stop U.S. troops already deployed on foreign soil, the solution is to draw clear Constitutional boundaries around the Executive's power, enforceable by the courts if necessary, and to find ways to force, commit or lure Congress to do the job it is supposed to do.

Leslie Gelb and I recently suggested ("Declare War", *The Atlantic Monthly,* November 2005) one approach to this: a new law that would restore the Framers' intent by restoring the declaration of war, and requiring Congress actually to declare war in advance of any commitment of troops that promises sustained combat. The president would be required to present Congress with critical information about war aims and plans; and Congress would in turn hold hearings to scrutinize for itself the intelligence justifying the recourse to war, the costs of fighting, and the administration's plans for the war's aftermath. A full floor debate and vote would follow. The lack of a Congressional declaration would automatically deny funds to that military operation. In Jefferson's words, "Congress must be called on to take it, the right of reprisal being expressly lodged with them by the Constitution, and not with the Executive." Congress must be called on, or must pre-commit itself, to take the same responsibility with respect to how we treat enemy prisoners and fight other critical fronts in the War on Terror.

Congressional participation in foreign affairs, however, is not an end in itself. The Framers' genius was to recognize the practical benefits of American democracy in conducting foreign affairs. In a world of shadowy and immeasurable threats, the real danger of getting war powers wrong is not simply the abuse of power by any one branch of government, but also the use of power without sufficient information, deliberation and imagination to succeed. As any global business recognizes, success today requires managing change and risk under conditions of uncertainty. So too with government. In this effort, many minds are better than one—to sift through and assess the quality of our information, to question and improve our strategies, and to brainstorm and troubleshoot so that tactics too narrowly conceived will not lead us astray.

The intelligence failures that enabled the attacks on September 11 and the rush to war in Iraq (leaving aside the accuracy of the limited intelligence presented to Congress) underscore the danger of leaving critical questions of war solely in the hands of the Executive. Congress' job is not simply to fund or not to fund. It is to question, to probe, to deliberate and to decide, together with the President, on behalf of the people whose sons and daughters will be sent to war and whose tax dollars will be spent. That is the originalist understanding of the Constitution, and the ensuing centuries have only strengthened the case for this interpretation of its text.

ANNE-MARIE SLAUGHTER is dean of the Woodrow Wilson School of Public and International Affairs and the Bert G. Kerstetter University Professor of Politics and International Affairs at Princeton University.

War Stories

Jeremy Rabkin

In the immediate aftermath of 9/11, most Americans wanted to fight the terrorists and the regimes that aided them. Even before that year ended, however, some voices warned that the impulsive, reckless policies of the Bush Administration would ultimately pose more of a danger to Americans and their way of life than the terrorists and their allies: We were, according to such critics, falling into the trap that clever terrorists always set, conspiring unwittingly in our own undoing. That opinion has gained ground as the shock of the initial terror attacks has receded. It is an opinion that owes far less to actual incursions on domestic liberties, however, than to insinuations and second thoughts about whether we need to be "at war" at all.

It is certainly possible to endorse a war while criticizing its conduct abroad and its policy repercussions at home. Such distinctions are not inherently illogical. But almost invariably, the loudest protests against wartime abuses come from those who reject the war in the first place. The fiercest critics of President Lincoln's war measures were the Copperheads, who opposed from the outset the effort to coerce the South by force of arms. The most outspoken critics of Cold War measures were those who dismissed the notion that communists or communism could threaten American security. And so it is with the War on Terror.

The current war has stimulated some measures that might be questioned in peacetime. They look altogether intolerable to those who reject the need for war. On the other hand, those who accept a "war" policy in current circumstances often hesitate to criticize particular security measures lest such criticism undermine general support for the war. It is hard in this setting to sort out competing claims about domestic security measures of the Bush Administration. The debate almost immediately shifts from actual experience to generalized claims about the Administration's posture in the world. After years of debate about the supposed excesses of the Patriot Act, for example, critics in Congress acquiesced earlier this year to its re-enactment with only minor changes. The Patriot Act seems to have been not so much a source of dispute in itself as a symbol of some wider, more amorphous complaint.

Several points about this larger debate do seem reasonably clear, however. The first is that, compared with our experience in past wars, the current war has been quite mild in its impact on domestic civil liberties. In World War II, the Federal government incarcerated more than 120,000 Japanese-Americans, including women, children and old people—all of them long-standing residents and most of them either citizens or immediate relatives of citizens. These unfortunates were held behind barbed wire in excess of two years, and the Supreme Court endorsed the practice essentially on the say-so of the President.

After 9/11 fewer than five thousand people were rounded up. All of them were aliens, almost all recent arrivals and unmarried males of suitable age for combat or terror operations. They were all released within a few weeks. Today's true legal counterpart of *Korematsu,* the 1943 case endorsing the mass detention of Japanese-Americans without any sort of due process, is the case of José Padilla—one person, who is now to be tried before an ordinary civilian court (though admittedly after years of military detention without trial or formal charges).

The same pattern holds regarding freedom of speech. In the Civil War, President Lincoln authorized military trials for antiwar agitators. He deployed the army to shut down an antiwar newspaper in New York and to suppress anti-conscription riots there. There was comprehensive official censorship during World War I and a Federal program to coach state universities on proper wartime curricula. The Cold War saw American Communist Party leaders prosecuted for conspiring to incite unspecified acts of disloyalty in unspecified future circumstances. The House Un-American Activities Committees hounded left-wing screenwriters. Some were ultimately sentenced to prison terms for refusing to testify about possible decades-old communist affiliations of associates in the movie industry. Yet the angriest charge against the Bush Administration is that it has used rhetoric that puts its critics on the defensive, as by ostensibly improper allusions to the 9/11 victims.

Today's legal counterpart to *Korematsu* is the case of José Padilla—*one person.*

So, too, with surveillance. There was a great uproar when it was revealed at the end of 2005 that the Bush Administration had, without proper judicial warrants, monitored phone calls between al-Qaeda suspects overseas and individuals in the United States. Yet President Roosevelt invoked national security to authorize wiretaps on domestic phone calls of suspicious individuals more than a year before the United States entered World War II. The practice continued during the Cold War. It was not until the late 1970s, amid revelations of abusive FBI surveillance activities, that Congress even attempted to regulate such practice with the Foreign Intelligence Surveillance Act.

In the recent dispute about when FISA procedures apply, a second point stands out: Even though the government is acting with greater restraint than in past wars, the clamor about threats to civil liberties is louder today because we now hold the government to higher standards. What critics now regard as outrageous was once regarded as more or less standard practice.

There are often good reasons for moving the goal posts in such ways. Past abuses prompt greater cautions in succeeding generations. No one wants to repeat Cold War abuses. J. Edgar Hoover himself cautioned during World War II against repeating the excesses committed by the Wilson Administration in World War I. Sometimes new technology raises new issues, as with the NSA surveillance systems that today allow immensely powerful computers to monitor vast volumes of telephone and Internet communication without direct human "listening."

Still, in an era in which so much constitutional debate proceeds on the basis of evolving standards, this particular debate has become disorienting. Those most indignant about threats to the Constitution tend to appeal not to traditional standards but to those that are recent or even heretofore unheard of. Over the past few years, for example, some of America's most distinguished law faculties have endorsed the claim that law schools have a First Amendment right to exclude military recruiters from their job fairs without forfeiting Federal funds, as current law requires. When the Supreme Court rejected this argument earlier this year, not a single justice offered so much as a sympathetic nod to this strange new constitutional theory. The harshest critics of constitutional abuses tend to be those who, in other contexts, champion the theory of a "living Constitution", one whose provisions are never quite settled. It is hard *not* to violate a "constitution" that keeps expanding in this way.

A third point follows from the second: Debates about civil liberties in wartime have now expanded to embrace standards regarded as global in scope, supposedly binding on America because they are "international law." Thus has a vast amount of debate centered on the treatment of captured terrorists at Guantánamo: Are they treated in accord with the Geneva Convention? Are they being interrogated in ways prohibited by the UN Convention Against Torture? Is the Bush Administration's disdain for these accepted international standards a threat to America's global leadership? Does the Administration's stance threaten Americans at home who rely on the protections of law?

and domestic critics that even overseas the U.S. military will follow what judges can certify as proper legal standards.

One can certainly argue that extreme brutality, even toward foreign prisoners in wartime, has a corrosive effect on military discipline, and that it may ultimately have poisonous moral consequences for any society that sponsors or tolerates such practices. But surely a lot depends on context. Stephen Ambrose's book about a company of paratroopers in World War II, *Band of Brothers,* reports that patrols were sent out behind enemy lines to capture low-ranking German soldiers whom American interrogators would then shoot or threaten to shoot to make others reveal information about enemy positions. It did not occur to Ambrose, author of many works on American military history, to denounce this tactic or to depict it as aberrant. Nor did the producers of the HBO mini-series based on the book feel obliged to suppress this unpleasant fact of history. Neither Ambrose nor his Hollywood adaptors even bothered to incorporate an acknowledgment that such tactics were in violation of the Hague Conventions and the applicable Geneva Convention at the time.

If one takes the idea of war seriously enough, one risks excusing almost anything in the interest of victory. That is the charge hurled most insistently at John Yoo, a professor of law at Berkeley who served as a top advisor in the Department of Justice in George W. Bush's first term. Yoo's internal memos, subsequently leaked by an Administration once thought to be strongly averse to leaks, have been denounced as authorizing torture and encouraging disregard of law.

No U.S. court has ever before presumed to judge military compliance with the Geneva standards.

The last question, though insistently posed by many critics, has scarcely anything to do with the others. The five hundred or so detainees in Guantánamo were taken to that naval base in the Caribbean precisely because it is not, technically, American soil. No American court had ever presumed to question U.S. military actions outside the United States. The Supreme Court had specifically repudiated such interference in a 1950 case about war prisoners held by the U.S. military in occupied Germany. The Court's exceedingly narrow, divided ruling in *Rasul v. Bush* in 2004 has left most questions about the status of Guantánamo detainees open, but assures that domestic courts will now, for the first time, have some role in monitoring external military actions. Some justices have indicated both in concurring opinions and in off-the-bench speeches that U.S. courts should indeed consider whether international standards have been properly applied in these settings. That would be another great novelty: No U.S. court has ever before presumed to judge military compliance with the Geneva standards. But many legal advocates now insist that the Court reassure foreign skeptics

Most past presidents have tacitly agreed with Yoo's constitutional constructions.

Now Yoo has published an academic study, *Powers of War and Peace: The Constitution and Foreign Affairs Since 9/11.* The book, however, says almost nothing about the convention against torture or the detentions at Guantánamo, and even less about domestic civil liberties. Instead, Yoo pursues seemingly legalistic questions about the separation of powers: Who decides when and whether the United States is at war? Who decides when and whether the United States is still bound by international treaties? Yoo argues that the Founders saw decisions about the resort to war just as they saw decisions about repudiating treaties as inherently an Executive branch prerogative. The power given to Congress to "declare" war simply entails the authority to announce a formality rather than control the strategic decision. Congress retains ultimate authority because it can finally deny funds to any presidential initiative, but the president retains broad powers of initiative in foreign affairs.

Conventional legal scholarship has run strongly in the other direction since the Vietnam War. But Yoo makes a very strong case for his interpretations based on the British practice familiar to the Framers, on what defenders of the Constitution said in ratification debates, and on what their opponents did not say. An honest reading of American history suggests that most past presidents have tacitly assumed the correctness of Yoo's constitutional constructions.

Still, the ultimate point at issue is not historical but philosophical. If one thinks that Congress is supposed to have the first word about the resort to war as well as the last, then one thinks that war must be, generally speaking, a legislative decision that we can adopt or reject like a tax cut. To think that, one must suppose that the world is fundamentally peaceful or at least that the United States is fundamentally at peace with the world, with conflict a rare and discretionary exception. Such a supposition makes it easy to embrace the notion of an international legal system that covers even the conduct of war in its smallest details. One can then suppose that such standards have great authority, even if some of the combatants in a conflict ignore them altogether, because the world remains in some way governed by a fine mesh of legal standards. Many advocates certainly want to live in a world of this kind. It happens, however, not to be the world in which we actually live.

L egal standards have value to the extent that they can be sustained. It does not promote law to ground it on merely wishful or fanciful premises. A proposal for law on such premises is offered in *Before the Next Attack: Preserving Civil Liberties in an Age of Terrorism,* a recent book by Yale law professor Bruce Ackerman. Ackerman acknowledges that terror attacks may indeed require emergency measures. He thinks, however, the responses of the Bush Administration were "disasters" for law and civil liberties because they have not been checked by adequate constraints. So Ackerman advocates a new scheme under which Congress could authorize suspensions of civil liberties for brief periods after an attack, but could only renew such emergency provisions contingent on successively higher majorities within Congress. Nothing in the Constitution warrants requiring Congress to abide by supermajority requirements in this way, but Ackerman argues that the courts could

nonetheless enforce something of the kind if Congress accepted the basic scheme.

Those who are familiar with Ackerman's work will not be surprised by this suggestion. He is best known for arguing that the Constitution can be amended not only by the formal process set out in Article V, but also by an informal political "process": When a contested new approach to the Constitution is defended by a political party or administration and the voters return them to office, that provides endorsement for the new approach. Ackerman's favorite example is, of course, the New Deal. He may now expect that his own constitutional doctrines will be ratified by voters in future elections. Ackerman is the quintessential cheerleader for a "living Constitution", stimulated by growth hormones slipped to it by attentive law professors.

Several times in *Before the Next Attack* Ackerman insists that we do not now face an "existential threat" comparable to that posed by Germany and Japan in the 1940s, and so we cannot now justify such significant abridgement of civil liberties in response. But was Germany really going to land an army in New England, or the Japanese in California? Was a German victory parade in Washington ever more likely than a mass-casualty terror attack today on an American city? No matter: If one wants to advance uniquely high standards of protectiveness toward supposed threats to civil liberties, it is easier to pretend that World War II was a unique exception and that the current war is more like the Cold War, when law professors could insist that the enemy was a figment of the imagination of McCarthyite demagogues.

I concede that war is always a potential threat to civil liberties. But so is defeat in war. Forced to choose between the risk of domestic abuses and the risk of defeat in war, most Americans will not harp on domestic legal standards. It is reasonable to worry about government excesses. It is escapist to pretend, at a time when terrorists plot new assaults on American cities, that our own government is the greatest threat to our security.

JEREMY RABKIN is a professor of government at Cornell University and serves on the board of directors of the Center for Individual Rights.

From *The American Interest,* Summer 2006, pp. 19–27. Copyright © 2006 by American Interest. Reprinted by permission.

Neo-Conservatives, Liberal Hawks, and the War on Terror

Lessons from the Cold War

Anatol Lieven and John C. Hulsman

Since 9/11, determined attempts have been made to resurrect the memory of the Cold War as an inspiration and model for the War on Terror. Proponents of this approach include neo-conservatives and others on the Right, and so-called "liberal hawks" in the Democratic camp. At a deeper, less evident level, the Cold War was also bound to have a profound impact on how America waged the War on Terror simply because the military, intelligence, bureaucratic, academic, ideological, and military-industrial institutions that have shaped U.S. strategy since 9/11 were created by the Cold War. They remained generally unreformed in the decade between the collapse of the Soviet Union and 2001.

Tragically, however, the Bush administration and dominant parts of the bipartisan U.S. establishment have, with almost deliberate perversity, ignored precisely those lessons of the Cold War that would have been most valuable. They have chosen instead to follow approaches that were rejected decades ago by the wisest American leaders and thinkers of the time.[1] The failure to heed the right lessons was demonstrated afresh by the response of the administration and the Democratic Party leadership to the war in Lebanon. Whatever Hezbollah's provocations, the Israeli response, and the way it was framed by most of the mainstream establishment, reflected historical amnesia.

This amnesia concerned the unwise and unethical character of preventive war except when truly and manifestly unavoidable; the extreme difficulty of suppressing guerrilla movements by military force, especially in a short campaign relying chiefly on bombardment; the fact that if guerrillas are joined to political parties with deep roots in a given society, they may well prove practically undefeatable; the critical role of local nationalism in empowering anti-American movements; and the central need to divide, rather than unite, hostile forces.

Perhaps most important, while paying lip service to the notion that the present struggle, like the Cold War, will inevitably be a "long war," far too many planners and analysts have in practice been focused on quick fixes (like "getting rid of Saddam Hussein") or unattainable ends (like "eliminating Hezbollah"). This has been combined with a shamefully short attention span when it comes to critically important long-term issues such as strengthening the fragile post-Taliban state in Afghanistan and supporting the Pakistan economy as a bulwark against Islamist extremism.

The Real Lessons

The Cold War leaders and thinkers who, in the late 1940s and early 1950s, authored a tough but restrained strategy of "containing" Soviet expansionism have been vindicated by events. They urged undermining communism through the force of the West's democratic and free-market example, and by massive economic support for key anticommunist states. This took longer than most of them hoped—but since the West triumphed completely, a few decades of mostly peaceful struggle were surely preferable to nuclear cataclysm.

By contrast, the "preventive war" and "rollback" schools of thought during the Cold War were proved wrong on just about everything. And a rolling river of wrongness has flowed down from them to their neo-conservative descendants, many of whose ideas derive directly from those of hardliners in the 1940s and 1950s.

In particular, the Bush administration and too many Democrats have not absorbed two critical Cold War lessons. The first, known to all the wisest Cold Warriors of the Truman and Eisenhower administrations, was that in the struggle between free-market democracy and communism, it was not enough to preach the virtues of democracy and freedom. Across the world, people looking to America had to see the real advantages in economic growth, jobs, services, education, and basic security. That was clearly perceived by everyone from former socialists like the theologian Reinhold Niebuhr to President Eisenhower himself. It has been too often ignored since 9/11.

Secondly, in much of the world, the struggle between American-backed, free-market democracy and Soviet-backed communism was only partly about their respective inherent virtues. It also mattered which side could appeal most successfully to local nationalism. Where America addressed the impassioned wish to escape Soviet domination, America ultimately won. Where communists were able to portray America as imperialist, and champion the continuing anti-colonial struggle for national independence, the communists won—at least for a while. The most intelligent advocates of containment, like George F. Kennan, and its most intelligent intellectual supporters, like Niebuhr and Hans Morgenthau, understood this from the start. Others in the U.S. establishment learned this lesson through America's ordeal in Vietnam.

The Bush administration's greatest mistake was to neglect the struggle with al Qaeda and instead pursue its irrelevant vendetta against Saddam Hussein. As of 2006, it risks repeating the same mistake even more disastrously by threatening conflict with Iran.

American foreign policy currently resembles a looking-glass version of policies pursued in Truman and Eisenhower's day, with a touch of Alice in Wonderland thrown in. Now, as then, after a season of bitter partisan strife over foreign policy, mainstream Republicans and Democrats have come to support what is basically the same program, though they themselves might fiercely deny this. Now, as then, those presenting real alternatives have been consigned to the fringes. The difference is that today the two parties have joined behind a somewhat moderated version of strategies put forward by the neo-conservatives in the Republican Party, and liberal hawks among the Democrats.

Today, exponents of utopian visions and over-ambitious uses of American power have moved center stage, and true centrists—the moderate, pragmatic descendants of Truman and Eisenhower—have been banished to the wings. Hence, it is vital to recall the values and positions for which Truman, Eisenhower, and their key advisors really stood.

Rollback Reborn

So completely has history vindicated containment that its opponents, the rollback and preventive war schools, have been not so much discredited as demolished. Just as nobody today seriously claims that Stalinism was basically benign and non-aggressive, so nobody seriously claims that it would have been right to launch a preventive nuclear war to destroy a Soviet Union that was always much weaker than it seemed and eventually crumbled of its own accord, as Kennan and Truman had predicted.

By the time Ronald Reagan assumed office, a generation after containment took root, the strategy had done its work: the communist economic, political, and ethical models were widely perceived as failures relative to the West. The credibility of communist ideology had ebbed throughout the Soviet bloc.

President Reagan sensed the inner rot in the Soviet bloc and increased U.S. pressure on Moscow. In doing so, he was also able to rally support from a majority of Americans of both parties. Although the most important factor in the Soviet collapse was internal decay, Reagan's policies certainly gave it an extra push.

But we should also remember that Reagan was heir not only of containment's results, but also of its philosophy. In his first term, Reagan adopted a tough posture that gave him the political cover in his second term to pursue an approach that was actually close to Kennan's philosophy of a mixture of containment and dialogue. He cooperated closely with Mikhail Gorbachev and Eduard Shevardnadze on international issues, implemented radical arms control measures, and conducted a peaceful wind-down of the Cold War. For doing this, he was attacked by some neo-conservatives.

By contrast, as historian Daniel Kelly said gently of one of the key intellectual works of the preventive war school, published by James Burnham in 1947, "the most obvious weakness of *The Struggle for the World* lay in the contrast between what it predicted and what actually happened."[2] (An example: Burnham's categorical statement that "if the communists succeed in consolidating what they have *already* conquered, then their complete world victory is certain. . . . We are lost if our opponent so much as holds his own."[3])

A question wisely raised by President Eisenhower in opposing preventive war: If the United States had destroyed Russia, or China, at low cost to itself, what would be the result? Instead of the troublesome but rational Russian and Chinese states of today, America would face hundreds of millions of ordinary people permanently possessed of a searing hatred of the United States and an implacable desire for vengeance.

We need to remember this when thinking about Iran. If we wait Iran out, then given the demographic reality of a youthful majority, there seems a good chance that in a generation we will have an Iran that is once again a basically pro-Western member of the international community (though we should never expect that this will make Iranians obedient followers of American strategy). To attack Iran, which is all too likely to lead to a major war with widespread destruction and civilian casualties, will gain us an implacable enemy for decades to come.

Yet the preventive war school remains alive and well in America among neo-conservatives, and even among leading Democrats. After 9/11, it enjoyed a rebirth; even under the false name of "preemption" it has been a central element of the Bush administration's National Security Strategies of both 2002 and 2006—with no acknowledgment that this approach had been proposed and carefully analyzed previously, and found hopelessly wanting.

The need to preempt a future Iraqi threat was the central justification for the attack on Iraq in 2003. The same rationale is being used today for an attack on Iran. But let us be clear: this is not "preemption" at all. The right of states to strike *preemptively* in the face of imminent attack by enemy states or coalitions—as Israel struck in 1967—has always been asserted as the right by all states, America included. A claim to the right of *preventive* war against a state that might possibly attack in the future is something altogether different. It represents a revolution in international affairs and a dismaying precedent for the behavior of others.

The supporters of preventive war today claim to be descendants of the containment school and, like Norman Podhoretz, in terms of personal lineage they sometimes are. But in terms of mentality, spirit, rhetoric, and understanding of the world, neo-conservatives like Podhoretz of *Commentary* magazine are the true descendants of James Burnham.

This can be seen in the tendency to grossly exaggerate the power both of America's enemies abroad and of real or alleged traitors at home. Burnham and Podhoretz both portrayed the Soviet Union as so strong, and American democracy as so pathetically weak, that unless America went to war quickly, doom beckoned. This recalls the old saying about the Austrian Empire's disastrous decision to go to war in 1914: "Out of fear of dying, we committed suicide." Burnham may have had some small cause for what he wrote in the late 1940s,[4] but Podhoretz was still repeating the same line in the early 1980s, a few years before the Soviet collapse.[5] Among neo-conservatives, an almost Teutonic obsession with power and will colors despair over America's "Athenian" democratic softness and respect for our enemies' "Spartan" authoritarian discipline. Burnham wrote that in the struggle with communism, "For us, international law can only be what it was at Nuremberg (and what it would have been at Moscow and Washington if the other side had conquered): a cover for the will of the more powerful."[6] A leading contemporary neo-conservative, Charles Krauthammer, writes:

America is no mere international citizen. It is the dominant power in the world, more dominant than any since Rome. Accordingly, America is in a position to reshape norms, alter expectations and create new realities. How? By unapologetic and implacable demonstrations of will.[7]

This obsession with will has had tragic effects on American policy. In its decision to escalate troop levels in Vietnam, the Johnson administration was heavily influenced by the belief that if it failed to do so, "it might as well give up everywhere else—pull out of Berlin, Japan, South America," as Johnson himself put it; a fantasy that helped cost the lives of 60,000 Americans and innumerable Vietnamese.[8]

Advocates of preventive war tend to portray pragmatists as Chicken Littles, but in fact it is they who forever warn that the sky is falling. For Burnham, a small mutiny of the Greek navy was "the beginning of World War III," and an Italian-Yugoslav squabble over the city of Trieste after World War II was the hinge on which hung the survival of the West.[9] For neo-conservatives throughout the 1990s, every petty ethnic clash in the ruins of the former Soviet Union heralded the restoration of that state as a mortal threat. Weak, isolated, and despised regional states with a tiny fraction of American power have been elevated into new equivalents of the Soviet superpower.

Burnham wrote that the idea of a Cold War persisting for decades was intolerable, because Western civilization could not stand the constant irritation. Yet constant itching is an inevitability in the international jungle—even during such comparatively peaceful times as the 1890s or the 1990s. In this sense, neo-conservatives, liberal hawks, and their ancestors are as utopian as communists used to be. They too believe in the possibility of what is in fact an impossibly stable world, a kind of global democratic nirvana under American hegemony.

Most dangerous of all has been this tradition's refusal to study individual nations and local conditions. Its exponents prefer instead to treat these realities with an ideological cookie-cutter, throwing away bits that don't fit. During the Cold War, all nations had to be neatly pro-Soviet or pro-American. Today they must be either pro-terrorist or pro-American. This near-racist contempt for the values, interests, identities, and politics of different nations—especially non-Western ones—led Burnham and others to predict in 1947 that, since the Indians were obviously incapable of governing themselves, once the British left, the country would fall into chaos and communism. He therefore urged Washington to assume quasi-imperial power over India, as an essential outpost of an American world if communism were to be resisted.[10]

Mercifully, America never attempted to rule India, and most of Burnham's wild prescriptions were rejected. But Burnham did contribute to an error which is being repeated in a new and disastrous form today: that all communist movements and states were an indissolubly unified threat to the West—a belief which survived Burnham once having dismissed Marshall Tito of Yugoslavia as being simply an agent of Stalin.

Kennan once wrote, "There seems to be a curious American tendency to search, at all times, for a single external center of evil, to which all our troubles can be attributed, rather than to recognize that there might be multiple sources of resistance to our purposes and undertakings, and that these sources might be relatively independent of each other."[11] This tendency stemmed, like so many others, from a desire to divide the world into black and white, good and evil. It has led above all to a determined refusal to study or understand the power of local nationalism, whether reflected in communism, Islamism, or whatever. This mistake led directly to America's tragic involvement in Vietnam, which was justified by fears of a united Sino-Soviet-North Vietnamese move to dominate Asia. In fact, even before the first Marine regiment set foot in Vietnam, the Sino-Soviet alliance had irretrievably broken up. Nevertheless, blinded by the vision of a united communism, many policy-makers declined to see the evidence before them. In a familiar pattern, lower level analysts in the State Department and the CIA who did see what was happening were forced to suppress or modify their views to suit the dominant consensus.[12]

Three years later, in 1968–69, while thousands of Americans were dying in Vietnam to resist a united communist threat, the two communist great powers were fighting in eastern Siberia, and coming close to a nuclear clash. Later, Vietnam and China fought their own border war. These clashes meant that America had no need to fight in Vietnam at all—it could, and eventually did, contain the spread of communism in the region by simply playing communist states against each other. Today, we see the equally absurd and potentially tragic risk of pursuing a policy of implacable hostility towards Muslim states like Iran and Syria that are among the fiercest enemies of the Sunni extremist camp from which al Qaeda springs.

Kennan predicted national divisions within the communist camp from the start. So did Reinhold Niebuhr, who drew a distinction between Soviet communism and the various communist movements of Asia, including the Chinese and Vietnamese. He saw Soviet Russia as an imperial power, dominating other nations by force and terror. In Europe, the West could justly represent itself as a force for liberation. In Asia, because of the legacy of European colonialism, circumstances were more complicated. Communist movements there, however ruthless, could present themselves as forces for national liberation from Western domination. This inspired mass support of a kind that did not exist in the Soviet empire, outside Russia itself.

Niebuhr, Kennan, and others understood the importance of nationalism and foresaw that communist states would sooner or later fall out among themselves. As Niebuhr wrote in 1948, "A Communist China is not as immediate a strategic threat as imagined by some. The Communism of Asia is primarily an expression of nationalism of subject peoples and impoverished nations. . . . It may take a long time to prove that we are better friends of China than Russia is. But if Russia should prove as heavy-handed in dealing with China as she has with the Eastern European nations, it may not take as long as it now seems."[13]

This prediction proved entirely accurate. It must be added that this did not require miraculous powers of prophecy. Even before the Korean War, the split between Tito's Yugoslavia and Stalin's empire had shown that this was likely to be a future pattern. Later, Niebuhr, Kennan, and other founders of the containment school opposed the U.S. involvement in Vietnam on the strength of their convictions of the power of anticolonial nationalism and of the differences between communist movements.[14]

Forces of Political Religion

Recently, neo-conservatives and liberal hawks have come together in a disastrous repetition of this self-evident reality. During the Cold War, Podhoretz continually referred to "the Communists" as if they were all the same. Today, he refers to "radical Islamism and the states breeding, sheltering, or financing its terrorist armory"—as wildly varied a bunch as one could well imagine—as "the enemy."[15] This is like a Briton in former times talking about "The Hun" and "Johnny Chinaman."

Neo-conservatives have been joined in this regard since 9/11 by leading intellectual representatives of the liberal hawk tendency in the Democratic Party. The confluence of the two streams is noticeable in a widely shared term, namely "Islamic totalitarianism" (also called Islamofascism), frequently reiterated by President Bush. In *Terror and Liberalism,* the leading liberal hawk Paul Berman argues that secular radical Arab nationalism and Islamic fundamentalism are essentially the same phenomenon, since both are supposedly expressions of an antiliberal, totalitarian, international ethos and tradition stemming originally from European fascism and communism. "The

Baathists and the Islamists were two branches of a single impulse, which was Muslim totalitarianism—the Muslim variation on the European idea," he writes. The "global war on terror" is therefore a continuation of America's past struggle against Nazism and communism, a parallel taken up by President Bush. In Berman's view:

> The totalitarian wave began to swell some 25 years ago and by now has swept across a growing swath of the Muslim world. The wave is not a single thing. It consists of several movements or currents, which are entirely recognizable. These movements draw on four tenets: a belief in a paranoid conspiracy theory, in which cosmically evil Jews, Masons, Crusaders and Westerners are plotting to annihilate Islam or subjugate the Arab people; a belief in the need to wage apocalyptic war against the cosmic conspiracy; an expectation that post-apocalypse, the Islamic caliphate of ancient times will reemerge as a utopian new society; and a belief that meanwhile, death is good, and should be loved and revered.[16]

Seeing Arab Baathism, Iranian Shiism, and Pan-Islamic Sunni extremism as part of the same movement, and the "political culture" of different Muslim countries as identical, enables Berman to portray the invasion of Iraq approvingly as part of the struggle against al Qaeda and the transformation not just of the Arab polity but of the entire Muslim world:

> The American strategists noticed that terrorism had begun to flourish across a wide swath of the Arab and Muslim world. And they argued that something had to be done about the political culture across the whole of that wide swath. The American strategists saw in Saddam's Iraq a main center of that political culture, yet also a place where the political culture could be redressed and transformed.[17]

With the exception of a common hostility to Israel, this is surreal. The ideological and theological roots of radical Islamism were laid down more than a thousand years before fascism was conceived. To suggest that Salafism, Shiism, and Baathism form part of the same basic "movement" is the equivalent of suggesting that in Europe past, communism, Catholic conservatism, fascism, and Russian czarism were all basically part of the same movement because they were all hostile to liberal democracy. The "Islamic totalitarianism" argument applied to all the current strains of radicalism in the Muslim world is no less historically illiterate.

In adopting this line, liberal hawks and neo-conservatives have had less excuse than American analysts during the Cold War. For whereas the different Communist parties did at least officially subscribe to the same Marxist-Leninist dogmas, the chief forces in the Muslim world are fundamentally opposed in their basic doctrines and view of history.

In the case of Sunnis, like al Qaeda and its allies, on the one hand, and the Shia on the other, this has been true for 1,300 years. Radical secular Arab nationalism, as represented at its most extreme by the Baath parties in Iraq and Syria, did indeed draw on roots in European fascism. But the roots of both Sunni and Shia religious radicalism are infinitely older—dating back to the first decades of Islam's existence. Even the religious culture of al Qaeda and its allies, Salafism, derives from ancient roots in Sunni Islam; and al Qaeda's specific theology, Wahabism, originated more than two centuries ago in eighteenth-century Arabia.

Baathism has always been deeply and often violently opposed to both Sunni and Shia fundamentalism, just as secular nationalist parties in Europe used to detest the Catholic Church. Baathist Arab nationalism is deeply opposed to any attempt to restore the "Islamic caliphate of ancient times"—as envisioned by al Qaeda and its Sunni radical allies—because this would embrace all Muslims, and the Baath want to create a united Arab secular state under their own fascistic rule.

In any case, the ideological founder of the Baath, Michel Affleq, was a Christian Arab, as were some of Saddam Hussein's leading minions. As modernizing nationalists, much like their former European equivalents, Baathists regard Sunni fundamentalists as dangerous opponents of Arab progress. As to the Shia, the Baath see them as not only culturally alien and retrograde, but as Iranian agents. In this, the Baath have followed the original Italian fascist model that so influenced Affleq.

The fascists had their roots in bitterly anticlerical Italian radical nationalism. When in power, Italian fascists made pragmatic deals with the Catholic Church; but in Italy and Germany, fascism was never influenced by or close to the Christian religion. This does not, of course, make Saddam's Baathists or the fascists more likable. It does define their difference with the forces of political religion.

By refusing to grasp the basic distinction between Arab nationalists and Islamists, Berman demonstrates the same ignorance that led the Bush administration into Iraq in the belief that overthrowing the Baathists would also strike a mortal blow at Islamist terrorism. Worse, Berman and others fail to make the critical distinction between Shiite and Sunni Islam, and between the national agendas of Iran and various Arab states.

In strategic terms, the liberal hawks' and neo-conservatives' line is equivalent to an argument that the United States and its allies should have fought Nazism and Soviet communism not sequentially, but simultaneously. This strategy was indeed weighed by Churchill in the winter of 1939–40. If it had been followed, it would have insured Britain's defeat and a dark age for the world. Similarly, the most dangerous aspect of the Bush administration's approach to the War on Terror is the desire to lump together radically different elements in the Muslim world into a homogeneous enemy camp.

Shades of Hawkishness

Since 9/11, some liberal hawks have tried to appropriate the memory and teachings of Reinhold Niebuhr in a way that radically misinterprets his real views on strategy and the greater part of his philosophy. To bolster this appropriation, some point to the Americans for Democratic Action (ADA), a movement which Niebuhr helped create in 1947. The ADA played a critical role in the late 1940s in rallying American liberals to support the Truman administration, oppose Soviet communism, and support its containment by firm American action. Among its founders were Eleanor Roosevelt, John Kenneth Galbraith, Arthur Schlesinger, and Hans Morgenthau.[18]

Many of ADA's founders had taken part in the earlier struggle to persuade Americans to abandon isolation and join in the fight against Nazi and Japanese aggression. They recognized earlier than most the essentially new and especially dangerous character of the mid-twentieth century totalitarianisms. As Schlesinger wrote, the ADA helped to "fundamentally reshape" American liberalism, dropping its former tendencies towards pacifism and isolationism and committing it to an international struggle against totalitarianism and aggression.[19]

Reviving the spirit of the ADA in the contemporary Democratic Party was the main theme of an essay by Peter Beinart, then editor of the *New Republic,* in December 2004, entitled "A Fighting Faith: An Argument for a New Liberalism." A book based on this essay was published in 2006.[20] Beinart and other liberal hawks have called on American liberals and Democratic Party supporters to fight a "worldwide crusade for democracy" against "totalitarian Islam," just as the ADA fought against totalitarian communism.[21]

Beinart supported the Iraq War, like Paul Berman, Leon Wieseltier, Thomas Friedman, Christopher Hitchens, and other leading Democratic intellectuals. Influential in their own right, these hawks are closely tied to the Democratic Leadership Council, and to the Democratic Party's foreign policy leadership, notably Senators Hillary Clinton and Joseph Biden, former secretary of state Madeleine Albright, and Ambassador Richard Holbrooke.[22]

In his new book, Beinart puts some new distance between himself and more hardline liberal hawks: he still uses the term "Islamist totalitarianism," but now makes clear that by this he means only the Salafi tradition from which al Qaeda is sprung. He no longer—in this book at least—attempts to extend this term to cover the Shia or radical Arab nationalists. In certain respects such distinctions are welcome, and form part of a desirable process of bridging an outdated, irrelevant, and damaging political divide over foreign policy. For the same reason, the recent more realist views of Francis Fukuyama, a semi-penitent from the neo-conservative camp, are also welcome. In an ideal world, these positions would gradually converge in a consensus that might provide real help in the struggle against al Qaeda and its allies.[23]

In the real world, however, Beinart—and even the more moderate and sensible liberal hawks—still have a long way to go. Commendably, Beinart now admits he was wrong to support the war in Iraq. This mistake he ascribes mainly to what the *American Observer* has rightly called "the incompetence dodge"—the argument that liberal hawks could not possibly have predicted the extent of the Bush administration's incompetence.[24] Beinart's new approach is also linked to a new and belated recognition of part of Niebuhr's message: the inherent limits on all human power and wisdom; and the particular need for America, although generally in the right, to recognize that it is also capable of great wrong, and to observe limits on its behavior accordingly. The problem is that when it comes to the recognition of limits, such liberal hawks are too representative of the U.S. establishment, in general. As a result of the Iraqi debacle, they have become more cautious, but not necessarily much wiser. Beinart writes of limits, but then, like the Bush administration's National Security Strategy of 2006, repeats his belief in America's mission to democratize the world.

This, however, is now to be done, according to Beinart, not by Washington acting unilaterally, but through an "alliance of democracies," which in real circumstances can only mean European democracies—with the possible addition of Turkey, Israel, and India. Here, Beinart reveals the central problem of the liberal hawk school when it comes to the War on Terror: an indifference verging on autism towards the views of the Muslim world in general, and the Arab world in particular.[25]

From the point of view of most Arabs, this "alliance of democracies" would simply mean replacing "American imperialism" with "Western imperialism." The addition of India and Israel would suggest to Muslims a global anti-Islamic alliance. And even the presence of Turkey would be problematic, given bitter Arab memories of Turkey's role as the former imperial power in the region. It is a strategy that completely ignores the role of nationalism in the countries concerned. As our analysis of the "Islamic totalitarianism" line

suggests, much of the liberal hawk and neo-conservative view of the Middle East—and, alas, of American perceptions in general—is overwhelmingly self-referential. Although ostensibly about backing Muslim liberals and extremists, it is not linked to real debates within the Muslim world.

In this too, the proponents of a Cold War—style struggle against Islamic totalitarianism, along the lines of the ADA's struggle against Soviet-backed communism, have been responsible for the creation, with bipartisan support, of the U.S. Arabic-language propaganda stations Al-Hurra Television (the "Free One") and Sawa Radio. These were founded on the explicit model of Cold War propaganda stations like Radio Liberty and Radio Free Europe—a model that is completely irrelevant to the Arab world.[26]

The early years of the Cold War were not only a struggle against Soviet expansionism; they were also an ideological civil war within Western Europe, and to a lesser extent within America. Let us not forget that Karl Marx was a German. Although communism triumphed spontaneously only within Russia and Yugoslavia, it came close to doing so at various times in Hungary, Germany, Spain, France, Italy, and Greece. For long periods, Communist parties had genuine mass appeal, and still more to the intelligentsia—especially when they were fighting against fascism. Even more dangerously, the communists often showed immense skill at forming "popular fronts" with Social Democratic and even Liberal parties—where communists used a democratic facade as cover for plans to seize power for themselves.

The ADA was founded precisely to counter moves towards such a "popular front" in America and to reach out to democratic forces in Western Europe to help them to resist communist blandishments. Instead of lumping all socialist movements together as enemies, the ADA appealed in particular to the non-communist European Left; this became the official strategy of the Truman administration, with the covert aid of the CIA.[27] In the 1940s and 1950s, the struggle for the soul of the progressive Western intelligentsia was critical to resisting communism.

The struggle with Sunni Islamist radicalism is very different. Beyond a few individual converts, Islam in general, and its extreme Salafi and Wahabi forms in particular, have little appeal to ordinary Westerners or the intelligentsia. Islamist extremism does have a threatening presence in the West, especially in Europe—but this stems from support for extremists among Muslim immigrants. Disaffection among these minorities is a serious problem, but unlike the communists, it does not pose a threat of revolution and the seizure of the state.

The ideological struggle against al Qaeda and Islamist radicalism is therefore one that can best be conducted by Muslims themselves. Unlike the leaders of the ADA in the Cold War, the liberal hawk intellectuals are irrelevant to this struggle—or even worse, insofar as they display arrogance and ignorance towards the Muslim world, and support U.S. and Israeli policies that even liberal Muslims generally find abhorrent. Thus, Washington's aid to Iranian liberal groups, far from helping them, is undermining their credibility in the eyes of most Iranians.

We must not allow the preaching of democracy, as advocated by neo-conservatives and liberal hawks alike and as embodied in the National Security Strategy of 2006, to become a substitute for tough but informed and enlightened diplomacy. We need the spirit that animates the philosophy of ethical realism, developed by Niebuhr, Morgenthau, and Kennan, as the philosophical basis for a radically new U.S. global strategy.

Notes

1. See, for example, Anatol Lieven, "Fighting Terrorism: Lessons from the Cold War," Carnegie Endowment for International Peace policy brief, no. 7, October 2001.

2. Daniel Kelly, *James Burnham and the Struggle for the World: A Life* (Wilmington, DE: ISI Books, 2002), p. 129. For a more sympathetic portrayal of Burnham's thought, see Samuel Francis, *Thinkers of Our Time: James Burnham* (London: Claridge Press, 1999).

3. James Burnham, *Containment or Liberation? An Inquiry Into the Aims of US Foreign Policy,* (New York: The John Day Co., 1952), pp. 251–54.

4. Kelly, p. 129.

5. Norman Podhoretz, *The Present Danger: Do We Have the Will To Reverse The Decline of American Power?* (New York: Simon and Schuster, 1980).

6. James Burnham, *The Struggle for the World* (New York: The John Day Co., 1947), p. 148.

7. Charles Krauthammer, "The Bush Doctrine," *Time,* March 5, 2001, vol. 157, iss. 9.

8. "Meeting on Vietnam," July 21, 1965, National Security File (LBJL), Country File, Vietnam; quoted in Steven M. Gillon, *Politics and Vision: The ADA and American Liberalism* (New York: Oxford University Press, 1987), p. 178.

9. Burnham, *The Struggle for the World,* pp. 1, 164.

10. Ibid, pp. 194–96; Kelly, pp. 168–70.

11. Kennan, *American Diplomacy,* p. 164.

12. See, for example, *Tracking the Dragon: National Intelligence Estimates on China During the Era of Mao, 1948–1976,* (Washington, DC: National Intelligence Council, 2004), pp. 215–48, in which the National Intelligence Estimate of August 9, 1960, on Sino-Soviet relations presents evidence of a deep and growing split but then concludes, strangely, that this will not amount to anything serious in the years to come.

13. *Chicago Sun-Times,* November 11, 1948, quoted in Alonzo L. Hamby, *Beyond the New Deal: Harry S. Truman and American Liberalism* (New York: Columbia University Press, 1973), p. 367. For similar views by other members of the ADA, see John K. Fairbank, "China: Three Lessons," in *ADA World,* September 22, 1949; ADA Board statement on Asia, *ADA World,* October 1950; David C. Williams, "Chinese Fanaticism Like Yugoslavs Prior to Break with Stalin," *ADA World,* November 1950.

14. David Halberstam, *The Best and the Brightest* (New York: Ballantine Books, 1992), p. 339.

15. Norman Podhoretz, "World War IV: How It Started, What It Means, and Why We Have to Win," *Commentary,* September 2004.

16. Paul Berman, *Terror and Liberalism* (New York: W. W. Norton, 2003).

17. Paul Berman, *Power and the Idealists: Or, The Passion of Joschka Fischer and Its Aftermath* (Brooklyn, NY: Soft Skull Press, 2005), quoted in Stephen Holmes, "The War of the Liberals," *The Nation,* November 14, 2005.

18. For the foundation of the ADA, see Gillon, *Politics and Vision,* pp. 16–24; Mark L. Kleinman, *A World of Hope, A World of Fear: Henry A. Wallace, Reinhold Niebuhr and American Liberalism* (Columbus, OH: Ohio State University Press, 1994), pp. 227–32; Kevin Mattson, *When America Was Great: The Fighting Faith of Postwar Liberalism* (New York: Routledge, 2004) pp. 45–46; Hamby, pp. 161–64.

19. Arthur Schlesinger, *The Vital Center: The Politics of Freedom* (first published 1949; republished Piscataway, NJ: Transaction Publishers, 1997).

20. Peter Beinart, "A Fighting Faith: An Argument for a New Liberalism," *New Republic,* December 13, 2004; Peter Beinart, *The Good Fight: How Liberals—And Only Liberals—Can Win the War on Terror and Make America Great Again* (New York: Harper Collins, 2006).

21. Peter Beinart, "Tough Liberalism," *Blueprint,* Progressive Policy Institute, October 21, 2005.

22. Ari Berman, "The Strategic Class," *The Nation,* August 29, 2005.

23. Anatol Lieven, "We Do Not Deserve These People," *London Review of Books,* vol. 27, no. 20 (October 20, 2005).

24. Sam Rosenfeld and Matthew Iglesias, "The Incompetence Dodge," *The American Prospect,* November 10, 2005.

25. Beinart, *The Good Fight,* p. 286.

26. Anatol Lieven and David Chambers, "The Limits of Propaganda," *Los Angeles Times,* February 13, 2006; Neil MacFarquhar, "Washington's Arabic TV Effort Gets Mixed Reviews," *New York Times,* February 19, 2004; Faye Bowers, "Al Hurra Joins Battle for Hearts and Minds," *Christian Science Monitor,* February 24, 2004; "US Voice in Arabia: Washington's Arabic Satellite TV Station Has Run Into Trouble," *Financial Times,* November 9, 2005; Anne Marie Baylouny, "Alhurra, the Free One: Assessing U.S. Satellite Television in the Middle East," *Strategic Insights,* vol. 4, no. 11 (November 2005).

27. See Schlesinger, p. 167, for an analysis of the "Non-Communist Left" strategy.

ANATOL LIEVEN is a senior research fellow at the New America Foundation covering American strategy and international relations. Formerly a journalist in South Asia and the former Soviet Union, his most recent book is *America Right or Wrong: An Anatomy of American Nationalism* (Oxford University Press, 2004). **JOHN C. HULSMAN** is the von Oppenheimer scholar in residence at the German Council on Foreign Relations in Berlin and a contributing editor to *The National Interest.* He was formerly a senior research fellow in international relations at the Heritage Foundation and has taught European security studies at the Johns Hopkins School of Advanced International Studies, and world politics and U.S. foreign policy at the University of St. Andrews, Scotland.

This essay is adapted from the authors' book, *Ethical Realism: A Vision for America's Role in the World,* published in September 2006 by Pantheon, New York.

From *World Policy Journal,* Fall 2006, pp. 64–74. Copyright © 2006 by John C. Hulsman. Reprinted by permission.

Securing the Information Highway
How to Enhance the United States' Electronic Defenses

WESLEY K. CLARK AND PETER L. LEVIN

During the July 4 holiday weekend, the latest in a series of cyberattacks was launched against popular government websites in the United States and South Korea, effectively shutting them down for several hours. It is unlikely that the real culprits will ever be identified or caught. Most disturbing, their limited success may embolden future hackers to attack critical infrastructure, such as power generators or air-traffic-control systems, with devastating consequences for the U.S. economy and national security.

As Defense Secretary Robert Gates wrote earlier this year in these pages, "The United States cannot kill or capture its way to victory" in the conflicts of the future. When it comes to cybersecurity, Washington faces an uphill battle. And as a recent Center for Strategic and International Studies report put it, "It is a battle we are losing."

There is no form of military combat more irregular than an electronic attack: it is extremely cheap, is very fast, can be carried out anonymously, and can disrupt or deny critical services precisely at the moment of maximum peril. Everything about the subtlety, complexity, and effectiveness of the assaults already inflicted on the United States' electronic defenses indicates that other nations have thought carefully about this form of combat. Disturbingly, they seem to understand the vulnerabilities of the United States' network infrastructure better than many Americans do.

It is tempting for policymakers to view cyberwarfare as an abstract future threat. After all, the national security establishment understands traditional military threats much better than it does virtual enemies. The problem is that an electronic attack can be large, widespread, and sudden—far beyond the capabilities of conventional predictive models to anticipate. The United States is already engaged in low-intensity cyberconflicts, characterized by aggressive enemy efforts to collect intelligence on the country's weapons, electrical grid, traffic-control system, and even its financial markets. Fortunately, the Obama administration recognizes that the United States is utterly dependent on Internet-based systems and that its information assets are therefore precariously exposed. Accordingly, it has made electronic network security a crucial defense priority.

But networks are only the tip of the iceberg. Not only does Washington have a limited ability to detect when data has been pilfered, but the physical hardware components that undergird the United States' information highway are becoming increasingly insecure.

Into the Breach

In 2007, there were almost 44,000 reported incidents of malicious cyberactivity—one-third more than the previous year and more than ten times as many as in 2001. Every day, millions of automated scans originating from foreign sources search U.S. computers for unprotected communications ports—the built-in channels found in even the most inexpensive personal computers. For electronically advanced adversaries, the United States' information technology (IT) infrastructure is an easy target.

In 2004, for example, the design of NASA's Mars Reconnaissance Orbiter, including details of its propulsion and guidance systems, was discovered on inadequately protected "zombie" computer servers in South Korea. Mimicking the tactics of money launderers, hackers had downloaded them there in order to pilfer the data from a seemingly legitimate source. Breaches of cybersecurity and data theft have plagued other U.S. agencies as well: in 2006, between 10 and 20 terabytes of data—equivalent to the contents of approximately 100 laptop hard drives—were illegally downloaded from the Pentagon's nonclassified network, and the State Department suffered similarly large losses the same year.

Russia has already perpetrated denial-of-service attacks against entire countries, including Estonia, in the spring of 2007—an attack that blocked the websites of several banks and the prime minister's website—and Georgia, during the war of August 2008. In fact, shortly before the violence erupted, Georgia's government claimed that a number of state computers had been commandeered by Russian hackers and that the Georgian Ministry of Foreign Affairs had been forced to relocate its website to Blogger, a free service run by Google.

The emergence of so-called peer-to-peer (P2P) networks poses yet another threat. These networks are temporary on-demand connections that are terminated once the data service has been provided or the requested content delivered, much like a telephone call. Some popular P2P services, such as Napster and BitTorrent, have raised a host of piracy and copyright infringement issues, mostly because of recreational abuse. From a security perspective, P2P networks offer an easy way to disguise illegitimate payloads (the content carried in digital packets); through the use of sophisticated protocols, they can divert network traffic to arbitrary ports. Data containing everything from music to financial transactions or weapons designs can be diverted to lanes that are created for a few milliseconds and then disappear without a trace, posing a crippling challenge to Washington's ability to monitor Internet traffic. Estimates vary, but P2P may consume as much as 60 percent of the Internet's bandwidth; no one knows how much of this traffic is legitimate, how much violates copyright laws, and how much is a threat to national security.

The commercially available systems that carry nearly all international data traffic are high quality: they are structurally reliable, globally available, and highly automated. However, the networking standards that enable cross-border electronic exchange were designed in stages over the last four decades to ensure compatibility, not security, and network designers have been playing catch-up for years. To the extent that they paid any attention to security, it was largely to prevent unauthorized, inauthentic, or parasitic access, not a widespread paroxysm of national or even international networks—the IT equivalent of a seizure that strikes suddenly and without warning.

The price of perpetrating a cyberattack is just a fraction of the cost of the economic and physical damage such an attack can produce. Because they are inexpensive to plan and execute, and because there is no immediate physical danger to the perpetrators, cyberattacks are inherently attractive to adversaries large and small. Indeed, for the most isolated (and therefore resource-deprived) actors, remote, network-borne disruptions of critical national infrastructure—terrestrial and airborne traffic, energy generation and distribution, water- and wastewater-treatment facilities, all manner of electronic communication, and, of course, the highly automated U.S. financial system— may be their primary means of aggression.

From isolated intrusions to coordinated attacks, the number of network-based threats is growing. Dan Geer, the chief information security officer at In-Q-Tel, the nonprofit private investment arm of the CIA, points out that the perpetrators are no longer teenagers motivated by lunchroom bragging rights but highly paid professionals. He also believes that after spending billions of dollars on commercial research and development, the United States will still have less, and perhaps much less, than 90 percent protection against network attacks—an unacceptably bad result. And this pessimistic estimate only considers software; it does not take into account the pernicious threat to hardware.

Hardware's Soft Spot

In 1982, a three-kiloton explosion tore apart a natural gas pipeline in Siberia; the detonation was so large it was visible from outer space. Two decades later, the *New York Times* columnist William Safire reported that the blast was caused by a cyber-operation planned and executed by the CIA. Safire's insider sources claimed that the United States carefully placed faulty chips and tainted software into the Soviet supply chain, causing the chips to fail in the field. More recently, unconfirmed reports in *IEEE Spectrum,* a mainstream technical magazine, attributed the success of Israel's September 2007 bombing raid on a suspected Syrian nuclear facility to a carefully planted "kill switch" that remotely turned off Syrian surveillance radar.

Although networks and software attract most of the media's attention when it comes to cybersecurity, chip-level hardware is similarly vulnerable: deliberate design deficiencies or malicious tampering can easily creep in during the 400-step process required to produce a microchip.

Integrated circuits are etched onto silicon wafers in a process that simultaneously produces tens, or even hundreds, of identical chips. In fact, each chip may contain as many as a billion transistors. At the rate of one transistor per second, it would take one person 75 years to inspect the transistors on just two devices; even a typical cell phone has a couple of chips with a hundred million transistors each. Finding a few tainted transistors among so many is an exceedingly tedious, difficult, and error-prone task, and in principle an entire electronic system of many chips can be undermined by just a few rogue transistors. This is why chip-level attacks are so attractive to adversaries, so difficult to detect, and so dangerous to the nation.

Modern automated equipment can test certain kinds of manufacturing fidelity within integrated circuits at the rate of millions of transistors per second. The problem is that such equipment is designed to detect deviations from a narrow set of specifications; it cannot detect unknown unknowns. An apparently perfect device can provide a safe harbor for numerous threats—in the form of old and vulnerable chip designs, embedded Trojan horses, or kill switches—that are difficult or impossible to detect. The theoretical number of potential misbehaviors and possible hardware alterations is simply too large, and no mathematical formulas to constrain the problem have yet been invented.

Moreover, the timeline of a hardware attack is altogether different from that of a software or network attack. With the important exception of infection by symbiotic malware (unauthorized software that depends on the host to survive), pervasive network infections are generally detectable, are mostly curable, and, until now, have been largely containable through the use of software patches, which are now ubiquitous. In contrast, compromised hardware is almost literally a time bomb, because the corruption occurs well before the attack—during design implementation or manufacturing—and is detonated sometime in the future, most likely from a faraway location. Sabotaged circuits cannot be patched; they are the ultimate sleeper cell.

Model Airplanes

Sadly, research in hardware security has been anemic, with relatively few institutions allocating very few dollars. But one researcher, the Stanford University aeronautics professor Per

Enge, has looked to the civilian aviation industry as a model for enhancing hardware security. Aircraft companies have historically focused intensely on systemic weakness and potential vectors of attack on the airframe of airplanes, its many components, and the flight-control infrastructure. It takes months or even years to assess danger in hardware-bound systems, which are common in the transportation industry. Therefore, the aviation sector has always preferred deliberate and quiet responses to vulnerabilities as they are revealed, in part to make sure that the vulnerabilities are not exploited and in part to maintain public trust in an otherwise excellent system. In contrast, the cryptography and software-development communities believe that full disclosure is the path to safety and security. In their view, a threat that is subject to the full scrutiny of academic, industrial, and governmental experts will be neutralized more quickly and mitigated more fully.

For many years, aviation companies believed they could not fully rely on such collaborative failure detection because the equipment they produced was not easily replaced, reused, or repaired. The cost of doing so was so prohibitive to those outside the industry that few even bothered to try. Today, however, with the advent of publicly available GPS technology, even the aviation community is beginning to absorb the lessons of open security standards.

Most computer hardware engineers have traditionally approached the problem in a similar manner: test, stress, and break, but keep discoveries low key so as to avoid exposing a weak flank to the public or to competitors. The long cycles of detection and remediation that characterize hardware, as opposed to software, are the fundamental reason why practically all large mainframe computer systems—from those on airplanes to those in hospitals—still require human intervention to detect and cope with failures.

The difference between a chip and an airplane is that an engineer's ability to absorb knowledge and reconfigure hardware in order to make it more secure is much greater in silicon than in aluminum, especially if the internal response is both adaptive and intelligent.

The need to endow U.S. networks, software, and even hardware with a digital immune system—one that is openly described and freely discussed—is one of the most important lessons to be learned from the open-source community, and it could help hardware engineers make their products more secure.

Immunization Drives

Comparing cyberthreats to biological diseases helps illustrate the potency of electronic attacks and point the way toward possible cures. As Stephanie Forrest and her colleagues at the University of New Mexico have shown, bodily immune systems work best when they are autonomous, adaptable, distributed, and diversified; so, too, with electronic security. Perhaps the biggest reason to focus on hardware assurance is that it provides a resilient form of immunoprotection and dramatically extends the range of potential responses to an attack.

As with their biological analogues, healthy electronic systems will focus protection at the gateways to the outside world (such as a computer's ports), rapidly implement sequential reactions to invading agents, learn from new assaults, remember previous victories, and perhaps even learn to tolerate and coexist with foreign intruders. In other words, healthy hardware can adapt to infection, but sick hardware is an incurable liability—a remote-controlled malignancy that can strike at any time.

Natural science also provides a framework to understand the dangerous implications of static thinking. The aphorism "nature abhors a vacuum" applies strikingly well to cybersecurity: if there is a weak point, whether it is there intentionally or unintentionally, a cybercriminal will find it. Because of its inherent complexity, modern electronic infrastructure is exposed to foreign intrusion. Eventually, the temptation to deliberately build in deficiencies—to leave the door unlocked, so to speak—will likely prove irresistible to professional saboteurs. And even when doors are not left unlocked, an adversary can still deliberately design all the locks to be fundamentally similar, making intrusion easier at some point in the future.

A hardware breach is more difficult to detect and much more difficult to defend against than a network or software intrusion. There are two primary challenges when it comes to enhancing security in chips: ensuring their authenticity (because designs can be copied) and detecting malevolent function inside the device (because designs can be changed). One could easily imagine a kill switch disabling the fire-control logic inside a missile once it had been armed or its guidance system had been activated, effectively disabling the tactical attack capability of a fighter jet. Inauthentic parts are also a threat. In January 2008, for example, the FBI reported that 3,600 counterfeit Cisco network components were discovered inside U.S. defense and power systems. As many as five percent of all commercially available chips are not genuine—having been made with inferior materials that do not stand up under extreme conditions, such as high temperatures or high speeds.

Even well-intentioned security efforts cannot provide ironclad safety. With only $10,000 worth of off-the-shelf parts, a research group led by Christof Paar at Ruhr-Universität Bochum, in Germany, built a code-breaking machine that was able to exploit a hardware vulnerability and, within ten seconds, crack the encryption scheme of the electronic passport chip in European Union passports. This breach could have exposed sensitive personal information to financial criminals and passport counterfeiters. The original design of the passport chip was not fundamentally flawed, but it was inadequately hardened, and no software upgrade could solve the problem.

Adversaries planning cyberattacks on the United States enjoy two other advantages. The first, and most dangerous, is Americans' false sense of security: the self-delusion that since nothing terrible has happened to the country's IT infrastructure, nothing will. Such thinking, and the fact that so few scientists are focused on the problem, undercuts the United States' ability to respond to this threat. Overcoming a complacent mentality will be as difficult a challenge as actually allocating the resources for genuine hardware assurance. Second, the passage of time will allow adversaries and cybercriminals to optimize the stealth and destructiveness of their weapons; the longer the U.S. government waits, the more devastating the eventual assault is likely to be.

The Technological Rain Forest

Seeking to completely obliterate the threats of electronic infiltration, data theft, and hardware sabotage is neither cost-effective nor technically feasible; the best the United States can achieve is sensible risk management. Washington must develop an integrated strategy that addresses everything from the sprawling communications network to the individual chips inside computers.

The U.S. government must begin by diversifying the country's digital infrastructure; in the virtual world, just as in a natural habitat, a diversity of species offers the best chance for an ecosystem's survival in the event of an outside invasion. In the early years of the Internet, practically all institutions mandated an electronically monocultural forest of computers, storage devices, and networks in order to keep maintenance costs down. The resulting predominance of two or three operating systems and just a few basic hardware architectures has left the United States' electronic infrastructure vulnerable. As a result, simple viruses injected into the network with specific targets—such as an apparently normal and well-trusted website that has actually been infiltrated—have caused billions of dollars in lost productivity and economic activity.

Recently, national intelligence authorities mandated a reduction in the number of government Internet access points in order to better control and monitor them. This sounds attractive in principle. The problem, of course, is that bundling the channels in order to better inspect them limits the range of possible responses to future crises and therefore increases the likelihood of a catastrophic breakdown. Such "stiff" systems are not resilient because they are not diverse. By contrast, the core design principle of any multifaceted system is that diversity fortifies defenses. By imposing homogeneity onto the United States' computing infrastructure, generations of public- and private-sector systems operators have—in an attempt to keep costs down and increase control—exposed the country to a potential catastrophe. Rethinking Washington's approach to cybersecurity will require rebalancing fixed systems with dynamic, responsive infrastructure.

In addition to building diverse, resilient IT infrastructure, it is crucial to secure the supply chain for hardware. This is a politically delicate issue that pits pro-trade politicians against national security hawks. Since most of the billions of chips that comprise the global information infrastructure are produced in unsecured facilities outside the United States, national security authorities are especially sensitive about the possibility of sabotage.

Some observers have pointed to the Clinton-era Information Technology Management Reform Act as a leaky crack in the levee of secure hardware infrastructure because it explicitly encouraged the acquisition of foreign-made parts. They are wrong. In fact, streamlining procurement of IT components is in no way related to the integrity of the components themselves; how the government purchases components is unrelated to what is actually delivered, tested, and deployed.

Moreover, the enormous cost of maintaining a parallel domestic production capability to match the tremendous manufacturing advances of the private sector abroad would never pass muster in even the most hawkish appropriations review; such dedicated production facilities would also make an easy target for sabotage or direct attacks. A disruption in the supply chain would exact an incalculable price, not least in terms of the United States' defensive readiness, and would violate the principle of having a layered, diversified response. It makes sense now—just as it made sense during the Clinton years—to purchase components, even those made offshore. The problem is not foreign sourcing; it is ensuring that foreign-made products are authentic and secure.

None of this will require a fundamental change in the way computer networks are currently configured and deployed. Because hardware itself can now be reconfigured—and is therefore adaptable—electronic defenses within actual devices can be augmented without domestic chip designers' revealing more than they already do to the foreign manufacturers who actually produce the chips.

Of course, adversaries could build in hardware deficiencies during production that could hurt the United States later. But there are some very elegant ways to detect those deficiencies without the adversaries' knowing that Washington is watching. Promising strategies in the near term, such as embedding compact authentication codes directly into devices and configuring anti-tamper safeguards after the devices are produced, will enhance protection by tightening control of the supply chain and making the hardware more "self-aware."

The Bush administration's classified Comprehensive National Cyber Security Initiative, which led to a reported commitment of $30 billion by 2015 to bolster electronic defenses and which the Obama administration is expected to support, is a solid first step toward managing the risk.

Unfortunately, much of the relevant information—such as the Defense Advanced Research Projects Agency's TRUST in Integrated Circuits program—is classified. Confidentiality will not necessarily help ensure that the nation's information assets are well protected or that its cyberdefense resources are well deployed. In fact, because many of the best-trained and most creative experts work in the private sector, blanket secrecy will limit the government's ability to attract new innovations that could serve the public interest. Washington would be better off following a more "open-source" approach to information sharing.

The cybersecurity threat is real. Adversaries can target networks, application software, operating systems, and even the ubiquitous silicon chips inside computers, which are the bedrock of the United States' public and private infrastructure.

All evidence indicates that the country's defenses are already being pounded, and the need to extend protection from computer networks and software to computer hardware is urgent. The U.S. government can no longer afford to ignore the threat from computer-savvy rivals or technologically advanced terrorist groups, because the consequences of a major breach would be catastrophic.

WESLEY K. CLARK, a retired four-star General, was Supreme Commander of NATO from 1997 to 2000, led the alliance of military forces in the 1999 Kosovo War, and is a Senior Fellow at the Ron Burkle Center for International Relations at UCLA. PETER L. LEVIN was the founding CEO of the cybersecurity company DAFCA and is now Chief Technology Officer and Senior Adviser to the Secretary at the Department of Veterans Affairs. The views expressed in this article do not necessarily represent the views of the U.S. government.

From *Foreign Affairs,* vol. 88, no. 6, November/December 2009, pp. 2–10. Copyright © 2009 by Council on Foreign Relations, Inc. Reprinted by permission of Foreign Affairs. www.ForeignAffairs.org

UNIT 6

U.S. International Economic Strategy

Unit Selections

Key Points to Consider

- Which type of international system: protectionist, global free trade, or regional trading blocs is in America's national interest? Explain.

- Rank order the United States' most important international economic partners? Defend your answer.

- Select a country in need of debt relief. What type of international economic strategy should the United States pursue toward that country? How does this compare with current U.S. debt relief programs?

- Design an economic strategy for ensuring that the United States has an adequate supply of oil and other natural resources in the future.

- Is American economic power more effective as a lever that attracts countries to the United States or as a weapon of denial or punishment against adversaries?

- What measures would you use to rank how powerful a country's economy is? How high would the United States rank?

Student Website
www.mhhe.com

Internet References

International Monetary Fund (IMF)
www.imf.org
United States Agency for International Development
www.usaid.gov/
United States Trade Representative
www.ustr.gov
World Bank
www.worldbank.org

As in so many areas of American foreign policy, the selection of U.S. international economic strategies during the Cold War seems to have been a rather straightforward process, and the accompanying policy debates fairly minor compared to the situation that exists today. At the most fundamental level, it was taken for granted that the American economy would best be served by the existence of a global free trade system. To that end, international organizations were set up whose collective task was to oversee the operation of the postwar international economic order. Foremost among them were the General Agreement on Tariffs and Trade (GATT), the International Monetary Fund (IMF), and the International Bank for Reconstruction and Development (the World Bank). It was also widely accepted that many states would not be able to resist pressure from the Soviet Union or from domestic communist parties, due to the weak state of their economies and military establishments. Thus, containing communism would require foreign aid programs designed to transfer American economic and military expertise, goods and services, and financial resources to key states.

Events of the 1960s and 1970s shook the international economic system at its political and economic foundations. There followed a period of more than 20 years in which the international economic system was managed through a series of ad hoc responses to crises and the continued inability of foreign aid programs to produce real growth in the less developed world existed. U.S. international economic policy during this period was often characterized as one of "benign neglect."

The adequacy of this response is questioned today. Policymakers and citizens today see the international economic order as highly volatile, perhaps even threatening. The focal point of their concern is the process of globalization. The IMF defines globalization as the growing economic interdependence of countries through the increasing volume and variety of border transactions in goods, services, and capital flows. Most fundamentally, globalization is change-inducing because of its ability to link activities around the world. From a policy perspective, the most significant aspect of globalization is that the international economic activity has become so large, rapid, and dense that it has outstripped the ability of governments and international organizations to manage it. Susan Strange described the situation as one of "casino capitalism" because, just as in a casino, a large element of luck determines the success or failure of international economic policies.

It is against this changed backdrop of globalization that American international economic policy is now made and carried out. We can identify two major dimensions to American international economic foreign policy. The first sees trade and investment as a way of strengthening the American economy.

Department of Defense/Lance Cpl. Christopher M. Carroll, U.S. Marine Corps.
(Released)

They are tools for creating and maintaining growth and prosperity. Subsumed within them are a host of challenging issues and trade-offs such as economic growth, worker's rights, environmental protection, and global equity. The second dimension of American international economic policy involves using its economic strength as an instrument of national security. Here it can be used either to reward or punish other countries for the policies they hold. The articles in this section highlight important issues that encompass questions in both of these two general areas.

The first reading, "America's Sticky Power," identifies economic power as a unique instrument of foreign policy having advantages that neither soft power nor military power possess. It attracts others to the United States voluntarily and then entraps them in a web of relations from which they cannot escape easily or without great cost. "The New Axis of Oil" examines how structural changes in the international oil market will impact on American economic prosperity and national security. The two key players in this new marketplace of buyers and sellers are Russia and China.

The next reading in this section looks at the growing problem in American financial markets and what it ultimately means for United States foreign policy. "The Coming Financial Pandemic" argues that the financial crisis in the United States will become global in scope before it ends. Key areas that will be affected by it are trade, the value of the dollar, and commodity prices.

The final essay, "Can Sanctions Stop Proliferation?," provides us with the tools needed to evaluate the potential for stopping countries such as Iran and North Korea from going nuclear or finding ways to reduce the degree to which they acquire a nuclear capability.

America's Sticky Power

U.S. military force and cultural appeal have kept the United States at the top of the global order. But the hegemon cannot live on guns and Hollywood alone. U.S. economic policies and institutions act as "sticky power," attracting other countries to the U.S. system and then trapping them in it. Sticky power can help stabilize Iraq, bring rule of law to Russia, and prevent armed conflict between the United States and China.

WALTER RUSSELL MEAD

Since its earliest years, the United States has behaved as a global power. Not always capable of dispatching great fleets and mighty armies to every corner of the planet, the United States has nonetheless invariably kept one eye on the evolution of the global system, and the U.S. military has long served internationally. The United States has not always boasted the world's largest or most influential economy, but the country has always regarded trade in global terms, generally nudging the world toward economic integration. U.S. ideological impulses have also been global. The poet Ralph Waldo Emerson wrote of the first shot fired in the American Revolution as "the shot heard 'round the world," and Americans have always thought that their religious and political values should prevail around the globe.

Historically, security threats and trade interests compelled Americans to think globally. The British sailed across the Atlantic to burn Washington, D.C.; the Japanese flew from carriers in the Pacific to bomb Pearl Harbor. Trade with Asia and Europe, as well as within the Western Hemisphere, has always been vital to U.S. prosperity. U.S. President Thomas Jefferson sent the Navy to the Mediterranean to fight against the Barbary pirates to safeguard U.S. trade in 1801. Commodore Matthew Perry opened up Japan in the 1850s partly to assure decent treatment for survivors of sunken U.S. whaling ships that washed up on Japanese shores. And the last shots in the U.S. Civil War were fired from a Confederate commerce raider attacking Union shipping in the remote waters of the Arctic Ocean.

The rise of the United States to superpower status followed from this global outlook. In the 20th century, as the British system of empire and commerce weakened and fell, U.S. foreign-policymakers faced three possible choices: prop up the British Empire, ignore the problem and let the rest of the world go about its business, or replace Britain and take on the dirty job of enforcing a world order. Between the onset of World War I and the beginning of the Cold War, the United States tried all three, ultimately taking Britain's place as the gyroscope of world order.

However, the Americans were replacing the British at a moment when the rules of the game were changing forever. The United States could not become just another empire or great power playing the old games of dominance with rivals and allies. Such competition led to war, and war between great powers was no longer an acceptable part of the international system. No, the United States was going to have to attempt something that no other nation had ever accomplished, something that many theorists of international relations would swear was impossible. The United States needed to build a system that could end thousands of years of great power conflicts, constructing a framework of power that would bring enduring peace to the whole world—repeating globally what ancient Egypt, China, and Rome had each accomplished on a regional basis.

To complicate the task a bit more, the new hegemon would not be able to use some of the methods available to the Romans and others. Reducing the world's countries and civilizations to tributary provinces was beyond any military power the United States could or would bring to bear. The United States would have to develop a new way for sovereign states to coexist in a world of weapons of mass destruction and of prickly rivalries among religions, races, cultures, and states.

In his 2002 book, *The Paradox of American Power: Why the World's Only Superpower Can't Go It Alone,* Harvard University political scientist Joseph S. Nye Jr. discusses the varieties of power that the United States can deploy as it builds its world order. Nye focuses on two types of power: hard and soft. In his analysis, hard power is military or economic force that coerces others to follow a particular course of action. By contrast, soft power—cultural power, the power of example, the power of ideas and ideals—works more subtly; it makes others want what you want. Soft power upholds the U.S. world order because it influences others to like the U.S. system and support it of their own free will [see sidebar: A Sticky History Lesson].

Nye's insights on soft power have attracted significant attention and will continue to have an important role in U.S. policy debates. But the distinction Nye suggests between two types of hard power—military and economic power—has received less consideration than it deserves. Traditional military power can usefully be called sharp power; those resisting it will feel bayonets pushing and prodding them in the direction they must go. This power is the foundation of the U.S. system. Economic power can be thought of as sticky power, which comprises a set of economic institutions and policies that attracts others toward U.S. influence and then traps them in it. Together with soft power (the values, ideas, habits, and politics inherent in the system), sharp and sticky power sustain U.S. hegemony and make something as artificial and historically arbitrary as the U.S.-led global system appear desirable, inevitable, and permanent.

Sharp Power

Sharp power is a very practical and unsentimental thing. U.S. military policy follows rules that would have been understandable to the Hittites or the Roman Empire. Indeed, the U.S. military is the institution whose command structure is most like that of Old World monarchies—the president, after consultation with the Joint Chiefs, issues orders, which the military, in turn, obeys.

Like Samson in the temple of the Philistines, a collapsing U.S. economy would inflict enormous, unacceptable damage on the rest of the world.

Of course, security starts at home, and since the 1823 proclamation of the Monroe Doctrine, the cardinal principle of U.S. security policy has been to keep European and Asian powers out of the Western Hemisphere. There would be no intriguing great powers, no intercontinental alliances, and, as the United States became stronger, no European or Asian military bases from Point Barrow, Alaska, to the tip of Cape Horn, Chile.

The makers of U.S. security policy also have focused on the world's sea and air lanes. During peacetime, such lanes are vital to the prosperity of the United States and its allies; in wartime, the United States must control the sea and air lanes to support U.S. allies and supply military forces on other continents. Britain was almost defeated by Germany's U-boats in World War I and II; in today's world of integrated markets, any interruption of trade flows through such lanes would be catastrophic.

Finally (and fatefully), the United States considers the Middle East an area of vital concern. From a U.S. perspective, two potential dangers lurk in the Middle East. First, some outside power, such as the Soviet Union during the Cold War, can try to control Middle Eastern oil or at least interfere with secure supplies for the United States and its allies. Second, one country in the Middle East could take over the region and try to do the same thing. Egypt, Iran, and, most recently, Iraq have all tried and thanks largely to U.S. policy—have all failed. For all its novel dangers, today's efforts by al Qaeda leader Osama bin Laden and his followers to create a theocratic power in the region that could control oil resources and extend dictatorial power throughout the Islamic world resembles other threats that the United States has faced in this region during the last 60 years.

As part of its sharp-power strategy to address these priorities, the United States maintains a system of alliances and bases intended to promote stability in Asia, Europe, and the Middle East. Overall, as of the end of September 2003, the United States had just over 250,000 uniformed military members stationed outside its frontiers (not counting those involved in Operation Iraqi Freedom); around 43 percent were stationed on NATO territory and approximately 32 percent in Japan and South Korea. Additionally, the United States has the ability to transport significant forces to these theaters and to the Middle East should tensions rise, and it preserves the ability to control the sea lanes and air corridors necessary to the security of its forward bases. Moreover, the United States maintains the world's largest intelligence and electronic surveillance organizations. Estimated to exceed $30 billion in 2003, the U.S. intelligence budget is larger than the individual military budgets of Saudi Arabia, Syria, and North Korea.

Over time, U.S. strategic thinking has shifted toward overwhelming military superiority as the surest foundation for national security. That is partly for the obvious reasons of greater security, but it is partly also because supremacy can be an important deterrent. Establishing an overwhelming military supremacy might not only deter potential enemies from military attack; it might also discourage other powers from trying to match the U.S. buildup. In the long run, advocates maintain, this strategy could be cheaper and safer than staying just a nose in front of the pack.

Sticky Power

Economic, or sticky, power is different from both sharp and soft power—it is based neither on military compulsion nor on simple coincidence of wills. Consider the carnivorous sundew plant, which attracts its prey with a kind of soft power, a pleasing scent that lures insects toward its sap. But once the victim has touched the sap, it is stuck; it can't get away. That is sticky power; that is how economic power works.

Sticky power has a long history. Both Britain and the United States built global economic systems that attracted other countries. Britain attracted the United States into participating in the British system of trade and investment during the 19th century. The London financial markets provided investment capital that enabled U.S. industries to grow, while Americans benefited from trading freely throughout the British Empire. Yet, U.S. global trade was in some sense hostage to the British Navy—the United States could trade with the world as long as it had Britain's friendship, but an interruption in that friendship would mean financial collapse. Therefore, a strong lobby against war with Britain always existed in the United States. Trade-dependent New England almost seceded from the United States during the War of 1812, and at every crisis in Anglo-American relations for the next century, England could count on a strong lobby of merchants and bankers who would be ruined by war between the two English-speaking powers.

A Sticky History Lesson

Germany's experience in World War I shows how "sticky power"—the power of one nation's economic institutions and policies—can act as a weapon. During the long years of peace before the war, Germany was drawn into the British-led world trading system, and its economy became more and more trade-dependent. Local industries depended on imported raw materials. German manufacturers depended on foreign markets. Germany imported wheat and beef from the Americas, where the vast and fertile plains of the United States and the pampas of South America produced food much more cheaply than German agriculture could do at home. By 1910, such economic interdependence was so great that many, including Norman Angell, author of *The Great Illusion,* thought that wars had become so ruinously expensive that the age of warfare was over.

Not quite. Sticky power failed to keep World War I from breaking out, but it was vital to Britain's victory. Once the war started, Britain cut off the world trade Germany had grown to depend upon, while, thanks to Britain's Royal Navy, the British and their allies continued to enjoy access to the rest of the world's goods. Shortages of basic materials and foods dogged Germany all during the war. By the winter of 1916-17, the Germans were seriously hungry. Meanwhile, hoping to even the odds, Germany tried to cut the Allies off from world markets with the U-boat campaigns in the North Atlantic. That move brought the United States into the war at a time when nothing else could have saved the Allied cause.

Finally, in the fall of 1918, morale in the German armed forces and among civilians collapsed, fueled in part by the shortages. These conditions, not military defeat, forced the German leadership to ask for an armistice. Sticky power was Britain's greatest weapon in World War I. It may very well be the United States' greatest weapon in the 21st century.

—W.R.M.

The world economy that the United States set out to lead after World War II had fallen far from the peak of integration reached under British leadership. The two world wars and the Depression ripped the delicate webs that had sustained the earlier system. In the Cold War years, as it struggled to rebuild and improve upon the Old World system, the United States had to change both the monetary base and the legal and political framework of the world's economic system.

The United States built its sticky power on two foundations: an international monetary system and free trade. The Bretton Woods agreements of 1944 made the U.S. dollar the world's central currency, and while the dollar was still linked to gold at least in theory for another generation, the U.S. Federal Reserve could increase the supply of dollars in response to economic needs. The result for almost 30 years was the magic combination of an expanding monetary base with price stability. These conditions helped produce the economic miracle that transformed living standards in the advanced West and in Japan. The collapse of the Bretton Woods system in 1973 ushered in a global economic crisis, but, by the 1980s, the system was functioning almost as well as ever with a new regime of floating exchange rates in which the U.S. dollar remained critical.

The progress toward free trade and economic integration represents one of the great unheralded triumphs of U.S. foreign policy in the 20th century. Legal and economic experts, largely from the United States or educated in U.S. universities, helped poor countries build the institutions that could reassure foreign investors, even as developing countries increasingly relied on state-directed planning and investment to jump-start their economies. Instead of gunboats, international financial institutions sent bankers and consultants around the world.

Behind all this activity was the United States' willingness to open its markets—even on a nonreciprocal basis—to exports from Europe, Japan, and poor nations. This policy, part of the overall strategy of containing communism, helped consolidate support around the world for the U.S. system. The role of the dollar as a global reserve currency, along with the expansionary bias of U.S. fiscal and monetary authorities, facilitated what became known as the "locomotive of the global economy" and the "consumer of last resort." U.S. trade deficits stimulated production and consumption in the rest of the world, increasing the prosperity of other countries and their willingness to participate in the U.S.-led global economy.

Opening domestic markets to foreign competitors remained (and remains) one of the most controversial elements in U.S. foreign policy during the Cold War. U.S. workers and industries facing foreign competition bitterly opposed such openings. Others worried about the long-term consequences of the trade deficits that transformed the United States into a net international debtor during the 1980s. Since the Eisenhower administration, predictions of imminent crises (in the value of the dollar, domestic interest rates, or both) have surfaced whenever U.S. reliance on foreign lending has grown, but those negative consequences have yet to materialize. The result has been more like a repetition on a global scale of the conversion of financial debt to political strength pioneered by the founders of the Bank of England in 1694 and repeated a century later when the United States assumed the debt of the 13 colonies.

In both of those cases, the stock of debt was purchased by the rich and the powerful, who then acquired an interest in the stability of the government that guaranteed the value of the debt. Wealthy Englishmen opposed the restoration of the Stuarts to the throne because they feared it would undermine the value of their holdings in the Bank of England. Likewise, the propertied elites of the 13 colonies came to support the stability and strength of the new U.S. Constitution because the value of their bonds rose and fell with the strength of the national government.

Similarly, in the last 60 years, as foreigners have acquired a greater value in the United States—government and private bonds, direct and portfolio private investments—more and more of them have acquired an interest in maintaining the strength of the U.S.-led system. A collapse of the U.S. economy and the ruin of the dollar would do more than dent the prosperity of the United States. Without their best customer, countries including China and Japan would fall into depressions. The financial strength of every country would be severely shaken should the United States collapse. Under those circumstances, debt becomes a strength, not a weakness, and other countries fear to break with the United States because they need its market and own its securities. Of course, pressed too far, a large national debt can turn from a source of strength to a crippling liability, and the United States must continue to justify other countries' faith by maintaining its long-term record of meeting its financial obligations. But, like Samson in the temple of the Philistines, a collapsing U.S. economy would inflict enormous, unacceptable damage on the rest of the world. That is sticky power with a vengeance.

The Sum of All Powers?

The United States' global economic might is therefore not simply, to use Nye's formulations, hard power that compels others or soft power that attracts the rest of the world. Certainly, the U.S. economic system provides the United States with the prosperity needed to underwrite its security strategy, but it also encourages other countries to accept U.S. leadership. U.S. economic might is sticky power.

How will sticky power help the United States address today's challenges? One pressing need is to ensure that Iraq's economic reconstruction integrates the nation more firmly in the global economy. Countries with open economies develop powerful trade-oriented businesses; the leaders of these businesses can promote economic policies that respect property rights, democracy, and the rule of law. Such leaders also lobby governments to avoid the isolation that characterized Iraq and Libya under economic sanctions. And looking beyond Iraq, the allure of access to Western capital and global markets is one of the few forces protecting the rule of law from even further erosion in Russia.

China's rise to global prominence will offer a key test case for sticky power. As China develops economically, it should gain wealth that could support a military rivaling that of the United States; China is also gaining political influence in the world. Some analysts in both China and the United States believe that the laws of history mean that Chinese power will someday clash with the reigning U.S. power.

Sticky power offers a way out. China benefits from participating in the U.S. economic system and integrating itself into the global economy. Between 1970 and 2003, China's gross domestic product grew from an estimated $106 billion to more than $1.3 trillion. By 2003, an estimated $450 billion of foreign money had flowed into the Chinese economy. Moreover, China is becoming increasingly dependent on both imports and exports to keep its economy (and its military machine) going. Hostilities between the United States and China would cripple China's industry, and cut off supplies of oil and other key commodities.

Sticky power works both ways, though. If China cannot afford war with the United States, the United States will have an increasingly hard time breaking off commercial relations with China. In an era of weapons of mass destruction, this mutual dependence is probably good for both sides. Sticky power did not prevent World War I, but economic interdependence runs deeper now; as a result, the "inevitable" U.S.-Chinese conflict is less likely to occur.

Sticky power, then, is important to U.S. hegemony for two reasons: It helps prevent war, and, if war comes, it helps the United States win. But to exercise power in the real world, the pieces must go back together. Sharp, sticky, and soft power work together to sustain U.S. hegemony. Today, even as the United States' sharp and sticky power reach unprecedented levels, the rise of anti-Americanism reflects a crisis in U.S. soft power that challenges fundamental assumptions and relationships in the U.S. system. Resolving the tension so that the different forms of power reinforce one another is one of the principal challenges facing U.S. foreign policy in 2004 and beyond.

WALTER RUSSELL MEAD is the Henry A. Kissinger senior fellow in U.S. foreign policy at the Council on Foreign Relations. This essay is adapted from his forthcoming book, *Power, Terror, Peace, and War: America's Grand Strategy in a World at Risk* (New York: Knopf, 2004).

The New Axis of Oil

FLYNT LEVERETT AND PIERRE NOËL

While Washington is preoccupied with curbing the proliferation of weapons of mass destruction, avoiding policy failure in Iraq and cheering the "forward march of freedom", the political consequences of recent structural shifts in global energy markets are posing the most profound challenge to American hegemony since the end of the Cold War. The increasing control that state-owned companies exercise over the world's reserves of crude oil and natural gas is, under current market conditions, enabling some energy exporters to act with escalating boldness against U.S. interests and policies. Perhaps the most immediate example is Venezuela's efforts to undermine U.S. influence in Latin America. The most strategically significant manifestation, though, is Russia's willingness to use its newfound external leverage to counteract what Moscow considers an unacceptable level of U.S. infringement on its interests. At the same time, rising Asian states, especially China, are seeking to address their perceived energy vulnerability through state-orchestrated strategies to "secure" access to hydrocarbon resources around the world. In the Chinese case, a statist approach to managing external energy relationships is increasingly pitting China against the United States in a competition for influence in the Middle East, Central Asia and oil-producing parts of Africa.

We describe these political consequences of recent structural shifts in global energy markets by the shorthand "petropolitics." While each of these developments is challenging to U.S. interests, the various threads of petropolitics are now coming together in an emerging "axis of oil" that is acting as a counterweight to American hegemony on a widening range of issues.[1] At the center of this undeclared but increasingly assertive axis is a growing geopolitical partnership between Russia (a major energy producer) and China (the paradigmatic rising consumer) against what both perceive as excessive U.S. unilateralism. The impact of this axis on U.S. interests has already been felt in the largely successful Sino–Russian effort to rollback U.S. influence in Central Asia. But the real significance is being seen in the ongoing frustration of U.S. objectives on the Iranian nuclear issue. This will likely be a milestone in redefining the post-Cold War international order—not merely because Iran is likely to end up with at least a nuclear-weapons option, but because of what that will imply about the efficacy of America's global leadership.

Structural Changes

The age of oil has clearly entered a new chapter, as strong demand and a shortage of productive capacity have generated a significantly higher trading range for crude oil than the world has experienced during the last twenty years. The dramatic rise in demand has been fed by high economic growth in emerging markets (where the increments of energy demand associated with specific increments of economic growth are usually greater than in OECD countries), particularly China and India. Overall, surging demand for crude oil from emerging economies has been the most immediate factor exerting upward pressure on prices.

A second element defining the recent structural shift in the international oil market is shrinking surplus productive capacity all along the supply chain. (Global oil supply has increased in recent years, but not as much as demand.) The degree that oil producers around the world expand their productive capacity is likely to be the most important factor affecting oil prices in the future. Not surprisingly, one finds a range of views about the possibilities for relieving the current supply "crunch."

There is significant evidence that there is, in fact, more oil to be discovered and produced, or recovered from already-producing fields, around the world—at the right price and with appropriate levels in investment. Thus, we do not share the unrelieved pessimism of those who argue we have reached the peak point of global oil supplies. However, we are also not inclined to accept the unrestrained optimism of some economists, who argue that high prices will, as they have in the past, necessarily attract the investment required to expand production relative to demand growth. Our skepticism flows primarily from the reality that the upstream oil sector—the exploration and production of crude oil—is far from an open and competitive environment. After 25 years of massive investment by multinational oil companies in exploration and development in oil-producing areas outside of OPEC and the former Soviet Union, the cost of replacing reserves in this "competitive fringe" of the oil industry, where the upstream sector has been relatively open, is now rising rapidly. Meanwhile, a high proportion of the remaining areas suitable for comparatively low-cost renewal of reserves, mostly in the Middle East and former Soviet Union, are off-limits to the international oil industry.

The next quarter-century of the oil age will therefore look quite different from the previous quarter-century: The rise in demand and the decline of several non-OPEC countries' production will have to be met by increased supplies of conventional oil from the Middle East and the former Soviet Union, as well as by unconventional oil (oil shale, tar sands and extra-heavy oil) and synthetic liquids (gas-to-liquids, coal-to-liquids and bio-fuels). Prices will likely be much higher on average and more unstable than in the past, with demand continuing to bump up against productive capacity.

There is an explicitly political dimension to these developments. As the "competitive fringe" of the upstream oil sector has been exploited by the multinational oil industry, the percentage of the world's oil reserves held by publicly traded international oil companies (IOCs) has declined, while the percentage held by state-owned national oil companies (NOCs) has increased. Currently, 72 percent of the world's proven oil reserves are held by NOCs. The ten-largest upstream companies in the world, measured by booked reserves (not market capitalization or production), are all NOCs. ExxonMobil—the largest publicly traded IOC in the world and the iconic symbol of "big oil"—is only the twelfth-largest upstream company in the world in terms of booked reserves. This means that NOCs and their parent governments, not IOCs and their shareholders, ultimately control the pace of development of upstream oil and gas resources.

Under current conditions of rising demand and tight supply, this is giving energy-exporting countries a more subtle but also more durable basis for enhancing their influence and generating new strategic options for themselves than that displayed by OPEC during and immediately after the 1973–74 oil embargo. Only now is the world seeing the full extent of the "OPEC revolution" of the early 1970s: Beyond an explicit cartel of oil producers, there is today an implicit cartel of resource-owning governments that control a large share of the world's known reserves of oil and natural gas. The power of this implicit cartel has been dormant for three decades; its actualization is an event of major economic and political significance that is generating critical challenges to America's regional interests and global standing.

Markets and the Russian Agenda

Russia stands as perhaps the leading exemplar of supply-side trends. After several years of uncertainty and contestation, President Vladimir Putin has successfully reasserted a definitive measure of state control over Russia's upstream oil and gas sectors, with NOCs like Gazprom and Rosneft playing increasingly important roles, the country's pipeline network firmly in government hands, Russian private-sector companies operating within parameters established by Moscow, and formidable barriers in place to large-scale foreign investment.

Suggestions just a few years ago that Russia could supplant Saudi Arabia as a swing producer for the global oil market were misplaced. There is no evidence that Putin or other senior leaders aspire to such a status, or that the Russian oil industry could muster what it would take to play such a role. Nevertheless, under Putin's presidency the internal conditions have been established for Russia to derive a significant measure of external leverage from its status as an important energy producer. In this regard, Putin wants to use Russia's presidency of the G-8 this year to transform Russia's international status from that of a mere (albeit major) energy supplier to that of a global supplier of energy security.

Moscow is using its market power to push back against the United States in arenas where it perceives U.S. infringement on its interests. Since the collapse of the Soviet Union, the list of accumulated Russian grievances over U.S. initiatives has grown ever longer: NATO enlargement, abrogation of the Anti-Ballistic Missile Treaty, basing of U.S. forces in Central Asia, the Iraq War and support for the "color revolutions" in states neighboring Russia. Through the late 1990s, Russia's ability to respond to these provocations was negligible. The Russian military was bogged down in Chechnya, and low oil and gas prices

contributed to economic weakness—epitomized by Russia's 1998 currency crisis—making Russia dependent on the United States and other international players for assistance. In recent years, however, Russia's autonomy has been reinforced by high energy prices, and Putin and his advisors have decided they can use this market power to "push back" against the United States.

Russia's unfolding strategy for bolstering its influence in the "near abroad" exemplifies this approach. In some cases, as in the recent controversy over Russian gas shipments through Ukraine, the Kremlin's initiatives seem heavy-handed and not particularly productive. But its approach has been quite effective in establishing a new sphere of influence in the Eurasian south.

Much Western commentary on Russian policy in Central Asia has focused on Moscow's recent successes in establishing military bases in Kyrgyzstan and Tajikistan and encouraging Uzbekistan to evict U.S. military personnel from the Karshi-Kanabad air base. The real story, however, is rooted in energy and Russia's rising market power. Since 2003, Moscow has worked assiduously to establish a new sphere of influence in Central Asia, using regional autocrats' interest in resisting U.S. pressure to democratize, and China's interest in avoiding "encirclement" by U.S. forces, to maximize pressure on America. Russia's status as a major energy producer has given it important tools for pursuing Putin's regional strategy: investment capital with which to assume a leading role in the development and marketing of Central Asian energy resources (with NOCs like Gazprom acting as effective agents of Kremlin policy) and control over access to Russia's state-owned pipeline system, which is essential for moving Central Asian oil and gas to markets in Europe.

Less directly, the oil boom of the last few years has fueled much higher rates of growth in the Russian economy, helping to turn the Russian service sector into a provider of jobs for Central Asian expatriates. Remittances from the expatriate workers constitute an increasingly important source of income for several Central Asian states—perhaps as much as 30 percent of GDP in Tajikistan, for example—which gives Moscow another lever of influence over these states.[2]

Russia has also used its energy-based market power to bolster its political influence in other strategically vital regions in ways that could potentially weaken America's international position. Perhaps most notably, Moscow has taken advantage of its market power to reinforce and enhance its otherwise sagging strategic position in East Asia. Although geopolitical legacies and existing transportation infrastructure orient Russian energy exports toward Europe, Moscow has used the prospect of substantial energy exports from eastern Siberia and the Russian Far East to markets in East Asia to make itself a major factor in the foreign policies of both China and Japan, playing on the interests of Beijing and Tokyo in balancing traditional sources of hydrocarbons from the Middle East in their energy profiles.

The Asian Challenge

Of course, the market power of energy suppliers like Russia is an outgrowth of escalating demand-side pressures. As noted earlier, increased demand, especially from emerging Asia, has been one of the most important factors exerting upward pressure on oil prices since 2003: According to the U.S. Department of Energy, 40 percent of oil-demand growth worldwide since 2001 has come from China alone. Despite a slowdown in China's oil-demand growth in 2005, many market forecasts show demand growth in Asia continuing at impressive rates for years to come.

In the current climate, the political impact of these demand-side pressures is exacerbated by consumer countries' increasing reliance on statist strategies to secure access to hydrocarbon resources on privileged bases, rather than relying solely on international markets to meet their energy needs. The best example of this approach is China's. In 2002, around the time that Hu Jintao became general secretary of the Communist Party, China formally adopted a "going out" (*zou chu qu*) policy of encouraging its three major NOCs—the China National Petroleum Corporation (CNPC), the China National Petrochemical Corporation (Sinopec), and the China National Offshore Oil Corporation (CNOOC)—to purchase equity shares in overseas exploration and production projects around the world, and to build pipelines, particularly to Siberia and Central Asia. The goal of the "going out" strategy is to secure effective ownership of energy resources and transportation infrastructure, measures that China perceives as essential to improving the country's energy security. The adoption of the policy was effectively a codification of long-standing practice, as Chinese energy companies had already engaged in these activities since the 1990s.

China has pursued the "going out" strategy in a wide range of oil-producing regions, including the Caucasus, Central Asia, East and South Asia, Africa and Latin America. In the Middle East, China has employed the strategy in various ways with a number of oil-producing states, including Algeria, Egypt, Iran, Libya, Oman, Saudi Arabia, Syria, Sudan and Yemen. Beijing supports the efforts of Chinese energy companies to win deals with regular high-level visits to and from regions in which the companies are seeking access. China also follows up its network of energy deals by increasing exports of manufactured goods and capital to countries where its NOCs are operating. In some cases, the Chinese appear willing to put expensive packages of side investments on the table in order to secure energy deals, as was recently the case in Angola and Nigeria. Chinese and other Asian NOCs participating in bidding rounds in a number of countries have shown a willingness to pay high prices in order to secure exploration and production contracts, sometimes overbidding IOCs.

However, while increased demand from Asian economies has a very direct effect on global oil prices, the impact of China's statist strategy on the market is probably not as dramatic as some assessments would suggest. It seems doubtful that Chinese NOCs' fledgling efforts to lock up petroleum resources will succeed in keeping a critical mass of oil reserves off an increasingly integrated and fluid global oil market. There is also no reason to anticipate that China's willingness to pay market premiums for privileged access to oil resources in various parts of the world will bolster upward pressure on prices generated naturally by rising demand. The opposite is more likely: The flow of "cheap" Chinese capital into global exploration and production is increasing competition among oil companies to access reserves and forcing IOCs to increase spending and take more risks. Other things being equal, this should bring *more* oil, not less, to market.

Arguably, the Chinese strategy of competing for access to hydrocarbon resources challenges the rules-based international order for trade and investment in energy that the United States has long championed. At a minimum, statist initiatives to secure effective ownership over hydrocarbon resources in foreign countries—with an attendant willingness toward corruption, offering soft loans, and making investments in unrelated sectors and infrastructure projects as part of these initiatives—undercut OECD standards for export financing and other good-governance criteria. And there is a risk that the Chinese approach will be taken as a model by others. This is already happening to some extent with India's Oil & Natural Gas Corporation (ONGC), which is pursuing equity oil deals in many of the same places as the Chinese NOCs—in some cases, as in Iran and Sudan, in consortium with them. Last year, for example, China and India announced an "agreement" aimed at preventing competition over hydrocarbon assets between Chinese NOCs and ONGC from driving up the prices of those assets, as happened in the contest to buy Canada-based PetroKazakhstan. There is also a resurgent debate in Japan as to whether it should take a more statist approach to external energy policy to meet the Chinese challenge. But we are still far from a turning point of massive defections from the market by major consumers and suppliers.

Nevertheless, while the market impact of statist strategies like China's may be minimal, Beijing's "going out" strategy is rapidly becoming a source of geopolitical tensions between China and the United States, with potentially significant implications for the development of the world's most important bilateral relationship during the first quarter of the 21st century. China's search for oil is making it a new competitor to the United States for influence, especially in the Middle East, Central Asia and Africa. China's energy-driven engagement in the Middle East is creating new foreign policy as well as commercial options for energy exporting states, including those at odds with U.S. foreign policy goals, like Iran, Sudan and Syria. (With regard to Sudan, Beijing went so far as to use its status as a permanent member of the Security Council to block the imposition of sanctions on Khartoum over the Darfur genocide.)

In Central Asia, China's interest in diversifying its external sources of energy to mitigate its reliance on the Persian Gulf has motivated Beijing's leading role in the Shanghai Cooperation Organization's campaign to undercut U.S. influence in Central Asia. In oil-producing African countries, Chinese and other Asian NOCs make available to host governments a supply of exploration and production capital that is free from any good-governance and transparency conditions. This, combined with high oil prices, is weakening the leverage that Western governments and international financial institutions can use to improve management of the oil sector and reduce corruption in these countries.

Additionally, Beijing's statist approach to energy security is raising geopolitical tensions with Japan, with prospectively a negative impact on the development of a regional political framework to anchor growing trade and financial interdependence in the world's most dynamic economic zone. Competition between Beijing and Tokyo for specific energy deals in a variety of settings, a bilateral dispute about sovereignty over possible natural gas reserves in the East China Sea, and jockeying over the ultimate destination of a projected Russian eastern oil pipeline have all contributed to the ongoing deterioration of Sino–Japanese relations. Unless these tensions can be ameliorated, it will be increasingly difficult for the United States to manage China's rise on the East Asian scene in a way that ensures long-term regional stability.

Over time, Russian oil and gas could be a major factor buttressing closer Sino–Russian strategic collaboration. Putin's recent meeting with Hu in Beijing, during which the two leaders concluded an agreement for Russia to begin exporting natural gas to China by 2012, was the fifth such meeting in the last year. In theory, a successful commercially grounded oil and gas relationship between Russia and China could be positive for at least some U.S. interests by mitigating China's sense of energy insecurity through reduced dependence on the Middle East (and U.S.-secured Asian maritime routes for their transport). But Moscow is clearly playing on Beijing's sense of energy insecurity to foster a closer geopolitical partnership.

The Axis of Oil and Iran

The implications of the new petropolitics and an emerging axis of oil for America's international influence are illustrated by the way these forces are frustrating U.S. objectives on the Iranian nuclear issue. The policies of key players on this issue are conditioned far more by calculations about the economics and geopolitics of energy than was the case during the run-up to the Iraq War. As the Western powers consider what sort of action against Iran they might collectively support, it is clear that their options in the Security Council are severely limited by Russian and Chinese resistance to the imposition of sanctions or other strongly punitive measures.

With growing market power increasing Russia's capacity for strategic initiative, its calculus of interests regarding the Iranian nuclear issue has become more complex than most Western analysts and policymakers understand. Moscow's policy agenda toward Iran has expanded significantly. Russia continues to have important economic interests in Iran. Moscow anticipates a substantial increase in high-technology exports (for example, civil nuclear technology) to Iran over the next decade. The Iranian market is also potentially lucrative for Russian exporters of conventional weaponry, one of Russia's main sources of foreign-exchange earnings alongside hydrocarbon exports. But over the last three years, Russia has also come to see Iran as an important geopolitical partner in its efforts to rollback U.S. influence, not only in Central Asia but in the Caucasus as well. Moscow's recent proposal to resolve the impasse between the Islamic Republic and the West over Iran's nuclear activities by establishing Iranian–Russian joint-venture entities for uranium enrichment was calculated to serve all of these interests. Such a scheme would allow Moscow to maintain and even expand an Iranian market for its nuclear technology, while also nurturing its developing strategic partnership with Tehran.

It is also increasingly evident that the current leadership in Moscow views the Iranian nuclear issue as an opportunity to frustrate the Bush Administration's unilateralist inclinations. Russian Foreign Minister Sergei Lavrov—formerly Russia's permanent representative to the UN for ten years and a master of Security Council politics and procedure—and his colleagues anticipate that, in the end, the United States may take unilateral military action against Iran, including the Russian-built reactor at Bushehr. They do not expect to be able to block such action anymore than they could block the invasion of Iraq, but they are working prospectively to impose serious costs on the United States for

a military strike against Iran by ensuring that Washington lacks international legitimacy for its actions.

For its part, China's approach to the Iranian nuclear issue is directly linked to its assessment of its requirements for energy security. Beijing has already put down a marker, in the form of its opposition to UN sanctions against Sudan, that it will oppose the imposition of multilateral sanctions on an energy-producing state in which Chinese companies operate. In private conversations, senior Chinese diplomats and party officials describe Beijing's policy on the Iranian nuclear issue as seeking to balance a range of interests: a secure supply of oil, nonproliferation and regional stability, the defense of important international norms (including the peaceful resolution of disputes and the sovereign right of states to develop civil nuclear capabilities), securing China's northwest border (meaning Xinjiang province, where there is a significant Muslim population), the development of Chinese–Iranian relations, the development of U.S.–Chinese relations, and the positions of the European Union and Russia. It seems increasingly clear that, in their efforts to balance this set of interests, Chinese officials will remain deeply resistant to the imposition of sanctions on Iran. And as long as Russian opposition provides China with political cover, Chinese officials seem to calculate that they will not have to choose between relations with Iran and relations with the United States.

China's willingness to protect Iran from international pressure would also complicate Western efforts to impose meaningful sanctions on Iran through a "coalition of the willing." Without Chinese participation, a voluntary ban on investment in Iran's energy sector by Western powers would, at this point, be little more than a symbolic gesture, as U.S. companies are already barred from doing business in Iran by U.S. law, and most European IOCs have put potential projects on hold because of the political uncertainties. In recent years, though, Chinese NOCs have committed themselves, at least in principle, to substantial investments in Iran's energy sector, thereby mitigating the impact of restrictions on Western investment.

With the Bush Administration having ruled out direct and broad-based strategic discussions with Iran aimed at a "grand bargain" that would include a resolution of the nuclear issue, the United States and its European partners are headed down an ultimately futile path in the Security Council. The Security Council's failure to deal effectively with the Iranian nuclear issue will confront the United States, during the last two years or so of the Bush Administration's tenure, with the choice of doing nothing as Iran continues to develop its nuclear capabilities or taking unilateral military action in the hope of slowing down that development. Each of these choices is likely to damage American leadership in the world: Doing nothing will highlight U.S. fecklessness, while unilateral action without international legitimacy will further strain America's international standing (and probably not meaningfully impede Iran's nuclear development).

Beyond speculating whether Iran might cut off oil exports in response to sanctions or military action, commentators tend to overlook the implications of the current controversy's outcome for the geopolitics of global energy. How the nuclear issue plays out will largely determine Iran's future as an oil and gas supplier. Iranian oil production relies heavily on a small number of old, "super-giant" fields, where output has plateaued and could soon start to decline. These old fields need massive infusions of investment and technology to increase their recovery rates. Iran is not Saudi Arabia and cannot make the investments itself. Since reopening its upstream oil sector in 1994, Iran has actually taken in only around $10 billion of foreign investment in oil exploration and production, due to a lack of political consensus on the country's oil policy, a difficult and opaque negotiating process, and unattractive contractual terms. Similarly, Iran needs large-scale investment and technology transfers to develop its gas-exporting potential. If the nuclear controversy leads to Iran's further isolation from Western IOCs, there would be a powerful incentive for Tehran to turn to Chinese and other Asian NOCs, supplement their investment capital with expertise from more technologically advanced Russian companies, and rely on government-to-government marketing deals. This would significantly reinforce the economic and political logic behind the axis of oil.

Possible Policies

One step Washington needs to take is to facilitate broader and deeper cooperation between the International Energy Agency (IEA) and China and India. Because these states are not members of the OECD, they are not formally eligible for membership in the IEA, and they have not yet built up the minimum levels of stockpiled oil and petroleum products defined by the IEA for its members. Notwithstanding these barriers, it is clearly in the interests of the United States and its Western partners to establish much closer coordination between emerging Asian economies and the IEA, especially to persuade these states to rely more on international markets and less on exclusive supply deals to meet their energy needs.

At the same time, the United States needs to change its approach to promoting expansion of global energy supplies. It will take more than exhortations about market logic to change elite attitudes and government policies regarding upstream resource development in key energy-producing states. These elites have, by and large, determined that values other than pure market efficiency have priority in their calculations about resource development. Traditional American advocacy of liberalization and internationalization of upstream oil and gas sectors needs to shift decisively toward encouraging NOCs in key producing states to increase investment in productive capacity.

The larger reality is that U.S. foreign policy is ill suited to cope with the challenges to American leadership flowing from the new petropolitics. Current policy does not take energy security seriously as a foreign policy issue or prioritize energy security in relation to other foreign policy goals.

The United States cannot change the course of Moscow's energy policy or foreign policy, but American diplomacy can mitigate Russian policymakers' threat perceptions in exchange for more cooperative Russian behavior. This would require the United States to reach a set of strategic understandings with Moscow encouraging mutual respect for each side's critical interests—and also to make clear privately that Washington and its Western partners will not recognize Russia as a provider of energy security as long as it plays geopolitically on the energy security of others. Vice President Cheney's recent public denunciation of Moscow, coupled with the Bush Administration's refusal to reconsider its strategic approach to Russia, is hardly likely to achieve positive results.

To deal more effectively with China, Washington must recognize that, despite some acknowledgment in Beijing that the "going out" strategy may prove a poor energy security policy, there is still a widely held perception within the Chinese establishment that the international oil market is a foreign (primarily American) construction, operated by Western IOCs in accordance with their interests, and that China cannot bet its energy security on that construction. U.S. policy should encourage Chinese and other Asian NOCs to move along their own paths of internationalization. In this regard, the U.S. Congress's resistance to CNOOC's potential acquisition of Unocal last year sent precisely the wrong message to China.

More broadly, U.S. policymakers need to remember that, even for a global hegemon, to govern is to choose. Washington cannot continue to disregard the impact of its foreign policy choices on the interests of key energy-producing states like Russia if it expects these states not to use their market power in ways that run counter to U.S. preferences. And, similarly, Washington cannot ignore the energy security interests and perceptions of rising consumer countries like China and avoid consequences reflected in these countries' foreign policy choices.

Notes

1. The term "axis of oil" is not new and has been used by various commentators to describe a number of oil-focused relationships, such as the U.S.–Saudi strategic partnership or a possible coordination between India and China in their quest to secure external energy resources. We use the term, in a manner similar to Irwin Stelzer, to describe a shifting coalition of both energy exporting and energy importing states centered in ongoing Sino–Russian collaboration.

2. The authors are grateful to their colleague Fiona Hill for this point.

FLYNT LEVERETT is senior fellow at the Brookings Institution's Saban Center for Middle East Policy and has been appointed visiting professor of political science at the Massachusetts Institute of Technology. **PIERRE NOËL** is research fellow at the French Institute of International Relations (IFRI) in Paris. He will join the Electricity Policy Research Group at Cambridge University's Judge Business School in September.

From *The National Interest,* Summer 2006, pp. 62–70. Copyright © 2006 by National Interest. Reprinted by permission.

The Coming Financial Pandemic

The U.S. financial crisis cannot be contained. Indeed, it has already begun to infect other countries, and it will travel further before it's done. From sluggish trade to credit crunches, from housing busts to volatile stock markets, this is how the contagion will spread.

NOURIEL ROUBINI

For months, economists have debated whether the United States is headed toward a recession. Today, there is no doubt. President George W. Bush can tout his $150 billion economic stimulus package, and the Federal Reserve can continue to cut short-term interest rates in an effort to goose consumer spending. But those moves are unlikely to stop the economy's slide. The severe liquidity and credit crunch from the subprime mortgage bust is now spreading to broader credit markets, $100 barrels of oil are squeezing consumers, and unemployment continues to climb. And with the housing market melting down, empty-pocketed Americans can no longer use their homes as ATMs to fund their shopping sprees. It's time to face the truth—the U.S. economy is no longer merely battling a touch of the flu; it's now in the early stages of a painful and persistent bout of pneumonia.

Meanwhile, other countries are watching anxiously, hoping they don't get sick, too. In recent years, the global economy has been unbalanced, with Americans spending more than they earn and the country running massive external deficits. When the subprime mortgage crisis first hit headlines last year, observers hoped that the rest of the world had enough growth momentum and domestic demand to gird itself from the U.S. slowdown. But making up for slowing U.S. demand will be difficult, if not impossible. American consumers spend about $9 trillion a year. Compare that to Chinese consumers, who spend roughly $1 trillion a year, or Indian consumers, who spend only about $600 billion. Even in wealthy European and Japanese households, low income growth and insecurities about the global economy have caused consumers to save rather than spend. Meanwhile, countries such as China rely on exports to sustain their high economic growth. So there's little reason to believe that global buyers will pick up the slack of today's faltering American consumer, whose spending has already begun to drop.

Because the United States is such a huge part of the global economy—it accounts for about 25 percent of the world's GDP, and an even larger percentage of international financial transactions—there's real reason to worry that an American financial virus could mark the beginning of a global economic contagion. It may not devolve into a worldwide recession, but at the very least, other nations should expect sharp economic downturns, too. Here's how it will happen:

Trade will drop. The most obvious way that a U.S. recession could spill over elsewhere in the world is through trade. If output and demand in the United States fall—something that by definition would happen in a recession—the resulting decline in private consumption, capital spending by companies, and production would lead to a drop in imports of consumer goods, capital goods, commodities, and other raw materials from abroad. U.S. imports are other countries' exports, as well as an important part of their overall demand. So such a scenario would spell a drop in their economic growth rates, too. Several significant economies—including Canada, China, Japan, Mexico, South Korea, and much of Southeast Asia—are heavily dependent on exports to the United States. China, in particular, is at risk because so much of its double-digit annual growth has relied on the uptick of exports to the United States. Americans are the world's biggest consumers, and China is one of the world's largest exporters. But with Americans reluctant to buy, where would Chinese goods go?

China is also a good example of how indirect trade links would suffer in an American recession. It once was the case that Asian manufacturing hubs such as South Korea and Taiwan produced finished goods, like consumer electronics, that were exported directly to American retailers. But with the rise of Chinese competitiveness in manufacturing, the pattern of trade in Asia has changed: Asian countries increasingly produce components, such as computer chips, for export to China. China then takes these component parts and assembles them into finished goods—say, a personal computer—and exports them to American consumers. Therefore, if U.S. imports fall, then Chinese exports to the United States would fall. If Chinese exports fall, then Chinese demand for component parts from the rest of Asia would fall, spreading the economic headache further.

A weak dollar will make matters worse. Already, the economic slowdown in the United States and the Fed's interest rate cuts have caused the value of the dollar to drop relative to many floating currencies such as the euro, the yen, and the won. This weaker dollar may stimulate U.S. export competitiveness, because those countries will be able to buy more for less. But, once again, it is bad news for other countries, such as Germany, Japan, and South Korea, who rely heavily on their own exports to the United States. That's because the strengthening of their currencies will increase the price of their goods in American stores, making their exports less competitive.

Housing bubbles will burst worldwide. The United States isn't the only country that experienced a housing boom in recent years. Easy money and low, long-term interest rates were plentiful in other countries, too, particularly in Europe. The United States also isn't the only country that has experienced a housing bust: Britain, Ireland, and Spain lag only slightly behind the United States as the value of their flats and villas trends downward. Countries with smaller but still substantial real estate bubbles include France, Greece, Hungary, Italy, Portugal, Turkey, and the Baltic nations. In Asia, countries including Australia, China, New Zealand, and Singapore have also experienced modest housing bubbles. There's even been a housing boom in parts of India. Inevitably, such bubbles will burst, as a credit crunch and higher interest rates poke holes in them, leading to a domestic economic slowdown for some and outright recession for others.

Commodity prices will fall. One need only look at the skyrocketing price of oil to see that worldwide demand for commodities has surged in recent years. But those high prices won't last for long. That's because a slowdown of the U.S. and Chinese economies—the two locomotives of global growth—will cause a sharp drop in the demand for commodities such as oil, energy, food, and minerals. The ensuing fall in die prices of those commodities will hurt the exports and growth rate of commodity exporters in Asia, Latin America, and Africa. Take Chile, for example, the world's biggest producer of copper, which is widely used for computer chips and electrical wiring. As demand from the United States and China falls, the price of copper, and therefore Chile's exports of it, will also start to slide.

Financial confidence will falter. The fallout from the U.S. subprime meltdown has already festered into a broader and more severe liquidity and credit crunch on Wall Street. That, in turn, has spilled over to financial markets in other parts of the world. This financial contagion is impossible to contain. A huge portion of the risky, radioactive U.S. securities that have now collapsed—such as the now disgraced residential mortgage-backed securities and collateralized debt obligations—were sold to foreign investors. That's why financial losses from defaulting mortgages in American cities such as Cleveland, Las Vegas, and Phoenix are now showing up in Australia and Europe, even in small villages in Norway.

> **Today, central banks' ability to stimulate their economies and dampen the effect of a global slowdown is far more limited than in the past.**

Consumer confidence outside the United States—especially in Europe and Japan—was never strong; it can only become weaker as an onslaught of lousy economic news in the United States dampens the spirits of consumers worldwide. And as losses on their U.S. operations hit their books, large multinational firms may decide to cut back new spending on factories and machines not just in the United States but everywhere. European corporations will be hit especially hard, as they depend on bank lending more than American firms do. The emerging global credit crunch will limit their ability to produce, hire, and invest.

The best way to see how this financial flu spreads is by watching global stock markets. Investors become more risk averse when their economies appear to be slowing down. So whenever there's bad economic news in the United States—say, reports of higher unemployment or negative GDP growth—there are worries that other economies will suffer, too. Investors sell off their stocks in New York and the Dow Jones plunges. You can expect a similarly sharp fall when the Nikkei opens in Tokyo a few hours later, and the ripple effect then continues in Europe when opening bells ring in Frankfurt, London, and Paris. It's a vicious circle; the market volatility culminates in a kind of panicky groupthink, causing investors to dump risky assets from their portfolios en masse. Such financial contagion was on prime display when global equity markets plummeted in January.

Money for Nothing

Optimists may believe that central banks can save the world from the painful side effects of an American recession. They may point to the world's recovery from the 2001 recession as a reason for hope. Back then, the U.S. Federal Reserve slashed interest rates from 6.5 percent to 1 percent, the European Central Bank dropped its rate from 4 percent to 2 percent, and the Bank of Japan cut its rate down to zero. But today, the ability of central banks to use monetary tools to stimulate their economies and dampen the effect of a global slowdown is far more limited than in the past. Central banks don't have as free a hand; they are constrained by higher levels of inflation. The Fed is cutting interest rates once again, but it must worry how the disorderly fall of the dollar could cause foreign investors to pull back on their financing of massive U.S. debts. A weaker dollar is a zero-sum game in the global economy; it may benefit the United States, but it hurts the competitiveness and growth of America's trading partners.

Monetary policy will also be less effective this time around because there is an oversupply of housing, automobiles, and other consumer goods. Demand for these goods is less sensitive to changes in interest rates, because it takes years to work out such gluts. A simple tax rebate can hardly be expected to change this fact, especially when credit card debt is mounting and mortgages and auto loans are coming due.

The United States is facing a financial crisis that goes far beyond the subprime problem into areas of economic life that the Fed simply can't reach. The problems the U.S. economy faces are no longer just about not having enough cash on hand; they're about insolvency, and monetary policy is ill equipped to deal with such problems. Millions of households are on the verge of defaulting on their mortgages. Not only have more than 100 subprime lenders gone bankrupt, there are riding delinquencies on more run-of-the-mill mortgages, too. Financial distress has even spread to the kinds of loans that finance excessively risky leveraged buyouts and commercial real estate. When the economy falls further, corporate default rates will sharply rise, leading to greater losses. There is also a "shadow banking system," made up of non-bank financial institutions that borrow cash or liquid investments in the near term, but lend or invest in the long term in nonliquid forms. Take money market funds, for example, which can be withdrawn overnight, or hedge funds, some of which can be redeemed with just one month's notice. Many of these funds are invested and locked into risky, long-term securities. This shadow banking system is therefore subject to greater risk because, unlike banks, they don't have access to the Fed's support as the lender of last resort, cutting them off from the help monetary policy can provide.

Beyond Wall Street, there is also much less room today for fiscal policy stimulus, because the United States, Europe, and Japan all have structural deficits. During the last recession, the United States underwent a nearly 6 percent change in fiscal policy, from a very large surplus of about 2.5 percent of GDP in 2000 to a large deficit of about 3.2 percent of GDP in 2004. But this time, the United States is already running a large structural deficit, and the room for fiscal stimulus is only 1 percent of GDP, as recently agreed upon in President Bush's stimulus package. The situation is similar for Europe and Japan.

President Bush's fiscal stimulus package is too small to make a major difference today, and what the Fed is doing now is too little, too late. It will take years to resolve the problems that led to this crisis. Poor regulation of mortgages, a lack of transparency about complex financial products, misguided incentive schemes in the compensation of bankers, wrongheaded credit ratings, poor risk management by financial institutions—the list goes on and on.

Ultimately, in today's flat world, interdependence boosts growth across countries in good times. Unfortunately, these trade and financial links also mean that an economic slowdown in one place can drag down everyone else. Not every country will follow the United States into an outright recession, but no one can claim to be immune.

NOURIEL ROUBINI is chairman of RGE Monitor and professor of economics at New York University's Stern School of Business.

Can Sanctions Stop Proliferation?

DINGLI SHEN

In contemporary international relations, sanctions are a means of settling disputes and attaining specific policy objectives,[1] often employed to reflect the dissatisfaction of certain members of the international community over another member's domestic or international behavior. Some argue that sanctions never work, whereas others think that they serve to moderate undesirable behavior, although often not entirely effectively.[2] In recent years, sanctions have been imposed against the Democratic People's Republic of Korea (DPRK) and Iran to compel these regimes to give up their nuclear weapons or suspected nuclear programs. How effective have these sanctions been, and what do these cases say about China's evolving attitudes toward sanctions as a nonproliferation tool?

Conditions of Effective Sanctions

Sanctions have historically been imposed when a state has domestically or internationally violated a code of conduct, for instance, regarding the protection of human rights or other generally accepted moral standards. The UN Charter allows for such action should massive abuses of human rights occur, even though the chief mission of the United Nations is to protect state sovereignty.[3] During the Cold War, for example, the apartheid system in South Africa was strongly and persistently condemned worldwide. Beginning in 1974, the UN excluded South Africa from participating in all international organizations and conferences under UN auspices.[4] Many countries participated in the sanctions regime against Pretoria as well.

Sanctions are also imposed after a state commits an act that violates established international law or is viewed as destabilizing regional order or global security. Theoretically, every country has sovereignty in deciding its own foreign and defense policy, and there is no requirement to mandate that certain or all countries participate in any particular international regimes, such as those related to nuclear nonproliferation. Nevertheless, under certain circumstances, the UN may decide that some countries may not be entitled to absolute sovereignty.[5] For example, UN Security Council Resolution 687 stripped Iraq of its right to possess certain categories of unconventional weapons after its disastrous 1991 invasion of Kuwait.[6]

In these cases, economic and political sanctions are designed to deliver enough harm or at least threat, short of warfare, to compel a state to refrain from undesirable behavior or actions.[7] Analyzing past and current sanctions cases suggests that the effectiveness of international sanctions is contingent on four factors: the legitimacy of sanctions through international law or moral standards, the impacts of the sanctions on sanction-imposing states, the degree of international participation, and the sanctions' strength as a deterrent.

The sanctions against apartheid in South Africa met all four criteria. Apartheid is generally considered to be a violation of human dignity and equality. The Universal Declaration on Human Rights provides a legal and moral basis for sanctions against such acts. A majority of world states boycotted Pretoria collectively, cutting off its economic lifeline. The political and economic pressures exerted by the sanctions, coupled with long-term, widespread domestic resistance, forced the white regime to end its reign in the early 1990s.

Sanctions are less successful when one or several of these components are absent. The boycott of the 1980 Moscow Olympics, although well conceived, did not achieve its purpose. The boycott demonstrated the displeasure of some members of the international community, including the United States and China, toward the military action of the Soviet armed forces in Afghanistan at that time, but it hardly affected the Soviet invasion. Rather, the sanctions sacrificed the rights of those nations' athletes to compete in the games and invited the Soviet bloc to retaliate by boycotting the 1984 Summer Olympics in Los Angeles. The sources of the 1980 failure were multitude: Its legitimacy was compromised by suspicions of simple Cold War competition; linking sports to politics is neither conducive nor effective; the cost of sanctions on those who boycotted was rather high, as athletes of the boycotting countries had trained intensely for the Games; only one-fifth of the world's states participated; and the Soviet Union tolerated the costs of the sanctions, which did not affect its core interests.

Iran's Intransigence

In 2002 the world learned of the existence of two nuclear facilities in Iran. Although its nuclear capabilities were not fully developed and Iran, like any other country, is entitled to undertake a full range of fuel cycle development, including uranium enrichment to fuel nuclear power reactors for civilian uses, it carried out this program without reporting it to the International Atomic Energy Agency (IAEA). Iran's failures to honor its obligations under the Nuclear Non-Proliferation Treaty (NPT) have been many. Despite Tehran gradually revealing some details of its nuclear program, the IAEA has identified additional undeclared matters and has encountered difficulty in securing Iran's cooperation in resolving a number of issues. For example, Tehran did not report importing centrifuges from Pakistan. When this fact was exposed, it initially made no effort to explain the sources of those centrifuges, the history of their use, and most importantly, why Tehran failed to report them and even tried to conceal certain facts.

The White House and U.S. intelligence community have long suspected that Iran's nuclear intentions are not innocent.[8] Despite subsequent IAEA inspections and U.S. intelligence efforts, however, Washington cannot conclude that Iran is developing nuclear weapons. To the contrary, the National Intelligence Council concluded with high confidence in November 2007 that Iran terminated its nuclear weapons program in the fall of 2003.[9] This latest judgment coincides with the latest resolution by the IAEA Board of Governors.[10]

Although the IAEA has asserted that Iran is not developing nuclear weapons now,[11] it still demands that Iran be more cooperative in clarifying the nature of parts of its past nuclear program. Given the murkiness of Iran's past historical development, two possible scenarios may explain Iran's nuclear past. Iran may be innocent but careless, developing civilian nuclear power but failing to report its activities, or alternatively, Iran has sought nuclear technology to have an immediate weapons capability or to possess the technical preparedness to create one later.

Iran has nevertheless violated its NPT commitment, even if it never had a weapons program. The international community has been disappointed by the fact that Tehran has not reported its nuclear program, later claimed as exclusively civilian, to the IAEA and has been frustrated by Iran's longstanding unwillingness or inability to clarify its past nuclear activities to the world's satisfaction. Various IAEA resolutions were passed to urge Iran to be cooperative. Because those failed to compel cooperation, on February 4, 2006, the IAEA brought Iran's nuclear issue to the UN Security Council, which passed three sanctions resolutions—Resolution 1737 on December 23, 2006; Resolution 1747 on March 24, 2007; and Resolution 1803 on March 3, 2008—to coerce Iran to immediately suspend or stop its ongoing uranium-enrichment programs until its past nuclear history is cleared.

Resolution 1737 demands that Iran "shall without further delay suspend proliferation-sensitive nuclear activities."[12] Until it complies, Resolution 1737 bans the supply of nuclear-related technology and materials, freezes the assets of key individuals and companies related to the enrichment program, and calls on countries to report travel into their territory by Iranian officials involved in that program. Resolution 1747 incrementally tightens these sanctions and imposes a ban on arms sales. Finally, Resolution 1803 extends financial sanctions to additional entities and travel bans to additional persons, calls on member states to inspect cargo bound to or from Iran, and urges countries to be cautious in providing trade incentives and guarantees to Iran.

In addition to the UN Security Council sanctions, the United States has imposed various sanctions on Iran. In October 2007, it enacted its harshest sanctions against Iran since the seizure of the U.S. embassy in Tehran in 1979. Washington launched financial sanctions against banking institutions and the Islamic Revolutionary Guard Corps and its associated companies, the first instance of sanctions against foreign armed forces.

The escalation of the UN and U.S. sanctions demonstrates that the sanctions imposed thus far have not met expectations.[13] Tehran has apparently not taken the Security Council's demands and the U.S. financial sanctions into serious consideration. It is pushing its uranium-enrichment program forward, and some of its cooperation with the IAEA under the terms of the Additional Protocol is still suspended. Iran has openly challenged the legality of the sanctions resolutions and has threatened to sue the Western countries imposing sanctions.

Why has this been the case? First, Iran has indeed violated international law for failing to meet its reporting obligations, but no solid evidence establishes yet that Iran was developing nuclear weapons in the past or at present, undermining the sanctions' perceived legitimacy. Both the IAEA and U.S. government have publicly ruled out the likelihood that Iran is currently developing nuclear weapons. Even though the U.S. National Intelligence Council concluded that Iran worked on nuclear weapons programs prior to late 2003, most countries will only take published U.S. intelligence estimates as a reference but depend more heavily on IAEA data for decisionmaking.

Such sanctions are thus legally controversial. As long as Iran is found not to have developed weapons now, it has full rights to carry out an independent civilian nuclear energy program with its own nuclear fuel cycle. The world community can be wary of the true nature of Iran's "civilian" program, but that concern should not deprive Tehran of its legitimate rights to peaceful uses of nuclear energy. The most balanced approach to addressing this question seems to be to allow Iran's enrichment program while closely monitoring its operation.

Also, some question the second criterion for the effectiveness of sanctions: the stakes for countries involved. How seriously would Iran's nuclear development hurt others if it went unsanctioned? Peaceful enrichment will certainly harm no one, assuming Iran does not develop weapons capabilities later on. If Iran is building a weapons program, however, some states could be affected, and some regional players and Muslim constituencies might be inspired to strike a balance of power in the Middle East by developing their own deterrent. This may ironically be a benefit for other regional states, providing the justification for those states that wish to pursue their own nuclear weapons to go ahead.

Third, the criterion of sanctions' strength has not been met. The sanctions so far have been weak, with the "tailored" sanctions targeting only Tehran's nuclear and missile programs. They are limited and focused in order to prevent Iran from quickly weaponizing its nuclear capabilities. Yet, given Iran's energy resources, the international community has been unwilling to impose any sanctions on Iran that would hurt energy trade between Tehran and many other capitals. Many countries will not embrace a comprehensive punitive package that undermines their overall economic partnership with Iran. The sanctions thus far do not threaten Iran's core interests and its most crucial and vulnerable sector: the export of petroleum and gas.

Punishing Iran has therefore been a self-contradictory mission, with some members of the international community declaring paramount nonproliferation concerns, whereas others sympathize with Tehran or need access to Iran's energy resources. Attempting to bypass those unwilling states would violate the third criterion: international participation. The means have not been sufficient to accomplish nonproliferation ends in Iran.

Sanctions have not been sufficient to accomplish nonproliferation ends in Iran.

The Empirical Record in North Korea

The North Korean sanctions case also involves a nuclear program long suspected of having a military dimension. Yet, the DPRK nuclear nightmare has already come true with Pyongyang conducting a nuclear test, exposing sanctions as insufficient.

Some would argue that the DPRK might have violated the NPT before it quit the treaty in 2003. That possibility aside, however, once it walked away from the NPT, the DPRK was no longer bound by it. In this sense, Pyongyang is free to choose its nuclear path.[14] Yet, North Korea cannot be completely free as it is still bound by a 1992 bilateral commitment with South Korea.[15] Under the Joint Declaration, North and South Korea agree not to test, manufacture, produce, receive, possess, store, deploy, or use nuclear weapons; to use nuclear energy solely for peaceful purposes; and not to possess facilities for nuclear reprocessing and uranium enrichment. In this context, Pyongyang's subsequent processing of plutonium and nuclear testing have violated that Korean peninsula bilateral commitment.

In September 2006, the Department of the Treasury imposed financial sanctions on Macau-based Banco Delta Asia, which was believed to have assisted North Korea's financial transactions. The U.S. action certainly undercut Pyongyang's international financial capability, as it forced various countries and financial agencies to distance themselves from Banco Delta Asia to avoid collateral damage. When the United States lifted the sanctions two years later, Chinese banks were reluctant to serve as conduits for bringing the frozen assets back to the DPRK for fear of damaging their reputation. The sanctions impacted North Korea financially. Nevertheless, Pyongyang responded with a nuclear test in October 2006 to demonstrate that the U.S. sanctions were not effective.

The DPRK's nuclear weapons and missile development is unwelcome at the least and possibly destabilizing. All of its neighbors are NPT members, with non–nuclear-weapon member states committing not to acquire nuclear weapons and China, its main nuclear neighbor, committing not to transfer nuclear weapons to non–nuclear-weapon states. North Korean nuclear weapons development upsets regional stability in Northeast Asia and could eventually harm Pyongyang's own peripheral security environment. Regional neighbors and the international community therefore swiftly responded to the DPRK's missile and nuclear tests in 2006.

Following the DPRK's July 5, 2006, missile test, the UN Security Council passed Resolution 1695 on July 15, condemning Pyongyang's missile launch and initiating missile-specific sanctions. After Pyongyang's announcement of a nuclear test on October 9, 2006, the Security Council quickly passed Resolution 1718 on October 14, condemning the DPRK's destructive action and launching nuclear-specific and wider sanctions. A few other countries also put forward unilateral sanctions against North Korea. For instance, Japan launched sanctions that denied port calls to North Korean ships and prevented Japanese ships from trading in open seas with DPRK ships.

These punitive actions were imposed as the denuclearization negotiations known as the six-party talks continued. Since the October 2006 nuclear test, Pyongyang has moved to a fundamentally different stance on its nuclear weapons capability. Given the DPRK's new bargaining chip and the U.S. overstretch in Afghanistan and Iraq, the United States was forced to moderate its position in the six-party talks. Since January 2007, Pyongyang and Washington have managed to negotiate a nuclear disablement scheme for the DPRK to follow and have overcome many unexpected difficulties not directly related to nuclear disablement, such as the imposition and subsequent lifting of the aforementioned financial sanctions against Pyongyang.

By the end of 2007, the DPRK had disabled most of its three Yongbyon-based nuclear facilities, including a five–megawatt electric experimental reactor, a reprocessing plant, and the nuclear fuel rod fabrication facility. Despite this significant progress, North Korea failed to submit a complete and correct declaration of all its nuclear programs by December 31, 2007.[16] Indeed, there is still a long way to go from nuclear disablement to nuclear dismantlement and then to nuclear disarmament.

Meeting the Criteria

Has the DPRK's progress in nuclear disablement been linked to the international sanctions placed on it? Without the external pressures of sanctions, the DPRK would not likely have voluntarily disabled its nuclear weapons capacity. These sanctions have more grounds for legitimacy than those against Iran. In the Iranian case, Tehran still claims to adhere to the NPT and vows not to develop nuclear weapons, and IAEA inspections have concluded that the nature of the ongoing uranium enrichment is peaceful. With the DPRK's clear case of weaponization, collective sanctions are more warranted, and international legal and moral support is more easily gathered.

Without sanctions, it is unlikely the DPRK would have disabled its nuclear weapons capacity.

On the second criterion, the stakes for sanction-imposing states, the complicated security environment in Northeast Asia means that Pyongyang's pursuit of nuclear weapons can hardly be accepted by any actors in the region. China is deeply concerned that Pyongyang's proliferation could have a domino effect, deteriorating the regional security situation. South Korea and Japan may be pressured to follow suit, and the United States will be even more preoccupied with maintaining the regional balance of power. All of these actors therefore share common stakes in reversing the DPRK's nuclear status, giving cohesive impetus to the six-party talks.

This regional collaboration in Northeast Asia contrasts with the case of nuclear proliferation in the Middle East. The threat of proliferation in each area is obviously very serious. Yet, international consensus on stemming Iran's nuclear development seems weaker than the consensus against the DPRK's program, as Iran has energy leverage and enjoys certain sympathy from some regional actors in Middle Eastern and Muslim constituencies.

Third, as relevant parties have their respective interests converging on disabling the DPRK's nuclear weapons program, the international efforts to dissolve Pyongyang's nuclear ambition have secured considerable participation, sending an authoritative message to the hermit kingdom's leadership. The six-party talks have brought three nuclear-weapon powers and two major industrialized countries to the table to share resources for the disablement endeavor. China's proactive role in hosting the talks, using its leverage and devising mutually acceptable compromises, has been instrumental in moving the initial discussions forward.

Finally, the adequacy of the sanctions' strength, the final criterion, matters. Resolution 1718 bars the DPRK's access to the international community in terms of nuclear and missile development and orders countries to restrict Pyongyang's access to heavy conventional weapons as well as some luxuries its leadership may be interested in continuing to acquire. Compared with the Iranian sanctions, those against North Korea are better organized, better designed, and heavier and wider in substance, although they are similarly limited primarily to specifically tailored areas without touching civilian and economic dimensions.[17] This carefully crafted sanctions strategy serves as effective leverage against Pyongyang. In the meantime, the Bush administration has adjusted its approach and is offering North Korea certain incentives, such as lifting financial sanctions without a North Korean apology and shipping heavy oil to North Korea before Pyongyang has disabled its nuclear facilities, enticing North Korea to reciprocate.

How Much Have They Mattered?

Yet, these sanctions measures are far from perfect. Once the DPRK quit the NPT, it indeed regained its freedom of action from an international legal standpoint, raising questions about the legitimacy of sanctions. Although members of the six-party talks share important common interests in seeing the Korean peninsula free of nuclear weapons, some of them have serious security issues with each other. For example, the distrust between China and the United States on the question of Taiwan

prevents them from carrying out even deeper cooperation. Moreover, U.S. policy toward North Korea seems fragmented and inconsistent from time to time, undercutting the effectiveness both of dialogue with and sanctions on the DPRK, while intensifying the fundamental distrust between North Korea and the United States. As a result, the lack of further progress on the North Korean nuclear program may not be so surprising.

Given this set of four criteria for effective sanctions, sanctions on Iran's nuclear behavior have not yet been effective, whereas sanctions against the DPRK's nuclear development have been more or less successful because of the degree of legitimacy, stakes for participants, international participation, and strength of the sanctions.

China's Changing Stance

China's perspective on the issue of sanctions has evolved significantly over time, culminating in its changing attitude toward sanctions and participation first in the sanctions against South Africa and now both sets of UN sanctions against Iran and North Korea. Historically, Beijing has asserted that exerting pressure on a state constitutes an unacceptable approach to resolving international disputes. China considers sovereignty to be a sacred ideal deserving to be safeguarded. For many years, Beijing thought that sovereignty should be absolute regardless of the nature of a state's internal affairs. In the 1950s, China and India proposed "five principles of peaceful coexistence," placing noninterference above all, based on the understanding that newly decolonized states tended to be particularly vulnerable to external pressures.

China's perspective on sanctions has evolved significantly.

Yet, China's contemporary stance toward sanctions is still evolving, reflecting its changing perspectives and interests in an increasingly interdependent world. To some extent, it has modified its traditional sovereignty rhetoric. Although China has been consistently and strongly opposed to any international interference, it condemned apartheid and distanced itself from South Africa during the Cold War. China did so because it believed that Pretoria's white supremacy was fundamentally against human rights and that the antiapartheid movement was part of a national independence and political liberation movement in Africa. In the meantime, Beijing had to compete with Taiwan over its policy toward South Africa. Mainland China had long supported Nelson Mandela and the African National Congress of South Africa. Although Taiwan recognized the apartheid regime, it eventually lost its official relationship with South Africa after Mandela took power.[18]

China's views on sanctions are also shaped by its own experiences on the receiving end of these measures. For the last two decades, the European Union and United States have had an arms embargo in place against China for its handling of the student demonstrations in Tiananmen Square in 1989. From a political standpoint, Beijing believes that sanctions render nations unequal and tend to suppress less developed countries. The sanctions launched in 1989 have made China unable to access EU and U.S. weapons markets for Chinese force modernization. Given its own experiences with foreign intervention in its affairs, China tends to find international sanctions objectionable.

China's views on sanctions are shaped by its own experiences on the receiving end.

With its economic reform over the last three decades, however, China is now heavily interdependent with the world and has diversified interests. It now looks to protect its sovereignty through one-on-one diplomacy and multilateral tactics on the international stage. The two nuclear cases of Iran and North Korea compel China to honor its own pledges under the NPT. Moreover, it is in China's interest to ensure that Iran and the DPRK do not develop nuclear weapons. Under these circumstances, dealing with Iran and the DPRK in certain multilateral settings adds to China's nonproliferation diplomacy with each of them. China, a sanctioned state, has joined the UN sanctions concerning North Korean and Iranian nuclear and/or missile development[19]—quite a significant development of China's move toward being a responsible stakeholder in the international system.

With interdependence, China has to adjust its traditionally held value of absolute sovereignty.

Traditionally, the development of such weapons of mass destruction and missiles has been the decision of a sovereign nation. China has developed its own nuclear weapons and missile capability according to this argument. Yet, Beijing now considers its commitment to regional stability and international nonproliferation regimes to be high priorities. In a time of globalization, China's economic and security interests have become intertwined with securing a stable peripheral environment and a peaceful world. Consequently, China has to adjust its traditionally held value of an abstract and absolute sovereignty.

Prospects for Progress

The effectiveness of sanctions is far from guaranteed. If they are to be used as a tool in international politics, their designers must make them legitimate, popular, and strong and balance their incentives and disincentives. The ongoing sanctions against Iran have not met such criteria well, and the chances of their success are limited so far. If a scheme could be developed in which these criteria are better met, it is possible to prevent Iran from pushing for non-peaceful uses of nuclear energy.

After many frustrations over finding a solution to the North Korean situation, however, a peaceful remedy may be possible down the road because a balance of incentives and disincentives has been in play. Sanctions against the DPRK's nuclear and missile development have been much better designed, with proper emphasis on legitimacy, stakes, popularity, and strength. Yet, this does not necessarily guarantee success. North Korea's eventual nuclear disarmament still demands a change in the leadership's security perceptions and in the statecraft of other involved parties. China has been adjusting its stance over the years regarding sanctions and now is playing a more proactive role in responsibly imposing sanctions to deal with issues of nonproliferation and regional stability.

Notes

1. Rose Gottemoeller, "The Evolution of Sanctions in Practice and Theory," *Survival* 49, no. 4 (Winter 2007–08): 99–110.

2. See Gary Clyde Hufbauer, Jeffrey J. Schott, and Kimberly Ann Elliott, *Economic Sanctions Reconsidered: History and Current Policy,* 2nd ed. (Washington, D.C.: Institute for International Economics, 1990), p. 123.

3. United Nations (UN), "Charter of the United Nations," www.un.org/aboutun/charter/ (hereinafter UN Charter).

4. See UN General Assembly, Resolution 3324 (XXIX), December 16, 1974, art. E8, www.un.org/documents/ga/res/29/ares29.htm.

5. UN Charter, art. 35(2).

6. UN Security Council, S/RES/687, April 8, 1991, www.un.org/Docs/scres/1991/scres91.htm.

7. David A. Baldwin, *Economic Statecraft* (Princeton: Princeton University Press, 1985), p. 9; Robert A. Pape, "Why Economic Sanctions Do Not Work," *International Security* 22, no. 2 (Fall 1997): 93; Gary C. Hufbauer, "Ineffectiveness of Economic Sanctions: Same Song, Same Refrain? Economic Sanctions in the 1990s," *American Economic Review,* no. 89 (May 1999): 403; Kimberly A. Elliot, "The Sanctions Glass: Half Full or Completely Empty?" *International Security* 23, no. 1 (Summer 1998): 53.

8. Yang Xingli, Ji Kaiyun, and Chen Junhua, *A Study on Iranian-U.S. Relations* [in Chinese] (Beijing: Shishi Publishing House, 2006), pp. 299–301; Fan Hongda, *The United States and Iran: A Friendly Period* [in Chinese] (Beijing: Social Science Academic Press, 2006).

9. Office of the Director of National Intelligence, "National Intelligence Estimate: Iran: Nuclear Intentions and Capabilities," November 2007, www.dni.gov/press_releases/20071203_release.pdf (press release).

10. IAEA Board of Governors, "Implementation of the NPT Safeguards Agreement and Relevant Provisions of Security Council Resolutions 1737 (2006) and 1747 (2007) in the Islamic Republic of Iran," GOV/2008/4, February 22, 2008, www.iaea.org/Publications/Documents/Board/2007/gov2007-58.pdf.

11. Ibid.

12. UN Security Council, S/RES/1737, December 23, 2006, para. 2, www.un.org/ Docs/sc/unsc_resolutions06.htm.

13. For debates over sanctions against Iran, see Vali Nasr and Ray Takeyh, "The Cost of Containing Iran: Washington's Misguided New Middle East Policy," *Foriegn Afairs* 87, no.1 (January/February 2008), www.foreignaffairs.org/20080101faessay87106/vali-nasr-ray-takeyh/the-costs-of-containing-iran.html; Joseph Cirincione and Andrew Grotto, "Contain and Engage: A New Strategy for Resolving the Nuclear Crisis With Iran," 2007, p. 46, www.americanprogress.org/issues/2007/02/pdf/iran_report.pdf; Ephraim Kam, "A Nuclear Iran: What Does It Mean, and What Can Be Done," *Institute for National Security Studies Memorandum,* no. 88 (February 2007), p. 84; Robert O. Freedman, "Russia, Iran and the Nuclear Question: The Putin Record," 2006, www.strategicstudiesinstitute.army.mil/pdffiles/PUB737.pdf; Shahram Chubin, *Iran's Nuclear Ambitions* (Washington, D.C.: Carnegie Endowment for International Peace, 2006), pp. 81–112.

14. Alexei Arbatov, "Withdrawal From the Non-Proliferation Treaty," in *At the Nuclear Threshold: The Lessons of North Korea and Iran for the Nuclear Non-Proliferation Regime,* ed. Alexei Arbatov (Moscow: Carnegie Moscow Center, 2007), pp. 77–89.

15. See "Joint Declaration of the Denuclearization of the Korean Peninsula," January 20, 1992, www.state.gov/t/ac/rls/or/2004/31011.htm.

16. See "Full Text of Joint Document of the Second Session of the Sixth Round Six-Party Talks," Chinaview.cn, October 3, 2007, http://news.xinhuanet.com/english/2007-10/03/content_6829017.htm.

17. Marcus Noland, "The Economic Implications of a North Korean Nuclear Test," *Asia Policy,* no. 2 (July 2006): 25–39; "Pyongyang Fears Regime Collapse Under Sanctions," *Times* (London), February 12, 2006, p. 22.

18. Qian Qichen, *Ten Episodes in China's Diplomacy* [in Chinese] (Beijing: World Affairs Press: 2006).

19. Dingli Shen, "Iran's Nuclear Ambitions Test China's Wisdom," *The Washington Quarterly* 29, no. 2 (Spring 2006): 55–66; John W. Garver, *China & Iran: Ancient Partners in a Post-Imperial World* (Seattle: University of Washington Press, 2006), pp. 281–301.

DINGLI SHEN is a professor and executive dean of the Institute of International Studies and director of the Center for American Studies at Fudan University in Shanghai. He may be reached at dlshen@fudan.ac.cn.

From *The Washington Quarterly,* Summer 2008, pp. 89–100. Copyright © 2008 by Taylor & Francis–Philadelphia. Reprinted by permission.

UNIT 7

U.S. Military Strategy

Unit Selections

Key Points to Consider

- Is military power an effective instrument of foreign policy today? What problems is it best and least capable of solving?

- Does arms control have a future? Can it make the United States more secure, or does it weaken U.S. security?

- How should we think about nuclear weapons today? What is their purpose? Who should they be targeted against? What dangers must we guard against?

- How great is the terrorist threat to the United States? What steps should the United States take to protect itself from terrorist attacks?

- Develop a list of "dos and don'ts" to guide American troops when they are called upon to act as occupation forces.

- Under what conditions should the United States engage in peace-keeping activities?

- Can nuclear proliferation be stopped? What strategy would you recommend?

Student Website

www.mhhe.com/cls

Internet References

Arms Control and Disarmament Agency (ACDA)
http://dosfan.lib.uic.edu/acda/

Counterterrorism Page
http://counterterrorism.com

DefenseLINK
www.defenselink.mil/news/

Federation of American Scientists (FAS)
www.fas.org

Human Rights Web
www.hrweb.org

During the peak of the Cold War, American defense planners often thought in terms of needing a two-and-a-half war capacity: the simultaneous ability to fight major wars in Europe and Asia, plus a smaller conflict elsewhere. The principal protagonists in this drama were well known: the Soviet Union and China. The stakes were also clear. Communism represented a global threat to American political democracy and economic prosperity. It was a conflict in which both sides publicly proclaimed that there could be but one winner. The means for deterring and fighting such challenges included strategic, tactical, and battlefield nuclear weapons; large numbers of conventional forces; alliance systems; arms transfers; and the development of a guerrilla war capability.

Until September 11, 2001, the political-military landscape of the post–Cold War world lacked any comparable enemy or military threat. Instead, the principal challenges to American foreign policymakers were those of deciding what humanitarian interventions to undertake and how deeply to become involved. Kosovo, East Timor, Somalia, Bosnia, Rwanda, and Haiti each produced its own answer, which presented American policymakers with a new type of military challenge in the form of humanitarian interventions. The challenge of formulating an effective military policy to deal with situations where domestic order has unraveled due to ethnic conflict and bottled-up political pressures for reform still remains unmet. However, they are no longer viewed as first order security problems in the post–Cold War era.

With the terrorist attacks on the World Trade Center and the Pentagon, a more clearly defined enemy has emerged. Formulating a military strategy to defeat this enemy promises to be no easy task. President George W. Bush acknowledged as much in defining his war against terrorism as a new type of warfare and one that would not end quickly. In his administration the war against terrorism led to two wars, one that brought down the Taliban government in Afghanistan and one that brought down Saddam Hussein in Iraq. It also brought forward a new national security strategy centered on preemption in place of deterrence. And, most unexpectedly from the point of view of the Bush administration, it has placed the American military squarely in the business of nation building and face-to-face with the problem of fighting counterinsurgencies. In the first year of the Obama administration, the war on terrorism entered into yet another new phase as U.S. forces returned to Afghanistan in large numbers.

The first essays in this unit deal with the use of military force. The lead essay, "The New Rules of War," argues that the United States has failed to make the necessary changes in its military strategy to fight "netwars." The author presents three rules of engagement for such wars: many and small beat few and large; finding matters more than flanking; and swarming is the new surging. The second essay moves to the opposite end of the force continuum by looking at "Space Wars." This article examines the

Department of Defense/U.S. Air Force photo by Airman 1st Class Laura Goodgame

potential for a new arms race in outer space. The third essay in this group looks at the history of preemptive military strikes. In "Preemption Paradox," Bennett Ramberg finds that such attacks only buy time and that they hold profound risks for the attackers. Lastly, Steve Metz looks at the problem of understanding 21st century insurgencies in "New Challenges and Old Concepts." He argues that today's insurgencies are different from the 20th century insurgencies that strategists turn to for lessons. Metz argues the goal now should be to deter insurgencies and end them quickly rather than try to fight and win in the long struggle.

Changes in the nature of the military threat confronting the United States have led to changes in the arms control agenda. The old arms control agenda was dominated by a concern for reducing the size of United States and Soviet nuclear inventories. While this problem remains, a much broader arms control agenda exists today. The problem is not just Russian nuclear forces, but those of other states, and it is not just nuclear forces but chemical and biological weapons as well. Collectively we now refer to them as weapons of mass destruction.

The essays in this section deal with arms control problems. The first essay, "Nuclear Disorder" by Graham Allison, provides us with a roadmap of the range and scope of the problems on the arms control agenda today. The second essay, "Nuclear Abolition" by long time arms control expert Fred Iklè, raises the question of whether nuclear abolition is a realistic goal or whether we need to focus, at least in the short run, on the challenge of maintaining a prohibition on the first use of nuclear weapons. The final essay, "Low-cost Nuclear Arms Races," alerts us to the fact that today's arms races may look very different from those of the past and any policies to stop them must take this into account if they are to succeed.

The New Rules of War

The visionary who first saw the age of "netwar" coming warns that the U.S. military is getting it wrong all over again. Here's his plan to make conflict cheaper, smaller, and smarter.

JOHN ARQUILLA

Every day, the U.S. military spends $1.75 billion, much of it on big ships, big guns, and big battalions that are not only not needed to win the wars of the present, but are sure to be the wrong approach to waging the wars of the future.

In this, the ninth year of the first great conflict between nations and networks, America's armed forces have failed, as militaries so often do, to adapt sufficiently to changed conditions, finding out the hard way that their enemies often remain a step ahead. The U.S. military floundered for years in Iraq, then proved itself unable to grasp the point, in both Iraq and Afghanistan, that old-school surges of ground troops do not offer enduring solutions to new-style conflicts with networked adversaries.

So it has almost always been. Given the high stakes and dangers they routinely face, militaries are inevitably reluctant to change. During World War I, the armies on the Western Front in 1915 were fighting in much the same manner as those at Waterloo in 1815, attacking in close-packed formations—despite the emergence of the machine gun and high-explosive artillery. Millions were slaughtered, year after bloody year, for a few yards of churned-up mud. It is no surprise that historian Alan Clark titled his study of the high command during this conflict *The Donkeys*.

Even the implications of maturing tanks, planes, and the radio waves that linked them were only partially understood by the next generation of military men. Just as their predecessors failed to grasp the lethal nature of firepower, their successors missed the rise of mechanized maneuver—save for the Germans, who figured out that blitzkrieg was possible and won some grand early victories. They would have gone on winning, but for poor high-level strategic choices such as invading Russia and declaring war on the United States. In the end, the Nazis were not so much outfought as gang-tackled.

Nuclear weapons were next to be misunderstood, most monumentally by a U.S. military that initially thought they could be employed like any other weapons. But it turned out they were useful only in deterring their use. Surprisingly, it was cold warrior Ronald Reagan who had the keenest insight into such weapons when he said, "A nuclear war cannot be won and must never be fought."

Which brings us to war in the age of information. The technological breakthroughs of the last two decades—comparable in world-shaking scope to those at the Industrial Revolution's outset two centuries ago—coincided with a new moment of global political instability after the Cold War. Yet most militaries are entering this era with the familiar pattern of belief that new technological tools will simply reinforce existing practices.

In the U.S. case, senior officials remain convinced that their strategy of "shock and awe" and the Powell doctrine of "overwhelming force" have only been enhanced by the addition of greater numbers of smart weapons, remotely controlled aircraft, and near-instant global communications. Perhaps the most prominent cheerleader for "shock and awe" has been National Security Advisor James Jones, the general whose circle of senior aides has included those who came up with the concept in the 1990s. Their basic idea: "The bigger the hammer, the better the outcome."

Nothing could be further from the truth, as the results in Iraq and Afghanistan so painfully demonstrate. Indeed, a decade and a half after my colleague David Ronfeldt and I coined the term "netwar" to describe the world's emerging form of network-based conflict, the United States is still behind the curve. The evidence of the last 10 years shows clearly that massive applications of force have done little more than kill the innocent and enrage their survivors. Networked organizations like al Qaeda have proven how easy it is to dodge such heavy punches and persist to land sharp counterblows.

The United States has come close to punching itself out since 9/11.

And the U.S. military, which has used these new tools of war in mostly traditional ways, has been staggered financially and gravely wounded psychologically. The Iraq war's real cost, for example, has been about $3 trillion, per the analysis of Nobel laureate Joseph Stiglitz and Linda Bilmes—and even "official" figures put expenditures around $1 trillion. As for human capital, U.S. troops are exhausted by repeated lengthy deployments against foes who, if they were lined up, would hardly fill a single division of Marines. In a very real sense, the United States has come close to punching itself out since 9/11.

When militaries don't keep up with the pace of change, countries suffer. In World War I, the failure to grasp the implications of mass production led not only to senseless slaughter, but also to the end of great empires and the bankruptcy of others. The inability to comprehend the meaning of mechanization at the outset of World War II handed vast tracts of territory to the Axis powers and very nearly gave them victory. The failure to grasp the true meaning of nuclear weapons led to a suicidal arms race and a barely averted apocalypse during the Cuban missile crisis.

Today, the signs of misunderstanding still abound. For example, in an age of supersonic anti-ship missiles, the U.S. Navy has spent countless billions of dollars on "surface warfare ships" whose aluminum superstructures will likely burn to the waterline if hit by a single missile. Yet Navy doctrine calls for them to engage missile-armed enemies at eyeball range in coastal waters.

The U.S. Army, meanwhile, has spent tens of billions of dollars on its "Future Combat Systems," a grab bag of new weapons, vehicles, and communications gadgets now seen by its own proponents as almost completely unworkable for the kind of military operations that land forces will be undertaking in the years ahead. The oceans of information the systems would generate each day would clog the command circuits so that carrying out even the simplest operation would be a terrible slog.

And the U.S. Air Force, beyond its well-known devotion to massive bombing, remains in love with extremely advanced and extremely expensive fighter aircraft—despite losing only one fighter plane to an enemy fighter in nearly 40 years. Although the hugely costly F-22 turned out to function poorly and is being canceled after enormous investment in its production, the Air Force has by no means given up. Instead, the more advanced F-35 will be produced, at a cost running in the hundreds of billions of dollars. All this in an era in which what the United States already has is far better than anything else in the world and will remain so for many decades.

These developments suggest that the United States is spending huge amounts of money in ways that are actually making Americans less secure, not only against irregular insurgents, but also against smart countries building different sorts of militaries. And the problem goes well beyond weapons and other high-tech items. What's missing most of all from the U.S. military's arsenal is a deep understanding of networking, the loose but lively interconnection between people that creates and brings a new kind of collective intelligence, power, and purpose to bear—for good and ill.

Civil society movements around the world have taken to networking in ways that have done far more to advance the cause of freedom than the U.S. military's problematic efforts to bring

democracy to Iraq and Afghanistan at gunpoint. As for "uncivil society," terrorists and transnational criminals have embraced connectivity to coordinate global operations in ways that simply were not possible in the past. Before the Internet and the World Wide Web, a terrorist network operating cohesively in more than 60 countries could not have existed. Today, a world full of Umar Farouk Abdulmutallabs awaits—and not all of them will fail.

But the principles of networking don't have to help only the bad guys. If fully embraced, they can lead to a new kind of military—and even a new kind of war. The conflicts of the future should and could be less costly and destructive, with armed forces more able to protect the innocent and deter or defend against aggression.

Vast tank armies may no longer battle it out across the steppes, but modern warfare has indeed become exceedingly fast-paced and complex. Still, there is a way to reduce this complexity to just three simple rules that can save untold amounts of blood and treasure in the netwar age.

Rule 1: "Many and Small" Beats "Few and Large"

The greatest problem traditional militaries face today is that they are organized to wage big wars and have difficulty orienting themselves to fight small ones. The demands of large-scale conflicts have led to reliance on a few big units rather than on a lot of little ones. For example, the Marines have only three active-duty divisions, the U.S. Army only ten. The Navy has just 11 carrier strike groups, and the Air Force about three dozen attack aircraft "wings." Almost 1.5 million active service members have been poured into these and a few other supporting organizational structures.

It is no wonder that the U.S. military has exhausted itself in the repeated deployments since the 9/11 attacks. It has a chronic "scaling problem," making it unable to pursue smaller tasks with smaller numbers. Add in the traditional, hierarchical military mindset, which holds that more is always better (the corollary belief being that one can only do worse with less), and you get massive approaches to little wars.

This was the case during the Vietnam War, too, when the prevailing military organizational structure of the 1960s—not much different from today's—drove decision-makers to pursue a big-unit war against a large number of very small insurgent units. The final result: 500,000-plus troops deployed, countless billions spent, and a war lost. The iconic images were the insurgents' AK-47 individual assault rifles, of which there were hundreds of thousands in use at any moment, juxtaposed against the U.S. Air Force's B-52s, of which just a hundred or so massed together in fruitless attempts to bomb Hanoi into submission.

The same problem persists today, the updated icons being the insurgents' thousands of improvised explosive devices and the Americans' relative handful of drones. It is ironic that the U.S. war on terrorism commenced in the Afghan mountains with the same type of B-52 bombers and the same problematic results that attended the Vietnam War.

The U.S. military is not unaware of these problems. The Army has incrementally increased the number of brigades—which typically include between 3,000 and 4,000 trigger-pullers—from less than three dozen in 2001 to almost 50 today. And the Marines now routinely subdivide their forces into "expeditionary units" of several hundred troops each. But these changes hardly begin the needed shift from a military of the "few and large" to one of the "many and small."

That's because U.S. military leaders have not sufficiently grasped that even quite small units—like a platoon of 50 or so soldiers—can wield great power when connected to others, especially friendly indigenous forces, and when networking closely with even a handful of attack aircraft.

Yet the evidence is there. For example, beginning in late 2006 in Iraq, the U.S. command shifted little more than 5 percent of its 130,000 troops from about three dozen major (i.e., town-sized) operating bases to more than a hundred small outposts, each manned by about 50 soldiers. This was a dramatic shift from few-large to many-small, and it soon worked wonders in reducing violence, beginning well before the "surge" troops arrived. In part this happened because the physical network of platoon-sized outposts facilitated social networking with the large numbers of small tribal groups who chose to join the cause, forming the core of the "Awakening" movement.

The Pentagon's reluctance to see the new possibilities—reflected in the shrilly repeated calls for more troops, first in Iraq, then in Afghanistan—stems in part from the usual generalized fear of change, but also from concern that a many-and-small force would have trouble against a traditional massed army. Say, like North Korea's.

Then again, perhaps the best example of a many-and-small military that worked against foes of all sizes was the Roman legion. For many centuries, legionary *maniples* (Latin for "handfuls") marched out—in their flexible checkerboard formations—and beat the massive, balky phalanxes of traditional foes, while dealing just as skillfully with loose bands of tribal fighters.

Rule 2: Finding Matters More than Flanking

Ever since Theban general Epaminondas overloaded his army's left wing to strike at the Spartan right almost 2,400 years ago at Leuctra, hitting the enemy in the flank has been the most reliable maneuver in warfare. Flank attacks can be seen in Frederick the Great's famous "oblique order" in his 18th-century battles, in Erwin Rommel's repeated "right hooks" around the British in North Africa in 1941, and in Norman Schwarzkopf's famous "left hook" around the Iraqis in 1991. Flanking has quite a pedigree.

Flanking also formed a basis for the march up Mesopotamia by U.S. forces in 2003. But something odd happened this time. In the words of military historian John Keegan, the large Iraqi army of more than 400,000 troops just "melted away." There were no great battles of encirclement and only a handful of firefights along the way to Baghdad. Instead, Iraqis largely waited until their country was overrun and then mounted an insurgency based on tip-and-run attacks and bombings.

Thus did war cease to be driven by mass-on-mass confrontation, but rather by a hider-finder dynamic. In a world of networked war, armies will have to redesign how they fight, keeping in mind that the enemy of the future will have to be found before it can be fought. To some extent this occurred in the Vietnam War, but that was a conflict during which the enemy obligingly (and quite regularly) massed its forces in major offensives: held off in 1965, defeated in 1968 and 1972, and finally winning in 1975.

In Iraq, there weren't mass assaults, but a new type of irregular warfare in which a series of small attacks no longer signaled buildup toward a major battle. This is the path being taken by the Taliban in Afghanistan and is clearly the concept of global operations used by al Qaeda.

At the same time, the U.S. military has shown it can adapt to such a fight. Indeed, when it finally improved its position in Iraq, the change was driven by a vastly enhanced ability to find the enemy. The physical network of small outposts was linked to and enlivened by a social network of tribal fighters willing to work with U.S. forces. These elements, taken together, shone a light on al Qaeda in Iraq, and in the glare of this illumination the militants were easy prey for the small percentage of coalition forces actually waging the campaign against them.

Today's terrorist swarm goes all the way back to traditional tribal warfare.

Think of this as a new role for the military. Traditionally, they've seen themselves largely as a "shooting organization"; in this era, they will also have to become a "sensory organization."

This approach can surely work in Afghanistan as well as it has in Iraq—and in counterinsurgency campaigns elsewhere—so long as the key emphasis is placed on creating the system needed for "finding." In some places, friendly tribal elements might be less important than technological means, most notably in cyberspace, al Qaeda's "virtual safe haven."

As war shifts from flanking to finding, the hope is that instead of exhausting one's military in massive expeditions against elusive foes, success can be achieved with a small, networked corps of "finders." So a conflict like the war on terror is not "led" by some great power; rather, many participate in it, with each adding a piece to the mosaic that forms an accurate picture of enemy strength and dispositions.

This second shift—to finding—has the potential to greatly empower those "many and small" units made necessary by Rule 1. All that is left is to think through the operational concept that will guide them.

Rule 3: Swarming Is the New Surging

Terrorists, knowing they will never have an edge in numbers, have pioneered a way of war that allows them to make the most of their slender resources: swarming. This is a form of attack undertaken by small units coming from several directions or hitting many targets at the same time. Since 9/11, al Qaeda has mounted but a few major stand-alone strikes—in Bali, Madrid, and London—while the network has conducted multiple significant swarming campaigns in Turkey, Tunisia, and Saudi Arabia featuring "wave attacks" aimed at overloading their targets' response capabilities. Such attacks have persisted even in post-surge Iraq where, as Gen. David Petraeus noted in a recent speech, the enemy shows "a sophistication among the militants in carrying out simultaneous attacks" against major government targets.

Perhaps the clearest example of a terrorist swarm was the November 2008 attack on Mumbai, apparently mounted by the Lashkar-e-Taiba group. The assault force consisted of just 10 fighters who broke into five two-man teams and struck simultaneously at several different sites. It took more than three days to put them down—and cost the lives of more than 160 innocents—as the Indian security forces best suited to deal with this problem had to come from distant New Delhi and were configured to cope with a single threat rather than multiple simultaneous ones.

In another sign of the gathering swarm, the August 2008 Russian incursion into Georgia, rather than being a blast from the Cold War past, heralded the possibility that more traditional armies can master the art of omnidirectional attack. In this instance, Russian regular forces were augmented by ethnic militias fighting all over the area of operations—and there was swarming in cyberspace at the same time. Indeed, the distributed denial of service attack, long a staple of cyberwarriors, is a model form of swarming. And in this instance, Georgian command and control was seriously disrupted by the hackers.

Simultaneous attack from several directions might be at the very cutting edge in conflict, but its lineage is quite old. Traditional tribal warfare, whether by nomadic horse archers or bush fighters, always featured some elements of swarms. The zenith of this kind of fighting probably came with the 13th-century Mongols, who had a name for this doctrine: "Crow Swarm." When the attack was not carried out at close quarters by charging horsemen, but was instead conducted via arrows raining down on massed targets, the khans called it "Falling Stars." With such tactics, the Mongols carved out the largest empire the world has ever seen, and kept it for a few centuries.

But swarming was eclipsed by the rise of guns in the 15th century, which strongly favored massed volley fire. Industrial processes encouraged even more massing, and mechanization favored large flank maneuvers more than small swarms. Now again, in an age of global interdependence replete with advanced information technologies, even quite small teams of fighters can cause huge amounts of disruption. There is an old Mongol proverb: "With 40 men you can shake the world." Look at what al Qaeda did with less than half that number on Sept. 11, 2001.

This point was made by the great British strategist B.H. Liddell Hart in his biography of T.E. Lawrence, a master of the swarm in his own right. Liddell Hart, writing in 1935, predicted that at some point "the old concentration of force is likely to be replaced by an intangibly ubiquitous distribution of force—pressing everywhere, yet assailable nowhere."

Now, swarming is making a comeback, but at a time when few organized militaries are willing or able to recognize its return. For the implications of this development—most notably, that fighting units in very small numbers can do amazing things if used to swarm—are profoundly destabilizing. The most radical change is this: Standing armies can be sharply reduced in size, if properly reconfigured and trained to fight in this manner. Instead of continually "surging" large numbers of troops to trouble spots, the basic response of a swarm force would be to go swiftly, in small numbers, and strike the attackers at many points. In the future, it will take a swarm to defeat a swarm.

Almost 20 years ago, I began a debate about networks that blossomed into an unlikely friendship with Vice Adm. Art Cebrowski, the modern strategic thinker most likely to be as well remembered as Alfred Thayer Mahan, the great American apostle of sea power. He was the first in the Pentagon power structure to warm to my notions of developing fighting networks, embracing the idea of opening lots of lateral communications links between "sensors and shooters." We disagreed, however, about the potential of networks. Cebrowski thought that "network-centric warfare" could be used to improve the performance of existing tools—including aircraft carriers—for some time to come. I thought that networking implied a wholly new kind of navy, one made up of small, swift vessels, many of them remotely operated. Cebrowski, who passed away in late 2005, clearly won this debate, as the U.S. Navy remains heavily invested in being a "few-large" force—if one that is increasingly networked. In an implicit nod to David Ronfeldt's and my ideas, the Navy even has a Netwar Command now.

Swarming has also gained some adherents. The most notable has been Marine Lt. Gen. Paul Van Riper, who famously used swarm tactics in the last great Pentagon war game, "Millennium Challenge 2002," to sink several aircraft carriers at the outset of the imagined conflict. But rather than accept that something quite radical was going on, the referees were instructed to "refloat" the carriers, and the costly game—its price tag ran in the few hundred millions—continued. Van Riper walked out. Today, some in the U.S. military still pursue the idea of swarming, mostly in hopes of employing large numbers of small unmanned aerial vehicles in combat. But military habits of mind and institutional interests continue to reflect a greater audience for surges than swarms.

What if senior military leaders wake up and decide to take networks and swarming absolutely seriously? If they ever do, it is likely that the scourges of terrorism and aggression will become less a part of the world system. Such a military would be smaller but quicker to respond, less costly but more lethal. The world system would become far less prone to many of the kinds of violence that have plagued it. Networking and swarming are the organizational and doctrinal keys, respectively, to the strategic puzzle that has been waiting to be solved in our time.

A networked U.S. military that knows how to swarm would have much smaller active manpower—easily two-thirds less than the more than 2 million serving today—but would be organized in hundreds more little units of mixed forces. The model for military intervention would be the 200 Special Forces "horse soldiers" who beat the Taliban and al Qaeda in Afghanistan late in 2001. Such teams would deploy quickly and lethally, with ample reserves for relieving "first waves" and dealing with other crises. At sea, instead of concentrating firepower in a handful of large, increasingly vulnerable supercarriers, the U.S. Navy would distribute its capabilities across many hundreds of small craft armed with very smart weapons. Given their stealth and multiple uses, submarines would stay while carriers would go. And in the air, the "wings" would reduce in size but increase in overall number, with mere handfuls of aircraft in each. Needless to say, networking means that these small pieces would still be able to join together to swarm enemies, large or small.

Is such a shift feasible? Absolutely. Big reductions in the U.S. military are nothing new. The massive demobilization after World War II aside, active forces were reduced 40 percent in the few years after the Vietnam War and by another third right after the end of the Cold War. But the key is not so much in cutting as it is in redesigning and rethinking.

But what happens if the status quo prevails and the potential of this new round of changes in strategic affairs is ignored or misinterpreted? Failure awaits, at ruinous cost.

The most likely form catastrophe could take is that terrorist networks would stay on their feet long enough to acquire nuclear weapons. Even a handful of warheads in Osama bin Laden's hands would give him great coercive power, as a network cannot be targeted for retaliation the same way a country can. Deterrence will lie in tatters. If there is ever to be a nuclear Napoleon, he will come from a terrorist network.

Within the U.S. military, the danger is that senior commanders will fall back on a fatalism driven by their belief that both congressional and industrial leaders will thwart any effort at radical change. I have heard this objection countless times since the early 1990s, repeated mantra-like, all the way up to the Joint Chiefs of Staff. Thus the mighty U.S. war machine is like a Gulliver trussed up by Lilliputian politicians and businessmen.

The irony, however, is that the U.S. military has never been in a better position to gain acceptance for truly transformational change. Neither party in Congress can afford to be portrayed as standing in the way of strategic progress, and so, whatever the Pentagon asks for, it gets. As for defense contractors, far from driving the agenda, they are much too willing to give their military customers exactly what they demand (rather than, perhaps, something better). If the U.S. armed forces call for smaller, smarter weapons and systems to support swarming, they will get them.

Beyond the United States, other countries' security forces are beginning to think along the lines of "many and small," are crafting better ways to "find," and are learning to swarm. Chinese naval thought today is clearly moving in this direction. Russian ground forces are, too. Needless to say, terrorist networks are still in the lead, and not just al Qaeda. Hezbollah gave quite a demonstration of all three of the new rules of war in its summer 2006 conflict with Israel, a virtual laboratory test of nation versus network—in which the network more than held its own.

It should not be assumed that the huge sums invested in national defense have been wisely spent.

For the U.S. military, failing a great leap forward in self-awareness of the need for radical change, a downward budgetary nudge is probably the best approach—despite President Barack Obama's unwillingness to extend his fiscal austerity program to security-related expenditures. This could take the form of a freeze on defense spending levels, to be followed by several years of, say, 10 percent annual reductions. To focus the redesign effort, a moratorium would be declared on all legacy-like systems (think aircraft carriers, other big ships, advanced fighters, tanks, etc.) while they are subjected to searching review. It should not be assumed that the huge sums invested in national defense have been wisely spent.

To most Americans who think that being strong on defense means devoting more resources and building bigger systems, this suggestion to cut spending will sound outrageous. But being smarter about defense might lower costs even as effectiveness improves. This pattern has held throughout the transformations of the last few decades, whether in farming or in industry. Why should the military be exempt?

There's real urgency to this debate. Not only has history not ended with the Cold War and the advent of commerce-driven globalization, but conflict and violence have persisted—even grown—into a new postmodern scourge.

Indeed, it is ironic that, in an era in which the attraction to persuasive "soft power" has grown dramatically, coercive "hard power" continues to dominate in world affairs. This is no surprise in the case of rogue nations hellbent on developing nuclear arsenals to ensure their security, nor when it comes to terrorist networks that think their essential nature is revealed in and sustained by violent acts. But this primary reliance on coercive capabilities is also on display across a range of countries great and small, most notably the United States, whose defense policy has over the past decade largely *become* its foreign policy.

From the wars in Iraq and Afghanistan, to simmering crises with North Korea and Iran, and on to longer-range strategic concerns about East Asian and Central European security, the United States today is heavily invested in hard-power solutions. And it will continue to be. But if the radical adjustments in strategy, organization, and doctrine implied by the new rules of war are ignored, Americans will go on spending more and getting less when it comes to national defense. Networks will persist until they have the capability to land nuclear blows. Other countries will leapfrog ahead of the United States militarily, and concepts like "deterrence" and "containment" of aggression will blow away like leaves in the wind.

So it has always been. Every era of technological change has resulted in profound shifts in military and strategic affairs. History tells us that these developments were inevitable, but soldiers and statesmen were almost always too late in embracing them—and tragedies upon tragedies ensued. There is still time to be counted among the exceptions, like the Byzantines who, after the fall of Rome, radically redesigned their military and preserved their empire for another thousand years. The U.S. goal should be to join the ranks of those who, in their eras, caught glimpses of the future and acted in time to shape it, saving the world from darkness.

JOHN ARQUILLA is professor of defense analysis at the U.S. Naval Postgraduate School and author of *Worst Enemy: The Reluctant Transformation of the American Military.*

Space Wars

Coming to the Sky Near You?

A recent shift in U.S. military strategy and provocative actions by China threaten to ignite a new arms race in space. But would placing weapons in space be in anyone's national interest?

THERESA HITCHENS

"Take the high ground and hold it!" has been standard combat doctrine for armies since ancient times. Now that people and their machines have entered outer space, it is no surprise that generals the world over regard Earth orbit as the key to modern warfare. But until recently, a norm had developed against the weaponization of space—even though there are no international treaties or laws explicitly prohibiting nonnuclear antisatellite systems or weapons placed in orbit. Nations mostly shunned such weapons, fearing the possibility of destabilizing the global balance of power with a costly arms race in space.

> **"In war, do not launch an ascending attack head-on against the enemy who holds the high ground. Do not engage the enemy when he makes a descending attack from high ground. Lure him to level ground to do battle."**
>
> —Sun Tzu, Chinese military strategist, *The Art of War,* circa 500 B.C.

That consensus is now in danger of unraveling. In October 2006 the Bush administration adopted a new, rather vaguely worded National Space Policy that asserts the right of the U.S. to conduct "space control" and rejects "new legal regimes or other restrictions that seek to prohibit or limit U.S. access to or use of space." Three months later the People's Republic of China shocked the world by shooting down one of its own aging Fengyun weather satellites, an act that resulted in a hailstorm of dangerous orbital debris and a deluge of international protests, not to mention a good deal of hand-wringing in American military and political circles. The launch was the first test of a dedicated antisatellite weapon in more than two decades—making China only the third country, after the U.S. and the Russian Federation, to have demonstrated such a technology. Many observers wondered whether the test might be the first shot in an emerging era of space warfare.

Critics maintain it is not at all clear that a nation's security would be enhanced by developing the means to wage space war. After all, satellites and even orbiting weapons, by their very nature, are relatively easy to spot and easy to track, and they are likely to remain highly vulnerable to attack no matter what defense measures are taken. Further, developing antisatellite systems would almost surely lead to a hugely expensive and potentially runaway arms race, as other countries would conclude that they, too, must compete. And even tests of the technology needed to conduct space battles—not to mention a real battle—could generate enormous amounts of wreckage that would continue to orbit Earth. Converging on satellites and crewed space vehicles at speeds approaching several miles a second, such space debris would threaten satellite-based telecommunications, weather forecasting, precision navigation, even military command and control, potentially sending the world's economy back to the 1950s.

"Star Wars" Redux

Since the dawn of the space age, defense planners have hatched concepts for antisatellite and space-based weaponry—all in the interest of exploiting the military advantages of the ultimate high ground. Perhaps the most notable effort was President Ronald Reagan's Strategic Defense Initiative (SDI)—derided by its critics as "Star Wars." Yet by and large, U.S. military strategy has never embraced such weapons.

Traditionally, space weapons have been defined as destructive systems that operate in outer space after having been launched directly from Earth or parked in orbit. The category includes antisatellite weapons; laser systems that couple ground-based lasers with airship- or satellite-mounted mirrors, which could reflect a laser beam beyond the ground horizon; and orbital platforms that could fire projectiles or energy beams from space. (It is important to note that all nations would presumably avoid using a fourth kind of antisatellite weapon, namely, a high-altitude nuclear explosion. The electromagnetic pulse and cloud of highly charged particles created by such a blast would likely disable or destroy nearly all satellites and manned spacecraft in orbit [see "Nuclear Explosions in Orbit," by Daniel G. Dupont; *Scientific American,* June 2004].)

But virtually no statement about space weapons goes politically uncontested. Recently some proponents of such weapons have sought to expand the long-held classification I just described to include two existing technologies that depend on passage through space: intercontinental ballistic missiles (ICBMs) and ground-based electronic warfare systems. Their existence, or so the argument goes, renders moot any question about whether to build space weapons systems. By the revised definition, after all, "space weapons" already exist. Whatever the exact meaning of the term, however, the questions such weapons raise are hardly new to think tanks and military-planning circles in Washington: Is it desirable, or even feasible, to incorporate antisatellite weapons and weapons fired from orbit into the nation's military strategy?

The new National Space Policy, coupled with the Chinese test, has brought renewed urgency to that behind-the-scenes debate. Many American military leaders expressed alarm in the wake of the Chinese test, worrying that in any conflict over Taiwan, China could threaten U.S. satellites in low Earth orbit. In April 2007 Michael Moseley, the U.S. Air Force chief of staff, compared China's antisatellite test with the launch of Sputnik by the Soviet Union in 1957, an act that singularly intensified the arms race during the cold war. Moseley also revealed that the Pentagon had begun reviewing the nation's satellite defenses, explaining that outer space was now a "contested domain."

Congressional reaction fell along predictable political lines. Conservative "China hawks" such as Senator Jon Kyl of Arizona immediately called for the development of antisatellite weapons and space-based interceptors to counter Chinese capabilities. Meanwhile more moderate politicians, including Representative Edward Markey of Massachusetts, urged the Bush administration to begin negotiations aimed at banning all space weapons.

International Power Plays

Perhaps of even greater concern is that several other nations, including one of China's regional rivals, India, may feel compelled to seek offensive as well as defensive capabilities in space. The U.S. trade journal *Defense News,* for instance, quoted unidentified Indian defense officials as stating that their country had already begun developing its own kinetic-energy (nonexplosive, hit-to-kill) and laser-based antisatellite weapons.

If India goes down that path, its archrival Pakistan will probably follow suit. Like India, Pakistan has a well-developed

The Players

Since the start of the space age, the list of countries, multinational entities and private commercial consortia that have demonstrated an ability to launch satellites into orbit—and thus potentially to shoot one down—has grown long. The chief worry among observers is that any effort by the U.S. to develop orbital weapons would drive the People's Republic of China, the Russian Federation and others to join in a costly arms race in space.

Demonstrated Ground-based Antisatellite Weapons

China, Russia, U.S.

Attained Geostationary Orbit (36,000 km above Earth)

European Space Agency (Austria, Belgium, Denmark, Finland, France, Germany, Greece, Ireland, Italy, Luxembourg, the Netherlands, Norway, Portugal, Spain, Sweden, Switzerland, U.K.), France, International Launch Services (Russia, U.S.), Japan, Sea Launch (Norway, Russia, U.S.)

Attained Only Low Earth Orbit (between 100 and 2,000 km above Earth)

India, Israel, Pakistan, Ukraine

ballistic missile program, including medium-range missiles that could launch an antisatellite system. Even Japan, the third major Asian power, might join such a space race. In June 2007 the National Diet of Japan began considering a bill backed by the current Fukuda government that would permit the development of satellites for "military and national security" purposes.

As for Russia, in the wake of the Chinese test President Vladimir Putin reiterated Moscow's stance against the weaponization of space. At the same time, though, he refused to criticize Beijing's actions and blamed the U.S. instead. The American efforts to build a missile defense system, Putin charged, and the increasingly aggressive American plans for a military position in space were prompting China's moves. Yet Russia itself, as a major spacefaring power that has incorporated satellites into its national security structure, would be hard-pressed to forgo entering an arms race in space.

Given the proliferation of spacefaring entities [see box The Players], proponents of a robust space warfare strategy believe that arming the heavens is inevitable and that it would be best for the U.S. to get there first with firepower. Antisatellite and space-based weapons, they argue, will be necessary not only to defend U.S. military and commercial satellites but also to deny any future adversary the use of space capabilities to enhance the performance of its forces on the battlefield.

Yet any arms race in space would almost inevitably destabilize the balance of power and thereby multiply the risks

Kinetic-Energy Interceptors

Feasibility: High

Cost Estimates*:

- Ground-based kinetic-energy interceptor (adapted from existing U.S. ballistic missile defense program): $0–$3 billion
- Airborne kinetic-energy interceptor: $3 billion

Apart from jamming the radio communications or attacking ground-control stations, probably the simplest way to disable a satellite is to launch a missile-borne payload and crash it into an orbital target. Medium-range ballistic missiles fielded by about a dozen nations can directly reach low Earth orbit (between 100 and 2,000 kilometers, or about 60 to 1,250 miles, high). Small air-launched kill vehicles can also attack satellites in low Earth orbit. Assaulting a target in the much higher geostationary orbit (about 36,000 kilometers, or 22,000 miles, high) requires a more powerful launch booster, now possessed by eight countries and space consortia. But the real technical challenge is to guide and maneuver the kill vehicle precisely onto its mark.

*Estimates generally include development and procurement costs associated with building a system and operating it for 20 years.

Source: Arming the Heavens: A Preliminary Assessment of the Potential Cost and Cost-Effectiveness of Space-Based, Weapons, *by Steven Kosiak. Center for Strategic and Budgetary Assessments, 2007.*

Directed-Energy Systems

Feasibility: Medium

Cost Estimates:

- Ground-based laser: $4 billion–$6 billion
- Space-based laser (low- to high-power capability): $3 billion–$60 billion
- Space-based microwave radiator: $200 million–$5 billion

Ground-based laser beams that are precision-guided onto their targets by adaptive optics (deformable mirrors that compensate for atmospheric distortions) could blind, disable or destroy satellites in low Earth orbit. Moderate-power lasers could "dazzle" optical-imaging satellites or damage their sensitive detectors. High-power lasers could "fry" satellites by damaging their electronics or even piercing their skin. Because fast-moving orbital targets lie mostly over Earth's horizon at any one time, ground stations could also direct laser beams at airships or satellite-borne transfer mirrors, which could redirect the beams toward their targets.

of global conflict. In such headlong competition—whether in space or elsewhere—equilibrium among the adversaries would be virtually impossible to maintain. Even if the major powers did achieve stability, that reality would still provide no guarantee that both sides would perceive it to be so. The moment one side saw itself to be slipping behind the other, the first side would be strongly tempted to launch a preemptive strike, before things got even worse. Ironically, the same would hold for the side that perceived itself to have gained an advantage. Again, there would be strong temptation to strike first, before the adversary could catch up. Finally, a space weapons race would ratchet up the chances that a mere technological mistake could trigger a battle. After all, in the distant void, reliably distinguishing an intentional act from an accidental one would be highly problematic.

Hit-to-Kill Interceptors

According to assessments by U.S. military and intelligence officials as well as by independent experts, the Chinese probably destroyed their weather satellite with a kinetic-energy vehicle boosted by a two-stage medium-range ballistic missile. Technologically, launching such direct-ascent antisatellite weapons is one of the simplest ways to take out a satellite [see box Kinetic-Energy Interceptors]. About a dozen nations

and consortia can reach low Earth orbit (between roughly 100 and 2,000 kilometers, or 60 to 1,250 miles, high) with a medium-range missile; eight of those countries can reach geostationary orbit (about 36,000 kilometers, or 22,000 miles, above Earth).

But the real technical hurdle to making a hit-to-kill vehicle is not launch capacity; it is the precision maneuverability and guidance technology needed to steer the vehicle into its target. Just how well China has mastered those techniques is unclear. Because the weather satellite was still operating when it was destroyed, the Chinese operators would have known its exact location at all times.

Ground-Based Lasers

The test of China's direct-ascent antisatellite device came on the heels of press reports in September 2006 that the Chinese had also managed to "paint," or illuminate, U.S. spy satellites with a ground-based laser [see box Directed Energy Systems]. Was Beijing actually trying to "blind" or otherwise damage the satellites? No one knows, and no consensus seems to have emerged in official Washington circles about the Chinese intent. Perhaps China was simply testing how well its network of low-power laser-ranging stations could track American orbital observation platforms.

Even so, the test was provocative. Not all satellites have to be electronically "fried" to be put out of commission. A 1997 test of the army's MIRACL system (for *mid*infrared *a*dvanced *c*hemical *l*aser) showed that satellites designed to collect optical images can be temporarily disrupted—dazzled—by low-power beams. It follows that among the satellites vulnerable to such an attack are the orbital spies.

The Case against

1. All satellites and space-based weapons are likely to remain highly vulnerable to attack.
2. Developing advanced antisatellite weapons will probably trigger a new international arms race.
3. The cost of space weaponry is huge.
4. Testing and using space weapons could leave enormous quantities of debris in orbit that would threaten all satellites and crewed spacecraft.

Co-orbital Satellites

Feasibility: Medium to high

Cost Estimates:

- Space-based (kinetic-energy and other) interceptor: $5 billion–$19 billion
- Space-based radio-frequency jammer: not available
- Space mine: $100 million–$2 billion

Small antisatellite weapons, or micro-satellites, could be lofted into the same orbits as their targets, where they could shadow or attach themselves to the targets. Once in place, such "space mines" could attack on command with explosives, small projectiles, radio-frequency jamming systems or high-powered microwave emitters—or they could simply smash into their targets. In one early design the resulting space debris was to be caught in a so-called flyswatter or large net.

The U.S. and the former Soviet Union began experimenting with laser-based antisatellite weapons in the 1970s. Engineers in both countries have focused on the many problems of building high-power laser systems that could reliably destroy low-flying satellites from the ground. Such systems could be guided by "adaptive optics": deformable mirrors that can continously compensate for atmospheric distortions. But tremendous amounts of energy would be needed to feed high-power lasers, and even then the range and effectiveness of the beams would be severely limited by dispersion, by attenuation as they passed through smoke or clouds, and by the difficulty of keeping the beams on-target long enough to do damage.

During the development of the SDI, the U.S. conducted several laser experiments from Hawaii, including a test in which a beam was bounced off a mirror mounted on a satellite. Laser experiments continue at the Starfire Optical Range at Kirtland Air Force Base in New Mexico. Pentagon budget documents from fiscal years 2004 through 2007 listed antisatellite operations among the goals of the Starfire research, but that language was removed from budget documents in fiscal year 2008 after Congress made inquiries. The Starfire system incorporates adaptive optics that narrow the outgoing laser beam and thus increase the density of its power. That capability is not required for imagery or tracking, further suggesting that Starfire could be used as a weapon.

Yet despite decades of work, battle-ready versions of directed-energy weapons still seem far away. An air force planning document, for instance, predicted in 2003 that a ground-based weapon able to "propagate laser beams through the atmosphere to [stun or kill low Earth orbit] satellites" could be available between 2015 and 2030. Given the current state of research, even those dates seem optimistic.

Co-orbital Satellites

Recent advances in miniaturized sensors, powerful onboard computers and efficient rocket thrusters have made a third kind of antisatellite technology increasingly feasible: the offensive microsatellite [see box Co-orbital satellites]. One example that demonstrates the potential is the air force's experimental satellite series (XSS) project, which is developing microsatellites intended to conduct "autonomous proximity operations" around larger satellites. The first two microsatellites in the program, the XSS-10 and XSS-11, were launched in 2003 and 2005. Though ostensibly intended to inspect larger satellites, such microsatellites could also ram target satellites or carry explosives or directed-energy payloads such as radio-frequency jamming systems or high-powered microwave emitters. Air force budget documents show that the XSS effort is tied to a program called Advanced Weapons Technology, which is dedicated to research on military laser and microwave systems.

During the cold war the Soviet Union developed, tested and even declared operational a co-orbital antisatellite system—a maneuverable interceptor with an explosive payload that was launched by missile into an orbit near a target satellite in low Earth orbit. In effect, the device was a smart "space mine," but it was last demonstrated in 1982 and is probably no longer working. Today such an interceptor would likely be a microsatellite that could be parked in an orbit that would cross the orbits of several of its potential targets. It could then be activated on command during a close encounter.

In 2005 the air force described a program that would provide "localized" space "situational awareness" and "anomaly characterization" for friendly host satellites in geostationary orbit. The program is dubbed ANGELS (for autonomous nanosatellite guardian for evaluating local space), and the budget line believed to represent it focuses on acquiring "high value space asset defensive capabilities," including a "warning sensor for detection of a direct ascent or co-orbital vehicle." It is clear that such guardian nanosatellites could also serve as offensive weapons if they were maneuvered close to enemy satellites.

And the list goes on. A "parasitic satellite" would shadow or even attach itself to a target in geostationary orbit. Farsat, which was mentioned in an appendix to the [Donald] Rumsfeld Space Commission report in 2001, "would be placed in a 'storage' orbit (perhaps with many microsatellites housed inside) relatively far from its target but ready to be maneuvered in for a kill."

Space Bomber

Feasibility: Low

Cost Estimate:

- Space bomber: $4 billion

The Pentagon's Common Aero Vehicle/Hypersonic Technology Vehicle is not by definition a space weapon, but it would travel through space to strike terrestrial targets within an hour or two of being deployed. It could be released in orbit from a hypersonic space plane, then glide unpowered into the atmosphere before delivering conventional munitions onto surface targets.

Other Antisatellite Systems

Most of the major military powers have probably experimented with ground-based radio-frequency systems that could disable the communications systems of satellites. Moreover, any country with nuclear-tipped ballistic missiles could explode an atomic weapon in orbit, which would wreak havoc on most of the satellites and spacecraft there.

Cost Estimates:

- Ground-based radio-frequency jammer: several tens of millions of dollars
- Nuclear weapon (for nations already possessing missiles with nuclear warheads): minimal

Finally, the air force proposed some time ago a space-based radio-frequency weapon system, which "would be a constellation of satellites containing high-power radio-frequency transmitters that possess the capability to disrupt/destroy/disable a wide variety of electronics and national-level command and control systems."

Air force planning documents from 2003 envisioned that such a technology would emerge after 2015. But outside experts think that orbital radio-frequency and microwave weapons are technically feasible today and could be deployed in the relatively near future.

Space Bombers

Though not by definition a space weapon, the Pentagon's Common Aero Vehicle/Hypersonic Technology Vehicle (often called CAV) enters into this discussion because, like an ICBM, it would travel through space to strike Earth-bound targets [*see box Space Bomber*]. An unpowered but highly maneuverable hypersonic glide vehicle, the CAV would be deployed from a future hypersonic space plane, swoop down into the atmosphere from orbit and drop conventional bombs on ground targets. Congress recently began funding the project but, to avoid stoking a potential arms race in space, has prohibited any work to place weapons on the CAV. Although engineers are making steady progress on the key technologies for the CAV program, both the vehicle and its space plane mothership are still likely decades off.

Some of the congressional sensitivity to the design of the CAV may have arisen from another, much more controversial space weapons concept with parallel goals: hypervelocity rod bundles that would be dropped to Earth from orbital platforms. For decades air force planners have been thinking about placing weapons in orbit that could strike terrestrial targets, particularly buried, "hardened" bunkers and caches of weapons of mass destruction. Commonly called "rods from God," the bundles would be made up of large tungsten rods, each as long as six meters (20 feet) and 30 centimeters (12 inches) across. Each rod would be hurled downward from an orbiting spacecraft and guided to its target at tremendous speed.

Both high costs and the laws of physics, however, challenge their feasibility. Ensuring that the projectiles do not burn up or deform from reentry friction while sustaining a precise, nearly vertical flight path would be extremely difficult. Calculations indicate that the nonexplosive rods would probably be no more effective than more conventional munitions. Furthermore, the expense of lofting the heavy projectiles into orbit would be exorbitant. Thus, despite continued interest in them, rods from God seem to fall into the realm of science fiction.

Obstacles to Space Weapons

What, then, is holding the U.S. (and other nations) back from a full-bore pursuit of space weapons? The countervailing pressures are threefold: political opposition, technological challenges and high costs.

The American body politic is deeply divided over the wisdom of making space warfare a part of the national military strategy. The risks are manifold. I remarked earlier on the general instabilities of an arms race, but there is a further issue of stability among the nuclear powers. Early-warning and spy satellites have traditionally played a crucial role in reducing fears of a surprise nuclear attack. But if antisatellite weapons disabled those eyes-in-the-sky, the resulting uncertainty and distrust could rapidly lead to catastrophe.

One of the most serious technological challenges posed by space weapons is the proliferation of space debris, to which I alluded earlier. According to investigators at the air force, NASA and Celestrak (an independent space-monitoring website), the Chinese antisatellite test left more than 2,000 pieces of junk, baseball-size and larger, orbiting the globe in a cloud that lies between about 200 kilometers (125 miles) and 4,000 kilometers (2,500 miles) above Earth's surface. Perhaps another 150,000 objects that are a centimeter (half an inch) across and larger were released. High orbital velocities make even tiny pieces of space junk dangerous to spacecraft of all kinds. And ground stations cannot reliably monitor or track objects smaller than about five centimeters (two inches) across in low Earth orbit (around a meter in geostationary

The Aftermath

When the Dust Won't Clear

A military conflict in space could release an enveloping cloud debris that could damage or destroy satellites and crewed spacecraft that circle the globe. At orbital speeds, even minuscule objects could deeply penetrate a vehicle and wreck vital equipment. The results of a nuclear detonation in space could be even worse: the electromagnetic pulse and blast of charged particles would degrade all but the most heavily shielded electronics systems in orbit. Space war could push the world economy back into the 1950s, as communications, navigation, weather and other advanced satellite services would be rendered impractical for years to come.

More To Explore

Report of the Commission to Assess United States National Security Space Management and Organization. Rumsfeld Space Commission report, 2001. Available at www.fas.org/spp/military/commission/report.htm

The U.S. Air Force Transformation Flight Plan. Future Concepts and Transformation Division, November 2003. Available at www.af.mil/library/posture/AF_TRANS_FLIGHT_PLAN-2003.pdf

The Physics of Space Security: A Reference Manual. David Wright, Laura Grego and Lisbeth Gronlund. American Academy of Arts and Sciences, 2005. Available at www.ucsusa.org/global_security/space_weapons/the-physics-of-space-security.html

China's ASAT Test: Motivations and Implications. Phillip C. Saunders and Charles D. Lutes. INSS Special Report, Institute for National Strategic Studies. National Defense University, 2007. Available at www.ndu.edu/inss/Research/SRjun07.pdf

The World Security Institute's Center for Defense Information: www.cdi.org

orbit), a capability that might enable satellites to maneuver out of the way. To avoid being damaged by the Chinese space debris, in fact, two U.S. satellites had to alter course. Any shooting war in space would raise the specter of a polluted space environment no longer navigable by Earth-orbiting satellites.

Basing weapons in orbit also presents difficult technical obstacles. They would be just as vulnerable as satellites are to all kinds of outside agents: space debris, projectiles, electromagnetic signals, even natural micrometeoroids. Shielding space weapons against such threats would also be impractical, mostly because shielding is bulky and adds mass, thereby greatly increasing launch costs. Orbital weapons would be mostly autonomous mechanisms, which would make operational errors and failures likely. The paths of objects in orbit are relatively easy to predict, which would make hiding large weapons problematic. And because satellites in low Earth orbit are overhead for only a few minutes at a time, keeping one of them constantly in range would require many weapons.

Finally, getting into space and operating there is extremely expensive: between $2,000 and $10,000 a pound to reach low Earth orbit and between $15,000 and $20,000 a pound for geostationary orbit. Each space-based weapon would require replacement every seven to 15 years, and in-orbit repairs would not be cheap, either.

Alternatives to Space Warfare

Given the risks of space warfare to national and international security, as well as the technical and financial hurdles that must be overcome, it would seem only prudent for spacefaring nations to find ways to prevent an arms race in space. The U.S. focus has been to reduce the vulnerability of its satellite fleet and explore alternatives to its dependence on satellite services. Most other space-capable countries are instead seeking multilateral diplomatic and legal measures. The options range from treaties that would ban antisatellite and space-based weapons to voluntary measures that would help build transparency and mutual confidence.

The Bush administration has adamantly opposed any form of negotiations regarding space weapons. Opponents of multilateral space weapons agreements contend that others (particularly China) will sign up but build secret arsenals at the same time, because such treaty violations cannot be detected. They argue further that the U.S. cannot sit idly as potential adversaries gain spaceborne resources that could enhance their terrestrial combat capabilities.

Proponents of international treaties counter that failure to negotiate such agreements entails real opportunity costs. An arms race in space may end up compromising the security of all nations, including that of the U.S., while it stretches the economic capacities of the competitors to the breaking point. And whereas many advocates of a space weapons ban concede that it will be difficult to construct a fully verifiable treaty—because space technology can be used for both military and civilian ends—effective treaties already exist that do not require strict verification. A good example is the Biological Weapons Convention. Certainly a prohibition on the testing and use (as opposed to the deployment) of the most dangerous class of near-term space weapons—destructive (as opposed to jamming) antisatellite systems—would be easily verifiable, because earthbound observers can readily detect orbital debris. Furthermore, any party to a treaty would know that all its space launches would be tracked from the ground, and any suspicious object in orbit would promptly be labeled as such. The international outcry that would ensue from such overt treaty violations could deter would-be violators.

Since the mid-1990s, however, progress on establishing a new multilateral space regime has lagged. The U.S. has blocked efforts at the United Nations Conference on Disarmament in Geneva to begin negotiations on a treaty to ban space weapons. China, meanwhile, has refused to accept anything less. Hence, intermediate measures such as voluntary confidence-building, space traffic control or a code of responsible conduct for spacefaring nations have remained stalled.

Space warfare is not inevitable. But the recent policy shift in the U.S. and China's provocative actions have highlighted the fact that the world is approaching a crossroads. Countries must come to grips with their strong self-interest in preventing the testing and use of orbital weapons. The nations of Earth must soon decide whether it is possible to sustain the predominantly peaceful human space exploration that has already lasted half a century. The likely alternative would be unacceptable to all.

THERESA HITCHENS directs the Center for Defense Information in Washington, D.C., and leads its Space Security Project, in cooperation with the Secure World Foundation. She is author of *Future Security in Space: Charting a Cooperative Course* (2004) and was editor of *Defense News* from 1998 until 2000. As a journalist, she has focused on the military, the defense industry and North Atlantic Treaty Organization affairs. Most recently, Hitchens served as director of research at the British American Security Information Council, a defense think tank.

Preemption Paradox

Using military force to destroy an adversary's nuclear program is a compelling option, so how come most nations have decided against it?

BENNETT RAMBERG

Twenty-five years ago, on a late spring afternoon, eight Israeli bombers streaked across the desert sky on a top-secret mission to destroy Osirak, Iraq's emerging nuclear reactor complex. A dramatic military action to prevent nuclear weapons proliferation, the June 7, 1981 strike left a legacy that echoes today in the "all options are on the table" drumbeat emanating from Washington and Jerusalem. The seemingly straightforward message to Iran and other would-be proliferators: Abrogate nonproliferation pledges in this post-9/11 era and risk being "Osiraked."

These aggressive declarations, however, butt against historical reality. Save for two major exceptions—the Allied effort to scuttle Nazi Germany's nuclear program, and attempts by Iran, Israel, and the United States to wipe out Saddam Hussein's nuclear ambitions—countries with incentives to use force to halt nuclear proliferation have spent more time conducting tabletop exercises than taking action. The result: nations such as the Soviet Union, China, and Pakistan produced the Bomb despite the interest and capacity of adversaries to stop them.

A Desperate Race

At the beginning of the nuclear age, there was no nonproliferation norm, no concept of nuclear deterrence, and no taboos against nuclear war. All that existed was an apparent race for the Bomb in the midst of history's bloodiest conflict.

Adolf Hitler's Third Reich lacked the resources, organization, scientific understanding, and even commitment to be in the pursuit.[1] But the United States did not know this early in the war. "At best, I do not see how we can catch up with the Germans unless they have overlooked some possibilities we recognize, or unless our military action should delay them," warned physicist Arthur Compton in a 1942 communiqué to Gen. Leslie R. Groves.[2]

In response, the Allies applied a two-pronged strategy: They would try to cross the nuclear finish line first, and simultaneously, they would destroy the Nazi effort. Planners targeted German-occupied Norway's Norsk Hydro hydrogen-electrolysis plant—marking the first instance of nuclear preemption.[3] With so much at stake, the hesitation that would characterize post-World War II coercive nonproliferation had no place in this decision.

The Allies targeted the Norsk Hydro plant because it was the world's only commercial processor of heavy water (deuterium oxide), which can be used in some reactors to turn natural uranium into weapons-usable plutonium. From late 1942 to February 1944, the Allies spared no effort to destroy the plant and its contents.[4]

In the first attempt, two gliders ferried 34 British commandos to their sabotage mission. But one glider crashed at sea, the other onto Norway's rocky terrain. The next Allied effort parachuted a team of Norwegian commandos into their native country; the nine saboteurs, scaling a steep, icy canyon wall, conducted a dramatic winter evening assault. The attack effectively destroyed eight weeks' worth of heavy water production, but the Germans rebuilt the installation in six weeks. The undertaking offered a cautionary note that would reverberate in post-war planning: Force can fall short; adversaries can absorb a blow and then recoup.

Desperate to finish the mission, Washington ordered hundreds of bombers to take out the plant in a single air raid. Only 12 of the 1,000 dropped bombs struck the target, but the attack was a success; Germany decided not to rebuild. A final act of sabotage sunk a transport ferry that was to carry remaining stocks of heavy water to Germany.

Though intelligence demonstrated that Germany's nuclear program had sputtered, Washington still worried. In its view, only the Reich's defeat combined with occupation, dismantlement, and destruction of nuclear facilities, and the incarceration of senior Nazi scientists would put an end to Hitler's nuclear ambitions. Preemptive military strikes alone were not enough.

The Reluctant Superpower

At war's end, the United States stood atop the nuclear pinnacle. But it could sense the Soviet Union striving to reach the same heights. In 1946, the Kremlin rejected the U.S.-proposed Baruch Plan that would have placed the most worrisome elements of the nuclear fuel cycle under the auspices of an International Atomic Development Authority. Coupled with tensions over occupation rights in Germany and the Soviet Union's consolidation of its hold on Eastern Europe, some public figures and members of the nuclear scientific establishment—including

Winston Churchill, Bertrand Russell, Leo Szilard, and John von Neumann—called for military action to stop the Kremlin before it got the Bomb.[5]

General Groves, the head of the Manhattan Project, reflected: "If we were ruthlessly realistic, we would not permit any foreign power with which we are not firmly allied . . . to make or possess atomic bombs. If such a country started to make atomic weapons, we would destroy its capacity to make them before it had progressed far enough to threaten us."[6] But President Harry S. Truman seemed resigned to the inevitability of proliferation. In a September 18, 1945 conversation with White House confidant Joseph E. Davis, Truman said, "Are we going to give up these [atomic] locks and bolts which are necessary to protect our house? . . . Clearly we are not. Nor are the Soviets. Nor is any country if it can help itself."[7]

The idea of preemption also found resistance in the military. "It might be desirable to strike the first blow, [but] it is not politically feasible under our system to do so or to state that we will do so," Pentagon planner George Lincoln acknowledged in 1945.[8] As Cold War historian John Lewis Gaddis has observed, U.S. reluctance was partly rooted in self-image: "America did not start wars."[9]

The practical question of whether the United States could actually "win" a preemptive war against the Soviet Union also loomed large. In a statement that presaged the dilemma currently confronting U.S. advocates of preemption, Truman's defense secretary, James Forrestal, observed, "Conquering the Russians is one thing, and finding what to do with them afterward is an entirely different problem."[10]

Truman's successor also contemplated the merits of preemption. President Dwight D. Eisenhower endorsed a December 1954 National Security Policy paper that concluded, "The United States and its allies must reject the concept of preventive war or acts intended to provoke it."[11] But the principle would never be as immutable as the policy document suggested. The Eisenhower administration generated a plethora of conflicting statements about the use of preemptive force against a coiled Soviet Union, suggesting a policy of ambiguity that neither embraced nor rejected the option.[12]

By 1962, the United States had learned to live with a nuclear-armed Kremlin for 13 years. But "geographic proliferation" on Washington's doorstep—the placement of Soviet nuclear missiles in Cuba—would be another matter.[13] While there would be no repetition of the Norsk Hydro attacks, during the Cuban Missile Crisis President John F. Kennedy forced Soviet leader Nikita Khrushchev to back down by crystallizing Washington's preemptive intentions. Given the balance of interests and military power favoring Washington—coupled to a side agreement to remove U.S. missiles from Turkey—the Soviets decided that they would not risk Moscow for Havana.

The idea of preemption found resistance in the military. U.S. reluctance was partly rooted in self-image: "America did not start wars."

No Good Options

China began its nuclear weapons research in the 1950s. By December 1960, U.S. satellite imagery and U-2 intelligence pieced together the fragmentary basis for a National Intelligence Estimate that forecast a Chinese nuclear weapon test by as early as 1963.[14]

That China might get the Bomb generated tremors among U.S. policy makers.[15] In June 1961, the Joint Chiefs of Staff warned that Beijing's "attainment of a nuclear capability will have a marked impact on the security posture of the United States and the free world."[16] In their subsequent review of diplomatic, economic, and military options—which included sabotaging nuclear facilities, an invasion by Chinese nationalists, a maritime blockade, renewing the Korean War, and U.S. conventional or tactical nuclear weapon strikes on the nuclear plants—the Joint Chiefs made no specific recommendation. Yet their aversion to preemption was evident. "Many of the [military] actions . . . above are obviously acts of war, [and] should be initiated only after all other means have been exhausted, and then only after full and careful consideration of the implications at the time," they argued in a 1963 memorandum.[17]

The State Department arrived at a similar cautionary conclusion. Robert Johnson, the department's leading analyst on the issue, sought to dampen the sense of mounting panic within the U.S. bureaucracy, arguing that the "great asymmetry in Chinese Communist and U.S. nuclear capabilities and vulnerabilities" made it unlikely that Beijing would ever contemplate nuclear first-use, except in the event of an attack that "threatened the existence of the regime."[18] And even if U.S. military strikes were successful—an uncertain outcome given incomplete intelligence on China's nuclear facilities—preemption would, at best, "buy some time."[19] If anything, such an attack could strengthen Beijing's resolve to obtain a nuclear deterrent, and a hardened successor program could be constructed in as few as four or five years.

Military action entailed other risks: It could prompt Chinese retaliation against Taiwan or U.S. allies in East Asia, entangle the Soviets (who were unwilling to join in such an attack), degrade Washington's international prestige and alliances, and reduce the prospects for arms control initiatives to constrain China. Johnson concluded, "Action with no justification other than a general argument that the U.S. was seeking to preserve the peace of the world through depriving a potential aggressor of nuclear weapons" could not be defended.[20]

The arguments resonated. On September 15, 1964, the secretaries of State and Defense and the national security adviser met with President Lyndon B. Johnson in the Cabinet Room to present their recommendation: "We are not in favor of unprovoked unilateral U.S. military action against Chinese nuclear installations at this time. We would prefer to have a Chinese test take place than to initiate such action now. If for other reasons we should find ourselves in military hostilities at any level with the Chinese Communists, we would expect to give very close attention to the possibility of an appropriate military action against Chinese nuclear facilities."[21] Johnson, running on a peace platform in the upcoming election, concurred. On October 16, 1964, China conducted its first nuclear test and became the world's fourth nuclear weapon state.

Israel's Gamble

In the 1960s, the United States was willing to adopt a "wait and see" approach with China. Decades later, Israel would not give Iraq the same benefit. On September 8, 1975, Iraqi Vice President Saddam Hussein declared publicly that Baghdad's purchase from France of a 70-megawatt test reactor called Osiris and a small Isis reactor—collectively called Osirak—would be "the first actual step in the production of an Arab nuclear weapon."[22]

Jerusalem's 1981 attack against Osirak marked the culmination of a failed multiyear campaign to halt the construction of Iraq's reactor by means other than military action. The government of Prime Minister Menachem Begin first lobbied Paris and Washington. Rebuffed, Israel tried assassination, but the deaths of three scientists affiliated with the nuclear program barely hindered Iraq's efforts. Israel attempted sabotage next, but the demolition of Osirak's core as it awaited shipment and the firebombing of an Italian firm contracted to provide reprocessing technology delayed Osirak only marginally.[23]

The decision to use military force was not made easily; Israel debated the option intensely. In cabinet discussions, Israel's deputy prime minister, defense minister, health minister, chief of military intelligence, and head of Mossad all preferred the "wait and see" approach.[24] They feared that an unprovoked attack could spark war, stimulate region-wide nuclear proliferation, and make Israel a global pariah. Furthermore, some doubted that Iraq even had the scientific ability to build the Bomb.

The preemption option itself posed serious logistical problems.[25] A commando raid in which agents were inserted into and extracted from hostile territory was too daunting. But an air strike was also risky, as demonstrated by a botched Iranian aircraft strike on the plant in September 1980, shortly after the start of the Iran-Iraq War. Some Israeli officials questioned whether Israel's Phantom or F-15 aircraft could travel 600 miles over hostile territory to do the job.

As it turned out, these aircraft did not have to take on the task. In the aftermath of the 1979 Iranian Revolution, Shah Reza Pahlevi's order of U.S. F-16s did not go through. Superior to Israel's Phantoms and F-15s, Jerusalem scooped up the F-16s after Washington put them on the block. Still, it was not the acquisition of the aircraft that tipped Israel's scales in favor of a preemptive strike; it was the determination of Prime Minister Begin.

Eight F-16s each carrying two 2,000-pound gravity bombs flew toward Osirak; a phalanx of F-15s hovered nearby to jam Iraqi radar, intercept Iraq's air force, and provide a communication link to Israel. Search and rescue helicopters were at the ready. The attack took place before Osirak went critical to avoid the release of the plant's radioactive contents. All but two bombs hit the plant, leaving the reactor in ruins.

Israel's assault sent shock waves through the world, garnering condemnation and grudging admiration. But despite the destruction the preemptive strike wrought, it did not extinguish Iraq's ambitions. Baghdad, which had committed 400 scientists and

$400 million to the nuclear program before the attack, enlarged its nuclear staff to 7,000 and upped its budget to $10 billion.[26]

South Asian Standoff

One country that took particular note of Israel's raid on Osirak was India. Throughout the 1970s and 1980s, India had watched apprehensively as Pakistan, its perennial adversary, followed a nuclear weapons path similar to its own. In addition to the acquisition of a "peaceful" heavy water reactor from Canada, the other telltale signs included an expanding number of reprocessing and enrichment installations. Given the diminutive size of Pakistan's nuclear power program, the fuel-cycle plants likely served only one purpose: nuclear weapons.

Adding to these concerns would be the program's principal political promoter. In 1971, in the aftermath of Pakistan's loss of Bangladesh to India's armed forces, Zulfikar Ali Bhutto became prime minister. Bhutto had been a patron of the atom as far back as 1960 when he became minister of minerals and natural resources. As foreign minister, in 1965, he laid the foundation for later nuclear weapons assistance from the Chinese. In the same year, he made his ambitions clear: "If India builds the bomb, we will eat grass or leaves, even go hungry, but we will get one of our own."[27] True to his word, as Pakistan's leader, he was determined to move forward. On January 24, 1972, he gathered the country's top scientists for a meeting in Multan, Punjab, to set the program in motion.

Although Bhutto would never see his ambition come to fruition—in 1977 the military overthrew and later executed him—his successors continued his efforts. India watched Pakistan's development at first with disdain—it couldn't possibly build the Bomb—but, in time, with mounting anxiety.[28] By the early 1980s, Indian analysts concluded that Pakistan had enriched sufficient uranium for one or two bombs.

Israel's bombing of Osirak provided inspiration for a military solution. The Indian Air Force—energized by the procurement of new British Jaguar strike aircraft—studied the application of Israel's example to Pakistan's Kahuta enrichment plant. Military planners concluded that the attack could succeed, but at a cost of half the bomber force. Such losses would not be the gravest risk. "What will happen next?" the chief of operations asked. "The international community would condemn us for doing something in peacetime, which the Israelis could get away with but India would not be able to get away with. In the end, it will result in a war."[29]

The specter of war prompted another concern. Pakistan's retaliatory response could include striking Indian nuclear reactors and reprocessing sites situated near urban settings—effectively mounting a devastating radiological attack upon India.[30] A high-ranking official commented, "We knew we would have to live with Pakistan's nuclear capability, and there was no way around it."[31]

But living together required some insurance; overcoming the temptation for nuclear preemption was in the interest of both parties. The two countries negotiated a 1985 accord (which was fully implemented in 1993) not to attack one another's nuclear facilities. However, as years passed, events would call into question whether the agreement would stand. The countries' tit-for-tat 1998 nuclear weapons detonations, coupled with the unresolved Kashmir dispute, periodically raised the preemption specter anew.

Targeting North Korea

As South Asia wrestled with its nuclear conundrum, another would-be nuclear power emerged in the Far East. North Korea's ambitions to obtain nuclear weapons lay rooted in U.S. threats to use the Bomb during the Korean War and the North's unease over the Soviet Union's retreat during the Cuban Missile Crisis. With assistance from Moscow, Pyongyang steadily expanded its indigenous nuclear program over the next couple of decades. However, in 1985, Moscow made it clear that further support was contingent upon North Korea joining the Nuclear Non-Proliferation Treaty (NPT).

From the beginning, signs were not good for international control. Seven years would pass before Pyongyang signed the International Atomic Energy Agency's (IAEA) Safeguards Agreement. And afterward, the North persistently denied IAEA inspectors access to sites of concern. In spring 1994, matters came to a head when North Korea began removing spent fuel from its five-megawatt reactor in Yongbyon.

Diplomacy was at the heart of the Clinton administration's effort to curb North Korea, but the president's advisers could not ignore the military option. The administration's senior national security staff evaluated the prospects in June 1994, against the backdrop of Pyongyang's announced intention to withdraw from the NPT and expel inspectors.[32] But armed force posed too many risks.[33] A commando or cruise missile attack might stop the future extraction of weapon-grade material, but it would not guarantee the destruction of material the North may have removed in advance. Attacking the reactor would substantially set back Pyongyang's program (albeit risking a radiological release), but doing so could prompt international opprobrium. Also, a strike against the North could spark a full-scale war. In the view of Gen. Gary Luck, commander of U.S. forces in South Korea, "If we pull an Osirak, they will be coming south." This could result in as many as 750,000 U.S. and South Korean military casualties alone.[34]

U.S. officials decided, at least for the time being, that sanctions offered a far more attractive option than preemption. Air Force Chief of Staff Gen. Merrill McPeak commented, "We can't find nuclear weapons now except by going on a house-to-house search," suggesting that, when it came to military options, he felt that only the occupation of North Korea, rather than limited preemptive strikes, would succeed.[35]

The matter became moot when former President Jimmy Carter visited Pyongyang in June 1994. Laying the foundation for what would become the Agreed Framework, the United States consented to lead an international consortium to provide the communist state with a light water reactor and heavy oil to meet its immediate energy needs.

In January 2003, confronted with U.S. intelligence that it had violated its nonproliferation vows by pursuing a secret enrichment program, President Kim Jong Il bolted from the NPT. On February 10, 2005, Pyongyang officially claimed that it had manufactured nuclear weapons.

Cautionary Tales

This recounting has summarized the "big" events in the history of nuclear preemption, save one: Washington's 2003 attack on Iraq.[36] Built on the false premise that Saddam had an active nuclear program, America's invasion was an exercise in preemptive overkill. Baghdad's nuclear program was already dead—not because of Saddam's aversion to the Bomb, but due to an earlier war that marked nuclear preemption by serendipity.[37] But for Iraq's defeat in 1991—or had Saddam delayed his invasion of Kuwait by a year or more—Baghdad might have joined the nuclear club.

While this and other cases are different from one another, viewed comparatively they suggest some tentative findings to answer a nonproliferation conundrum: Why has history not witnessed more consistent application of the Osirak template?

First, nuclear preemption in peacetime poses profound political risks. In confronting the prospects of a nuclear-armed Soviet Union and China, the United States was reluctant to be seen as the aggressor. India had similar reservations. Even Israel's security establishment—well aware of Iraq's declared ambition to obtain nuclear weapons—was mindful of the potential political costs of instigating an unprovoked attack.

A second lesson is that nuclear states appear reluctant to preempt emerging nuclear powers if the latter have a significant capacity to strike back. The geographic proximity of adversaries has long accentuated this dilemma. India feared ruinous reprisals from neighboring Pakistan. U.S. military planners worried that China would lash out across the Taiwan Straits and that North Korea would head south against Seoul. In today's world, strike-back could also include spectacular surrogate terrorist acts or military counterattacks against vital economic lifelines, such as petroleum production or distribution.

Radiological risks add novel concerns. India was not alone in its apprehension about retaliation against its nuclear sites. Japan, for example, feared that U.S. preemption of North Korea could result in attacks on its nuclear power plants.[38] Even without this prospect, successful destruction of Pyongyang's plants risked radioactive releases.[39] (By contrast, anxiety over nuclear contamination actually accelerated Israel's decision to bomb Osirak. Prime Minister Begin pressed for the strike before the reactor became "hot.")

The use of an atomic weapon by a preemptor would have even greater consequences. Even the lowest-yield nuclear "bunker buster" promises significant local damage and contamination.[40] The National Academy of Sciences estimates that high-yield nuclear attacks on hardened sites could result in hundreds of thousands of casualties depending on the depth of the burst, weather patterns, and the proximity of populations.

The resulting fallout—which would be even greater if the target were a nuclear facility—could reach beyond the borders of the country that was attacked to include a neighboring initiator or its allies.[41]

Facilities that have been destroyed can be rebuilt. As former U.N. weapons inspector David Kay once pointedly asked, "How do you roll back knowledge?"

In Israel's raid on Osirak, geography played a different role. The distance separating the adversaries made Jerusalem's decision easier, since Baghdad could not easily retaliate. However, in the 2003 Iraq War, geography was less important for another reason: the proximity of Washington's regional allies to Baghdad did not deter preemption because American planners believed that U.S. military superiority and destructiveness would more than compensate.

Another lesson from history is that preemptive military strikes are a logistical nightmare. Absent complete intelligence, a nation cannot be certain that a military attack will sufficiently devastate a rival country's nuclear program. In that respect, Osirak was an anomaly, in that the key elements of Iraq's nuclear infrastructure were clustered within one site. Other would-be nuclear proliferators have learned that lesson well, and today an adversary's nuclear program is likely to be scattered across several hardened facilities. As General McPeak acknowledged regarding North Korea in the early 1990s, nothing less than a "house-to-house search" would suffice. The effectiveness of international inspectors in Iraq after the 1991 war demonstrated that point.

But, even then, another dilemma remains: What has been destroyed can be rebuilt, a fact first evidenced in the initial "successful" sabotage of Norsk Hydro. As former U.N. weapons inspector David Kay once pointedly asked, "How do you roll back knowledge?"[42] During the Cold War, U.S. analysts recognized that China could reconstitute a nuclear program within a few years. Israeli bombers were able to destroy Osirak, but they could not destroy Iraq's technical and scientific infrastructure. Consequently, Iraq was able to reconstitute its nuclear program by the beginning of the 1990s.[43]

If nations are unable to deny adversaries the means and know-how to develop nuclear weapons, then the preemptive option with the best chance of long-term success is the World War II template of regime change. Yet, as the current U.S. occupation of Iraq reveals, this is not an option to be considered lightly. The costs of foreign rule and nation building—in terms of lives and economic resources—can be daunting.

The final lesson from the history of preemption is that surgical military strikes can only buy time. That said, buying time should not be as readily dismissed as some argue.[44] Israel's 1981 attack clearly set back Iraq's program. Indeed, time bought by military or other means allows international incentives, disincentives, and/or domestic political changes to curtail nuclear

ambitions. Libya's 2003 nuclear surrender proves that, given sufficient time, a country can decide to relinquish its nuclear ambitions.[45] But as North Korea and Iraq in 1981 demonstrated, time purchased, either through diplomacy or coercion, is no sure path to stem nuclear ambitions.

Ultimately, the legacy of Osirak lies in the fact that it effectively legitimized military means as a way to halt proliferation if other measures fail. But as history reveals, preemption is no easy solution. It is just one of many competing tactics in dealing with a predicament that has proven time and again to have few good options.[46]

Notes

1. Thomas Powers, *Heisenberg's War: The Secret History of the German Bomb* (New York: Knopf, 1993).

2. Quoted in Dan Kurzman, *Blood and Water: Sabotaging Hitler's Bomb* (New York: Henry Holt & Co., 1997), p. 17.

3. I use the term "preemptive" rather than "preventive" throughout to reflect the temporal opportunity to eliminate an adversary's nuclear program. See Alan Dershowitz, *Preemption* (New York: W. W. Norton, 2006), p. 96.

4. Ibid., pp. 195–202, 211–213; and Kurzman, *Blood and Water.*

5. George H. Quester, *Nuclear Monopoly* (New Brunswick: Transaction Publishers, 2000), pp. 37–56.

6. Ibid., quoted on p. 42.

7. Quoted in John Lewis Gaddis, *The United States and the Origins of the Cold War, 1941–1947* (New York: Columbia University Press, 1972), p. 273.

8. Quoted in John Lewis Gaddis et al., eds., *Cold War Statesmen Confront the Bomb* (New York: Oxford University Press, 1999), p. 88.

9. John Lewis Gaddis, *We Now Know* (New York: Oxford University Press, 1997), p. 88.

10. Ibid., quoted on p. 89.

11. David Alan Rosenberg, "The Origins of Overkill: Nuclear Weapons and American Strategy, 1945–1960," *International Security,* Spring 1983, p. 34.

12. Ibid.; Marc Trachtenberg, *A Constructed Peace: The Making of the European Settlement, 1945–1963* (Princeton: Princeton University Press, 1999), chap. 5; Marc Trachtenberg, "A Wasting Asset: American Strategy and the Shifting Nuclear Balance, 1949–1954," *International Security,* Winter 1988/89, p. 34, fn. 121; private communication from David Alan Rosenberg, March 2006.

13. White House tapes on the Cuban Missile Crisis reveal different views on the significance of Moscow's geographic proliferation. Robert McNamara reported that the Joint Chiefs believed the presence of Soviet nuclear weapons in Cuba would "substantially" change the strategic balance. McNamara's opinion: "Not at all." The first view dominated decision making. Marc Trachtenberg, "The Influence of Nuclear Weapons in the Cuban Missile Crisis," and "White House Tapes and Minutes of the Cuban Missile Crisis," *International Security,* Summer 1985, pp. 137–203.

14. William Burr and Jeffrey T. Richelson, "Whether to Strangle the Baby in the Cradle: The United States and the Chinese

Nuclear Program, 1960–64," *International Security,* Winter 2000/01, p. 59.

15. Ibid., pp. 54–99.

16. Ibid., p. 61.

17. Joint Chiefs of Staff, "Memorandum for the Secretary of Defense: Study of Chinese Communist Vulnerability," JCSM-343-63, April 29, 1963, p. 3.

18. Robert H. Johnson, "A Chinese Communist Nuclear Detonation and Nuclear Capability: Major Conclusions and Key Decisions," State Department, October 15, 1963, p. 1.

19. Burr and Richelson, "Whether to Strangle the Baby in the Cradle," p. 80.

20. Robert H. Johnson, "The Chinese Communist Nuclear Capability and Some Unorthodox Approaches to the Problem of Nuclear Proliferation," June 1, 1964; Burr and Richelson, "Whether to Strangle the Baby in the Cradle," pp. 78–80.

21. McGeorge Bundy, "Memorandum for the Record," White House, September 15, 1964.

22. Dan Reiter, "Preventive Attacks Against Nuclear Programs and the Success at Osirak," *Nonproliferation Review,* July 2005, p. 357.

23. Rodger W. Claire, *Raid on the Sun* (New York: Broadway Books, 2004), pp. 40– 41, 47–50, 61–65, 81, 97.

24. Ibid., p. xvii.

25. Claire's book provides the best insider account of the attack; see chap. 4–7.

26. Reiter, "Preventive Attacks," p. 263.

27. Quoted in Carey Sublette, "Pakistan's Nuclear Weapons Program," Nuclear Weapon Archive, January 2, 2002 (nuclearweaponarchive.org/Pakistan/PakOrigin.html).

28. George Perkovich, *India's Nuclear Bomb* (Berkeley: University of California Press, 1999), pp. 275–276.

29. Ibid., quoted on p. 240.

30. Ibid., p. 241.

31. Ibid.

32. Joel Wit et al., *Going Critical: The First North Korean Nuclear Crisis* (Washington: Brookings Institution, 2004), p. 210.

33. Ibid., pp. 210–211, 244–245, 410. See also Don Oberdorfer, *The Two Koreas* (New York: Basic Books, 1997), pp. 306–326 for a more pessimistic view of the odds of war.

34. Wit, *Going Critical,* p. 102.

35. Ibid., p. 104.

36. There are a number of lesser-known cases involving contemplation of preemption. For instance, in 1969, Sino-Soviet border clashes prompted Moscow to contemplate a preemptive strike against China. See Lyle J. Goldstein, "Do Nascent WMD Arsenals Deter? The Sino-Soviet Crisis of 1969," *Political Science Quarterly,* vol. 118, no. 1, 2003, pp. 53–79. In 1976, the Soviet Union approached the United States to consider cooperating in a joint effort to preempt South Africa's nuclear weapons program. See David Albright, "South Africa and the Affordable Bomb," *Bulletin of the Atomic Scientists,* July/August 1994.

37. While the United States did not use Iraq's nuclear program to justify the 1991 Gulf War, some in Congress did seek to rationalize the war on these grounds. See Michael J. Mazarr et al., *Desert Storm: The Gulf War and What We Learned* (Boulder: Westview, 1993), p. 85.

38. Wit, *Going Critical,* p. 178.

39. Ibid., p. 211.

40. Robert W. Nelson, "Low-Yield Earth Penetrating Nuclear Weapons," *Science and Global Security,* vol. 10, no. 1, 2002, pp. 1–20.

41. Committee on the Effects of Nuclear Earth-Penetrator and Other Weapons, "Effects of Nuclear Earth-Penetrator and Other Weapons" (Washington, D.C.: National Research Council, 2005), pp. 2, 6. For a depiction of the radioactive plume generated by a 300-kiloton earth-penetrator on North Korea, see Christopher Paine et al., "The Bush Administration's Quest for Earth-Penetrating and Low-Yield Nuclear Weapons" (Washington: Natural Resources Defense Council, 2003), p. 8. In Bennett Ramberg, *Nuclear Power Plants as Weapons for the Enemy: An Unrecognized Military Peril* (Berkeley: University of California Press, 1984), pp. 51, 54–56, the author illustrates the consequences of nuclear strikes against civil reactors.

42. David Kay, "With More at Stake, Less Will Be Verified," *Washington Post,* November 17, 2002.

43. Jeremy Bernstein, "Atomic Secrets," *New York Review of Books,* May 25, 2006, p. 43.

44. See, for example, Richard Betts, "The Osirak Fallacy," *The National Interest,* Spring 2006, p. 22.

45. Bruce W. Jentleson and Christopher A. Whytock, "Who 'Won' Libya? Force-Diplomacy Debate and Its Implications for Theory and Policy," *International Security,* Winter 2005/06, pp. 47–86; Judith Miller "How Gadhafi Lost His Groove," *Wall Street Journal,* May 16, 2006, p. A14; and Judith Miller, "Gadhafi's Leap of Faith," *Wall Street Journal,* May 17, 2006, p. A18.

46. The author wishes to thank Michael Intriligator, Kent Harrington, George H. Quester, and Robert Pendley for their helpful comments.

BENNETT RAMBERG, author of *Nuclear Power Plants as Weapons for the Enemy* (1984), served in the State Department's Bureau of Politico-Military Affairs in the first Bush administration. He can be reached at bennettramberg@aol.com.

New Challenges and Old Concepts
Understanding 21st Century Insurgency

STEVEN METZ

From the 1960s to the 1980s stopping Communist-backed insurgents was an important part of American strategy, so counterinsurgency was an important mission for the US military, particularly the Army. Even when most of the Army turned its attention to large-scale warfighting and the operational art following Vietnam, special operation forces preserved some degree of capability. In the 1980s American involvement in El Salvador and a spate of insurgencies around the world linked to the Soviets and Chinese sparked renewed interest in counterinsurgency operations (as a component of low-intensity conflict). By 1990 what could be called the El Salvador model of counterinsurgency, based on a limited US military footprint in conjunction with the strengthening of local security forces, became codified in strategy and doctrine.[1]

Interest then faded. Policymakers, military leaders, and defense experts assumed that insurgency was a relic of the Cold War, posing little challenge in the "new world order." With the demise of the Soviet Union and the mellowing of China, insurgency—even though it persisted in the far corners of the world—was not viewed as a strategic challenge to the world's sole superpower. With American involvement in Somalia, Bosnia, Kosovo, and Haiti, multinational peacekeeping—a previously unimportant role for the military—moved to the fore. In a burst of energy, the military revamped its peacekeeping doctrine and concepts. Professional military education and training shifted to accommodate these missions. Wargames, conferences, and seminars proliferated. Counterinsurgency was forgotten by all but a tiny handful of scholars.

Then, one clear September morning, the world turned. Al Qaeda and its affiliates adopted a strategy relying heavily on the methods of insurgency—both national insurgency and a transnational one.[2] Insurgency was again viewed as a strategic threat and the fear grew that insurgent success would create regimes willing to support and protect organizations like al Qaeda. The global campaign against violent Islamic extremists forced the United States military to undertake counterinsurgency missions in Iraq and Afghanistan. Once again, the Department of Defense was required to respond to a major strategic shift. The military services scrambled to develop new concepts and doctrine.[3] Counterinsurgency reentered the curriculum of the professional military educational system in a big way. It became a centerpiece for Army and Marine Corps training. Classic assessments of the conflicts in Vietnam and Algeria became required reading for military leaders. Like the mythical phoenix, counterinsurgency had emerged from the ashes of its earlier death to become not just a concern of the US military but the central focus.

This is all to the good. Augmenting capabilities to respond to new strategic threats is exactly what the Department of Defense is supposed to do. There is a problem, however: As the American military relearned counterinsurgency strategy and doctrine, it may not have gotten them right. During the 1970s America's national security strategy was shaped by what became known as the "Vietnam syndrome"—a reluctance to intervene in internal conflicts based on the assumption that some disaster would ensue. Ironically, while the United States eventually overcame the Vietnam syndrome, a new one emerged. Vietnam has been treated as a universal model, the Viet Cong as the archetypical foe. Defense experts even concluded that insurgents who did not use the Vietnamese approach (derived from the teaching of Mao Zedong) stood little chance of success.[4]

This tendency to look back to the classic insurgencies of the twentieth century was pervasive. For instance, as the Army sought to understand the conflict in Iraq, the books most recommended for its officers were John Nagl's *Learning to Eat Soup with a Knife* (which dealt with the British involvement in Malaya and the American experience in Vietnam) and David Galula's *Counterinsurgency Warfare* (drawn from the French campaigns in Indochina and Algeria).[5] Both were excellent choices. But both deal with wars of imperial maintenance or nationalistic transition, not with complex communal conflicts where armed militias and organized crime play a key role.

In a sense, the United States has once again derived new strategies from old conflicts, while again preparing to fight the last war. Rather than rigorously examining twenty-first century insurgencies, America simply assumed that their logic, grammar, organization, and dynamics were the same as the classic insurgencies of the twentieth century. Such assumptions may be dangerously misguided. In many ways contemporary insurgencies are more like their immediate forebears—the complex internal conflicts of the 1990s—rather than twentieth century insurgencies. Somalia, Bosnia, Sierra Leone, Congo, Colombia, and Kosovo are possibly better models than Vietnam or Algeria. If that is true, the military and the defense analytical community need to rethink the insurgency challenge once again, this time seeking to distinguish its persisting elements from its evolving ones.

The Dynamics of Contemporary Insurgencies

Normally a twentieth century insurgency was the only game in town (or at least the most important one). Nations facing serious insurgencies such as South Vietnam or, later, El Salvador, certainly had other security problems, but they paled in comparison to the insurgent threat. Insurgencies were organizationally simple. They involved the insurgents, the regime, and, sometimes, outside supporters of one side or the other. When the United States finally engaged in counterinsurgency operations, many government agencies played a supporting role, but it was primarily a military effort. After all, Americans now viewed counterinsurgency as a variant of war. In war, the military dominates and the objective is the decisive defeat of the enemy. Why should counterinsurgency operations be any different?

This perception was always problematic, leading the United States to pursue military solutions to threats that could only be solved politically. This disconnect is even more dangerous today, largely because twenty-first century insurgencies have diverged significantly from their forebears. Rather than being discrete conflicts between insurgents and an established regime, they are nested in complex, multidimensional clashes having political, social, cultural, and economic components. In an even broader sense, contemporary insurgencies flow from systemic failures in the political, economic, and social realms. They arise not only from the failure or weakness of the state, but from more general flaws in cultural, social, and economic systems. Such complex conflicts involve a wide range of participants, all struggling to fill the voids created by failed or weak states and systemic collapse. In addition to what might be labeled "first forces" (the insurgent and the regime) and "second forces" (outside sponsors of the insurgents or the regime), there are "third forces" (armed groups such as militias, criminal gangs, or private military corporations) and "fourth forces" (the international media and nongovernmental organizations) all with the capability to impact the outcome.[6] The implications are stark; in the face of systemic failure, simply crushing insurgents and augmenting local security forces may not be enough to stem instability.

Contemporary insurgencies are less like traditional war where the combatants seek strategic victory, they are more like a violent, fluid, and competitive market. This circumstance is the result of globalization, the decline of overt state sponsorship of insurgency, the continuing importance of informal outside sponsorship, and the nesting of insurgency within complex conflicts associated with state weakness or failure. In economic markets, participants might dream of strategic victory—outright control of the market such as that exercised by Standard Oil prior to 1911—but seldom attained it. The best most can hope for is market domination. Even these trends tend to be transitory. Most businesses have more limited objectives—survival and some degree of profitability. This phenomenon of limited objectives also describes many insurgencies, particularly those of the twenty-first century. Competition and the absence of state sponsors mitigate against outright conquest of states in the mode

of Fidel Castro or Ho Chi Minh. It is nearly impossible for a single entity, whether the state or a nonstate player, to monopolize power. Market domination and share are constantly shifting.

In contemporary complex conflicts, profitability often is literal rather than metaphorical. There is an extensive body of analytical literature that chronicles the evolution of violent movements such as insurgencies from "grievance" to "greed."[7] The idea is that political grievances may instigate an insurgency but, as a conflict progresses, economic motives may begin to play a greater role. While combatants "have continued to mobilize around political, communal, and security objectives," as Karen Ballentine and Jake Sherman write, "increasingly these objectives have become obscured and sometimes contradicted by their more businesslike activities."[8] Conflict gives insurgents access to money and resources out of proportion to what they would have in peacetime. As Paul Collier, one of the pioneers of this idea, explains:

> Conflicts are far more likely to be caused by economic opportunities than by grievance. If economic agendas are driving conflict, then it is likely that some groups are benefiting from the conflict and these groups, therefore, have some interest in initiating and sustaining it.[9]

The counterinsurgents—the regime or its supporters—also develop vested political and economic interests in sustaining a controllable conflict. A regime facing an armed insurgency is normally under somewhat less outside pressure for economic and political reform. It can justifiably demand more of its citizens and, conversely, postpone meeting their demands. Insurgency often brings outside financial support and provides opportunities for corrupt members of the regime to tap into black markets. Even though internal conflict may diminish economic activity overall, it may increase profit margins by constraining competition. This too can work to the advantage of elites, including those in the government or security services. Collier continues:

> Various identifiable groups will "do well out of the war." They are opportunistic businessmen, criminals, traders, and the rebel organizations themselves. The rebels will do well through predation on primary commodity exports, traders will do well through the widened margins on the goods they sell to consumers, criminals will do well through theft, and opportunistic businessmen will do well at the expense of those businesses that are constrained to honest conduct.[10]

Internal wars "frequently involve the emergence of another alternative system of profit, power, and protection in which conflict serves the political and economic interests of a variety of groups."[11] Hence the insurgents, criminals, militias, or even the regime have a greater interest in sustaining a controlled conflict than in attaining victory.

The merging of armed violence and economics amplifies the degree to which complex conflicts emulate the characteristics and dynamics of volatile, hypercompetitive markets. For instance, like all markets, complex conflicts operate according to rules (albeit informal, unwritten ones). In the most basic sense, these rules dictate what is and is not acceptable as participants compete for market domination or share. Participants may violate the rules, but doing so entails risk and cost. The more risk averse a participant the less likely it is to challenge the rules—and governments are normally more risk averse than nongovernment participants, and participants satisfied with their market position and with a positive expectation about the future are more risk averse than those who are unsatisfied and pessimistic. These rules are conflict- and time-specific; they periodically evolve and shift. This year's rule or "road map" might not be next year's.

As in commercial markets, participants in a complex conflict may enter as small, personalistic companies. Some may resemble family businesses built on kinship or ethnicity. As in a commercial market, the more successful participants evolve into more complex, variegated corporate structures. Insurgencies then undertake a number of the same practices as corporations:

- Acquisitions and mergers (insurgent factions may join in partnerships, or a powerful one may integrate a less powerful one).
- Shedding or closing unproductive divisions (insurgencies may pull out of geographic regions or jettison a faction of the movement).
- Forming strategic partnerships (insurgencies may arrange relationships with internal or external groups— political, criminal, etc.—which share their objectives).
- Reorganizing for greater effectiveness and efficiency.
- Developing, refining, and at times abandoning products or product lines (insurgencies develop political, psychological, economic, and military techniques, operational methods, or themes. They refine these over time, sometimes dropping those which prove ineffective or too costly).
- Advertising and creating brand identity (insurgent psychological activities are akin to advertising. Their "brands" include political and psychological themes, and particular methods and techniques).
- Accumulating and expending capital (insurgents accumulate both financial and political capital, using it as required).
- Subcontracting or contracting out functions (contemporary insurgents may contract out tasks they are ineffective at or which they wish to dis-associate themselves from).
- Bringing in outside consultants (this can be done by physical presence of outside advisers or, in the contemporary environment, by "virtual" consultation).
- Entering and leaving market niches.
- Creating new markets and market niches.
- Creating and altering organizational culture.
- Professional development and establishing patterns of career progression.

As in commercial markets, a conflict market is affected by what happens in other markets. Just as the automobile market is affected by the petroleum market, or the American national market by the European market, the Iraq conflict market is affected by the Afghan conflict market or by the market of political ideas in the United States and other parts of the Arab world.

That contemporary insurgents emulate corporations in a hyper-competitive (violent) market shapes their operational methods. Specifically, insurgents gravitate toward operational methods which maximize desired effects while minimizing cost and risk. This, in conjunction with a profusion of information, the absence of state sponsors providing conventional military material, and the transparency of the operating environment, increases the value that terrorism provides the insurgent. Insurgents have always used terrorism. But one of the characteristics of this quintessentially psychological method of violence is that its effect is limited to those who know of or are impacted by the act. When, for instance, the Viet Cong killed a local political leader, it may have had the desired psychological effect on people in the region, but the act itself did little to shape the beliefs, perceptions, or morale of those living far away. Today, information technology amplifies the psychological effects of a terrorist incident by publicizing it to a much wider audience. This technology includes satellite, 24-hour media coverage, and, more importantly, the Internet which, Gordon McCormick and Frank Giordano believe, "has made symbolic violence a more powerful instrument of insurgent mobilization than at any time in the past."[12]

So terrorism is effective. It is easier and cheaper to undertake than conventional military operations. It is less costly and risky to the insurgent organization as a whole (since terrorist operations require only a very small number of personnel and a limited investment in training and material). It is efficient when psychological effects are compared to the resource investment. It allows insurgents to conjure an illusion of strength even when they are weak. Terrorism is less likely to lead to outright victory, but for an insurgency which does not seek victory, but only domination or survival, terrorism is the tool of choice.

As the second decade of the twenty-first century approaches, there are still a few old-fashioned insurgencies trying to militarily defeat established governments, triumphantly enter the capital city, and form their own regime. The more common pattern, though, is insurgencies satisfied with domination of all or part of the power market in their particular environment. The insurgents in Iraq, Colombia, India, Sri Lanka, Uganda, and even Afghanistan have little hope of or even interest in becoming an established regime—whether for their entire country or some breakaway segment. To continue conceptualizing contemporary insurgency as a variant of traditional, Clausewitzean warfare, where two antagonists each seek to impose their will and vanquish the opponent in pursuit of political objectives, does not capture the reality of today's geostrategic environment. Clausewitz may have been correct that war is always fought for political purposes, but not all armed conflict is war.

Rethinking Counterinsurgency

In today's world it is less the chance of an insurgent victory which creates a friendly environment for transnational terrorism than persistent internal conflict shattering any semblance of control and restraint in the state. During an insurgency, both the insurgents and the government focus on each other, often leaving parts of the country with minimal security and control.

Transnational terrorists exploit this phenomenon. Protracted insurgency tends to create a general disregard for law and order. Organized crime and corruption often blossom. A significant portion of the population also tends to lose its natural aversion to violence. A society brutalized and wounded by a protracted insurgency is more likely to spawn a variety of evils, dispersing violent individuals around the world long after a particular conflict ends.

Such actions suggest that the US military and broader defense community need a very different way of thinking about and undertaking counterinsurgency strategies and operations. At the strategic level, the risk to the United States is not that insurgents will "win" in the traditional sense, gain control of their country, or change it from an American ally to an enemy. The greater likelihood is that complex internal conflicts, especially ones involving an insurgency, will generate other adverse effects: the destabilization of regions; reduced access to resources and markets; the blossoming of transnational crime; humanitarian disasters; and transnational terrorism. Given these possibilities, the US goal should not automatically be the direct defeat of the insurgents by the established regime (which often is impossible, particularly when a partner regime is only half-heartedly committed), but, rather, the rapid resolution of the conflict. A quick and sustainable outcome which integrates most of the insurgents into the national power structure is less damaging to US national interests than a protracted conflict that may lead to the total destruction of the insurgent base. Protracted conflict, not insurgent victory, is the threat.

Because Americans consider insurgency a form of warfare, US strategy and doctrine are based on the same beliefs that are associated with a general approach to warfare: War is a pathological action which evil people impose on an otherwise peace-loving society. It is a disease which sometimes infects an otherwise healthy body politic. This metaphor is a useful one. Today, Americans consider a body without parasites and pathogens "normal." When parasites or pathogens invade, medical treatment is required to eradicate them and restore the body to its "normal" condition. Throughout human history, persistent parasites and pathogens were, in fact, normal. Societies and their members simply tolerated them. Today, this analogy characterizes conflict in many parts of the world. Rather than an abnormal and episodic condition which should be eradicated, it is viewed as normal and tolerated.

Because Americans see insurgency as a form of war and, following Clausewitz, view war as quintessentially political, they focus on the political causes and dimensions of insurgency. Certainly insurgency does have an important political component. But that is only part of the picture. Insurgency also fulfills the economic and psychological needs of the insurgent. It provides a source of income out of proportion to what the insurgent could otherwise earn, particularly for the lower ranks. It provides a source of identity and empowerment for those members with few sources for such things. Without a gun, most insurgent soldiers are simply poor, uneducated, disempowered people with no prospects and little hope. Insurgency changes all that. It makes the insurgent important and powerful and provides a livelihood. Again, the economic metaphor is useful; so

long as demand exists, supply and a market to link supply and demand will appear. So long as there are unmet human needs that can be addressed by violence, markets of violence will be created.

The tendency of insurgencies to evolve into criminal organizations suggests that counterinsurgency strategy itself needs to undergo a significant shift during the course of any conflict. If an insurgency has reached the point that it is motivated more by greed than grievance, addressing the political causes of the conflict will not prove effective. The counterinsurgency campaign needs to assume the characteristics of a program to defeat organized crime or gangs. Law enforcement should replace the military as the primary manager of a mature counterinsurgency campaign. This evolving cycle of insurgency also implies that there may be a window of opportunity early in the insurgency before its psychological, political, and economic dynamics are set. For the outsiders undertaking counterinsurgency operations, a rapid, large-scale security, political, law enforcement, intelligence, or economic effort in the nascent stages of an insurgency has the potential for providing greater results than any incremental increase in assistance following the commencement of conflict. Timing does matter.

Because Americans view insurgency as political, American counterinsurgency strategy and doctrine stress the need for political reform in those societies threatened by the insurgency. This is in fact necessary but not always sufficient. A comprehensive counterinsurgency strategy requires the simultaneous raising of the economic and psychological costs and risks for those participating in the insurgency (or other forms of conflict) while providing alternatives. David Keen explains:

> In order to move toward more lasting solution to the problem of mass violence, we need to understand and acknowledge that for significant groups this violence represents not a problem but a solution. We need to think of modifying the structure of incentives that are encouraging people to orchestrate, fund, or perpetuate acts of violence.[13]

Economic assistance and job training are as important to counterinsurgency as political reform. Businesses started and jobs created are as much "indicators of success" as insurgents killed or intelligence provided. Because the margins for economic activity tend to widen during conflict, counterinsurgency should attempt to make markets as competitive as possible.[14] Because economies dependent on exports of a single commodity or a few commodities are particularly vulnerable to protracted conflict, counterinsurgency operations need to include a plan for economic diversification.[15] A comprehensive counterinsurgency strategy should offer alternative sources of identity and empowerment for the bored, disillusioned, and disempowered. Simply providing low-paying, low-status jobs or the opportunity to attend school is not enough. Counterinsurgents—including the United States when it provides counterinsurgency support—need to recognize that becoming an insurgent gives the disenfranchised a sense of belonging, identity, and importance. Counterinsurgency cannot succeed unless it finds alternative sources of power and worth. It is in this environment where the military and other government agencies involved with counterinsurgency support need to look beyond their normal sources of inspiration and motivation. For starters, counterinsurgent planners should consult law enforcement personnel associated with antigang units, inner-city community leaders, social psychologists, and cultural anthropologists.

Counterinsurgency cannot succeed unless it finds alternative sources of power and worth.

Women's empowerment—a brake on the aggression of disillusioned young males—should also be a central component of a successful counterinsurgency strategy. This illustrates one of the enduring problems and paradoxes of any counterinsurgency: What are foreign or external counterinsurgency supporters to do when some element of a nation's culture directly supports the conflict? Evidence suggests that cultures based on the repression of women, a warrior ethos, or some other social structure or factor are more prone to violence. Should counterinsurgency operations try to alter the culture or simply accept the fact that even once the insurgency is quelled, it may reappear?

The core dilemma, then, is that truly resolving an insurgency requires extensive social reengineering. Yet this may prove to be extremely difficult and expensive. This problem has many manifestations. In some cases, it may be impossible to provide forms of employment and sources of identity that are more lucrative than those offered by the insurgency. Regimes and national elites—the very partners the United States seeks to empower in counterinsurgency operations—often view actions necessary to stem the insurgency as a threat to their own power. They may view the conflict itself as a lesser evil. For many regimes, the insurgents pose less of a threat than a unified and effective security force. It is a basic fact that more regimes have been overthrown by coups than by insurgencies. Hence threatened governments will deliberately keep their security forces weak and divided. Alas, those with the greatest personal interest in resolving the conflict—the people—have the least ability to create peace.[16] Yet American strategy and doctrine are based on the assumption that our partners seek the same objective we do: the quickest possible resolution of the conflict. The United States assumes its partners will wholeheartedly pursue political reform and security force improvement. We are then often perplexed when insurgencies like the ongoing one in Colombia fester for decades; we are unable to grasp the dissonance between our objectives and those of our allies.

The implications of this are profound. If, in fact, insurgency is not simply a variant of war, if the real threat is the deleterious effects of sustained conflict, and if such actions are part of a systemic failure and pathology where key elites and organizations develop a vested interest in the sustainment of the conflict, the objective of counterinsurgency support should be systemic reengineering rather than simply strengthening the government so that it can impose its will more effectively on the insurgents. The most effective posture for outsiders is not to be viewed as an ally of the government and thus a sustainer of the flawed sociopolitical-economic system, but rather to be seen as a neutral mediator and peacekeeper, even when the outsiders may have a greater ideological affinity for the existing regime than the insurgent.[17] If this is true, the United States should only undertake support of counterinsurgency operations in the most pressing instances.

When considering such support, we cannot assume that the regime of a particular nation views the conflict as we do. We need to remember that our allies often consider the reforms which the United States defines as key to long-term success as more of a threat than the insurgency itself. Elites in states faced with an insurgency do not want a pyrrhic victory in which they defeat the insurgents only to lose their own grip on power. The cure may be worse than the disease. America has to understand that many of its friends and allies view their own security forces with as much apprehension as they do the insurgents. So while the United States may press for strengthening of local security forces political leaders may resist. Ultimately, this dissonance may be irresolvable. Where the United States, viewing insurgency as a variant of war, seeks "victory" over the enemy, our allies often find that a contained insurgency which does not threaten the existence of a particular nation or regime is perfectly acceptable.

Conclusion

What, then, does all this mean? Outside of America's historic geographic area of concern (the Caribbean basin), the United States should only consider undertaking counterinsurgency operations as part of an equitable, legitimate, and broad-based multinational coalition. Unless the world community is willing to form a neo-trusteeship such as those in Bosnia, Eastern Slavonia, Kosovo, or East Timor in order to reestablish a legitimate administration, security system, or stable society, the best that can be done is ameliorating the human suffering associated with the violence.[18] In most cases, American strategic resources are better spent in the prevention of the insurgency or its containment. Clearly, systemic reengineering is not a task for the United States acting unilaterally. Nor is it a task for the US military. When America is part of a coalition, the primary role for the US military should be the protection of noncombatants until other security forces, preferably local ones, can assume that mission.

Rather than a "one size fits all" American strategy for counterinsurgencies, the United States should recognize three distinct insurgency environments, each demanding a different response:

- A functioning and responsible government with some degree of legitimacy in a nation with significant US national interests or traditional ties can be rescued by foreign internal defense (El Salvador model).
- There is no functioning or legitimate government but there is a broad international and regional consensus favoring the creation of a neo-trusteeship until systemic reengineering is complete. In such instances, the United States should provide military, economic, and political

support as part of a multinational force operating under the auspices of the United Nations.

- There is no functioning and legitimate government and no international or regional consensus for the formation of a neo-trusteeship. In such cases, the United States should pursue containment of the conflict through the support of regional states and, in cooperation with friendly states and allies, creating humanitarian "safe zones" within the region of the conflict.

In the long term, counterinsurgency operations may or may not remain a mission for the US military. It is possible that Iraq and Afghanistan were unique events caused by a combination of political factors not likely to be repeated. It is possible that future political leaders will decide that the control of ungoverned spaces or support to fragile regimes will not constitute a central pillar in American foreign policy or military strategy.

Counterinsurgency may, in fact, remain a key mission. If it does, continued analysis of insurgencies by the US military and—perhaps even more importantly, other agencies of the government—is essential. We cannot assume that twenty-first century insurgency is so like its twentieth century predecessor and that old solutions can simply be dusted off and applied. Perhaps we need to transcend the idea that insurgency is simply a variant of conventional war and amenable to the same strategic concepts. Such a conceptual and strategic readjustment will not come easily. It will be hard to simply contain an insurgency and possibly witness the ensuing humanitarian costs when no salvageable government or multinational consensus exists that is capable of reengineering the failed social, political, or economic system. It will be particularly difficult to conform to the notion of serving as mediators or honest-brokers rather than as active allies or supporters of a regime. But to not do so—to confront new security problems with old ideas and strategies—is a recipe for disaster.

Notes

1. Field Manual 100-20/Air Force Pamphlet 3-2, *Military Operations in Low Intensity Conflict* (Washington: Headquarters, Department of the Army and Department of the Air Force, 1990).

2. The most important treatment of this is David Kilcullen, "Countering Global Insurgency," *Journal of Strategic Studies,* 28 (August 2005), 597–617.

3. Field Manual 3-24/Marine Corps Warfighting Publication 3-33.5, *Counterinsurgency* (Washington: Headquarters, Department of the Army and Headquarters, United States Marine Corps, December 2006). Joint counterinsurgency doctrine is under development.

4. For instance, see Gary Anderson, "The Baathists' Blundering Guerrilla War," *The Washington Post,* 26 June 2003, A29.

5. John A. Nagl, *Learning to Eat Soup with a Knife: Counterinsurgency Lessons from Malaya and Vietnam*

(Westport, Conn.: Praeger, 2002), reprinted in paperback by the Univ. of Chicago Press, 2005; and David Galula, *Counterinsurgency Warfare: Theory and Practice* (Westport, Conn.: Praeger, 1964), reprinted 2006. Also popular is Galula's *Pacification in Algeria 1956–1958* (Santa Monica, Calif.: RAND, 1963), reprinted 2006. Nagl is a US Army officer who served multiple tours in Iraq after writing the book (which was derived from his Ph.D. dissertation). Galula was a French Army officer who based his analysis on his experience in Indochina and Algeria.

6. I explain this idea of "third" and "fourth" forces in *Rethinking Insurgency* (Carlisle, Pa.: US Army War College, Strategic Studies Institute, June 2007), 15–42.

7. Paul Collier and Anke Hoeffler, "Greed and Grievance in Civil War," *Policy Research Working Paper* No. 2355 (Washington: The World Bank, 2000).

8. Karen Ballentine and Jake Sherman, "Introduction," in Karen Ballentine and Jake Sherman, eds., *The Political Economy of Armed Conflict: Beyond Greed and Grievance* (Boulder, Colo.: Lynne Rienner, 2003), 3.

9. Paul Collier, "Doing Well Out of War: An Economic Perspective," in Mats Berdal and David M. Malone, eds., *Greed and Grievance: Economic Agendas in Civil Wars* (Boulder, Colo.: Lynne Rienner, 2000), 91.

10. Ibid., 103–104.

11. Mats Berdal and David Keen, "Violence and Economic Agendas in Civil Wars: Some Policy Implications," *Millennium,* 26 (No. 3, 1997), 797.

12. Gordon H. McCormick and Frank Giordano, "Things Come Together: Symbolic Violence and Guerrilla Mobilisation," *Third World Quarterly,* 28 (No. 2, 2007), 312.

13. David Keen, "Incentives and Disincentives for Violence," in Berdal and Malone, 25.

14. Collier, 107.

15. Ballentine and Sherman, 3.

16. Collier, 105.

17. James Fearon described and advocated such an approach in "Iraq's Civil War," *Foreign Affairs,* 86 (March/April 2007), 2–15.

18. On "neo-trusteeships," see James D. Fearon and David D. Laitin, "Neotrusteeship and the Problem of Weak States," *International Security,* 28 (Spring 2004), 4–43; and Richard Caplan, "From Collapsing States to Neo-Trusteeships: The Limits of Solving the Problem of 'Precarious Statehood' in the 21st Century," *Third World Quarterly,* 28 (No. 2, 2007), 231–44.

DR. STEVEN METZ is Research Professor and Chairman of the Regional Strategy and Planning Department at the US Army War College Strategic Studies Institute. This article is based on his monograph *Rethinking Insurgency* (Carlisle, Pa.: US Army War College, Strategic Studies Institute, June 2007).

From *Parameters,* Winter 2007/2008. Published in 2008 by U.S. Army War College. Reprinted by permission.

Nuclear Disorder
Surveying Atomic Threats

GRAHAM ALLISON

The global nuclear order today could be as fragile as the global financial order was two years ago, when conventional wisdom declared it to be sound, stable, and resilient. In the aftermath of the 1962 Cuban missile crisis, a confrontation that he thought had one chance in three of ending in nuclear war, U.S. President John F. Kennedy concluded that the nuclear order of the time posed unacceptable risks to mankind. "I see the possibility in the 1970s of the president of the United States having to face a world in which 15 or 20 or 25 nations may have these weapons," he forecast. "I regard that as the greatest possible danger." Kennedy's estimate reflected the general expectation that as nations acquired the advanced technological capability to build nuclear weapons, they would do so. Although history did not proceed along that trajectory, Kennedy's warning helped awaken the world to the intolerable dangers of unconstrained nuclear proliferation.

His conviction spurred a surge of diplomatic initiatives: a hot line between Washington and Moscow, a unilateral moratorium on nuclear testing, a ban on nuclear weapons in outer space. Refusing to accept the future Kennedy had spotlighted, the international community instead negotiated various international constraints, the centerpiece of which was the 1968 Nuclear Nonproliferation Treaty (NPT). Thanks to the nonproliferation regime, 184 nations, including more than 40 that have the technical ability to build nuclear arsenals, have renounced nuclear weapons. Four decades since the NPT was signed, there are only nine nuclear states. Moreover, for more than 60 years, no nuclear weapon has been used in an attack.

In 2004, the secretary-general of the UN created a panel to review future threats to international peace and security. It identified nuclear Armageddon as the prime threat, warning, "We are approaching a point at which the erosion of the nonproliferation regime could become irreversible and result in a cascade of proliferation." Developments since 2004 have only magnified the risks of an irreversible cascade.

The current global nuclear order is extremely fragile, and the three most urgent challenges to it are North Korea, Iran, and Pakistan. If North Korea and Iran become established nuclear weapons states over the next several years, the nonproliferation regime will have been hollowed out. If Pakistan were to lose control of even one nuclear weapon that was ultimately used by terrorists, that would change the world. It would transform life in cities, shrink what are now regarded as essential civil liberties, and alter conceptions of a viable nuclear order.

Henry Kissinger has noted that the defining challenge for statesmen is to recognize "a change in the international environment so likely to undermine a nation's security that it must be resisted no matter what form the threat takes or how ostensibly legitimate it appears." The collapse of the existing nuclear order would constitute just such a change—and the consequences would make nuclear terrorism and nuclear war so imminent that prudent statesmen must do everything feasible to prevent it.

The Nuclear Cascade

Seven story lines are advancing along crooked paths, each undermining the existing nuclear order. These comprise North Korea's expanding nuclear weapons program, Iran's continuing nuclear ambitions, Pakistan's increasing instability, al Qaeda's enduring remnant, growing cynicism about the nonproliferation regime, nuclear energy's renaissance, and the recent learning of new lessons about the utility of nuclear weapons in international affairs.

Most of the foreign policy community has still not absorbed the facts about North Korean developments over the past eight years. One of the poorest and most isolated states on earth, North Korea had at most two bombs' worth of plutonium in 2001. Today, it has an arsenal of ten bombs and has conducted two nuclear weapons tests. It is currently harvesting the plutonium for an eleventh bomb and restoring its reactor in Yongbyon, which has the capacity to produce a further two bombs' worth of plutonium a year. In addition, Pyongyang has repeatedly tested long-range missiles that are increasingly reliable, has proliferated nuclear technology (including the sale of a Yongbyon-style reactor to Syria), and may be developing a second path to nuclear weapons by building a facility to enrich uranium.

From the perspective of the nuclear nonproliferation regime, two questions jump off the page. First, does Kim Jong Il imagine that he could get away with selling a nuclear weapon to Osama bin Laden or Iran? The fact that he sold Syria a plutonium-producing reactor suggests that he does. Second, what are the consequences for the NPT if one of the world's weakest states can violate the rules of the regime with impunity and defy the demands of the strongest states, which are those that are charged with its enforcement?

Already, North Korea's nuclear advances have triggered reflections in Seoul, Tokyo, and other regional capitals about options that were previously considered taboo. Although Japan's political culture is unambiguously against nuclear weapons, in 2002 then Prime Minister Junichiro Koizumi demonstrated how quickly that could change when he observed publicly, "It is significant that although we could have them, we don't." And because Japan has a ready stockpile of nearly 2,000 kilograms of highly enriched uranium and a well-developed missile program (for launching satellites), if Tokyo were to conclude that it required a credible nuclear deterrent of its own, it could adopt a serious nuclear weapons posture virtually overnight.

Meanwhile, Iran's nuclear odyssey is a moving target. Developments in the current negotiations may offer glimmers of hope. But it is unlikely that Iran will prove less obstinate and devious than North Korea has been. All the evidence suggests that Iran is methodically building up a widely dispersed array of mining, uranium-conversion, and uranium-enrichment facilities that could provide the infrastructure for nuclear weapons. At this point, it has mastered the technologies to indigenously manufacture, build, and operate its own centrifuges. Already, Iran is spinning 4,500 centrifuges, which produce an average of six pounds of low-enriched uranium per day, and has installed an additional 3,700 centrifuges that are ready to begin operation. The country now has a stockpile of over 3,000 pounds of low-enriched uranium—enough, after further enrichment, to make two Hiroshima-type nuclear bombs. Moreover, as the outing of a previously secret enrichment facility at Qom makes evident, Iran has thought carefully about the threat of a military strike on its declared facility at Natanz. To hedge against that risk, it has likely constructed more than one covert enrichment plant—facilities that would also provide a potential sneak-out option.

If Iran conducts a nuclear weapons test sometime in the next several years, it is probable that over the decade that follows, it will not be the only new nuclear weapons state in the Middle East. Saudi Arabia, for example, has insisted that it will not accept a future in which Iran—its Shiite, Persian rival—has nuclear weapons and it does not. Given the technical prerequisites, Saudi Arabia would much more likely be a buyer than a maker. Indeed, some in the U.S. intelligence community suspect that there have already been conversations between Saudi and Pakistani national security officials about the sale or transfer of an "Islamic bomb." In the 1980s, Saudi Arabia secretly purchased from China 36 CSS-2 missiles, which have a range of 1,500 miles and no plausible military use other than to carry nuclear warheads.

Egypt and Turkey could also follow in Iran's nuclear footsteps. As former U.S. National Security Adviser Brent Scowcroft testified to the Senate Foreign Relations Committee in March 2009, "We're on the cusp of an explosion of proliferation, and Iran is now the poster child. If Iran is allowed to go forward, in self-defense or for a variety of reasons, we could have half a dozen countries in the region and 20 or 30 more around the world doing the same thing just in case."

The Nuclear Terrorist

As Mohamed ElBaradei, director general of the International Atomic Energy Agency (IAEA), has noted, nuclear terrorism is "the most serious danger the world is facing." In 2007, the U.S. Congress established the Commission on the Prevention of Weapons of Mass Destruction Proliferation and Terrorism. The commission, of which I am a member, issued its report to Congress and the new administration in December 2008. It included two provocative judgments: first, that if the world continued on its current trajectory, the odds of a successful nuclear or biological terrorist attack somewhere in the world in the next five years were greater than even, and second, "Were one to map terrorism and weapons of mass destruction today, all roads would intersect in Pakistan."

Over the past eight years, the Pakistani government has tripled its arsenal of nuclear weapons.

Over the past eight years, as its stability and authority have become increasingly uncertain, the Pakistani government has tripled its arsenal of nuclear weapons and nuclear weapons material. During this same period, the leadership of al Qaeda has moved from Afghanistan to ungoverned areas inside the Pakistani border, the Taliban have become a much more effective insurgent force within Pakistan, and the military leader who ruled Pakistan, Pervez Musharraf, has been replaced by a fragile, fledging, splintered democracy.

Pakistan's military has grown increasingly reliant on its nuclear arsenal to deter India's overwhelming superiority in conventional arms. This strategy requires the dispersal of nuclear weapons (to prevent Indian preemption) and, especially in crises, looser command and control. In 2002, India and Pakistan went to the brink of war—a war that both governments thought might go nuclear. After Lashkar-e-Taiba terrorists with links to Pakistani intelligence services killed 173 people in a dramatic attack in Mumbai in November 2008, Indian Prime Minister Manmohan Singh displayed exquisite restraint. But he has warned unambiguously that the next major terrorist attack supported or sponsored by Pakistan will trigger a sharp military response.

In October 2009, Taliban extremists wearing Pakistani army uniforms occupied the government's military headquarters in Rawalpindi. Had they instead penetrated a nuclear weapons storage facility, they could have stolen the fissile core of a nuclear bomb. More troubling is the question of what would happen to Pakistan's estimated 100 nuclear bombs, and even larger amount of nuclear material, if the government itself were to fall. When asked about this, U.S. officials suggest that Pakistan's arsenal is secure: Secretary of Defense Robert Gates recently stated, "I'm quite comfortable that the security arrangements for the Pakistani nuclear capabilities are sufficient and adequate." History offers a compelling counter to these claims. In 2004, the father of Pakistan's nuclear bomb, A. Q. Khan, was arrested for selling nuclear weapons technology and even bomb designs to Iran, Libya, and North Korea. Khan created what the head of the IAEA called the "Wal-Mart of private-sector proliferation." Khan was enabled by an extended period of instability in Pakistan. Could uncertainty and instability in Pakistan today provide similarly propitious opportunities for mini-Khans to proliferate nuclear technology?

That al Qaeda has been significantly weakened by the U.S. military's focused Predator and Special Forces attacks on its leadership in the ungoverned regions of Pakistan is good news. The bad news is that bin Laden and his deputy, Ayman al-Zawahiri, remain alive, active, and desperate. On 9/11, al Qaeda demonstrated the capacity to organize and execute a large-scale terrorist attack more operationally challenging than detonating a nuclear weapon. As the 9/11 Commission documented, al Qaeda has been seriously seeking nuclear weapons since the early 1990s. The commission's report provides evidence about two Pakistani scientists who met with bin Laden and Zawahiri in Afghanistan to discuss nuclear weapons. These scientists were founding members of Ummah Tameer-e-Nau, which is ostensibly a charitable agency that was created to support projects in Afghanistan. But the foundation's board included a fellow scientist knowledgeable about nuclear weapons construction, two Pakistani air force generals, one Pakistani army general, and an industrialist who owned Pakistan's largest foundry.

Bin Laden has called the acquisition of nuclear weapons al Qaeda's "religious duty" and has announced the movement's aspiration to "kill four million Americans." As former CIA Director George Tenet wrote in his memoir, "The most senior leaders of al Qa'ida are still singularly focused on acquiring WMD [weapons of mass destruction]." "The main threat," he argued, "is the nuclear one. I am convinced that this is where [Osama bin Laden] and his operatives desperately want to go." As the noose tightens around al Qaeda's neck, its motivation to mount a spectacular attack to demonstrate its prowess and rally its supporters grows. Bin Laden has challenged his followers to "trump 9/11." Nothing could realize that aspiration so successfully as a mushroom cloud over a U.S. city.

Regime Fatigue

Growing cynicism about the nonproliferation regime also threatens to undercut the global nuclear order. It is easy to see why non-nuclear-weapons states view the regime as an instrument for the haves to deny the have-nots. At the NPT Review Conference in 2000, the United States and other nuclear weapons states promised to take 13 "practical steps" toward meeting their NPT commitments, but later, at the Review Conference in 2005, John Bolton, then the U.S. ambassador to the UN, declared those 2000 undertakings inoperable and subsequently banned any use of the word "disarmament" from the "outcome document" of the UN's 60th anniversary summit. In preparation for the 2010 Review Conference, which will convene in

May, diplomats at the IAEA have been joined by prime ministers and presidents in displaying considerable suspicion about a regime that permits nuclear weapons states to keep their arsenals but prevents others from joining the nuclear club. Those suspicions are reflected in governments' unwillingness to accept additional constraints that would reduce the risks of proliferation, such as by ratifying the enhanced safeguards agreement known as the Additional Protocol or approving an IAEA-managed multinational fuel bank to ensure states access to fuel for nuclear energy plants.

At the same time, rising concerns about greenhouse gas emissions have stimulated a growing demand for nuclear energy as a clean-energy alternative. There are currently 50 nuclear energy plants under construction, most of them in China and India, and 130 more might soon be built globally. Concern arises not from the nuclear reactors themselves but from the facilities that produce nuclear fuel and dispose of its waste product.

The hardest part of making nuclear weapons is producing fissile material: enriched uranium or plutonium. The same setup of centrifuges that enriches uranium ore to four percent to make fuel for nuclear power plants can enrich uranium to 90 percent for nuclear bombs. A nuclear regime that allows any state with a nuclear energy plant to build and operate its own enrichment facility invites proliferation. The thorny question is how to honor the right of non-nuclear-weapons states, granted by the NPT, to the "benefits of peaceful nuclear technology" without such a consequence. The answer is to provide an IAEA-governed international fuel bank that would guarantee a supply of nuclear fuel for states that would agree not to pursue enrichment and reprocessing activities. But persuading countries to forgo something others have for the greater good remains a stumbling block.

The Nuclear Weapons States

Finally, recent lessons about the utility of nuclear weapons in international affairs have also eroded the global nuclear order. U.S. President Barack Obama has endorsed President Ronald Reagan's vision of a world free of nuclear weapons and has enlisted the endorsement of many other leaders, including Russian President Dmitry Medvedev. Most realists in the international security community, however, regard such thinking as a hazy, long-term, and probably unachievable aspiration.

In the meantime, France is modernizing its nuclear arsenal, which President Nicolas Sarkozy has called "the nation's life insurance policy." China continues the modernization and expansion of its limited nuclear arsenal. With the collapse of its conventional forces, Russia has renewed its reliance on nuclear weapons. In the United States, the release of this year's Nuclear Posture Review, these reviews being a process meant to assess whether the U.S. nuclear arsenal is "reliable," will spark debates about whether the United States is building a stealth version of the earlier proposed "reliable replacement warhead."

Even more important than proposals for future programs are lessons learned from recent actions. The George W. Bush administration designated Iran, Iraq, and North Korea as "an axis of evil" and then proceeded to attack the one state that demonstrably had no nuclear weapons and give a pass to the state that had two bombs' worth of plutonium. The British strategist Lawrence Freedman summarized the lessons drawn by national security analysts around the world this way: "The only apparently credible way to deter the armed force of the US is to own your own nuclear arsenal." Many Iranians, and even a few Iraqis, have wondered whether the United States would have invaded Iraq in 2003 had Iraq been armed with a nuclear arsenal as large as North Korea's current one.

The George Marshall Question

After listening to a compelling briefing for a proposal or even in summarizing an argument presented by himself, Secretary of State George Marshall was known to pause and ask, "But how could we be wrong?" In that spirit, it is important to examine the reasons why the nonproliferation regime might actually be more robust than it appears.

Start with the bottom line. There are no more nuclear weapons states now than there were at the end of the Cold War. Since then, one undeclared and largely unrecognized nuclear weapons state, South Africa, eliminated its arsenal, and one new state, North Korea, emerged as the sole self-declared but unrecognized nuclear weapons state.

One hundred and eighty-four nations have forsworn the acquisition of nuclear weapons and signed the NPT. At least 13 countries began down the path to developing nuclear weapons with serious intent, and were technologically capable of completing the journey, but stopped short of the finish line: Argentina, Australia, Brazil, Canada, Egypt, Iraq, Italy, Libya, Romania, South Korea, Sweden, Taiwan, and Yugoslavia. Four countries had nuclear weapons but eliminated them: South Africa completed six nuclear weapons in the 1980s and then, prior to the transfer of power to the postapartheid government, dismantled them. Belarus, Kazakhstan, and Ukraine together inherited more than 4,000 strategic nuclear weapons when the Soviet Union dissolved in December 1991. As a result of negotiated agreements among Russia, the United States, and each of these states, all of these weapons were returned to Russia for dismantlement. Ukraine's 1,640 strategic nuclear warheads were dismantled, and the highly enriched uranium was blended down to produce low-enriched uranium, which was sold to the United States to fuel its nuclear power plants. Few Americans are aware that, thanks to the Megatons to Megawatts Program, half of all the electricity produced by nuclear power plants in the United States over the past decade has been fueled by enriched uranium blended down from the cores of nuclear warheads originally designed to destroy American cities.

Although they do not minimize the consequences of North Korea's or Iran's becoming a nuclear weapons state, those confident in the stability of the nuclear order are dubious about the prospects of a cascade of proliferation occurring in Asia, the Middle East, or elsewhere. In Japan, nuclear neuralgia has deep roots. The Japanese people suffered the consequences of the only two nuclear weapons ever exploded in war. Despite their differences, successive Japanese governments have remained confident in the U.S. nuclear umbrella and in the cornerstone of the United States' national security strategy in Asia, the U.S.-Japanese security alliance. The South Koreans fear a nuclear-armed North Korea, but they are even more fearful of life without the U.S. nuclear umbrella and U.S. troops on the peninsula. Taiwan is so penetrated and seduced by China that the terror of getting caught cheating makes it a poor candidate to go nuclear. And although rumors of the purchase by Myanmar (also called Burma) of a Yongbyon-style nuclear reactor from North Korea cannot be ignored, questions have arisen about whether the country would be able to successfully operate it.

In the Middle East, it is important to separate abstract aspirations from realistic plans. Few countries in the region have the scientific and technical infrastructure to support a nuclear weapons program. Saudi Arabia is a plausible buyer, although the United States would certainly make a vigorous effort to persuade it that it would be more secure under a U.S. nuclear umbrella than with its own arsenal. Egypt's determination to acquire nuclear weapons, meanwhile, is limited by its weak scientific and technical infrastructure, unless it were able to rent foreign expertise. And a Turkish nuclear bomb would not only jeopardize Turkey's role in NATO but also undercut whatever chances the country has for acceding to the EU.

Looking elsewhere, Brazil is now operating an enrichment facility but has signed the Treaty of Tlatelolco, which outlaws nuclear weapons in Latin America and the Caribbean, and has accepted robust legal constraints, including those of the Brazilian-Argentine Agency for Accounting and Control of Nuclear Materials. Other than South Africa, which retains the stockpile of 30 bombs' worth of highly enriched uranium that was once part of its nuclear program, it is difficult to identify other countries that might realistically become nuclear weapons states in the foreseeable future.

Such arguments for skepticism have a certain plausibility. The burden of evidence and analysis, however, supports the view that current trends pose unacceptable risks. As the bipartisan Congressional Commission on the Strategic Posture of the United States, which was led by former Secretaries of Defense William Perry and James Schlesinger, concluded in 2009, "The risks of a proliferation 'tipping point' and of nuclear terrorism underscore the urgency of acting now."

The Fierce Urgency of Now

Obama has put the danger of nuclear proliferation and nuclear terrorism at the top of his national security agenda. He has called it "a threat that rises above all others in urgency" and warned that if the international community fails to act, "we will invite nuclear arms races in every region and the prospect of wars and acts of terror on a scale that we can hardly imagine." Consider the consequences, he continued, of an attack with even a single nuclear bomb: "Just one nuclear weapon exploded in a city—be it New York or Moscow, Tokyo or Beijing, London or Paris—could kill hundreds of thousands of people. And it would badly destabilize our security, our economies, and our very way of life."

Obama's mission is to bend the trend lines currently pointing toward catastrophe.

Obama's mission is to bend the trend lines currently pointing toward catastrophe. Most of the actions required to achieve this mission must be taken not by Washington but by other governments around the world, which will act on the basis of their own assessments of their interests. But in an effort to encourage them to act and to demonstrate U.S. leadership, Obama has pledged to reduce the role of nuclear weapons in the United States' national security strategy, negotiate a follow-on arms control agreement with Russia to decrease U.S. and Russian nuclear armaments, ratify the Comprehensive Nuclear Test Ban Treaty, endeavor to ban the production of fissile material worldwide, and provide additional authority and resources to the IAEA. In the hope of rolling back North Korea's arsenal and stopping Iran short of building a nuclear bomb, he has opened negotiations with both countries, signaling a willingness to live with their regimes, however ugly, if they forgo nuclear weapons.

These steps mark the most substantial effort to revitalize the nuclear order since Kennedy. From his first major address abroad, when he spoke to the EU's 27 heads of state in Prague, to his chairmanship of the UN Security Council in September, Obama has been attempting to transform conceptions of the challenge.

This is an extraordinarily ambitious agenda—easy to say, hard to do. And this important work will encounter serious obstacles and stubborn adversaries. As Obama noted at the UN, "The next 12 months could be pivotal in determining whether [the nonproliferation regime] will be strengthened or will slowly dissolve." Indeed, the year ahead is crowded with dates and events that will move this agenda forward or leave it floundering. Optimists can take heart from the much more positive attitudes toward the United States evident in capitals around the world recently. Skeptics, however, can point to the objective forces propelling dangers along, as well as the disconnect between the aspirations and the daily actions of the president and of the cabinet officers charged with realizing these goals.

The international community has crucial choices to make, and the stakes could not be higher. Having failed to heed repeated warning signs of rot in the U.S.-led global financial system, the world dare not wait for a catastrophic collapse of the nonproliferation regime. From the consequences of such an event, there is no feasible bailout.

GRAHAM ALLISON is Douglas Dillon Professor of Government and Director of the Belfer Center for Science and International Affairs at Harvard University's Kennedy School of Government. For an annotated guide to this topic, see "What to Read on Nuclear Proliferation" at www.foreignaffairs.com/readinglists/nuclear-proliferation.

From *Foreign Affairs*, vol. 89, no. 1, January/February 2010, pp. 74–85. Copyright © 2010 by Council on Foreign Relations, Inc. Reprinted by permission of Foreign Affairs. www.ForeignAffairs.org

Nuclear Abolition

A Reverie

FRED C. IKLÉ

Sixty-two years ago, Dean Acheson warned President Truman that nuclear weaponry was "a discovery more revolutionary in human society than the invention of the wheel" and that "if the invention is developed and used destructively there will be no victor and there may be no civilization remaining." Dean Acheson was certainly no woolly-eyed disarmer. He promoted the Atlantic alliance as a bulwark against Soviet expansion. Yet, he recommended approaching Stalin to explore international controls for a global ban on nuclear weapons.

Two months later, U.S. and British officials reached the extraordinary decision that international controls must be the responsibility of the United Nations—a new and yet-untested organization. Dean Acheson chaired a committee which recommended an international authority to restrict the use of atomic energy to entirely peaceful purposes. The United States and its allies were convinced our world should never have nuclear weapons and indeed at the time there were none. Alas, because of Stalin's opposition to intrusive verification and his distrust of the United States, this well-intentioned American transformation of the international order reached a dead end.

But this idea of abolishing nuclear weapons has now been revived. Distinguished American statesmen and strategic experts have begun to advocate a world free of nuclear weapons as a long-term goal. In fact, when President Obama and Russian President Dmitry Medvedev met in London on April 1, 2009, their joint statement said: "We committed our two countries to achieving a nuclear free world . . ."

I have long been a proponent of the abolition of ballistic missiles. As then–Secretary of State George Shultz explains in his autobiography, I originated this idea before the Reagan-Gorbachev summit at Reykjavik in 1986. Reagan was more interested in his Strategic Defense Initiative, and zero missiles rather than zero nuclear weapons. Yet, for Americans who are promoting a nuclear-free world, it is tempting to allege—wrongly—that the Gipper had endorsed their goal.

One might well wonder, how can all nuclear states be persuaded to believe in a nuclear-free world? And how can states without atomic weapons—Iran comes to mind—be convinced not to build them? Advocates of nuclear abolition often assert that the nations with the largest nuclear arsenals can lead the way by reducing their stockpiles to a few hundred weapons. But once the largest arsenals have been shrunk so much, the small arsenals of North Korea, Iran and other countries will become a powerful military asset. Making matters worse, decommissioning nuclear-weapons stockpiles is complex. Nuclear weapons must be carefully dismantled and their plutonium or enriched uranium must be safeguarded. This process is costly and takes time. The United States already has a fifteen-year backlog of weapons to be dismantled.

Unfortunately, most proponents of zero nuclear weapons ignore important facts, forget the lessons of similar arms-control proposals and disregard insurmountable obstacles. With such a cavalier approach, the idea of a nuclear-weapons-free world becomes a mere reverie.

To achieve a nuclear-free world we would need an international organization so powerful that it can implement, supervise, protect and enforce the dispensation of zero nuclear weapons. This will not be an easy task. The organization would have to accomplish five exceedingly difficult missions. First, it would have to generate irresistible political pressure to convince all nations with nuclear weapons that they must ratify the new treaty obligating them to abolish all of their nuclear armaments. Second, it would have to control all fissionable materials that could be used to build nuclear bombs. Third, it would have to verify that no nation has kept nuclear weapons or has started to produce them. Fourth, in the event a nation has embarked on massive violations that would put an end to a nuclear-free world, the body must be authorized to call on the United Nations Security Council to intervene with military force, and to defeat this violator. Fifth, to cope with the threat of terrorists who might acquire nuclear weapons, the organization would have to be authorized to request that the International Criminal Court punish every one of these terrorists for war crimes, plus all of their supporters and providers of weapons technology. Moreover, the organization would need a Praetorian Guard endorsed by the United Nations to annihilate terrorists who prepare, or who have carried out, an attack with a nuclear weapon.

Creating such an organization would be far more difficult than was the creation of the United Nations at the end of World War II. And hard facts are aplenty to spoil the fantasy that this organization will be successful. For example, North Korea does not allow the United States or other nations to verify its commitments regarding nuclear weapons. Neither massive bribes nor significant sanctions have given us access to North

Korea's nuclear facilities. As the Congressional Research Service revealed, the United States donated over $1 billion during the last ten years to propitiate North Korea. All in vain. Rogue nations and repressive dictatorships pose a virtually intractable barrier to global nuclear disarmament.

On top of this, the assumption that this international organization could control all of the fissionable material usable for nuclear weapons is not supported by intelligence experts. Leon Panetta, director of the Central Intelligence Agency, said the United States does not know the location of Pakistan's nuclear weapons: "We don't have, frankly, the intelligence to know where they all are located. . . ." If this holds true even for Pakistan, a country with which the United States has active military links, think how much harder it would be to control fissionable material in Syria, Burma or Iran.

The persistent lack of success in managing inspection regimes and arms-control agreements should serve as a lesson. The Hague Convention of 1899 prohibited the use of asphyxiating gases. Fifteen years later, horrible gases were used on the battlefields of Flanders. In 1974, the U.S. Senate ratified President Nixon's convention prohibiting the stockpiling and production of biological weapons. Yet, the Soviet Union started to violate this convention immediately following U.S. ratification. Proponents of a nuclear-free world like to assert that we are already committed to abolition because the Treaty on the Non-Proliferation of Nuclear Weapons requires in Article VI that each party "undertakes to pursue negotiations" for nuclear disarmament. But this article also obligates the parties to "general and complete disarmament" which is the most drastic arms-control measure ever proposed. It requires the destruction of all armaments except those needed to maintain internal order. By being so all-encompassing and unrealistic, the treaty merely makes nuclear abolition seem an idyll. The sad history of arms-control agreements provides an important lesson. It must be studied by those proposing we attempt nuclear abolition.

Despite the many obstacles, a world free of nuclear weapons is a noble cause, provided it can be realized in a way that will protect political freedom and will do no harm. It is a cause that deserves serious effort, exploring how the political order would need to be transformed before nuclear abolition could be implemented.

After the atomic attacks on Hiroshima and Nagasaki, in June 1946 Albert Einstein asserted that world government had become "necessary for survival," and that Great Britain, the United States and the Soviet Union must draft a constitution for world government. Also in 1946, the Federation of American Scientists published a best seller, *One World or None*. In 1947, the United World Federalists (a new national organization with considerable influence at that time) agreed that world government will be needed.

Today, many promoters of zero nuclear weapons also see world government as necessary to maintain and secure a global order free of nuclear bombs. Though we have no experience building a world government, the European Union offers a potential model for success. The creation of the EU effectively changed the political structure of Europe. Ever since the Middle Ages, Europe has been plagued by war. Now, thanks to this supranational governing body, violent conflict among the major powers on the Continent is extremely unlikely. Certainly, within the European Union nuclear weapons have no strategic function.

Instead, today's internal conflicts within the EU are primarily about economic issues, changes in its political structure or the Union's further expansion, and occasionally about human rights and migration. Given time, we might be able to create a worldwide governance structure similar to the European Union.

The fact that nuclear weapons have not been used for sixty-four years gives us hope. This tradition of nonuse is almost miraculous. In at least four wars a nuclear-armed power fought against an enemy who had no nuclear weapons, and yet the nuclear power accepted defeat or a stalemate instead of using its nuclear dominance to win the war. This was the case in the Korean War, America's invasion of Vietnam, the Soviet occupation of Afghanistan and China's cross-border attack on Vietnam in 1979. This is a tradition we can build upon. If it lasts at least a hundred years, say until 2050—and if we are lucky—a global version of the EU may be possible.

If president Obama is truly committed "to achieving a nuclear free world," as his joint statement with President Medvedev says, he might want to order some preparatory studies so that we will know what steps should be taken when the time seems ripe for nuclear abolition. Technical studies are needed about the best ways to dismantle all atomic weapons. Better nuclear-detection instruments must be developed and deployed to intercept smuggled nuclear bombs.

Beyond technical concerns, the most difficult problems could arise from regional conflicts which would dissuade nations from giving up their nuclear weapons. Our diplomacy might have to insulate states from nuclear warfare. And in the event of nuclear use, we must strive to restore the dispensation of nonuse. If the United States aspires to lead the long and hazardous march toward a world free of nuclear weapons, it must not reduce its nuclear forces too fast.

In any event, as long as nuclear use can be prevented, abolition is less important. Preserving the tradition of nonuse is vital to the international community. Let us do all we can to maintain this dispensation. It is the most important tacit consensus among all nuclear powers, essential for the survival of a civilized world. It has lasted more than six decades and has taken us safely through all the crises of the cold war and the dramatic changes that followed.

Meanwhile, the abolition of nuclear weapons can wait until its time has come.

FRED C. IKLÉ is a distinguished scholar at the Center for Strategic and International Studies. He was undersecretary of defense for policy in the Reagan administration and director of the Arms Control and Disarmament Agency in the Nixon administration. He is also a member of The National Interest's Advisory Council.

From *The National Interest*, no. 103, September/October 2009, pp. 4–7. Copyright © 2009 by National Interest. Reprinted by permission.

Low-cost Nuclear Arms Races

The United States and the Soviet Union spent hundreds of billions of dollars trying to out duel each other during the Cold War. Today, nuclear arms races would cost considerably less.

DAN LINDLEY AND KEVIN CLEMENCY

In two research articles, scholars Keir Lieber and Daryl Press suggested in Spring 2006 that the United States had achieved nuclear primacy over Russia and China.[1] The United States could conduct a nuclear first strike on either country and remain virtually unscathed in the aftermath, argued Lieber, an associate professor of political science at the University of Notre Dame, and Press, an associate professor of government at Dartmouth College. Their analysis met a great deal of skepticism within the international security community. U.S. and Soviet/Russian strategic calculations had indeed changed since the end of the Cold War, as had calculations between the United States and China, but most, if not all, observers believed both nations had sufficient nuclear forces to deter the United States.

Despite this initial skepticism, the idea that the United States had gained a dominant strategic position over Russia and China lingered, raising the tantalizing question: What if Lieber and Press were right? How easily might Russia and China expand their nuclear arsenals and challenge U.S. superiority? And how should U.S. thinking on arms control and nonproliferation change as a consequence to avoid further destabilizing arms races?

These concerns are vital. Since its post-Cold War decline, Russia has been making a bid to regain its global power and standing, and its recent military buildup includes new nuclear forces. Further to the east, China continues its rise to superpower status. While Chinese actions have remained relatively pacific in recent years, its economy financed yearly double-digit percent increases in its defense spending during the past decade.[2] And new nuclear arms races may not be limited to just the United States, China, and Russia. With the prospect of an Iranian nuclear capability looming on the horizon, a number of countries including Egypt, Saudi Arabia, and Turkey may also develop nuclear weapons.

The following analysis demonstrates that cost would not be a barrier to nuclear weapons states, including Russia and China, looking to increase their deployment of nuclear weapons. Indeed, cost also would not be a barrier for many states that currently don't deploy nuclear weapons but have or are

contemplating developing the infrastructure to support nuclear energy generation. These findings make it easy to contemplate renewed arms races.

The greatest obstacles for states looking to build nuclear weapons remain the challenges of obtaining fissile materials and maintaining the political will to do so. Efforts to limit both vertical and horizontal proliferation should thus continue to focus on restricting access to fissile materials and reducing the incentives for nations to build nuclear weapons.

A Cold War Baseline

To begin understanding how Russia and China can afford to expand their nuclear arsenals beyond today's totals, we needed a benchmark for cost. We decided to use U.S. spending on its nuclear program in the early Cold War. We measured the aggregate costs of U.S. nuclear weapons during this period and then broke down these costs as a percent of GDP and calculated what they represented in per capita spending. The 1950s and early 1960s marked the most active period in the Cold War nuclear arms race, especially in terms of U.S. production. In just 15 years, the United States and the Soviet Union produced a total of 37,737 nuclear weapons (31,613 for the United States and 6,124 for the Soviet Union). To build its strategic forces to this level cost the United States a little more than $1 trillion from 1951 to 1965, or an average of $74 billion annually in 2007 dollars (see "Costs of U.S. Nuclear Weapons and Strategic Forces, 1951–1965").

An average cost of $74 billion a year would be daunting to many states seeking to build a nuclear arsenal. However, this average includes the development costs for the *entirety* of U.S. strategic forces, including research, development, the mass production of nuclear arms, and everything from building hardened ICBM silos to maintaining a fleet of nuclear-armed bombers. We refer to these as "deployed weapons" expenses to reflect the costs of the weapons, the delivery systems, etc. The cost of building only the warheads will be referred to as "warhead only" expenses.

Costs of U.S. Nuclear Weapons and Strategic Forces, 1951–1965

Year	Gross Increase in Nuclear Weapons	Estimated Cost of Nuclear Weapons (Billions of Dollars)	Percent of GDP	Estimated Cost of Strategic Forces (Billions of Dollars)	Percent of GDP
1951	271	11.3	0.51	67.12	3.02
1952	365	5.4	0.23	97.32	4.18
1953	431	20.6	0.84	83.89	3.43
1954	627	7.0	0.29	41.95	1.72
1955	994	6.8	0.27	58.73	2.32
1956	1,561	7.4	0.28	75.51	2.83
1957	1,826	8.6	0.32	90.61	3.34
1958	3,378	9.7	0.36	83.89	3.11
1959	5,646	10.6	0.38	87.25	3.08
1960	4,966	10.8	0.37	75.51	2.56
1961	3,692	10.2	0.34	90.61	3.04
1962	3,261	10.2	0.32	83.89	2.66
1963	2,072	10.1	0.31	70.47	2.15
1964	1,597	9.2	0.26	60.40	1.74
1965	926	8.1	0.22	41.95	1.15
Total	**31,613**	**146.1**	—	**1,109.09**	—
Average	**2,108**	**9.7**	**0.35**	**73.94**	**2.69**

Notes: All spending is presented in 2007 U.S. dollars. As the number of weapons produced increased, the per unit cost of each bomb decreased.

Sources: Estimated annual AEC/ERDA/DOE Spending on Nuclear Weapons Materials (Operating Expenses, Materials Procurement, Construction, and Capital Equipment) and Estimated Annual AEC/ERDA/DOE Spending on Nuclear Weapons Research, Development, Testing, and Production (R&D, Testing, Production, Operating Expenses, Construction, and Capital Equipment) from Stephen I. Schwartz, *Atomic Audit: The Costs and Consequences of U.S. Nuclear Weapons Since 1940* (Washington D.C.: Brookings Institution Press, 1998), pp. 560, 562. Total estimated costs of U.S. strategic forces are derived from Kevin N. Lewis, *Historical U.S. Force Structure Trends: A Primer* (Santa Monica, California: RAND Corporation, 1989), p. 16. Population figures are drawn from U.S. Bureau of Census, *Urban and Rural Population: 1900 to 1990* and *Projected Population of the United States, by Race and Hispanic Origin: 2000 to 2050.*

This distinction is worth making, because not all nuclear weapons states have a full array of nuclear delivery systems, yet their nuclear forces are sufficient to maintain deterrence. Britain eliminated its land-based platforms in 1963, retired its nuclear-bomber fleet in 1994, and currently relies solely on its submarine fleet to provide a nuclear deterrent. France eliminated its land-based program, reduced its fleet of nuclear bombers, and continues to maintain its nuclear-armed navy. Other states such as India, Pakistan, and Israel have adapted current aircraft systems to deliver nuclear weapons rather than develop single-purpose bombers.[3]

To provide a low-end estimate for states looking to build nuclear weapons, we also looked at what the United States spent to produce each warhead during the same period. "Costs of U.S. Nuclear Weapons and Strategic Forces, 1951–1965" summarizes these expenses, which include costs for warheads deployed on tactical nuclear weapons. These calculations suggest that with an average annual expenditure of $9.74 billion, states with access to nuclear materials could produce massive numbers of nuclear weapons. It should be noted that these figures do not include the research and development costs of the Manhattan Project and immediate post-war follow-on work. However, much of this research and investment is no longer necessary for states looking to build nuclear weapons, due to the diffusion of technology and knowledge. The key barrier for states today is obtaining highly enriched uranium and

plutonium, the fissile materials that fuel nuclear weapons. The United States and Soviet Union developed the infrastructure to produce these materials, but many other states have not.

While we would prefer to offer comparable cost figures for the early days of the Soviet nuclear program, providing reliable estimates is exceedingly difficult, as "the political and the heavily militarized economic system that the Soviets followed provided no way to accurately measure these costs."[4] Despite these difficulties, scholars Noel Firth and James Noren place annual Soviet spending on strategic offensive and defense weapon systems at $28.53 billion a year from 1951 to 1959.[5] Estimates of Chinese nuclear spending on just warheads place the costs at $3.56 billion a year in the 10 years prior to Beijing's 1964 nuclear test.[6] Observers estimate that the initial 10 years of the Indian nuclear weapons program cost between $820 million and $2 billion a year, a period that saw the Indians produce roughly 150 warheads.[7] Although the totals in the latter two cases are relatively small, these costs make up 39 percent, 5 percent, and between 8 and 21 percent, respectively, of U.S. spending on similar programs.[8]

Cost Is No Barrier

Using early–Cold War U.S. spending levels as rough indicators, we calculated what it would cost other countries to produce either 100 or 2,000 nuclear weapons a year. Our calculations are conservative as U.S. costs were likely much greater than

Estimated Costs of Building 2,000 Weapons Annually

	GDP (Billions of Dollars)	Deployed Weapons		Warheads Only	
		Cost Per Capita (Dollars)	Percent of GDP	Cost Per Capita (Dollars)	Percent of GDP
U.S annual average 1951–1965	2,749	430	2.7	57	0.4
Argentina	524	1,835	14.1	242	1.9
Brazil	1,838	389	4.0	51	0.5
China	7,043	56	1.0	7	0.1
Egypt	432	920	17.1	121	2.3
France	2,067	1,154	3.6	152	0.5
Germany	2,833	897	2.6	118	0.3
India	2,965	65	2.5	9	0.3
Iran	853	1,131	8.7	149	1.1
Israel	185	11,505	40.0	1,516	5.3
North Korea	40	3,173	184.9	418	24.4
Pakistan	446	449	16.6	59	2.2
Russia	2,076	523	3.6	69	0.5
Saudi Arabia	572	2,679	12.9	353	1.7
South Korea	1,206	1,508	6.1	199	0.8
Syria	83	3,831	89.1	505	11.7
Taiwan	690	3,235	10.7	426	1.4
Turkey	668	1,039	11.1	137	1.5
Britain	2,147	1,217	3.4	160	0.5

Notes: All spending is presented in 2007 U.S. dollars.

Sources: *CIA World Factbook*. We used the CIA's method of calculating GDP based on purchasing power parity, not exchange rate. U.S. averages drawn from "Costs of U.S. Nuclear Weapons and Strategic Forces, 1951–1965."

the costs to states today because of the relatively small size of the U.S. economy at the time. And yet these estimates show that it would be surprisingly cheap for many countries to produce large numbers of nuclear weapons. Of the 17 countries we focused on, only Israel and North Korea would have to spend more than 1 percent of their GDP to produce 100 weapons a year, assuming they had the requisite fissile materials.

This U.S. buildup between 1951 and 1965 cost an average of 2.7 percent of U.S. GDP, whereas today, China, Germany, and India could build a huge arsenal of strategic forces by spending less than 3 percent of their national GDP (see "Estimated Costs of Building 2,000 Weapons Annually"). Four more states—Brazil, France, Russia, and Britain—could do so for between 3 and 4 percent of their GDP. Keep in mind, the $74 billion average yearly U.S. price tag used to draw these comparisons represents a very high-end cost baseline for building and maintaining a full-fledged nuclear triad.

When looking at just the cost of building warheads, more than half the states we examined could afford to build approximately 2,000 warheads per year by spending just 1.5 percent or less of their GDP, matching the annual U.S. warhead development rates of the early Cold War. Using our metrics, this rate of warhead development would cost each Russian citizen $68.89 per year. The annual per capita costs for China and India would be $7.37 and $8.62, respectively. It is unlikely, however, that any state would want or need to build thousands of nuclear warheads a year, even if they wanted to establish a state of mutually

assured destruction with the United States. The costs of a slower buildup, say 100 weapons per year, would be even more doable for states, and building at this rate would, for example, give both India and Pakistan parity with China in three years.

By taking 5 percent of the U.S. cost estimate for a 2,000-per-year buildup of weapons and warheads, we can estimate the cost of building 100 weapons and warheads (see "Estimated Costs of Building 100 Weapons Annually"). We recognize that this may underestimate costs, as costs per unit do not scale down linearly. Yet, the diffusion of knowledge and technology since the 1950s, as well as the relatively high degree to which U.S. officials valued safety and manufacturing standards during the weapons production process, suggests that other states could build nuclear weapons with lower unit costs. In any case, these are rough illustrative estimates. Considering the great uncertainty about cost estimates for the Russian, Chinese, and Indian programs, any cost baseline for manufacturing facilities and technology development is imprecise, as would be cost estimates for scaling up. We simply suggest that cost is not a significant barrier for many states if they should choose to build nuclear weapons.

A Return to Proliferation?

By spending less than 1 percent of its GDP, all but two of the states we analyzed could afford to produce and maintain a small strategic force. For less than $25 per capita, all but Israel

Estimated Costs of Building 100 Weapons Annually

	GDP (Billions of Dollars)	Deployed Weapons		Warheads Only	
		Cost Per Capita (Dollars)	Percent of GDP	Cost Per Capita (Dollars)	Percent of GDP
Argentina	524	91.73	0.71	12.08	0.09
Brazil	1,838	19.46	0.20	2.56	0.03
China	7,043	2.80	0.05	0.37	0.01
Egypt	432	46.02	0.86	6.06	0.11
France	2,067	57.71	0.18	7.60	0.02
Germany	2,833	44.87	0.13	5.91	0.02
India	2,965	3.27	0.12	0.43	0.02
Iran	853	56.53	0.43	7.45	0.06
Israel	185	575.26	2.00	75.78	0.26
North Korea	40	158.66	9.24	20.90	1.22
Pakistan	446	22.44	0.83	2.96	0.11
Russia	2,076	26.15	0.18	3.44	0.02
Saudi Arabia	572	133.94	0.65	17.64	0.09
South Korea	1,206	75.38	0.31	9.93	0.04
Syria	83	191.53	4.45	25.23	0.59
Taiwan	690	161.73	0.54	21.30	0.07
Turkey	668	51.95	0.55	6.84	0.07
Britain	2,147	60.83	0.17	8.01	0.02

Notes: All spending is presented in 2007 U.S. dollars.

Sources: *CIA World Factbook.* We used the CIA's method of calculating GDP based on purchasing power parity, not exchange rate.

could afford to produce 100 warheads a year. This suggests that efforts to stem proliferation must focus on providing incentives for states not to build weapons, as well as preventing states from obtaining the full range of nuclear fuel-cycle facilities and obtaining fissile materials.

We would do well to remember the fear of nuclear annihilation that enshrouded the Cold War. Our analysis suggests that at least as far as costs are concerned, those fears could easily return, and not just for the United States but also for many regions of the world. The prospect of new and renewed arms races should make national leaders more cautious about adopting bellicose or inflammatory policies. Why start a nuclear arms race unless we really have to?

Notes

1. Keir A. Lieber and Daryl G. Press "The Rise of U.S. Nuclear Primacy," *Foreign Affairs,* vol. 85, no. 2; and Keir A. Lieber and Daryl G. Press, "The End of MAD?" *International Security,* vol. 30, no. 4.

2. China's official defense budget for 2008 is $59 billion; for 2007 it was roughly $45 billion. U.S. estimates of China's 2007 defense expenditures ranged from $95 billion to $140 billion.

3. P. K. Ghosh, "Economic Dimension of the Strategic Nuclear Triad," *Strategic Analysis,* vol. 26, no. 2. While Russia

continues to maintain its nuclear triad, its scale has been significantly drawn down since the fall of the Soviet Union. China relies predominantly on its land-based missiles while maintaining an antiquated submarine fleet. For a more detailed account on the current status of the Russian and Chinese nuclear forces see previously cited articles by Lieber and Press.

4. Ibid.

5. Noel E. Firth and James H. Noren, *Soviet Defense Spending: A History of CIA Estimates 1950–1990* (College Station: Texas A&M University Press, 1998), p. 111.

6. George Perkovich, *India's Nuclear Bomb: The Impact on Global Proliferation* (Berkeley: University of California Press, 1999), p. 80.

7. Ibid., p. 283. Figures converted by the authors to 2007 U.S. dollars. Note that *India Today* reported an arsenal of 150 weapons, about three times most current estimates of the Indian arsenal.

8. We used the full U.S. program costs to calculate these percentages for the Soviet Union and China, and the U.S. warhead-only costs when comparing to India.

DAN LINDLEY is an associate professor in the Department of Political Science at the University of Notre Dame. **KEVIN CLEMENCY** graduated with a degree in political science from Notre Dame in 2008 and works on local political campaigns in New York City.

UNIT 8

The Iraq War, Afghanistan, and Beyond

Unit Selections

Key Points to Consider

- How important are allies and the United Nations in the reconstruction of Iraq and Afghanistan?

- How important are Iraq and Afghanistan to the security interests of the United States?

- Make a list of dimensions along which you would measure the success or failure of the U.S. foreign policy toward Iraq and Afghanistan? Is the list the same for both countries?

- How would you rate the present situation along these dimensions?

- What words of advice about using military force would you give policy makers given the experience in Iraq and Afghanistan?

- Can we have an exit strategy in place at the start of a conflict or escalation?

- How would you rate the terrorist threat to the United States today compared to September 10, 2001? What about five years from now?

Student Website
www.mhhe.com/cls

Internet References

Army Knowledge Online
www.us.army.mil
White House: Renewal In Iraq
www.whitehouse.gov/infocus/iraq/

The Iraq War, right from its planning and conduct, to postwar occupation and reconstruction, was the single defining feature of the George W. Bush administration's foreign policy. Now, observers have begun to refer to Afghanistan as Obama's war, but it remains to be seen whether Afghanistan will be the defining foreign policy undertaking of his administration. Much will depend upon how successful that war is and its costs. Also figuring prominently in any such historical judgment will be how his administration handles foreign policy problems, particularly those involving the use of force, that lie in the future.

The Iraq War came to sharply divide the American public. To its supporters, the Iraq War is the second campaign of the first war of the 21st century, the war against terrorism. For its detractors, the Iraq War detracted the United States from more critical threats that are emanating from terrorist groups such as al Qaeda, and has isolated the United States from its traditional allies. Conflicts of opinion extended beyond the war to questions about the handling of intelligence and decision-making procedures prior to the terrorist attacks of September 11, 2001. As the Bush administration ended, debate over the Iraq War lessened. The tide of battle had turned in the favor of U.S. forces and the political situation in Iraq appeared to have stabilized.

These developments changed the nature of the public discourse on the Iraq War. Talk now turned to how and when the U.S. could leave Iraq as well as sending U.S. military forces into Afghanistan to deal with a resurgent Taliban and continued al Qaeda operations along the Afghanistan-Pakistan border. After lengthy internal debate, President Obama decided in December 2009 to significantly increase the American military presence in Afghanistan in order to complete the task begun in October 2001 when U.S. military forces entered Afghanistan and helped force the Taliban from power.

The first reading in this section, "Lifting the Veil," provides findings from recent public opinion polls from the Middle East. The author concludes that defeating terrorism will require defeating the rage that fuels it. The next essay, "How We'll Know When We've Won," focuses on Iraq but has applicability to Afghanistan as well. It presented definitions and measures of success that might be applied to these conflicts. The next two essays examine the merits of the war in Afghanistan. Stephen Biddle in "Is It Worth It?" argues in the positive but sees significant costs and risks in the effort. Michael Daxner, "Afghanistan: Graveyard of Good Intent," argues that success will require a fundamental mindset in U.S. thinking. Much more attention, he argues, must be given to Afghani concerns than to U.S. security priorities. One of the key driving forces behind the U.S. military involvement in both Iraq and Afghanistan is the terrorist threat to U.S. national security. Thomas Rid, "Cracks in the Jihad," discusses the evolving nature of al Qaeda as an organization and security threat. The final essay, "Exit Lessons," takes up the question of how one leaves a conflict that one has grown tired of. He examines several options and concludes that, short of victory, all present problems.

In order to better understand the chain of events that led the authors of these essays to take the positions that they did, a timeline of key events in the U.S. involvement in these wars is presented below.

Department of Defense/U.S. Air Force photo by Staff Sgt. Nicholas Pilch

September 11, 2001: Nineteen al Qaeda terrorists strike in the United States by hijacking commercial aircraft and flying them into the World Trade Center and Pentagon killing 2,973.

October 7, 2001: The United States launches Operation Enduring Freedom in Afghanistan after the Taliban government refuses to turn over Osama bin Laden, al Qaeda's leader.

December 20, 2001: The United Nations establishes the NATO-led International Security Assistance Force to help stabilize Afghanistan.

January 29, 2002: In his State of the Union address, Bush identifies Iraq, North Korea, and Iran as an "axis of evil" and promises that the United States would not allow "the world's most dangerous regimes to threaten us with the world's most destructive weapons."

September 12, 2002: Bush addresses the opening session of the United Nations and challenges it to confront the "grave and gathering danger" of Iraq or become irrelevant.

September 17, 2002: The Bush administration releases its national security strategy that replaces deterrence with preemption.

October 10, 2002: Congress authorizes the use of force against Iraq.

December 21, 2002: Bush approves deployment of U.S. forces to the Persian Gulf.

February 14, 2003: UN Weapons Inspector, Hans Blix, asserts that progress has been made in Iraq.

February 24, 2003: The United States, Great Britain and Spain introduce a resolution at the Security Council, authorizing the use of military force against Iraq. France, Germany and Russia oppose the resolution.

March 17, 2003: Bush presents Saddam Hussein with a 48 hour ultimatum to leave Iraq.

March 19, 2003: Operation 'Iraq Freedom' begins with a decapitation strike, aimed at Iraqi leadership targets in Baghdad.

March 21, 2003: Major fighting in Iraq begins.

April 9, 2003: Baghdad falls.

May 1, 2003: President Bush declares an end to major combat operations.

May 19, 2003: Thousands in Baghdad peacefully protest U.S. presence.

May 23, 2003: UN Security Council lifts sanctions and gives United States and Great Britain authority to control Iraq until an elected government is in place.

July 9, 2003: Secretary of Defense, Donald Rumsfeld, admits that the cost of the war was underestimated by one-half. He now places it at $3.9 billion/month and acknowledges that far more troops than anticipated will be needed for the occupation.

December 13, 2003: Saddam Hussein is captured.

April 29, 2004: Photos of torture and mistreatment of Iraqi prisoners by U.S. personnel at the Abu Ghraib prison.

June 8, 2004: UN Security Council passes resolution ending formal occupation and outlining a role for the UN in post-transition Iraq.

June 28, 2004: The United States transfers power to the new Iraqi government.

October 6, 2004: U.S. top weapons inspector issues a report concluding that Iraq destroyed its illegal weapons months after the 1991 Persian Gulf War.

December 1, 2004: The United States announces that it plans to expand its military presence in Iraq to 150,000 troops.

January 30, 2005: Iraq holds first multiparty election in 50 years.

October 15, 2005: Iraqi's vote on new constitution.

December 15, 2005: Iraq holds parliamentary elections.

March 15, 2006: Saddam Hussein testifies for the first time at his trial.

April 22, 2006: Nuri al-Maliki of the Shiite Dawa Party is approved as Prime Minister, breaking a long political deadlock.

June 8, 2006: Abu Musab al-Zarqari, head of al Qaeda in Iraq, is killed in a U.S. air strike.

June 22, 2006: Republican controlled Senate rejects a Democrat proposal to start a withdrawal of troops from Iraq.

December 6, 2006: The Iraq Study Group Report [Baker-Hamilton Report] calling for disengagement from Iraq is released.

December 30, 2006: Saddam Hussein is executed.

January 2007: President Bush announces a surge of U.S. forces into Iraq to stem the violence and create conditions for peace.

March 19, 2008: Fifth anniversary of the start of the Iraq War.

March 24, 2008: 4,000th U.S. combat death in Iraq War.

December 1, 2009: President Obama indicates he will increase the U.S. military presence in Afghanistan by 30,000 and proposes a withdrawal date for U.S. forces in July, 2011.

March 7, 2010: Elections are held in Iraq.

Lifting the Veil
Understanding the Roots of Islamic Militancy

HENRY MUNSON

In the wake of the attacks of September 11, 2001, many intellectuals have argued that Muslim extremists like Osama bin Laden despise the United States primarily because of its foreign policy. Conversely, US President George Bush's administration and its supporters have insisted that extremists loathe the United States simply because they are religious fanatics who "hate our freedoms." These conflicting views of the roots of militant Islamic hostility toward the United States lead to very different policy prescriptions. If US policies have caused much of this hostility, it would make sense to change those policies, if possible, to dilute the rage that fuels Islamic militancy. If, on the other hand, the hostility is the result of religious fanaticism, then the use of brute force to suppress fanaticism would appear to be a sensible course of action.

Groundings for Animosity

Public opinion polls taken in the Islamic world in recent years provide considerable insight into the roots of Muslim hostility toward the United States, indicating that for the most part, this hostility has less to do with cultural or religious differences than with US policies in the Arab world. In February and March 2003, Zogby International conducted a survey on behalf of Professor Shibley Telhami of the University of Maryland involving 2,620 men and women in Egypt, Jordan, Lebanon, Morocco, and Saudi Arabia. Most of those surveyed had "unfavorable attitudes" toward the United States and said that their hostility to the United States was based primarily on US policy rather than on their values. This was true of 67 percent of the Saudis surveyed. In Egypt, however, only 46 percent said their hostility resulted from US policy, while 43 percent attributed their attitudes to their values as Arabs. This is surprising given that the prevailing religious values in Saudi Arabia are more conservative than in Egypt. Be that as it may, a plurality of people in all the countries surveyed said that their hostility toward the United States was primarily based on their opposition to US policy.

The issue that arouses the most hostility in the Middle East toward the United States is the Israeli-Palestinian conflict and what Muslims perceive as US responsibility for the suffering of the Palestinians. A similar Zogby International survey from the summer of 2001 found that more than 80 percent of the respondents in Egypt, Kuwait, Lebanon, and Saudi Arabia ranked the Palestinian issue as one of the three issues of greatest importance to them. A survey of Muslim "opinion leaders" released by the Pew Research Center for the People and the Press in December 2001 also found that the US position on the Israeli-Palestinian conflict was the main source of hostility toward the United States.

It is true that Muslim hostility toward Israel is often expressed in terms of anti-Semitic stereotypes and conspiracy theories—think, for example, of the belief widely-held in the Islamic world that Jews were responsible for the terrorists attacks of September 11, 2001. Muslim governments and educators need to further eliminate anti-Semitic bias in the Islamic world. However, it would be a serious mistake to dismiss Muslim and Arab hostility toward Israel as simply a matter of anti-Semitism. In the context of Jewish history, Israel represents liberation. In the context of Palestinian history, it represents subjugation. There will always be a gap between how the West and how the Muslim societies perceive Israel. There will also always be some Muslims (like Osama bin Laden) who will refuse to accept any solution to the Israeli-Palestinian conflict other than the destruction of the state of Israel. That said, if the United States is serious about winning the so-called "war on terror," then resolution of the Israeli-Palestinian conflict should be among its top priorities in the Middle East.

Eradicating, or at least curbing, Palestinian terrorism entails reducing the humiliation, despair, and rage that drive many Palestinians to support militant Islamic groups like Hamas and Islamic Jihad. When soldiers at an Israeli checkpoint prevented Ahmad Qurei (Abu al Ala), one of the principal negotiators of the Oslo accords and president of the Palestinian Authority's parliament, from traveling from Gaza to his home on the West Bank, he declared, "Soon, I too will join Hamas." Qurei's words reflected his outrage at the subjugation of his people and the humiliation that Palestinians experience every day at the checkpoints that surround their homes. Defeating groups like Hamas requires diluting the rage that fuels them. Relying on force alone tends to increase rather than weaken their appeal. This is demonstrated by some of the unintended consequences of the US-led invasion and occupation of Iraq in the spring of 2003.

On June 3, 2003, the Pew Research Center for the People and the Press released a report entitled *Views of a Changing World June 2003*. This study was primarily based on a survey of nearly 16,000 people in 21 countries (including the Palestinian Authority) from April 28 to May 15, 2003, shortly after the fall of Saddam Hussein's regime. The survey results were supplemented by data from earlier polls, especially a survey of 38,000 people in 44 countries in 2002. The study found a marked increase in Muslim hostility toward the United States from 2002 to 2003. In the summer of 2002, 61 percent of Indonesians held a favorable view of the United States. By May of 2003, only 15 percent did. During the same period of time, the decline in Turkey was from 30 percent to 15 percent, and in Jordan it was from 25 percent to one percent.

Indeed, the Bush administration's war on terror has been a major reason for the increased hostility toward the United States. The Pew Center's 2003 survey found that few Muslims support this war. Only 23 percent of Indonesians did so in May of 2003, down from 31 percent in the summer of 2002. In Turkey, support dropped from 30 percent to 22 percent. In Pakistan, support dropped from 30 percent to 16 percent, and in Jordan from 13 percent to two percent. These decreases reflect overwhelming Muslim opposition to the war in Iraq, which most Muslims saw as yet another act of imperial subjugation of Muslims by the West.

The 2003 Zogby International poll found that most Arabs believe that the United States attacked Iraq to gain control of Iraqi oil and to help Israel. Over three-fourths of all those surveyed felt that oil was a major reason for the war. More than three-fourths of the Saudis and Jordanians said that helping Israel was a major reason, as did 72 percent of the Moroccans and over 50 percent of the Egyptians and Lebanese. Most Arabs clearly do not believe that the United States overthrew Saddam Hussein out of humanitarian motives. Even in Iraq itself, where there was considerable support for the war, most people attribute the war to the US desire to gain control of Iraqi oil and help Israel.

Not only has the Bush administration failed to win much Muslim support for its war on terrorism, its conduct of the war has generated a dangerous backlash. Most Muslims see the US fight against terror as a war against the Islamic world. The 2003 Pew survey found that over 70 percent of Indonesians, Pakistanis, and Turks were either somewhat or very worried about a potential US threat to their countries, as were over half of Jordanians and Kuwaitis.

This sense of a US threat is linked to the 2003 Pew report's finding of widespread support for Osama bin Laden. The survey of April and May 2003 found that over half those surveyed in Indonesia, Jordan, and the Palestinian Authority, and almost half those surveyed in Morocco and Pakistan, listed bin Laden as one of the three world figures in whom they had the most confidence "to do the right thing." For most US citizens, this admiration for the man responsible for the attacks of September 11, 2001, is incomprehensible. But no matter how outrageous this widespread belief may be, it is vitally important to understand its origins. If one does not understand why people think the way they do, one cannot induce them to think differently.

Similarly, if one does not understand why people act as they do, one cannot hope to induce them to act differently.

The Appeal of Osama bin Laden

Osama bin Laden first engaged in violence because of the occupation of a Muslim country by an "infidel" superpower. He did not fight the Russians in Afghanistan because he hated their values or their freedoms, but because they had occupied a Muslim land. He participated in and supported the Afghan resistance to the Soviet occupation from 1979 to 1989, which ended with the withdrawal of the Russians. Bin Laden saw this war as legitimate resistance to foreign occupation. At the same time, he saw it as a *jihad,* or holy war, on behalf of Muslims oppressed by infidels.

When Saddam Hussein invaded Kuwait in August 1990, bin Laden offered to lead an army to defend Saudi Arabia. The Saudis rejected this offer and instead allowed the United States to establish bases in their kingdom, leading to bin Laden's active opposition to the United States. One can only speculate what bin Laden would have done for the rest of his life if the United States had not stationed hundreds of thousands of US troops in Saudi Arabia in 1990. Conceivably, bin Laden's hostility toward the United States might have remained passive and verbal instead of active and violent. All we can say with certainty is that the presence of US troops in Saudi Arabia did trigger bin Laden's holy war against the United States. It was no accident that the bombing of two US embassies in Africa on August 7, 1998, marked the eighth anniversary of the introduction of US forces into Saudi Arabia as part of Operation Desert Storm.

Part of bin Laden's opposition to the presence of US military presence in Saudi Arabia resulted from the fact that US troops were infidels on or near holy Islamic ground. Non-Muslims are not allowed to enter Mecca and Medina, the two holiest places in Islam, and they are allowed to live in Saudi Arabia only as temporary residents. Bin Laden is a reactionary Wahhabi Muslim who undoubtedly does hate all non-Muslims. But that hatred was not in itself enough to trigger his *jihad* against the United States.

Indeed, bin Laden's opposition to the presence of US troops in Saudi Arabia had a nationalistic and anti-imperialist tone. In 1996, he declared that Saudi Arabia had become an American colony. There is nothing specifically religious or fundamentalist about this assertion. In his book *Chronique d'une Guerre d'Orient*, Gilles Kepel describes a wealthy whiskey-drinking Saudi who left part of his fortune to bin Laden because he alone "was defending the honor of the country, reduced in his eyes to a simple American protectorate."

In 1996, bin Laden issued his first major manifesto, entitled a "Declaration of Jihad against the Americans Occupying the Land of the Two Holy Places." The very title focuses on the presence of US troops in Saudi Arabia, which bin Laden calls an "occupation." But this manifesto also refers to other examples of what bin Laden sees as the oppression of Muslims by infidels. "It is no secret that the people of Islam have suffered from the oppression, injustice, and aggression of the alliance of Jews and Christians and their collaborators to the point that the blood of the Muslims became the cheapest and their wealth was loot in the hands of the enemies," he writes. "Their blood was spilled in Palestine and Iraq."

Bin Laden has referred to the suffering of the Palestinians and the Iraqis (especially with respect to the deaths caused by sanctions) in all of his public statements since at least the mid-1990s. His 1996 "Declaration of Jihad" is no exception. Nonetheless, it primarily focuses on the idea that the Saudi regime has "lost all legitimacy" because it "has permitted the enemies of the Islamic community, the Crusader American forces, to occupy our land for many years." In this 1996 text, bin Laden even contends that the members of the Saudi royal family are apostates because they helped infidels fight the Muslim Iraqis in the Persian Gulf War of 1991.

A number of neo-conservatives have advocated the overthrow of the Saudi regime because of its support for terrorism. It is true that the Saudis have funded militant Islamic movements. It is also true that Saudi textbooks and teachers often encourage hatred of infidels and allow the extremist views of bin Laden to thrive. It is also probably true that members of the Saudi royal family have financially supported terrorist groups. The fact remains, however, that bin Laden and his followers in Al Qaeda have themselves repeatedly called for the overthrow of the Saudi regime, saying that it has turned Saudi Arabia into "an American colony."

If the United States were to send troops to Saudi Arabia once again, this time to overthrow the Saudi regime itself, the main beneficiaries would be bin Laden and those who think like him. On January 27, 2002, a *New York Times* article referenced a Saudi intelligence survey conducted in October 2001 that showed that 95 percent of educated Saudis between the ages of 25 and 41 supported bin Laden. If the United States were to overthrow the Saudi regime, such people would lead a guerrilla war that US forces would inevitably find themselves fighting. This war would attract recruits from all over the Islamic world outraged by the desecration of "the land of the two holy places." Given that US forces are already fighting protracted guerrilla wars in Iraq and Afghanistan, starting a third one in Saudi Arabia would not be the most effective way of eradicating terror in the Middle East.

Those who would advocate the overthrow of the Saudi regime by US troops seem to forget why bin Laden began his holy war against the United States in the first place. They also seem to forget that no one is more committed to the overthrow of the Saudi regime than bin Laden himself. Saudi Arabia is in dire need of reform, but yet another US occupation of a Muslim country is not the way to make it happen.

In December 1998, Palestinian journalist Jamal Abd al Latif Isma'il asked bin Laden, "Who is Osama bin Laden, and what does he want?" After providing a brief history of his life,

bin Laden responded to the second part of the question, "We demand that our land be liberated from the enemies, that our land be liberated from the Americans. God almighty, may He be praised, gave all living beings a natural desire to reject external intruders. Take chickens, for example. If an armed soldier enters a chicken's home wanting to attack it, it fights him even though it is just a chicken." For bin Laden and millions of other Muslims, the Afghans, the Chechens, the Iraqis, the Kashmiris, and the Palestinians are all just "chickens" defending their homes against the attacks of foreign soldiers.

In his videotaped message of October 7, 2001, after the attacks of September 11, 2001, bin Laden declared, "What America is tasting now is nothing compared to what we have been tasting for decades. For over 80 years our *umma* has been tasting this humiliation and this degradation. Its sons are killed, its blood is shed, its holy places are violated, and it is ruled by other than that which God has revealed. Yet no one hears. No one responds."

Bin Laden's defiance of the United States and his criticism of Muslim governments who ignore what most Muslims see as the oppression of the Palestinians, Iraqis, Chechens, and others, have made him a hero of Muslims who do not agree with his goal of a strictly Islamic state and society. Even young Arab girls in tight jeans praise bin Laden as an anti-imperialist hero. A young Iraqi woman and her Palestinian friends told Gilles Kepel in the fall of 2001, "He stood up to defend us. He is the only one."

Looking Ahead

Feelings of impotence, humiliation, and rage currently pervade the Islamic world, especially the Muslim Middle East. The invasion and occupation of Iraq has exacerbated Muslim concerns about the United States. In this context, bin Laden is seen as a heroic Osama Maccabeus descending from his mountain cave to fight the infidel oppressors to whom the worldly rulers of the Islamic world bow and scrape.

The violent actions of Osama bin Laden and those who share his views are not simply caused by "hatred of Western freedoms." They result, in part at least, from US policies that have enraged the Muslim world. Certainly, Islamic zealots like bin Laden do despise many aspects of Western culture. They do hate "infidels" in general, and Jews in particular. Muslims do need to seriously examine the existence and perpetuation of such hatred in their societies and cultures. But invading and occupying their countries simply exacerbates the sense of impotence, humiliation, and rage that induce them to support people like bin Laden. Defeating terror entails diluting the rage that fuels it.

HENRY MUNSON is Chair of the Department of Anthropology at the University of Maine.

From *Harvard International Review,* Winter 2004, pp. 20–23. Copyright © 2004 by the President of Harvard College. Reprinted by permission.

How We'll Know When We've Won

A Definition of Success in Iraq

FREDERICK W. KAGAN

The president's nomination of generals David Petraeus and Raymond Odierno to take command of U.S. Central Command and Multinational Force-Iraq, respectively, was obviously the right decision. By experience and temperament and demonstrated success, both men are perfectly suited to these jobs. Given the political climate in Washington, however, their nominations are likely to be attacked with the same tired arguments war critics used to try to drown out reports of progress in Iraq during the recent Petraeus-Crocker hearings. So before the shouting begins again, let us consider in detail one of the most important of these arguments: that no one has offered any clear definition of success in Iraq.

Virtually everyone who wants to win this war agrees: Success will have been achieved when Iraq is a stable, representative state that controls its own territory, is oriented toward the West, and is an ally in the struggle against militant Islamism, whether Sunni or Shia. This has been said over and over. Why won't war critics hear it? Is it because they reject the notion that such success is achievable and therefore see the definition as dishonest or delusional? Is it because George Bush has used versions of it and thus discredited it in the eyes of those who hate him? Or is it because it does not offer easily verifiable benchmarks to tell us whether or not we are succeeding? There could be other reasons—perhaps critics fear that even thinking about success or failure in Iraq will weaken their demand for an immediate "end to the war." Whatever the explanation for this tiresome deafness, here is one more attempt to flesh out what success in Iraq means and how we can evaluate progress toward it.

Success Defined

A Stable State

An unstable Iraq is a recipe for continued violence throughout the Middle East. Iraq's internal conflicts could spread to its neighbors or lure them into meddling in its struggles. An unstable Iraq would continue to generate large refugee flows, destabilizing vulnerable nearby states. An unstable Iraq would enormously complicate efforts by the United States or any other state to combat terrorists on Iraqi soil. An unstable Iraq would invite the intervention of opportunist neighbors.

The Middle East being an area of vital importance to the United States and its allies, all these developments would harm America's interests.

A Representative State

Some war critics (and even some supporters) argue that the goal of "democratizing" Iraq is overoptimistic, even hopeless. So what are the alternatives? Either Iraq can be ruled by a strongman, as it was in the past, or it can be partitioned into several more homogeneous territories, each ruled according to its own desires. Before settling for either of these, we should note that the overwhelming majority of Iraqis continue to manifest their desire for representative government, as evidenced by the 8 million who voted in the last elections, the 90 percent of Sunni Arab Iraqis who tell pollsters they will vote in the upcoming provincial elections, and the sense on the streets that anyone who tries to eliminate representative government will do so at his peril. Beyond that, we must note that neither of the two suggested alternatives is compatible with stability. Nevertheless, let us examine them.

A Strongman

Iraq is a multiethnic, multisectarian state just emerging from a sectarian civil war. How could a strongman rule it other than by oppression and violence? Any strongman would have to come from one or another of the ethno-sectarian groups, and he would almost certainly repress the others. Although he might, in time, establish a secure authoritarian regime, the history of such regimes suggests that Iraq would remain violent and unstable for years, perhaps decades, before all opposition was crushed. This option would not sit well with American consciences.

Partition

Partitioning Iraq would generate enormous instability for the foreseeable future. Again, virtually no Arab Iraqis want to see the country partitioned; the Sunni, in particular, are bitterly opposed. But their desires aside, could a partitioned Iraq be stable? The Kurds, after all, already have their region. What would happen if the Shia got all nine provinces south of Baghdad, and the Sunni got Anbar, Salah-ad-Din, and whatever part of Ninewa the Kurds chose to give them? Well, there would be the problem of Baghdad and Diyala, the two mixed provinces, containing mixed cities. Despite the prevailing mythology, Baghdad has not been "cleansed" so as to produce stable sectarian borders. The largely Sunni west contains the Khadimiyah shrine, which the Shia will never abandon, while the largely Shia east contains the stubborn Sunni enclave in Adhamiya. The Sunni in Adhamiya have just gone through many months of hell to hang on to their traditional ground. And there are other enclaves on both sides of the river. Any "cleansing" of them would involve the death or forced migration of tens or possibly hundreds of thousands. Attempts to divide Diyala and even Ninewa would produce similar results. If ethno-sectarian conflict restarted in Iraq on a large scale, cleansing might make this solution more feasible, but at enormous human cost. In the current context, even to seriously propose it threatens Iraq's stability.

A State that Controls Its Territory

We already have an example of a sovereign, quasi-stable state confronting terrorist foes that is theoretically allied to the United States but has no American troops and does not control all of its own territory. It is Pakistan, whose ungoverned territories in the Federally Administered Tribal Areas and the Northwest Frontier Province have become safe havens for the leaders of the global al Qaeda network. If the United States abandoned Iraq before Iraq could control all of its territory with its own forces, we might make way for similar safe havens in the heart of the Middle East. It is clearly not in America's interests to create a Pakistan on the Euphrates.

A State Oriented toward the West

It is also clearly against America's interests for Iraq to become an Iranian puppet. Some in the United States, however, see that development as inevitable; they point to geography and religious ties. Some even say that the United States should not only acquiesce in the inevitable but embrace it, reaching out to the Iranians for their assistance in smoothing our withdrawal as they establish their domination. But why? Iran has not dominated Iraq in centuries. True, the Sunni-Shia divide is profound, but so is the Arab-Persian divide. Iraq's Shia, remember, enthusiastically supported Saddam Hussein's war against their Iranian co-religionists in the 1980s—a sectarian "betrayal" for which the Iranians have never forgiven them. Again, American troops and civilians who live day to day with Iraqis throughout the country report a dramatic rise in anti-Persian sentiment, coincident with a rise in Iraqi Arab nationalism. But back in the United States, the debate over Iraq is scarcely tethered to reality on the ground. In the simple terms suitable to that debate, then, suffice it to say that neither shared Shia faith nor a shared border has historically led to Iranian domination of Iraq. There is no reason to assume it will do so now.

An Ally in the Struggle against Militant Islamism

Whatever Saddam Hussein's ties were to al Qaeda before the invasion, the reality today is that an important al Qaeda franchise has established itself in Iraq. It initially had the support of a significant portion of Iraq's Sunni Arab community, but that community—with critical American support—has rejected al Qaeda and united with Iraq's Shia and Kurds to fight it.

As a result, there is no state in the world that is more committed than Iraq to defeating al Qaeda. None has mobilized more troops to fight al Qaeda or suffered more civilian casualties at the hands of al Qaeda—or, for that matter, taken more police and military casualties. Iraq is already America's best ally in the struggle against al Qaeda. Moreover, the recent decision of Iraq's government to go after illegal, Iranian-backed Shia militias and terror groups shows that even a Shia government in Baghdad can be a good partner in the struggle against Shia extremism as well.

Much has been made of the inadequacy of the Iraqi Security Forces' performance in Basra. If the Pakistani army had performed half as well in its efforts to clear al Qaeda out of the tribal areas, we would be cheering. Instead, Pakistani soldiers surrendered to al Qaeda by the hundreds, and Islamabad shut the operation down; it is now apparently on the verge of a deal with the terrorist leader who killed Benazir Bhutto. Iraqi Security Forces who underperformed were fired and replaced, and operations in Basra and elsewhere continue. The United States has given Pakistan billions in aid since 9/11 so that it could fight al Qaeda in the tribal areas. To be sure, it has spent far more billions on the Iraq war. Still, one may wonder which money has produced real success in the war on terror, and which has been wasted.

Progress Measured
Stability

Violence is the most obvious indicator of instability and the easiest to measure. The fact that violence has fallen dramatically in Iraq since the end of 2006 is evidence of improving stability. But critics are right to point out that areas tend to be peaceful both when government forces control them completely and when insurgents control them completely. Violence can drop either because the government is winning or because insurgents are consolidating their gains. So in addition to counting casualties and attacks, it is necessary to evaluate whether government control has been expanding or contracting. In fact, it has expanded dramatically over the past 15 months.

At the end of 2006, Sunni Arab insurgents controlled most of Anbar province, large areas of Salah-ad-Din and Diyala, southern Baghdad and northern Babil provinces (the "triangle of death"), and large areas of Baghdad itself including the Ameriya, Adhamiya, Ghazaliya, and Dora neighborhoods, which were fortified al Qaeda bastions. Shia militias controlled Sadr City almost completely—American forces could not even enter the area, and virtually no Iraqi forces in Sadr City operated independently of the militias; the militias also controlled the nearby districts of Shaab and Ur, from whence they staged raids on Sunni neighborhoods; they operated out of bases in Khadimiyah and Shula in western Baghdad; they owned large swaths of terrain in Diyala province, where they were engaged in an intense war against al Qaeda; they fought each other in Basra and controlled large areas of the Shia south.

Today, al Qaeda has been driven out of Dora, Ameriya, Ghazaliya, and Adhamiya; out of Anbar almost entirely; out of the "southern belt" including the former triangle of death; out of much of Diyala; and out of most of Salah-ad-Din. Iraqi and coalition operations are underway to drive al Qaeda out of its last urban bastion in Mosul. Remaining al Qaeda groups, although still able to generate periodic spectacular attacks, are largely fragmented and their communications partially disrupted. Iraqi Security Forces have been on the offensive against Shia militias in the "five cities" area (Najaf, Karbala, Diwaniya, Hilla, and Kut) and have severely degraded militia capabilities and eliminated militia control from significant parts of this area; the attack in Basra resulted in a reduction of the militia-controlled area, including the recapture of Basra's lucrative ports by government forces; tribal movements in Basra and Nasiriya are helping the government advance and consolidate its gains against the militias; and Iraqi Security Forces, with Coalition support, are moving through parts of Sadr City house by house and taking it back from the militias.

The fall in violence in Iraq, therefore, reflects success and not failure. Enemy control of territory has been significantly reduced, and further efforts to eliminate enemy control of any territory are underway. Spikes in violence surrounding the Basra operation reflect efforts by the government to retake insurgent-held areas and are, therefore, positive (if sober) indicators.

As for the argument that this stability is based solely on the increased presence of U.S. forces, which will shortly end, or that it is merely a truce between the Sunni and the Shia as they wait for us to leave—we shall soon see. Reductions of U.S. forces by 25 percent are well underway. The commanding general has recommended that after we complete those reductions in July, we evaluate the durability of the current stability, and President Bush has accepted his recommendation.

Representative Government

The Iraqi government is the product of two elections. The Sunni Arabs boycotted the first, with the result that Iraq's provincial councils and governors do not reflect its ethno-sectarian make-up. The second saw a large Sunni Arab turnout and the seating of a multiethnic, multisectarian government in Baghdad. The Iraqi government recently passed a law calling for provincial elections later this year, and the United Nations special envoy to Iraq, Steffan de Mistura, has been consulting with Baghdad about the details of the election, including efforts to ensure that the various committees overseeing it are not unduly influenced by militias or political parties. Surveys show that the Iraqis are nearly unanimous in their desire to vote, particularly in Sunni areas. The Anbar Awakening has turned into a political movement, introducing political pluralism into Sunni Arab politics for the first time. Similar movements, including the splintering of Moktada al-Sadr's "Sadrist Trend," are underway more haltingly among the Shia.

Each of Iraq's elections has been more inclusive than the last. Each has seen more enthusiasm for voting among all groups. Political pluralism is increasing within both sects. Whatever the popularity of the present government of Iraq, the overwhelming majority of Iraqis see elections as the correct way to choose their leaders, believe that their votes will count, and want to participate. The provincial elections this fall—and the national legislative elections next year—will be important indicators of the health of representative government in Iraq, and we should watch them closely. So far, all indications in this area are positive.

Control of Territory

The restoration of large urban and rural areas formerly held by insurgents and militias to government control is a key indicator of Iraqi progress. And there are others: the Maliki government's determination to clear Basra and Sadr City of militia influence; Iraqi operations to clear Mosul of al Qaeda fighters; the dramatic growth of the Iraqi Security Forces in 2007 and the further growth underway in 2008. There is anecdotal confirmation of this progress, such as the dramatic decline in the number of illegal militia-controlled checkpoints, most of them set up in and around Baghdad in 2006 for purposes of control, extortion, and murder. Although some war critics claim that the Anbar Awakening has simply put the province into the hands of a new militia, the truth is that the first stage of the movement saw more than 10,000 Anbaris volunteer for the Iraqi Security Forces. Two divisions of the Iraqi army remain in Anbar, and they are mixed Sunni-Shia formations. The Iraqi police force in Anbar, paid for, vetted, and controlled by the Iraqi government, has also grown dramatically. The "Sons of Iraq," who are the security component of the awakening movement, are auxiliaries to these government forces, supplemented by the presence of American troops. In Baghdad's neighborhoods, Sons of Iraq are dwarfed in number by the two Iraqi army divisions stationed in the city (in addition to the mechanized division based just to the north in Taji) and the numerous police and national police formations, all supported by American combat brigades. The Iraqi government is steadily extending its control of its own territory, and has demonstrated a determination to retake insurgent-held areas even from Shia militias.

Orientation toward the West

Iranian president Mahmoud Ahmadinejad visited Iraq in March 2008 and was warmly received, prompting concern in the United States that the Iraqi government was tilting toward Tehran. War critics, attempting to spin the Iraqi government's offensive against Shia militias in Basra, argued that Iran "supports" both the militias and the principal Shia parties fighting them—the entire operation, they claimed, was simply "Shia infighting" among groups already devoted to Tehran.

A closer examination shows this to be false. While it is true that Iran "supports" both ISCI and Dawa, the two leading Shia parties in the government, with money, and it provides the Sadrist militia not only with money, but with lethal weapons, training, trainers, and advisers inside Iraq to support the militia's fight against the United States and the Iraqi government—nevertheless, Iran does not provide such support to the government of Iraq or to the Iraqi Security Forces, which the United States and its allies have worked hard to develop into effective fighting forces, at the behest of the United Nations and the request of the legitimate government of Iraq. This is not simply "Shia infighting" in which the United States has no stake.

More to the point, we might ask what the Iraqi government itself has done to show its preferences. It has asked the United Nations to endorse the Multinational Force mission supporting it, a mission that includes American forces—but not Iranian ones. It has requested a bilateral security agreement with the United States—and not with Iran. It has determined to purchase American weapons and equipment for its armed forces, to replace the Warsaw Pact gear it had been using—and has not requested equipment from Iran or its principal international suppliers, Russia and China. Baghdad is organizing, training, and equipping its military and police forces to be completely interoperable with the United States—and not with Iran. For a government accused of being in Tehran's thrall, the current Iraqi government appears to have demonstrated repeatedly a commitment to stand with the United States, at least as long as the United States stands with Iraq.

An Ally in the War on Terror

Al Qaeda has killed many more Iraqis than Americans. Iraq has eight army divisions—around 80,000 troops—now in the fight against al Qaeda, and another three—around 45,000 troops—in the fight against Shia extremists. Tens of thousands of Iraqi police and National Police are also in the fight. Thus, there are far more Iraqis fighting al Qaeda and Shia militias in Iraq than there are American troops there. Easily ten times as many Iraqi as Pakistani troops are fighting our common enemies. At least three times as many Iraqi soldiers and police as Afghan soldiers and police are in the fight. And many times more Iraqi troops are engaged in the war on terror than those of any other

American ally. In terms of manpower engaged, and sacrifice of life and limb, Iraq is already by far America's best ally in the war on terror.

These facts will surely not put to rest the debate over definitions and measures of success in Iraq. Certainly, the American people have a right to insist that our government operate with a clear vision of success and that it develop a clear plan for evaluating whether we are moving in the right direction, even if no tidy numerical metrics can meaningfully size up so complex a human endeavor. As shown here, supporters of the current strategy do indeed have a clear definition of success, and those working to implement it are already evaluating American progress against that definition every day. It is on the basis of their evaluation that we say the surge is working.

The question Americans should ask themselves next is: Have the opponents of this strategy offered a clear definition of their own goals, along with reasonable criteria for evaluating progress toward them? Or are they simply projecting onto those who have a clear vision with which they disagree their own vagueness and confusion?

Here is a gauntlet thrown down: Let those who claim that the current strategy has failed and must be replaced lay out their own strategy, along with their definition of success, criteria for evaluating success, and the evidentiary basis for their evaluations. Then, perhaps, we can have a real national debate on this most important issue.

FREDERICK W. KAGAN is a resident scholar at the American Enterprise Institute.

From *The Weekly Standard*, May 5, 2008, pp. 19–23. Copyright © 2008 by Frederick W. Kagan. Reprinted by permission.

Is It Worth It?

The Difficult Case for War in Afghanistan

STEPHEN BIDDLE

The war in Afghanistan has been nearly invisible to the American public since its initial combat phase ended in early 2002, but it has rapidly come once again into view. Indeed, the war is now poised to become perhaps the most controversial and divisive issue in U.S. defense policy.

Managing this war will pose difficult problems both in Afghanistan and here at home. The strategic case for waging war is stronger than that for disengaging, but not by much: The war is a close call on the merits. The stakes for the United States are largely indirect; it will be an expensive war to wage; like most wars, its outcome is uncertain; even success is unlikely to yield a modern, prosperous Switzerland of the Hindu Kush; and as a counterinsurgency campaign its conduct is likely to increase losses and violence in the short term in exchange for a chance at stability in the longer term.

But failure is not inevitable. The U.S. military is now a far more capable counterinsurgency force than the Soviets who lost to the *mujaheddin* in the 1980s; the Obama Administration is committed to reforming a corrupt government in Kabul that the Bush Administration mostly accepted; and perhaps most important, the United States has the advantage of a deeply flawed enemy in the Taliban. The stakes, moreover, are important even though indirect: Failure could have grave consequences for the United States.

On balance, then, reinforcement is a better bet than withdrawal. But neither option is unassailable, and if presented with all costs and benefits appended, neither looks very appealing—and that will make for very contentious politics in the United States.

A war effort that is costly, risky and worth waging—but only barely so—will be hard to sustain politically; it would be just as hard to end. The Obama Administration wisely wants to avoid unrealistic overpromising or the hyping of threats, but for Afghanistan this means promising smaller benefits in exchange for greater exertions, yielding a net cost-benefit calculus perilously close to a wash. By ruling out clarion calls to great sacrifice for transcendent purpose, a sober approach to Afghanistan makes for a very hard sell and exposes the Administration to criticism from all sides. Yet disengagement, a weaker policy on the merits, courts blame, too, if circumstances in Afghanistan, abandoned to its fate, take a darker turn.

Public opinion is beginning to sour on the war, but for now most voters prefer reinforcement to withdrawal. As public attention shifts from Iraq, the domestic political salience of the Afghan war will grow, however, and public opinion could shift. Given that the rationale for war is such a close call, it will make for a daunting challenge in political management regardless of the Administration's policy choice. There is no easy way out of Afghanistan, no clear light at either end of the tunnel, for President Obama.

Stakes, Costs and Prospects

Analytically, the merits of the Afghan war turn on three questions: What is really at stake? What will it cost to pursue those stakes? And what is the likelihood that the pursuit will succeed?

The Stakes: The United States has two primary national interests in this conflict: that Afghanistan never again become a haven for terrorism against the United States, and that chaos in Afghanistan not destabilize its neighbors, especially Pakistan. Neither interest can be dismissed, but both have limits as *casus belli*.

The first interest is the most discussed—and the weakest argument for waging the kind of war we are now waging. The United States invaded Afghanistan in the first place to destroy the al-Qaeda safe haven there—actions clearly justified by the 9/11 attacks. But al-Qaeda is no longer based in Afghanistan, nor has it been since early 2002. By all accounts, bin Laden and his core operation are now based across the border in Pakistan's Federally Administered Tribal Areas (FATA). The Taliban movement in Afghanistan is clearly linked with al-Qaeda and sympathetic to it, but there is little evidence of al-Qaeda infrastructure within Afghanistan today that could directly threaten the U.S. homeland. If the current Afghan government collapsed and were replaced with a neo-Taliban regime, or if the Taliban were able to secure political control over some major contiguous fraction of Afghan territory, then perhaps al-Qaeda could re-establish a real haven there.

But the risk that al-Qaeda might succeed in doing this isn't much different than the same happening in a wide range of weak states throughout the world, from Yemen to Somalia to Djibouti to Eritrea to Sudan to the Philippines to Uzbekistan, or even parts of Latin America or southern Africa. And of course

Iraq and Pakistan could soon host regimes willing to put the state's resources behind al-Qaeda if their current leaderships collapse under pressure.

Many of these countries, especially Iraq and Pakistan, could offer al-Qaeda better havens than Afghanistan ever did. Iraq and Pakistan are richer and far better connected to the outside world than technologically primitive, landlocked Afghanistan. Iraq is an oil-rich Arab state in the very heart of the Middle East. Pakistan is a nuclear power. Afghanistan does enjoy an historical connection with al-Qaeda, is well known to bin Laden, and adjoins his current base in the FATA. Thus it is still important to deny al-Qaeda sanctuary on the Afghan side of the Durand Line. But the intrinsic importance of doing so is no greater than that of denying sanctuary in many other potential havens—and probably smaller than many. We clearly cannot afford to wage protracted warfare with multiple brigades of American ground forces simply to deny al-Qaeda access to every possible safe haven. We would run out of brigades long before bin Laden ran out of prospective sanctuaries.

The more important U.S. interest is indirect: to prevent chaos in Afghanistan from destabilizing Pakistan. With a population of 173 million (five times Afghanistan's), a GDP of more than $160 billion (more than ten times Afghanistan's) and a functional nuclear arsenal of perhaps twenty to fifty warheads, Pakistan is a much more dangerous prospective state sanctuary for al-Qaeda.

Furthermore, the likelihood of government collapse in Pakistan, which would enable the establishment of such a sanctuary, may be in the same ballpark as Afghanistan, at least in the medium to long term. Pakistan is already at war with internal Islamist insurgents allied to al-Qaeda, and that war is not going well. Should the Pakistani insurgency succeed in collapsing the state or even just in toppling the current civilian government, the risk of nuclear weapons falling into al-Qaeda's hands would rise sharply. In fact, given the difficulties terrorists face in acquiring usable nuclear weapons, Pakistani state collapse may be the likeliest scenario leading to a nuclear-armed al-Qaeda.

Pakistani state collapse, moreover, is a danger over which the United States has only limited influence. We have uneven and historically fraught relations with the Pakistani military and intelligence services, and our ties with the civilian government of the moment can be no more efficacious than that government's own sway over the country. The United States is too unpopular with the Pakistani public to have any meaningful prospect of deploying major ground forces there to assist the government in counterinsurgency. U.S. air strikes can harass insurgents and terrorists within Pakistan, but the inevitable collateral damage arouses harsh public opposition that could itself threaten the weak government's stability. U.S. aid is easily (and routinely) diverted to purposes other than countering Islamist insurgents, such as the maintenance of military counterweights to India, graft and patronage, or even support for Islamist groups seen by Pakistani authorities as potential allies against India. U.S. assistance to Pakistan can—and should—be made conditional on progress in countering insurgents, but if these conditions are too harsh, Pakistan might reject the terms, thus removing our leverage in the process. Demanding

conditions that the Pakistani government ultimately accepts but cannot reasonably fulfill only sets the stage for recrimination and misunderstanding.

If we cannot reliably influence Pakistan for the better, we should at least heed the Hippocratic Oath: Do no harm. With so little actual leverage, we cannot afford to make the problem any worse than it already is. And failure in Afghanistan would make the problem in Pakistan much harder.

The Taliban are a transnational Pashtun movement active on both sides of the Durand Line and are closely associated with other Pakistani insurgents. They constitute an important threat to the regime in Islamabad in rough proportion to the regime's inherent weaknesses (which are many and varied). If the Taliban regained control of the Afghan state, their ability to use the state's resources to destabilize the secular government in Pakistan would increase the risk of state collapse there. Analysts have made much of the threat that Pakistani Taliban base camps pose to the stability of the government in Kabul, but the danger works both ways: Instability in Afghanistan also poses a serious threat to the secular civilian government in Pakistan. This is the single greatest U.S. interest in Afghanistan: to prevent it from aggravating Pakistan's internal problems and magnifying the danger of an al-Qaeda nuclear-armed sanctuary there.

These stakes are important, to be sure, but they do not merit an infinitely high price tag. Afghanistan's influence over Pakistan's future is important, but it is also incomplete and indirect. A Taliban Afghanistan would make a Pakistani collapse more likely, but it would not guarantee it. Nor does success in Afghanistan guarantee success in Pakistan: There is a chance that we could struggle our way to stability in Afghanistan at great cost and sacrifice, only to see Pakistan collapse anyway under the weight of its own elite misjudgments and deep internal divisions.

The Cost: What will it cost to defeat the Taliban? No one really knows. War is an uncertain business. But it is very hard to succeed at counterinsurgency (COIN) on the cheap. Current U.S. Army doctrine is clear on this point:

> [M]aintaining security in an unstable environment requires vast resources, whether host nation, U.S., or multinational. In contrast, a small number of highly motivated insurgents with simple weapons, good operations security, and even limited mobility can undermine security over a large area. Thus, successful COIN operations often require a high ratio of security forces to the protected population. For that reason, protracted COIN operations are hard to sustain. The effort requires a firm political will and substantial patience by the government, its people, and the countries providing support.[1]

In fact, the doctrinal norm for troop requirements in COIN is around one security provider per fifty civilians. Applied to the population of Afghanistan, this would mean about 650,000 trained soldiers and police. If one assumes that only half the country requires active counterinsurgency operations (the south and east at the present time), this still implies a need for about 300,000 counterinsurgents.

Ideally, most of these forces would be indigenous Afghans, but there is reason to doubt that the Afghan government will ever be able to afford the necessary number of troops. If any significant fraction of this total must be American or NATO-based, then the resources needed would be very large in relation to total force availability.

The commitment could also be very long; successful counterinsurgency campaigns commonly last ten to 15 years or more.[2] And, at least initially, casualties could be heavy. An extrapolation from the 2007 experience in Iraq could imply more than fifty U.S. fatalities per month during active pacification.[3]

Prospects of Success: In general, the historical rate of great power success in COIN is not encouraging—around 25 percent.[4] And some important features of Afghanistan today are enough to give anyone pause. Orthodox COIN theory puts host-government legitimacy at the heart of success and failure, yet the Karzai government is widely seen as corrupt (even by local standards), inept, inefficient and en route to losing the support of the population. Ultimate economic and political development prospects are constrained by Afghanistan's forbidding geography, lack of infrastructure and political history. The Taliban enjoy a cross-border sanctuary in the FATA that the Pakistani government seems unwilling or unable to eliminate. Violence is up, perceptions of security are down, casualties are increasing, and the Taliban enjoys freedom of movement, access to the population and financial support from a thriving drug trade.

Worse perhaps, we can affect only some of these challenges directly. We can increase security by deploying more troops, we can bolster the economy to a degree with U.S. economic aid, we can put some pressure on poppy production, and we can pressure Karzai to reform. But only the Afghans can create a legitimate government, and only the Pakistanis can shut down the safe havens in the FATA. We can influence Afghanistan and Pakistan to a much greater degree than we have so far, but we cannot guarantee reform ourselves. To date, neither ally seems ready to do what it takes.

This does not make failure inevitable, however. Great powers' poor track record in COIN is due partly to the inherent difficulty of the undertaking but also to poor strategic choices. We can learn from experience, and we can change strategies and methods. Indeed, the U.S. military has learned a great deal about COIN in recent years. The new Army-Marine counterinsurgency doctrine is the product of a nearly unprecedented degree of internal debate, external vetting, historical analysis and assessment of recent experience.

The new Administration, moreover, seems determined to address one of the Afghan effort's most important remaining shortcomings. The new doctrine assumes a close alignment of interests between the United States and its host government: The manual assumes that our role is to enable the host government to realize its own best interest by making itself into a legitimate defender of all its citizens' well-being. If this is indeed what the host wants, U.S. aid will bring improvement in a direct, unproblematic way—and this is largely what the Bush Administration assumed in providing aid to Afghanistan and Pakistan with few strings attached. But if local leaders put self-interest ahead of public interest and rank currying favor with local elites above economic development or broad political legitimacy, then unconditional aid will often be misdirected and governing legitimacy sacrificed in favor of short-term personal expediency. Many see Hamid Karzai and Pervez Musharraf as precisely the kind of leaders who put their own tenure first and real legitimacy second. Such problems lead some students of counterinsurgency to emphasize the need for conditionality in aid in order to encourage behavior that broadens a host government's legitimacy and weakens the insurgency. The Obama Administration has made it clear that it intends to combine bigger carrots with real sticks by withdrawing aid should recipients fail to adopt needed reforms. This is an important step forward.

The forces implementing COIN doctrine are also much improved over their Vietnam-era predecessors—and even over their immediate predecessors in Iraq in 2003–04. The U.S. military of 2009 has become uncommonly proficient at counterinsurgency, combining stronger doctrine with extensive COIN combat experience, systematic training and resources that dwarf most historical antecedents. More should be done to improve U.S. COIN capability, but we are now vastly better at this than, for example, the Soviets were in the 1980s, and much more proficient than most historical great power counterinsurgents have been.

Perhaps most important, we are blessed in Afghanistan with deeply flawed enemies. Afghans remember what life was like under Taliban rule, and few want to return to their brand of medieval theocracy. Of course, these preferences are secondary to the need for security, and often to the desire for basic services such as courts free of corruption or police who enforce the laws without first demanding bribes. But because most Afghans oppose Taliban rule, we enjoy a strong presumption in favor of the government, as long as that government provides at least basic services competently.

The Taliban are also far from a unified opposition group. Contrast them with the Viet Cong of 1964, for example, a force in which a common ideology bound the leadership together and linked it to its fighters. The neo-Taliban of 2009 are a much more divided coalition of often fractious and independent actors. There is a hard core of committed Islamist ideologues centered on Mullah Omar and based in Quetta, but much of the Taliban's actual combat strength consists of an array of warlords and other factions who often side with the Taliban for reasons of profit, prestige or convenience. Depending on the circumstances, they may not follow orders from the leadership in Quetta. We often lament the challenges to unity of effort flowing from a divided NATO command structure, but the Taliban face difficulties on this score at least as severe as ours and potentially much worse. No NATO member would ever switch sides and fight for the Taliban, but one or more component factions of the Taliban might well leave the alliance for the government side. This makes it difficult for the Taliban to mount large-scale, coordinated offensives of the kind needed to conquer a defended city, for example.

In addition, the Taliban face major constraints in extending their influence beyond their ethnic base in southern and eastern Afghanistan. They are a Pashtun movement, but Pashtuns make up less than 45 percent of Afghanistan's population overall and constitute only a small fraction of the population in the north and west, where the Taliban have very little popular following.[5] The Afghanistan war is mainly about ideology, not ethnicity (the government is itself run in large measure by Pashtuns such as Hamid Karzai). Nevertheless, the Taliban's narrow ethnic base makes it hard for them to conquer the north and west of the country. It acts as a limit on their expansion in the near term.

Taking all this into account, advocates for withdrawal from Afghanistan certainly have a case. The stakes are not limitless, the costs of pursuing them are high, and there is no guarantee that even a high-cost counterinsurgency effort in Afghanistan will succeed. But success is possible all the same, given our strengths and our opponents' limitations. And failure could have potentially serious consequences for U.S. security.

The Taliban's weaknesses make it hard for them to overthrow a U.S.-supported government while large Western military forces defend it. But without those Western troops, the Afghan state would offer a much easier target. Even with more than 50,000 Western troops in its defense, the Karzai government has proven unable to contain Taliban influence and prevent insurgents from expanding their presence. If abandoned to its fate the government would almost surely fare much worse. Nor would an orphaned Karzai regime be in any position to negotiate a compromise settlement that could deny the Taliban full control. With outright victory in their grasp, it is hard to see why the Taliban would settle for anything less than a complete restoration.

A Taliban restoration, as noted, could restore to al-Qaeda a sanctuary for attacking the United States. And even if a Taliban 2.0 regime vetoed al-Qaeda attacks on the United States, it would almost certainly provide Pashtun militants and their allies in Pakistan a massive launching pad for efforts to destabilize the regime in Islamabad. Even without a haven in Afghanistan, Pakistani insurgents might ultimately topple the government, but that threat clearly grows with the additional resources of an openly sympathetic state across the Durand Line. And this raises the specter of Pakistani nuclear weapons falling into al-Qaeda's hands in Pakistan.

The danger of a nuclear al-Qaeda should not be exaggerated, however. For a U.S. withdrawal to lead to that result would require a networked chain of multiple events: a Taliban restoration in Kabul, a collapse of secular government in Islamabad, and a loss of control over the Pakistani nuclear arsenal (or deliberate transfer of weapons by sympathetic Pakistanis). These events are far from certain, and the compound probability of all of them happening is inherently lower than the odds of any one step alone. But a U.S. withdrawal would increase all the probabilities at each stage,

and the consequences for U.S. security if the chain did play itself out could be severe. During the Cold War, the United States devoted vast resources to diminishing an already-small risk that the USSR would launch a nuclear attack on America. Today, the odds of U.S. withdrawal from Afghanistan yielding an al-Qaeda nuclear weapon next door in Pakistan may be relatively low, but the low risk of a grave result has been judged intolerable in the past and perhaps ought to be again. On balance, the gravity of the risks involved in withdrawal narrowly make a renewed effort in Afghanistan the least-bad option we have.

U.S. Politics and Afghanistan

Barack Obama's presidential campaign promised to de-emphasize Iraq and refocus on Afghanistan. At the time, his Afghan hawkishness drew little opposition. The dovish wing of the Democratic Party feared they might hand John McCain the presidency if they undermined support for their nominee. Republicans saw the Iraq war and the Afghan war as important on the merits and also as Republican political legacies, discouraging opposition to either war.

Today the political landscape is different. The Obama Administration put its stamp on Afghanistan policy by boosting troop levels and contrasting this approach with Bush's COIN-lite methods there. But by putting his seal on the current strategy, Obama has freed Republicans to criticize the conduct of a war that will now be waged with a distinctively Democratic strategy and led by a new commanding general. At the same time, some left-leaning Democrats, increasingly frustrated with the Administration's centrism on other issues, see escalation in Afghanistan as a further demotion of the progressive agenda they expected Obama to push forward.

Meanwhile, the American public, which has focused mostly on Iraq for the past six years, has begun to rediscover Afghanistan—and it is uncomfortable with what it sees. A March 17, 2009 *USA Today*/Gallup poll, for example, found that 42 percent of those polled believed it was a mistake for the United States to send troops to Afghanistan, up from 30 percent in February and just 6 percent in January 2002. The percentage of those saying the war is going well dropped to 38 percent in March from 44 percent just two months earlier.[6]

For now, the public still supports both the war and the Obama Administration's approach to it: A February 20–22 Gallup poll found 65 percent of respondents favoring the President's decision to send an additional 17,000 U.S. troops to Afghanistan, with only 17 percent favoring a total withdrawal. But that support is fragile. Indeed, a nascent Afghan antiwar movement is already visible, and it includes both Democrats and Republicans. It is small now, but if history is any guide, it will grow as losses do, which they surely will. Even a successful counterinsurgency campaign looks bad in the early going. Classical COIN trades higher losses early on for lower casualties later, which will make the coming year in Afghanistan a hard one, regardless of the strategy's ultimate merits. Many of the announced reinforcements will be used to clear areas now held by the Taliban and hold them against counterattack, both of which will increase near-term casualty rates. As the U.S. troop count increases, so will the violence, and many will associate the former with the latter. Expect the calls for withdrawal to grow apace with the body count.

The coming Afghanistan debate is unlikely to get as vitriolic as the one over in Iraq in 2006–07. That affair erupted from a potent mix of partisanship and anger at perceived deceit, and so is unlikely to recur. But the political problems the new anti-war movement will pose for Obama could actually be harder to overcome than those the Iraq opposition posed for Bush. After all, Bush was able to circle the wagons, rally his base, and push an unpopular position through Congress by holding the Republican Party together, thereby forcing congressional Democrats to either unite behind a different approach to Iraq or acquiesce in Republican policies. Democrats chose the latter, giving President Bush the freedom to conduct the war as he wished.

Obama, by contrast, heads a Democratic Party that is already divided on the Afghan war and likely to grow more so over time. He also faces a series of domestic crises that will require him to spend political capital in order to win support for his governing agenda. Republicans have shown little willingness to cooperate on anything else, and the Administration's new ownership of the Afghanistan war gives the GOP another opportunity to retreat into opposition as the news from the front gets worse. Obama could face a situation in which a bipartisan antiwar coalition threatens the majority he will need to maintain funding for an increasingly unpopular war. His ability to impose party discipline could be limited by competing priorities, depending in part on how long and how deep the economic crisis turns out to be.

These challenges will likely get harder over time. If U.S. forces reach a positive military turning point in the Afghan campaign soon enough, political opposition in the United States will wither, as it mostly has with regard to Iraq since late 2007. But if the conflict proves as long and arduous as many counterinsurgencies have, votes on many budgets over several years will be needed to bring this war to a successful conclusion. These votes will take place against the backdrop of mounting casualties, increasing costs and growing pressure to restrain Federal budgets in the face of unprecedented deficits. The result could be a slow bleeding of support as a protracted COIN campaign goes through its inevitable darkest-before-the-dawn increase in casualties and violence.

Even if the Afghan war were an unambiguous necessity, the political challenge of holding a congressional coalition together through a long period of apparent gloom would be hard enough. But a war whose merits skirt the margin of being worthwhile makes this harder still, especially for an Administration that seeks to be restrained and realistic about expectations in Afghanistan. Moreover, the strongest part of the Administration's case for war, the link between Afghanistan and al-Qaeda, is ultimately indirect. The link is real, but with Osama bin Laden in Pakistan and with the strategic importance of Afghanistan lying chiefly in its effect on its neighbor, a candid, realistic appraisal of Afghanistan's stakes for the United States requires both modesty and the articulation of a more complicated causal chain than is normal in wartime appeals for U.S. public support. This is an honest leader's nightmare and his speechwriter's greatest challenge.

However, reversing policy and disengaging would be no easier for Obama. It would be the wrong course on the merits. Politically, it would commit the Administration to a policy now supported by only 17 percent of the electorate. It would play into the traditional Republican narrative of Democratic weakness on defense, facilitate widespread if ill-founded Republican accusations of the Administration's leftist radicalism, and risk alienating moderate Democrats in battleground districts whose support the President will need on other issues. However bad the news may look if the United States fights on, withdrawal would probably mean a Karzai collapse and a Taliban victory, an outcome that would flood American TV screens with nightmarish imagery.

Withdrawal would also gamble the Democratic Party's future—not to mention the nation's—on the hope that the worst potential consequences of withdrawal and collapse can be averted safely. If the United States pulls out, the Karzai government falls, the Taliban establishes an Afghan state haven, Pakistan collapses and a Pakistani nuclear weapon falls into bin Laden's hands, then a decision to walk away from Afghanistan would be seen as one of the greatest foreign policy blunders of the modern era. Unlikely as this chain of events may be, to withdraw from Afghanistan while success is still possible is to accept this gamble voluntarily. It is to stake potentially enormous consequences on a decision that need not have been taken. Therein lies the dilemma: *Neither* course, staying or leaving, is politically easy or strategically safe.

The best policy, therefore, is to defend an expensive, risky, potentially unpopular war with an argument that is sound but ultimately indirect and a close call on the merits. And this will need to be done by the leader of a divided party in the face of rising antiwar sentiment and a host of competing demands, political and financial. Barack Obama is a perhaps uniquely skilled political communicator, and his policy for Afghanistan is the right one. But even the right policy for Afghanistan is going to be a very hard sell indeed.

Notes

1. *The U.S. Army-Marine Corps Counterinsurgency Field Manual* (University of Chicago Press, 2007), p. 4.

2. Seth Jones, *Counterinsurgency in Afghanistan,* (RAND Corporation, 2008), p. 10.

3. The financial costs are also likely to be high. The Congressional Research Service estimates that the war in Afghanistan cost $34 billion in FY 2008 and projects that this figure will increase in coming years. See Amy Belasco, *The Cost of Iraq, Afghanistan and other Global War on Terror Operations Since 9/11* (Congressional Research Service, October 15, 2008).

4. See Jason Lyall and Isaiah Wilson, "Rage Against the Machines: Explaining Outcomes in Counterinsurgency Wars," *International Organization* (Winter 2009); and Ivan Arreguin-Toft, *How the Weak Win Wars: A Theory of Asymmetric Conflict* (Cambridge University Press, 2005), which finds "strong

actors" winning only 45 percent of asymmetric conflicts between 1950 and 1998.

5. This is why, even in their first rule, the Taliban never completely secured the north. Indeed, it was the unconquered Northern Alliance's hold over contiguous territory in that part of Afghanistan that provided the allies a jumping-off point for U.S. Special Forces, which teamed with them to topple the Taliban in 2001.

6. Tom Vanden Brook, "Afghan War Hits Peak of Disfavor," *USA Today,* March 17, 2009; Jeffrey Jones, "In U.S., More Optimism About Iraq, Less About Afghanistan," *Gallup.com,* March 18, 2009.

STEPHEN BIDDLE is senior fellow for defense policy at the Council on Foreign Relations.

Afghanistan: Graveyard of Good Intent

MICHAEL DAXNER

Not long ago, in a remote Afghan village, a well was drilled by a civilian aid group in the heart of the marketplace in the center of town. The team leader had observed that there was no easy access to clean, potable water and undertook the project, assuming it would be welcomed by the residents, not to mention the village elders. It would, he reasoned, shorten the trip women and children would need to make as the old wells were far outside the village.

This largesse was not well received. Women complained that this goodwill gesture had deprived them of their traditional meeting place, where they could talk without being overheard by their husbands. It was not the only tale involving water—that most precious of Afghan commodities. In a brand new female student dormitory built by a European aid organization, I visited in Parwan province, not far from Kabul, the faucets were fixed so high up in the wall that the short Afghan women could not reach them at all.

Afghanistan today is a series of unanswered prayers—a succession of failures to listen to the people, while their traditional leaders speak of unsatisfied hopes and failed aspirations.

Today, eight years after allied forces "liberated" the nation from the vicious, tyrannical rule of the Taliban, this is the land of failed dreams.

The golden hour after the U.S.-led invasion of 2001 was remarkable. I walked through the remnants of what had been downtown Kabul before the war. Parts of the city looked like the last remnants of Stalingrad, just a few chimneys left in a sea of debris. But it didn't feel like a war zone. I could inhale the sweet air of relief. I could flag down a taxi, or buy what I liked in the shops on Chicken Street and Flower Street. Most people were beaming. Ostentatious signs of liberation were seen not only in the offices of government and in the classrooms of the reopened universities, but also on the dusty, rubble-strewn streets. The many encounters I had with ordinary people were inspiring, and the mood was spreading across the country.

But as a United Nations officer in the Kosovo intervention after 2000 and a long-term observer of peacekeeping operations, I knew too well that it would only take a few months for liberation without liberty to descend slowly into a disgruntled impatience. There would be calls for foreign troops to leave the country, opposition from both traditionalists and fundamentalists, and the spirit of liberation would be replaced by the perception of occupation and humiliation. Sadly, I could see the storm clouds coming. In the haste to make war, Washington (and NATO) had obviously not thoroughly learned its lessons from previous interventions such as those in Kosovo and the rest of the Balkans.

The war in Afghanistan and the overflow into the wider Central Asian region will become the toughest test for the new foreign policy of President Barack Obama. After barely a half year in office, the president cannot be expected to provide any comprehensive and coherent strategy—nor can we expect an immediate shift in the fortunes of a war that has gone from bad to worse. But what we can see already from the Obama administration is disquieting. The focus on the security of America and its allies is too narrow, as it excludes Afghans and other people in the region from playing an active part in building a peaceful, functioning civic society.

Afghanistan has been the West's "good war," until now. In recent history, there has rarely been another intervention with so much institutional legitimacy and so little questioning of strategy and perspective as there has been with Operation Enduring Freedom and the International Security Assistance Force (ISAF). The immediate numbness and anger after 9/11 created its own logic. The "war on terror" overshadowed all rhetoric and good intentions. In the immediate aftermath of the invasion and rousting of the Taliban, the George W. Bush administration abused the trust of the Afghan people by using the first, halting steps of the new society for its own purposes, mainly to bolster the legitimacy of his 2004 reelection campaign.

The coordination of our strategies with the needs of the people in the region has been incomplete, false or, at best, superficial. Some strategies serve the people and the Afghan government, but many ongoing operations bypass both. Even our understanding of our enemies has been flawed. Only now can we see that the Taliban have been lumped together with Al Qaeda, and insurgents and terrorists have become synonymous. However, some Taliban depend on the masterminds of Al Qaeda for survival; many do not. Likewise, some insurgents are terrorists; many are not. These fundamental misunderstandings have, perhaps irrevocably, damaged the halting process of reconstruction.

Indeed, for allies of the United States, such as Canada or Germany, the reconstruction of the country has become "the unexpected war," a phrase coined by Janice Stein of Toronto's

Munk Center. Washington's allies had constituencies quite willing to commit military forces to protect reconstruction efforts, but not to fight a war that has had little if any relation to rebuilding Afghanistan.

Security Pretexts

Though I understand the broad range of domestic and international priorities of the new Obama administration, I am concerned that there has been only a halfhearted gesture toward a new strategy for Afghanistan, and that Washington seems to be at risk of sinking into a new quagmire, as potentially devastating as Vietnam. President Obama has promised to change the entire approach towards stabilizing this region. In his first accounts before Congress and the public, he pledged a political rather than a military outcome for Afghanistan and the region. He then stressed very clearly that security will still be his absolute priority. "We are not in Afghanistan to control that country and to dictate its future," Obama said on March 27, "but to disrupt and defeat Al Qaeda in Pakistan and Afghanistan."

Yet only the day before, Obama once again mentioned "our security" in disclosing his plans for conducting the warfare and civil reconstruction of Afghanistan, noting that it shall never again serve as a "safe haven for terrorists." The implication is clear. If we take as valid the pretext that "our security" (meaning that of the United States and the West) is at stake, then we can assume that the safety and security of the Afghans is not the core strategy in the Central Asian theater—and never was.

My years of travel through the region and through a score of other post-conflict locales, from Bosnia to Kosovo to Guatemala, suggest to me that this self-serving focus may lead us down a troubled and dangerous path. We, the interveners, frankly care less about how renewed insurgent attacks may run rough-shod over the human rights of Afghans and the remarkable achievements of civil society since the intervention brought an end to the last Taliban regime than we do about the continued threat to *our* societies.

It is true that President Obama's new policy towards American engagement in the region is likely to lead to some constructive changes. Human rights, co-ordination between civil reconstruction and military protection, and a stronger voice for the Afghan civil society are among the new American goals. Early hints from the State Department's Policy Planning Staff and United States Agency for International Development (USAID) are promising.

But what we have seen during the last three months also indicates that the new strategy does not yet affect day-to-day tactical ground operations. At best, the broad strategy is incomplete, at worst, already beginning to show signs of failing. The number of civilian casualties attributable to air raids has not been reduced. Diplomatic efforts—largely stalemated—still focus on corruption and drugs instead of reconstruction and delivery of public assistance. And the policy of punishing those accused of collaborating with the Taliban continues, rather than rewarding those who resist them peacefully.

A Mosaic of Inconsistencies

Numerous visits as a member of human rights groups, mainly for the Observatory of the Magna Charta, an academic freedom advocacy group, and as an investigator into the effectiveness of measures in the education sector and in refugee projects, have taught me some important lessons. Much of what I learned was confirmed by members of United Nations Assistance Mission in Afghanistan (UNAMA) and United Nations Educational, Scientific, and Cultural Organization (UNESCO) teams. Many mistakes are made under the pressure of time and security considerations and because, in the end, the Afghan people are all too often not our fundamental concern. Quite simply, we do not take the time to come to a deep understanding of their needs and hopes, despite the best intentions of America's hearts-and-minds-campaign. All this may change under President Obama's new doctrine, which includes broader measures for civil reconstruction, institution building, and humanitarian aid. Change may also develop as American forces close ranks with European allies.

In the beginning of the military engagement, German leaders claimed that Western values of security and freedom were being defended in Afghanistan. Now, however, the rhetoric has changed. After the Taliban's bloody attacks on German units in northern Afghanistan on April 2, Foreign Minister Frank-Walter Steinmeier said that German engagement will "continue to serve the tormented people of Afghanistan." The small shift in rhetoric—from defending Western values to defending the people of Afghanistan—is important.

Afghans want their collective integrity and dignity restored; they want and need the traumas from 30 years of terrible violence eased.

There have been many differences over the binary question of whether *their* interest equals *our* security. But I insist on the basic assumption that we can protect ourselves better against terrorist attacks in ways other than fighting the Afghan Taliban. Quite simply, and underlying the entire problem, we have been neither able nor willing to recognize the demand of the Afghan citizenry to be taken seriously. As a whole, Afghans want their collective integrity and dignity restored; they want and need the traumas from 30 years of terrible violence to be eased with food, justice, and employment. They want their long efforts toward modernity revived. Indeed, though it may be difficult for Westerners to imagine that Afghanistan even remotely resembles a modern nation, there have been significant attempts to modernize the state and society, stretching back nearly a century from King Amanullah Khan, who assumed the throne in 1919, through President Daoud Khan, who initiated progressive rule from 1973 to 1978, and on through the Soviet occupation. Even the last 30 years of war effectively continued the process of modernizing the country—in its own rather cynical, but apparently irreversible, way. Stinger missiles, satellite phones, guerrilla warfare

249

tactics, and the ever-present Toyota HiLux (a 4x4 vehicle favored by the Taliban) are all vestiges of this modern era. We must understand that decades of conflict have created enormous tensions between traditional lifestyles and modern attitudes. Now, all these elements must be disentangled—beginning with a consensus as to how the people in this country want to create a new relationship among tribes, local powers, and statehood.

When the majority of Afghans say openly that "we should not let them down again," as we did in 1988–89 following the withdrawal of Soviet occupation forces, they also implicitly complain that the West has acted out of solidarity with the United States—not out of any solidarity with the Afghan people. Instead, Afghans were left alone to pursue an atrocious series of factional, often tribal, fights—in many cases with open support from Western players in a succession of dirty games.

Afghans recall clearly all of the escapades that took place before the American-led invasion in 2001. American support for the Taliban first began in the mid-1990s, when Washington became impatient with the corrupt and agonizing rule of the *mujaheddin*. The latter comprised a conglomerate of victorious warlords left over from the war against the Soviets. The Taliban, by contrast, were a complex network of traditionalist and extreme Islamists who vowed to purge the society of Western and secular influence and are still trying to establish a strict regime based on *sharia* law. There was also well-organized support of Pashtun tribes against the Northern Alliance by the Directorate for Inter-Services Intelligence (ISI), Pakistan's secret service; Iranian support of some western Afghan tribes; and assistance from Uzbekistan for their ethnic counterparts in northern Afghanistan. Additionally, but by no means finally, there were intricate dealings by commercial and state agencies with Afghan tribes that lived along the route of a planned strategic oil pipeline from Turkmenistan to Pakistan.

My observation on several missions since 2003 has been that most Western officials have been blind to the obvious grievances of many of these parties. No one likes to be meddled with, and Afghanistan's history is one of almost constant foreign interference. The educated Afghan elites who returned from abroad with the ouster of the Taliban, and the more politically aware new generation who have grown up amid the now seven-plus-year American war on their soil, must learn about their nation's history, lest they idealize the time before the Soviet occupation. So must we in the West. Some lessons—like the moment in 1988–89 when strong foreign aid directed toward nation building could have been helpful in persuading the nation to turn its back on the Taliban—are unfailingly bitter.

Shortcomings

From the outset of the war, there were many shortcomings in Western perceptions of the social and cultural circumstances peculiar to this artificial, patchwork nation comprised of a host of tribes and nationalities. One critical error made by Western experts has been our desire to lump Al Qaeda with the Taliban and other insurgents who want to hamper the state-building process. But fighting the Taliban does not mean fighting Al Qaeda. They share links and idiosyncrasies, but the two organizations are only very loosely coupled.

During the war against the Soviets, Pakistan's ISI encouraged the expansion of Al Qaeda in order to internationalize the war against the Soviets while destabilizing Afghanistan. The geographic and logistic circumstances were certainly inviting at that moment, and in the years that followed, when the Taliban allowed Osama bin Laden to plan for the 9/11 attacks under the umbrella of hospitality. But cozy relations do not necessarily suggest twins. Thus it is troubling that military leaders of Operation Enduring Freedom, NATO forces and, most recently, President Obama have all too frequently equated Al Qaeda with the Taliban. While the two organizations may occasionally share a common cause, they do not share a religious doctrine. The extreme Saudi form of Sunni Wahhabism is traditionally not attractive to most Afghan tribes. In fact, from the tenth century on, the Afghan interpretation of the Koran differed from the Arabic. And Afghans, especially from the northern parts of the country, have long considered Arabs inferior to their own Iranian/Aryan ancestry.

Moreover, by contrast with Al Qaeda's terrorist cells, the Taliban are especially heterogeneous, comprising networks ranging from highly trained military forces to "afternoon volunteers," as one Kabul friend who had served with the Taliban called them. Thus the Taliban, with their ability to blend in with the larger Afghan populace, are an insurgency that can and will only be defeated by the Afghans themselves—not by any external force. As for Al Qaeda, we can diminish its ability to recruit in Afghanistan if we support the building of an effective national security structure instead of importing such forces.

Certainly, we must continue to fight the Taliban and strengthen the capabilities of the Afghan National Police (ANP) and Afghan National Army (ANA). If the international military forces, led by the United States—but not under its exclusive command—were able to coordinate more effectively with their Afghan counterparts, local indigenous forces would be in a position to take up the security roles more quickly and effectively. But, as Tom Koenigs, the former United Nations Special Representative for Afghanistan, has repeatedly explained, securing stable and adequate pay, and ensuring that indigenous forces are given respect and responsibility, are critical elements to success. While an Afghan police officer may earn $50 a month as a representative of the state, the Taliban now are offering $200, plus what they describe as "social protection" for one's family—a form of extortion that has often proved remarkably effective. Beyond the issue of salary, the training of army and police officers must also encompass human rights and rule of law. Without such training it will be more difficult to restore the reputation of the police as an incorruptible and effective force of the state, or to displace the challenge from local and irregular security providers—warlords, drug-barons, militias, and the Taliban.

At the same time, we must avoid weakening the central government, notably the president, Hamid Karzai, and his democratically elected government. Karzai may not be a perfect leader, but other contenders for the presidency in the August elections are worse—either weak and disconnected from local elites or lacking a sufficient constituency to challenge the incumbent. Karzai supporters also point out that the president is quite a charismatic leader among the Pashtun majority. I am persuaded that it is too early to present a non-Pashtun leader at a time when most Pashtuns are rather discontented with the present leadership of the tribal groups. It appears that Barack Obama, in the wake of Karzai's visit to Washington in May, is taking a similar position—reversing the view of the Bush administration and the early days of Obama's own tenure in office, when it was the vogue in Washington to criticize Karzai for incompetence and corruption. There is no real alternative option for the position, which seems to account for the recent improvement of relations between him and Washington.

A Desire for Respect

The fundamental problem is that the West seems to be unable to understand Afghans, above all their deep need for respect. Indeed, there are tens of thousands of citizens in Afghanistan who have studied or worked in Western countries—and who know us better than we know them. We in the West think we know much about the Afghans and pride ourselves on a new, non-colonialist attitude, but we do not know enough even about ourselves to understand the people in Afghanistan. By this I mean that we are still rather unclear—after seven years of war—whether we are liberators, friends, protectors, or simply concerned with our own homeland security and role on the international scene.

The fundamental problem is that the West seems to be unable to understand Afghans, above all their deep need for respect.

My own experience on four continents suggests that cultures of intervention are the result of incomplete attempts to rebuild society after war. There is no way to rebuild a state in a single, coherent approach. The post-war culture will dominate many stages of state-building and the cultural account of each political step should be considered. Afghanistan is a country with many tribal, ethnic, religious, and local points of fragmentation. It is by no means a homogenous and coherent nation with a unified government and citizenry. If the West is truly to commit its energies to rebuilding this fractured nation, we must endeavor to understand the rich complexities of the Afghan life and its deep traditions.

Simply tasking an American official to distribute Viagra to husbands in scores of villages will not win hearts and minds. In a similar vein, I recall a conversation with a young army captain who proudly recalled to me in 2007 how his Provincial Reconstruction Team (PRT) built a bridge for villagers in a central Afghan town, because "he just had the heavy gear" lying unused at his camp. It seemed a generous act, but when I spoke to a local village elder later that day, I was told that while a bridge might certainly have been welcome, it was all but useless where it was built, and would have been far more effective elsewhere. None of the village elders had ever been consulted.

In Herat Province, a highly sophisticated yet traditional irrigation system had been developed over centuries, only to be destroyed during the recent wars. Today, U.S. forces are at work developing a new water distribution system (with the assistance of expensive foreign consultants) when a cheaper and indigenous alternative merely needs rebuilding. Ismail Khan, former governor of Herat and current Minister of Water and Energy, expressed the same frustrations. "Why do we allow private and public development agencies to build public toilets at $20,000 apiece," he asked me, when his constituents would be happy for the work and could do it almost for free. Such examples speak not of friendship but of misunderstanding.

But the desire for respect is not unique to Afghanistan. In all the post-conflict landscapes I have visited in my career, there is a constant: enormous damage can be done by seemingly minimal acts of negligence or condescension. Take, for instance, the dangers that are shouldered by local employees of foreign civilian or military personnel in Afghanistan—all too often ignored or dismissed out of hand. Do we, as a society, concern ourselves with how our interlocutors, our interpreters, will get home tonight? Or what the neighbors might do to a woman who continues working for an international organization despite warnings from a traditionalist local clergy? There are ways to protect or to support these persons, but it is important to appreciate the concepts of honor and dignity in each case. Armed guards won't work indefinitely.

Adapting Reality

If we in the West have chosen for ourselves the task of nation building, we must do it properly. A primary responsibility must be to adapt the structures of the Afghan government to realities on the ground. Indeed, the Afghan nation cannot be (and perhaps never has been) centrally controlled. Yet some form of federal organization is required. Moreover, legitimacy—that most elusive currency—is critical to the long-term success of the federal system. In Afghanistan, in particular, given the massive decentralization and heterogeneity of the populace, this is not an easy task. That said, a weaker president or government in Kabul is not necessarily a good thing. But it is difficult to imagine how a central government with appointed governors can effectively pay tribute to the multitude of differences between the disparate provinces and regions in Afghanistan. Without a stronger and more convincing constitution, it will be difficult, if not impossible, to tune the dissonance of differing religious streams, traditions, local circumstances, and customary laws into harmony.

Yet, though I do not fear a break-up of the state along ethnic lines, civil society needs to reinforce the central government with robust, local, legal pluralism and conflict resolution in order to satisfy Afghans' need for more security and certainty. Such decentralization would inevitably require that similar structures are built into a two- or three-layer federal system—where district councils and development agencies have a serious role. As of now, a coherent vision of this is but a mirage.

> **Though I do not fear a break-up of the state along ethnic lines, civil society needs to reinforce the central government with robust, local, legal pluralism.**

As Sayed Hussain Anwari, the successor to Ismail Khan as governor of Herat province, told a UN-sponsored conference in Kabul, we also must deal with the compound problem of "second victimization"—our reflexive urge to blame Afghans for their failure to put to good use the aid Western nations have offered. Not only had his countrymen been the victims of a long and terrible war, said the governor, but now they have again become victims—of our prejudice that their corruption and ineptitude will hamper the West's best efforts to deliver peace, security, and prosperity to their country. Afghan leaders know well their own flaws and are certainly aware of the corruption, but they also are aware of ours. Indeed, we risk humiliating the Afghans even further by importing Western consultants and experts, Anwari explained, without first asking the locals for advice. Eventually, the West will leave Afghanistan, and if we do so without developing the capacity of the local populace to govern its own affairs, we risk total failure in the region. All in all, we do not pay enough respect to the rights of Afghans to discuss their vision of the future.

Incidentally, a few hours after the governor's speech, the civilian NATO representative, Daan Everts, gave an address at the same conference. He had not been present for the governor's earlier remarks, and to my ears, his speech reflected the same tired, old, Western prejudices—a litany of accusations and warnings, a disregard for respect and understanding toward Afghans—that the governor had so eloquently denounced. The atmosphere was polite, but icy.

We have now come full circle. The West has replaced the reality of liberation with the ephemera of a move toward Afghan ownership. Ownership means shifting responsibilities to the society where we have intervened, while preparing an exit for the interveners. If the Afghans "own" their own governance, it is they who are responsible, not us, who only have provided the means and will continue to steer the process. I know this risks sounding sarcastic, but it is more a question of helplessness now—observing how well-intended actions become the unintentional opposite.

But since we have never established a trusteeship, or a formal protectorate, it is not really fair to claim now that we advocate Afghan ownership—a full transfer of political, economic, and military responsibility. President Karzai has demanded a stronger say in American operations in his country. Of course, this should be taken with a grain of salt. Karzai is not immune to the temptations of political rhetoric, but ownership is critical to the success of any post-conflict society. In the end, we have no desire to own and occupy a country we had helped to "liberate," and thus we must openly explain to Afghans our stakes in co-governance. Here lies a big chance for American diplomacy. It is clear that the interests of the United States, NATO, and other regional players go beyond supporting a national government in Afghanistan.

We may want to include Afghanistan—and the region—in a partnership of peaceful development that includes a stable relationship with all its neighbors. If this is accepted and will not merely lead to extending our military operations there, then our intent must be communicated to the Afghans in a way that allows a more realistic understanding of what our role will continue to be. Only then can we allow Afghans themselves to deliberate the terms of our responsibility and set in place a fair, honest, and shared trusteeship.

Who's in Charge?

Certainly there is the expectation that the Afghans should soon handle their own affairs without Western supervision. But the basis of our arguments have focused on state-building, not the equivalent on the social level. Without a doubt, the goal is an enduring and sustainable formal Afghan statehood—but only on the rarest of occasions have the Afghan people been given the opportunity to ask themselves how they want to live. Society-building must be given priority over state-building.

Society building starts with soft sectors, such as education, public health, and clean water. It also requires rule of law to provide basic and uncompromised human rights, leaning heavily on a system of legal pluralism. By this, I mean a system under which conflict resolution, penal and civil actions, and court decisions respect fundamental principles of law, but with different methods and while respecting a range of customary traditions and procedures. Not surprisingly, in a society as pluralistic as Afghanistan (and with centuries-old customs and traditions), this is already proving a very complicated task.

You may ask whether the efforts thus far should have shown some progress in this direction. Indeed, there are hundreds of governmental and non-governmental organizations operating in the theater, and many programs are already quite well established—particularly in the refugee and repatriation sectors. Some have proved quite successful, others are clearly failing, but most have in common an almost total lack of local institutional backing—legal or bureaucratic. The reorganization of Afghan ministries and the civil administration cannot be imposed from the outside. While soft sectors function better if the personal relations between foreign actors and their local counterparts are good, they can sour if maintained over too long a period.

Foreign "experts" are prone to develop a sense of unintended ownership and even the most benign efforts to befriend local aid recipients are a poor substitute for effective disinterested institutions. Only the latter can create lasting trust and confidence in the renewal of Afghan statehood and social structures. The liberation from our ownership over the Afghan lifestyle and future takes time, however, and we must help them through the transition, while also protecting them from the Taliban and other dangers to free civil society in Afghanistan.

First and foremost, the mistakes of our security-first approach cannot be corrected by a simple shift of strategy. The integrated approach of President Obama's new strategy appears to be a step in the right direction, but the integration should quickly shift to an Afghans-first policy. In short, we cannot continue to fight Al Qaeda in Afghanistan and blithely accept that the reconstruction of Afghan society will be a welcome spinoff. Instead, the reverse is far more realistic. Building a peaceful Afghan society will better serve our interests and reduce the chances that Al Qaeda will be able to manipulate the Taliban for their destructive aims. When the majority of Afghans feel confident that their lives will not improve with a Taliban return to power, the militant cause will wither.

Some Humble Recommendations

To make this more concrete, I recommend a few substantial changes in today's strategy:

- Allow the Afghans to build their own institutions and an effective governance. By building their infrastructure with our contractors, we ignore the substantial manpower and expertise already in the country.
- Support the Afghan military in its fight against the Taliban, though it will take some time until the ANA will be able to assume these responsibilities alone. The United States and other allied forces must deploy protective detachments wherever a village or a region has been cleared of Taliban. This implies, of course, a long-standing visible presence of foreign troops, but it will narrow the Taliban's ability to attack with impunity at a time or place of their choosing.
- Use Provincial Reconstruction Teams and other civil-military coordination to protect the Afghan security forces, mainly police. PRTs should not act as a stand-alone and often alienating development agency. In concert, they can effectively replace illegitimate forces such as warlords and local commando units with secure, honest government enforcement.
- Allow no compromise in the education of girls and proactively protect schools. This is a field where our responsibility must be shared. It must be demonstrated clearly that this particular aspect of human rights cannot depend on imagined cultural traditions or a Taliban interpretation of *sharia* law.
- Stop arming local tribes. Build citizen militias instead, or we will continue the failure to build trust in the only legitimate institutions for security—the police and army.

- Understand that building institutions to enforce the rule of law is a difficult and long-term process. The routines and procedures of effective and efficient courts requires years of training, which has not yet begun to take practical root in Afghanistan, and exist only on the theoretical level.
- Stop using international forces for counter-narcotics policy, especially eradicating poppy-seed agriculture. Afghans argue quite convincingly that the harsh measures produce more insurgents among farmers. Meanwhile, we are losing the war on drug users in our own countries. Massive development aid, alternative food production, and non-agrarian employment options in the countryside will be more promising—and less costly.

The Culture of Intervention

These recommendations may seem obvious, but the main—and sorely misunderstood—issue is the culture of intervention. One hopes that the Obama administration and its allies will agree that their intervention should neither produce a protectorate nor keep the Afghans in the subordinate role they were obliged to accept immediately after their liberation from the Taliban. At that time, however, there was hope for a quick recovery. It has been a long eight years since.

However, we are not intending to rule as colonial powers and we do not need to win the "hearts and minds" of the Afghan people. If we are serious in attaining the goal of a free, unified, self-reliant Afghanistan, corrections are needed in our approach. A new integrated strategy must have room for improving both development aid and institutional support.

It is also essential that obvious wrong-doing—collateral damage and civilian casualties, the unnecessary humiliation of local populations by military and international forces, the abusive interrogation techniques in Bagram and other prisons—are publicly renounced and come to an immediate end. Sadly, our perception of how deeply these injustices affect public opinion in Afghanistan is widely underestimated.

The Sociologist in Me

You may have noticed that, in this essay, I have frequently used the first-person plural—the "we"—instead of enumerating the concrete actors. But a sociologist cannot be an observer without being an accomplice to the events and the reality behind them. As an active intervener and researcher in Afghanistan, I am inherently an actor, caught in the dual role of observer and co-conspirator. Yet the "we" is neither good nor bad: it comprises not only actors like the alliance forces of Operation Enduring Freedom and NATO, but also a community of individuals who care deeply for the Afghan people, and feel responsible for what happens there.

However, the situation in Afghanistan is deteriorating, and will deteriorate further, if we continue to only consider the hard security side of the equation. Today, attacks on intervention forces are occuring more frequently in all parts of the country and progress that had been celebrated not long ago is now at risk. Too many deficiencies and errors have occurred to allow us to continue to plod along in the same manner.

Yet I am optimistic for three reasons. First, President Obama's new strategy will add substantial support to the civil sectors, thus strengthening and eventually expanding the existing islands of peace in a landscape of war. Second, we seem increasingly aware that the conflict is regional. While that risks creating a much larger field of operations, it clearly shows that the United States and its allies understand that more is at stake than nation building in Afghanistan alone. Third, and most singularly important, the shortcomings and obvious faults of our efforts can still be remedied.

We have erred terribly in strategic and tactical approaches, but we can still correct our mistakes. When Afghans tell me that we should not let them down, it is clear that they, too, are desperate for change. It would be a tragedy if we lost the peace in an intervention where we are still wanted and needed.

MICHAEL DAXNER is professor of sociology and president emeritus of the University of Oldenburg, Germany, and has served as special counselor to United Nations missions in Kosovo and Afghanistan.

From *World Policy Journal,* Summer 2009, pp. 13–23. Copyright © 2009 by MIT Press Journals. Reprinted by permission.

Cracks in the Jihad

Al Qaeda and the Taliban are at odds, and even Internet jihadis are taking fewer cues from Osama bin Laden. Yet it is only growing more difficult to defeat the global jihad.

THOMAS RID

"Get ready for all Muslims to join the holy war against you," the jihadi leader Abd el-Kader warned his Western enemies. The year was 1839, and nine years into France's occupation of Algeria the resistance had grown self-confident. Only weeks earlier, Arab fighters had wiped out a convoy of 30 French soldiers en route from Boufarik to Oued-el-Alèg. Insurgent attacks on the slow-moving French columns were steadily increasing, and the army's fortified blockhouses in the Atlas Mountains were under frequent assault.

Paris pinned its hopes on an energetic general who had already served a successful tour in Algeria, Thomas-Robert Bugeaud. In January 1840, shortly before leaving to take command in Algiers, he addressed the French Chamber of Deputies: "In Europe, gentlemen, we don't just make war against armies; we make war against interests." The key to victory in European wars, he explained, was to penetrate the enemy country's interior. Seize the centers of population, commerce, and industry, "and soon the interests are forced to capitulate." Not so at the foot of the Atlas, he conceded. Instead, he would focus the army's effort on the tribal population.

Later that year, a well-known military thinker from Prussia traveled to Algeria to observe Bugeaud's new approach. Major General Carl von Decker, who had taught under the famed Carl von Clausewitz at the War Academy in Berlin, was more forthright than his French counterpart. The fight against fanatical tribal warriors, he foresaw, "will throw all European theory of war into the trash heap."

One hundred and seventy years later, jihad is again a major threat—and Decker's dire analysis more relevant than ever. War, in Clausewitz's eminent theory, was a clash of collective wills, "a continuation of politics by other means." When states went to war, the adversary was a political entity with the ability to act as one body, able to end hostilities by declaring victory or admitting defeat. Even Abd el-Kader eventually capitulated. But jihad in the 21st century, especially during the past few years, has fundamentally changed its anatomy: Al Qaeda is no longer a collective political actor. It is no longer an adversary that can articulate a will, capitulate, and be defeated. But the jihad's new weakness is also its new strength: Because of its transformation, Islamist militancy is politically impaired yet fitter to survive its present crisis.

In the years since late 2001, when U.S. and coalition forces toppled the Taliban regime and all but destroyed Al Qaeda's core organization in Afghanistan, the bin Laden brand has been bleeding popularity across the Muslim world. The global jihad, as a result, has been torn by mounting internal tensions. Today, the holy war is set to slip into three distinct ideological and organizational niches. The U.S. surge in Afghanistan, whether successful or not, is likely to affect this development only marginally.

The first niche is occupied by local Islamist insurgencies, fueled by grievances against "apostate" regimes that are authoritarian, corrupt, or backed by "infidel" outside powers (or any combination of the three). Filling the second niche is terrorism-cum–organized crime, most visible in Afghanistan and Indonesia but also seen in Europe, fueled by narcotics, extortion, and other ordinary illicit activities. In the final niche are people who barely qualify as a group: young second- and third-generation Muslims in the diaspora who are engaged in a more amateurish but persistent holy war, fueled by their own complex personal discontents. Al Qaeda's challenge is to encompass the jihadis who drift to the criminal and eccentric fringe while keeping alive its appeal to the Muslim mainstream and a rhetoric of high aspiration and promise.

The most visible divide separates the local and global jihadis. Historically, Islamist groups tended to bud locally, and assumed a global outlook only later, if they did so at all. All the groups that have been affiliated with Al Qaeda either predate the birth of the global jihad in the early 1990s or grew later out of local causes and concerns, only subsequently attaching the bin Laden logo. Al Qaeda in the Islamic Maghreb, for example, started out in 1998 as the Salafist Group for Preaching and Combat, an offshoot of another militant group that had roots in Algeria's vicious civil war during the early 1990s. Pakistan's Lashkar-e-Taiba, the force allegedly behind the 2008 attacks in Mumbai, India, that killed more than 170 people, was formed in the 1990s to fight for a united Kashmir under Pakistani rule. In Somalia, Egypt, Saudi Arabia, and other countries, the Al Qaeda brand has been attractive to groups born out of local concerns.

By joining Al Qaeda and stepping up violence, local insurgents have long risked placing themselves on the target lists of governments and law enforcement organizations. More recently, however, they have run what may be an even more consequential risk, that of removing themselves from the social mainstream and losing popular support. This is what happened to Al Qaeda in Iraq during the Sunni Awakening, which began in 2005 in violence-ridden al-Anbar Province and its principal city, Ramadi. Al Qaeda had declared Ramadi the future capital of its Iraqi "caliphate," and by late 2005 it had the entire city under its control. But even conservative Sunni elders became alienated by the group's brutality and violence. One prominent local leader, Sheikh Sattar Abdul Abu Risha, lost several brothers and his father in assassinations. Others were agitated by the loss of prestige and power to the insurgents in their traditional homelands. In early 2006, Sattar and his sheikhs decided to cooperate with American forces, and by the end of the year they had helped recruit nearly 4,000 men to local police units. "They brought us nothing but destruction and we finally said, enough is enough," Sattar explained.

The awakening (*sahwa* in Arabic) was not limited to al-Anbar. One after another, former firebrand imams, in so-called revisions, have started questioning the theological justifications of holy war. The trend may have begun with Gamaa al-Islamiya, Egypt's most brutal terrorist group, which was responsible for the assassination of Egyptian president Anwar el-Sadat in 1981 and the slaughter of 58 foreign tourists in Luxor in 1997. As the Iraq war intensified during the summer of 2003, several of Gamaa al-Islamiya's leaders advised young men not to participate in Al Qaeda operations and accused the organization of "splitting Muslim ranks" by provoking hostile reactions against Islam "and wrongly interpreting the meaning of jihad in a violent way."

Former firebrand imams have started questioning the theological justifications of holy war.

Another notable revision came in September 2007, when Salman al-Awda, an influential Saudi cleric who had previously declared that fighting Americans in Iraq was a religious duty, spoke out against Al Qaeda. He accused bin Laden in an open letter of "making terror a synonym for Islam." Speaking on a popular Saudi TV show on the sixth anniversary of 9/11, al-Awda asked, "My brother Osama, how much blood has been spilt? How many innocent people, children, elderly, and women have been killed . . . in the name of Al Qaeda?"

Other ideologues have followed, including Sajjid Imam al-Shareef, one of Al Qaeda's founding leaders, who used the nom de guerre Dr. Fadl. "Every drop of blood that was shed or is being shed in Afghanistan and Iraq is the responsibility of bin Laden and Zawahiri and their followers," he wrote in the London-based newspaper *Asharq Al Awsat*.

In Afghanistan, coalition soldiers see the global-local split replicated as a fissure between what they call "big T" Taliban and "small t" Taliban. The "big T" ideologues fight for more global spiritual or political reasons; the "little t" opportunists fight for power, for money, or just to survive, to hedge their bets. A family might have one son fighting for the Taliban and another in the Afghan National Army; no matter which side prevails, they will have one son in the right place. U.S. Marines in Helmand Province say that 80 to 85 percent of all those they fight are "small t" Taliban. The U.S. counterinsurgency campaign aims to co-opt and reintegrate many of these rebels by creating secure population centers and new economic opportunities, spreading cleared areas like "inkblots." But the Taliban have long been keen to spread their own inkblots, with a similar rationale: attracting more and more "accidental" guerrillas, in the famous phrase of counterinsurgency specialist David Kilcullen, not just hardliners.

Yet even Afghanistan's "big T" Taliban, the ideologues, cannot simply be equated with Al Qaeda. Last fall, Abu Walid, once an Al Qaeda accomplice and now a Taliban propagandist, ridiculed bin Laden in the Taliban's official monthly magazine *al-Sumud,* for, among other things, his do-it-yourself approach to Islamic jurisprudence. A number of veterans had criticized bin Laden in the past, among them such towering figures as Abu Mus'ab al-Suri, one of the key architects of the global jihad. But Abu Walid's criticism was more biting. Bin Laden's organization lacks strategic vision and relies on "shiny slogans," he told Leah Farrall, an Australian counterterrorism specialist, in a much-noted dialogue she reported on her blog. Consequently the Taliban would no longer welcome the terrorists in Afghanistan, he said, because "the majority of the population is against Al Qaeda."

At the root of the disagreement between the two groups is the question of a local, or even national, popular base. Last September, Mullah Omar, the Taliban's founding figure and spiritual overlord, issued a message in several languages. He called the Taliban a "robust Islamic and nationalist movement" that had "assumed the shape of a popular movement." Probably realizing that pragmatism and a certain amount of moderation offer the best chance of a return to power, Omar vowed "to maintain good and positive relations with all neighbors based on mutual respect."

Al Qaeda's reaction was swift and harsh. Turning the jihad into a "national cause," in the purists' view, was selling it out. Prominent radicals, in a remarkable move, compared the Taliban's turnabout to the efforts by Hezbollah in Lebanon and Hamas in Gaza to distance themselves from Al Qaeda. Hamas in particular, perhaps because it is, like Al Qaeda, a Sunni organization, has been the subject of "relentless" criticism in Al Qaeda circles, says Thomas Hegghammer of the Institute for Advanced Study in Princeton, New Jersey. When a self-proclaimed Al Qaeda faction appeared in Gaza, Hamas executed one of its leading imams and many of his armed followers. Jihadi ideologues were aghast. The globalists shuddered at the thought that local interests could compromise their pan-Islamic ambitions. "Nationalism," declared Ayman al-Zawahiri, Al Qaeda's number two, "must be rejected by the *umma* [Muslim community], because it is a model which makes jihad subject to the market of political compromises and distracts the *umma* from the liberation of Islamic lands and the establishment of the Caliphate."

A few weeks later, Mullah Omar pointedly reiterated his promise of good neighborliness and future cooperation with Afghanistan's neighbors, including China, Uzbekistan, and Turkmenistan—all of whom face their own jihadi insurgencies and are on Al Qaeda's target list.

The Taliban is moderating its tone and throwing an "ideological bridge" to parts of the Kabul elite.

The Taliban's new tactics are throwing an "ideological bridge" not only to nearby countries but to parts of the current Kabul elite, most notably politically mobilized university students, notes Thomas Ruttig of the Afghanistan Analysts Network. Even the newly moderate Taliban, it should be clear, remains wedded to inhumane and medieval moral principles. Yet Omar's pragmatism immediately affects the question of who and what is a desirable target of attacks.

Perhaps the greatest tension between the local and global levels of the jihad grows out of a divide over appropriate targets and tactics. Classical Islamic legal doctrine sees armed jihad as a defensive struggle against persecution, oppression, and incursions into Muslim lands. In an attempt to mobilize Muslims around the world to fight the Soviets in Afghanistan, Abdallah Azzam, an influential radical cleric who was assassinated in 1989, helped expand the doctrine of jihad into a transnational struggle by declaring the Afghan jihad an individual duty for all Muslims. Azzam also advocated *takfir*, a practice of designating fellow Muslims as infidels (*kaffir*) by remote excommunication in order to justify their slaughter. Al Qaeda ideologues upped the aggressive potential of such arguments and expanded the defensive jihad into a global struggle, effectively blurring the line between the "near" enemy—the Arab regimes deemed illegitimate "apostates" by the purists—and the "far" enemy, these regimes' Western supporters.

In the remote areas of Pakistan and Afghanistan that produce many of today's radicals, however, local and tribal affiliations are powerful. One U.S. political adviser who worked in Afghanistan's Zabul Province, a hotbed of the insurgency, describes prevailing local sentiment as "valleyism" rather than nationalism. It is a force that drives the tribes to oppose

anybody who threatens their traditional power base, foreign or not—a problem not just for the Taliban and Al Qaeda but for any Afghan government. Al-Zawahiri complained of this in a letter after the invasion of Afghanistan: "Even the students (*talib*) themselves had stronger affiliations to their tribes and villages . . . than to the Islamic emirate." The provincial valleyists, to the distress of Al Qaeda's more cosmopolitan agitators, are selfishly eyeing their own interests, with little appetite for international aggression and globe-spanning terrorist operations.

The contrast with the character of jihad in the Muslim diaspora could not be starker. For radical Islamists in Europe, the local jihad doesn't exist. And they understand that toppling governments in, say, London or Amsterdam is a fantasy. These radicals are less interest driven than identity driven. Many young European Muslims are out of touch with their ancestral countries, yet not fully at home in France or Sweden or Denmark. For some, the resulting identity crisis creates a hunger for clear spiritual guidelines. The ideology of global jihad, according to a report by EUROPOL, the European Union's police agency, "gives meaning to the feeling of exclusion" prevalent among the second- and third-generation descendants of Muslim immigrants. For these alienated youth, the idea of becoming "citizens" of the virtual worldwide Islamic community may be more attractive than it is for first-generation immigrants, who tend to retain strong roots in their native countries.

The identity problems of these young people seem to have affected the character of the jihad itself. Like the disoriented Muslim youth of the diaspora, the global jihad has loose residential roots and numb political fingertips. One sign of this disconnection from the local is that Al Qaeda's rank and file does not include many men who could otherwise join a jihad at home: There seem to be few Palestinians, Chechens, Iraqis, or Afghans among the traveling jihadis, who tend to come from countries where jihad has failed, such as Egypt, Saudi Arabia, Libya, and Syria.

Al Qaeda's identity crisis is also illustrated by how it treats radicalized converts, often people without religious schooling and consolidated personalities. Olivier Roy, one of France's leading specialists on radical Islamism, has pointed out that convert groups assume responsibilities "beyond all comparison with any other Islamic organization." Roy has put the proportion of converts in Al Qaeda at between 10 and 25 percent, an indicator that the movement has become "de-culturalized."

These contrary trends, in turn, create chinks in Al Qaeda's recruitment system. The most extreme Salafists, deprived of identity and cultural orientation, have an appetite for utopia, for extreme views that appeal to the margin of society, be it in Holland or Helmand. Recruitment in the diaspora, as a result, follows a distinctive pattern, not partisan and political but offbeat and outré. The grievances and motivations of European extremists and the rare American militants tend to be idiosyncratic, the product of unstable individual personalities and a history of personal discrimination. Many take the initiative to join the movement themselves, and because they are not recruited by a member of the existing organization, their ties to it may remain loose. In 2008 alone, 190 individuals were sentenced for Islamist terrorist activities in Europe, most of them in Britain, France, and Spain. "A majority of the arrested individuals belonged to small autonomous cells rather than to known terrorist organizations," EUROPOL reports.

Al Qaeda's latest recruits look more like a self-appointed elite than representatives of the Muslim "masses."

As a result of the change in its membership, the global Al Qaeda movement is encountering strong centrifugal forces. The rank and file and the center are losing touch with each other. The vision of Abu Mus'ab al-Suri, who laid much of the ideological foundation for Al Qaeda's global jihad, blends a Marxist-inspired focus on popular mass support with 21st-century ideas of networked, individual action. Al-Suri's aim was to devise a method "for transforming excellent individual initiatives, performed over the past decades, from emotional pulse beats and scattered reactions into a phenomenon which is guided and utilized, and whereby the project of jihad is advanced so that it becomes the Islamic Nation's battle, and not a struggle of an elite." The global jihad was to function like an "operative system," without vulnerable, old-fashioned organizational hierarchies. That method is intuitively attractive for a Facebook generation of well-connected young sympathizers, but the theory contains an internal contradiction. Self-recruited and "homegrown" terrorists present a wicked problem for Al Qaeda. As a bizarre type of self-appointed elite, they undermine the movement's ambition to represent the Muslim "masses."

The problem is embodied in the online jihad. For Al Qaeda, Web forums operated by unaffiliated Islamists have been the most important distribution platform for jihadi materials. But after the arrest of a top-tier online activist in London two years ago, the connection between the forums and Al Qaeda's official media center, al-Sahab, began to loosen. Al Qaeda has lost more and more control of the online jihad. And, just like others online, jihadi Web administrators face increasingly tough competition for visibility. Within the forums the tone has become harsher. Brynjar Lia, a specialist on Salafism at the Norwegian Defense Research Establishment, says that "interjihadi quarrels seem to have become more common and less 'brotherly' in tone in recent years."

Some far-flung jihadi groups are enjoying newfound independence of another kind, as a result of criminal ventures they have established to fund their efforts. This too is intensifying the centrifugal forces within the global movement. Some groups are tipping into a more purely criminal mode.

A cause is what distinguishes an insurgency from organized crime, as David Galula, an influential French author on counterinsurgency, noted decades ago. Organized crime does not have to be incompatible with jihad. It may even be justified in religious terms: Baz Mohammed, an Afghan heroin kingpin and the first criminal ever extradited from Afghanistan, bragged to his co-conspirators that selling heroin in the United States was jihad because it killed Americans while taking their money.

A budding insurgency has only a limited window of opportunity to grow into a serious political force. If the cause withers and loses its popular gloss, what remains as a rump may be nothing but a criminal organization, attracting a following with criminal energy rather than religious zeal, thus further damaging jihad's status in the eyes of the broader public. For some groups, this already appears to be happening. Al Qaeda in the Islamic Maghreb funds itself through the drug trade, smuggling, extortion, and kidnappings in southern Algeria and northern Mali. Indonesia's Abu Sayyaf Group and the Philippines' Jamiyah Islamiyah engage in a variety of criminal activities, including credit card fraud. The terrorist cell behind the 2004 Madrid bombings earned most of its money from criminal activities; when Spanish police raided the home of one of the plotters, they seized close to $2 million in drugs and cash, including more than 125,000 Ecstasy tablets, according to *U.S. News and World Report.* The Madrid bombings had cost the terrorists just $50,000.

The goal of leading Islamists has always been to turn their battle into "the Islamic Nation's battle," as al-Suri wrote. Far from reaching this goal, the jihad is veering the other way. Eight years after 9/11, support for Islamic extremism in the Muslim world is at its lowest point. Support for Al Qaeda has slipped most dramatically in Indonesia, Pakistan, and Jordan. In 2003, more than 50 percent of those surveyed in these countries agreed that bin Laden would "do the right thing regarding world affairs," the Pew Global Attitudes Project found. By 2009 the overall level of support had dropped by half, to about 25 percent. In Pakistan, traditionally a stronghold of extremism, only nine percent of Muslims have a favorable view of Al Qaeda, down from 25 percent in 2008. Even an American failure to stabilize Afghanistan and its terror-ridden neighborhood would be unlikely to ease Al Qaeda's crisis of legitimacy.

But it would be naive to conclude that the cracks in Al Qaeda's ideological shell mean that the movement's end is near. Far from it. Islamist ideology may be losing broad appeal, and the recent global crop of extremists may be disunited and drifting apart. Yet in the fanatics' own view, the ideology remains a crucial cohesive force that binds together an extraordinarily diverse extremist elite. Salafism, despite its crisis, continues to be attractive to those at the social margins. One of the ideology's most vital functions appears to be to resolve the contradictions of jihad in the 21st century: being a pious Muslim, yet attacking women and children; upholding the authority of the Qur'an, yet prospering from crime; depending on Western welfare states, yet plotting against them; having no personal ties to any Islamic group, yet believing oneself to be part of one.

Al Qaeda's altered design has a number of immediate consequences. The global jihad is losing what David Galula called a strong cause, and with it its political character. This change is making it increasingly difficult to distinguish jihad from organized crime on the one side and rudderless fanaticism on the other. This calls into question the notion that war is still, as

Clausewitz said, "a continuation of politics by other means," and therefore whether it can be discontinued politically. Second, coerced by adversaries and enabled by the Internet, the global jihadi movement has dismantled and disrupted its own ability to act as one coherent entity. No leader is in a position to articulate the movement's will, let alone enforce it. It is doubtful, to quote Clausewitz again, whether war can still be "an act of force to compel the enemy to do our will." And because jihad has no single center of gravity, it has no single critical vulnerability. No matter what the outcome of U.S.-led operations in Afghanistan and other places, a general risk of terrorist attacks will persist for the foreseeable future.

In combating terrorism, therefore, quantity matters as much as quality. But some numbers matter more than others. How many additional American and European troops are sent to Afghanistan matters less than the number of terrorist plots that don't happen. Success will be found subtly in statistics, in data curves that slope down or level off, not in one particular action, one capitulation, or even one leader's death. It will be marked not by military campaigns and other events but by decisions not taken and attacks not launched. Because participation in the holy war in both its local and global forms is an individual decision, these choices have to be the unit of analysis, and influencing them must be the goal of policy and strategy. As in crime prevention, measuring success—how many potential terrorists did not join an armed group or commit a terrorist act—is nearly impossible. Success against Islamic militancy may wear a veil.

THOMAS RID is a visiting scholar at the Shalem Center in Jerusalem and coauthor of *War 2.0* (2009). He was a public policy scholar at the Woodrow Wilson Center in 2009.

Exit Lessons

The search is on for graceful strategies for exiting Iraq and Afghanistan. Apart from victory, history suggests, there are none.

DAVID M. EDELSTEIN

I n the midst of negotiating the Soviet withdrawal from Afghanistan in the mid-1980s, a Western diplomat confided to United Nations mediator Diego Cordovez, "The Russians would like to get out of Afghanistan, but they don't know how. And we in the West would like to cooperate and help them, but we don't know how either." The Soviet experience is not unique. Historically, it has always been easier to launch a military intervention than to end one, especially when the effort has not gone well. From the United States in Vietnam to the Soviet Union in Afghanistan to Israel in Lebanon, intervening powers have often found it exceedingly difficult to extricate themselves from bad situations. As the United States is learning in Iraq, even when you are determined to make an exit, it is easier said than done.

The debate over exit strategies originated in America's painful experience during the Vietnam War, which led some foreign-policy thinkers to conclude that an exit plan should be a prerequisite for any military intervention. The debate intensified in the 1990s, after the end of the Cold War, as the United States undertook interventions that appeared to be matters of choice more than necessity. In laying down what came to be called the Powell Doctrine, then-chairman of the Joint Chiefs of Staff Colin Powell included an exit strategy on his list of conditions that should be met before the United States committed forces overseas. But from Somalia to the Balkans and Haiti, none of the subsequent conflicts to which U.S. forces were committed in the 1990s met this condition, much less Powell's chief principle that interventions must be directly tied to the long-term security of American interests. These costly and inconclusive efforts led critics to put even greater emphasis on questions about how the story was going to end. A year before he was elected president, George W. Bush questioned President Bill Clinton's 1999 decision to intervene in Kosovo: "Victory means exit strategy, and it's important for the president to explain to us what the exit strategy is."

Yet for all the talk of exit strategies, there has been little attempt to review their history and assess their effectiveness. The results of such a study are chastening. Since the end of World War II, the United States has been very active in the world, but it has had no monopoly on large-scale intervention.

The Soviet Union was the other obvious player in the postwar period, but there were also interventions by Egypt (in Yemen), Cuba (in Angola and Ethiopia), and India (in Sri Lanka), among others. The majority of these states' interventions did not end well. (Among the notable exceptions, at least from the perspective of the intervening power, were the U.S. defense of South Korea from 1950 to '53, the Soviet Union's 1956 invasion of Hungary, and the American overthrow of President Manuel Noriega's corrupt Panamanian regime in 1989.) A survey of nearly two dozen major military interventions since the end of World War II reveals that intervening powers were able to craft effective exit strategies in only about a third of the cases—and those happen to be the cases in which the goals of the interventions had already been met. Both the successes and the failures yield a handful of clear lessons about getting out.

Lesson 1: How You Leave Doesn't Matter Very Much

During the 2008 presidential campaign, former U.S. national security advisers Zbigniew Brzezinski, a Democrat, and Brent Scowcroft, a Republican, published a much-noted book in which they debated the future of U.S. foreign policy, strongly disagreeing on Iraq. Brzezinski called for a rapid withdrawal, arguing that it would encourage the Iraqi people to take responsibility for their own governance. Scowcroft contended that a quick pullout would have disastrous consequences for Iraq, the region, and the United States.

The assumption by both these eminent foreign-policy thinkers that it matters a great deal how you leave is widely shared, and it has a surface logic. An abrupt departure could unleash a civil war or create a power vacuum that adversaries could exploit. Leaving according to a considered plan, on the other hand, could allow an intervening power to withdraw with stability intact and its reputation unscathed.

What might such a smart exit strategy look like? It might be conditional on the creation of credible institutions that could govern the post-intervention state. It could require a slow-and-gradual withdrawal of troops rather than cutting and running, as the United States supposedly did in leaving Somalia in 1993 after the "Blackhawk Down" incident. Perhaps it involves leaving behind a residual force to keep the peace, as the United States did after the Korean War and as a number of states did in Bosnia and Kosovo in the 1990s.

There is no such thing as a failed intervention capped by a successful exit strategy.

The evidence suggests that these choices do not much matter. Whether or not an exit leads to instability or the erosion of the intervening power's reputation depends much more on the conditions under which the intervention ended than on the character of the pullout. There is no such thing as a failed intervention capped by a successful exit strategy. This is not to say that exit strategies are completely inconsequential–some clearly are executed better than others. But exit strategies are far less important than the overall success of the interventions that precede them. America's intervention in South Korea produced good results because it ended reasonably well—in stalemate, if not victory—not because of a brilliant exit strategy. The residual forces left in place there, and later in Bosnia and Kosovo, would not have been effective if the intervention had not established a degree of underlying stability. Exits of all shapes and sizes—from the hasty U.S. departure from Somalia to the prolonged Soviet withdrawal from Afghanistan—have failed to achieve much in the way of results that suggest that the particular form of exit strategy can have a significant impact.

Lesson 2: It's Hard to Make a Defeat Look Like a Victory

Leaders sometimes recognize Lesson 1, but they still spend a great deal of time debating exit strategies. Even if a struggling military campaign cannot be transformed into a success, appearances can be manipulated, they hope, so that the nation's (and the leader's) honor, reputation, and status can be salvaged. Nobel Prize winner Thomas Schelling lent weight to this argument in *Arms and Influence* (1966), contending that "face" is not merely a matter of a "country's 'worth' or 'status' or even 'honor,' but . . . its reputation for action. If the question is raised whether this kind of 'face' is worth fighting over, the answer is that this kind of face is one of the few things worth fighting over."

Attempts to save face usually take the form of arduously negotiated pre-withdrawal agreements that allow all sides to claim that they have accomplished something positive in the course of the fighting. That is what happened in Vietnam, Angola, and Afghanistan, where negotiations over pre-withdrawal agreements dragged on for years. Facesaving agreements include elaborate plans for post-withdrawal governance and security institutions as well as economic support and other aid to a fledgling local government. What is most striking about these agreements is that they are rarely credible, rarely last very long, and are almost always known to be flawed by the signatories. Two years after the endlessly negotiated 1973 Paris

Peace Accords, North Vietnamese tanks rolled into Saigon. The Tripartite Accord, signed by Angola, South Africa, and Cuba, concluded Cuba's 13-year presence in Angola in 1988 with a withdrawal stretched over another 18 months, yet Angola's civil war continued for a decade. The 1988 Geneva Accords, which brought an end to the Soviet intervention in Afghanistan, proved equally ineffective, as the country slipped into chaos and then, in 1996, the hands of the Taliban.

It should not be surprising that such agreements quickly fall apart. Once the outside force has departed, the balance of power on the ground shifts, opening up opportunities for some contending groups and leaving others vulnerable. Opposition groups that may have been biding their time can also find fresh opportunities in the wake of evacuation, as the Taliban did in Afghanistan.

If face-saving agreements are rarely credible and the signatories know it, why do they continue to pursue them? History gives two answers. First, the agreements offer short-term domestic rewards to political leaders. Even if the pacts are likely to collapse eventually, extricating forces in a way that appears honorable may offer enough cover to allow a leader to get reelected or stay in power. Second, an agreement may hold together long enough to allow leaders to disclaim any responsibility for violence that recurs after their troops have left.

Both of these logics were evident in the strategy the Nixon administration adopted in Vietnam: The United States would withdraw from South Vietnam in such a way that a "decent interval" would be guaranteed before things fell apart, as National Security Adviser Henry Kissinger famously put it. In June 1972, he told Chinese premier Zhou Enlai, "While we cannot bring a communist government to power . . . if, as a result of historical evolution it should happen over a period of time, we ought to be able to accept it." Ultimately, the accords were signed too late to aid in Richard Nixon's reelection—he still swamped Senator George McGovern in their 1972 contest—but they allowed him to claim he had achieved "peace with honor." It was left to others to cope with the hollowness of those words.

Face-saving requires a sleight of hand. Sometimes a clever leader can buy a bit of time in domestic politics, but that kind of magic is harder to pull off on the international stage. In the end, the truth will out. While a prolonged exit may generate an immediate perception that a withdrawal has been carefully planned and conducted on the intervening power's terms, the long-term attempt to convince others that a defeat is actually a victory is not likely to succeed.

Lesson 3: When in Doubt, Leave

The only good reason to prolong a struggling military intervention is if a change in strategy can bring victory. Of course, few politicians believe their strategy is going to fail, but it is very rare for leaders who lack the ability to be honest with themselves to succeed. There are no sure things. Any strategy is going to be highly debatable, as the Bush administration's "surge" strategy was in 2007. The point is that leaders must evaluate strategies based on whether they are likely to produce a successful outcome, not just whether they may yield some political advantage.

If a plausible strategy for victory is unavailable, it is best to withdraw sooner rather than later. This reality is often difficult for leaders to recognize. They fear the domestic political costs of leaving without victory, but prolonging matters promises to increase human and material costs without concomitant gains. Some 20,000 American lives were lost in Vietnam as the Nixon administration searched for a way out after 1970.

There are reasonable things an intervening power can and should do when it is leaving to reduce the chances of a catastrophic outcome. It can press other powers in the region to refrain from meddling in the power vacuum created by its departure, and it can appeal to the United Nations and other institutions to step in to protect vulnerable minorities and preserve the peace. But the fact is that such institutions are rarely eager to clean up the mess left by an unsuccessful intervention, and the record when they try to do so is not encouraging. The UN forces that took over from departing Americans in Somalia in 1994 and Haiti in 1995, for example, were helpless to prevent worsening violence and political chaos. Somalia today is an anarchic haven for pirates, and Haiti, despite the presence of 9,000 UN troops, is plagued by political instability and violence.

Leaving sooner rather than later may be the best available option, but that is not to say it will produce a good outcome. The damage caused by a misguided intervention is not easily repaired, and it is usually layered on top of nasty preexisting conditions. The notion that the people of an occupied country will get their political act together once the intervening power threatens to leave is based more on hope than experience. Political instability is often what draws in an outside power in the first place. In many cases, the underlying tensions can only be resolved over the long haul, after considerable bloodshed.

Lesson 4: Beware the Domestic Politics of Exit

The key motivating forces behind exit strategies are as often domestic political considerations as they are military or diplomatic ones. Consider the end of Israel's 1982–85 intervention in Lebanon, marred from the beginning by the 1982 massacres at Sabra and Shatila, which saw more than a thousand Palestinian and Lebanese civilians killed by Phalangist militia as Israeli troops stood by. The primary impetus to withdraw came from Israeli political groups that were critical of what they saw as their government's lack of strategic clarity in Lebanon and unhappy about the human and moral costs of the occupation.

Two kinds of domestic political pressure usually appear, pushing in opposite directions. One kind of pressure comes in the form of demands to cut costs and reduce the human suffering caused by an intervention, reflected in highly visible poll numbers and protest marches. The other is less obvious and thus less discussed by analysts: the imperative to avoid appearing to be the author of failure. Leaders face a strong temptation to "kick the can down the road" and pass on the dilemma of how to get out to a subsequent government.

In the end, it is impossible to disentangle the domestic politics of exit from strategic decisions, but good leaders put more emphasis on the likelihood of military victory than the likelihood of their own political survival. Concerns about the domestic political consequences of withdrawal have more often pushed leaders to drag out interventions than to end them quickly.

Lesson 5: Concerns about How to Get Out Shouldn't Preclude Intervention, but They Must Be a Consideration

Public demands for an exit strategy are often simply camouflage for a particular speaker's opposition to the intervention. When President Bill Clinton announced plans to send 20,000 U.S. troops to serve as peacekeepers in Bosnia in 1995, for example, Senate Republican leader Robert Dole quipped, "If Bill Clinton is going to have the entry strategy, the rest of us should have the exit strategy."

Requiring a solid advance plan for getting out would amount to precluding almost any intervention. Yet there are cases in which intervention makes sense, including some humanitarian ones. It is usually impossible to fix the terms of exit in advance; they must be shaped by conditions on the ground. In any case, an *ex ante* exit strategy is not likely to be credible, because battlefield realities will inevitably require strategic adjustments.

That is not to say that political leaders do not need to consider scenarios for withdrawal before taking the plunge. It may be politically impossible to publicly contemplate defeat, but good strategists plan for the possibility. Leaders should be expected to establish the conditions under which they would consider disengagement, and they should have contingency plans in place should a speedy pullout be necessary. The time for a leader to think about the cost of losing face in a hasty retreat is emphatically before the fighting starts.

The implications of the five lessons can be applied across a wide range of cases, but especially in Iraq and Afghanistan. Barack Obama promised as a presidential candidate to withdraw U.S. troops from Iraq, and under the plan he has adopted, U.S. forces have already moved out of Iraqi city centers and are scheduled to leave the country entirely by the end of 2011. The framework for the withdrawal, the U.S.-Iraqi Status of Forces Agreement (SOFA), was actually negotiated by the Bush administration in 2008, at a moment of optimism about Iraq. The level of violence had fallen, and though progress on the political front was halting, there was hope that sound political and security institutions would be in place before the United States left the country.

In pushing his exit strategy, President Obama seems to have avoided most of the pitfalls that have tripped up other leaders. The SOFA and the Obama administration's subsequent withdrawal plan appear to reflect a genuine hope for a positive outcome in Iraq rather than an effort simply to save face. The real test of this strategy, however, will come if the situation in Iraq deteriorates. Will the United States remain committed to its plan or will it prolong its intervention? If the Obama administration extends the U.S. presence, will its decision be driven by sound strategic logic or by a desire to save face? The history of interventions suggests that a turn for the worse in Iraq should be met with a continued determination to pull out. The United States should do whatever it can to minimize the risk of catastrophic events in Iraq as its troops depart, but if the situation turns sour, its speedy withdrawal, however bloody, could very well be the best option for both the United States and Iraq.

In Afghanistan, the United States does not yet have an exit strategy. It remains committed to that intervention, with Obama calling in February for an immediate increase of 17,000 troops on the ground, bringing the total to 62,000. And military commanders may soon ask for more reinforcements. If the increase does not generate signs of progress toward stability, then it will likely be in everybody's best interest for the United States to ratchet down its goals, withdraw its troops, and reorient its military effort to very specific counterterrorism missions designed to contain future threats that may germinate on Afghan soil.

It is time to recognize that history does supply useful exit lessons. In January 1973, Henry Kissinger discussed the Paris Peace Accords with his assistant John Negroponte (U.S. ambassador to Iraq from 2004 to '05) and John Ehrlichman,

a top aide to President Nixon. "How long do you figure the South Vietnamese can survive under this agreement?" Ehrlichman asked. "I think that if we're lucky they can hold out for a year and a half," Kissinger replied. Negroponte asked whether such an agreement was in the best interest of South Vietnam. Kissinger's response: "Do you want us to stay there forever?"

That question is familiar to students of military intervention. There is no easy way out of an intervention gone awry. There are no clever exit strategies that can convert failure into success, and not even the most detailed agreements can effectively alter others' perceptions of an effort that simply has not accomplished its goals. The lesson of past military interventions is that it is almost always better to leave sooner rather than later. Leaving is not likely to produce a pretty result, but international politics often necessitates choosing between bad options. When things go wrong, door number one—the exit door—is likely to be the least bad option.

DAVID M. EDELSTEIN is an assistant professor in the Edmund A. Walsh School of Foreign Service, the Security Studies Program, and the Department of Government at Georgetown University, and the author of *Occupational Hazards: Success and Failure in Military Occupation* (2008). This article is drawn from his research on exit strategies as a fellow at the Woodrow Wilson Center during 2008–09.

Test-Your-Knowledge Form

We encourage you to photocopy and use this page as a tool to assess how the articles in *Annual Editions* expand on the information in your textbook. By reflecting on the articles you will gain enhanced text information. You can also access this useful form on a product's book support website at www.mhhe.com/cls

NAME: _____ DATE: _____

_____

TITLE AND NUMBER OF ARTICLE:

_____

BRIEFLY STATE THE MAIN IDEA OF THIS ARTICLE:

_____

LIST THREE IMPORTANT FACTS THAT THE AUTHOR USES TO SUPPORT THE MAIN IDEA:

_____

WHAT INFORMATION OR IDEAS DISCUSSED IN THIS ARTICLE ARE ALSO DISCUSSED IN YOUR TEXTBOOK OR OTHER READINGS THAT YOU HAVE DONE? LIST THE TEXTBOOK CHAPTERS AND PAGE NUMBERS:

_____

LIST ANY EXAMPLES OF BIAS OR FAULTY REASONING THAT YOU FOUND IN THE ARTICLE:

_____

LIST ANY NEW TERMS/CONCEPTS THAT WERE DISCUSSED IN THE ARTICLE, AND WRITE A SHORT DEFINITION:

We Want Your Advice

ANNUAL EDITIONS revisions depend on two major opinion sources: one is our Advisory Board, listed in the front of this volume, which works with us in scanning the thousands of articles published in the public press each year; the other is you—the person actually using the book. Please help us and the users of the next edition by completing the prepaid article rating form on this page and returning it to us. Thank you for your help!

ANNUAL EDITIONS: American Foreign Policy 11/12

ARTICLE RATING FORM

Here is an opportunity for you to have direct input into the next revision of this volume.
We would like you to rate each of the articles listed below, using the following scale:

1. **Excellent: should definitely be retained**
2. **Above average: should probably be retained**
3. **Below average: should probably be deleted**
4. **Poor: should definitely be deleted**

Your ratings will play a vital part in the next revision.
Please mail this prepaid form to us as soon as possible.
Thanks for your help!

RATING	ARTICLE	RATING	ARTICLE
	1. From Hope to Audacity: Appraising Obama's Foreign Policy		25. Lost for Words: The Intelligence Community's Struggle to Find Its Voice
	2. The World Still Needs a Leader		26. Arrested Development: Making Foreign Aid a More Effective Tool
	3. Hegemony on the Cheap: Liberal Internationalism from Wilson to Bush		27. When Congress Stops Wars: Partisan Politics and Presidential Power
	4. The Eagle Has Crash Landed		28. Law, Liberty and War: Originalist Sin
	5. Pillars of the Next American Century		29. Neo-Conservatives, Liberal Hawks, and the War on Terror: Lessons from the Cold War
	6. Grand Strategy for a Divided America		30. Securing the Information Highway: How to Enhance the United States' Electronic Defenses
	7. Enemies into Friends: How the United States Can Court Its Adversaries		31. America's Sticky Power
	8. Will Moscow Help with Trouble Spots?		32. The New Axis of Oil
	9. Russia and the West: Mutually Assured Distrust		33. The Coming Financial Pandemic
	10. Emerging Strategic Dilemmas in U.S.-Chinese Relations		34. Can Sanctions Stop Proliferation?
	11. China's Challenge to U.S. Hegemony		35. The New Rules of War
	12. Let's Make a Deal		36. Space Wars: Coming to the Sky Near You?
	13. Requiem for the Monroe Doctrine		37. Preemption Paradox
	14. Mirror-Imaging the Mullahs: Our Islamic Interlocutors		38. New Challenges and Old Concepts: Understanding 21st Century Insurgency
	15. After Iran Gets the Bomb: Containment and Its Complications		39. Nuclear Disorder: Surveying Atomic Threats
	16. U.S. Africa Command: A New Strategic Paradigm?		40. Nuclear Abolition: A Reverie
	17. Bottom-Up Nation Building		41. Low-cost Nuclear Arms Races
	18. The War We Deserve		42. Lifting the Veil: Understanding the Roots of Islamic Militancy
	19. The Evangelical Roots of US Africa Policy		43. How We'll Know When We've Won: A Definition of Success in Iraq
	20. Waiting Games: The Politics of US Immigration Reform		44. Is It Worth It?: The Difficult Case for War in Afghanistan
	21. The Carter Syndrome		45. Afghanistan: Graveyard of Good Intent
	22. National War Powers Commission Report		46. Cracks in the Jihad
	23. The Homeland Security Hash		47. Exit Lessons
	24. Coming Soon: A Crisis in Civil-Military Relations		

NO POSTAGE
NECESSARY
IF MAILED
IN THE
UNITED STATES

BUSINESS REPLY MAIL
FIRST CLASS MAIL PERMIT NO. 551 DUBUQUE IA

POSTAGE WILL BE PAID BY ADDRESSEE

McGraw-Hill Contemporary Learning Series
501 BELL STREET
DUBUQUE, IA 52001

ABOUT YOU

Name

Date

Are you a teacher? ☐ A student? ☐
Your school's name

Department

Address   City   State   Zip

School telephone #

YOUR COMMENTS ARE IMPORTANT TO US!

Please fill in the following information:
For which course did you use this book?

Did you use a text with this ANNUAL EDITION? ☐ yes ☐ no
What was the title of the text?

What are your general reactions to the Annual Editions concept?

Have you read any pertinent articles recently that you think should be included in the next edition? Explain.

Are there any articles that you feel should be replaced in the next edition? Why?

Are there any World Wide Websites that you feel should be included in the next edition? Please annotate.

May we contact you for editorial input? ☐ yes ☐ no
May we quote your comments? ☐ yes ☐ no